Generalist Social Work Practice with Families

Stephen J. Yanca

Saginaw State University

Louise C. Johnson

University of South Dakota

PEARSON

Boston   New York   San Francisco
Mexico City   Montreal   Toronto   London   Madrid   Munich   Paris
Hong Kong   Singapore   Tokyo   Cape Town   Sydney

Senior Series Editor: *Patricia Quinlin*
Series Editorial Assistant: *Nakeesha Warner*
Marketing Manager: *Laura Lee Manley*
Editorial Production Service: *Omegatype Typography, Inc.*
Composition Buyer: *Linda Cox*
Manufacturing Buyer: *Debbie Rossi*
Electronic Composition: *Omegatype Typography, Inc.*
Photo Researcher: *Omegatype Typography, Inc.*
Cover Administrator: *Kristina Mose-Libon*

For related titles and support materials, visit our online catalog at www.ablongman.com.

Portions of this text first appeared in *Social Work Practice: A Generalist Approach,* 9th ed., by Louise C. Johnson and Stephen J. Yanca, published by Allyn and Bacon. Copyright © 2007 by Pearson Education, Inc.

To obtain permission(s) to use material from this work, please submit a written request to Allyn and Bacon, Permissions Department, 75 Arlington Street, Boston, MA 02116 or fax your request to 617-848-7320.

Between the time Website information is gathered and then published, it is not unusual for some sites to have closed. Also, the transcription of URLs can result in typographical errors. The publisher would appreciate notification where these errors occur so that they may be corrected in subsequent editions.

ISBN-13: 978-0-205-47010-5
ISBN-10:   0-205-47010-6

Library of Congress Cataloging-in-Publication Data

Yanca, Stephen J.
    Generalist social work practice with families / Stephen J. Yanca, Louise
C. Johnson. — 1st ed.
        p.   cm.
    ISBN-13: 978-0-205-47010-5
    ISBN-10: 0-205-47010-6
    1. Family social work—United States.   I. Johnson, Louise C.   II. Title.
    HV699.Y36   2007
    362.82'530973—dc22

                                                        2007007038
Printed in the United States of America

Photo credits: p. 3, Tony Freeman/PhotoEdit; p. 23, Ariel Skelley/Corbis/Bettmann; p. 53, Getty Images Inc. PhotoDisc; p. 65, Deborah Davis/PhotoEdit; p. 71, Ariel Skelley/Corbis/Stock Market; p. 78, Esbin-Anderson/The Image Works; p. 82, Will Hart; p. 87, Bob Daemmrich/PhotoEdit; p. 120, Michelle D. Bridwell/PhotoEdit; p. 157, Will Hart; p. 180, Bill Aron/PhotoEdit; p. 214, Kayte M. Deioma/PhotoEdit; p. 231, Myrleen Ferguson Cate/PhotoEdit; p. 256, David Young-Wolff/PhotoEdit; p. 288, Michael Newman/PhotoEdit; p. 325, Tony Freeman/PhotoEdit; p. 352, Bob Daemmrich/PhotoEdit

CONTENTS

■ CHAPTER 4

PART II

■ CHAPTER 5

■ CHAPTER 11

Generalist Practice with Parents   288

PREFACE

■ ■

We are pleased to present the first edition of *Generalist Social Work Practice with Families.* In many ways this is a family version of our text *Social Work Practice: A Generalist Approach,* ninth edition. We have converted portions of the practice text into material that is specific to working with families using our Johnson/Yanca model for generalist social work practice. The conversion was quite easy as we found that our model can readily be applied to working with families and family subsystems. At the same time, we are cognizant of the need to emphasize that in generalist social work practice the social worker must be prepared to work with any size system as a client system, as a target for change, or as part of the support system. This text has been written to fill a gap in terms of providing an in-depth approach to working with families from a generalist perspective. We provide a means for determining the appropriate size for a client system along with assistance in determining whether a subsystem might be appropriate. The text assumes that once it has been determined that family work is needed, the generalist social worker will need to have an effective approach to providing services.

The text is intended for use by BSW students and practitioners, first-year MSW students, MSW programs that offer a generalist degree, and practitioners looking for a text about working with families using a generalist approach. Most other family texts seem to be oriented toward providing family therapy with the entire family system present. And yet, our research and practice indicate that this is relatively rare. Most social work practice with families is comprised of other services that we see as falling under the umbrella of generalist practice. A unique feature of this text is the inclusion of the application of our model to social work practice with family subsystems. Again, our research and practice indicates that the predominant form of generalist social work practice with families is with parents and parent–child subsystems. We use the term *family work* very broadly to include any kind of social work practice with any part of the family system. This can range from the entire family system to subsystems, dyads, triads, and so forth to individuals where their membership in the family is a concern or where the family or some part of the family system is the target for change.

Although it is helpful to have used our generalist practice text before or along with this text, it is not necessary. For those who have read the practice text, some of the material will sound familiar and will serve as a refresher with a concentration on applying concepts to working with families. We hope that instructors, students, and practitioners find it useful to have two texts that use the same model. Typically, texts by different authors use different approaches leaving it to the reader to bridge the gaps between approaches or make the translation from one to the other.

For those who have not read an edition of our practice text but have been exposed to other versions of generalist practice, this text will add to that understanding by presenting an approach to family work from a generalist perspective. Foundation material provided in Part One serves as a base for understanding our perspective on generalist social work practice in preparation for understanding this presentation of generalist practice with families. It is assumed that students and practitioners will have had some exposure to or understanding of generalist social work practice and are using this text to gain a more thorough understanding of how to work with families using a generalist approach.

As with our practice text, generalist social work as developed in this text begins with the need of a client system. This might be an individual, a family, a family subsystem, or a social system. The social worker explores or assesses the situation in which the need exists with the client system and significant others. Based on the findings of this exploration, a plan for work to alleviate the situation is developed and an agreement between the worker and the client system is drawn up. The focus of the plan can be an individual, a small group, a family, an organization, or a community. Once the plan is developed, the worker and client system, and perhaps other persons, work to carry out the plan. At some point, the worker and client system decide whether to terminate their relationship or continue to work together on further plans.

Students should have certain prerequisites before using the material covered in this book. These include the following:

1. At least one introductory course covering the history and development of social welfare and an introduction to the profession.
2. A broad liberal arts base providing a wide variety of knowledge pertaining to the human situation, an appreciation of history, and some understanding about the nature of knowledge.
3. Courses providing an understanding of human behavior and the social environment, such as those in psychology, sociology, anthropology, political science, and economics. Courses that include understandings of human development and human diversity, including racial and ethnic differences, are particularly important.
4. Some exposure to generalist social work practice either through academic experiences or practice that uses a generalist approach.

The book presents our model for generalist practice with families; however, it does not attempt to present any one approach to social work practice with families but rather synthesizes material from a number of sources into a coherent whole. Also, no attempt is made to consider practice with any particular population or social problem area. Rather, the assumption is made that the generalist approach with families can be used in a wide variety of situations, such as with older people, those who have medical and mental health problems, those who are discriminated against because of diversity, and those who suffer because their social situation does not provide for their basic needs. We also provide an approach that is readily applied to social work practice in any setting from rural to urban.

One more important note—we have chosen to use both male and female pronouns throughout the text with some preference to using female pronouns. We have done this because the majority of readers are likely to be females. We hope that our male readers will understand this and will join us in an effort to be more inclusive with regard to using female pronouns. We think that the overuse of male pronouns in almost every other area of our society, including most texts, more than compensates for any concerns about using fewer male pronouns here.

Plan for the Text

Part I provides an overview of foundation material that will assist the reader in understanding our approach to generalist social work practice with families. A more thorough presentation of our approach to generalist social work practice can be found in our companion text *Social Work Practice: A Generalist Approach.* The first chapter introduces the reader to family work and develops the concept of family ecosystem. The second provides background material on generalist social work practice along with an overview of the Johnson/Yanca model. Chapter 3 is vital to understanding diversity and the concept of diversity competent practice. Of course no single chapter, or book for that matter, can make someone diversity competent. Diversity competence is a lifelong learning process that is never really fully achieved. This chapter provides a means of organizing that process and presents some foundation material on understanding some of the diverse families social workers typically encounter in their practice. Other chapters throughout the text provide suggestions about working with diverse families using the approach introduced in this chapter. Chapter 4 is adapted from our practice text and provides a vital understanding of relationship, interaction, and engagement with families.

Part II is comprised of five chapters that represent the family version of the Johnson/Yanca model for generalist practice. It is also adapted from our practice text. The chapters cover assessment, planning, direct practice actions, indirect practice actions, and evaluation and termination with families. The focus in Part II is work that tends to be with the entire family as a system. This is probably the most complicated version of family work and so we have chosen to use it as the focus as we present the use of our model in working with families. However, most of the material presented in Part II is also used when working with family subsystems.

Part III applies our model to working with each of the four family subsystems, the couple subsystem, the parent subsystem, the parent–child subsystem, and the sibling subsystem. As we mentioned earlier, this is a unique feature of this text and we hope that instructors, students, and practitioners find it useful to consider how to apply the generalist approach to working with these family subsystems. The first section of the Appendix is adapted from our practice text and presents our version of "best practices," which we call "good practice." We apply this to working with families who face special challenges including substance abuse, violence, the need for child welfare services, crime and delinquency, physical disability, mental disability, and aging.

The organization chosen for this text seems most appropriate to the authors, who have based it on years of experience in teaching generalist social work practice. As the concepts are developed, attention is given to building on material presented in earlier sections of the book. Repetition is used to reinforce learning. The authors assume that the present cannot be understood apart from the past, thus historical as well as contemporary aspects of the material covered are noted.

An attempt has been made to minimize the use of jargon yet to introduce the reader to professional language. Charts and schemas are provided to help the reader organize considerable amounts of information into a coherent whole to maximize understanding.

The book contains many case examples. Major sections of some chapters contain vignettes or case examples that depict the major concepts in action. In addition, longer case examples are provided. An attempt has also been made to use case examples from practice in a variety of settings. Although much can be learned from a textbook, thorough learning takes place only as the conceptualizations are applied in actual practice experiences. Most chapters contain summaries, statements of learning expectations, study questions, and suggested readings for use by students and teachers. An appendix with chapter notes, a glossary of key terms, and indexes are included at the end of the text.

Acknowledgments

In the ninth edition of our practice text, we gave special recognition to several practitioners and students whose assistance should also be recognized here because some of the material from that text has been adapted to family work in this text. Thanks go out to Karen Pabalis for her feedback on good practice in health care settings and to Jeanne Yonke and her colleagues for their contributions to good practice in domestic violence services. Several students at Saginaw Valley State University provided research materials on working with diverse populations, including Stacie Buszka, Renee Oberski, Roshell Watley-Thomas, Mark Ciacuia, Tunya Hottois, and Eddie Payne.

For this first edition of *Generalist Social Work Practice with Families* special recognition is given to Kim Sawatzki and Tony Moore who worked on the research project on generalist practice with families. Their contributions were invaluable in confirming our practice experience with generalist practice with families. Thanks to Dr. Lucy Mercier of Saginaw Valley State University for reviewing material on diversity. At this time, we would also like to thank the individuals who reviewed this book: Cynthia Bishop, Meredith College; Deborah E. Bowen, University of North Carolina–Wilmington; and Sara Sanders, University of Iowa.

We would like to dedicate this text to our families: the families in which we grew up and the families we helped create along with our extended families. Their support and encouragement made us who we are and in many ways, both large and small, they helped us to write this text by teaching us about families.

S.J.Y.
L.C.J.

PART I

Foundations of Generalist Social Work Practice with Families

Social workers have been working with families since the beginning of the profession. The earliest social workers, who were called friendly visitors, visited families hoping to help them escape from poverty and other social problems. As the profession of social work matured, so did social workers engagements with families. We now see social workers providing everything from marital and family therapy to referrals and assistance with accessing resources. Therapy is typically provided by specialists with masters of social work (MSW) degrees and specialized training. However, even generalist social workers can find themselves counseling couples and families when access to specialized services is not available.

The generalist social worker provides a wide range of services to families in a wide range of settings. Anywhere generalist social work is practiced, we can find that working with some part of the family system is an important piece of the work either directly as **client systems** or indirectly as a significant aspect of the environment.

Part I provides an overview of foundation material that is necessary for understanding our approach to generalist social work practice with families. A more thorough presentation of generalist social work practice can be found in our companion text *Social Work Practice: A Generalist Approach*. Some material from that text has been adapted for and appears throughout this text. Although it is helpful to have used that text before or together with this text, it is not necessary. For those who have read the practice text, some of the material in this text will sound familiar and will serve as a refresher. For those who have not read the practice edition but have been exposed to other versions of generalist practice, the foundation material presented in this text provides a base for understanding our perspective on generalist social work practice in preparation for understanding generalist practice with families. It is assumed that students will have had some exposure to generalist social work practice and are using this text to gain a more thorough understanding of how to work with families using a generalist approach.

Let us share our view of generalist practice. As we indicate in Chapter 1, a generalist approach requires that the social worker assess the situation with the client system, then together they decide which systems are the appropriate *units of attention,* or focus of the work, for the change effort. The client system may be an individual, a family, a small group, an agency or organization, or a community. The units of attention may be any of these systems or the transactions among these systems. Thus, the generalist approach emphasizes knowledge that can be applied to a variety of systems.

Chapter 1 begins with a look at families and family work. We consider the various forms of families in U.S. society. These forms frequently are different from the image of the intact nuclear family that may be seen by some as the "ideal family." One of the authors, Louise Johnson, has compiled a brief history of family work. Louise has lived a major part of this history during her career as a social worker and later as a social work educator. The chapters lay a foundation for studying generalist practice with families by presenting some of the major theories and approaches that are necessary to understanding this work. The fundamental approach that we use comes from family systems theory. We have combined ecosystems and strengths approaches with problem solving to form an **ecosystems strengths approach** to change. An increasingly important aspect of social work practice is understanding diversity and becoming more competent in serving diverse families.

Chapter 2 provides a foundation for understanding our approach to generalist social work practice. It includes a brief history of generalist practice. Once again Louise has compiled this and lived much of it in her roles as social worker and social work educator. This is followed by a description of the Johnson/Yanca model of generalist practice.

Chapter 3 lays a foundation for generalist social work practice with diverse families. It includes a description of an approach to diversity competent practice that extends the concept of cultural competence to all forms of diversity. A particularly important aspect of family work is gender competent practice, which is discussed along with diversity competent practice with gay and lesbian families. A schema for studying families from diverse ethnic groups has been developed and is applied to African American, Hispanic/Latino, and Native American families.

Finally, Chapter 4 is a family-focused version of material from our practice text that is essential to forming an action system with families. The focus is on interaction and engagement with families. We also discuss relationships, especially the formation of a helping relationship and the use of the interview process with the family.

1

Generalist Practice with Families

LEARNING EXPECTATIONS

1. Understanding of the importance of working with the family in generalist social work practice.
2. Understanding of the variation in family forms in modern U.S. society.
3. Understanding of the use of social systems theory and family systems theory in generalist social work practice with families.
4. Understanding of the importance of an ecological perspective and a strengths approach in generalist social work practice with families.
5. Understanding of the importance of developing a diversity approach in generalist social work practice with families.

The experience of growing up in a family is something that nearly all human beings have in common with each other. At the same time, this experience is actually quite unique for each person. The uniqueness of each human being means that we experience each other in unique ways. When culture and diversity are considered, family life becomes even more diverse.

Social workers have worked with families since the very beginnings of the profession. Friendly visitors visited families in an effort to free them from the grips of poverty and other social problems. Settlement houses served immigrant families seeking a new life in the United States. The challenge in finding effective ways of working with families has always been to understand the commonality of experiences in family life while also appreciating its uniqueness. The development of theories and approaches to working with people are predicated on the assumption that common needs and concerns will lend themselves to common solutions. Without this we would be left with pure guesswork as to what is most likely to be effective. However, the uniqueness of the human experience must be considered even as we rely on the assumption of commonality.

In this text, we present a model for working with families for generalist social workers that seeks to incorporate both the commonality of family life and its uniqueness. We refer to our approach as an ecosystems strengths approach to change. It includes diversity competent practice with families. The assumptions we have made in developing this approach are that all families interact with an environment that has resources to meet needs. We assume that all families have strengths. We assume that diversity means different approaches are needed in meeting family needs. We also assume that the social worker can discover the approach that is more likely to be effective by listening to the stories that family members tell. The basic model provides a framework for understanding commonality and uniqueness. Our diversity competent approach provides a process for uncovering uniqueness while preserving the ability to understand commonality.

As we stated, most people start out life in a family. Of course, families may look quite different from the nuclear family that has been the image of what a family is for white society in the United States. Even this image is more of an ideal than a reality. The middle-class family with an intact marriage, with the husband as breadwinner and the wife as homemaker, and two children only existed in significant numbers during the 1950s. The absence of a family experience can be devastating for human beings unless a suitable replacement is provided. This discussion centers on the family as the first and most important multiperson interaction human beings have.

Another basic assumption guiding this consideration of the family is that the fundamental issue for all human beings is answering the question, Can I be an individual and still be loved and accepted by others? The tension between acting on one's own needs while preserving relationships with others is basic to human relations. Initially, this tension is played out in the family between a young child and the parents. The child vacillates between the search for autonomy and independence and the desire for meaningful attachment. When parents successfully communicate the message that the child is loved and accepted unconditionally for himself, then attachment is secure and provides a base from which the child can establish individual autonomy. When the message is something else or if it does not get through, then doubts begin to occur and self-confidence is more tenuous.

In simple terms, if the answer to the question is or seems to be "yes," then the child can internalize this answer and feel more secure about loving and accepting himself. This is the essence of self-image, self-esteem, self-worth, and self-respect—what one thinks or feels about oneself. If the answer to the question was a conditional "yes" (I love you if . . . or I love you when . . .), then the child begins to look outside the self for the approval of others and for his value and worth. If the answer was "no," then the child may conclude he is not worthwhile or may reject others as the source of influence on his behavior.

This last circumstance is what generally happens when children are abused or neglected. These children often have extremely low self-worth. They may learn to treat others as objects just as they were treated as objects. In the case of feelings of low self-worth, the person thinks, "If my parent(s) did not love me, who will? I must be unlovable." In treating others as objects, the person thinks, "If my parents did not care about me, why should I care about anyone else?" This is the reasoning of the majority of people who go to prison, many of whom were abused or neglected as children. These individuals conclude that acting on self-interest is the only way to survive.

Whatever our experience was as a child, we are likely to carry it with us outside of the family and reflect it in our expectations of ourselves and others. This is fundamental to family work and affects the client, the social worker, and the people in the systems with whom we have contact. Understanding who we are means understanding the impact our family had on us. Before undertaking work with clients, especially with families, the social worker should first have insight into her own background and how it influences self-perceptions and the perceptions of clients and of the world. Self-awareness and a healthy self-esteem are necessities in developing oneself as a competent professional social worker.

When working with individuals, families, and groups, it is important to keep in mind how the client's self-image and relationships with others have been shaped by family experiences. Working with clients in families or groups provides opportunities to help them find positive responses to the question of acceptance and individuality. In fact, the social work value of belief in the inherent value and worth of every human being represents a positive response to this question. Thus, if the social worker is successful in communicating this value to others and in getting the family or group to experience it, then individuals can re-experience the question of self-worth in a more positive way. A more positive experience can have a profound impact on a client's future experiences.

Understanding the influence of family on self-esteem and on relationships with others is fundamental to assessment and intervention with individuals, families, and groups. The ways in which families influence individual development and relationships provide a key to what the worker needs to focus on in multiperson interaction. It is important to view the family as a system and to understand its structure, functioning, and development or history. It is also important to understand the needs of each member and the system as a whole. Examining strengths and challenges provides a basis on which to build strategies for change.

In this chapter, we present a foundation for generalist practice with families. Most texts on families are oriented toward family therapy. Generalist practitioners do not typically provide therapy unless they are MSWs from an advanced generalist practice program. The chapter begins by considering the family forms in U.S. society. It moves on to look at a brief history of family work. Next, we discuss family systems theory along with other theories that underlie our approach. Finally, the concept of the family ecosystem is outlined.

■ FAMILY FORMS IN AMERICAN SOCIETY ■

When working with the family, social workers may encounter difficulty because they either are not aware of or have not resolved some of their own concerns and feelings about their families of orientation (the families in which they grew up). Workers may also make unfounded assumptions about the functioning of families based on their personal experiences. Thus, an important prerequisite to working with families is recognition and resolution of how the worker has been affected by her own family.

Often the assumption is made that a family consists of two parents and two or more children. In contemporary U.S. society, this is frequently not the case. Many couples choose to remain childless; some parents have multiple divorces; some have children outside of marriage; more couples are living longer after their children have left home; and the number of single-parent families, families with grandparents raising grandchildren, and blended families has grown. Social workers need to adapt models for work with families to these varied situations. Couple or marital therapy can provide a basis for working with a family made up of only a husband and wife. When working with older persons, either as couples alone or with their adult children and their families, consideration must be given to the developmental tasks of the later years. Unresolved or poorly resolved issues from the past may need to be addressed. Two tasks that often are important for families with older persons are (1) helping the family find and use community resources that will allow older persons to live in the least restrictive environment possible and (2) helping families maintain supportive, helpful relationships that do not overburden any family member.

When working with single-parent or blended families, it is important to consider the influence of the absent parent. Different concerns may be present if the absent parent is dead, a divorce has taken place, or there has never been a marriage. The father or mother may be the custodial parent, or there may be a joint-custody agreement. When working with the single-parent family, it is particularly important to consider role overload and the needs of the single parent. There may be unresolved feelings or issues resulting from death or divorce. Inappropriate expectations of family members may be present. Children may be filling the role of the absent parent in a way that places too much stress or responsibility on the child. This type of family often has a need for supportive community resources.

Blended families present special challenges for the social worker. In the **blended family** the parents have had previous marriages or relationships and have children from these marriages or relationships. There may be children from the current marriage or union, along with children from other relationships. Some of the children may be "half siblings." Everyone in the family has a "step" relationship with at least one other member. Some of the children may leave to visit their other biological parent. Some children may come to visit their noncustodial parent. All of this can be very confusing for the family as well as the worker. One of the fundamental issues that all blended families face is how to adjust to living together as a family, given all of these various types of relationships. Most second marriages fail because family members are not able to adjust. Thus, the work to be done generally revolves around the development of appropriate relationships in the face of what are often difficult circumstances. It is especially important that children be assisted in accepting their parents' decisions regarding divorce and remarriage. The work also should include helping the family to restructure itself around the current reality and to adapt its communication and functioning to meet each member's needs.

Some of the families that social workers work with may be seen as multiproblem or chaotic families. Child abuse, spouse abuse, and substance abuse are often what bring these families to the social agency. These families usually do not come to social workers voluntarily but are ordered by the court or some other authority to seek service. When working in these difficult situations, a first step must be the development of a relationship based on trust of the worker. To do this, the worker must be consistent and flexible and avoid any type of retaliation. The worker must be honest with the family about why they are there and what the consequences of lack of cooperation may be. Concern and empathy expressed in a nonjudgmental manner are very important. In many of these cases, the worker will find a history of difficulties that goes back to previous generations. In addition, the worker will generally find individuals who are unable to get their needs met in socially acceptable ways or who simply do not know how to get their needs met. Often the family's interactions with its environment are limited or fraught with conflict. These families often need help in setting priorities and developing skills for social functioning. Their communication skills may be limited. It is most important that these families develop a sense of competency.

The worker must understand the differences in family functioning and structure within different cultural groups. When working with families from a minority cultural group, workers should not presume an understanding of family function until they have determined with the family how it operates within its cultural group. Usually, meeting with families in their homes and using short-term, action-oriented modes is a successful approach. The worker helps the family work out its own solution in a manner that is supportive of the extended family and immediate ethnic community system. Often, work with minority group families involves helping them deal with the external dominant society system and its institutions. This is when an ecosystems strengths approach is especially beneficial. Advocacy or mediation with individuals, groups, and institutions within the majority culture may be needed. An important goal when working with all families, but particularly with families who have experienced discrimination, is to enable the family and its members to take control of their own lives and work toward changing their situation by influencing the transactions with their environment. The social worker needs to develop understanding of the various forms families take in our society. Workers need to develop skill in assessing a family and its situation and then creatively develop a means for working with the family. Skill is necessary in interacting with the family to provide the needed information and to enable participation in the planning and work necessary for need fulfillment and enhanced social functioning.

Finally, the worker assesses the strengths of the family and of the systems in the family's environment. There is a tendency to see families who are different from the traditional nuclear family as being inferior. In reality, all families have strengths, regardless of their structure, function, development, ethnicity, or culture. Even chaotic families are able to provide for most of the needs of their members. There is also a tendency to focus on what is missing rather than what is already there. If the worker and the family are able to see the strengths of the family system and its ecosystem, then growth and change can be built on these strengths and on the transactions within the ecosystem instead of undertaking a major overhaul of the whole system. If people decide to make a change, they need to do so from a position of strength, not a position of weakness. It is more likely that change will occur and be sustained if it is based on existing strengths the system already possesses. It is up to the worker to identify and point out the strengths when the family is not able to do so.

■ A BRIEF HISTORY OF FAMILY WORK ■

The Charity Organization Society (COS) and particularly the writings of Mary Richmond from about 1890 are generally considered the beginning of the profession of social work. The private welfare movement called for "scientific philanthropy" or help based on rational understandings of the nature of poverty. Mary Richmond was the foremost person identified with social work at that time. She saw that it was essential for a very careful social diagnosis to take place as a part of the helping process. She is often seen as the "mother of social case work." She saw study of both the individual and family as essential. She also saw that to improve a situation, change in both the individual and the immediate situation (the family) are to be sought.[1] Thus, we see that in the early practice of social work, work with families was considered essential.

However, very soon inclusion of concern for the family in social case work was strongly questioned. Psychology and psychiatry with their focus on individuals became influential in social case work thinking. The primary focus became the individual as the unit of attention. Mary Jarrett, the first psychiatric social worker who practiced at Boston Psychiatric Hospital strongly spoke out for a primary emphasis on individuals using psychological understandings from about 1918. Other social workers including those employed in the so-called family agencies followed suit. In the 1930s, with the advent of Freud's psychoanalytical approach, social case workers began to adopt this approach in their practice. The switch from the family to the individual as the focus of practice seemed complete.

Ann Hartman and Joan Laird have suggested four reasons for the switch. First, the impact of both the mental hygiene movement and psychoanalytical psychology focused attention on the individual. Second, the family focus was lost when social work became split between an "inner" and an "outer" focus. Third, limitations in the knowledge and theory base made integration of a family focus with the new psychological emphasis difficult, if not impossible. Finally, the organizational arrangement of practice by method and field of practice made the family focus difficult to categorize appropriately.[2]

However, the change was not universal. As early as 1919, Porter Lee, director of the New York School of Social Work, questioned the shift away from a family focus.[3] There were social workers in the trenches who knew that families were important and continued to consider the family in their "diagnosis and treatment." What was lacking was a knowledge and theoretical base to underlie their work. What existed might be characterized as "practice wisdom," knowledge gained from experience and knowledge passed from worker to worker in an informal manner. At least some of the knowledge that these social workers drew from was probably the developing discipline of sociology. The discipline of sociology had its early development in the late 1800s and early 1900s, although it was not until the 1920s that family sociology became a low-status subdiscipline of sociology.

Another indication of the continued concern for the family is evident in the first professional social work journal entitled *The Family,* later known as *Social Casework.* The successor organization to the COS became known in 1946 as The Family Service Association even though members of this organization tended to use an individual approach based in Freudian psychology. Thus, it appears that although an emphasis on the individual was considered the emphasis in social casework, there remained a thread of practice that saw work with the family unit not only as appropriate but also as essential in some situations.

In 1938, Herbert Aptekar noted that it was impossible for a worker to work with more than one person. The writings of Florence Hollis (from 1949) strongly reflect the psychoanalytical approach and became a leading expression of social casework. The mental hygiene movement of the 1920s gave rise to the Child Guidance Clinic where it was the usual custom for psychiatrists to see the child and social workers to work with the mothers.[4] The title "psychiatric social worker" became prestigious within the social work profession, although the term only meant that the social worker worked with psychiatrists.

Another development of the late 1800s was the social settlement movement.[5] This movement is considered the precursor of another stream of social work, the social group work method. James Leiby sees this movement as more closely tied to the developing discipline of sociology. Jane Addams who is closely identified with the settlement movement is also considered one of the early sociologists. The *American Journal of Sociology* was established in 1895 at the University of Chicago. Many of its early articles were on the stockyards, Hull House, and other subjects that now would be considered social work.[6]

Until the 1930s, sociology and social work were often considered one discipline, and the relationship between sociology and social work in academia remains close to this day. In the early 1970s, undergraduate social welfare programs became baccalaureate social work programs. These programs provided the workers for the public social welfare services that developed as a result of the Depression and later public policy, and for those who served the rural areas. The "social welfare programs" tended to be in land grant universities and in the southeastern United States. They also provided settings that saw the family as an important unit of attention.

It can be assumed that those who had been educated in programs closely aligned with sociology programs gained understandings about the family, its influence on the individual, and its relationships to the larger community and used them in their practice, probably under the "practice wisdom" way of knowing. What seems to have happened during the 1930s, 1940s, 1950s, and even into the 1960s was that the psychiatric social workers (today's clinicians) and academicians dominated the profession with their thinking, which was heavily based in psychoanalytical thinking. The sociological knowledge base used in work with the family unit was hidden. Social group workers made considerable use of sociological concepts and came to consider the family as a special case of the small group. The understanding of the influence of the family on the individual was important to most social group workers.

During the 1950s, psychiatry began to explore methods for working with a total family unit, particularly as it related to families of schizophrenics. The work of Dr. Murray Bowen of the National Institute of Mental Health and Lyman Wynne and Theodore Lidz of Yale University provide examples of this work. In a 1969 monograph, Joan Stein of the Region IX Rehabilitative Research Institute at the University of Washington identified three approaches to working with families.[7] These approaches were psychoanalytic, integrative, and communicative–interactive. Ivan Boszormenyi-Nagy and James L. Framo described the psychoanalytic approach as "intensive working through of unconscious transference distortions which pervade close family relationships."[8] The integrative model was heavily influenced by the work of Nathan Ackerman, of New York's Jewish Family Service. It too was based on psychoanalytical theory but placed emphasis on the ego and on role. Frances H. Scherz, a social worker, also was involved in developing the social work use of this approach.[9] The communicative–interactive approach developed from the work of Don Jackson at the Palo Alto Medical Research Foundation. As the title indicates, this approach is concerned with communication and interaction processes within the family unit. Virginia Satir, a social worker, wrote about this model.[10]

During the 1950s, concern for what came to be called "multiproblem families" began to develop. In 1952, Bradley Buell published the results in what is known as "the St. Paul Study." In this study, Buell found that 6 percent of the families studied suffered from such a compounding or vicious circle of problems that they absorbed more than half of the combined services of all agencies.[11] He called for a focus on families rather than individuals, as well as a public health approach. Based on Buell's work, the concept of the multiproblem family became widely discussed. In 1956, Congress amended the Social Security Act to provide for public assistance beyond income maintenance and services with particular emphases on connecting people with services. Although there was encouragement for states to accept this provision, no money was provided to use in carrying out this service provision.[12] There was also increased concern for families in health settings and in services for those with mental retardation and chronic mental illness.

During the 1960s, the tide began to turn regarding the domination of psychoanalytic theory. One of the authors, as a second-year graduate student in 1962, enrolled in an addition to the curriculum: a course on the nature of the family. New and innovative practice models began to appear, such as crisis intervention and Reed and Epstein's task approach. Of particular interest was a model developed by Elizabeth McBroom for working with multiproblem families.[13]

Also of importance was the introduction of what was at first known as integrative practice and is now know as generalist practice. In the beginning, the thrust of integrative social work was to identify the commonalities of casework, group work, and community organization. If family work was considered, it was seen as a subset of group work. The family was seen as a special case of the small group. As generalist models developed, it became apparent that work with families needed to be given equal status with that of work with individuals, groups, and communities.

In the fall of 1969, the University of Chicago School of Social Administration hosted a conference on family treatment. This conference was a memorial to Charlotte Towle, a long-time member of Chicago's faculty. The papers from that conference were published by Columbia University Press with Eleanor Reardon Tolson and William Reid as editors. Some of the perspectives included were a small-group approach, a structural approach, a behavioral approach, an ecological model, a family systems model, and a model focused on brief therapy. Presenters included Sanford N. Sherman, John Elderkin Bell, Eileen D. Gambrill, John P. Spiegel, Ann Hartman, and Lynn Segal. There was a therapy emphasis with most of the models assuming that family treatment would include total family groups in the work together. This work can be seen as representing the clinical/academic strand of social work.[14]

During the 1970s, numerous articles and books were published that pointed to an integrative approach to practice and also began to incorporate systems thinking as a way to gain an understanding of "**person in situation.**" These would include Carol Meyer, *Social Work: A Response to Urban Crisis* (1970); Carel Germain, *Social Work Practice: People and Environments* (1979); and Allen Pincus and Anne Minahan, *Social Work Practice: Model and Method* (1973). All used a systems approach.

In the 1970s, Ann Hartman became a leading social work figure in the area of family treatment. In 1982, she co-authored, with Joan Laird, *Family Centered Social Work Practice.* This book is still a major resource for social workers working with families. Although most of the case examples presented in the book seem to be taken from what might be identified as clinical practice, the authors make it very clear that this approach can be used when working in a wide variety of fields of practice and in situations where the total family is not physically present during service. This book provides information on social policy as it affects families and very usable assessment and intervention tools. It looks at the total family system and its environment. It can be considered an eclectic systems approach with a strong ecological emphasis. It provides a knowledge base for nonclinical social workers to assess and intervene into transactions of family units in a broad range of situations. It makes it possible to truly consider the family a single intervention point when using a generalist approach to practice.[15]

■ FOUNDATIONS OF GENERALIST PRACTICE WITH FAMILIES ■

To begin our discussion of generalist practice with families, it is important to understand what is meant by the term *generalist practice.* In using a generalist approach, the social worker assesses the situation with the client system and together they decide which systems are the appropriate focus of the work or change effort. The client system of a generalist social worker may be an individual, a family, a small group, an agency or organization, or a community. The focus of the change effort may be any of these systems or the transactions among these systems. Thus, the generalist approach requires knowledge that can be applied to a variety of systems.

The generalist social worker works with families in many different ways and in many different settings. Sometimes the work is focused on the family itself. Other times most of the work involves the family's environment. Most of the time the worker works with both the family and elements of the family's environment, including interactions among these. In order to provide this wide array of services to families, the generalist practitioner needs to understand several important aspects of families and their environments. In this portion of the chapter, we introduce a foundation for understanding these aspects. We have included family systems theory, an ecological perspective, a strengths approach, an introduction to diversity competence, and the family ecosystem. In the next chapter we examine foundations of generalist practice along with the concept of family ecosystems.

Family Systems Theory

A consideration of family systems theory should begin with an understanding of social systems theory. Human need cannot be considered apart from the larger systems in which humans function. These include the family; small groups; the community; and various social institutions, such as the school, the church, and the social agency. All people belong to several larger systems, which often make conflicting demands. These systems are a part of each individual's environment. The demands of these systems are called **environmental demands.** Social systems theory provides a means of understanding these systems and identifying their needs.

Ann Hartman described the social systems approach as a "means of ordering the . . . world in terms of its relatedness. . . . A system would be a whole composed of interrelated and interdependent parts. . . . It has boundaries."[16] The system of focus has a relationship to individuals and systems outside its boundary. The relationships across the boundary are not as intense as those within it and do not have the strength of influence that the parts (subsystems) have on one another. The environment affects the social system. This approach calls for a kind of thinking that considers parts, wholes, and environments and the relationships that exist among them.[17]

Social systems theory is useful to social workers because it provides a means for conceptualizing linkages and relationships among seemingly different entities—individuals, families, small groups, agencies, communities, and societies. This theory notes similarities and differences among different classifications of systems and aids social workers in considering private troubles and public issues within both the nurturing system and the sustaining system of the situation being assessed.

For a **social system** to be able to maintain itself and fulfill its function, the subsystems or parts (individuals and groups) must make adjustments in their own functioning to meet the needs of the larger systems. When these adjustments are supportive of the need fulfillment of individuals, no problem exists. However, often this is not the case. The task of the social worker then is to focus on both the personal trouble (individual need) and the public issues (system need). The response identifies the needs of all persons and systems involved and seeks to enable each to function in such a manner that need fulfillment is complementary and the needs of all are fulfilled. This response calls for identification of all the component parts (systems) of a situation in which need exists. It also calls for consideration of the need of each system in relation to the situation. A social systems analysis of human functioning demonstrates the great complexity of that functioning and thus leads to responses that consider this complexity. Social systems theory is conceptualized in a variety of ways. The conceptualization used in this book sees any system as having structural, functional, and developmental aspects.

When considering the structure of a social system, the relationships among parts and wholes are of prime interest. Usually a **focal system,** or **holon,** is identified. This system is itself made up of parts, or subsystems, and it is also a part of other systems. All systems are more than the sum of their parts. The parts are interacting and interdependent. The relationships among parts and wholes are relatively stable. Sometimes the relationship between systems is referred to as a *network.* Systems theory focuses on communication patterns, on the transactions among the parts, and on the relationships among parts. The **boundary** of any system is an important structural concept—an imaginary line drawn around the focal system. It may be relatively open or relatively closed. **Openness** and **closedness** refer to the ease with which ideas, energy, resources, people, or information can enter or leave the system. Closely related to the concept of boundary are *environment, situation,* and *frame of reference.* These all refer to the larger systems within which a focal system exists. Other structural considerations include **steady state, equilibrium,** and **homeostasis.** Although each carries a slightly different meaning, they all refer to the balance that exists among the various parts of the system. This balance is not fixed or static but is maintained within a range of change that allows the system to function and maintain itself.

The functioning aspects of the system are related to the use of energy, the manner in which a system carries out its purpose, and the way it maintains itself. Terms from communication theory such as **input, throughput, output,** and **feedback** are used. **Equifinality,** the capacity of two systems to achieve identical goals when starting from different conditions, and **multifinality,** beginning from similar conditions and achieving different end states, are also used. System needs are fulfilled by means of communication among the parts or across the systems boundary, by means of a decision-making process, and by using resources both inside and outside the system to carry out the tasks necessary to accomplish its functions. A means of task distribution (specialization) often develops. In order to be functional, each system develops these processes over time, not only as a way of accomplishing the necessary tasks but also as a means of maintaining itself. Goals and norms for functioning are established, and roles and relationships are created. The system develops its unique way of functioning.

Developmental aspects of a system relate to the continuous process of change in any system. Each system progresses through identifiable stages of development. If this does not occur, the system becomes less capable of using its energy and carrying out its function, which is known as **entropy. Negative entropy**—or efficient use of energy and the development of means for adding new energy from across the system boundary—results in greater specialization and complexity in the organization of a system. No system can maintain a status quo; the system either tends toward entropy or toward negative entropy. The process of development is continuous, and systems are in a constant process of change. Change in any part of a system brings about change in the system itself.

When we apply social systems theory to families, we need to consider the family itself as a system and we also need to consider the family as part of larger systems. The application of social systems theory to the family is referred to as **family systems theory.** The family as a system is seen as having structure, functioning, and development. The structure of the family includes its subsystems, which are classified by types of relationships. The marital or couple subsystem is made up of the adults who head the household. This can be a marital pair, an unmarried couple, or a single person without a partner. This relationship subsystem is considered separately from any role they might have as parents. The subsystem is generally responsible for organizing and running the household. The parent subsystem can be comprised of married or unmarried biological parents, married or unmarried stepparents, a single parent who is divorced or unmarried, or adoptive or foster parents. As parents, this subsystem is responsible for making decisions and carrying them out regarding child-rearing practices and tasks. The parent–child subsystem is made up of the relationships between parents and children, stepparents and stepchildren, adoptive parents and adopted children, or foster parents and foster children. It may also include grandparents or guardians raising children. The fourth subsystem is the sibling subsystem. This can include full and half siblings, stepsiblings, adopted siblings, and various combinations of sibling relationships in foster care.

In addition to considering the relationship subsystems in the family, the structure of the family considers family cohesion. This includes its internal and external boundaries and how open or closed they are. Internal boundaries are boundaries between subsystems. External boundaries are those between the family system and the environment. Cohesion also refers to separateness or connectedness among family members. Within the family there are family rules and roles that are also part of the structure of the family system. Family rules refer to prescribed expectations for behavior. Roles are sets of behavior that can be expected from certain family members.

In terms of functioning, the family system develops patterns of communicating, decision making, conflict resolution, and adaptive and coping mechanisms. Functioning also includes how roles are performed and how the family maintains itself as a system.

Family development involves the way in which the family is structured and how it functions over time. Some theories of family development have been proposed that consider stages of development that families experience. These theories are primarily organized around having and raising children and cycles of marriage and divorce. However, the various forms of family life we identified in this chapter do not lend themselves well to any single aspect of development.

These elements of family subsystems are developed further in Chapter 5, in which family assessment is examined and in Part III where we consider generalist practice with the four family subsystems.

An Ecological Perspective

Closely related to systems theory is an **ecological perspective.** The term *ecology* comes from the biological theory that studies the relationship between organisms and the environment. An ecological perspective includes the environment in the change process and encompasses human development, human diversity, and social systems theory. This approach bridges some of the gap between focusing on the person and focusing on the environment. In an ecological view, the environmental side is made more relevant to people's everyday lives by including it in a comprehensive manner. Carol Meyer and Carel Germain are generally considered major contributors to the development of this perspective.[18]

From an ecological perspective, need is a condition of the relationship between a person or people and their environments. People and their environments have needs and resources. Needs are met when the environment responds to a person in a way that satisfies a need and the person responds to the environment in a way that satisfies needs in the environment. A mutually beneficial interaction between person and environment is desired. When needs are met, a state of **congruity** exists. There is agreement or harmony—a "fit"—between the person and the environment.

Unmet need reflects an imbalance between the responses of the person and the environment. Sometimes needs are not met because there are insufficient resources available. More often, the interaction between the person and the environment is not balanced in a way that can sustain the needs of either one or both over time. This results in a state of **incongruity**—that is, a lack of agreement or harmony between the person and the environment.

An **ecosystems perspective** is a subset of the ecological perspective and involves all the systems in a person in environment approach, including the physical environment. It examines the exchange of matter, energy, and information among these systems over time, including past, present, and future. These exchanges are also called **transactions.** Changes in these exchanges in one part of the ecosystem will affect other parts of the ecosystem.

In planning for change, an ecosystems approach considers the impact of change on all the systems involved. Meeting needs is not simply a matter of meeting the needs of one person at one moment in time. If needs are met at the expense of other people or systems in the environment, and if transactions between systems are not balanced in a way that results in mutual benefit, then, over time, the client will have difficulty in maintaining any benefits from the social work endeavor. If a balance is not found, there is the likelihood that the situation will either return to its previous state or perhaps worsen. Using this perspective to assist clients in meeting needs means facilitating changes in the person, the environment, and the transactions between person and environment in a way that ensures a balance between needs and resources over time.

A Strengths Approach

In a **strengths approach** the worker moves from looking at deficits to looking at abilities and assets. This approach recognizes the importance of empowerment, resilience, healing, and wholeness in working with people. Membership (or belonging) is seen as essential to well-being. The development of this approach has been led by the social work faculty at the University of Kansas, in particular Dennis Saleeby.[19] Two of the basic tenets of this approach are that (1) "every individual, group, family, and community has strengths"[20] and (2) "every environment is full of resources."[21]

In responding to need, social workers should assist the client in identifying strengths and resources in herself and in her environment and then use these to create an appropriate response to the need. There are some critical reasons for incorporating a strengths approach into the process of meeting needs. Policy changes in human services have resulted in limitations on the length of service available to clients and an emphasis on brief, **solution-focused intervention.** Interventions that focus on deficits and dysfunction and look at the past to understand pathology do not lend themselves well to brief intervention. A strengths approach is focused on the future and fits much better with shortened time frames. This approach builds on strengths and capacities that the client and the environment already have rather than relying on the acquisition of new skills and resources. Thus, a more solid foundation for changes that do occur is ensured. In addition, the worker can identify and build a support system in the existing environment designed to maintain a new balance in the person in environment ecosystem.

In this text, an ecosystems approach and a strengths approach are combined with the problem-solving process to form an approach in which the social worker facilitates growth and change as a response to need. The focus is on the concerns and needs of the family in interaction with the environment. In responding to need, the worker develops an understanding of person or family in environment and then assists the family in developing and carrying out a plan for meeting needs. In accomplishing this, the strengths, abilities, assets, and capacities of family members, family, neighborhood, and community are included.

Human Diversity

Although there are common human needs, people fulfill those needs in different ways. The way in which needs are fulfilled is greatly influenced by cultural factors, as well as by physical and mental disabilities, socioeconomic factors, age, gender or sexual orientation, and discriminatory practices against certain groups in our society. The human diversity approach is useful in considering human need in a multicultural society.

A **human diversity approach** brings together understandings about the nature of culture, disability, gender, age, and sexual orientation and their effects on the development and functioning of human beings. Given the power differential inherent in a structured society, this perspective is specifically concerned with the effects of social institutions on human behavior.

The concept of human diversity is based on the premise that U.S. society is composed of a wide variety of cultures and diverse groups. Members of some cultural and diverse groups have difficulties in meeting needs because they differ from the dominant cultures or groups of U.S. society. Some of these groups have experienced prejudice and discrimination; some have experienced poverty and institutional racism—the built-in characteristics of societal institutions that have a negative effect on certain segments of society. These segments of society are further affected because they tend to be rendered less powerful in modifying societal institutions to better provide culturally or diversity congruent means for meeting human need.

A human diversity approach considers human behavior from the position of cultural relativity. It sees normal behavior as an irrelevant concept and behavior as appropriate or inappropriate relative to the social situation in which a person is operating. What may be appropriate in one situation may be inappropriate in another. Differences in developmental patterns found in different cultures should not be considered as necessarily abnormal. According to this approach, the response to need is not to measure norms but to determine the meaning of perceptions, experiences, and events as they affect the growth and functioning of individuals in their own cultural contexts.

Ronald Federico, discussing the concept of human diversity, believed behavior was influenced by three factors: (1) genetics, (2) culture, and (3) society. Genetic influences include both mental and physical growth potential, the ability to tolerate stress, and ways of responding to stress. Cultural influences include life goals, behavior patterns, resource utilization patterns, self-concepts and attitudes, and ways of perceiving events. Social influences include the social institutional structure, which comprises systems of socialization, social control, social gratification, and social change. These three sets of influences—genetic, cultural, and social—interact in a complex manner.[22] This conceptualization can also be applied to conditions that are not cultural in source, such as developmental disability, blindness, or chronic physical illness.

Dolores Norton, who developed a similar concept, "the **dual perspective,**" sees each person as part of two systems: (1) the nurturing system, which includes the family and immediate community environment (the culture of an individual), and (2) the sustaining system, which includes the organization of goods and services, political power, economic resources, educational system, and larger societal systems. If the perspective of the two systems is such that there are broad areas of incongruence between the two, then individuals are prone to difficulties in functioning.[23] Such individuals will have unique needs. In our society, this incongruence is particularly evident in the situation of women and people of color. The dual perspective provides another way of considering human development and functioning in a diverse society. The response to need lies in helping individuals and groups find ways of living together in such a way that maximizes opportunities to meet the needs of all.

In order to understand human need, the social worker must also have significant knowledge about the role of environmental factors as they affect the development and functioning of individuals. Environmental factors include social, economic, geographical, and climactic conditions that are a part of the immediate surroundings of the individual. Discriminatory attitudes toward the person, extremes of climate, and sociocultural expectations all influence individual behavior. The worker should also understand the effect of disabling conditions on individual functioning and development, including physical and mental disabilities as well as prejudice and discrimination. The causes as well as the nature and effects of prejudice and discrimination should be understood, as should differences in lifestyle patterns among socioeconomic groups.

To understand such environmental factors, a social worker needs to have considerable knowledge of the culture of the ethnic and racial groups with which he is working. This involves knowledge of a cultural group's history, values, mores, family and community patterns, attitudes and thinking patterns, religious traditions, child-rearing practices, and ways of coping with change and stress. Also important are the group's experiences in relating to the dominant culture, which involves social and economic factors and acculturation experiences and their results. The worker needs to be cognizant of the different subgroups that exist within any cultural group. This knowledge may be used to identify special needs of individuals and groups of individuals that arise in relation to their development and functioning because of human diversity.

Some workers substitute the term **special populations** for human diversity. There is a risk that this term can lead to stereotyping people according to the population groups to which they belong. In contrast, the concept of human diversity encourages social workers to look at diversity in an individual manner and recognizes that diversity is more than identification with a specific population group.

Diversity Competence

Diversity competence is the ability to provide services to families in a manner that is acceptable within their diverse group. Before a worker can understand the influence of diversity on any specific client or family, she must understand that diversity group generally. It takes special effort to gain such understanding, but social workers are responsible for knowing the general characteristics of any group with whom they are working. Acquiring this knowledge can be accomplished in several ways. One approach involves undertaking formal study through coursework or reading books and articles about a diversity group. Another way to gain understanding is to seek out members of the group or people with expertise working with a particular group. However, the most important approach is to recognize that the client is an expert, not only with respect to his or her diversity but also in how he or she experiences that diversity. The worker should encourage clients to teach her about their diversity. It is also important to understand the individuality of each person in the context of his or her diversity. As important as this understanding is, it is not sufficient; the worker must also understand how the dominant society has affected individuals of a particular group. A person's needs arise from the expectations of the cultural group and from the attitudes of, and relationships with, the dominant society. In addition, restrictions on the diverse group that arise from the dominant society must be understood. It is also important to consider the range of differences that exist in any cultural group. Cultural understanding recognizes that persons in situations operate uniquely within the diverse group just as they operate uniquely in the larger social setting.

The influence of social class is another factor that must be taken into account in understanding the individual within a culture. In considering an ethnic culture, it is important to separate culture from social class. In other words, how much of the diversity is the result of membership in a cultural group, and how much is because the person lives in poverty? According to John Longres, minority status is not simply a matter of cultural difference but also is related to relative power, privilege, advantage, and prestige of a group within society (social class is an important consideration here). He pointed out that these factors lead to the individual's perception of her place in society and her identity. This leads to help-seeking and help-using behaviors and influences the ways people of minority status perceive problems.[24] Kenneth L. Chau noted that unless "impediments to individual progress are taken into consideration in needs assessment, the meaning and significance of the client's attempt to solve problems may not be properly understood."[25]

Human diversity is not only ethnic or racial but also involves age, gender, physical or mental ability, physical appearance, religious affiliation, sexual orientation, and socioeconomic standing. When diverse persons form an identifiable group with a common culture, factors of cultural diversity exist, and worker understanding of that culture is important.

Race, color, national origin, religion, and ethnicity are aspects of, or factors related to, culture. Although the United States professes to be a nation that welcomes people with diverse roots or backgrounds, the actual experience of most of these groups has been quite different. Historically, the group that has been dominant politically, economically, and socially in the United States has been males of white northern European Protestant heritage. The signers of the Declaration of Independence were nearly all in this category, along with most of our presidents and our early state and federal leaders. In addition to sharing this heritage, many of our founding fathers were also among the wealthier members of society. People who have not shared this heritage have experienced a long history of discrimination and oppression. Most African Americans are descended from slaves and have had difficulty in gaining political, economic, or social justice and influence. These individuals continue to struggle against prejudice and discrimination, despite laws outlawing them.

Native Americans have also had a difficult experience with the dominant U.S. culture. Some would categorize past U.S. policy toward various Native American tribes as genocidal. At the very least, history shows a pattern of broken treaties and promises. Today, many Native American tribes live on reservations where poverty, unemployment, alcoholism, and hopelessness are epidemic. Hispanics have seen nearly half of their native country, Mexico, taken from them as a result of the Mexican-American War. Many of those who remained after the war were deprived of their property and not given the full rights of citizenship that were promised. Today, changes in immigration policy are often aimed at restricting Hispanic immigration. The attacks on bilingual programs launched by certain groups in the United States are aimed at Hispanics, as are the "English only" movements. Asians have also had a long history of unfair and discriminatory practices with regard to immigration laws. World War II, the Korean War, and the war in Vietnam were fought against Asian countries, and, as a result, a considerable amount of prejudice and stereotyping toward Asian Americans lingers. In a more extreme example of discrimination against Asians, during World War II, many Japanese Americans living on the West Coast were incarcerated in detention camps. German and Italian Americans did not experience this fate.

In terms of religion, although the practice of most religions has been tolerated for the most part, opportunity for economic, political, and social equality has been limited. Catholics are the largest denomination in the United States, but they have had to fight for a share of political power. As of 2007, the only president of the United States who was

Catholic was John F. Kennedy. No one has ever been either president or vice president who is not male, white, and Christian. With the terrorist attacks on September 11, 2001, people of the Islamic faith have increasingly been targeted for prejudice, discrimination, and various forms of hate crimes, including murder. It is regrettable that some people have responded to the events of 9/11, which represented one of the most terrible hate crimes in our history, by perpetrating more hate and hate crimes.

This history of prejudice, discrimination, and oppression of groups that are not made up of white Protestant males creates a suspicion and distrust of people who are white in most members of diverse groups. These attitudes present significant barriers to developing the knowledge and skills needed for diversity competent practice. In addition, most students in the United States are taught a Eurocentric view of U.S. history that primarily concentrates on the exploits of white American males of European descent and is nearly devoid of any negative aspects of our history. Thus, the average student knows very little of the struggles that people of color, members of non-European ethnic groups, and members of non-Christian faiths have had to face in fighting for their rights. Instead, many students have been indoctrinated with the conservative view that equal opportunity has been available to all and that those who are not doing well have only themselves to blame.

Elaine P. Congress developed the culturagram as a tool in understanding culturally diverse families. This tool can also be used to understand the culturally diverse individual. Aspects of the culturagram include various circumstances for the individual or the family related to immigration, along with "language spoken at home and in the community, contact with cultural institutions, health beliefs, holidays and special events, impact of crisis events, and values about family, education, and work."[26] The worker can use the construction of the culturagram to understand the culturally diverse family.

Some types of diversity do not exist as a cultural group. For example, a person with a physical disability may not identify with other persons with physical disabilities; nevertheless, that person may be subject to discrimination, stereotyping, expectations, exploitation, opportunity restriction, and the like. The societal attitudes and behaviors toward the person with diversity are important in identifying need because of diversity; also important is the person's attitude toward self as a person with diversity. It is important to consider the impact labels can have on people with diversity. It is preferable to say the word *person* or *people* first so that the emphasis is on the person rather than on the "differentness" or diversity. Thus, it is better to say "person with a disability" rather than "disabled person" or "handicapped person."

Age is also classified as a diversity factor. People who are at the extremes of age are often marginalized in U.S. society. Children and people who are older find it difficult for their voices to be heard. They do not typically find themselves valued. Children have limited rights. The predominant view is that parents have the right to raise their children as they see fit. Child poverty and child abuse and neglect are major social problems that seem to make the news only when a child dies. On the other end of the spectrum, workers who are older may find themselves without jobs when companies downsize. Middle managers and employees with higher salaries are the most likely targets, as opposed to younger workers with lower salaries. Adults who are older, particularly women, too often find themselves living on limited incomes and with inadequate health care coverage. In the United States, people who are older do not typically enjoy the high regard that older individuals have in many other countries. Issues related to age generally are attributed to overvaluing young adulthood and to the U.S. economic system, which places a high value on wealth and productivity. Children and people who are retired are not participating in the production side of the economy and are even seen by some as economic liabilities. Similar attitudes occur regarding people with physical or mental disabilities. In the not-so-distant past, people with disabilities were isolated in institutions. Before that, many were hidden away by their families in cellars, attics, or sheds. Although attitudes toward people with physical disabilities have improved somewhat, attitudes toward people who are mentally ill continue to be predominantly negative.

One group that has received considerable attention in terms of diversity is women. Women are not a cultural group, although there is a sense of culture in subgroups of women such as feminist groups. It is important to see women as having a particular kind of diversity and as having been affected by social factors that can undermine their capabilities, opportunities, and self-perceptions.[27] During times of social change, it is particularly important to determine an individual's orientation toward that change by identifying attitudes and self-image in relation to change issues. Major social change has been taking place with respect to the role and function of women. Thus, social workers should be aware of a particular female client's orientation toward this change, of how she perceives society affecting her as an individual, and of her view of her role and function as a woman. It is especially important that female social workers not assume that all women have or should have the same attitudes toward the women's movement that they may hold.

Two other groups that have experienced considerable discrimination and oppression are gays and lesbians. There is generally a moralistic or religious basis used to rationalize this discrimination. The assumption is that gays and lesbians have chosen to be attracted to the same sex. Given the overwhelmingly negative attitude of the dominant society toward homosexuality, one might wonder about using the words *choice* or *preference*. Increasingly, research indicates that human sexuality is much more complex and that people cannot really be dichotomized into heterosexual and homosexual beings. Biological and genetic factors seem to play important roles in sexuality, along with environment. Thus, the term sexual orientation seems more appropriate. Even if it were legitimate to use the term *choice* regarding sexuality, there is no room in social work or in a truly democratic society for discrimination against or oppression of gays and lesbians or against any individual or group.

If the worker is to become diversity competent, he must be able to understand his clients from the client's perspective. Applying Dolores Norton's dual perspective to working with all forms of diversity, the worker needs to understand the effects of both the nurturing and the sustaining systems on the individual.[28] The response of the family and the immediate community environment to the individual's diversity is important to the individual's self-worth and sense of personal well-being. People can face a considerable amount of negative messages from the sustaining systems (organizations and larger societal systems) if there are messages of support, acceptance, and love from the nurturing systems. A good example of this is the "black is beautiful" message. African Americans who receive this message from within their family systems can develop healthy self-esteem even in the face of continuing prejudice and discrimination from the larger society. However, negative messages from the nurturing systems can be devastating even if the larger society is accepting of the diversity. Of course, if the larger society is also negative, the destructive messages can be overwhelming. A good example of this would be the reaction to the coming-out process for gays or lesbians. Although there may be increased tolerance for, and even some acceptance of, gays and lesbians in the larger society, there can be negative consequences from the nurturing system. If the family is rejecting, the person may feel totally cut off from his nurturing system. If he is fortunate enough to have a substitute nurturing system, such as friends or a gay community, he may be able to receive enough support and acceptance to weather these negative reactions.

Social workers must be attuned to current and past experiences of members of groups that have suffered prejudice, discrimination, and oppression. Some workers may be reluctant to consider historical facts regarding prejudice, discrimination, and oppression toward diverse groups. However, current attitudes are based on and reflect these past practices. The vestiges of these past practices can be found in attitudes held by diverse groups toward people from the dominant group and those held by the dominant group toward the diverse group.

The Family Ecosystem

In ecological terms, person in environment represents an ecosystem. For families, we refer to this as family in environment or a family ecosystem. An **ecosystem** includes the person(s), all of the systems with which the person(s) interacts, and the larger environment, along with the transactions among the person(s) and systems.[29] Thus, a family and its environment are seen as a unified whole in which the various parts are interdependent. Families and family members are influenced by their environment and, in turn, influence the environment by their actions. In developing an understanding of a family ecosystem, the worker seeks to understand the feelings, thoughts, and actions of family members, the human systems in the environment, and the transactions of family members and systems in the environment, along with understanding the effects of diversity on the ecosystem.

A combination of ecosystems and strengths approaches gives the worker a powerful means to assist families in meeting their needs beyond the immediate situation. This approach also brings the environment into play in a positive way and dramatically expands potential resources for change well beyond the worker or the family. Instead of limiting the possibilities to whatever the worker or family brings to the helping situation, the worker and family can seek other possibilities by tapping into resources in the environment. In addition, as the family is able to experience this expanded range of resources with the worker, family members are empowered to use this approach in working to meet other needs, now and in the future.

In understanding the ecosystem, the worker who is striving to become diversity competent also considers the attitudes toward diversity in her community and agency. She looks at each of the groups identified from her understanding of diversity. She looks for signs that indicate that diversity is valued by the community. She looks at patterns of race and ethnicity in the community. She considers to what extent these patterns represent current or past discrimination toward various groups. She observes how people of color, women, children, and people who are older or disabled are valued and respected. She evaluates community attitudes toward gays and lesbians. Some of these indicators are apparent in the institutions and services available to various groups. Some cannot be seen but can be heard in the stories of people who live in the community. As she becomes more diversity competent, the worker learns to look at the environment from a diversity perspective and to be an active listener.

SUMMARY

This chapter provides an introduction to generalist social work practice with families. In understanding practice with families, it is important that the worker have an appreciation for the variety of families in the United States. In addition to nuclear families made up of husband, wife, and children, families may include those with extended family members, childless couples, families that are the products of one or more divorces, families with unmarried parents, single-parent families, families with grandparents raising grandchildren, and blended families.

In order to work with families, the social worker needs to understand the history of family work and foundation concepts and theories. These include family systems theory, including an ecological perspective, a strengths approach, diversity and diversity competent practice, and the family as an ecosystem. These concepts and theories provide the worker with the fundamental tools necessary to understand the family as a system along with the systems in its environment. These are also tools for helping families to bring about change.

QUESTIONS

1. With what family forms are you familiar? With what forms are you not familiar? How could you learn more about those with which you are not familiar?
2. Describe the various elements that make up a system and apply these to a family system.
3. What is meant by the term *ecosystem*? Describe your family's ecosystem.
4. What does it mean to be diversity competent?
5. What knowledge and skills do you possess that would be strengths in working with families? What knowledge and skills do you need to acquire? How might you get these?

SUGGESTED READINGS

Johnson, Louise C., and Yanca, Stephen J. *Social Work Practice: A Generalist Approach,* 9th ed. Boston: Allyn & Bacon, 2007 (Chapters 1–4 and 13).

Fong, Rowena, and Furuto, Sharlene, Eds. *Culturally Competent Practice: Skills, Interventions, and Evaluations.* Boston: Allyn & Bacon, 2001.
Lum, Doman. *Culturally Competent Practice: A Framework for Understanding Diverse Groups and Justice Issues,* 3rd ed. Pacific Grove, CA: Brooks/Cole, 2007.
Saleeby, Dennis, Ed. *The Strengths Perspective in Social Work Practice,* 4th ed. Boston: Allyn & Bacon, 2007.

2

Foundations of Generalist Social Work Practice

LEARNING EXPECTATIONS

1. Understanding of the foundations of generalist social work practice.
2. Understanding of the history of generalist social work practice.
3. Understanding of the Johnson/Yanca model for generalist social work practice.
4. Understanding of the environment as an ecosystem.

We will begin by considering some of the fundamentals of social work practice from the generalist perspective. As we indicated in the introduction to Part I, a more thorough presentation of generalist social work practice can be found in our companion text *Social Work Practice: A Generalist Approach*. Some material from that text has been adapted and appears throughout this text. It is important for the reader to understand what it means to be a generalist social worker and how generalist practice has evolved over time. This background information gives some direction to the work that is done with various client systems in the wide variety of settings in which generalist social workers practice. The foundation material in this chapter provides a base for understanding our perspective on generalist social work practice in preparation for understanding our approach to generalist practice with families. It is assumed that the reader has had some exposure to generalist social work practice and that this text is being used to gain a more thorough understanding of how to work with families using a generalist approach.

As we indicated in the introduction to Part I and in Chapter 1, in a generalist approach the social worker assesses the situation with the client system and together they decide which systems are the appropriate *units of attention*, or focus of the work, for the change effort. The client system and the unit of attention may be an individual, a family, a small group, an agency or organization, or a community. The units of attention may also be any of the transactions among these systems. Thus, the generalist social worker needs to have knowledge that can be applied to a variety of systems.

This chapter considers important aspects of social work practice that form a foundation for professional practice as a social worker. This is intended to provide a common base for any student using this text. The first part of the chapter presents a brief history of generalist practice. The next part of the chapter considers generalist practice from our perspective. Finally, it is important to understand our blending of an ecosystems and a strengths approach to change and the environment as an ecosystem.

■ A BRIEF HISTORY OF GENERALIST PRACTICE IN SOCIAL WORK ■

The more formal development of generalist practice as an approach to social work practice took place in the 1960s and 1970s. This is the same time that bachelor of social work (BSW) programs began to become accredited. Generalist practice was adopted as the required curriculum for accredited BSW programs. During this time, most MSW programs were organized by sequences such as casework, group work, and community organization. More recently, the Council on Social Work Education (CSWE) which accredits both BSW and MSW programs has required that the BSW and the first year of the MSW curriculums be generalist practice. Although the formal development of generalist practice is more recent, the basic practices associated with generalist practice have been used since the very beginnings of social work. It is a blending of the two major approaches that evolved in early social work practice. Charity organization societies and settlement houses were developed during the late 1800s and early 1900s.

The early practice of social work can generally be characterized as pretheoretical. Workers saw needs and responded. They were caught up in the pragmatic philosophy of the times. They had preconceived views of the causes of poverty from individual defects such as laziness, mismanagement, or alcoholism. Workers used a "friendly visitor" approach to model what people needed to do to overcome their difficulties. The first major statement of social work practice theory was Mary Richmond's *Social Diagnosis*[1] in which she developed the original framework for assessment. However, rather than the term *assessment,* she used the term **diagnosis,** borrowing medical terminology from the **medical model.**

It was assumed that a cause–effect relationship existed; in other words, the social worker was looking for the cause of the problem. The cause was generally assumed to be either moral inadequacy or lack of appropriate use of social resources. The process of careful, thorough, systematic investigation of the evidence surrounding those in need of service and then the putting together of that evidence so that the worker gained an accurate picture of the situation were the heart of the social work process. This was **scientific philanthropy,** the study of the social situation. The information to be gathered was comprehensive and specific. The sources to be used included not only the client but also the family, other relatives, schools, medical sources, employers, neighbors, and pertinent documents.[2]

There seems to have been an assumption that the painstaking gathering of information would lead to an understanding of the cause of the problem. Further, it was assumed that if the cause were known, the remedy would be simple to apply. This idea, which grew out of the Charity Organization Society, assumed that the problem lay primarily within the individual. For example, poverty was considered a result of immorality, misuse of money, laziness, or excessive drinking. The Charity Organization Societies tended to focus on individuals and families and later developed into the casework approach.

Settlement houses, the originators of the group work and community organization methods, responded to the same social conditions differently. The source of problems was in the environment and in a lack of understanding about how to cope with one's surroundings. Workers used educational and enriching group activities and worked within the political system to bring about change.

The Charity Organization Society saw the cause of poverty as lying with the person, representing the conservative perspective. Settlement houses saw people who were poor as caught in situations that were not of their own doing. Economic and political conditions, including discrimination, oppression, and exploitation, left many people powerless to change their circumstances. Settlement workers sought to empower people through collective action to bring about change in the system. The radical version of this view was that a complete change in the system was needed. The liberal view held that radical change was unlikely but that amelioration of some social problems was possible by making the system more humane and responsive to people's needs.

The beginning of professional social work was a response to the social milieu of the early twentieth century, a time when new immigrants, with their different cultures and lifestyles, were of concern to the larger society. Progressives were working for reforms they believed would eliminate poverty. The developing social sciences were rooted in the belief that application of a scientific method could identify the causes of poverty and deviance. It was felt that if these causes could be identified, solutions would be apparent and social ills eliminated.

The early theory about the practice of social work reflected efforts to work with the new immigrants in ways that would enable them to live "moral lives" and thus avoid poverty. This theory was strongly based on the new sociological understandings and called for meticulously searching for facts that would illuminate the causes of deviance. This reflected the conservative perspective of the Charity Organization Society, which also sought to make helping more scientific. Science was seen as based on facts; facts led to answers. Thus, the answers as to how to help lay in the collection of facts. A strong emphasis on diagnosis (assessment) developed and remains an important legacy in contemporary social work practice.

In the late 1950s, a new statement of casework was presented by Helen Harris Perlman in *Social Casework: A Problem-Solving Process.*[3] She saw the casework endeavor as "a person with a problem comes to a place where a professional representative helps him by a given process."[4] Perlman continued using the term *diagnosis,* but her meaning seems closer to that of the term *assessment,* as used in contemporary social work literature. She saw diagnosis as dynamic, as "a cross-sectional view of the forces interacting in the client's problem situation."[5] Diagnosis was seen as an ongoing process that gives "boundary, relevance, and direction"[6] to the work. It was considered to be the thinking in problem solving.

Perlman saw casework as a process—a problem-solving process—and she developed the **process** or movement idea throughout her book. She held that the caseworker–client relationship was essential to the movement or work of problem solving. The professional relationship was perceived as being purposeful, accepting, supportive, and nurturing. Underlying Perlman's work is the assumption of human competence, with a goal of developing this competence. **Problems** are seen not as pathological but as part of life. The social-functioning focus of social work began to emerge.

Another trend of that era was the emergence of literature that began to identify and specify the theory base underlying practice. This base included not only the casework method but also group work and community organization, which drew heavily from a sociological theory base. Knowledge of small-group process was a major interest, and the assessment of group interaction was a major concern. The focus of these two methods was in part on growth as a process. Relationship with nonclients began to be considered. The groundwork was being laid to identify the common base of social work practice—those concepts that applied to practice regardless of the system being worked with.

The era was rich in theory development, just as it was rich in the development of new service possibilities, concern for new problem areas and new client groups, and the use of old methods in new ways. Theory development in that era focused on (1) the continuing development of traditional methods, (2) the development of generic or integrated approaches to practice, and (3) the development of new approaches to practice using new underlying assumptions for use in service to specific groups of clients.

During the 1960s, both the **diagnostic approach** (now called the **psychosocial approach**) and the **functional approach** were expanded and updated.[7] Both were approaching the stage of well-developed theory. Use of social systems theory and communications theory began to appear.[8]

During this period, important formulations of group work and community organization became available. These not only continued to develop the practice theory of these methods but also made it possible to identify the concepts that were universal to casework, group work, and community organization. Thus, the theoretical commonalities of all types of social work practice could be distilled.

Of particular interest is the movement from the use of the medical terms *diagnosis* and *treatment* to the more general terms *assessment* and *intervention.* As community organization theory developed, the use of the terms *assessment* and *intervention* was given additional support as commonalities were found.

Examination of the concept of **problem-solving process** during the early part of the era indicates that it was being used in all three traditional methods of social work: casework, group work, and community organization. The casework use of the problem-solving process is reflected in the continued importance of Perlman's approach during that era. Process came to imply movement through time.

The concepts of person in situation and client–worker relationship were again expanded in the period by the application of new social science theory. The 1970s saw a rapid rise in the use of social systems theory as important supportive knowledge for all social work. The concept of relationship enlarged. Relationship was seen as important for work with the client. The importance of many other relationships was noted in group work and community organization literature. There began to be discussion of **interactional skill.**

In 1970, two early attempts to conceptualize social work from an integrative point of view were published. Carol Meyer's *Social Work Practice: A Response to the Urban Crisis* stressed the need for a new conceptual framework because of limitations of current theory in relating to urban turmoil in the 1960s.[9] Harriett Bartlett's *The Common Base of Social*

Work Practice was written out of the need of the social work profession for specification about the nature of practice.[10] Both books reflected the development of the concepts of assessment, intervention, person in environment, relationship, and process. Although the books focused on the problems of integration rather than on the development of theory, they did introduce several useful concepts. Bartlett identified *social functioning, professional judgment in assessment,* and *interventive action.* Meyer noted *process of individualization, interventive points,* and *plan of action.* She saw the diagnostic process as a tool of assessment and intervention as having a variety of possibilities known as the **interventive repertoire.** These two books marked a turning point in theory development. No longer was theory to be developed for the traditional methods of casework, group work, and community organization. It was to be developed for the unified social work profession and to respond to particular problems and needs.

During the early 1970s, several textbooks appeared that presented conceptualizations that were integrative in approach.[11] A text by Allen Pincus and Anne Minahan received the widest acceptance. In their approach, social work was seen as a planned change, with the intervention plan being based on problem assessment. The assessment "identified problems, analyzed dynamics of the social situation, established goals and targets, determined tasks and strategies, and stabilized the change effort."[12] One major aspect of the approach was the use of influence—"effecting the condition of development of a person or system."[13] The use of **relationship** was seen as part of this process. The developing profession was moving toward new ways of thinking about practice, toward new practice conceptualizations.

Given the growing commonality of social work practice, it is not surprising that an important contribution of this era was the effort to develop what came to be known as *integrated methods* or **generalist practice.** New services were evolving and new groups of clients were being served. It was discovered that these clients did not fit nicely into traditional casework, group work, or community organization categories. Instead, a combination of methods was needed to respond to the complex problems and situations these clients presented. The efforts of the National Association of Social Workers and others toward the unification of the profession provided a milieu in which efforts toward identifying the commonality of theory could go forward. The federal legislation of the Great Society and the War on Poverty provided training funds that increased the capacity for knowledge building. The rediscovery of rural social work called for a generalist approach. The time was right, both in a societal and a professional sense, for this forward movement in the development of the theory base of social work.

A third trend of this era was the development of new approaches to practice that focused on specific needs. This trend began in the 1960s as the family became a unit of attention and as approaches for work with the family developed. Interest in short-term casework, particularly crisis intervention, also contributed to this trend. As social workers began to work with new problems and new client groups, approaches with more specific focus were needed for action with and for clients after a generalist approach had been used in the early stages of service. Concurrently, examination of current group work and community organization practice yielded the understanding that more than one approach had developed in each of these traditional methods.[14] The 1969 Charlotte Towle Memorial Symposium was a presentation of major theoretical approaches to casework practice.[15]

In this era, there was not as much agreement about practice approaches as there once had been. For example, social workers no longer agreed that the conceptual framework of person in situation underlay professional practice. Some of the important new practice approaches that evolved were crisis intervention, task-centered casework, solution-based interventions, and social–behavioral social work.

A social work practice was emerging in which a general theory base was used for the original response to need and for the assessment of client in situation. Then, using a relationship developed in the process, an intervention based on one of the more specific approaches was chosen from the intervention repertoire. The essence of generalist practice began to appear. Since that time a number of texts have been published on generalist social work practice. The first such text devoted to practice at the BSW level was the first edition of our companion text, *Social Work Practice: A Generalist Approach* by Louise C. Johnson in 1982. Since then, the text has been adapted for use in the first year of an MSW program now that generalist practice is the required curriculum.

The philosophy underlying generalist practice is best exemplified by practices that arose in the settlement houses. While practice in the Charity Organization Societies saw the need for change as lying with the individual, the settlement houses saw the need for environmental change. This broadened the arena for social work practice considerably. Although collective action was preferred, workers in settlement houses worked at whatever level was most appropriate. They would work with individuals, families, groups, organizations, or the community to bring about change. This is the basic approach used by the modern generalist social worker.

■ THE JOHNSON/YANCA MODEL ■ OF GENERALIST PRACTICE

In this chapter we present a summary of the Johnson/Yanca model of generalist practice.[16] It is important for the reader to be familiar with this generalist model of social work practice for two reasons. First, generalist practice with families assumes that a generalist approach to the situation has chosen to focus on the family or a subsystem of the family. It is recommended that the reader have an understanding of and use this model to determine whether the family or one of its subsystems is the appropriate unit of attention or focus for the intervention. Second, the practice with families as presented in this text uses the Johnson/Yanca model for work with a family or a family subsystem. In this chapter the Johnson/Yanca model is presented in summary form.

The Johnson/Yanca model of generalist practice is continually evolving. It was first developed in the 1970s when Louise Johnson began to specify the nature of integrated practice, which was a developing conceptualization of social work practice at that time. It looked at practice with individuals, small groups, and communities for concepts that were used in practice with all of these systems. In doing this, five concepts were identified in an historical context: assessment, relationship, person in environment, process, and intervention. As the integrative model became the generalist model of social work practice, two other systems were included: families and organizations or institutions. This work resulted in the publication of *Social Work Practice: A Generalist Approach* by Allyn & Bacon in 1983. The model continued to evolve with each subsequent edition of the book, based on teaching, practice experience, and developing trends within the profession. With the seventh edition published in 2001, Stephen Yanca joined Louise Johnson as co-author. He has contributed to the work by providing material on newer understandings used in generalist practice: an eco systems approach to practice; a strengths consideration; and, most recently, diversity competence. Another assumption made in developing the model was that it would focus on the learning needs of the undergraduate (BSW) student. Because the Council on Social Work Education required a generalist approach for the first-year curriculum for graduate programs, the text has been modified so it can also be used at the foundation level of masters practice.

Discussion of the major concepts of concern or need; creative blending of knowledge, values, and skills; and a change process focused on intervention into human transactions contained in the model follow. Also discussed are the two interwoven processes of the model: the interactional process and the social work process.

Concern or Need

In the model, a concern or need is brought to a worker or an agency. *Concern* is defined as a feeling that something is not right. It is interest in, regard for, and care about the well-being of oneself or other individuals. *Need* is that which is necessary for a person or a social system to function within reasonable expectations in a given situation. "They need" is need identified by others. "**Felt need**" is need identified by the client. The worker starts with need identification.

The identification of the need is considered by using several points of view representing the complexity of the human situation. These points of view include human development, human diversity, an ecosystems perspective, and a strengths approach. The **human development perspective** includes social, emotional, cognitive, physical, and moral or spiritual development. The human diversity point of view brings together understandings about the nature of culture, disability, gender, age, and sexual orientation and their effects on the development and functioning of human beings and other systems. An ecosystem point of view considers environmental factors (including the physical environment) and the exchange of matter, energy, and information over time—past, present, and possibly future. In the early consideration of conceptualizations that helped to explain concern and need, we used social systems theory. Now we believe that the ecosystems approach encompasses social systems theory. Important is the focus on change because change in one part of the environment affects change in other systems in the environment (family, small groups, organizations, and communities) and influences individual functioning. Social systems theory also brings to ecosystems theory the knowledge that all systems have structural, functional, and developmental aspects. A strengths approach calls for an assessment with emphasis on abilities and assets rather than on deficits and uses an ecosystems approach. This recognizes the importance of empowerment, resilience, healing, and wholeness in working with people. It reduces the emphasis on deficits and pathology and sees a focus on strengths and resources that can be used to facilitate growth and change. It places less emphasis on problems and problem solving than was true in earlier conceptualizations of the model.

Finally, a concern/needs approach to social work practice considers social functioning, which is seen as people coping with environmental demands.[17] Thus, a focus of the social work endeavor as it considers concern and need is on helping individuals and systems to cope and to deal with environmental factors impinging on social functioning.

Creative Blending of Knowledge, Values, and Skills

Social work has thinking, feeling, and doing aspects. In some ways these three elements relate to knowledge (thinking), values (feeling), and skills (doing). The Johnson/Yanca model identifies **knowledge** as a picture of the world and the humans in it. The ideas and beliefs about this world are based on reality, which is confirmable or probably so. The knowledge base used by social workers is a broad one. It is obtained from the liberal arts with emphasis on the social sciences and human biology. It contains knowledge about persons, their interactions, and social situations; knowledge about practice theory, which involves the nature of helping interactions, the process of helping, and a variety of intervention strategies; specialized knowledge needed to work with specific groups of clients; and the capacity to be reflective, imaginative, and creative in the use of the knowledge base. To have a sufficiently broad knowledge base, a social worker needs the following:

1. *A broad liberal arts base*—This includes a knowledge of the social sciences (sociology, psychology, anthropology, history, political science, and economics) to provide explanations about the nature of human society and the human condition. Study of the natural sciences provides tools for scientific thinking and an understanding of the physical aspects of the human condition. Study of the humanities aids in the development of the creative and critical thought processes; it provides an understanding of the nature of the human condition through the examination of creative endeavors and of the cultures of human society. The latter is especially important for diversity competence. A social worker is a person with a developed and expanded personal capacity gained by exposure to a broad, liberal educational experience.

2. *A sound foundation knowledge about persons, their interactions, and the social situations within which they function*—This includes knowledge about persons from emotional, cognitive, behavioral, spiritual, and developmental points of view. Such knowledge must consider the diversity of the human condition and the effect of diversity on functioning and development. Understanding of human interaction in depth is also essential. This knowledge includes one-to-one relationships, family relationships, and small-group relationships and the variety of these relationships in diverse populations. It also includes an understanding of the societal organizations and institutions that are a part of contemporary society and of the social problems that affect human functioning, especially those that are exacerbated by prejudice and discrimination.

3. *Knowledge about practice theory, with concern for the nature of helping interactions, of the process of helping, and of a variety of intervention strategies appropriate for a variety of situations and systems*—This includes knowledge of professional and societal structures and institutions for delivery of service to individuals in need of help and of methods

of adapting and developing the service structure for more adequate need fulfillment.[18] It also includes knowledge about effective ways of providing service to diverse individuals and families.

4. *Specialized knowledge needed to work with particular groups of clients and in partic-ular situations*—The choice of knowledge each worker includes in this area depends on the practice situations and on career aspirations. In diversity competent practice, the worker needs to be knowledgeable about the values and beliefs of the population, its experience with the dominant society, the manner in which help is given and received, and good prac-tices that need to be used with each group.

5. *The capacity to be reflective, imaginative, and creative in the use of knowledge ob-tained from a variety of sources*—It is especially important to be able to see the strengths in people and in their environments and to be able to use those strengths to build a vision for the future. To become diversity competent, the worker must be able to reflect on her knowl-edge about herself and knowledge about each diverse group. She must be willing to criti-cally examine her knowledge and be open to considering distortions that might be present as a result of prejudices and stereotypes. She must be able to acquire and use new knowl-edge about diversity from her clients and from professional sources such as articles, books, professional training, colleagues, and other sources.

6. *The ability to learn new and different ways of acquiring and using knowledge*—In diversity competent practice, the worker needs to become more familiar with the different ways of knowing that each diverse group may use in acquiring knowledge. In white male Eurocentric society, great value is placed on knowledge that is gained by the scientific method. Other groups value knowledge that is more experiential and passed on from earlier generations. Women may value knowledge that is acquired through relationships.

Values are not provable. They are what is desirable. They identify what is preferred. They act as guides for behavior. The social work endeavor considers several sets of values, including the client's, those of the community and agency, the worker's and those of the so-cial work profession. The latter have been clearly spelled out in the *NASW Code of Ethics*. (The *Code of Ethics* is available online at www.socialworkers.org/pubs/code/code.asp.) These values have often been expressed as principles of worth and dignity of the individ-ual, the right to self-determination, and the right to confidentiality. The social work en-deavor is based on the dual values of the worth and dignity of individuals and of social responsibility. These values can be expressed in the following principles for action:

1. People should be free to make choices.
2. Individuals are important; individual needs and concerns cannot be totally subjected to community needs.
3. Workers should use a nonjudgmental approach to persons and their concerns, needs, and problems.
4. The social work role involves helping or enabling, not controlling.
5. Feelings and personal relationships are important.
6. People have responsibility for others, for their needs and concerns.

Diversity competent practice requires the recognition and valuing of diversity. It does not recognize differences as superior or inferior resulting in value judgments of good or bad but rather simply as different. Good and bad judgments lead to prejudice, discrimination, and oppression. This in turn negates the worth and dignity of individuals and cultural groups and is counter to the social work value system.

Skill brings knowledge and values together and converts them to action, which is a response to concern or need. Skill may be defined as a complex organization of behavior directed toward a particular goal or activity. Social workers need both cognitive and interactive skills. Betty Baer and Ronald Federico have organized the skill component into four areas: (1) information gathering and assessment; (2) the development and use of the professional self; (3) practice activities with individuals, groups, and communities; and (4) evaluation.[19]

The *Educational Policy and Accreditation Standards* of the Council on Social Work Education[20] provide the official statement of the skill level expected of baccalaureate- and master's-level social work graduates. Two types of skills are called for (although it is impossible to completely separate them): cognitive skills and interactive or relationship skills. *Cognitive skills* are those used in thinking about persons in situations, in developing understanding about person and environment, in identifying the knowledge to be used, in planning for intervention, and in performing evaluation. *Interactive skills* are those used in working jointly with individuals, groups, families, organizations, and communities; in communicating and developing understanding; in joint planning; and in carrying out the plans of action. A social worker must be proficient in both types of skills.

This model sees the three elements, knowledge, values, and skill, as a creative choosing of what is applicable to a particular situation and creatively blending them for use in responding to the clients' and others' concerns and needs. The ability to combine appropriately and creatively the elements of knowledge, values, and skills calls not only for choosing and applying appropriate knowledge, values, and skills but for blending the three elements in such a manner that they fit together and become a helping endeavor that is a consistent whole. It involves identifying and choosing appropriate, often unrelated, bits of knowledge and using not only social work values but also those of the client and the agency as a screen for tentatively chosen knowledge. It calls for skillful application of the knowledge and values. Because each person and situation is different, the knowledge, values, and skills are different in any situation. There are no cookbooks or standardized procedures, only generalized ways of approaching persons in situations.

The Change Process

The blending of an ecosystems perspective and a strengths approach with problem solving creates a change process that allows the social worker to be creative and allows for the organization of a complex array of knowledge into a cohesive whole. It calls for moving from understanding need to identifying assets, abilities, and capacities of all systems involved in the situation. This process facilitates growth. It also sees the primary interventions as intervention into human transactions rather than change focused on interior systematic change. Originally, we conceptualized the change process as a problem solving process. Newer thinking focuses on strengths, resources, and growth rather than on deficits. Thus, we now talk about the change process. We then conceptualize the change process (social work process) as having four phases: assessment, planning, action, and evaluation and termination. The assessment process includes: identification of the concern or need, identification of the nature of concern or need, identification of potential strengths or resources in the ecosystem, selection and collection of information, and analysis of available information. The change process then involves two types of activities: (1) working within a relational/interactional framework with clients and others and (2) carrying out the helping process. Both are essential concerns of the model and are described as we envision them in subsequent sections of this chapter.

A strengths approach has contributed to practice theory by reducing the emphasis on deficits and pathology and focusing on strengths that can be used to facilitate growth and change.[21] An ecosystems perspective offers a way to organize and understand the environment and the transactional nature of person in environment. In our model, a strengths approach and an ecosystems perspective are blended with the traditional problem-solving process to form an ecosystems strengths approach to change. This approach views the change process as meeting needs in a way that facilitates natural growth and change in the person, the environment, and the transactions between person and environment. It sees the social work endeavor as aimed at identifying and utilizing the assets that are available in the person, the environment, and the transactions between person and environment to bring about change that fits with what the client's desires and the reality of the situation.

Ecological and strengths approaches have a health-based orientation. Both see growth and change as natural parts of human development over time and consider healthy functioning as a goal and as a reality for most areas of the client's life. It is not necessary to change everything about the person or the situation, only the area in which a need is not being met. In general, people are able to meet the majority of their needs in socially accepted ways.

An ecosystems approach sees need as arising out of an imbalance or incongruity in the transactions among systems. Person in environment is viewed as a system of systems in which the client and his natural environment are all a part of one ecosystem. The social worker and the client work together to identify the transactions that are out of balance. Using a strengths approach, they seek to rebalance the transactions based on the abilities, capacities, and resources available within both the client and the environment. The knowledge, values, and skills of social work, along with the strengths and resources within the client and the client's environment, are used in understanding the situation and in identifying possible goals.

Contributions from a strengths approach can become an integral part of the change process used in social work practice when (1) the focus of the helping process is on the unique individual or client system involved and on the possibilities for positive growth and change, (2) the strengths and competencies of the client system are respected and valued by the social worker and used as a major resource in the helping process, and (3) the client is involved in all phases of the helping process and is given maximum opportunity for self determination. Social workers who incorporate these principles in their work with client systems will discover that the change process is a useful tool to help the client reach his goals and objectives.

Blending these two approaches into assessment, planning, action, and evaluation allows the worker and the client to build on environmental and personal strengths in discovering ways to meet unsatisfied needs.

Diversity Competence

A recent addition to the model, although this way of thinking has been implicit for some time, is the concept of diversity competence. We use the term *diversity competence* rather than *ethnic* or *cultural competence* because there is great diversity in U.S. society; there is diversity beyond that related to ethnic or cultural groups. That diversity relates to socioeconomic class, political beliefs, religious beliefs, age, education, and culture of origin, to name a few of the differences that exist in modern society. Diversity competence calls for the use of **naturalistic inquiry.** That is, workers assume that they do not know what they do not know. It is a form of **inductive learning** and calls for the worker to learn from the client or others and not make assumptions based on preconceived notions. This makes clients and others equal partners in the change process. The client or other is expected to provide the understandings of her way of functioning, her cultural history, and her view of what is important in the change process. Diversity competence calls for the worker to seek from the diverse group understandings about culture, values, expectations, and other things that affect the use of help. It calls for the worker to develop a level of self-knowledge so that he does not bring expectations and beliefs to the helping situation that preclude gaining the necessary understandings for diversity competent practice. Chapter 3, "Diversity Competent Practice with Families," develops this aspect of the model to a greater extent.

In terms of the phases of the change process, a diversity competent approach is used throughout the process. The diversity competent worker incorporates her learning from the family into each phase of the process. She is careful to consider diversity as she conducts her assessment. She works with the family to develop a plan that is consistent with the diversity of the family. She uses direct and indirect practice actions that are comfortable for the family. She considers diversity in evaluation and is knowledgeable about the termination process for diverse groups.

Two Intertwined Processes

The separation of the interactional and the social work processes is artificial at best. Both take place at the same time. Each depends on the other. However, for purposes of understanding, we have chosen to discuss each process separately.

The Interactional Process

In its simplest form the **interactional process** involves a worker and a client working together on a concern or need in an environment. However, there are other interactional forms as well. Several clients may make up a family or small group. The "worker" may be a **team** of several helpers, all social workers, an interdisciplinary team, or a worker and other interested people. For a social worker to be most able to use the interactional process, she must have begun the lifelong task of self-understanding from a number of view points, including lifestyle and philosophy of life, her moral code and value system, her family and cultural roots, and personal needs, to name a few of the view points. (See Table 2.1, "A Guide for

Table 2.1   A Guide for Thinking about Personal Need

My Common Human Needs

1. What are my needs for food, shelter, and clothing? How do I meet these needs?
2. What are my needs for safety and to avoid pain and physical damage to self? How do I meet these needs?
3. What are my health care needs? How do I meet these needs?
4. What are my needs for love and belongingness? How do I meet these needs?
5. What are my needs for acceptance and status? How do I meet these needs?
6. What are my needs for developing my capacity and potentiality? How do I meet these needs?
7. What are my needs for understanding myself and the world in which I live? How do I meet these needs?
8. What other biological needs do I have?
9. How do I describe my spiritual development? What are major sources for this development? What are my present needs in this area?

My Developmental Needs

1. What are my needs based on my physical development? How do I meet these needs?
2. What are my needs in relation to my cognitive development? How do I meet these needs?
3. What is my present stage of psychosocial development?
4. What are my needs based on the development tasks of my current stage of development?
5. How well have I accomplished the tasks of earlier developmental stages?
6. What present needs do I have because of challenges related to not accomplishing these tasks?

My Needs Arising from Human Diversity

1. What in my lifestyle is "diverse" from the dominant lifestyle of my community?
2. What is the basis of the diversity? Is it race, culture group, gender, religion, disabling condition, or other?
3. What is the meaning of this diversity to me? How do I feel about myself in relation to this diversity?
4. What is the meaning of this diversity to my immediate environment? How does the environment deal with me as a diverse person?
5. How do I deal with the stresses and strains that exist because of diversity?
6. What strengths or special needs do I have because of my diversity?

My Needs Arising from Social Systems of Which I Am a Part

1. What expectations do the various social systems of which I am a part have of me? (These include family, peer group, school or work, organizations of which I am a member, neighborhood or cultural group, etc.).
2. What do I see as my responsibility toward the social systems of which I am a part?
3. What needs do I have in relation to these social systems, including the expectations and responsibilities related to them?

Thinking about Personal Need.") She also must have a sense of the use of self in professional activities, being able to use responsibility and authority appropriately. She needs to have developed skill as a diversity competent social worker. Furthermore, it is important to have skills for working with multiperson helping persons. This includes skill in collaboration, referral, and consultation.

The social worker understands what it means to become a client and how to develop a workable social history. (See Table 5.2, "Schema for Development of a Social History: Individual.") He recognizes the place of motivation, capacity, and opportunity in the helping endeavor and how to assess stress levels and crisis situations. Clients are always seen as individuals who are unique and have strengths. When the client or focus of service is a larger system, a systemic assessment is used to understand and work with that system.

All interaction takes place within an environment or ecosystem. This environment includes the client's personal life system, the agency providing the service, and the community of client and agency. (See Table 2.2, "Schema for the Study of a Geographic Community," later in this chapter.) Social workers need to develop skill in assessing and understanding the structure, functioning, and development of agencies, institutions, and various kinds of communities. (See Table 2.3, "Schema for the Study of a Social Agency," later in this chapter.) They need an understanding of how to work in bureaucratic settings.

Of prime importance for use of the interactional process with worker and client in an ecosystem are communication skills. These are necessary for the development of helping relationships. Communication skills are the heart of the interview and for work with families and small groups. They are the prime tools of the social worker.

Thus, the interactional process involves client (one or multiple persons), worker (one or multiple persons), and an environment, with communication as a primary tool. This is one of two major processes within the social work endeavor as seen in the Johnson/Yanca model.

The Social Work Process
The second process, which, as noted, is intertwined with the interactional process, is what we call the **social work process.** This is the process that encompasses the work that the worker(s) and client(s) do together. In the Johnson/Yanca model it has four phases: assessment, planning, action, and evaluation and termination. Although it is recognized that usually it is important to return to an earlier phase at some point during the process and sometimes the phases seem to be overlapping, for developing understanding each part is considered separately.

The assessment phase is carried out with the client(s). Clients are prime sources of information and will verify conclusions that are drawn based on that information. This is the viewpoint of the culturally competent social worker. There is a progression within the assessment process: (1) identification of the concern or need, (2) identification of the nature of the concern or need, (3) identification of the potential strengths and resources in the ecosystem, (4) selection and collection of information, and (5) analysis of the available information.

The work then begins to move into the planning phase of the process. Of prime importance again is the involvement of the client in this process. As assessment and planning progress, the worker and client identify the most appropriate target for developing change possibilities. It is here that individual, family, small group, organization, or community systems become the focus, and the work returns to the assessment process applied to the chosen focus for attention.

The planning phase not only involves identification of the most appropriate unit of attention based on client desires, worker competence, and the usual way of work of the agency but also identification of the strategy to be used. Strategy is an overall approach that specifies roles for worker and client, tasks to be carried out, and methods and techniques to be used. Of great importance is the specification of goal—the overall, long-range expected outcome of the process. As with assessment the client is involved in the planning process, and the plans developed are within the diversity context of the situation. Thus, we conceptualize a plan as having a unit of attention, goals, objectives (intermediate steps in reaching a goal), tasks, and a specified strategy for the work to be done. If the assessment yields desirability for a plan beyond the competence of the worker or the scope of the agency, then referral to another source for help should be considered. If such a resource is unavailable, then worker and client return to the assessment or planning process and seek a workable plan.

The action phase can be direct or indirect. Direct action is action with clients. It focuses on transactions of individuals within their environments or actions with families or small groups.

Direct practice action strategies, which fall within the purview of the generalist practitioner, include action taken to enable the development of relationships, action taken to enable the development of understanding of person in environment, action taken in the planning process, action taken to enable the client to know and use available resources, action taken to empower or enable clients, action taken in crisis situations, action taken to support the social functioning of clients, action taken that uses activity with clients as the basis for help, and action taken to mediate between clients and a system in their environments. Generally, generalist social workers, particularly at the BSW level of practice, do not use a clinical model of practice.

Indirect practice action strategies are used with persons or systems other than clients in order to help clients. The actions include those that use mediation, those that use influence in service of clients, those designed to change the environment, and those used to coordinate services. Case management is one approach to coordination of services.

The fourth phase of the social work process is evaluation and termination. Although it is assumed that evaluation will be a part of the termination phase, it is also recognized that evaluation is an ongoing part of the social work process. Termination, it is hoped, will come as a result of meeting the goals of the plan of action, of resolving the concern or need that initiated the work together. This kind of termination is planned for from the beginning of the social work process. However, it is recognized that termination can take place in an unplanned manner if a client decides to discontinue the endeavor. It can also take place when a worker leaves agency employment. Three components of termination work are disengagement, stabilization of change, and evaluation. As in all parts of the social work process, clients are heavily involved.

The social work process usually begins with a **feeling** of concern about something. This concern arises because a need is not being met. After **thinking** about the situation in a particular way—a process called assessment—some **action** is taken. This response—feeling, thinking, acting—is cyclical in nature. As the worker and client think and act together, new feelings of concern arise and new needs become apparent. As they act, they think about what is happening and gain new insights into the situation. The worker's knowledge about human development, human diversity, social systems theory, ecosystems, and a strengths approach is used in thinking about the situation. (See Figure 2.1.)

What has been presented in this chapter is the current formulation of the Johnson/Yanca model for generalist social work practice. It is assumed that this model will continue to

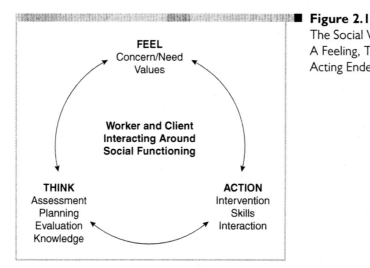

Figure 2.1
The Social Work Process:
A Feeling, Thinking,
Acting Endeavor

develop as new understanding of social work practice emerges. It is a model developed for use by BSW workers and is also used by the MSW worker, especially because it comprises the first year of the MSW curriculum. It is a model that can be adapted for use in a variety of social work practice settings and for use when the individual, family, small group, organization, or community become the unit of attention. It is used with clients to determine the appropriate unit of attention. It stresses a naturalistic approach, involving the client heavily in assessment, planning, action, and evaluation and termination. It is the model on which work with a family or a subsystem of a family is used in this text. Reader understanding of the model is essential for the family work discussed in the text.

THE ENVIRONMENT AS AN ECOSYSTEM

Environmental aspects of the ecosystem have not been as well developed as theories and understandings about systems. We know a lot more about the person or client side of the concept of person in environment. The environment as an ecosystem is introduced here to lay a foundation for understanding the environment as we discuss generalist practice with families.

In using an ecosystems approach that encompasses person in environment or family in environment, the *in* can serve as the focal point for social work services. The *in* can represent the *in*terface between the family as a system and the environment. **Interface** is the point of contact between two systems. At the *in*terface there are *in*teractions that occur. To the extent that both the family and the environment exchange resources, energy, or *in*formation via these *in*teractions, transactions take place. When these *in*teractions or transactions are balanced, both the family and the environment benefit. *In*terrelationships are formed, and a certain level of *in*terdependence exists. Change in one part of the ecosystem will *in*fluence other parts of the ecosystem. When the *in*teractions or transactions are out of balance, an *in*congruity exists between the needs of the family and the environment and resources available to meet those needs. This imbalance or *in*congruity gains the attention of the social worker and is the reason for and focal point of social work *in*tervention.

Combining ecosystems and strengths approaches with the change process gives the worker a powerful tool to assist families to meet their needs beyond the immediate situation. Using this approach brings the environment into the process in a positive way and expands potential resources for change. The worker and family can tap into resources in the environment. In addition, the family is empowered to use this approach in meeting other needs in the current situation and in the future.

The Community

The **community** is the environment of the worker, the family, and the agency. Different units of the community will have different impacts and influences on each other. The interactions of worker and family members are influenced by the transactions of the community. Service delivery is a part of the community system. Understanding these impacts and influences is an important aspect of generalist social work knowledge. To gain this understanding, it is first necessary for the worker to see the community as a social system. This knowledge is important not only because the environment influences the worker–family interaction but also because the community may be the client or it may be the target for intervention. In either of these cases, the worker usually works with individuals and small groups to bring about change in the community structure and functioning. For the generalist social worker, effort is usually focused on changing or developing a community resource that will in turn enhance the functioning of individuals and families. Whether the community or some element of it is the client or is the target of change, it is important to understand the community as a social system so that its strengths and resources can be included in promoting growth and change. Particular attention needs to be paid to these elements as the worker studies the community.

At a minimum, such knowledge calls for an awareness of the boundaries of the community, its component parts (individuals, families, associations, neighborhoods, organizations, institutions, etc.), and its environment. The worker also needs to be aware of the way the community functions and of its historical development.

The identification of a community's boundaries poses a substantial problem in a society of large cities and multiple institutional catchment areas. Is an agency's community a geographic place, the catchment area from which the clients come? Is a group of persons who support and sanction the agency its community? Is it the immediate geographic neighborhood in which it is located? Should the entire metropolitan area be considered a community? Or are community and neighborhood the same? Each of these questions may be answered affirmatively under certain circumstances.

There is also a time element in the concept of community. The *community system* functions in relation to issues and to provide services (e.g., education). The *community units* may interact only when dealing with those issues and in providing services. Community units are groups (both formal and informal), organizations, institutions, and other social systems that function within the boundaries of the community. Thus, the community system also may have a time element; it may exist only under certain circumstances.

The community may be seen as a geographic place. *Community* is a term also used to describe "nonplace" associations, such as the professional community or the religious community. When considering the kinship group, the extended family, or certain cultural groups, community is a related concept. The community system can have a wide variety of forms that can influence the transactions among individuals, families, and small groups.

Sociology furnishes us with several ways of considering a community. Ferdinand Tönnies saw a change in the relationships among people with the industrialization of society. He described this change as one from **Gemeinschaft** (rural "we-ness") to **Gesellschaft** (individuals related through structures in the community).[22] These differences among communities still exist. Rural or small communities function rather informally; urban or large communities tend to function more through formal structures. In searching for understanding of a community, a worker will find it useful to determine the kinds of relationships that exist in the community. Usually, there are different kinds of relationships, depending on the community functions involved.

Understanding the use of land adds another dimension to the study of a community. One method of using this concept is to draw maps of a community showing retail stores; wholesale businesses; industry (light and heavy); schools, churches, and other institutions; various types of residential dwellings; and the locations of various ethnic and socioeconomic groups.

Floyd Hunter's studies of community power are also useful.[23] The location of the community power structure is particularly important when trying to develop new services or to change existing services. This power structure may be formal or informal, elected or assigned. The impact of the power varies, depending on how the power holder and others perceive the power. It is exercised through initiating activity, legitimizing activity, giving approval to ideas and plans, implementing decisions, or blocking discussions of issues and of decisions. Usually, the impact of a particular power holder depends on the issue at hand. Some in power tend to have greater influence over economic issues than over social welfare issues. In larger communities, where power is more dispersed, there is a greater chance that power is related to specific segments of community life. In smaller communities, power tends to reside with one small group of people. Identification of not only the individuals in the power structure but also how they exercise that power and over what issues they have significant influence is another important ingredient of any community assessment.

Eugene Litwak's work on the significance of the neighborhood points out the neighborhood's importance for the family in meeting need. He identified several types of neighborhoods and their effectiveness in meeting need. The *mobile neighborhood* manages to retain its cohesion despite a rapid turnover of residents. In the *traditional neighborhood*, residents stay long term and that maintains stability. The *mass neighborhood* is one in which there is no mechanism of integration.[24] Understanding the kind of neighborhood a client lives in helps a worker understand a client and the resources that may be available for that client.

Roland Warren's work, which considers the community as a social system, is especially useful. He identified the locally relevant functions of a community as (1) production–distribution–consumption, (2) socialization, (3) social control, (4) social participation, and (5) mutual support. Each community has community units that carry out these functions. The business community has a major responsibility for production, distribution, and consumption. The schools are involved in socialization. Government is concerned with social control. Various clubs and organizations fulfill social participation needs. Social welfare organizations are involved in mutual support. Warren also noted that many community units have ties with structures and systems outside the community. These links are known as *vertical patterns;* relationships within the community are known as *horizontal patterns.* An example of this conceptualization as it relates to a church (a community unit) would be that the horizontal link would be a local council of churches or ministerial group; the vertical link would be to a denominational body. Warren saw the exploration of these patterns as a primary means for studying a community.[25]

There are differences among communities, just as there are among any category of social system. It is almost impossible to develop a scheme for classifying communities because of the many variables involved. Dennis Poplin identified three areas that seem important when considering differences among communities: size, the nature of a community's hinterland, and social–cultural features.[26]

Differences in size usually have been discussed on a rural–urban continuum. The U.S. Census Bureau uses a population of 2,500 as the division point between rural and urban. This leaves many different types of communities in the urban category. Another division point frequently used is 50,000, the population necessary for a Standard Metropolitan Statistical Area. In looking at nonmetropolitan community service delivery systems, Louise Johnson identified four types of communities: the small city, the small town, the rural community, and the reservation community.[27]

In subsequent work, Johnson identified two additional types of small communities: the bedroom community and the institutional community. The bedroom community is found near a larger community that furnishes jobs and often a variety of services for residents of the bedroom community. The institutional community contains a large institution, such as a state mental hospital, an educational institution, or a government site (state capital), which is the major employer in that community. She found that community characteristics are heavily influenced by the distance between communities that contain services (e.g., medical, social, and retail): Small communities that are at considerable distance from services in another community have a richer service system than do communities of the same size that are near communities from which they can obtain services.[28]

Metropolitan areas contain communities that differ: There are the central city, the suburban community, and the satellite city. In addition, some communities are inhabited by the upper class (Grosse Point, Michigan, for example). Some may have a reputation for being inhabited by bohemian, intellectual, or artistic persons, such as Greenwich Village in New York City; others are middle-class communities. There also are the ghettos and the barrio communities that have always been of particular concern to social workers. Ethnic communities have particular characteristics derived in part from the cultures of the groups occupying them. A social worker should possess an understanding of the characteristics of the particular kind of community with which he is working.

A community, then, can be considered as a social system that has a population, shared institutions and values, and significant social interactions among individuals and institutions. The institutions perform major social functions. A community usually, but not always, occupies space or a geographic area and has many forms. In modern society, several communities may overlap. Communities differ in the amount of autonomy they have and the extent to which persons living in the community identify with their community. When considering the community as a social system, understanding from many sources can be used to provide a theoretical base or to point to characteristics that should be considered in specific communities. In other words, different communities, because of differing characteristics, often call for different choices as to what is important to include in a community study.

In trying to attain understanding about a community and its impact on people, agencies, and institutions, a social worker faces two major problems. First is the identification of the system itself, which varies depending on the situation. Often a political unit is the defined system; this is a fairly easy way to define boundaries, but it is artificial and does not really consider parts of the community system that may lie outside the political boundaries. When looking at the neighborhood system, it is difficult to define boundaries.

Understanding a community calls for identifying the boundaries of the unit to be considered. Too large an area makes the study unwieldy; too small an area makes it too limited. In nonmetropolitan areas, the choice may be a small city or town. In metropolitan areas the choice may better be a neighborhood or some other manageable unit. Creativity is necessary in deciding how to define the community.

Social workers function in many different kinds of communities: large metropolitan areas, neighborhood settings, small cities, rural communities, large institutions, Native American reservations, and so on. Each kind of community has different characteristics. The study of any community as a social system provides understandings that can lead to greater degrees of client-congruent culture, to better use of available resources, to identification of when the community should be the focus of change, and to better identification of which work strategy is best suited to a particular situation.

Of special concern to social workers are diversity factors that exist in the community. The racial and ethnic makeup of the community are important to know. With regard to race and ethnicity, the worker should have knowledge about the degree to which various groups are integrated or segregated. He should note the attitudes of various groups toward each other. Is there respect or valuing of differences? Are there coalitions that have been formed? Are there adversarial relationships? How tolerant or intolerant are these groups toward each other? What groups hold power? Who has little or no power, and how does this reflect the general population? Similar questions should also be asked with respect to gender, age, and sexual orientation.

Some information about diversity can be obtained from census data or community surveys. However, much of this information is obtained more informally, through observation and discussion with key informants who know the history and have personal knowledge about various populations. For instance, knowledge about the gay or lesbian community may only be available from someone who is a member of the gay or lesbian community or from someone who works with these individuals.

The diversity competent social worker tunes in on the attitudes and stereotypes toward diverse groups and the affect that these have on members of each population. She is also aware of the values that each group holds and is alert to value conflicts and their affect on relationships. The worker identifies ways of helping that each group uses and seeks to improve her skills so that she can serve members of each group in a manner with which they are comfortable.

Second, the information that can be collected about any community is vast. It is never possible to obtain complete information. Some decisions must be made as to when there is sufficient information for understanding. Care needs to be taken to ensure that the information is representative of all units in a community. Some information can be found in a library in local history books, census reports, directories, and the like. Other helpful written material can be obtained from chambers of commerce, local government units, and volunteer organizations. Some information is not as easy to obtain; it may be known within the community but not shared with outsiders. This includes information about relationships among people and institutions and the community's decision-making and power structure. Information about norms and values may be obtainable only after observing and being a part of the community for some period of time.

In order to understand community interaction, gathering information from many individuals and small groups is essential. The generalist social worker uses both formal and informal interviews and observes and participates in small groups. The worker carefully observes a wide range of community interactions in order to develop understanding about the community and its impact on the functioning of individuals, groups, and families.

Because of the amount of material, in terms of both volume and variety, it is helpful if an organized plan is developed for gathering such material. Social workers can begin to gather some material before entering a new community. They also need to add to this material as long as they work in the community. As with all social systems, the community system continues to change. In Table 2.2 one means of organizing a community study considers major subsystems related to Warren's locally relevant functions. The table provides a means to identify possible impacts, influences, and resources in the community

Table 2.2 Schema for the Study of a Geographic Community

I. Setting, history, demography
  A. Physical setting
    1. Location, ecology, size
    2. Relationship to other geographic entities
      a. Ecological, political, economic, social
      b. Transportation, mass media from outside the community
  B. Historical development
    1. Settlement, significant events, change over time, cultural factors
  C. Demography
    1. Population
      a. Age and sex distribution
      b. Cultural, ethnic, racial groups
      c. Socioeconomic distribution
    2. Physical structure
      a. Who lives where?
      b. Location of businesses, industry, institutions
    3. Other
      a. Mobility
      b. Housing conditions
  D. Cultural setting
    1. Community norms, values, and expectations
    2. Community traditions and events

(continued)

Table 2.2   Continued

II. Economic system
    A. Employment
        1. Industry: nature, who employed, number of employees, influence from outside community, relationship to community and employees
        2. Distribution–consumption: retail and wholesale business, kind, location, ownership, employees, trade territory
        3. Institutions that employ large numbers of persons: nature, number of employees, types of employees, relationship to community, influence from outside community
    B. Other economic factors
        1. Stability of economy
        2. Leading business persons
        3. Organizations of business or organizations that influence the economic system

III. Political system
    A. Government units (structure and functioning)
        1. Span of control
        2. Personnel, elected and appointed
        3. Financial information
        4. Way of functioning—meetings, etc.
    B. Law enforcement, including court system
    C. Party politics: dominant party and history of recent elections
    D. Influence on social service system
    E. Services provided

IV. Educational system
    A. Structure and administration (all levels)
    B. Financing, buildings
    C. Students
        1. Numbers at each level or other divisions
        2. Attendance and dropout rates
    D. Instructional factors
        1. Teacher–student ratio
        2. Subjects available, curriculum philosophy
        3. Provisions for students with special needs
    E. Extracurricular activity
    F. Community relations

V. Social–cultural system
    A. Recreational–cultural activities, events
        1. Parks, public recreation programs
        2. Cultural resources: libraries, museums, theaters, concerts
        3. Commercial recreation
    B. Religious institutions and activities
        1. Churches: kind, location, membership, activities, leadership
        2. Attitudes: values, concern for social welfare issues, concern for own members
        3. Influence on community
    C. Associations and organizations
        1. Kind, membership, purpose, and goals
        2. Activities, ways of functioning, leadership

      3. Intergroup organizations and linkage within and without the community
      4. Resources available
   D. Mass media in community
      1. Radio, television, newspapers
   E. Ethnic, racial, and other diverse groups
      1. Way of life, customs, child-rearing patterns, etc.
      2. Relationship to larger community
      3. Structure and functioning of group
   F. Community persons
      1. Power persons; how power is manifest
      2. Leadership and respected persons

VI. Human service system
   A. Health care services and institutions
      1. Doctors, dentists, and other professionals
      2. Hospitals, clinics, nursing homes
      3. Public health services
      4. Responsiveness of health care system to needs of people
   B. Formal social welfare system
      1. Agencies in community: function, persons eligible for service, how supported and how sanctioned, staff, location
      2. Agencies from outside that serve community: location, services available, conditions of service, control of agency
      3. Conflicts among, overlaps, complementary factors of social welfare agencies
   C. Informal helping system
      1. Individuals and organizations
      2. How help is given, to whom
      3. Relationship to formal system
   D. Planning bodies
      1. Fundraising, regulatory, consultative

VII. General considerations
   A. Current concerns of community. Who is concerned? Why? What has been done about the concern?
   B. Customary ways of solving community problems. Who needs to be involved?
   C. Community decision-making process
   D. How autonomous is the community? Do various service areas coincide or are they different? How strong is the psychological identification with the community?
   E. Strengths of community in terms of "quality of life"
   F. Limitations of community in terms of "quality of life"

system and looks for both horizontal and vertical relationships. Table 2.2 provides a social worker with a guide for developing a working understanding of a community. The community study represents the assessment document for community practice.

    Once a social worker has the necessary information, it becomes possible to identify and understand current concerns in the community, the community decision-making process, and the manner in which that community usually solves its problems. Issues relative to community autonomy become clearer, as do differing service areas for different community agencies and institutions. For instance, the school district, the political boundaries, and the shopping service area are often different. Also, at this point it is possible to identify strengths and limitations of the community system. Because of the size and diversity of the units (subsystems) within the community system, different parts of the system will show different strengths and different limitations. One way of focusing the consideration of strengths and limitations is to consider the overall quality of life as perceived by community residents.

A community study should include at least some consideration of the strengths and limitations of the community system, the manner in which that community solves its problems, and the capacity and motivation for change. Communities that seem most able to fulfill their functions and meet people's needs have the following characteristics:

1. At least some primary relationships exist.
2. They are comparatively autonomous (not overly impacted by outside influences).
3. They have the capacity to face problems and engage in efforts to solve those problems.
4. There is a broad distribution of power.
5. Citizens have a commitment to the community.
6. Citizen participation is possible and encouraged.
7. There are more homogeneous than heterogeneous relationships.
8. They have developed ways of dealing with conflict.
9. There is tolerance for and valuing of diversity.

It is difficult for a community to meet citizen need when (1) the problems lie beyond the capacity of the community to solve, (2) the organizations and institutions of the community lack sufficient autonomy, and (3) the citizens lack identification with the community. These community characteristics should be considered when identifying strengths and limitations of any community system.

The community can be a nebulous entity that is often understood only intuitively. It can also be a defined system understood through organized study. In fact, through organized study a social worker is most apt to grasp the impacts and influences the community has on the social work endeavor. Skill in understanding a community includes the following:

1. A framework to organize information
2. The ability to locate information and resources
3. The ability to identify the information needed in specific situations
4. The ability to analyze the information obtained and to identify linkages and relationships among information and among subsystems in the community system
5. The ability to interact with individuals and small groups for purposes of developing relationships and gathering information about a community
6. The ability for careful observation of community functioning

It is also through organized study that the social worker gains knowledge about the resources a community provides for all members of that community. Knowledge of impacts, influences, and resources lead to effective practice with individuals, families, and small groups. They also lead to a practice that considers interventions into the system of the community and its subsystems when these larger systems impact on individuals, families, and small groups. Negative impacts, then, may become legitimate targets for change.[29]

The community is a social system. Like any social system, it has a structure, a way of functioning, and a history. It has energy and organization. The functioning of the helping system cannot be fully understood apart from the environment in which it functions, the community.

The Agency

Social work is an agency-based profession. The **agency** is the immediate environment of the worker–client interaction. This interaction often takes place in an office or building identified as "the agency." The influence of the agency is strong even when the interaction takes place elsewhere in the community. As an employee, the worker is a part of the agency system, and because of this, the worker is accountable to the agency. The form and content of the service offered must be within the agency's purview and guidelines. The manner in which the agency is structured and functions greatly influences the nature of the worker–client interaction. The agency also provides resources for both the worker and the client. To work in and use the agency in service of the client, the social worker must first understand the agency and its way of functioning.

Social workers not only need to understand the agency in which they are employed but they also need to be able to understand other social agencies. This is important if the worker is to help clients use the resources and services of other agencies. In addition, where needed resources are not available or usable, an understanding of the agency is a prerequisite to bringing about needed change.

From an ecosystems strengths perspective, the agency is a part of the worker's ecosystem and also becomes a temporary part of the client's ecosystem as the helping process develops. In addition, the agency has an ecosystem that is made up of the community. An important component of the agency's ecosystem is the human service delivery system within the community of which the agency is a part. Understanding the agency as a system and as a part of the larger ecosystem is essential to maximizing access to important resources for growth and change.

Agencies in which social workers are employed vary as to type and organization. Some are exclusively social work agencies. They provide social services delivered by professional social workers (MSW or BSW). A family service agency might be an example of this. The family service agency may, however, have a homemaker service or use nonprofessional workers in other ways. A family service agency is a voluntary agency; that is, it has a governing board of citizens and raises money for its support in the community (either separately or with other agencies). Once voluntary agencies did not use governmental funds, but because public funds have been used to purchase service from private agencies, this is no longer true.

Other social workers are employed by a variety of governmental agencies. They are in what is known as the *public sector.* These agencies are often state and/or federally funded. The worker is regulated by law and by governmental policies and regulations. Other social workers are employed in what is known as *host* or *secondary* settings. In this kind of setting, the primary function of the setting is not social service; social services are used to enhance the primary service. The social worker in a hospital is an example of this kind of setting. In other settings the social worker is part of an interdisciplinary team. The prime focus may be social service, or it may be some other service. Work in a community mental health center is an example of this kind of setting.

Barbara Oberhofer Dane and Barbara L. Simon pointed out that social workers in host settings have predictable issues that they must address. These include value discrepancies between social workers and the primary discipline in an agency, an often marginal status assigned to social work in such settings, devaluing social work as woman's work, and role ambiguity and role strain.[30] Thus, agencies vary with respect to several dimensions: size, means of support and governance, nature of the primary service offered, and range of people who are employed.

Before a worker can effectively deliver service as a professional in a bureaucratic organization, the worker must first understand the organization. A social systems approach, again, is a means for developing that understanding.

The first task in understanding an agency is to define its boundaries. The entity that operates with a great enough degree of autonomy so that a unique structure and ways of functioning have developed—in which the influences within the structure are stronger than those without—might be identified as the agency. In a Veterans Administration hospital, the social services department might be the choice as the primary system for focus if interaction among departments is limited largely to department heads. If the interaction is greater within a team of doctor, nurse, and social worker, then the unit team might be considered the agency. Because both kinds of interaction are important, however, the total institution might be the better choice. None of these answers is completely adequate. Whatever set of boundaries is used, it should be one that defines the entity with the greatest influence on the worker–client interaction.

The second task is to determine environmental factors that influence the structure and functioning of the agency. These influences involve other social systems and broad socioeconomic factors, including those that impact the agency either by providing resources or by placing expectations.

Some of the social systems that may need to be considered include (1) any organization or system of which the agency is part (e.g., a national membership organization, a statewide organization, or an institution of which the social services department is a part); (2) the community (or communities) from which clients come or that provides support for the agency; (3) professional organizations to which the workers belong; (4) foundations or other sources of support; (5) community planning and funding bodies; (6) governmental bodies that regulate or supply support for the services; (7) colleges and universities that educate for the professions employed; (8) other social agencies; (9) individuals and families who are clients or potential clients; and (10) organizations, such as churches and service clubs, that may be resources to the agency or its clients.

Socioeconomic forces that should be considered include (1) economic trends, (2) societal trends, (3) community expectations, (4) community need, (5) political forces, (6) governmental policies or regulations, and (7) cultural and diversity needs within the community.

The third task is to understand the structure and functioning of the agency system. The factors involved include the following:

1. *The purposes, objectives, and values of the system*—These are spelled out in articles of incorporation, enabling legislation, agency handbooks, and other official documents. Also important is how these formal expressions are interpreted and implemented in actual service delivery. The agency's value priorities influence this interpretation and implementation. The history of the agency is important in determining how the purposes, objectives, and values developed.

2. *Agency resources, including financial resources*—Resources include the funds provided by the community, through either gifts or tax money; the building or other physical structures the agency leases or owns; and the people resources, both paid and volunteer, including professional and support staff.

3. *The traditional ways of working*—Each agency tends to use particular approaches in its service (such as long-term counseling, crisis intervention, provision of specific resources, group work activity). This can also include specific theoretical approaches, such as task-centered, psychoanalytical, and so on. Agencies tend to work with particular systems, individuals, families, groups, or communities. They tend to hire workers with particular educational backgrounds for specific tasks (e.g., MSW, BSW, college graduates, persons indigenous to the community). They have particular patterns of work (e.g., teams, cotherapy).

4. *Boards or other governing bodies*—An important consideration is the method of sanctioning the agency (public or private). If public, the laws, policies, and other regulations that govern the agency and the organizational structure of the larger organization of which the agency is a part should be identified. If private, the structure and functioning of the board of directors is the focus. Members of the board and their motivations and needs are also important, as is the relationship of the governing body to the agency and its staff. Another element is the committee structure and functioning. This structure can be one of the board, the staff, or a combination of the two. It is often in committees that new ideas are formulated and that the work of the organization is carried out.

5. *The organizational structure*—This includes both the formal and informal structure, the administrative style, the accepted norms and values, the decision-making and communication processes, and the power and control patterns.

6. *The staff*—Important considerations include who they are as both persons and professionals; the relationships among staff (formal and informal); and the relationship of staff, clients, administration, and governing body. The professional identification and qualifications of staff should also be considered.

7. *The clients*—Often clients are overlooked as a part of the agency system. Without them, the agency would have no reason for existence. In an age of consumer advocacy, this aspect of agency functioning takes on new importance. Consideration should be given to client needs, expectations, and ways of relating to the agency. The status, designation (patient or student, etc.), and values relating to clients should also be considered.

8. *Diversity*—Diversity within the agency and other agencies is an important consideration. Some questions to consider are, What are the hiring practices of the agency that assure a diverse staff? Are there inappropriate attitudes and stereotypes? How do policies and procedures affect service to diverse groups? Do some groups feel excluded because of expectations for receiving help?

Table 2.3   Schema for the Study of a Social Agency

A. Identify the boundaries of the agency.
B. Discuss the history of the agency.
C. Discuss the structure and function of the agency.
   1. The purposes, objectives, and value priorities of the agency
   2. The agency resources: financial (sources and amount), physical property, staff (paid and volunteer)
   3. The traditional way of working with clients
   4. The sanctioning of the agency (public or private). If public, identify the laws, policy, and regulations that impact on the agency functioning. Identify the organizational structure of any larger organization of which the agency is a part. Note means of citizen involvement and input. If private, describe the structure and functioning of the board of directors. Who serves on the board? (Describe them as persons.) What are the roles and responsibilities of the board (both internal to the board and with the rest of the agency)? Describe committee structure and functioning.
   5. The organizational structure of the agency. Describe formal and informal functioning of the agency. What are the accepted norms and values? How are decisions made? What is the communication process? Describe power and control aspects.
   6. The staff, as persons and as professionals, their relationships, diversity, roles, and ways of working with each other, clients, administration, and governing boards. Identify formal and informal staff groups and describe their functioning.
   7. The clients, their diversity, needs, characteristics, expectations, role, and status
   8. Diversity issues regarding clients and staff
D. Identify the strengths and limitations of the agency.
   1. What are the strengths of the agency in terms of serving clients?
   2. What are the limitations of the agency in terms of serving clients?

Each of these aspects of the structure and functioning of the agency system may overlap with other aspects. In developing understanding of an agency, workers should be aware of these overlaps and of the relationships and linkages between the various aspects. Workers also need to be aware of any special aspects of their agency that affect its structure and functioning. In order to gather the information needed for understanding an agency, an organized framework is often useful, such as that presented in Table 2.3.

SUMMARY

This chapter provides a foundation for understanding generalist social work practice. It includes a description of the Johnson/Yanca model of generalist practice on which this text is based. In generalist practice, the social worker and the client system together decide on the appropriate client system and the target for change. Either of these may be an individual, a family, a group, an organization, or a community.

The Johnson/Yanca model of generalist practice starts with an understanding of the concern or need. The model is based on a creative blending of knowledge, values, and skills for social work practice. The change process is characterized as moving through phases that include assessment, planning, action, and evaluation and termination. Included in the model is an approach identified as diversity competent practice.

This chapter also considers the environment of the helping endeavor, including the community and the agency. Both can be understood from a social systems perspective. The transactional nature of human functioning makes it essential that social workers understand the strengths and resources of the community and the agency and the influence of these two systems on the functioning of both the worker and the family.

If the worker is to be a generalist, this understanding is essential in making decisions as to the target for change and the mode of intervention. If the target is to be the community or agency system, the worker needs in-depth understanding of that target. Communities and agencies are complex systems that must be understood in some depth before they become a target for change.

QUESTIONS

1. Describe generalist social work practice and give an example.
2. Describe the Johnson/Yanca model of generalist social work practice.
3. Describe the concept of the environment as an ecosystem.
4. Using a community with which you are familiar and the material presented in this chapter, identify information you should obtain if you are to develop a greater understanding of the community. Pay special attention to strengths and resources. Where would you go to obtain that information?
5. How would you go about gathering the information needed to understand any agency in which you might be employed?

SUGGESTED READINGS

Johnson, Louise C., and Yanca, Stephen J. *Social Work Practice: A Generalist Approach,* 9th ed. Boston: Allyn & Bacon, 2007 (Chapters 5–13).

Edwards, Richard L., Ed. *Encyclopedia of Social Work,* 19th ed. Washington, DC: NASW Press, 1995 ("Community"; "Community Needs Assessment"; "Community Organization"; "Community Practice Models"; and "Ecological Perspective").

Homan, Mark S. *Promoting Community Change: Making It Happen in the Real World,* 2nd ed. Pacific Grove, CA: Brooks/Cole, 2004.

Kettner, Peter M. *Achieving Excellence in the Management of Human Service Organizations.* Boston: Allyn & Bacon, 2002 (Chapter 3).

Meyer, Carol. "The Ecosystems Perspective: Implications for Social Work Practice," in *The Foundations of Social Work Practice,* Carol Meyer and Mark Mattaini. Eds. Washington, DC: NASW Press, 1995 (pp. 16–27).

Netting, Ellen F., Kettner, Peter M., and McMurtry, Steven L. *Social Work Macro Practice,* 2nd ed. Boston: Allyn & Bacon, 2004.

Netting, Ellen F., and O'Connor, Mary K. *Organization Practice: A Social Worker's Guide to Understanding Human Services.* Boston: Allyn & Bacon, 2003.

Rubin, Herbert J., and Rubin, Irene S. *Community Organizing and Development*, 3rd ed. Boston: Allyn & Bacon, 2001 (Chapter 5).

Sheaford, Bradford W., and Horejsi, Charles R. *Techniques and Guidelines for Social Work Practice*, 7th ed. Boston: Allyn & Bacon, 2006 (Chapters 9 and 16).

Tropman, John, E., Erlich, John L., and Rothman, Jack. *Tactics and Techniques of Community Intervention*, 4th ed. Itasca, IL: F. E. Peacock, 2001.

3

Diversity Competent Practice with Families

LEARNING EXPECTATIONS

1. Understand diversity competence and the process of becoming diversity competent.
2. Understand gender competent practice with families.
3. Understand diversity competent practice with gay and lesbian families.
4. Understand the development and use of a schema for studying families from diverse ethnic groups.
5. Understand diversity competent practice with African American families.
6. Understand diversity competent practice with Hispanic/Latino families.
7. Understand diversity competent practice with Native American families.

Diversity competence is an important aspect of social work practice. The great majority of clients are members of populations whose diversity places them at risk of experiencing prejudice, discrimination, and oppression. At one time, diversity was seen as a barrier to be overcome. More recently, theories evolved that called for ethnic sensitive practice in which the worker respected and valued the ethnicity and culture of the client. However, being sensitive does not necessarily mean that the worker makes fundamental changes to the manner in which services are delivered. Thus, the next step in this evolution has been to develop **cultural competence** that calls for the worker to be able to practice in ways that are consistent with expectations in the client's culture. In the previous two editions of our text, *Social Work Practice: A Generalist Approach*, we extended this a step further by considering diversity competent practice skills. This extends the concept of cultural competence to all forms of diversity. The Council on Social Work Education identifies diversity as differences related to age, class, gender, color, culture, disability, ethnicity, marital status, family structure, race, national origin, religion, sex, and sexual orientation. The National Association of Social Work (NASW) includes most of these populations in its standards for cultural competence. However, we believe that diversity competent practice is a more descriptive term. The lists of populations for both organizations extend well beyond culture and recognize that people can be different from each other in many ways, and in multiple ways, as well.

The diversity competent social worker explores ways to serve diverse clients in a manner that is expected within their diverse group. For instance, a white worker might need to be able to use an Afrocentric approach in working with some of her African American clients or a feminist approach in working with some of her female clients. The professional worker realizes that it is her responsibility to adapt her skills to meet the needs of her client. She meets that responsibility by engaging in lifelong learning activities throughout her career. She reads materials and attends relevant training programs. She seeks to learn from knowledgeable colleagues and members of the community. She realizes the value of learning from her clients about how they would like to be served and incorporates this into her repertoire of skills. She uses diversity-appropriate skills in engagement and relationship building, assessment, planning, action, and evaluation and termination with every client she serves. She realizes that diversity competence is a lifelong process that is never really achieved, but she seeks to add to her competence with every client she serves.

The importance of diversity competence can be seen in the demographic changes occurring in the United States. During the first half of the twenty-first century, sweeping demographic changes will alter the face of the United States. Population projections indicate that the number of people who are older will increase in the United States and in other industrialized countries. The United States will also experience dramatic changes in its ethnic and racial composition. It appears that sometime in the middle of this century, people of color will surpass whites in population, and we will become a nation of minority groups. By that time, more than half of our high school graduates will be children of color, as will half of our working-age adults. Martha Ozawa studied these trends and raised concerns about the high rate of poverty among children, especially African American and Hispanic children. She pointed out that federal spending has been eleven times greater for people who are elderly than for children. She concluded that child poverty, especially among children of color, will lead to a decline in our economic and social well-being unless we dramatically increase our investment in children.[1]

Nowhere is diversity competent practice more important than when the social worker works with families. Families are primary sources of culture and diversity. They are the purveyors of culture and the incubators of diversity. For most people they are both refuges from prejudice, discrimination, and oppression and support systems in the battle against these ills. Culture and diversity are always on the table when the social worker works with families.

■   DIVERSITY COMPETENT PRACTICE   ■

In order for the social worker to develop diversity competence, she must take a comprehensive approach to understanding the effects of diversity on herself, her clients, the environment, and the interactions among these. Table 3.1 presents an outline for developing a diversity competent approach to practice. There are two important aspects to this work. The

Table 3.1 Outline for Developing Diversity Competence

I. Understanding self
   A. Understand the social worker's own attitudes and beliefs about diverse groups
   B. Understand the influence of attitudes and beliefs of the worker's family on the social worker's own attitudes and beliefs about diverse groups
   C. Understand the influence of attitudes and beliefs of the worker's ecosystem on the social worker's own attitudes and beliefs about diverse groups
   D. Understand the influence of societal attitudes and beliefs on the social worker's own attitudes and beliefs about diverse groups

II. Understanding societal influences
   A. Understand the history of each diverse group in the United States
   B. Understand historical and current stereotypes, prejudice, discrimination, and oppression
   C. Understand formal and informal mechanisms in U.S. society that cause or reinforce discrimination or oppression (past and present)
   D. Understand privileges and advantages that dominant groups have over the population (male privilege, white privilege, heterosexual privilege, wealth or class privilege, etc.)

III. Understanding a diverse group
   A. Understand the particular culture and circumstances that make each group diverse
   B. Understand the values, beliefs, and customs of each diverse group
   C. Understand strengths of diverse groups and resources available in their ecosystems
   D. Understand the social, psychological, economic, and political effects of historical and current stereotypes, prejudice, discrimination, and oppression on diverse groups

IV. Developing diversity competent practice skills
   A. Develop knowledge regarding relationship building, assessment, planning, action, evaluation and termination that are necessary to provide services in a manner that is expected within each diverse group
   B. Develop a personal and professional value system that values diversity
   C. Develop skills in providing direct and indirect services in a manner that is expected within each diverse group

first is the need for the social worker to develop her ability to acquire and use knowledge, values, and skills in a way that makes diversity competent practice possible. This requires developing a view of the world and an attitude toward professional social work practice that is inclusive rather than exclusive, that seeks to include everyone rather than excluding anyone, that genuinely values differences, and variation, that taps one's natural curiosity about difference, and that truly values every human being. This means developing a system of thinking, feeling, and acting that opens the door to actively seeking new knowledge, to developing values that are consistent with this approach, and to trying new skills that may be uncomfortable for awhile. It means becoming a true professional by giving up the safety of what we know and risking to reach out and learn about what we do not know. This task also involves learning how to acquire knowledge in a variety of ways. It involves learning about values that are different from our own and respecting those values. It involves learning how to use new skills while coping with discomfort that may be associated with doing something different.

The second aspect is to actually acquire and use appropriate knowledge, values, and skills in practice with diverse groups. It means learning how to learn about others. It includes learning where to look, who to ask, what it means, and how to use new knowledge about others. It requires the social worker to learn about his own values and those of others without preconceived notions or judgments that prevent including the client's value system in the work to be done. It means becoming adept at altering one's approach or even abandoning it in favor of one with which the client is comfortable.

To become diversity competent, the worker must be able to reflect on his knowledge about himself and knowledge about each diverse group. He must be willing to critically examine his knowledge and be open to considering distortions that might be present as a result of prejudices and stereotypes. He must be able to acquire and use new knowledge about diversity from his client and from professional sources, such as articles, books, professional training, colleagues, and other sources.

In diversity competent practice, the worker needs to become more familiar with the different ways of knowing that each diverse group may use in acquiring knowledge. In white, male, Eurocentric society, great value is placed on knowledge that is gained by the scientific method. Other groups value knowledge that is more experiential and passed on from earlier generations. Women may value knowledge that is acquired through relationships.

In diversity competent practice, the worker needs to be aware of her own values and the influence these have on her attitudes toward various diverse groups. She needs to be able to change those values that are based on or lead to prejudices and stereotypes so that she is free to accept every client as a valuable human being. This brings her value system in line with the cardinal value of social work, which holds that all human beings have inherent value and worth. She needs to be able to reconcile conflicts between her personal values and those of her profession. The diversity competent worker actively explores her client's values with an open mind. She is aware of how the larger society values or devalues certain groups. For instance, the dominant culture values males over females, heterosexuals over homosexuals, Caucasians over people of color, youth over age, Christianity over other religions, and so on. The diversity competent worker understands how this affects diverse clients and her work with them. She seeks to ameliorate these affects and to reduce the barriers that result. She is constantly aware of the importance of values in her work. She seeks to develop an awareness of her own values in every situation she encounters. She explores her client's values and incorporates appropriate values into the work. She is aware of value conflicts that may arise between her values, her client's values, the values of the social work profession, and those of the larger society. She actively searches for mutually acceptable ways to resolve these conflicts and engages in lifelong learning to improve her appropriate use of values in diversity competent practice.

The diversity competent social worker tunes in on the attitudes and stereotypes toward diverse groups and the affect that these have on members of each population. He is also aware of the values that each group holds and is alert to value conflicts and their affect on relationships. The worker identifies ways of helping that each group uses and seeks to improve his skills so that he can serve members of each group in a manner with which they are comfortable.

In diversity competent practice, the worker needs to be knowledgeable about the values and beliefs of the population, its experience with the dominant society, the manner in which help is given and received, and good practices that need to be used with each group.

In understanding the environment, it is essential that the worker develop an understanding of responses to diversity from people and systems in the environment. The dual perspective proposed by Dolores Norton is especially relevant. Her discussion of the nurturing environment included family and the immediate community environment.[2] The latter refers to the neighborhood in which the person lives. Norton's sustaining environment consists of the organization of goods and services, political power, economic resources, educational system, and larger societal systems.

In understanding the ecosystem, the worker who is striving to become diversity competent also considers the attitudes toward diversity in his community and agency. He looks at each of the groups identified from his understanding of diversity. He looks for signs that indicate that diversity is valued by the community. He looks at patterns of race and ethnicity in the community. He considers to what extent these patterns represent current or past discrimination toward various groups. He observes how people of color, women, children, and people who are older or disabled are valued and respected. He evaluates community attitudes toward gays and lesbians. Some of these indicators are apparent in the institutions and services available to various groups. Some cannot be seen but can be heard in the stories of people who live in the community. As he becomes more diversity competent, the worker learns to look at the environment from a diversity perspective and to be an active listener.

Of special concern to social workers are diversity factors that exist in the community. The racial and ethnic makeup of the community are important to know. With regard to race and ethnicity, the worker should have knowledge about the degree to which various groups are integrated or segregated. She should note the attitudes of various groups toward each other. Is there respect or valuing of differences? Are there coalitions that have been formed? Are there adversarial relationships? How tolerant or intolerant are these groups toward each other? What groups hold power? Who has little or no power, and how does this reflect the general population? Similar questions should also be asked with respect to gender, age, and sexual orientation.

Becoming diversity competent may seem like an insurmountable challenge, especially for a student or a new social worker. But this work is not done over a semester or over a year. It is done over a lifetime. In fact, it is never really finished. However, the social worker can become more diversity competent if she is open to learning from each and every client she meets and if she accepts the responsibility to engage in the lifelong learning that is expected of a professional. In this chapter and those that follow, we address some of the knowledge, values, and skills that are needed for diversity competent practice, keeping in mind that no single text can do it all. What we seek to do instead is to learn about the process of becoming more diversity competent so that the student or practitioner has the knowledge, values, and skills to begin this endeavor as she experiences diversity in field placement and beginning professional practice. We begin this process in this chapter by considering diversity competent practice with various types of families. An outline is presented for studying families from diverse ethnic groups in Table 3.2 (see page 69).

Becoming Diversity Competent

Often students have difficulty in identifying their own diversity. Marty Dewees cited an unpublished paper by W. Nichols that found that "many students from White, dominant, middle-class status, particularly in geographical areas with limited racial diversity, regard themselves as having *no* culture or ethnicity."[3] This observation is consistent with the authors' experiences in teaching BSW students. Some of this lack of cultural identity may be attributed to the mixing of cultures and ethnic groups in U.S. society. However, the inability to identify one's own culture or ethnicity does not mean that one does not have any cultural or ethnic influences. What it means is that one is not aware of these influences. In addition, the authors have consistently observed that many female students have difficulty in recognizing discrimination they have experienced as women. Often, this begins to slowly change when there are discussions about male privilege and who did what around the house when they were growing up or in their current living arrangements. Unfortunately, this type of discrimination is only the tip of the iceberg.

The danger here is that the worker will not recognize or be open to the affects of diversity on the helping relationship and will not be prepared to deal with issues his client experiences that arise out of diversity. To become competent as a social worker, the student must become "diversity competent," or competent in working with diverse clients, especially those who are different from oneself. Competence in working with diversity begins with an awareness of one's own diversity and the affect that diversity has in one's personal life. James W. Leigh suggested that knowing one's own cultural influences is critical to developing cultural competence. He points out that we all carry unconscious cultural influences that either are directly prejudicial toward certain other cultures or lead us in that direction because of cultural differences.[4] Barbara Okum, Jane Fried, and Marcia Okum have discussed the need to develop self-awareness first before being able to develop an awareness of others.[5] Doman Lum cited a number of references that reinforce the need for self-awareness.[6] Jerry V. Diller stated, "It is impossible to appreciate the impact of culture on the lives of others, particularly clients, if one is out of touch with his or her own cultural background."[7] Yuhwa Lu, Doman Lum, and Sheying Chen have developed a conceptual framework for cultural competency that begins with "awareness of cultural and ethnic experiences which are part of the personal and professional socialization of the worker."[8] They included the need to evaluate one's own experiences and reactions to "racism, sexism, homophobia, and other forms of prejudice/discrimination."[9] Two out of the four steps that Marty Dewees proposed for cultural competence with families are related to the need for students to identify their own cultural influences.[10]

Thus, the preponderance of work that is being done on developing models for cultural competence in social work practice points out the need for the student or worker to develop cultural awareness of herself. We propose to extend this requirement beyond culture to all forms of diversity in society. To become diversity competent, the student or worker must begin with an examination of her own diversity, along with an examination of how her experiences have shaped her attitudes toward her own diversity and the diversity of others. Cultural influences play a major role in both of these endeavors. It is not enough to be "color-blind" or "culture blind" or "diversity blind." Assertions of tolerance will not ensure the development of trust in clients who are different from oneself. In fact, it is more likely to lead to mistrust because clients get the idea that diversity does not matter when indeed they know that it does. Professing tolerance for diversity can easily come across as insensitivity toward diversity. Diversity competence calls for an active listening approach to diversity that seeks to know more. It uses diversity to create a dialogue with the client that will lead to a better understanding of the client and his environment.

All of the authors in the sources previously cited point to the need for the student or worker to obtain knowledge about the culture to which the client belongs and skills in working within the client's cultural system. Gargi Sodowsky, Richard Taffe, Terry Gutkin, and

Steven Wise have added another dimension to the skills related to cultural competence, namely, the multicultural counseling relationship.[11] Again, the requirement to develop knowledge and skills must be extended beyond culture to all forms of diversity in society.

Lu, Lum, and Chen suggested that the worker "engage in inductive learning that promotes investigation and inquiry."[12] Doman Lum also included this idea in his work on culturally competent practice.[13] The inductive approach is different from **deductive learning** that uses the scientific method. The deductive process involves moving from theory to hypothesis to testing the hypothesis to determine whether the theory is supported. The inductive process involves moving from making observations of phenomena to searching for patterns that may lead to theory development. Applying the inductive learning approach to becoming competent in working with diversity means adopting an open-minded inquisitive approach, laying aside preconceived notions, and listening to the experiences of the client. Self-knowledge must come first so that the worker can move away from experiencing the client's story out of her own experience and instead hear the client's story out of his experience.

As a professional, the social worker has a responsibility to engage in a process of lifelong learning. An important area of lifelong learning is learning about diversity. The student begins this process through coursework, research, assignments, reading, class discussions, and examining himself as a person and as a developing professional. He learns to use inductive learning and natural inquiry in his approach to diversity. In field placement, the student is frequently put in a position of working with people who are diverse, often for the first time. Many of these people have experienced considerable prejudice and discrimination related to their diversity. The student learns how to work with diverse clients by applying what he has learned from his academic experiences along with his new field experiences. He learns from his field instructor and from others with expertise who may be available in his agency, community, or university. Most important, he learns to learn from his clients. They are the experts on their own experiences with diversity. As a professional social worker, he learns to continue this learning, and he seeks out additional training through in-service training, conferences, and other continuing education activities.

Becoming "diversity competent" means developing self-knowledge—developing knowledge about one's own diversity. Learning about diversity continues as the student or worker takes an active, inductive approach to learning about diversity in others. This learning lasts for a lifetime as the professional social worker engages in a lifelong process of self-examination, seeks out knowledge about diversity, and develops skills in working with people who are different from her.

The number of families that are biracial or multiracial have increased substantially during the past several decades and will continue to increase as the United States becomes a more multicultural, multiethnic, and multiracial society. Some of these families are produced by biracial couples. Others are a product of couples who adopt children of another race. In some cases, these are children from foreign adoption. Despite becoming more common, biracial and multiracial families face the same kinds of prejudice and discrimination as families and children of color. In addition, some of these families find that they are not accepted by either culture or racial group. The children may experience these same attitudes. Biracial parents need to bolster their child's self-image and self-esteem in order to withstand these negative attitudes. Social workers need to support these families in fighting and coping with the consequences of negative attitudes and actions. Social workers must stand up and fight prejudice, discrimination, and oppression in all its forms.

Families with same-sex partners are a special form of family that has gained greater recognition as gays and lesbians have advocated for legal status as couples. Children in these families may be a product of prior heterosexual relationships, adoption, surrogate mothers, or donor insemination. In heterosexual families, roles are often assigned by gender and culture. For same-sex couples, there is a need to establish a communication system that can be used to discuss the roles that each partner will take or how these roles will be shared. Egalitarian heterosexual couples have this same need. In many cases, discussing each day who will do what tasks—such as cooking, childcare, errands, housework, and the like—is necessary. Same-sex couples and their children often face a great deal of prejudice and discrimination. Children in same-sex families need assistance from their parents in establishing a healthy identity that can withstand these negative social attitudes, along with positive descriptions of their family and family members. For example, in a lesbian family, the child might be encouraged to see himself as having two mothers. It is important that he see this as a strength and that he feel he is just as worthwhile as a child of a heterosexual couple. Families are also headed by single parents who are gay or lesbian. In some respects, these parents become somewhat invisible in terms of their sexual orientation because it is more difficult to tell someone is gay or lesbian if he or she is single. Families may have members who are bisexual or transgendered. People who are bisexual are attracted to both males and females. People who are transgendered feel that they are actually the opposite sex from the one that they are biologically. They frequently describe themselves as being a man trapped in a woman's body or a woman trapped in a man's body. These individuals are people who may seek out a sex change in order to resolve this dilemma. Social workers need to provide support for gay, lesbian, bisexual, and transgendered families to counteract and cope with the consequences of negative attitudes and actions from society. Social workers must be advocates and fight prejudice, discrimination, and oppression in all its forms, regardless of personal values and beliefs.

When considering the ethnic family there are two levels of understanding that are needed by the worker: first is the more general level, which provides overall knowledge, second is the specific level, which provides understanding of a specific family. Table 3.2 presents an outline for studying families from diverse ethnic groups. We use this outline to examine important factors in working with each ethnic family. However, first we consider the role of gender in families and examine how the generalist social worker develops and implements a gender competent approach to practice.

■ GENDER COMPETENT PRACTICE WITH FAMILIES ■

Gender is an especially important consideration in working with families. Expectations for males and females are interwoven into the fabric of nearly every society. These expectations are reinforced by various social institutions. Perhaps the strongest messages about these expectations come from within the family.

During the twentieth century, women in the United States were able to gain the right to vote nationally, have access to higher education, obtain many jobs from which they were formerly excluded, own property, and have other rights that had been denied. However, full equality has still eluded women. Gender-based roles carry the expectation that women will do most of the domestic chores around the home including childcare and elder care. Women have not gained access to real power in the economic and political arenas. There are only a very few women who head major corporations or serve on their boards, and there has never been a female president or vice president of the United States. Women are more likely than men to be poor and to be victims of rape and domestic violence.

The plight of women internationally is not much better and in most regards is much worse than in the United States The exception is western Europe where in most countries women not only enjoy the same or better social and economic well-being but also have achieved real political power that is much greater than that of U.S. women. Globally, women own a very small percentage of the world's wealth. This demonstrates the extent to which women are oppressed.

In developing gender competent practice, it is important to understand feminist practice. A paradigm that is suggested by some social workers as applicable to many populations is the **feminist perspective.**[14] This paradigm is based on five principles: (1) the elimination of false dichotomies and artificial separations, (2) the reconceptualization of power, (3) the valuing of process equally with product, (4) the validity of renaming, and (5) the personal is political. In other words, this approach calls for a holistic view; a wide distribution of power; attention to how goals are implemented; the renaming of action so as to purge discriminatory language; and the recognition that personal problems are often the result of political injustice, requiring that the focus of intervention be on change in large systems. This paradigm seems useful in any situation in which discrimination is of major concern, such as in working with women or minority groups.

Feminist social workers stress the need for teaching clients how to empower themselves as well as how to work with systems that affect them. They also emphasize the importance of working with clients as equals in order to avoid replicating the "one-up" position common in other environmental interactions. Feminist workers attempt to link clients with others who face similar issues in order to build systems that can be used for networking, support, and education. The feminist perspective and method seem particularly relevant in addressing social injustice in that it acknowledges that many of the difficulties faced by populations at risk of discrimination are a result of their interactions with the environment or with the surrounding systems rather than within the clients themselves.

Feminist practice was developed by practitioners as an attempt to integrate feminist theory, commitments, and culture with conventional approaches to social work practice. It goes beyond a "nonsexist" or "women's issues" orientation. The underlying assumptions include the following: (1) The inherent purpose and goal of human existence is self-actualization, which is a collective endeavor involving the creation of material and ideological conditions that enable it; (2) systems and ideologies of domination/subordination, exploitation, and oppression are inimical to individual and collective self-actualization; (3) given the structural and ideological barriers to self-actualization, practice is explicitly political in intent; and (4) women have unique and relatively unknown histories, conditions, developmental patterns, and strengths that must be discovered and engaged by practitioners.[15]

Some aspects of practice theory for feminist practitioners have some similarity to the approach we use in our texts, including this one. For instance, assessment focuses on preferred and available patterns of strength in intellectual, emotional, social, cultural, physical, and spiritual domains. Special emphasis is given to basic, concrete needs, safety, and perceptions of personal power. An underlying principle informing practice is that healing, health, and growth are the purpose of the social work endeavor. Feminist practice sees these as functions of validation, consciousness, and transformative action, which are supported and sustained through resources to meet basic human needs. Feminist practitioners seek the creation of validating environments and relationships that preserve and nurture uniqueness and wholeness. They use a range of conventional and nonconventional approaches. Feminists frequently use groups, which are seen as favorable for developing validation and raising consciousness. They encourage and facilitate individual and collective action and work for open, egalitarian, and collegial relationships with clients. Feminist practice can be used in all kinds of settings, with all populations. Particular attention is focused on women.

The oppression of women around the world presents many challenges for social workers in practicing gender competence with various cultural groups. There are numerous cultures that seek to perpetuate paternalism and have substantial power imbalances between men and women as major cultural constructs for gender roles and expectations. The challenge for gender competent social workers is to engage and work with members of these cultural groups without sacrificing the principles of good gender competence. The risk is that if the worker comes on too strong, the family may be alienated or feel that the worker's values and views are being imposed on the family members.

In diversity competent practice, the worker explores with the family actions that are consistent with the diversity of the family. She does not impose her own or society's view of what the family should do but seeks to find what fits with the family system. One of the difficulties in working with families from certain cultures is the strict boundaries between male and female role expectations. This generally results in the male being in the role of head of the household, called a patriarchal system. This system may be viewed as oppressive toward women. Most of these cultures define a "good husband" or a "good father" as a man who incorporates the needs and best interests of his wife and children into his decision making. He is obligated to see that the needs of his wife and family are met. This places tremendous pressure on him when faced with limited resources. Some men use their dominant position to meet their own needs or suppress the needs of other family members. Within their culture, this is a deviation from the "good husband and father" role. The worker can assist the husband to define this role within his culture and then work with him to obtain the resources that are necessary to carry this out. The worker might also help him to see that sharing his power is not necessarily a sign of weakness but may indeed be a sign of strength.

There are some substantial dilemmas for the gender competent social worker to resolve in her practice with families, especially those from patriarchal cultures. These are probably best expressed in terms of several questions: How does the worker respect the family's culture when some of the culture's values conflict with her personal and professional value system? How does the worker support power sharing and egalitarian relationships without imposing her views on the family? How does she maintain her personal and professional value system of valuing all human beings equally while working with a family whose culture does not reflect this value? How does she maintain her personal and professional value system of valuing self determination while working with a family whose culture does not reflect this value?

A feminist-informed approach appears to hold some promise for developing successful gender competent practice. Shelley A. Haddock, Toni Schindler Zimmerman, and David MacPhee from the Human Development and Family Studies Department at Colorado State

University have developed the Power Equity Guide to assist in assessing attention to gender in family therapy. They see a feminist-informed approach to working with families as mainly a philosophical and political perspective rather than a model or set of techniques.[16] The Guide can be used by family workers at all levels of development.

Using the basic philosophy behind feminist-informed practice, the gender competent practitioner would focus on both process and content that reflected gender equity. Process refers to the way in which he works with families. Content is what is actually said and done in his work. Because many cultures perceive differences in males and females, especially with respect to specific and overall competence, there are going to be differences in how male and female social workers are perceived. This also influences how male and female social workers are able to work with families. This includes both the content and process of working with families. Because of gender differences within the family system, male and female social workers may use techniques that are different from each other but have the same effect, and they may use the same techniques but have different effects. For example, a female worker who supports gender equity may be perceived differently by the husband than a male worker may be perceived. The husband may interpret the female worker as being culturally insensitive or threatening to his culturally determined status as head of the family. The husband might interpret the same approach by a male worker in the same way as he interpreted the female worker's approach or he might view it as acceptable because it is coming from another male.

Cross-cultural work with families is much more complicated when the work is also cross-gender. If the worker is female and the family system is patriarchal, it can be very difficult for the worker to gain credibility. Naturalistic inquiry can be especially helpful in these cases. Asking questions and giving the role of cultural guide to the family allows the process to unfold. The family will be more comfortable with a discussion of its cultural background if there is a focus on strengths. Actively incorporating cultural customs and values into the plan is vital. This lays the groundwork for action that is culturally appropriate. It is important for the family to take pride in its cultural heritage and to use that heritage as a source of strength.

The worker needs to be constantly aware of gender differences while also seeking ways to rebalance those differences toward greater gender equity. This is the essence of gender competent practice. It begins with working with couples to develop more egalitarian relationships. This includes encouraging equality in communication, problem solving, decision making, and conflict resolution. Under no circumstances, regardless of the cultural background of the family, should the worker show any tolerance for violence or the threat of violence.

An important point to be made here is the need for the worker to allow adult female members of the family to decide how to proceed with encouraging gender equity. This is not a decision for the worker to make independently. It is her client's choice. Feminist practitioners may see this as "selling out," but if the worker is to respect her client's right to self determination, she is compelled to respect her client's right to make a decision with which the worker disagrees. This does not mean that the worker cannot model gender equity in her work with the family. However, in working with families on making decisions about family structure and functioning, the worker needs to respect their right to decide how they wish to do this.

It is also important to consider the involvement of male family members in this decision-making process, especially those in positions of power in the family. Because they are in the position of exerting power over female members and female members are thereby placed in a powerless or less powerful position, the worker should give preference to the choice of the female members. This generally means that the worker uses influence, persuasion, and encouragement to move the family toward greater gender equity if that is what the female members choose.

In promoting gender equity, the worker should encourage sharing responsibility for parenting and household tasks. The worker can point out how men are often deprived of the pleasures of child-rearing and forming close relationships with their children. It is also important for parents to prepare their children for life in a free and democratic society that values independence. This means that children of both sexes need to learn how to take care of themselves by learning and doing all forms of household chores. The worker also encourages parents to support children of both sexes in pursuing education and careers that are growth enhancing and take advantages of opportunities that may not have been available in the home country of their culture. Many immigrants come to the United States for greater economic opportunity. Convincing them to allow their female members to take advantage of those opportunities may not be as difficult as one might expect. Certainly, the greater the opportunities for more family members, the more likely the family will become more prosperous more quickly.

Probably, the area that is of greatest concern for ethnic groups, especially for first-generation immigrants, is retention of their cultures. However, it is almost inevitable that some cultural influences will be diluted as their children are exposed to the dominant culture. In fact, this is often an area of great turmoil and conflict between earlier and later generations. Parents need to be realistic about this and select those aspects of cultural heritage that have the highest value for them. These are usually customs and traditions such as holidays and religious or spiritual beliefs. In order to preserve these, parents will likely have to yield some latitude in other areas. This is where gender-based roles may be loosened. In essence, the worker helps the family become bicultural and seeks to do so in a rational way that preserves important aspects of both cultures.

Many culturally diverse families have experienced prejudice, discrimination, and oppression both in their countries of origin and here in the United States. Another approach to use in encouraging more egalitarian relationships is to discuss these experiences and point out the parallels to the treatment of females. Raising consciousness and awareness of these experiences allows the family to decide what aspects of their culture will serve them best in this country. This is an empowering approach. In many respects, empowering the family as a system can lead to freeing it from cultural constrictions. It can empower them to make choices about a bicultural style that is in the best interests of the family as a whole as well as each member.

Some techniques the gender competent social worker can use in his work with families include both verbal and nonverbal. Verbally, the worker encourages everyone to tell their own stories and gives equal credibility to them. He addresses the parents jointly regarding parenting and child-rearing and is careful to initiate and maintain eye contact with both. Workers who are not gender conscious will tend to look at the mother first when it comes to these issues. The worker moves cultural influences from the nonverbal to the verbal level, openly discussing cultural issues and concerns and raising the possibility of decision making and choice. As much as possible, he assists the family through mediation and negotiation in settling disagreements in an equitable manner that is free from power and control.

Most importantly, the worker is careful to model egalitarianism in his actions and relationships with families. He demonstrates the advantages of an egalitarian approach and points out the disadvantages of power imbalances and control. He discusses the larger social context in which the family finds itself and looks for ways to empower the family and its members to overcome negative aspects of that social context.

Resources

Affilia: Journal of Women and Social Work.

Bricker-Jenkins, Mary, and Hooyman, Nancy. *Not for Women Only: Social Work Practice for a Feminist Future.* Silver Spring, MD: NASW Press, 1986.

Bricker-Jenkins, Mary, Hooyman, Nancy, and Gottlieb, Naomi. *Feminist Social Work Practice in Clinical Settings.* Newbury Park, CA: Sage, 1991.

Silverstein, Louise B., and Goodrich, Thelma Jean, Eds. *Feminist Family Therapy: Empowerment in Social Context.* Washington, DC: American Psychological Association, 2005.

Valentich, Mary. "Feminism and Social Work Practice" in *Social Work Treatment: Interlocking Theoretical Approaches,* 4th ed., Francis J. Turner, Ed. New York: Free Press, 1996, pp. 282–318.

Van Den Bergh, Nan. *Feminist Practice in the 21st Century.* Washington, DC: NASW Press, 1995.

Van Den Bergh, Nan, and Cooper, Lynn. *Feminist Visions for Social Work.* Silver Spring, MD: NASW Press, 1986.

■   DIVERSITY COMPETENT PRACTICE WITH   ■
GAY AND LESBIAN FAMILIES

In some respects, the description of feminist and feminist-informed practice described in the previous section on gender competent practice also applies to working with gay and lesbian families. This is especially the case regarding the need for empowerment and the principle

that the personal is political. People who are gay or lesbian are probably the object of more hatred than any other groups in the United States, especially by conservative right-wing religious groups and by people who are homophobic. The most common reasons given for negative attitudes are based on religious beliefs.

Recent political battles have been fought over gay and lesbian marriage and gay and lesbian rights. Some states have moved toward recognizing gay and lesbian marriages or civil unions, whereas other states have passed constitutional amendments prohibiting them. This population is the only one that can be legally discriminated against under federal law. In fact, people can be fired for being gay or lesbian without any protection by the federal government. The only protections afforded people who are gay or lesbian are under state and local laws prohibiting discrimination based on sexual orientation. Fortunately, overall prejudice, discrimination, and oppression toward this group have been reduced considerably during recent years. Unfortunately, those who are prejudiced toward people who are gay or lesbian have become more intense in their opposition. Younger generations seem much more tolerant of diversity in sexual orientation, and it would appear that recognition of gay and lesbian marriage and preservation of rights for people who are gay or lesbian is inevitable.

On a professional level, social workers are committed to valuing all human beings and treating everyone with dignity and respect. On a personal level some social workers have religious beliefs that view people who are gay or lesbian negatively. Some may feel conflicted about working with people who are gay or lesbian. However, regardless of the client, social workers should set aside their personal values and act on their professional value system. Generally speaking, when asked, most people say that they would change negative attitudes they have toward people who are gay or lesbian if it were proven that being gay or lesbian was biologically determined. Most studies point in this direction. It is important that social workers use the term *sexual orientation* rather than *sexual preference*. Sexual orientation places sexuality in the biological realm. Sexual preference refers to choice. The term "lifestyle" should also be avoided.

Working with gay and lesbian families involves using similar approaches to those social workers use with other families. The main differences lie in areas related to dealing with the social and political ramifications of their sexual orientation. Prejudice, discrimination, and oppression along with homophobia and heterosexism on the part of others result in social and political reactions that affect people who are gay or lesbian and their families. Socially, these negative reactions range from stares and negative comments to hate crimes that include assaults and murders. Politically, most states do not give legal recognition or status to gay and lesbian relationships. This goes beyond the issue of gay and lesbian marriage. It creates difficulties with insurance coverages, inheritance, adoption, medical consents, child custody, and so on. Rights that are taken for granted by heterosexuals are routinely denied to gay and lesbian couples. Thus, advocacy and empowerment are often needed to overcome some of these issues.

Social workers are often unaware of the extent to which heterosexuality is assumed in society at large and even within the practice of social work itself. Estimates of the percentage of people who are gay or lesbian run as high as 10 percent. This means that as many as one out of ten clients are likely to be gay or lesbian. Many of these clients will not reveal their sexual orientation if they do not know that it is safe to do so. Social workers need to become comfortable in working with clients who are gay and lesbian. They should also communicate to their clients that it is safe to reveal this to them. Some subtle ways of doing this are to display materials related to gay and lesbian services or issues. The rainbow is a symbol for gays and lesbians. There are also stickers and other materials that state that the worker or the agency is a safe place for people who are gay or lesbian.

Social workers should not assume that clients are heterosexual. They should incorporate this into their assessment both verbally and in the type of documentation that is used. Most agency materials including assessment documents are biased toward heterosexuality. Social workers should work to change this to an unbiased approach.

Focusing on family work with gay and lesbian families, there are three primary areas we examine here. These are concerns related to coming out, especially with families of origin; working with gay and lesbian couples; and assisting gay and lesbian parents and their children with social issues related to sexual orientation.

Concerns related to coming out as a gay man or a lesbian woman are quite common when working with gay and lesbian families. The dilemma is typically described as a need to be open about being gay or lesbian and to be accepted. The fear is that acceptance will be lost or rejection will occur if others know the person is gay or lesbian. This fear has a great deal of reality to it as many people who are gay or lesbian experience rejection from their families and friends and may even be fired from their jobs if they reveal their sexual orientation. This causes stress for many people who are gay or lesbian. Having to hide an important aspect of one's true identity can cause a great deal of stress and strain. It can also be quite complicated for couples because if one of them comes out the other person's sexual orientation is also revealed.

Working with adolescents who are gay or lesbian is quite challenging because of the extreme reactions by their peers, negative reactions by their families, and the volatility of adolescence itself. Both suicide attempts and completions are much higher for youth who are gay and lesbian as compared to heterosexual teens. The social worker must be vigilant about depression and suicidal thinking when she works with this population. It is best if these youth can work with a trained therapist in dealing with these issues. However, generalist social workers also work with this population. They need to be sensitive to the possibility that as many as 10 percent of their youthful clients are struggling with their sexual identity and the social stresses related to it.

Working with gay and lesbian couples and their families involve all of the same issues and approaches that are identified in Parts II and III of the text. What is different is the issue of gender-based roles. In heterosexual relationships, various cultures may prescribe certain roles to the male and others to the female. This will not work for same-sex couples. A common myth about same-sex couples is that one of the partners assumes the male role and the other the female role. Some same-sex couples do this, but the majority do not. It appears that many are able to develop egalitarian relationships and may even provide good models for heterosexual couples who are struggling with developing shared-role relationships. The key to developing shared-role relationships is communicating effectively and using an efficient and effective decision-making process. Roles cannot be assumed and need to be discussed every day to determine who is going to do what. Communication is discussed in the next chapter and throughout the rest of the text. Various aspects of decision making are covered in Parts II and III. As with any couple, disagreements can and do arise with same-sex couples. Helping them to develop and use effective conflict resolution skills is important. This is also covered in Chapters 7 and 8 and in Part III.

Social workers may become involved with assisting gay and lesbian parents and their children with social issues related to sexual orientation. Dealing with the reactions of others can be quite challenging. Fortunately, there are books and materials that are becoming available to help same-sex couples and their children with these issues. First, let us look at how same-sex couples become parents. Some were formerly in a heterosexual relationship in which children were produced. Some people who are gay or lesbian have been able to adopt children, although only one of them is typically a legal parent to the child. Some same-sex couples use formal and informal fertility options, including artificial insemination and surrogate mothers. Those couples who produced children in previous heterosexual relationships often experience a great deal of difficulty with the legal system regarding custody and visitation if their sexual orientation is revealed. The same can be true for adoption.

Negative reactions by peers toward children in gay and lesbian families can be very difficult challenges. Negative reactions by the general public toward the family as a whole or toward same-sex couples can also be quite challenging. Some same-sex parents will hide their sexual orientation to avoid these challenges. Many find that they have to be very selective about where they live and where their children attend school. They look for neighborhoods or communities where there is either tolerance for their sexual orientation or tolerance for diversity in general. Groups have been formed to assist with these issues and to offer gay and lesbian families opportunities to share time with other gay and lesbian families in order to escape from these challenges and to experience acceptance. These groups offer vacations, trips, cruises, and social events especially for gay and lesbian families.

Resources

Laird, Joan, and Green, Robert-Jay, Eds. *Lesbians and Gays in Couples and Families.* San Fransisco, CA: Jossey-Bass, 1996. A "must have" text for anyone practicing with gay and lesbian couples and families.

Mallon, Gerald P. "Practice with Families Where Sexual Orientation Is an Issue: Lesbian and Gay Individuals and Their Families" in *Multicultural Perspectives in Working with Families,* 2nd ed. Elaine P. Congress and Manny J. Gonzales, Eds. New York: Springer, 2005, pp. 199–227.

Morrow, Deana F., and Messinger, Lori, Eds. *Sexual Orientation and Gender Expression in Social Work Practice: Working with Gay, Lesbian, Bisexual, and Transgender People.* New York: Columbia University Press, 2006.

Silverstein, Louise B., and Goodrich, Thelma Jean, Eds. *Feminist Family Therapy: Empowerment in Social Context,* Washington, DC: American Psychological Association, 2005.

Walters, Karina L., Longres, John F., Han, Chong-suk, and Icard, Larry D. "Cultural Competence with Gay and Lesbian Persons of Color" in *Culturally Competent Practice: A Framework for Understanding Diverse Groups and Justice Issues,* 2nd ed. Doman Lum, Ed. Pacific Grove, CA: Brooks/Cole, 2003.

■ A SCHEMA FOR STUDYING FAMILIES FROM ■ DIVERSE ETHNIC GROUPS

Table 3.2 displays a schema for studying families from diverse ethnic groups. It is intended to be broad enough to be used with any family, regardless of ethnicity. It can be adapted for use with families with mixed ethnic backgrounds by using it multiculturally and covering each

Table 3.2 Schema for Studying Families from Diverse Ethnic Groups

I. Overall knowledge of diverse ethnic group
  A. History of the particular ethnic group
    1. Significant information about the point of origin
    2. Immigration patterns, when, why
    3. Experience(s) with the dominant society, any legal events, prejudice/discrimination concerns
    4. Experience in coping or integrating with dominant society
  B. Significant cultural patterns
    1. Spiritual considerations, experiences, beliefs
    2. Relationship beliefs about the physical world
    3. Significant values/value system(s)
    4. Attitudes toward things, time and its use, age, authority, work, display of feeling or emotions
    5. Change and its meaning to group
    6. Past, present, and future orientation
    7. Ceremonies, rituals
    8. Traditional art forms—music—use of in daily or ceremonial life
    9. Taboos
  C. Family patterns and structure
    1. Relationships of importance
      a. Within cultural group
      b. With larger society
    2. Decision-making processes
    3. Generational factors, age, sex considerations
    4. Child-rearing and housekeeping practices
    5. Expectations within the family
  D. Communication patterns
    1. Language usage; concepts, values, philosophies
    2. Nonverbal expression
  E. Traditional coping patterns and mechanisms
    1. Adaptation, compensation, reaction to stress, stigmatization, stereotyping
  F. Community structures
    1. Traditional forms and ways of functioning
    2. Community provision for help
    3. Contemporary society structures relative to this ethnic group
  G. Current issues of the group or regarding the group
    1. Quality of life issues
    2. Economic, educational, spiritual
    3. Group identity
    4. Opportunity provision or restriction
    5. Discrimination, prejudice concerns
  H. Resources for gaining understanding of group

II. Knowledge of the individual family
  A. History
    1. Experience of this particular family
    2. Migration, movement within the United States

(continued)

Table 3.2   Continued

> a. Social–economic mobility
> b. Identification with ethnic group
> 3. Note urban–rural experience
> 4. Fit within larger ethnic group
> B. Value concerns
> 1. What of traditional ethnic patterns is important to this family? What is not? How do they deal with discrepancies?
> 2. Spirituality within the family
> 3. Traditions
> C. Family
> 1. How does this family define itself (nuclear, extended, etc.)?
> 2. Relationships in this family
> 3. How does this family relate to larger ethnic group? To their heritage?
> D. Communication patterns
> 1. Within this particular family
> 2. With larger society
> E. Coping in this particular family
> F. Community
> 1. Relationships to ethnic community, to dominant community
> 2. Resources available, usable by this family, experience with
> G. Issues concerning this family

cultural background that is relevant. The use of the schema forms the framework for our studies of diversity competent practice with African American, Hispanic/Latino, and Native American families. It can also be used in learning about families from various parts of Europe, Asia, and the Pacific Islands as well as those who are immigrants from Central and South America and from Africa. Space prohibits us from covering every type of family, but three main types in which social workers are likely to encounter cross-cultural relationships are covered here.

When considering the ethnic family there are two levels of understanding that are needed by the worker: first is the more general level, which provides overall knowledge, second is the specific level, which provides understanding of a specific family. At the general level, it is important to consider the history of the ethnic group, including information about the point or country of origin. The worker should gather information about immigration patterns and reasons for the immigration of the ethnic group as a whole. Did this group experience discrimination and oppression in their country of origin? Religious persecution? Economic deprivation? Political persecution? The worker should also seek to uncover experiences the group has had with the dominant group in U.S. society and how they have coped with those experiences or have been integrated into the dominant group.

Significant cultural patterns provide the next area for examination. Spirituality, values, art forms, taboos, and attitudes and beliefs, including those regarding change and time, should be explored. Ceremonies and rituals are also important aspects of culture.

Within each culture are family patterns and structure. It is important to know about significant relationships, how decisions are typically made, child-rearing and housekeeping practices, and expectations that families typically have of their members. There are also generational factors and age and sex considerations. These latter factors refer to inter- and intragenerational relationships and statuses, attitudes toward aging and the aged, and sex- or gender-based role expectations.

The diversity competent social worker needs to pay close attention to communication patterns, especially as these relate to language and to nonverbal communication. Because interaction is the staple of both family life and the social work endeavor, this aspect of culture takes on great significance.

Another area for study are the coping mechanisms that are typically used by members of the ethnic group. How do they respond to stress or to prejudice and stereotyping? What is accepted within the culture and what is not?

Looking beyond the family, the worker needs to be familiar with community structures that are typical for the ethnic group. How does the community typically function within the culture? How is help usually offered and received? What kinds of societal structures are constructed within this ethnic community? Some ethnic groups rely on neighborhood communities or clubs to preserve their identity and their culture. Others rely on religious institutions. Still others have little in the way of formal or informal structures, and, as a result, their ethnic identity may be quickly absorbed into the dominant culture provided they are not identified by skin color or some other recognizable feature that makes them a target for exclusion.

The worker should be familiar with current issues that are important for the ethnic group. For instances, the status of illegal immigrants is an important consideration within the Mexican American community. Other issues relate to the group's quality of life, economic and educational opportunities or restrictions, identity, and prejudice and discrimination. What are the important issues for this population and why are these important?

Finally, in the area of general or overall knowledge the worker needs to be aware of resources that are available for gaining an understanding of the ethnic group. These range from formal to informal sources of information. Formal sources come from census data, library resources, histories, educational institutions, community resources for the family ethnic group, and other community structures. Informal resources tend to be verbal and include colleagues, indigenous workers, experts, and members of the ethnic group, including the family system with whom the worker is working.

The second area of knowledge is at the specific level, which provides understanding of a specific family. This area recognizes that, although families may share a common ethnic identity, each family is unique in terms of how it experiences and expresses its identity. The information for this area of study comes mainly from the family itself. The worker seeks to have the family tell its story and she listens without any preconceived notions about what she will hear.

The first area for exploration is the unique history of this family. What were their experiences and those of their ancestors? What is their history of migration and their movement within the United States? What is their socioeconomic status and how mobile have they been in terms of increasing their status? What is the family's identification with their ethnic group and how strong is this? Have they lived in rural or urban areas and what affect has this had on the family system?

Next, the worker should look at values and how the family experiences or adheres to values from its ethnic roots. What has been retained and what has not? How does the family feel about discrepancies between its values and those of its ethnic heritage? What are the spiritual or religious practices within the family and how do these reflect traditional ethnic practices? What ethnic traditions have been retained and what traditions are no longer practiced?

For the family itself, the worker should explore how they see themselves as a family. Who are considered members? How important is the extended family? What characterizes relationships within the family? How does the family relate to the larger ethnic group? How does it relate to their ethnic heritage? What are the communication patterns within the family and between the family and the larger society? What are the typical coping patterns and mechanisms used by this family and how do these relate to those that are typical for its ethnic group? What relationships are there between the family and its ethnic community? How does the family relate to the larger society? What resources are available to this family and how are these accessed and used? What has been the family's experiences with those resources? What are the main issues that concern this family?

The worker uses naturalistic inquiry as he explores these unique areas of family life. He draws out their story and takes the position that he does not know what he does not know. He respects the family as experts on their own lives and their cultural heritage and experience. The diversity competent worker is aware of his own attitudes toward the particular ethnic group and attempts to set those aside so he can be as nonjudgmental as possible. He is also aware of attitudes and stereotypes of the larger society toward the ethnic group and the effects of these on that group. As the worker explores these areas, he builds a meaningful relationship with the family that will carry them through the work to be done.

■   DIVERSITY COMPETENT PRACTICE WITH   ■
AFRICAN AMERICAN FAMILIES

Diversity competent practice with African American families begins with the understanding that African American families are diverse while also sharing common experiences. African Americans have diverse roots and histories that create diversity within their culture. At the same time, African Americans share the experience of living in a society that is racist and has continued to marginalize them, even in the face of legal challenges to discrimination and oppression. Diversity within the African American culture exists because of variation in their roots. Although most African Americans have their roots in areas of West Africa, some are descendants of former slaves who lived in the Caribbean and

West Indies. In addition, there was a great deal of variation in their ancestral experiences in the United States during slavery and afterward.

Diversity competent practice with African American families generally means using an Afrocentric approach. This approach evolved primarily during the twentieth century. Jerome H. Schiele described three basic assumptions regarding Afrocentric social work: "1) that individual identity is conceived as a collective identity; 2) that the spiritual aspects of humans is just as legitimate as the material component; and 3) that the affective approach to knowledge is epistemologically valid."[17] The first two of these assumptions are particularly important in working with African Americans and their families. Whereas individual identity and materialism are highly prized in Eurocentric cultures, individual identity is tied to family, culture, community, and creator for African Americans, and people are seen as being spiritually connected with each other and with the world around them.

Historical Considerations

Most African Americans are descendents of the only non–Native American group that did not immigrate as such; they were brought to the United States against their will to be used as slaves. African American history during slavery and afterward is the predominant issue when it comes to understanding working with African American families. Although most slaves were brought to the United States from West Africa, there was a great deal of cultural and language diversity among the tribes to which they belonged. In addition, many African Americans are descended from former slaves who lived in the Caribbean and West Indies and had developed a rich and varied culture that was different from African American slaves.

The experiences of African Americans after slavery ended are also important historical considerations. Most former slaves remained in the South and were eventually subjugated again, especially after Reconstruction ended. Few owned any land and the system of sharecropping ensured that they remained poor and in debt. In addition to economic subjugation, African Americans were systematically excluded from voting and holding office. A social and legal system known as "Jim Crow" reinforced their status as second-class citizens. This economic, political, and social oppression was enforced by groups such as the Ku Klux Klan and various vigilante groups who beat, murdered, and lynched African Americans who dared to challenge the system. Some former slaves migrated to the North and the West where they were free but still experienced prejudice, discrimination, and oppression in various forms. With the collapse of the cotton and tobacco economies, especially during the Great Depression, many African Americans migrated to cities in the South, the North, and the West looking for work. They were typically concentrated in poor neighborhoods with overcrowded substandard housing.

More recently, many African Americans have become economically successful and have been able to move to other areas with better housing and more opportunities. Unfortunately, a disproportionate number of African American families have not enjoyed the same success and are still mired in poverty in our inner cities. What is remarkable is that the progress that African Americans have made since slavery has been almost entirely at their own hands. Little if any assistance has been given by the dominant culture. In fact much of the progress made by African Americans has actually occurred in spite of barriers that have been and continue to be erected by the dominant culture.

Cultural Patterns

Efforts were made to eliminate African culture as part of the subjugation of slavery. However, African Americans were successful in using their African culture to survive both the ravages of slavery and the further oppression that has followed it. Afrocentricity gives us a view of various aspects of African culture that have survived and contributed to survival. Schiele's description refers to collective identity and spirituality. These two assumptions are intertwined in that spirituality includes a belief that all human beings are interconnected with each other, with the environment, and with the creator, which is the web that connects everything together. Thus, individual identity does not exist separate from the environment, but as a part of the collective identity of the community, the nation, and the world.[18]

In many traditional African cultures, the community is the most important social entity. This is captured in the African proverb "It takes a village to raise a child." Kinship extended beyond the nuclear family and included both extended family and nonfamily members of the community. Responsibility for child-rearing, preparation for adulthood, and rites of passage were the responsibilities of the entire village. This collective identity resulted in African Americans forming similar communities of related and unrelated kinship networks during slavery and afterward. The community made sure that the elderly, children, and widows were cared for regardless of how poor members were themselves.

The essence of Afrocentricity is best illustrated by the Nguzo Saba of Kwanzaa, which is an Afrocentric value system made up of seven principles. There are numerous renditions of this. The following is from an article by Vanessa D. Johnson regarding its use as a foundation for African American college student development theory:

> *Umoja* (unity): To strive for and maintain unity in the family, community, nation, and race.
>
> *Kujichagulia* (self-determination): To define ourselves, name ourselves, create for ourselves, and speak for ourselves instead of being defined, named, created for, and spoken for by others.
>
> *Ujima* (collective work and responsibility): To build and maintain our community together and make our sisters' and brothers' problems our problems and to solve them together.
>
> *Ujamma* (cooperative economics): To build and maintain our own stores, shops, and other businesses and profit from them together.
>
> *Nia* (purpose): To make our collective vocation the building and developing of our community in order to restore our people to their traditional greatness.
>
> *Kuumba* (creativity): To do always as much as we can, in the way we can, in order to leave our community more beautiful and beneficial than we inherited it.
>
> *Imani* (faith): To believe with all our hearts in God, our people, our parents, our teachers, our leaders, and the righteousness and victory of our struggle.[19]

The values that are expressed in these seven principles reflect values that have been preserved from African heritage. They could easily be used by any group that has experienced oppression.

Given the varied history of African American families, there are also variations in the extent to which families have retained and practice elements of their African heritage. Peter Bell and Jimmy Evans suggested four interpersonal styles they associated with the degree of acculturation. Those who are fully acculturated have assimilated into mainstream white culture and do not typically identify with or express their African American heritage. On the opposite side of the spectrum are those who reject white culture and identify with and express only their African American heritage. In between these are those who are bicultural and who are comfortable with both white and African American culture. A fourth group are traditional. They tend to value their African American heritage and have limited contact outside the African American community. They may show some of the effects of their history under slavery and Jim Crow such as deference to whites.[20]

Family

As indicated under the Nguzo Saba, the family plays a critical role in the life of African Americans.[21] The African American family is an extended family that may also include fictive kin or members who are not related by blood or marriage. This reflects the African cultural heritage in which the community was considered the most important social unit. Unrelated family members may be referred to using the terms *brother, sister, aunt, uncle,* or *cousin.* Grandparents who raise their grandchildren or informal guardians who informally adopt children to raise may be called *mother* or *father.*

Probably one of the greatest impacts on African American families has been the effects of economic deprivation and oppression. Employment opportunities have been extremely limited. One could argue that the only legitimate economic roles readily afforded African Americans by the dominant white society were those associated with slavery, sharecropping, and domestic services. In addition, African American males have generally found it more difficult than females to acquire and maintain employment. Thus, one of the effects of economic oppression on the African American family has been to undermine the role of provider for African American males. From the emasculation of males during slavery and Jim Crow to the collapse of the cotton and tobacco economy, which relied on sharecropping, to the exportation of manufacturing jobs under globalization, many African American males have been robbed of the role of provider. These experiences have contributed to a situation in which the majority of African American families today are headed by females, whereas many of those incarcerated in prison or jail are African American males.

Communication Processes

Although African American families speak English, a form of English has evolved that is referred to as *Black English* or *African American language.* Valerie Borum differentiates between this and "Standard English" and points out that some families speak only one or the other and some will switch back and forth and are bilingual.[22] She describes African American language as allowing for flexibility and including "highly meaningful nonverbal communication and expression via body language."[23] She sees it as "dramatizing that which Standard English fails to communicate."[24] It "might be regarded as a 'highly exquisite form of pantomime.'"[25]

Accompanying this variation in language are variations in culture and worldviews, which are reflected in the principles of the Nguzo Saba, especially regarding collective identity, unity, and creativity.[26] Relationships are highly prized and are generally valued over the materialism that is seen as characterizing white culture.

Coping Patterns

The coping patterns of African Americans is also reflected in Afrocentricity and the seven principles of the Nguzo Saba.[27] Collective identity, a strong sense of community, and spirituality make for a strong base from which members can deal with adversity. The whole history of African Americans has been fraught with adversity beginning with the diaspora and slavery and continuing through pervasive prejudice, discrimination, and oppression that continues to this day. Through all of this African Americans have persevered and many are quite prosperous in spite of their mistreatment by the dominant white society.

Collective identity gives African Americans a means of overcoming negative messages from the dominant culture, which devalues people of color. By relying on their families, communities, and culture for self-esteem and respect, many African Americans are able to develop healthy self-images despite the actions of white society. Their strong sense of community and the high value placed on mutual aid provided their own safety net during slavery and the following hard times when there were no such structures in the U.S. social welfare system for African Americans. A strong belief in spirituality is the third leg of their coping system. A belief in a creator and a universe where everything is connected has given African Americans the will and determination to persevere.

Community Structure

The word *community* for African Americans means much more than the physical surroundings or place where they live. It is a network of relationships that connect them to each other, to all other human beings, to the world, and to the creator.

Using the Eurocentric concept of community, the physical structure and geography of the African American community varies based on their history. The majority in the North and the West live in urban areas, and traditionally they were restricted by discriminatory practices to the inner city where housing was old and frequently substandard. Most of the rest live in rural areas in the southeastern United States. Some of those living in the North or urban areas of the South have gradually migrated to suburban areas as they have been able to achieve a level of economic prosperity. However, they have generally not been welcomed by their white neighbors who often engage in "white flight" when an African American family moves into the neighborhood. Some of these African American families have experienced various forms of harassment including threats, racist graffiti or publications, or having a crosses burned on their lawns.

Most African Americans try to maintain close family ties by either living in close proximity to relatives or by maintaining contact by phone, Internet, and frequent family reunions. Even when close relatives are not nearby, African Americans are able to build their own family networks through the adoption of fictive kin wherever they may live.

The migration of African Americans to urban areas has probably undermined to some extent the strong sense of community that was built in rural areas. Social scientists who study human behavior in crowded communities typically see a breakdown in social structures when people are overwhelmed with a large number of relationships caused by overcrowding. When people are not familiar with their neighbors, they are less likely to establish mutual aid systems.

Current Issues

Current issues for African Americans involve those that typically would be expected. Overcoming prejudice, discrimination, and oppression continues, only in somewhat different forms. On paper it is illegal, but in reality these barriers still exist. Recently, a backlash has developed and there are attacks on such programs as affirmative action, which have opened doors for women and minorities. Poverty remains a reality for a disproportionate percentage of families, especially for a substantial minority of African American children. Substance abuse and incarceration are also overrepresented in the African American community.

Resources

Borum, Valerie. "An Afrocentric Approach in Working with African American Familes" in *Multicultural Perspectives in Working with Families,* 2nd ed. Elaine P. Congress and Manny J. Gonzales, Eds. New York: Springer, 2005, Chapter 12.

Boyd-Franklin, Nancy. *Black Families in Therapy: Understanding the African American Experience,* 2nd ed. New York: Guilford Press, 2003.

Fong, Rowena, and Furuto, Charlene, Eds. *Culturally Competent Practice: Skills, Interventions, and Evaluations,* 2nd ed. Boston: Allyn & Bacon, 2001. (See Chapters 3, 8, 9, 16, 17, 24, and 25.)

McRoy, Ruth. "Cultural Competence with African Americans" in *Culturally Competent Practice: A Framework for Understanding Diverse Groups and Justice Issues,* 2nd ed. Doman Lum, Ed. Pacific Grove, CA: Brooks/Cole, 2003, Chapter 9.

Schiele, Jerome H. *Human Services and the Afrocentric Paradigm.* New York: The Haworth Press, 2000.

Willis, Winnie. "Families with African American Roots" in *Developing Cross-Cultural Competence: A Guide to Working with Children and Their Families,* 2nd ed. Eleanor W. Lynch and Marci J. Hanson, Eds. Baltimore, MD: Paul H. Brookes, 1998, Chapter 6.

■ DIVERSITY COMPETENT PRACTICE WITH ■ HISPANIC/LATINO FAMILIES

Hispanic/Latino families represent a wide variation in race, culture, and roots. We use the term *Hispanic/Latino* to refer to those people whose language is predominantly Spanish and whose culture is at least partially influenced by the cultures that evolved in regions of North and South America that came under Spanish rule during and after the 1500s. This is a vast area with many variations in culture. The most common cultures found in the United States are Mexican, Central and South American, Puerto Rican, and Cuban. There are variations in language among these as well as culture.

Historical Considerations

The Spanish approach to exploration and settlement can probably best be described as one of conquest. Priests often accompanied the conquistadors, and religion, language, and culture were imposed on those who were conquered, often under the penalty of death. Spanish and indigenous populations intermingled, leaving a wide variation of racial and ethnic groups. Skin color ranged from light-skinned, blond-haired and blue-eyed descendants of Spanish origin to those descended from North and South American First Nations tribes and

from African slaves. Portugese language and culture is a major influence in Brazilian culture. Many people in the United States think of those who are Hispanic/Latino as a race, but they are really an ethnic group that includes various combinations of white, Native American, and African American genetic backgrounds.

The Spanish influence in the United States began in the 1500s mainly in the Southeast and the Southwest. The United States acquired Spanish and Mexican territory primarily through force or the threat of it. Florida was ceded to the United States to avoid a confrontation over its acquisition. Texans won their independence from Mexico. Texans included both immigrants from the United States and local residents of Mexican descent. Later, the Mexican-American War was fought so the United States could acquire Texas and California and the lands in between. This represented nearly half of what had formerly been Mexico. After the War, residents of Mexican descent were promised citizenship and property rights, but there were numerous instances in which this was not what ensued. Periodic mass deportations have taken place along with the seizure of land. Cuba was captured from Spain during the Spanish-American War at the end of the 1900s and was later given its independence. Puerto Rico was also captured but has remained a U.S. territory. Puerto Ricans are considered U.S. citizens and they do not need passports or visas to move back and forth between the island and the mainland.

Descendants of Mexican descent are either long-term residents of territory seized from Mexico or they are immigrants from Mexico. People of Central American descent are primarily relatively recent immigrants, mainly either refugees fleeing various civil wars in that region or those seeking improved economic prospects. Most Cubans have settled in the Miami area and are political and economic refugees who left Cuba after the regime of Fidel Castro began in the late 1950s. Most of the immigration policy in the United States during the past century has been aimed at controlling the immigration of Hispanic/Latino populations. Undocumented immigration is a major issue with estimates of as many as 11 million people living in the United States without proper documentation.

Cultural Patterns

Cultural patterns are influenced by the area from which the family comes. However, there are some common patterns of note. *Familismo* is a cultural value that is held by many Hispanic/Latino families. It places a high value on the family and family relationships and sees individual identity as a product of family relationships.[28] Another value that is closely associated with the family is *machismo,* which values traditional gender-based roles and a patriarchal structure within the family.[29] *Personalismo* is a cultural value that emphasizes closeness in interpersonal relationships, which includes valuing people over material objects and emphasizing relationships over individual achievement.[30] Religion plays an important role in the culture, with most families adhering to Roman Catholic beliefs. Pentecostal religions have made strong inroads into this traditional pattern of beliefs in some areas, especially along the Mexican border.

Families experience a wide range of acculturation, which determines the degree to which cultural heritage and language are retained. Many families are bicultural and bilingual. However, language skills are frequently lost by younger generations who grow up speaking English at school.

Family

As mentioned previously, familismo places a high value on the family. Individual identity depends heavily on family relationships. Many people of Hispanic/Latino heritage would not consider making individual decisions without family input or considering the effects of the decision on the family. Patriarchy and traditional gender-based roles are prominent in most families. The family is generally considered the most important social unit, and cultural values are primarily family centered.

Communication Processes

There are a wide variety of patterns in Hispanic/Latino families with regard to the use of Spanish and English. Some families have a pattern of speaking Spanish within the home and English or Spanish outside of the home depending on the setting. Family members who are older may not speak or understand much, if any, English. This may also be the case for recent immigrants from Spanish-speaking countries. Children may become the first truly bilingual family members as they encounter English when they enter school. This may also be the case for adults who work and acquire English through their work setting. Generally, the latter remain more comfortable with Spanish. Younger Hispanic/Latino families may have lost their Spanish-speaking abilities and may speak only English although they might understand some Spanish.

Coping Patterns

Religion and spirituality are very important for coping for many Hispanic/Latino families. Celia Jaes Falicov describes how most Latinos attribute adversity to sources that are beyond one's control. She points out that many Latinos will add the phrase "God willing" when discussing the future, which is an indication of the belief that one's life is not under one's control.[31] Falicov describes several coping mechanisms that result from these beliefs. Controlarse is "control of the self," which refers to controlling one's mood or emotions as a way of mastering adversity.[32] This concept includes ". . . *aguantarse* (endurance), or the ability to withstand stress in times of adversity; *no pensar* (don't think of the problem), or avoidance of focusing on disturbing thoughts or feelings . . . ; *resignarse* (resignation), or the passive acceptance of one's fate; and *sobreponerse* (to overcome), a more active cognitive coping that allows for working through or overcoming adversity."[33]

The combination of deep religious belief and conviction along with the coping mechanisms mentioned previously give many Hispanic/Latino families incredible fortitude when they are faced with adversity. At the same time, these coping mechanism may not be understood by members of the dominant culture and are easily misinterpreted or stereotyped.

Community Structure

There is variation in the community structure for Hispanic/Latino families. Some of this variation is caused by differences among the cultural groups described earlier. For instance, Puerto Ricans are more likely to be found in New York City and several urban areas along the Atlantic Coast. Cubans tend to be clustered in south Florida. People of Mexican descent have large populations in rural and urban areas along the southern boundaries of the border states of Texas, New Mexico, Arizona, and California. They are also found in both urban and rural areas where migrant workers settled.

Wherever they live Hispanic/Latino families form community networks. The Hispanic/Latino community typically comes together several times each year to celebrate traditional holidays. Some of these are religious and others are related to events from their native countries, such as Cinqo de Mayo which celebrates Mexican independence. In rural areas, many families travel to the nearest community with a Hispanic/Latino population. Some will celebrate with only their families or with some close neighbors. In urban areas, people who are Hispanic/Latino often live close together in certain areas. Mexican American communities in larger cities of the Southwest are typically referred to as *barrios*.

Current Issues

Most of the current issues for people who are Hispanic/Latino revolve around immigration, preserving their heritage, and overcoming economic hardship. Most recent changes in immigration law in the United States are aimed at people who are Hispanic/Latino. There is a great deal of disparity regarding experiences between various groups. Puerto Ricans are able to enter the United States legally because they are considered U.S. citizens. Cubans have generally been accepted as political refugees, although some were identified as mentally ill or former prisoners who were criminals in Cuba, and many of these were detained for some time. Immigrants from Mexico and Central American have not been able to immigrate quite as easily. The poverty and lack of opportunity to improve their economic well-being in their own countries lead many to immigrate illegally or without proper documentation. This has become a major political issue with intense debate about what to do to stem the tide of illegal immigrants along with the question of what to do with undocumented workers and illegal immigrants who are already here.

To some extent, the desire to preserve their language, culture, and heritage is reflected in the community networks that Hispanic/Latino families form. At the same time, they have been criticized for not assimilating into the larger culture when they do so. Within the family, including the extended family, it is not unusual to see conflicts over cultural preservation arising between older and younger generations.

Economic hardship is a primary reason for immigration for many Hispanic/Latino families. However, economic prosperity is not guaranteed, especially for undocumented workers. They are easily exploited by employers. This exploitation can go beyond financial to include sexual exploitation as well. Many Hispanic/Latino families have learned to cope with economic hardship by working hard for long hours and pooling their resources within the family. So, even though several family members may be working at very low wages, the family may be able to experience some prosperity from their combined incomes.

Resources

Falicov, Celia Jaes. *Latino Families in Therapy: A Guide to Multicultural Practice.* New York: Guilford Press, 1998. This book provides a good base for understanding Hispanic/Latino families. Although it uses the term *therapy,* it is written in a way that can be used by generalist social workers working with this population.

Fong, Rowena, and Furuto, Charlene, Eds. *Culturally Competent Practice: Skills, Interventions, and Evaluations,* 2nd ed. Boston: Allyn & Bacon, 2001. (See Chapters 4, 10, 11, 18, 19, 26, and 27.)

Romero, Mary, and Hondagneu-Sotelo, Pierette. *Challenging Fronteras: Structuring Latina and Latino Lives in the U.S.: An Anthology of Readings.* New York: Routledge, 1997. Another look at the lives of Hispanic/Latino families in the United States.

Suarez-Orozco, Marcelo M., and Paez, Mariela. *Latinos: Remaking America.* Berkeley: University of California Press, 2002. A comprehensive look at experiences of Latinos and issues they face.

Zuniga, Maria. "Families with Latino Roots" in *Developing Cross-Cultural Competence: A Guide to Working with Children and Their Families,* 2nd ed. Eleanor W. Lynch and Marci J. Hanson, Eds. Baltimore, MD: Paul H. Brookes, 1998, Chapter 7.

Zuniga, Maria E. "Cultural Competence with Latino Americans" in *Culturally Competent Practice: A Framework for Understanding Diverse Groups and Justice Issues,* 2nd ed. Doman Lum, Ed. Pacific Grove, CA: Brooks/Cole, 2003, Chapter 10.

■ DIVERSITY COMPETENT PRACTICE WITH ■ NATIVE AMERICAN FAMILIES

When working with the Native American[34] families, two understandings are central: First, there are many tribes, each with its own culture, and each considered by most Native Americans as a sovereign nation. Second, each family as it lives in a world dominated by a majority group has its particular ways of dealing with dual perspectives of functioning. This makes it essential that any social worker rely on the Native American family to provide the understandings needed for effective work. An understanding of a family's ties to its culture are of prime concern. The ways in which a family functions is usually closely tied to this cultural base. Rural and urban context is also important. Educational policies and practices are important to understand. The impact of boarding schools, with their emphases, had great implications for the family in the past. This all supports the use of a diversity competent mode of practice that uses the client as the expert in determining what is important and what is to be done in the work together. However, a diversity competent worker strives to understand the client in the culture to the best of her ability. This, of course, suggests that a worker should concentrate learning about the tribes to which her client families belong. That understanding is far too diverse for this text to provide.[35] However, there are more general understandings that can be provided.

Historical Considerations

First of importance is an understanding of the historical relationship of Native Americans to the U.S. government. Zimmerman and Molyneaux describe this as "dispossession." To quote them, "There were three types of European invasion: physical (the occupation of territory by immigrants), spiritual (the imposition of Christianity), and material (the introduction of goods such as guns and alcohol). Native people were driven out, swindled by unobserved treaties, subjugated, shattered, plied with alcohol and confined to reservations."[36] Vine Deloria, Jr., describes this as "Promises Made, Promises Broken."[37] Continual changing federal policy regarding removal, resettlement, assimilation, land allotment, and termination have left native peoples with feelings of distrust of the majority society and great uncertainties when relating to a majority person. These practices and policies have also had two major effects on native peoples: the breakdown or even destruction of traditional ways of functioning and the extreme poverty that many Native Americans experience. Land is sacred to Native Americans, thus experiences that interfere or destroy the traditional relationship to the land are particularly destructive to society and family.

Cultural Patterns

Native American cultural patterns, although specific to a tribe or clan, also have some general characteristics. The Native American way of thinking, rather than being linear, tends to be circular or systemic, everything is related to everything else. Past, present, and future are very much intertwined. One means for depicting the native life concept is the circle, which encompasses nature or everything that comes from Mother Earth. Mind, spirit, and body are all seen as major parts yet a part of the whole. All life is sacred and all aspects of nature, as well as all things, all events, and people, are related.

Family is very important and it is the extended family that is the focal point. Children are valued and belong to the tribe and the extended family. Grandparents are of great importance in the raising of children; in fact, they often are of greater importance than parents. Elders are greatly respected. Sharing and giving are important. There is a sense that time is to be used in showing respect and caring for others, not the importance of "being on time."

There is usually a belief in a higher being. Creation stories are important but vary from tribe to tribe. All life is sacred. Spirituality is encompassed in all of daily living. It tends to be more of an individual expression rather than a group expression. Specifics relate to particular tribes' beliefs and experiences. Assimilation of Christianity is related to the historical policy of assigning particular denominations to specific areas. Where Christian beliefs and practices have been accepted, they have a denominational element blended with the native traditions and beliefs. Communal land is sacred. It is tied to the health of the tribe. It is a place to which to periodically return.

Each tribe has its own rituals and ceremonies. Each usually have traditional art forms, crafts, dances, and so on. Workers would do well to gain appreciation for the meaning of these art forms to the group. Each have various taboos. Many of these relate to relationships among people. Workers must have knowledge of these so as not to offend those for whom they are providing service. In many tribes, eye contact is to be avoided. It is seen as a sign of disrespect.

Family

As has been indicated, the traditional Native American family is an extended one. All members are responsible for one another. All share in childcare. They are expected to share what they have with this extended group. This sometimes become problematic when some members of the extended family gain opportunities to better themselves through education or other options and are then expected to share with members of the extended family who are poverty stricken, addicted to alcohol and other drugs, or otherwise not providing for their basic needs. It is expected that decision making will also be shared among family members. Elders are looked to for advice and guidance.

It should be noted that the more isolated the tribe, the less change there will be in family life from traditional ways. Native families in urban area have been most affected by majority ways of functioning. However, many keep close ties with the "homeland/reservation" or live within an urban enclave of Native Americans. These families tend to relate to two worlds with the tensions inherent in such situations.[38]

Communication Processes

Although most Native Americans speak English, there is a tendency to have a somewhat limited vocabulary and to word sentences somewhat differently from that which majority workers are used to. It is most important to listen carefully and use feedback techniques to be sure that there is mutual understanding. Native culture is strongly an oral culture. Truths and culture are passed along by means of storytelling. It is important to gain an appreciation for this means of communication and develop skill in interpreting the meaning of the stories.

Relationships take time to develop. Time needs to be spent in small talk, in letting a Native American person get to know who you are as a person. Often the provision of some small concrete service will further the development of a relationship.[39]

Coping Patterns

There is a strong emphasis on bringing situations into balance. Ceremonies are used to create or restore harmony with nature that reflects Native American beliefs in a holistic world in which all things are interconnected and interrelated. There is strong reliance on beliefs and sacred wisdom. Because of historical experiences with the majority culture, there are themes of conflict, resistance, and survival.

Native persons are very skilled at hiding emotions. Attitudes toward authority are important because the worker is considered an authority person. Particularly older Native Americans respect authority and often express this respect by agreeing with the worker, although they have no intent to carry out what seems to have been agreed on. Younger Native Americans often display hostility toward workers or other authority figures.

Socialization is of great importance to these people. Each person is valued. When sanctions become necessary, shame and disapproval are the primary methods used.

Community Structure

Tribal structures have been compromised by the imposition of the majority culture's way of governing. Sometimes, the official governmental structure, the tribal government, may be corrupt, and care needs to be taken in assessing its usefulness to the Native American. The strengths of the natural community with its elders, medicine folk, and other natural helpers are often overlooked. In urban areas, this type of strength is often found in the Native American community that has formed.

There are special Native American resources administered by the federal government under the Bureau of Indian Affairs (BIA) and Indian Public Health Services. There are also resources, particularly educational resources, in community colleges, which have developed on many reservations. Religious groups still provide resources, particularly educational resources. State and federal social welfare systems also provide Supplemental Security Income (SSI), child welfare, and other resources. The Indian Child Welfare Act of 1978 gives tribes jurisdiction over all native children in civil placement. Tribal courts usually carry out this responsibility. Education is today primarily in the public school system, but, as noted, tribal schools and religious schools provide for some students. Today some Native Americans are reaching out to the majority world through the gambling industry and through other recreation opportunities. Social workers can participate in cultural activities but they should avoid tribal politics.

Current Issues

A primary concern is the maintenance of the native culture in contemporary society. Extreme poverty, especially on some reservations, is widespread. Alcoholism and the use of other addictive substances is prevalent, especially where there is significant unemployment. There are many health problems. Tuberculosis, diabetes, and high blood pressure are quite high. The plight of urban Native Americans is concerning as they attempt to live in two cultures. Economic opportunity for those who choose to remain on reservations deserves attention. Educational opportunities in modes that are congruent with native cultures deserve attention at elementary, secondary, and higher education levels. The delivery of health and social services in diversity competent modes is another issue.

Resources

As has been indicated, a primary source must remain the Native American community and individual. If not the client, then other Native Americans become the source.

Brown Miller, Nancy, "Social Work Services to Urban Indians" in *Cultural Awareness in the Human Services*. James W. Green, Ed. Englewood Cliffs, NJ: Prentice Hall, 1993.

Fong, Rowena, and Furuto, Charlene, Eds. *Culturally Competent Practice: Skills, Interventions, and Evaluations*, 2nd ed. Boston: Allyn & Bacon, 2001. (See Chapters 5, 12, 13, 20, 21, 28, and 29.)

Joe, Jennie R., and Malach, Randi Suzanne, "Families with Native American Roots" in *Developing Cross-Cultural Competence: A Guide to Working with Children and Their Families*, 2nd ed. Eleanor W. Lynch and Marci J. Hanson, Eds. Baltimore, MD: Paul H. Brookes, 1998, Chapter 5.

McMaster, Gerald, and Trafzer, Clifford E., Eds. *Native Universe: Voices of Indian America*. Washington DC: National Museum of the American Indian, Smithsonian Institution. This magnificent book, done in cooperation with the National Geographic Society, contains multiple essays by native writers with scholarly recognition. These essays provide contemporary understandings about Native American people.

Riley, Patricia. *Growing Up Native American*. New York: HarperCollins, 1993. This is a compilation of stories by Native American writers about their growing up. It encompasses a number of tribal backgrounds and historical and contemporary experiences.

Weaver, Hilary N., "Cultural Competence with First Nations Peoples" in *Culturally Competent Practice: A Framework for Understanding Diverse Groups and Justice Issues*, 2nd ed. Doman Lum, Ed. Pacific Grove, CA: Brooks/Cole, 2003, Chapter 8.

Zimmerman, Larry, and Molyneaus, Brian Leigh. *Native North America*. Norman: University of Oklahoma Press, 1996. This small, readily available book written by anthropologists who have had considerable experience with the Native American world provides an excellent overview of the variety of tribes and cultural aspects of this world.

In addition there should be a search for tribal-specific literature. Also there are very usable bibliographies on the Internet.

SUMMARY

It essential for social workers to become as diversity competent as possible so that we can serve families in a manner with which they are comfortable. All social workers are called on to serve people who are different from themselves in some way. Differences include race, ethnicity, age, gender, physical or mental ability, physical appearance, religious affiliation, sexual orientation, and socioeconomic standing.

The diversity competent professional social worker seeks to gain knowledge and skills in working with diverse families. She begins with a thorough examination of her own diversity and an awareness of her knowledge about and attitudes toward various diverse groups. She seeks to add to her knowledge and skills by conducting research, discussing diversity with colleagues who have expertise in this area, and learning from her clients as she uses naturalistic inquiry.

The chapter discusses gender competent practice, especially while working with patriarchal families. Practice with gay and lesbian families is presented along with a schema for studying ethnic families. This schema is applied to African American, Hispanic/Latino, and Native American families.

Diversity competence is never fully achieved and is a lifelong process. Diversity competent social workers continuously work to learn more about serving diverse families.

QUESTIONS

1. List as many diverse groups as you can that have experienced prejudice, discrimination, or oppression at some time during U.S. history. Briefly describe their experiences.
2. Discuss attitudes and beliefs of your family, your peers, or other sources about each diverse group from item 1 to which you have been exposed.
3. Discuss your experiences with any of the groups from item 1.
4. Applying Table 3.2 to a cultural group different from your own and with which you have not had considerable contact, identify factors that you need to find out about to have sufficient knowledge to work as a social worker with people from that culture group.
5. Discuss your current level of diversity competence using Table 3.1. Where would you like to be? How might you get there?
6. What knowledge and skills do you possess that make you diversity competent in working with various families? With what kind of families would you feel comfortable working? With what kind of families would you feel uncomfortable working? How could you become more comfortable?

SUGGESTED READINGS

In addition to the resources identified in this chapter, the following readings are suggested:

Johnson, Louise C., and Yanca, Stephen J. *Social Work Practice: A Generalist Approach,* 9th ed. Boston: Allyn & Bacon, 2007 (Chapters 1, 3, 5, 6, and 13).

Fong, Rowena, and Furuto, Sharlene, Eds. *Culturally Competent Practice: Skills, Interventions, and Evaluations.* Boston: Allyn & Bacon, 2001.

Lum, Doman. *Culturally Competent Practice: A Framework for Understanding Diverse Groups and Justice Issues,* 3rd ed. Pacific Grove, CA: Brooks/Cole, 2007.

Saleeby, Dennis, Ed. *The Strengths Perspective in Social Work Practice,* 4th ed. Boston: Allyn & Bacon, 2007.

Interaction and Engagement with Families

LEARNING EXPECTATIONS

1. Understanding of the action system as one context for delivering social work services to families.

2. Understanding of the concepts of engagement and relationship and of their importance in the action system with families.

3. Understanding of the specific characteristics of a professional relationship.

4. Appreciation of the complexity of cross-cultural relationships in generalist practice with families.

5. Knowledge about developing and using effective communication.

6. Knowledge about the use of the interview as a tool in social work practice with families.

Social work practice takes place in an interpersonal, interactional process. This interaction is more than an exchange between a worker and a client; the worker also interacts with colleagues, community persons, professionals, and people who are significant to the helping situation (significant others). The interaction can be one-to-one, between the worker and another person, or it can take place in multiperson situations such as a family, a team, or a small group. Although there are similarities between the process of interaction between one individual and another and the interactions among multiperson systems, there are also differences. This chapter focuses on the interaction of the social worker and family members. The interaction may take place with individual family members, members of family subsystems, or the family as a whole.

In an ecosystems strengths approach, the work that is done by the worker and the family also involves other relevant parts of the family's ecosystem. In most cases, the family mobilizes

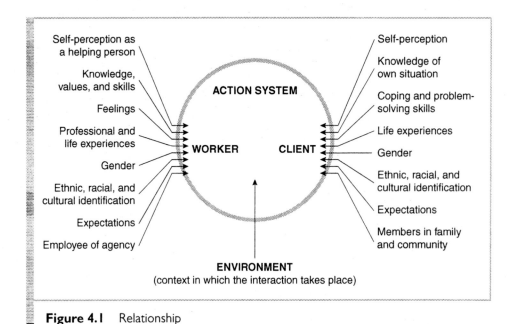

Figure 4.1   Relationship

the strengths and resources available in their ecosystem. This approach empowers the family and its members to take control of their lives and get their needs met while meeting the needs of others in the environment. In some cases, the worker may need to assist the family and its members in developing skills. When the family is unable to mobilize resources or there is a major obstacle to doing so, the family and the worker may decide that the worker should intervene more directly either with or on behalf of the family and its members. Most of the skills covered in this chapter are important for such interventions. Because the worker–client system interaction is the core of the social work endeavor, it will receive primary focus; however, interactions among family members and with members of the family's ecosystem also are discussed. Much of the knowledge base relative to the worker–client system interaction also applies to the interactions a worker has with other persons.

As discussed in Chapter 2, in an ecosystems approach to working with families there is an emphasis on the interactions and transactions that take place among systems and subsystems. Figure 4.1 depicts the transactional nature of an ecosystem. Transactions among people and within an ecosystem can influence the feelings, thoughts, and actions of people and systems and can also be influenced by the feelings, thoughts, and actions of other people and systems. In developing an understanding of the family's environment as an ecosystem, the worker seeks to understand the feelings, thoughts, and actions of people; the human systems in the ecosystem; and the transactions within the ecosystem, as well as to understand the effects of diversity on the ecosystem. The family system is considered a part of the ecosystem, and matter, energy, and information are exchanged among various systems that make up the ecosystem. When there is congruity or balance in these exchanges, all of the systems function in a manner that results in needs being met for family members and the family system and for other systems in their ecosystem. However, when there is an unmet need, there is imbalance or incongruity in the ecosystem. The work of the social worker and family focuses on restoring balance or developing a new balance. This does not necessarily mean that fundamental changes will be needed in family members, the family system, or in systems in the environment. Instead, the emphasis is on bringing about a change in the interactions and transactions among systems (including the family system and subsystems). This approach is more realistic than approaches that hope to restructure or change a persons's personality or change the basic structure and functioning of a family, an organization, or a community.

The social worker may temporarily provide needed matter or energy either directly or by linking the family with other human services. However, much of the work to be done represents exchanges of information. This includes information that flows from family members to worker, from worker to family members, from family members to other systems in their ecosystem, from worker to other systems in the family's ecosystem, and from worker to other work-related systems in her ecosystem. The purpose of exchanging information is to influence growth and change in various parts of the ecosystem with the purpose of meeting needs and restoring balance. Much of this process involves changing interactions.

Because the exchange of information is the focus of most of the social work endeavor, issues that are important in understanding interactions are (1) engagement and formation of an action system, (2) the nature of relationship, and (3) communication. Techniques to enhance relationship and communications are also important because they can improve the quality of interactions. As discussed earlier, the worker striving to become diversity competent uses naturalistic inquiry and intuitive learning regarding culture and diversity as he builds a relationship with his client and proceeds through the phases of the change process.

■ ENGAGEMENT AND FORMATION ■ OF AN ACTION SYSTEM

An **action system** is formed based on the work to be done and because the tasks to be carried out require more than one person. In order for an action system to be formed, the worker must engage the client system (an individual, family, group, organization, or community). **Engagement** occurs when a helping relationship is established between the worker and the client system. In addition, an ecosystem strengths approach is based on the theory that needs are met through interaction. The worker collaborates with a colleague because each may have special areas of expertise relative to the work at hand or because the worker may profit from another view of the situation. The worker interacts with other family members when they have some information needed for helping another family member or can serve as a support or resource for the family's efforts in meeting needs.

In worker–client systems interaction, the efforts of all parties are necessary in the helping endeavor. The worker brings to the interaction a professional knowledge base and a professional set of values and skills for helping. The worker also brings the total self, finely tuned, to be used with the family as is appropriate to the needs of the helping situation and the worker's capacity. The worker brings skill in understanding situations, identifying needs, focusing on strengths, and facilitating growth and change. The family and its members bring needs, a perception of the situation, life experiences that influence this perception, and a capacity for growth and change. The family also brings motivational forces for work in meeting needs or for changes in the family, its members or subsystems, or the situation. In the work to be done, the roles of the worker and of the family and its members emerge from what each brings to the interaction.

Engagement

The first encounter is crucial in forming the action system because it determines much that will happen in subsequent sessions. The nature of the interaction, its kind and quality, begins to form at this point. The family will be making decisions as to whether the worker can provide the needed help, can be trusted, and has the capacity to understand the family and their situation.

Typically, the initial contact takes place when one or more family members come to the agency for help, either with regard to a personal need or with a concern about someone else; or it occurs when the worker reaches out to one or more family members to help with a need. Throughout this section we use the term *family* to refer to one or more family members.

Social workers disagree about whether new workers should read records of a previous worker before meeting the client system. Records may present stereotypes or invalid assumptions that can influence the thinking of the new worker. Records may focus on problems or deficits rather than strengths and resources. But if records can be read with an open mind and an eye for facts, they can be good preparation for meeting with a family for the first time. The worker needs to be careful not to develop unsupported preconceptions about the family and the situation. Unsupported preconceptions can endanger the formation of the action system.

In preparation for the first contact, the worker may decide to collect and review any available information to determine what is known about the family. Consideration of possible needs this family might bring as well as potential strengths in the family and its ecosystem is also useful. The worker can also get in touch with feelings he might have about the family in situation and about possible feelings of the family and its members. If the ethnicity, race, or culture of the family is known, the worker should be aware of his knowledge and attitudes regarding their diversity. Although prior knowledge of ethnicity, race, or culture can be helpful in understanding the family, the worker needs to listen to how the family has experienced this diversity.

Based on the preliminary understanding of family in situation, the worker can structure the first encounter to make the family or family members feel comfortable. This structuring will also involve environmental factors related to the time and place of the encounter— for example, the nature of the worker's greeting as the family enters the agency and meets the worker, the placement of desks so as not to be barriers between worker and family members, and comfort in terms of temperature and privacy for the encounter. The worker should use formal forms of address, such as Mr., Mrs., and Ms., until or unless she is asked to address adults in the family by their first names. If the worker is familiar with the family's ethnicity, she might greet them in a way that reflects their culture. This could include using a greeting in their language. For instance, if the family is Latino, the worker might use a greeting in Spanish. In addition, the worker is sensitive to other cultural expectations as were pointed out in Chapter 3. For example, in many patriarchal systems, it is customary to address the male head of the family first and then he introduces his family.

Choice of time for the family is also important, especially because the more members involved, the more difficult it may be to schedule a time when everyone can meet. When working with families, it is usually best to decide ahead of time who should attend the first session, if it is possible. Generally, this will be a parent or parents. However, this may already be decided by the family or by circumstances when the first contact is made. For example, the parent may bring a child in because she is concerned about his behavior or the worker may have to make a home visit without an appointment because the family does not have a telephone.

At the point of contact the worker will attempt to make the family as comfortable as possible. Cultural factors need to be taken into consideration. If the family comes from a culture in which small talk is used before getting on with the task at hand, the worker should engage in a bit of small talk. If the worker is not proficient in the language that the family uses at home, she should apologize for not being bilingual and recognize the fact that they are. If the family is not bilingual, then the worker needs to arrange for a professional interpreter if possible. If the family is anxious about the purpose of the interaction and comes from a culture that wastes few words, the worker will quickly explain what is to be done together. In other words, it is important to structure the initial contact from the interactional framework of the family, not from the worker's framework. The reader should review Chapter 3 to gain a better understanding of relevant aspects of understanding diverse families.

The worker should demonstrate to the family what will happen in the work together as soon as possible and to the extent possible. The worker does this by

1. Being attentive to what family members are saying and being receptive to their feelings
2. Demonstrating a real desire to help the family and giving them some indication that the worker knows how to help
3. Actively asking family members to share their perceptions of the situation (asking them about the significance of the need, about the onset and attempts at meeting the need, and about the solutions desired are other ways to involve family members and demonstrate the way of working together)
4. Attempting to answer any unspoken questions family members may have (e.g., they may not be sure if the information being shared will be available to anyone else)
5. Explaining something about the way the agency delivers service, the kind of help it gives, and the procedures for using that help
6. Focusing on strengths and potential resources within the family and within its ecosystem (this reduces feelings of blame and of helplessness or hopelessness and communicates a positive "can do" approach to meeting needs)
7. Trying to reach for the feelings family members are having about what is happening

In other words, the worker does as much as possible to enable the family to become engaged in helping themselves in the need-meeting, problem-solving activity. In addition, attention should be given to supporting and developing self-esteem in family members. Partly, this can happen through the realization by family members that they are capable of participating in the search for solutions. Under no circumstances should the worker give unrealistic assurances about the outcome of the service.

Formation of an Action System with the Family

As the worker is demonstrating to the family the way in which they can work together, she is also gathering information, understanding family functioning and the need as seen by the family, and enabling the family to think about the situation and perhaps see it in a new perspective. The social history is begun. This may be an individual or a family social history or it may be one that is focused on a family subsystem. Schemas for each of these are presented in later chapters. The type of social history is determined by the client system. Typically, the worker and the family or family members decide who the appropriate client system is during this engagement process or during assessment. The worker encourages a climate of trust to develop. Until the family can trust the worker, the relationship is tenuous and the interaction is influenced by the family's concerns about the trustworthiness of the worker. As the family experiences the concern, understanding, and expertise of the worker, there is usually a reduction of these concerns and a strengthening of the relationship. This is further facilitated when the worker uses an ecosystems strengths approach because the focus is on resolving the situation in a positive way rather than an examination of what is wrong.

During this exploratory phase of the initial contact, the worker's task is to test out ideas about the nature of the need and the potential strengths and resources; to gather information about family in situation, with an emphasis on the strengths of the family and its ecosystem; to identify who should be involved in the work to be done; and to define expectations for the family and its members about the nature of service, relationships, and behaviors. The worker is nonauthoritarian, genuine, accepting, and empathic. The family is gathering information about the agency, its services, and the helping process and is also providing information needed to give the worker understanding. The goal is to develop what Nick F. Coady identified as a "therapeutic alliance." He defined this as "an observable ability of the worker and client to work together in a realistic collaborative relationship based on mutual liking, trust, respect, and commitment to the work of counseling."[1]

Sometimes the family or a certain member presents an angry, hostile, and resistive front. Carl Hartman and Diane Reynolds noted that this front is used when people are frightened and hurting and lack trust in the worker and in the process of help. They suggested using an approach that they identify as confrontation, interpretation, and alliance. After searching for the source of the feelings and associated behaviors, the worker first confronts the family member about the behavior with questions or other means that communicate that the worker recognizes the feelings and the resistance to help. This is not a hostile, personal confrontation but one that lets the family member know that the worker is willing to accept the family member's anger and hear him out. Immediately thereafter, the worker provides an interpretation of the meaning or source of the feelings and associated behaviors. Then the worker provides support and encouragement.[2] This approach often allows the family member to feel accepted, which leads to a trusting and working relationship.

When the worker decides that sufficient understanding has developed, she refocuses the discussion to service delivery. During this next stage, the worker and the family discuss whether the need as the family sees it is one that the worker, agency, and family can work on meeting. They discuss whether the family is willing to work on meeting the need in the way expected by the agency or if the diversity of the family indicates that another approach is needed that would make them more comfortable. The diversity competent worker is sensitive to the need to deliver services in a manner that is comfortable for the family. As much as possible, she tries to learn about this beforehand, but she allows the family to take the lead with this. Some families may choose to receive services in the usual way the agency delivers services. Other families may wish to receive services in a way that is customary in their culture. For instance, an African American family may wish to be served in a manner that reflects an Afrocentric approach as described in Chapter 3. Using this approach, the worker would incorporate a sense of collective identity and connectedness rather that emphasizing individuality. She would help the family use available community resources and help them strengthen ties with the community. She would explore the family's spirituality as a strength that could be used in helping them to cope and to overcome barriers. She would pay close attention to affect and respect the view that affective ways of knowing are important. When the worker encounters a family whose diversity is unfamiliar to her, she seeks to learn from them about the way in which help is received within that diversity or culture. If the family decides to receive services, the worker explores this using formal and informal resources as we described in Chapter 3.

The worker and family discuss other possibilities for need fulfillment. The worker attempts to break down the situation into parts for the family and identify potential strengths so that it does not seem overwhelming. The worker outlines the realities of what the family can expect from the service and discusses adaptations or alternative ways of delivering services in a diversity competent manner.

During this phase, the worker and family decide whether (1) they can work together on the concern or need brought by the family, (2) some other need should be worked on, (3) the service needed by the family is better delivered by another resource, (4) another agency or service is more culturally appropriate for the family, or (5) the family desires not to use further services. There are times when all a family needs is to discuss a situation and gain a new perspective or knowledge of unthought-of resources. The family can then cope without further service.

In deciding whether to continue to work together (to form an action system), the worker and family need to make explicit the expectations of each person, the possible goals and expected outcomes of the service, the role of each person, and the ways of working together. In particular, it is important to identify the client system. In families, this might be individual family members, a family subsystem, or the family as a whole. The worker looks for feelings family members may have and brings negative feelings and disagreements out into the open so they can be examined and discussed. It is very important to discuss the limits of confidentiality connected with the service. Also, the worker should be sure that all terms being used are understood by family members.

If the decision is made to work together, an agreement or preliminary contract may be developed that states the next steps of the work as well as the responsibilities of both the worker and the family members and time frames for accomplishing the needed task. The contract or agreement should also indicate hoped-for outcomes of the service. (The concept of contract is developed in Chapter 6.)

During the negotiation and contract stage, the worker openly faces and deals with resistance. Edith Ankersmit, in discussing contracting in probation settings, has suggested that, in dealing with resistance, it is useful to help the client discuss two questions: Why am I here? How do I feel about being here? This discussion will allow the client to ventilate hostile feelings. The worker must not deny the existence of such feelings; rather, the worker should actively listen and point out the reality of such feelings. According to Ankersmit, it is important to point out the power the worker has in the situation, particularly noting its limits and the power the client maintains. This discussion can communicate to clients that they do have responsibility for their own behaviors.[3] It should be noted that in most situations where there is more than one person in the client system there will be differences in levels of resistance among the members of the system. It is not unusual for one member to be participating under some form of duress. For instance, a child may be brought in by a parent because of his behavior or one spouse may threaten to leave if the other spouse does not come in to work on their relationship.

Charles Horejsi called for a motivation, capacity, and opportunity approach in working with clients on probation. He pointed out that it is particularly important to try to identify the problem from the client's point of view and then decide with the client if the problem can be worked on together. He stated that the client must believe that there is hope for a solution and recognize a feeling of discomfort about the problem. The balance between hope for relief and recognition of discomfort is important; both must be present, yet neither should overwhelm the other. He pointed out that there is discomfort in change. This must be considered when determining the client's capacity for change. Workers should attempt to reduce the discomfort concerning change as one means of lowering resistance.[4] One source of resistance may be environmental factors. For example, if a person's peers support delinquent behavior, it can be difficult for him to give it up. The discomfort of losing the companionship of one's peers may be so great that the change carries too great a price for the client. Another source may be diversity factors that create concerns about being able to work together. When the worker uses a strengths approach along with naturalistic inquiry, she has a much better chance to reduce resistance that is based on diversity.

During this stage, the worker attempts to provide a climate that allows for productive discussion and a focus for the work together, and to identify behavioral, cognitive, spiritual, and emotional responses of family members to the work at hand and possible future work together. The worker also needs to keep in touch with her own feelings and to share these, as appropriate, with the family.

When agreement about the work together is reached, engagement is established. The worker should summarize what has happened in the previous stages of exploration and negotiation. It is also important to be sure that the next steps, the next session together, and any tasks to be accomplished before the next session are clearly understood.

The formation of the action system or engagement may be accomplished in one session or several sessions. During this formation, the worker attempts to bridge gaps in understanding; set the tone for the work; develop involvement of family members in the work to be done; maintain a focus on the work; tune in to family members' feelings, way of functioning, and concerns; develop an understanding of diversity and establish an open dialogue regarding diversity; and identify potential strengths and resources in the family and its ecosystem. In carrying out the worker role, the worker is sensitive to the readiness of family members to move from one stage of work to another.

Blocks to Formation of an Action System

Several blocks can prevent the formation of a functional worker–client system. The worker should be aware of these and attempt to prevent them from interfering with the system's functioning. First, there is the complexity of human functioning. Relationships between persons with different life experiences and cultural backgrounds are particularly difficult. Misunderstandings happen easily. Bias and prejudice are often present. These lead to differences in perceptions of what is happening in the work together. This is especially the case between couples from different backgrounds or in blended families with different histories and various combinations of race and ethnicity. It is also a reality that relationships between parents and children change over time as the child grows into adolescence and adulthood and as parents age.

A second block can be family members' fears. They may fear depersonalization, powerlessness, being judged, having irrelevant goals placed on them, or being treated differently or misunderstood as a result of their diversity. These fears can lead to feelings of anger. Family members may keep distance between themselves and the worker or avoid appropriate involvement in the work together. The fears may result from prejudices and unrealistic expectations on the part of family members.

A third block can be the worker as an employee of a bureaucratic organization. The complexity of rules and regulations and the inability of an organization to individualize clients often get in the way of providing the needed service. The worker may have feelings of powerlessness and may not feel appreciated by the agency, leading to frustrations that hamper responding to the family appropriately.

A fourth block can be inadequate communication, which is also related to the differing cultures of worker and family. There may be language barriers if the family's primary language is not English or the worker is not proficient in the family's language. There can also be misunderstandings about the use of slang or idioms that are unfamiliar to the family or the worker. Because of poor communication, the family may not understand what is expected in the work together. The family also may not be able to sense the worker's interest and readiness to help or may see the worker as incompetent.

A fifth block relates to the worker's sense of purpose. If he has unrealistic expectations for self and family members, the family may sense this and avoid engagement in the tasks at hand. Workers sometimes aspire to heal all, know all, and love all; this leads to unrealistic expectations. Other workers have strong nurturing drives and tend to place clients in overly dependent relationships. Still other workers may avoid conflict, anger, and aggressive behavior. This stifles the expression of feelings that need to be considered in the development of the action system.

A final block is the underlying assumptions or theory base chosen by the worker for explaining the situation. For example, if the assumptions label the family as sick or dysfunctional, the worker may be hesitant to demand work from the family, and this may lead to more dependency in the relationship than is merited. If the assumptions assign blame, as might occur with a family of a child that is acting out at school, this will influence the worker's relationship with that family.

When working with nonvoluntary family members, it is particularly important to pay attention to these blocks. Unwilling family members often do not see the need for service, do not believe help is possible, or have difficulty developing a relationship with the worker. In this situation, workers can sometimes overcome resistance by pointing out the reason for the concern or the consequences of a lack of change. A caring, nonjudgmental approach that focuses on the family member's concerns and desires can often provide the nonvoluntary family members with a unique helping experience and reduce resistance to help. The nonvoluntary family member can be very sensitive to any hint of blame. Thus, using an ecosystems strengths approach can be very helpful in working with a nonvoluntary family members because the focus is on changing interactions and transactions in a positive way as opposed to looking for causes.

The worker has a responsibility to attempt to engage resistant family members when services have been mandated by a societal institution or when the family member or a person for whom the family member is responsible is in danger of significant harm. This might be a child, an elderly parent, or an adult family member with a significant disability. In doing this, the worker should try to relate as much as possible to the family member's frame of reference. She should attempt to use their communication patterns and should not catch them unaware. She should say why there is a concern and what the consequences of not resolving the situation might be. She should openly deal with either hostility or quiet inertia and should support the family member's strengths. In working with a resistive family member, the worker must be reasonably comfortable with the authority she carries and be reasonable and supportive in its use. Often the resistant family member misunderstands the nature of the service, has unmet needs that mitigate against dealing with the situation, has inadequate cognitive capacity to deal with the situation, or is influenced by the environment in a way that prevents need fulfillment. In working with a resistant family member, the worker should determine the source of the resistance and attempt to overcome it if possible; otherwise, a functioning action system may not form. It is difficult enough to form a functioning action system with an individual client who is resistant. It is even more challenging when there is more than one family member or, in some cases, an entire family that is resistant.

Often a bargaining strategy can be used. The worker can make family members who are resisting services aware of benefits from working with the social worker. For example, a neglecting mother can come to understand that cooperation with the worker may prevent removal of her children from her care. A juvenile delinquent can come to see that cooperation with the worker can prevent placement in an institution. A teen can see that by adhering to certain rules and carrying out prescribed tasks he can gain desired privileges.

In using these strategies, it is important that the worker acknowledge the family member's anger and resentment and develop with him a plan that incorporates the object of his concern. For instance, if a family or family member has been ordered by a court to receive services, they are likely to be angry, hostile, and resistant. The worker might begin by asking how they feel about working with him. This will likely bring their anger to the surface. At some point, they will express a desire to not be there. Instead of trying to talk them out of their anger and into liking the situation, the worker should accept these feelings and seek to form an alliance by finding ways in which they will not have to come for service. Of course, this generally means reaching a point at which the family is functioning at a level that will satisfy the court that the situation is resolved. The worker may help the family to see that because they have to be there it is better to work on their concerns than to waste their time.

It is unlikely that all members of the family will be equally resistant to working with the social worker. Typically, there is a range of resistance. The worker should note this and attempt to form a working relationship with less resistant family members. If more resistant members notice that positive changes are occurring, they may be willing to participate later on.

The development of the action system may be limited by the time available to the worker and family members, by the skill of the worker, by ethical considerations, by the agency function, and by the family's desires. The worker and family must decide together on the desirability and the ways of working together.

Forming an Action System with Other Members of the Ecosystem

Another type of action system that social workers are often involved in is one made up of a social worker and a person who is not a client. This is a common arrangement when using an ecosystems strengths approach because mobilizing potential resources and changing interactions and transactions are the focus of the work. The nonclient is generally a member of the family's ecosystem or a significant other in a family member's life, a resource provider, or an individual who is or could be involved in a helping endeavor. In using an ecosystems approach, the worker uses resources in the community and within his work-related ecosystem. In this case, the nonclient might be another service provider, an influential community member, a person who is or could be involved in action plans focused on community or organizational change, or a person whom the worker is seeking to educate about some aspect of service delivery or the social welfare system.

Although worker–nonclient relationships are somewhat different, the worker still must pay attention to the formation of the action system. The same principles apply to these systems as apply to worker–client systems. If a worker uses the process of precontact, exploration, negotiation, and agreement, both parties are more aware of the reason for working together and of the responsibility of each party for that work. Nonclient individuals may also display resistance. Exploration of the resistance is the first step in overcoming it and in deciding if it is possible to form a functional action system. A positive, strengths-based approach tends to result in less resistance than an approach that focuses on deficits or problems.

■ RELATIONSHIP ■

Relationship is the cohesive quality of the action system. It is the product of interaction between two or more persons. *Relationship* is a term of considerable historical significance in social work practice. It has often been expressed as "good rapport" or engagement with the client system. The development of a good relationship is a necessary ingredient of the helping endeavor. Helen Harris Perlman has provided a description of relationship and its importance: "Relationship is a catalyst, an enabling dynamism in the support, nurture and freeing of people's energies and motivation toward problem solving and the use of help."[5] In her view, relationship is an emotional bond and is the means for humanizing help. Further, she stated, "'Good' relationship is held to be so in that it provides stimulus and nurture. . . . [It] respects and nourishes the self-hood of the other. . . . [It] provides a sense of security and at-oneness."[6]

The social work relationship is both a professional and a helping relationship. A **professional relationship** is one in which there is an agreed-on purpose; one that has a specific time frame; one in which the worker devotes self to the interests of the client system; and one that carries the authority of specialized knowledge, a professional code of ethics, and specialized skill. In addition, a professional relationship is controlled in that the worker attempts to maintain objectivity toward the work at hand and to be aware of and in charge of her own feelings, reactions, and impulses.[7]

The Helping Relationship

A great deal has been written about the nature of *helping relationships*.[8] The characteristics that appear most often in these discussions include the following:

1. *Concern for others*—An attitude that reflects warmth, sincere liking, friendliness, support, and an interest in the client. It communicates a real desire to understand person in situation.

2. *Commitment and obligation*—A sense of responsibility for the helping situation. Dependability and consistency are also involved. The worker must have a willingness to enter into the world of others, with its hurts and joys, its frustrations and commitments.

3. *Acceptance*—A nonjudgmental, noncritical attitude on the part of the worker, as well as a realistic trust of the client and respect for the client's feelings. Belief that the client can handle her own problems and can take charge of her own life.

4. *Empathy*—An ability to communicate to the client that the worker cares, has concern for the client, is hearing what the client is perceiving, wants to understand, and is hearing and understanding.

5. *Clear communication*—The capacity to communicate to the client in ways that enable the client to fully understand the message being sent.

6. *Genuineness*—The worker's honesty about self and personal feelings. An ability to separate the experiences and the feelings of the worker from those of the client. Genuineness on the part of the worker allows the client to become what the client wants to be. It is present when the worker's communication is understood and comfortable for the client. The worker's personal style of helping should not be an inflexible use of technique.

7. *Authority and power*—The expectation that the client will work to fulfill needs and responsibilities and will want to resolve the situation. This involves encouraging the client to go beyond the present level of functioning and providing guidance and resources so that goals can be reached. It involves insistence that the client do what she can for herself. The worker's knowledge and skills are a base for authority and power. The client must know that the worker's power and authority are not to be used to dominate or control her but to assist her in having her needs, and those of others around her, met in a positive, mutually beneficial manner.

8. *Purpose*—The helping relationship has a purpose known to, and accepted by, both worker and client. According to Beulah Compton and Burt Galaway, this is the most important characteristic of all.[9]

There is some disagreement about the place of advice giving in helping. Traditionally, social workers have thought it unhelpful to give advice; advice was seen as the worker's solution for the client and not the product of mutual problem solving and thus was not useful for the client. Clients, however, often indicate that they expect and are looking for advice.[10] Advice is tangible evidence of help. If advice is given, it should be done selectively and as a result of mutual problem solving by worker and family. It should be presented in a nondemanding manner as something that might be tried, leaving the final decision for its use to the family. When given in this manner, advice may well be a useful tool for helping. However, it is essential that the advice be given by the worker and received by the family in a way that ensures that family members see it as one of several options. Generally, it is best to use advice as a last resort when family members are truly stuck or if they seem headed for a situation that is harmful to themselves or others or if they are overwhelmed by a crisis.

Another characteristic of the helping situation is that help can be given by family members to the worker. The family helps the worker understand the situation or culture or diversity. This is help and should be recognized as such. When the family evaluates the usefulness of means of help and the appropriateness of goals, this is help. Such a view of help enables the family to see the roles as interdependent rather than as superordinal to subordinal. An interdependent relationship encourages growth rather than dependency and is more helpful to the family.

Biestek's classic seven principles of a casework relationship and the worker's role in using each principle are one way of defining the responsibility of the social worker in a worker–client interaction or action system. His principles included individualizing the client system, encouraging expression of feelings that is purposeful, responding to the client's feelings in a controlled and purposeful way, communicating acceptance, maintaining a nonjudgmental attitude, respecting the client's right to self determination, and preserving confidentiality.[11]

These principles are used to guide the professional helping relationship. They help promote a climate in which the client–worker action system can work toward fulfilling client needs. The principles can also be applied selectively to other action systems.

Special Influences on the Helping Relationship

Any difference in diversity between the family and the worker has an influence on the action system's functioning. These include situations in which the worker and the family or its members come from different ethnic or racial backgrounds and those in which the gender of the worker affects the interaction with family members and the environment in which the action takes place. Several obstacles seem to be prevalent in cross-diversity helping relationships:

1. *Mutual unknowingness*—Because of a lack of knowledge about the other's culture or diversity on the part of both the worker and the family, there is a tendency toward stereotyping. Fear of the other is also a result of lack of knowledge and understanding. Inappropriate "good" or "bad" judgments may be made. Social distance that does not allow for the sharing and the trust necessary in the helping endeavor is often present. Of particular importance is lack of knowledge about a family's traditional communication patterns.

2. *Attitudes toward the other culture or diversity*—Negative attitudes may have developed from limited knowledge about a different culture or diverse group. These attitudes may also have developed from negative experiences with persons who belong to the same cultural or ethnic or diversity group as the person being interacted with.

3. *Availability of different opportunities*—Members of different cultural or diversity groups have different opportunities. When the social worker does not understand this difference of opportunity, she can have unrealistic expectations about how families should use the help offered. This fact also can relate to the use of appropriate resources. Some resources are not usable for a particular diversity group. For example, a culture that does not allow expression of feeling or that uses limited verbal expression and is action oriented will have considerable difficulty with traditional talk therapy. Some resources are available to, and traditionally useful for, particular ethnic groups. For example, Native Americans traditionally use the tribe's medicine man or elders as resources. They also may have the support and financial aid resources of the Bureau of Indian Affairs.

4. *Conflicts between societal and cultural expectations*—These often are difficult to resolve around the helping situation. Families may have difficulty in identifying these conflicts, and the worker may not be aware of them.

In addition, family members of various diversity groups may have a low sense of self-worth as a result of chronic and acute oppression and discrimination. This can result in low expectations for resolution of situations, in special relationship needs, and in lack of appreciation of their own diversity. There may be a different worldview, different expectations for the use of time, and different expectations of male and female behavior. These can get in the way of developing working relationships. The family may have a low trust level toward persons of other cultures or diversity; this may be the result of past relationships that produced pain and anger. A family member with a low level of trust may use concealment mechanisms that hinder the helping endeavor. Different mechanisms for showing respect can result in misunderstandings. Different mechanisms for expressing ideas and feelings and different communication patterns can be particularly troublesome. Ann Brownlee has identified some of the areas in which communication differences may exist in cross-cultural relationships, including situations appropriate for the communication of specific information; tempo of communication; taboos; norms for confidentiality; ways of expressing emotions, feelings, and appreciation; meaning of silence; form and content of nonverbal communication; and style of persuasion or explanation.[12] In order to work effectively in cross-cultural situations, the worker should develop an understanding of diverse needs, of the complexities of cross-cultural communication, and of his own biases and prejudices, and must also develop considerable skill in accurate perception and tolerance for difference.

In using an ecosystems strengths approach, it essential that the worker be diligent, flexible, and creative in uncovering strengths and resources within the family and its ecosystem. Contrary to its professed belief in freedom and tolerance, the United States has a history of oppression and discrimination toward minorities, especially people of color. The basis of prejudice and discrimination is viewing other cultures as weak, inferior, and undesirable. Thus, members of the dominant culture, as well as nondominant cultures, are not accustomed to finding strengths in other cultures. In spite of the social worker's efforts to be nonjudgmental, it will be impossible to avoid all prejudice and stereotyping because these are pervasive and embedded in the dominant culture. Even if the worker has a predisposition toward seeing strengths, it is unlikely that she will thoroughly know these strengths unless she has had considerable exposure to or conducted research about other cultures. Nonetheless, if the worker and family make a real effort to see strengths and positive opportunities, they can overcome the negative effects of cultural bias.

Gender is another factor that affects relationships. Social work literature contains little discussion of the influence of the worker's gender on the helping endeavor. There seems to be an assumption that a skilled worker should be able to work with both male and female clients. Although this is probably true, social workers should become more aware of gender factors in professional relationships. One study has found that when male and female workers make assessments about female clients, male workers see these clients as less mature and less intelligent than do female workers. Female workers see women as having greater need for emotional expression and less need of home and family involvement than do male workers.[13] Differences in perceptions between male and female social workers, then, seem to exist. These different perceptions are probably a result of sex-role socialization and can affect professional relationships.

Joanne Mermelstein and Paul Sundet have found differences in client expectations in rural areas based on gender factors. In the female worker–female client situation, the client expects nurturing, mothering, and friendship. In the female worker–male client situation, the client sees taking help from a woman as counter to his definition of manhood. The interaction is also affected by taboos about what is to be discussed with women. In the situation of male worker and female client, the male worker is seen as performing a traditional female nurturing role. The female client expects the male worker to support her, to give her moral guidance and clear direction. In the male client–male worker situation, the male client expects the male worker to prove his masculinity.[14]

Louise Johnson, Dale Crawford, and Lorraine Rousseau found that in traditional Sioux Native American culture it is a mistake for a male worker to go alone to a female client's home. The male worker should go with a male relative because in traditional culture a female speaks through a male relative.[15]

Social workers should examine the expectations for male and female behaviors from the family's perspective and take these into consideration in developing action systems and in understanding and using relationships within these systems. Attention also must be given to the influence of gender of both worker and family members on practice, that is, on the functioning of the action system. Workers also need to develop an understanding of how their own gender expectations influence their professional relationships.

Other differences that may exist between worker and family are young workers with older family members; unmarried workers with experienced parents; well-educated, middle-class workers with illiterate, poor families; heterosexual workers with homosexual clients, or vice versa; and upright, well-behaved workers with norm violators. These and other differences all influence the functioning of the action system—the helping relationship.

Little attention has been given to how the context of the social work endeavor affects practice, particularly the relationship factors of practice. A growing body of literature relative to the practice of social work in rural areas has pointed out the need to pay attention to the context of practice. Again, the work of Sundet and Mermelstein provides an indication of the influence of context on practice. They found that social work roles that call for little risk on the part of the client system are most effective when an outside worker enters a new rural community.[16] It may be that this experience provides a useful principle for situations in which cultural distance exists between the worker and the client. Confidentiality is an aspect of relationship that takes on new features when examined in a rural setting. People are more visible in rural settings. In some situations, it is in the family's best interest that certain aspects of the service be known so that misinterpretations about the service do not develop.[17]

Social workers have given little attention to the understanding of the relationship in an action system that does not involve a client system—for example, relationships with other professionals such as a teacher or a pastor or relationships with community leaders. Yet workers often use this type of action system in serving families, especially when using an ecosystems strengths approach. In discussing this type of system from an interactional viewpoint, Yvonne Fraley has suggested that mutual problem solving is more effective if this type of relationship is assessed using these six variables: (1) the position of the worker ("actor one")—that is, the location of actor one in an agency or community system; (2) the goal of actor one in the relationship; (3) the position of the other ("actor two"); (4) the goal of the other; (5) the form of communication being used (verbal, written, nonverbal media, etc.); and (6) the method of influence being used by each actor (problem solving, teacher–learner, helper–helpee, etc.).[18] This kind of analysis points out that in the nonclient action system there needs to be some reason for the two actors to work together. If the goals of each are compatible, if one actor does not feel threatened by the position of the other, and if the form of communication and the method of influence are carefully chosen, there is a better chance for gaining the desired outcome.

Regardless of the nature of the action system, the characteristics of the actors (worker–client or other), and the situation in which the interaction is taking place, the relationship of the two persons is a crucial factor in whether the work together produces the desired outcomes. Each person brings much to the system that can aid in, or detract from, the relationship and the work to be done. The social worker must be aware of these factors and use them to further the work by developing functional working relationships with other people. (See Figure 4.1.)

Relationship is not the end-state goal of the helping endeavor or the action system; it is the glue that holds the action system together and as such is a necessary ingredient of a well-functioning action system. It is not a relationship in which there is no conflict and all is happiness and goodwill, nor is it an overly dependent relationship. It is a relationship in which conflict is open and examined and in which there is respect for the position of the other. It is a working relationship, and the purpose of the relationship is the accomplishment of tasks needed to fulfill client need and promote growth and change.

COMMUNICATION

Because effective communication is such an important ingredient of the functioning action system as well as a functioning family, it is important for all social workers to develop good communication skills and to develop skills in facilitating good communication. When working with families, facilitating good communication within the family is often a major focus. Communication is the sending and receiving of messages between two or more persons. Effective communication occurs when the persons involved in a situation accurately perceive the messages of the other person and when the messages are sent in a way that allows the receiver to take action or respond to the sender in ways that facilitate the purposes of the communication. The purposes of communication in the social work interaction include the following:

1. Gathering information needed for the helping endeavor, including strengths and resources
2. Exploring ideas, feelings, and possible ways to meet need based on the strengths and resources within the client and the ecosystem
3. Expressing feelings or thoughts

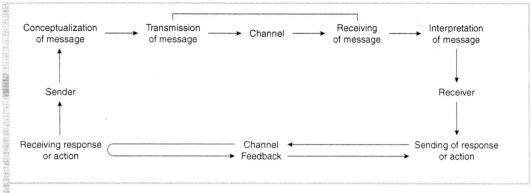

Figure 4.2 Communication

4. Structuring the work of the action system
5. Providing support, informing, advising, encouraging, and giving necessary directions

Communication is a process. The *sender* conceptualizes the message and through a *transmitter* (the voice or visual production) sends the message through a *channel* (sensory and modern technological means) to a *receiver* who interprets the message cognitively and affectively. This results in a *response,* another message, or an action. The response may result in *feedback,* a means for the sender to evaluate the effectiveness of the message. One other factor of the process is *interference* or noise. Interference consists of those influences from outside the process that affect the message while it is in the channel and cause *distortion* of the message as it reaches the receiver. (See Figure 4.2.)

Each part of the process has a particular function, and special problems can interfere with the effectiveness of the communication. The sender must conceptualize the message in a way that is understandable to the receiver. This requires understanding how the receiver deals with and interprets ideas and information. The transmission of the message takes place not only through verbalization but also through nonverbal means. Nonverbal communication takes place through vocal tone and behaviors, such as gestures, facial expression, and body position. The motivation, needs, feelings, and attitudes of the sender influence the manner in which the message is transmitted. The message has content—the specific words used—and it has meaning—how that content is treated. The choice of words, the order of ideas and words, the use of humor and silence all contribute to the quality of the message.

Special attention needs to be paid to cultural and personal differences in the meaning of words. Different cultures can have different attitudes, values, and beliefs that influence how words are interpreted and the meaning of nonverbal communication. Beyond the cultural aspect, each of us has unique and individual life experiences. For example, take the word *mother.* For someone who has had a warm, loving relationship with his mother, the word will evoke positive feelings. However, if a person had experienced the death of his mother at an early age, the word *mother* will probably be associated with grief and loss. Even siblings can have different ideas of their mother based on their individual perceptions.

As the message travels through the channel, the possibility of distortion is great. Previous experiences, cultural and societal demands, and attitudes and feelings of the receiver can distort the message. Distractions such as additional stimuli, concerns, and responsibilities can distort the message. The recognition of distortion and noise is a recognition of the transactional nature of communication.

The manner in which the message is received also influences the effectiveness of the message. The receiver may perceive or interpret the message in a manner different from the intention of the sender. The receiver may not comprehend the meaning of the message as intended or may receive only a part of the message. These influences can occur between any individuals but are especially important when communication occurs between two people who are different in terms of diversity. Feedback is the means of ascertaining whether the message received and the message intended by the sender are sufficiently similar to make the communication effective. Feedback is sending a message about a received message to the sender of that message. The feedback is also subject to the problems of the original message.

Effective communication is communication in which the outcome is the accomplishment of the purpose intended by the sender. Messages that have the best chance of being effective are those in which

1. The verbal and nonverbal messages are congruent
2. The message is simple, specific, and intelligible to the receiver
3. The receiver can understand what is meant by the sender
4. There is sufficient repetition for the receiver to sense the importance of this message from among other messages being received simultaneously
5. There has been sufficient reduction of both psychological and actual noise
6. Feedback has been solicited from the receiver and sufficient time taken to ensure that the original message was received

Effectiveness in communication is affected by the credibility and honesty of the sender of the message. The receiver who has reason to trust the competence and reliability of the sender will tend to be receptive to the message and its expectations. Effective communicators tune into and are sensitive to the feelings and situations of those with whom they are communicating. They are assertive without being overly aggressive or confrontational.

Often, communication is not with the client system but with other professionals, with significant others in the environment, or with people who may in some way be involved in situations that are blocking need fulfillment. These relationships are particularly important when the focus is on organizational or community change. The principles of communication discussed in this section (regarding clients) apply to interactions with nonclients even though communication may be of a bargaining or adversarial nature. When social workers find themselves in situations where the viewpoint of the other may be different from their own, clear communication is imperative. Sometimes the differences can be resolved through clarification of messages. Other times a clear understanding of the differences allows work to progress. Brett Seabury has identified several problems that confront social workers in their communications with clients and significant others:

1. *Double messages*—Two contradictory messages are received simultaneously or in close succession.

2. *Ambiguous messages*—These messages have little meaning or several possible messages for the receiver.

3. *Referent confusion*—The words have different meanings to each person, or they may be professional jargon not understood by the other person involved in the communication.

4. *Selective attention and interpretation*—This causes distortion of the message or confusion as to meaning.

5. *Overload*—This is the receiving of more messages than a receiver can interpret and respond to at any one time.

6. *Ritual or order incongruence*—This is the failure of the message sequence to follow expected or habitual behavioral patterns.

7. *Regulator incompatibility*—The use of eye contact and patterns of speaking and listening that regulate the communication of one party in the interchange are not known to, used by, or are unacceptable to another party in the interchange.[19]

Other barriers to effective communication are inattentiveness, assuming the understanding of meanings, and using the communication for purposes different from those of others in the interchange (having hidden agendas). Cross-cultural communication is particularly problematic because the structure of messages differs from culture to culture. Even if the same language is used, words are used differently or have different meanings. Each culture has its own idioms and expressions, and the syntax (form) of the language may be different. The differences make it difficult to listen to the messages and make the likelihood of misunderstanding great. The social worker must overcome the barriers to effective communication if the action system is to function to reach its goals. In social work, communication is dialogue. The worker and client openly talk together and seek mutual understanding. Floyd Matson and Ashley Montagu, in the introduction to *The Human Dialogue*, described communication as not to "command" but to "commune" and indicated that knowledge of the highest order (whether of the world, of oneself, or of other) is to be sought and found not through detachment but through connection, not by objectivity but by intersubjectivity, not in a state of estranged aloofness but in something resembling the act of love.[20]

When the social worker works with a family or any multiperson client system, there is often a need to work on the communication within the family or client system. The worker uses her knowledge about effective communication to facilitate good communication among members of the family or system and with others in their ecosystems. She models good communication and shares her knowledge with them. She encourages and coaches them to improve their communication with each other and with others.

This is the essence of communication in its most effective form. This kind of communication adds vitality to, nourishes, and sustains the process of working together, the interaction.

■   THE INTERVIEW: AN INTERACTIONAL TOOL   ■

The **interview** is a primary tool of the social worker. It is the structure for operationalizing the interaction between a worker and a family or family members. Each social worker develops his own interviewing style. Interviewing is an art and a skill, and learning how to interview is accomplished by doing it. Some guides to interviewing can be helpful to the person learning to interview. These guides include preparing for an interview, knowing the stages of an interview, and developing interviewing skills.

Each interview should have a specific purpose or goal. Generally, this purpose may be to obtain the information needed for carrying out some task or function or to work together to meet a family's need or solve a family's problem. The purpose of a specific interview will depend on the stage of work together, the agency function and the method of service, and the family's needs or the nature of the situation at hand. In addition to purpose, several types of variables, listed next, affect the nature of the interview:

1. *How the interview is initiated*—Is it a voluntary activity on the part of the family or family members? Is it a formal, planned, regular interview or a walk-in request? Or is it a life-space contact (one that takes place in the process of the family's daily activities)?

2. *Where the interview takes place*—Does the interview take place in an office, a home, a hospital room, or some other setting?

3. *The experience of the worker and family with each other*—Have this worker and this family had previous contact with each other? Is this encounter a part of a time-limited or long-term plan?

Each interview will be different. The worker needs to be flexible in structuring and guiding the interview, depending on the interview's purpose and the needs of the family or family members. It should be carried out in a manner that encourages interaction and relationship.

Limited or shrinking resources and the advent of managed care have brought about a greater emphasis on brief and solution-focused intervention. The results are limitations on the amount of time available to work with a client system. Some settings still provide unlimited or open-ended services. However, the wave of the future is clearly toward some form of time-limited service throughout the human service delivery system.

Time limits mean that the social worker must place a high premium on the efficient use of time in accomplishing maximum effectiveness. This applies to each interview that is undertaken with a family. It means that the worker must be focused on developing and accomplishing goals and objectives that will bring about necessary change. This might seem to be contrary to the idea of encouraging interaction and relationship. However, if the worker is able to empathize with the family, she would come to realize that the family's needs are met best by moving toward resolution of the concerns that brought them to the worker. In the process, the family is also well served by learning to bring about change without assistance. This is in line with the social work value of maximizing self determination for clients. Thus, families can benefit from a solution-focused approach that builds on their strengths and that results in improved problem-solving skills. It is not so much the amount of time that is spent in building a relationship but the manner in which the worker interacts with the family. When the worker makes it clear to family members that they are valued and respected as human beings and that they are capable of making their own decisions, the foundation for a sound helping relationship has been established. This is not separate from the change process but rather a fundamental part of it.

Preparing for an Interview

In preparing for any interview the worker has three tasks: (1) planning the environment for the interview, (2) planning the content of the interview, and (3) "tuning in." Each of these tasks is carried out before contact with the family.

The worker thinks about the physical conditions of the interview. If the interview takes place in an office, the worker arranges the office so as to encourage the work together. This can be done by giving some thought to the placement of desk and chairs (sitting behind a desk may place a barrier between worker and family). An office that is comfortable and does not have too many distracting features is ideal. If the office is too small for the family to sit comfortably, the worker arranges to meet in an area that will accommodate the family while maintaining confidentiality. The worker tries to prevent interruptions such as phone calls and knocks on the door. If the worker plans to take notes or use a tape recorder, arrangements are made so this can be done with full knowledge of the family but in a manner that does not distract from the work at hand. The worker tries to provide a place for the interview where the conversation will not be overheard by others. Attention is given to the time of the interview so that neither worker nor family will be hurried, but the interview will also not be overly long. The worker will think about the impact of his dress on the family. If the interview is held outside the office, the worker will choose a time that is convenient for the family and when the fewest interruptions are likely to take place. For instance, an interview with a mother in the home might best take place when the children are in school.

In planning for the content of the interview, the worker will recall the goal and the purpose of the service and will identify the goal for this particular interview. The tasks to be accomplished will be considered. Any additional knowledge or information needed will be obtained. The worker might review notes about the previous interview if there has been one. The structure of the interview and questions to be asked will be considered. This planning is done to give form and focus to the interview, but the worker is prepared to be flexible and make changes if the family has unanticipated needs.

In tuning in, the worker first tries to anticipate the family's needs and feelings in the interview and to think about her own response to those feelings and needs.[21] The worker tries to become aware of her own feelings and attitudes that might interfere with effective communication. Such awareness should minimize the impact of these feelings and attitudes on the interview. The worker also needs to prepare to help by dealing with personal needs and any work-related attitudes that might interfere with the work of the interview.

Preparation for the interview is one way to promote worker readiness, which communicates to family members that they are important and that the work to be done together is important. Worker readiness prepares the way for effective interviewing.

The Stages of an Interview

All interviews have three stages: (1) the opening or beginning stage, (2) the middle or working-together stage, and (3) the ending stage. Each stage has a different focus and different tasks. In each interview some time is spent in each stage, but the amount of time spent in each stage may differ depending on the work at hand and the relationship of the worker and family. The stages represent steps in what might be called a "mini" change process. In Part II of this text, we examine the social work process as a change-oriented approach. The phases are assessment, planning, action, and evaluation and termination. However, these phases are not limited to the overall process but are included during each contact the social worker has with the family.

The opening, or beginning, stage of interviewing corresponds to the relationship-building and assessment phases. The middle, or working-together, stage involves evaluation, planning, and action. It includes evaluating success and barriers to success in carrying out the plan, deciding whether to continue with the plan or to modify it, and taking action to continue success or to remove barriers to success. The ending stage involves termination of the interview.

During the first few interviews with a new family, more emphasis might be needed on the first phases of relationship building and assessment, with planning and action limited to meeting needs that require immediate attention. Likewise, the last few interviews might focus more on termination. However, elements of each phase of the change process should be built into each interview. Besides helping to maintain a focus on the work to be done, this has the added benefit of reinforcing the steps necessary for successful change.

The beginning stage starts when the worker greets the family members by name and does whatever seems in order to make them comfortable. In working with adults, it is important that the worker address them formally as we mentioned earlier unless they ask to be addressed by their first names. This is especially important for people of color, such as African Americans, who have experienced situations where the use of their first name is a sign of inferiority or control. Generally, in Hispanic culture, the use of first names with adults is reserved for those who have been accepted into the family system. The worker tries to reduce any tensions and discuss any hostilities that may exist and reaches out to family members to help them become active participants in the interview. This can be done by asking the family to share any significant events since the last session. This keeps the worker in tune and current with the family and its concerns. In working with families, the worker is conscious of the need to reinforce appropriate family roles. When addressing parents as a couple, the worker should use their formal titles, Mr., Mrs., and so on. When addressing them as parents, the worker might call them father, mother, stepfather, stepmother, mom, dad, and so on. This has the effect of reinforcing those respective roles and strengthening them in the family.

During the beginning stage, the worker defines the purpose of the interview or recalls plans made in a previous session. The family is given an opportunity to discuss this purpose and any special needs they might have at this time. The worker elicits family member's feelings about the work to be done and accepts the family's sense of purpose and need by modifying the purpose and plan of the interview if necessary. Thus, an assessment of the current situation is made while the worker establishes or reestablishes a relationship by demonstrating care and concern and empathy.

If this is an initial interview, much of the time may need to be devoted to building relationships and making an initial assessment of the situation. The worker asks the family to identify needs and concerns. Diversity issues may be especially prominent during the first few interviews. The worker should communicate a respect for diversity and a valuing of difference while also seeking to learn about diversity from the family. However, some of the time should be spent in getting started with the work to be done. At the least, the worker should ask the family what they might do during the next week that might make a difference in meeting their needs. A plan for carrying this out should be included.

When the worker senses that the family is ready to proceed with the work to be done, the worker changes the focus of the interview. According to Lawrence Shulman, the worker may have to "demand this work."[22] This is not done in a harsh or demeaning manner, but in a firm manner that helps the family accept the need to begin working on the situation at hand. The middle phase has then begun. The content of this phase depends on the task at hand but should include evaluation of the success of the plan, decisions regarding continuation or modifications of the plan, and actions needed to carry out the plan or to remove barriers. The worker needs to maintain a sense of timing attuned to the family's pace of work as well as time limits that may be relevant to refocus if the content strays from the task or to renegotiate the purpose if this is indicated. The worker also should monitor communication for its effectiveness.

Before the agreed-on time for ending an interview is reached or when the purpose of the interview has been fulfilled, the worker again shifts the focus. In bringing the interview to an end, the worker summarizes what has happened during the interview and how it fits into the service being offered. The worker and the family together plan the next steps, which include work to be done by each family member before the next interview and the purpose, goal, time, and place of the next interview. If this is a single interview or a final interview, the family is helped to say good-bye and given permission to come again if other needs develop.

If the worker has been successful in incorporating termination at the end of each interview, the family may be well prepared for the termination of service when it comes. However, even if the worker is able to do this, some family members may have difficulty with termination. This is covered in greater detail in Chapter 9.

Skills Used by the Worker during the Interview

As a means of guiding and supporting the work together and of promoting relationship and effective communication, the worker uses six groups of skills during an interview: inductive learning and naturalistic inquiry skills; climate-setting skills; observation skills; listening skills, especially reflective listening; questioning skills; and focusing, guiding, and interpreting skills. The skill of interviewing is, in part, skill in selecting and using the appropriate response at the appropriate time. Like all skills, these must be developed through use over a period of time. The student or worker can improve his communication skills by using them in his everyday life. In addition, many exercises have been developed that are useful in beginning to acquire these skills, but it is only in actual client situations that skill development reaches the professional level. Each of these skills should be utilized in a way that is sensitive to cultural and individual differences.

The case example is from Chapter 5 with the Perez family involving two Hispanic teens and their parents. The teens are in a runaway shelter and refuse to return home and stay. Mr. and Mrs. P came to a session at the shelter. They left their younger children at home with Mrs. P's mother.

■ Beginning Stage

Jane met with Mr. and Mrs. Perez and with their son and daughter at the runaway shelter. Carmen is fourteen and ran away to be with a new boyfriend. Juan went with her to protect her, but he has also had an issue with his parents about wanting to quit school to go to work. Jane began by introducing herself and the purpose of the meeting. Mr. P introduced himself and his wife. Jane asked if the family would be able to discuss the situation in English or if they needed to arrange for a translator. She apologized for not being bilingual. Mr. P thanked her but said it would be best for them to use English because Juan and Carmen have not maintained their Spanish. Jane was careful to address the parents as Mr. and Mrs. and she addressed her questions to Mr. P first. She indicated that she had talked with Juan and Carmen earlier in the day and informed Mr. and Mrs. P about the gist of their conversation. Mr. P confirmed the issues of a boyfriend with Carmen and school with Juan and added his concern about Juan running with the wrong crowd and getting into trouble. Jane noted that Juan had left out these last two concerns. She asked Mr. P how his wife felt about what was going on. He invited Jane to ask her directly. When Jane asked Mr. P about concerns his son and daughter might have, he again invited her to ask them. Jane took this as a sign that the family was opening up some and that she could address some questions directly to each member.

■ Middle Stage

During the middle of the interview, Jane discussed what the family might need to do to have Juan and Carmen return home. It was obvious that neither side was willing to yield at this point, so she redirected the interview toward having each family member talk about what they liked best about the family and what their concerns were. This opened up some areas for discussion that allowed them to let their guard down. Jane used naturalistic inquiry to listen to each person's story. As the discussion unfolded, she was able to get them to discuss Juan's school issues. Juan stated that he did not like school except for his friends and pointed out that Mr. P had dropped out in ninth grade and he had already surpassed that. Besides, he was aware of the family's financial hardship and wanted to try to make it better by working. Mr. P expressed how he wanted more for Juan and his children than he was able to accomplish and he pointed out that although he was proud of his work his lack of education had limited his opportunities. Juan said that he had not thought of it that way and was quiet for awhile. The issue with Carmen seemed much more volatile. Mr. P stated that she was absolutely forbidden from dating until after she was fifteen and then it would be chaperoned. He folded his arms indicating that he would not yield on this issue. Mrs. P spoke up, saying to Carmen that she understood what Carmen was feeling and that she herself had wanted to go out before she was permitted, but that she was glad she had waited otherwise she might not have met Mr. P. Mrs. P expressed her concern that although Carmen was becoming a woman, she did not think that Carmen was ready for an adult relationship. Mrs. P wanted to see Carmen enjoy high school and become the first woman in Mrs. P's family to graduate high school and go on to college. As she listened to her mother, Carmen began to cry softly. She looked down at the floor and began to sob. Her brother reached over and put his arm around her shoulder. Mrs. P got up and reached out to her daughter who collapsed into her arms sobbing loudly, saying she was sorry for causing them so much worry. Mr. P stood back unsure of what to do. Jane allowed the family time to express their feelings as Mrs. P held Carmen in a close hug. Juan and Mr. P stood by and then sat down. Carmen stopped crying and sat down, pulling her chair closer to her mother so she could hold her hand. Carmen stated that one reason why she had wanted to date was because she felt good about the attention. She explained that there was a group of girls at school who were attractive and very popular and they had been mean to her and made fun of her dark hair and complexion. Carmen thought that having a boyfriend who was a senior might prove to them that she could be popular too. Jane tried to put into words what she had observed, that it was obvious that this family loved and cared very deeply for each other. She asked a question about what they wanted to do at this point. Carmen said she wanted to go home. Juan held back for awhile but later said that he was not fond of the food at the shelter and missed his mother and grandmother's cooking. Jane mapped out a plan to meet with the family until they could start with a family specialist at Catholic Family Services across town.

■ Ending Stage

As Jane was wrapping up the session, Carmen and Mrs. P expressed some reluctance to work with another worker at the family service agency, but Jane explained that her role was more temporary regarding providing counseling and that the agency she was referring them to would have staff that could help them on a longer-term basis. She indicated that she would work with them until they could get an appointment and would contact the school and coordinate services until the situation was resolved. Jane asked them if there was anything they needed to do this evening before they sent Carmen and Juan home. Juan agreed to attend school for now until they could discuss future plans. Carmen said she would abide by her parents wishes and would work on ways to deal with the other girls at school. Mr. and Mrs. P thanked Jane and the staff for keeping their children safe and returning them to the family. They set a follow-up appointment for later in the week.

Inductive Learning and Naturalistic Inquiry

These approaches are important to becoming culturally and diversity competent. Inductive learning refers to three important concepts. According to Doman Lum, the worker must first take a lifelong learning approach to becoming culturally competent. This means that learning does not stop but is built into professional development throughout one's career. Second, the worker should use inductive learning as she comes to know each client. This requires an openness to new knowledge as the worker discovers similarities and differences in how each client experiences diversity. Similarities serve to confirm earlier observations of members of her diversity group. Observing differences allows new learning to take place. Thus, the worker never closes the door to the possibility of advancing her knowledge about diversity. The third concept involves having the family assume the role of teacher while the worker assumes the role of learner each time the worker encounters diversity. This promotes the recognition that each client is an expert in his or her own diversity and that he or she experiences that diversity in an individual way.[23] Lum suggested the use of the "Essential Question," which is, "What does X mean to you?" where "the symbol X can refer to a family or social experience, to feelings, beliefs or cultural meanings."[24] Open-ended questions and facilitative communication skills are used to deepen the family member's narrative.[25]

Naturalistic inquiry comes out of ethnography. It involves the use of the inductive process to learn about a culture. James W. Leigh described this as beginning with the position that one does not know what one does not know. This is different from traditional social work, which uses a deductive process in which the worker uses prescribed guidelines for gathering knowledge, formulates a hypothesis about the current situation, and then designs a plan based on this hypothesis. The emphasis in traditional social work is on knowing what one does not know and then using this knowledge to guide the process of acquiring knowledge about the client system. To not know what one does not know means leaving oneself open to whatever unfolds in the interaction with the client system. Knowledge acquisition is not prescribed ahead of time but unfolds from the interaction with the client system.[26] The worker asks what Leigh described as global questions designed to uncover the client system's experiences.[27] The role of the client system is as "culture guide," and the role of the worker as "stranger."[28] From this open interaction, the plan and actions emerge.[29]

These approaches fit very well with an ecosystems strengths approach. In fact, Lum pointed out the need to use a strengths approach in becoming culturally competent.[30] In addition, the need to observe the family in the context of their culture brings an ecosystem approach into play.

Climate-Setting Skills

Three attributes have been identified as characteristics of interpersonal situations that seem to produce understanding, openness, and honesty, which are enabling factors in the work of the action system. These three characteristics are empathy, genuineness, and nonpossessive warmth.[31]

Empathy is the capacity to communicate to the family that the worker accepts and cares for them. Empathy communicates that at this point in time the family and each family member's welfare is to be considered before the worker's. Empathy is expressed by openly receiving and recognizing the feelings of family members, by accurately perceiving the family members' messages, and by providing the family with concrete feedback about messages.

Genuineness is the capacity of the worker to communicate to the family that the worker is trustworthy. It is expressed by being willing to let the family know the worker as a person in ways that meet the family's need for such information. It also reflects congruence between the worker's verbal and nonverbal messages. In addition, genuineness involves informing family members when the worker disagrees with them and when their behavior and communication are inconsistent. This skill calls for honesty but honesty communicated in a manner that is sensitive to the family member's feelings and concerns.

Nonpossessive warmth is the capacity to communicate to the family both a concern and a desire for intimacy; this allows the family to make decisions, to have negative and positive feelings, and to feel worthwhile. It has qualities of nonblame, closeness, and nondefensiveness. A warmth that is nonpossessive is displayed through positive regard and respect for family members and through thoughtfulness and kindness as well as appreciation for, and pleasure at, the family's growth and well-being. When working with families, this also has the added benefit of modeling family relationships that need to be founded on nonpossessive warmth and acceptance. Family relationships in which this is absent pose a great challenge. Family relationships that have this quality are stronger and are sources of strength for the work to be done.

These three attributes are tied to social work values. One of the cardinal values of social work is the belief in the value and worth of every human being. This leads the worker to respect each family member as an individual. This does not mean that the worker approves of all of the family member's behavior. Some family members will have done things that are wrong, either morally or legally. The worker accepts family members as human beings even with their faults and mistakes. When the worker is able to do this, then he can listen to the family member's story without judging her as a person. This helps the worker put himself in his client's shoes and leads to empathy. A genuine belief in the value and worth of every human being allows the worker to be more genuine in treating family members with dignity and respect. It allows the worker to care about each person as a human being even though he may find things about her that he does not like.

The climate of all interpersonal endeavors greatly affects the nature of the relationship and the quality of the communication. Skills in developing and maintaining an accepting, growth-producing climate are an important part of the worker's repertoire.

Interviewing is only one form of communication. The skills used in the interview can also be used in less formal social work interactions. They are the same skills that encourage relationships to form and to be used and maintained. In the social work endeavor, in the action system, it is the responsibility of the social worker to move toward the family so that relationships may form and a common ground for communication may be established. To do this, the social worker must understand the family and be willing to work with them in meeting their needs and in resolving the situation. Improved communication and relationships are central to success in the ecosystems strengths approach. The focus of growth and change is on the interactions and transactions among family members, within family subsystems, and between the family and its members and the environment. Success is often determined by the family's ability to change their interactions with others and their interactions with the worker. Thus, the worker frequently will be in a position to assist family members to acquire these skills in order to bring about growth and change.

Observation Skills

People give information and express feeling in nonverbal, behavioral ways. They also provide information and express feelings in the way in which other information is given and discussed. Sensitivity to this nonverbal material is useful for tuning in to where the family member really is in relation to the material being discussed, for checking the validity of the family member's verbal expression, and for feedback purposes. Workers should observe the following:

1. *Body language*—What is the family member communicating by the way she sits, by behaviors such as thumping on the desk with the fingers, by facial expression?

2. *The content of opening and closing sentences*—These sentences tend to contain particularly significant material. They also may give cues about the family member's attitudes toward self and the environment.

3. *Shifts in conversation*—These shifts, particularly when always related to similar topics, can indicate that a particular topic is painful, taboo, or something the family member does not want to discuss.

4. *Association of ideas*—Observing which ideas family members seem to associate with which other ideas can often give the worker an indication of unspoken feelings.

5. *Recurrent references*—When family members continue to bring up a subject, this indicates that it is a subject of importance to them or one with which they would like help.

6. *Inconsistencies or gaps*—When these are present, it is an indication either that the material being discussed is threatening to family members or that they are unwilling to openly share in this area.

7. *Points of stress or conflict*—In cross-cultural action systems, stress and conflict may indicate areas of inadequate knowledge about cultural aspects of the family's functioning. This may also indicate misunderstanding on the part of family members or areas of family members' bias or prejudice.

Listening Skills

Listening is of vital importance in any interview situation. The worker listens to what family members have to say and how they respond to questions and responses. Beginning workers often place primary emphasis on what they have to say and on the questions to be asked. Good questioning enables family members to provide necessary information, consider alternatives, and work on the situation at hand. If the worker's listening skills are deficient, the full value of the interview will not be realized. Active listening—being with family members in their struggle to deal with difficulties and problems—is the appropriate response at many points in the interview.

Developing listening skills is also important because social workers often communicate with persons whose language expression is somewhat different from their own. In listening, it is important to try to understand what the family member is attempting to communicate. To do this, the worker seeks to understand what the words mean to the family member. The worker maintains focus on what the family member is saying even though there is a tendency to shut out the communication because it seems strange and is difficult to listen to. It is important to note feeling words and how they are expressed. Listening should reflect an attitude of openness and acceptance. Effective listening involves a sense of timing that allows the worker to focus on the family member and what is being said and does not shut off communication by premature evaluation or advice.

It is much easier to obtain cooperation from others if they know that we are paying attention to what they are saying and experiencing. This demonstrates care and concern for others in a way that has real meaning for them. It is not simply lip service but demonstrates interest in a genuine way.

Questioning Skills

The essence of this group of skills is knowing the various types of questions to ask and the usefulness of each type of question. A first category of questions includes open- and closed-ended questions. A closed-ended question calls for a specific answer. An example would be, What is your age? These questions are used to gain factual information. An open-ended question is one that enables the client to define, discuss, or answer the question in any way he chooses. An example would be, What do you think is the reason your child is doing poorly in school? The open-ended question allows expression of feeling and gives the worker the family member's perception of the subject at hand. In developing a social history, it is usually advisable to mix open- and closed-ended questions; this allows for discussion between the worker and the family about the facts as well as about the family's life experiences.

There are also leading and responding questions. A leading question is used when it is desirable for a family member to continue to explore the subject at hand. An example would be, You have tried to cope with this problem, haven't you? A responding question follows the lead of the family member's response. An example would be when a family member has been discussing how he has tried to cope and the worker responds, Could you tell me more about how you went about helping your child?

In an answer-and-agree question, the family member is expected to answer in such a way as to agree with the worker. An example would be, You are feeling much better today, aren't you? This usually is not a good form of questioning to use because it blocks discussion and imposes the worker's ideas on the family member.

With most family members, it is better to ask questions so that they contain single, rather than several, ideas. A question with a number of ideas might be used when the worker is attempting to help the family recognize connections between the ideas. Whether to ask very broad questions or very specific ones depends on the work at hand and on the worker's style. Some workers like to gain a broad picture first and then explore details. Other workers believe it is more helpful for clients to consider small parts of the situation and then look at the broader picture later. Questioning is one of the means used by a social worker to enhance relationships and communication.

In general, it is better for the worker to avoid asking too many questions; otherwise, the family may feel bombarded or put on the spot. Questions also tend to set an agenda that is worker centered rather than client centered. In many respects, questions can be used to control the interview in that the family can end up talking about what the worker wants to discuss, as opposed to discussing their concerns. In addition, questions tend to be one-sided and offer little opportunity for feedback, interaction, or give and take in the interchange. There are other ways to provide guidance or focus that do not use questions but do incorporate family member's concerns.

Focusing, Guiding, and Interpreting Skills

This group of skills is used by the worker to enable the action system to accomplish the tasks necessary to reach the agreed-on objectives. It includes the capacity to use encouragers; to paraphrase and summarize what has been said; and to reflect feelings, meaning, and ideas. These are skills that incorporate what the family member says or does into the worker's response. Thus, they are client centered, but they can be used to guide or focus the interview on what is important to the family or family member and what the worker needs to know about the family or family member, their diversity, the environment, and their needs. The capacity to confront and to elaborate are important in terms of moving the work toward difficult areas and reaching an understanding of the situation or the work to be done. The effective use of these skills includes a sense of timing as to when to listen, when to focus, when to interpret, and when to direct.

Paraphrasing and summarizing often clarify what has been said. Clarification and elaboration enhance understanding. With understanding of issues and facts, the work can progress as a truly joint effort.

Confrontation and silence are often difficult for the worker. Confrontation is the bringing out into the open of feelings, issues, and disagreements. It involves looking at these elements and attempting to find ways to deal with them. If feelings, issues, and disagreements remain hidden, they may interfere with the work at hand. Silence may indicate resistance, frustration, or anger, but it also can provide a time for worker and client to be reflective. Instead of being uncomfortable with silence, the worker can attempt to understand the nature of the silence and use it appropriately. Times of reflection are useful in the work together. Silence related to resistance can be used to develop sufficient discomfort on the part of the family member so that she will have to do something. This can help in focusing on the work together. The worker who senses frustration and anger can bring it out into the open, confront the family or family member, and thus deal with it so that the work can proceed.

It is the worker's responsibility to guide the interview but not to control it. The worker takes whatever material and expression of feeling are given by the family or family member and, by listening, questioning, focusing, guiding, and directing, enables the process of the work together to proceed toward the desired outcome.

SUMMARY

The emphasis in this chapter is on interaction and engagement that takes place in an action system and with the family and members of their ecosystem. The formation of the action system requires understanding of the family and skill on the part of the worker. Special consideration must be given in developing action systems with resistant family members.

Relationship is the cohesive quality of the family and the action system. The helping relationship is for the purpose of assisting families in meeting their needs. It is influenced by the life experiences of both the family and the worker. Cross-diversity relationships have special characteristics that the worker must understand.

The same principles and skills used in interaction with families are also used when working with significant persons in the situation, with those who may be able to provide resources for the family, or with a variety of community persons. The capacity for forming and using one-to-one relationships is a core social work skill.

Communication is an important ingredient of the action system. The process of communication can become blocked in a variety of ways. Social workers need to be aware of these blocks and of the means for dealing with them.

The interview is an important interactional tool for use in the action system. It is important to prepare for interviews and to make them goal directed. Each interview has three stages: a beginning, a middle, and an ending. Workers use a variety of skills in the interview. These include inductive learning and naturalistic inquiry; climate setting; observation; listening; questioning; and focusing, guiding, and interpreting.

QUESTIONS

1. What are some of the ways to facilitate the development of a helping relationship?
2. Why is the development of a relationship so essential to the helping situation?
3. What are some ways to encourage nonvoluntary clients to engage in the helping process?
4. How should resistance be viewed in any helping situation?
5. Why is it difficult to communicate across cultural boundaries? How can social workers facilitate such communication?
6. Discuss the needed balance between questioning and listening in a social work interview.

SUGGESTED READINGS

Johnson, Louise C., and Yanca, Stephen J. *Social Work Practice: A Generalist Approach,* 9th ed. Boston: Allyn & Bacon, 2007 (Chapter 8).

Anderson, Joseph, and Carter, Robert Wiggins. *Diversity Perspectives for Social Work Practice.* Boston: Allyn & Bacon, 2003.

Ivey, Allen E., and Ivey, Mary Bradford. *Intentional Interviewing: Facilitating Client Development in a Multicultural Society,* 6th ed. Belmont, CA: Wadsworth, 2007.

Lum, Doman. *Culturally Competent Practice: A Framework for Understanding Diverse Groups and Justice Issues,* 3rd ed. Belmont, CA: Wadsworth, 2007.

Perlman, Helen Harris. *Relationship: The Heart of Helping People.* Chicago: University of Chicago Press, 1979.

Poorman, Paula B. *Microskills and Theoretical Foundations for Professional Helpers.* Boston: Allyn & Bacon, 2003.

Ragg, D. Mark. *Building Effective Helping Skills: The Foundation of Generalist Practice.* Boston: Allyn & Bacon, 2001.

Sheafor, Bradford W., and Horejsi, Charles R. *Techniques and Guidelines for Social Work Practice,* 7th ed. Boston: Allyn & Bacon, 2006 (Chapter 8).

Shulman, Lawrence. *The Skills of Helping: Individuals and Groups,* 5th ed. Belmont, CA: Wadsworth, 2006.

Generalist Social Work Practice with Families

The content of the service process, or the work of the family and the worker in meeting need, is the focus of Part II. This process of the work can be separated from the interactional process presented in Chapter 4 only for purposes of study. Interaction and service are two ways of looking at the professional response to need. The generalist social work process, as developed in this book, is a change process based on knowledge, values, and skill. It is intervention into the transactions of human systems. The material in Part II has been adapted from the material in Part III of our companion text *Social Work Practice: A Generalist Approach* and is a family-focused version of it.

The process can be conceptualized as having four major components: assessment, planning, action, and evaluation and termination. Although assessment precedes planning, planning precedes action, and action precedes termination, the process is cyclical in nature. Planning often leads to the need for a new or different understanding (assessment) of family in environment or the family ecosystem. Action often produces new information for use in understanding or demonstrates the need for additional planning. Evaluation, the assessment of what has happened as a result of action, is ongoing in the process and leads to new understanding and sometimes to new plans and action. Thus, all four phases are always present, but at various points in the work one or more may be the focus and receive the most attention.

All four phases as well as the interactional process constitute intervention. All can influence change in the transactions between families and the systems in their environment. All can influence the social functioning of individuals, families, and social systems. Figure II.1 depicts the social work process.

The generalist social worker is prepared to work with individuals, families, groups, organizations, and communities at any point during the change process either as client systems or as the focus of the change process. The generalist social worker keeps an open mind about working with various size systems. She is free to initiate change that is needed at whatever level is most efficient and effective. Table 5.1 in Chapter 5 provides a guide for determining the appropriate client system. For Part II it is assumed that the family system as a whole is either the client system or the target for change. Part III presents an application of this model

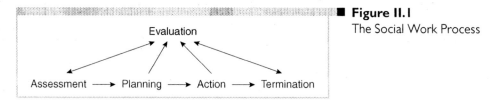

■ Figure II.1
The Social Work Process

with various subsystems in the family. Studying the change processes with the family as a system and with subsystems of the family are separated in this text for learning purposes. We have done this so that the student or practitioner can achieve a better understanding of how to work with family subsystems; which is likely to be the focus of most of their work with families. However, the material on family subsystems in Part III is also used in working with the family as a system, especially when subsystems and relationships are part of the focus of the work. Similarly, working more exclusively with a family subsystem does not exclude the need to understand the family as a system. In fact, the schemas for development of a social history for each subsystem in Part III includes the information from the schema for the family social history. In addition, the units of attention for parts of the plan for a family system may be parts of a subsystem, the whole subsystem, or the interactions that occur with members of subsystems. Direct and indirect practice actions that are identified with working with the family system may also be used when working with subsystems and vice versa. On those occasions when the worker is working with all or most of the family system, issues related to family subsystem structures, functioning, and development are likely to arise and the worker will need to use the relevant material in Part III. Thus, it is important to view the material in Parts II and III as integrated with each other and only separated here for learning purposes. This should not be construed as encouraging separate methodologies for practicing social work as a generalist practitioner.

Chapter 5 considers the assessment phase with an emphasis on the family as a system. Attention is given to the stages in assessment, to the nature of transactional assessment, and to strengths and resources available in the ecosystem.

Chapter 6 discusses planning with an emphasis on the family as a system, including the means for developing a plan of action that includes goals and objectives based primarily on strengths and resources in the ecosystem. Units of attention, strategy, roles, tasks, and techniques are also discussed. Factors that affect the plan of action are explored, including diversity and at-risk populations. In addition, there is a discussion of the agreement between worker and client about the plan.

Chapter 7 identifies and discusses important actions used in direct practice with the family by the generalist social worker. The specific direct practice actions identified and discussed are (1) diversity competent practice actions; (2) actions to develop relationships; (3) use of resources, including a discussion of the nature of the service delivery system, referral, and broker and advocate roles; (4) empowering and enabling clients; (5) crisis intervention; (6) supportive social work; (7) use of activity; and (8) mediation within the family.

Chapter 8 examines indirect practice actions with families, including (1) mediation between the family and the environment; (2) the use of influence; (3) action to change the environment; and (4) coordination of services, including the strategy of case management.

Chapter 9 discusses evaluation and termination with families. The chapter includes a look at kinds of evaluation, the use of single system design and research techniques in evaluation, and evaluation during the phases of the change process. It ends with an examination of the kinds of termination, planned termination with individual family members, and components of termination.

5

Family Assessment

LEARNING EXPECTATIONS

1. Understanding of family assessment as a complex process and beginning skill in assessing families in generalist practice.

2. Ability to decide on the most appropriate client system to be served.

3. Ability to choose and apply appropriate knowledge to the family assessment process.

4. Skill in judgment or decision making in family assessment.

5. Skill in identifying needs in families and blocks to their fulfillment.

6. Skill in identifying strengths and resources in the family ecosystem and in transactional assessment with families.

Assessment with families can be a complex process. The complexity is associated with the need to assess both the family as a system and individuals within the family system. This is further complicated by factors such as family structure, including single parent, unmarried couples, and various forms of blended families. Diversity presents an additional factor in assessment. This was introduced in Chapter 3 and should be noted and reviewed as we consider various aspects of family assessment. In addition, family work is often done with subsystems. In fact, our research as well as our practice experience indicates that most work with families involves working with family subsystems (marital, parent, parent–child, or sibling) as opposed to working with the family as a whole. Having the family meet as a whole is actually relatively rare compared to meeting with subsystems. However, family texts generally assume that family work is performed with the entire family present. Assessment, planning, action, and evaluation and termination are generally presented as if the entire family is present. The change process with the family as a system is presented in the chapters for Part II. The change process with marital, parent, parent–child, and sibling subsystems of the family is the focus of Part III. This chapter presents schemas for assessing the family as a system and individuals within the family. Schemas for assessing family subsystems are presented in chapters in Part III. Relevant portions of the family and individual schemas are also used in schemas for family subsystems.

■   SELECTION OF THE CLIENT SYSTEM   ■

One of the most important decisions to be made is the appropriate client system to be served. The generalist approach calls for the worker to be prepared to work with individuals, families, groups, organizations, and communities. The generalist social worker may work with individuals or systems as clients, or they may be the focus of the change efforts on behalf of any size client system. Table 5.1 can be used as a guide for deciding when the worker and the client should select various client systems or units of attention. (See Table 10.1 for selecting family subsystems.) The selection of the client system generally occurs during the assessment phase, although it can also occur during planning. The selection of the focus of the change efforts or the unit of attention is part of the planning process. The selection of the client system determines the focus of the assessment process and the type of assessment to be used (individual, family, group, organization, or community).

The term *client* refers to the person or system that either seeks the help of a social worker or is served by an agency employing a social worker. For students in field placement and for most social workers, an individual is the most frequent type of client system encountered. The next most frequent is the family or subsystems of the family. Groups can be fairly frequent in some settings, such as residential care, day programs, and prevention and growth and development services for children and youth. The least frequently served client system for the typical social worker, especially BSWs would be an organization or community. The type of client served is determined primarily by the nature of the service delivered by the agency in which the student is placed or the worker employed. It is also determined by the role and the status the worker has in the agency. For example, MSW social workers are more likely to be employed in agencies that provide family work or group work to families or individuals with complicated problems that require therapy. BSW social workers provide counseling and support services to families or in groups, but they are not trained to do therapy. In most agencies, administrators and supervisors who are social workers are more likely to be MSWs. Part of their responsibility is to plan and implement changes in the agency. Professional community organizers are also more likely to be MSWs. However, BSW social workers will have opportunities to participate in change at the organizational or community level and at times may actually initiate those changes. Thus, the worker must be prepared to work with all of these systems.

Even when the worker has an opportunity to work with systems larger than the individual client, the initial request for service frequently involves an individual or individuals. As the assessment of the need or concern proceeds, the worker may find that the most appropriate client system is the family or a subsystem of the family (marital, parent, parent–child, or sibling subsystems). The worker might believe that the person would be served better in a group, especially one that is made up of members who have similar needs or concerns. He might observe that service delivery or meeting client needs could be improved by changing how an agency functions. He may find that a segment of the community is affected by a situation and that collective action is needed. Table 5.1 outlines several common indications and counterindications for selecting various size client

Table 5.1   Indications and Counterindications with Client Systems and Units of Attention

	Indications	**Counterindications**
Individuals	Information giving Information gathering Concrete service Referral service Need relates primarily to an individual without significant family No other involvement feasible Intrapsychic difficulties Individual who with help can involve significant systems in the change process Individual choice	Cannot function in a one-to-one helping relationship Action-oriented service needed Focus on interactional aspects of family or peer group needed Need fulfillment best reached by change in larger system
Family	Major difficulties seem to exist in family interaction One family member undercuts change efforts of other members Family needs to respond to individual need Need for understanding family interaction to understand individual functioning Family needs to examine role functioning or communication Chaotic families where there is a need to restore order Family choice	Irreversible trend toward family breakup Significant impairment of individual family member prevents participation Need for individual help precludes work with family No common concern or goal Worker cannot deal with destructive interactions
Small group	Individuals face similar situations and can benefit from interchange Group influence on the individual is great Development of socialization skills is indicated Use of activity is desirable Focus on environmental change Usable natural groups	Individual overwhelmed by the group Individual destructive to group A common purpose or goal does not exist Sufficient cohesive factors do not exist Environment will not allow the group to function Environment will not allow the group to reach its goal to at least some extent
Organization	Difficulty related to organizational functioning Number of individuals are affected and needs not being met because of organizational factors Workers are overconstrained from providing service to clients	Dangers of further negative results to clients are great Client service will be neglected or negated
Community	Lack of needed resources and services Lack of coordination of services Community influence on organization or family prevents meeting of need Community functioning affects a large number of individuals and families negatively	Same as organization

systems and units of attention. Units of attention refers to systems that are the focus of the change efforts.

As the worker begins to discuss the initial need or concern, she maintains an open mind about the appropriate level for service delivery. This will determine the client system with whom she will be working. She focuses first on person in environment. She is knowledgeable about the nature of the service delivery system within her agency and for other organizations in the community. She is also aware of issues that concern various segments of the community. The decision about the appropriate client system to be served is a joint decision involving the worker and the client. It is made within the context of person in environment, the service delivery system, and the community.

■   THE ASSESSMENT PROCESS WITH FAMILIES   ■

In the assessment process with families, the worker identifies needs and concerns and makes assumptions about the nature of the need or concern and about potential strengths and resources in the family ecosystem. Information is selected and collected that may or may not support these assumptions. The worker analyzes the available information to understand family in environment and to build a foundation for change based on the strengths of the family and resources in the ecosystem. When the client system is the family, then the primary assessment document is the family **social history,** which also uses relevant portions of the individual social history to understand individual members. When the client system is an individual and the family is the unit of attention, then the individual social history is the primary assessment document, and relevant portions of the family social history are used to understand the family.

When the client is a multiperson system, the worker must understand not only the persons who are members of the system but also the subsystems that exist within the system and the system itself. This includes understanding the relationships among the individuals and subsystems. Social systems theory provides one means for describing **multiperson client systems.** All social systems have structural, functional, and developmental aspects. An analogy from photography helps to differentiate these three aspects. Structure may be seen as a snapshot; it describes the parts and their relationship to one another at a given point in time. Functioning may be seen as the movie; functioning describes the nature of the process of the system. Development may be seen as time-lapse photography; development describes stages of family functioning and is also concerned with roots and history and with significant past events in the life of the system.

The family is the system most apt to influence the functioning of the individual; it is the primary system responsible for providing for needs of individuals. Challenges to individual functioning often arise from family functioning, past or present. Often, without change in the family system, the needs of individuals cannot be provided for and the challenges that the individual faces cannot be met. To bring about this change in the family system, it is necessary to understand the family as a social system. Knowing about an individual's place in the family system is also often necessary for understanding that individual. When the change needed is in transactions among members of the family system, the family may be either the unit of attention or the client system. The social worker determines the family system's strengths, motivation, capacity, and opportunity for change and engages the family system in the helping process. The family goes through the process of becoming a client.

The individual social history is the assessment document for working with individuals. The family social history is the assessment document for working with the family system. (See Table 5.2 for a schema for an individual social history and Table 5.3 for a schema for a family social history.) The family schema contains four parts: (1) necessary identifying information, (2) a description of the family as a system, (3) the identification of concerns and needs of the family system, and (4) identification of the strengths and challenges of the family system and the environment for meeting needs.

Table 5.2   Schema for Development of a Social History: Individual

I. The person
   A. Identifying information (as needed by agency): name, address, date and place of birth, marital status, religion, race, referred by whom and why
   B. Family
      1. Parents: names, dates of birth, dates of death, place or places of residence, relationship
      2. Siblings: names, dates of birth, places of residence, relationships
      3. Spouse: names, ages, dates of marriages and divorces, relationships
      4. Children: names, ages, dates of birth, places of residence, relationships
      5. Resources in the family for client—expectations for client
   C. Education and work experience
      1. Last grade of school completed, degrees if any, special knowledge or training; attitudes toward educational experiences; resources and expectations of educational system for client
      2. Work history—jobs held, dates, reasons for leaving; attitudes toward work experiences; resources and expectations of work system for client
   D. Diversity
      1. Disabling factors—physical, mental health history, current functioning
      2. Cultural and ethnic identification, importance to client
      3. Other diversity factors (include religious affiliation or spiritual factors, if any)
      4. Resources and expectations related to diversity characteristics of client
   E. Environmental factors
      1. Significant relationships outside family; resources and expectations for client
      2. Significant neighborhood and community factors; resources and expectations for client

II. The concern or need
   A. Reason for request for service
   B. History of concern or need; onset of concern or need; nature and results of coping attempts; factors that seem to be contributing to concern or need
   C. Capacity to carry out "vital roles"
   D. Needs of client (general)
      1. Needs based on common human need/development
         a. Stage of physical, cognitive, and psychosocial development
         b. Adequacy of need fulfillment in previous stages
         c. Present needs (needs for developmental stage and compensation for previous stage deficiency)

2. Needs based on diversity factors
   a. What dominant societal factors and attitudes affect the way people of this diversity meet common human/developmental needs?
   b. What cultural group factors affect the way people of this diversity meet common human/developmental needs?
   c. Individualize client within the diverse group. What are this client's attitudes toward diversity, means of coping with diversity, adaptation or lifestyle within diverse group, coping or adaptation relative to dominant societal expectations?
   d. What incongruities exist between this client's way of functioning and societal expectations based on this diversity?
   e. What needs does this person have as a result of dominant societal attitudes and expectations, cultural factors related to common human need/human development, individual factors of attitudes toward the diversity and dominant societal expectations and impingements, or incongruities between the client's way of functioning and societal expectations based on this diversity?
3. Needs based on environmental expectations
   a. Client's responsibilities toward family, peer group, work, organizations, community
   b. Other environmental expectations of client; client's attitudes toward these expectations
   c. Are responsibilities and expectations of the client realistic?
   d. Client needs because of the responsibilities and expectations
4. Needs of client in relation to the request for service
   a. What general needs of the client have bearing on the request for service?
   b. What is the specific need of the client in relation to the request?
   c. What factors seem to be blocking the fulfillment of that need?

III. Strengths and challenges for helping
   A. What does the client expect to happen during and as a result of the service to be provided?
   B. What are the client's ideas, interests, and plans that are relevant to the service?
   C. What is the client's motivation for using the service and for change?
   D. What is the client's capacity for coping and for change? What might impinge? What are the individual's internal resources for change?
   E. What are the client's strengths?
   F. What are the environmental resources and the environmental responsibilities and impingements that could support or mitigate against coping or change?
   G. Are there any other factors that affect the client's motivation, capacity, or opportunity for change?
   H. What is the nature of the stress factor?
   I. Are the client's expectations realistic?
   J. Summary of strengths and challenges of client in situation as they relate to meeting need

In studying the structure of the family, it is useful to understand each family member in considerable depth. Use of appropriate parts of Table 5.2 (a schema for an individual social history) would be helpful for development of such understanding. In addition, families

Table 5.3 Schema for Development of a Social History: Family

I. Identifying information (as needed by agency)
 A. Names and birth dates of family members, dates of death
 B. Dates of marriage, dates of previous marriages
 C. Religion, race, cultural background
 D. Language spoken in the home
 E. Date of first contact, referred by whom

II. The family as a system (note the strengths, resources, and challenges for each section)
 A. Family structure
  1. Identify all persons within the functioning family system. Include members of extended family and nonrelated persons if they function as part of the system. Describe each person using appropriate parts of "Schema for Development of a Social History: Individual" (Table 5.2).
  2. Subsystems—describe the relationships and functioning of the marital, parental, sibling, and parent–child subsystems or other subsystems
  3. Family cohesiveness—describe the manner in which the family maintains its system, boundary, and relatedness; include the issues of connectedness and separateness among family members, specification of family rules and norms, and emotional climate
  4. The family's environment—describe the family's
   a. Living situation
   b. Socioeconomic status
   c. Community or neighborhood and the family's relationship with the community or neighborhood. Include community organizations and institutions important for the family and the nature of relationships with these. Describe community and neighborhood resources and responsibilities and impingements for this family in this community
   d. Extended family: involvement with; significant persons in the extended family; strength of the influence of this family system; and resources, responsibility, and impingements from it
 B. Family functioning
  1. Communication patterns
  2. Decision-making patterns
  3. Role performance
   a. Work and housekeeping standards and practices
   b. Parenting and childcare standards and practices
   c. System member support; growth encouragement, care, and concern
  4. Family's customary adaptive and coping mechanisms
  5. Construct an eco-map for the family
 C. Family development—history
  1. Roots, influence of cultural group and previous generations on the family system
  2. Significant event in the life of the family
  3. Developmental stage of family life
  4. Construct a genogram

III. The concern or need
 A. Why did this family come to the agency? What service is requested?
 B. Needs of individual family members (see Table 5.2)

C. Needs of subsystems within the family. (Particular attention should be paid to the marital system and the parental system.) Identify resources and other assistance or change needed for appropriate functioning.

D. Needs of the family system. Consider how the needs of individuals and subsystems impact on the family system. Also consider environmental responsibilities, expectations, and any diversity factors that impact on the family as a system. Identify blocks to the family system's meeting these needs.

IV. Strengths and challenges for meeting needs

A. What does this family want to happen as a result of the service provided?

B. What are the family's ideas, interests, and plans that are relevant to the service?

C. What is the family's motivation for using the service or for change?

D. What is the family's capacity for coping and change? What might impinge?

E. What are the family's resources for change (internal to the system)?

F. What are the environmental resources, responsibilities, and impingements on this family that could support or mitigate against change?

G. Are there any other factors that affect the family system's motivation, capacity, or opportunity for change?

H. Are the system's and the environment's expectations realistic for this family?

I. What are the strengths and challenges for family in situation as they relate to meeting need?

need to be understood within the context of their diversity. Table 5.4 ("Assessment of the Individual Family from a Diverse Ethnic Group") is an excerpt from Table 3.2 in the chapter on diversity competent practice with families. When the worker is working with an ethnically diverse family, he should incorporate this into his assessment and the family social history.

The family should be considered as a system. System members are those persons who have stronger relationships among themselves than with other persons. The boundary of the family—the separation of the family from the environment—should be drawn so as to include other significant persons and reflect the family's view of itself.

Thus, the family system may include some members of the extended family who may or may not be living in the home, such as a grandparent or an aunt. It may include an unrelated person living in the home or a neighbor. The children who have left the home for whatever reason need to be considered, depending on the nature of their functioning within the family system. Attention should be paid to absent family members—those who have died or left the family through divorce. Their influence on the family system and its functioning should be ascertained. The determination of who is in a family system is particularly difficult in the case of a blended family. Often, in blended families, custody and visitation of children from previous marriages create a changing mix of individuals and relationships that results in a state of flux. In addition, relationships between stepparents and stepchildren and between stepsiblings may be tenuous or conflicted. These family relationships may be even more complicated by multiple divorces, live-in partners, and children born out of wedlock.

Table 5.4 Assessment of the Individual Family from a Diverse Ethnic Group

I. Knowledge of the individual family

A. History
  1. Experience of this particular family
  2. Migration, movement within the United States
     a. Social–economic mobility
     b. Identification with ethnic group
  3. Note urban–rural experience
  4. Fit within larger ethnic group

B. Value concerns
  1. What of traditional ethnic patterns is important to this family? What is not? How do they deal with discrepancies?
  2. Spirituality within the family
  3. Traditions

C. Family
  1. How does this family define itself (nuclear, extended, etc.)?
  2. Relationships in this family
  3. How does this family relate to larger ethnic group? To their heritage?

D. Communication patterns
  1. Within this particular family
  2. With larger society

E. Coping in this particular family

F. Community
  1. Relationships to ethnic community, to dominant community
  2. Resources available, usable by this family, experience with

G. Issues concerning this family

Defining the family and determining who is considered part of the family system is heavily influenced by culture. This was pointed out in Chapter 3. Many cultures consider the extended family as part of the family system. In fact, most cultures outside of European and European American cultures do so. Many African American and Hispanic/Latino families include fictive kin in their families but in different ways. African American families may include unrelated members of the community with whom they feel a close bond. Informal adoption, or raising unrelated children without legally adopting them, is also an accepted practice. Hispanic/Latino families often include godparents as family members, especially regarding matters that involve their children.

Another part of the structure of the family is its subsystems—the marital, the parental, the sibling, and the parent–child subsystems. The marital subsystem includes the husband and wife or the couple as partners. Their relationship should be described in terms of separation from each partner's family of origin and the ability of each partner to support and validate the other partner. The parental subsystem includes the mother and father or couple and their interactions as parents or stepparents. The understanding of the sibling subsystem is concerned with how the children relate to one another. The parent– child subsystem is intergenerational in nature; of particular concern is how limits of authority and responsibility are drawn between the generations.[1] Other subsystems may exist in a family, and these should be identified and the nature of relationships described. Ann Hartman and Joan Laird pointed out that an intergenerational perspective is very helpful in developing understanding of the family system, which can be aided by the use of a **genogram.**[2]

A third consideration in describing family structure is cohesiveness. This is what binds the family together. It is the emotional or feeling tone of the family, the we-ness of the family; it is the connectedness of family members with one another. Healthy family relationships allow for both connectedness and separateness.[3] The mechanisms for both connectedness and separateness should be described. Family rules and norms (the way this family does things or behaves) are means of expressing cohesiveness. A description of what is allowed and under what circumstances is another means of discovering the interrelatedness of family members. This is another area that is heavily influenced by culture. Most cultures outside of Europe and European American culture place an exceptionally strong emphasis on family ties and relationships. This could be seen as an emphasis on connectedness. In these families, rules and norms reflect the centrality of the family. In addition, many cultures prescribe certain rules and norms that are based on gender. Some of this was discussed in Chapter 3.

The family system is part of a larger environment. That environment has expectations for the family, which involve the functioning of the family as a system internally and responsibility toward other systems in the environment. In a society of cultural diversity, there are often conflicting expectations that should be identified. Impacts of prejudice and discrimination because of family diversity should be identified. It is important to determine the nature and extent of the influence of systems such as church, school, cultural group, extended family, and the like that impinge on the family or have expectations of responsibility for the family. The importance of spirituality and religion for African American and Hispanic/Latino was identified in Chapter 3. Churches with large populations made up of these families typically have rather extensive support systems that can be quite beneficial in meeting needs. In addition, there are often informal support and helping systems in their communities for these families along with organizations that may specialize in providing services to the population. It is useful to identify environmental systems that may be a resource to the family. As one way of gathering this information, Hartman and Laird developed the technique of using an eco-map. (An illustration of this technique is found in the case example.)[4]

Important features to consider regarding family functioning are the communication patterns, the manner in which decisions are made, and the way in which roles delegated to family members are carried out. (See Figure 5.1, "Eco-Map.") Families having difficulty often have communication patterns that do not serve the needs of their members. Some of these patterns may involve parents communicating through children, lack of freedom to communicate, and conflicting messages.[5] Identification of these patterns is important in understanding the functioning of the system.

In understanding the functioning of any social system it is important to know how decisions are made. This includes identifying which decisions are individual ones, which are made in the subsystem, and which belong to the total system. It includes influences on the decisions and how those decisions are communicated, performed, and enforced. In most families, there are communication patterns that meet the needs of various members; however, these patterns may be limited to certain relationships. For example, a child may have a pattern of positive interactions with one parent but may not have such a relationship with

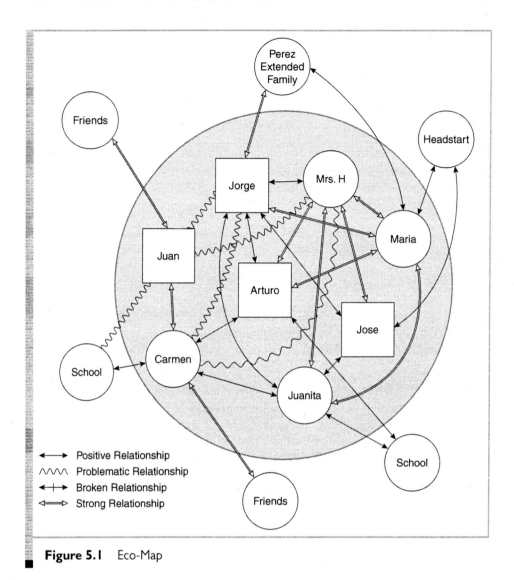

Friends

Perez
Extended
Family

Headstart

Jorge

Mrs. H

Maria

Juan

Arturo

Jose

School

Carmen

Juanita

School

Friends

⟷ Positive Relationship
⋀⋀⋀ Problematic Relationship
⟵⊦⟶ Broken Relationship
⟺ Strong Relationship

Figure 5.1   Eco-Map

the other parent. A positive pattern of communication is a strength, and the goal is to extend this pattern to other relationships in the family.

The family is one of the major institutions of society. For any society to function, families must carry out the roles delegated to them by society. These functions include the primary provision of common human needs for individuals, the care and nurturing of children, and the continuance of the culture. In order to perform these functions, the adult members of the family perform work roles, including the homemaking role, the income-providing role, the parenting role, and the childcare role. These are vital roles in meeting the common human needs and the developmental needs of all family members. Through the carrying out of work, parenting, and marriage roles, the family provides the support, encouragement for growth, and care of and concern for all family members. Knowing how these roles are filled provides an understanding of family functioning. These roles are often important sources of strength in the family, even when one or more of these roles present challenges. In fact, meeting challenges in fulfilling these roles is a sign of resilience and strength.

Communication, decision making, and roles were examined for various diverse families in Chapter 3. For many ethnic groups, decision making and roles are heavily influenced by their cultures and are often based on gender. For instance, traditional Hispanic/Latino families are generally patriarchal and most decisions are made by the father. Males tend to be in breadwinner roles and females in the roles of wife and homemaker. In these families, females may participate in bringing income into the family, but they are still expected to fulfill these roles. On the other hand, African American couples tend to be more egalitarian in their relationships and share more of the decision making and roles.

Change is a part of all human functioning. The family is subject to change in several ways: (1) growth of family members; (2) birth, children leaving the family home, death, and divorce; (3) changed functioning of family members as a result of illness or disability; (4) changed environmental resources, impacts, or responsibilities; and (5) environmental change resulting from immigration and migration. All systems develop mechanisms for coping with changes or for adapting to changing conditions. These adaptive and coping mechanisms should be identified and examined for their contribution to appropriate flexibility of the family system in meeting changes both within the social system and in the environment. Again, these are important indications of strength and resilience. As indicated in Table 5.4, it is important to assess the history of the family in terms of immigration or migration patterns along with understanding how the family has coped. In addition, the worker should assess the extent to which the family has been integrated or acculturated into the larger society.

A final area for understanding the family as a social system is the development of the family, which begins in a family's roots. Current structure and functioning are, in part, a product of its roots. The genogram (see Figure 5.2) is a useful tool to use with a family in considering these roots. Also important is an understanding of the family's cultural background. Events that have called for significant change, adaptation, and coping within the family system are also important in understanding a family's development. Family culture is part of a family's roots, and pride in one's culture and family heritage can be a foundation for growth and change. Self-knowledge begins with knowing where we came from and how our values, beliefs, and lifestyles reflect our past and that of our family and our culture. Understanding and appreciating family and cultural heritage strengthens the family and its members.

All families experience stages as the composition and needs of family members change. Sonya Rhodes identified seven stages of family life:

1. *Intimacy vs. idealization or disillusionment*—The dyadic relationship of husband and wife is formed. Developmental task involves developing a realistic appreciation of one's partner.

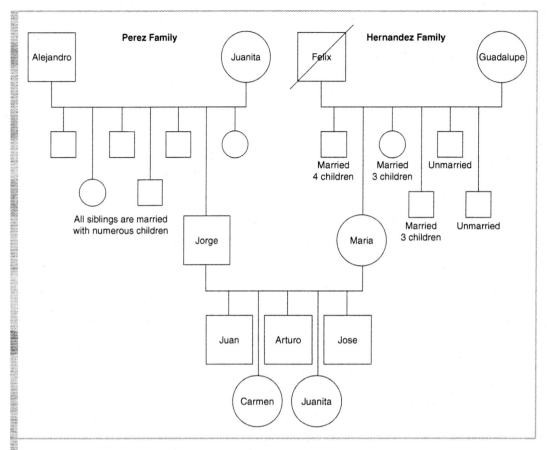

Figure 5.2   Abbreviated Genogram

2. *Replenishment vs. turning inward*—The stage between the birth of the first child until the last child enters school. Developmental task involves developing nurturing patterns for family members.

3. *Individualization of family members vs. pseudomutual organization*—The stage where the family has school-age children. Tasks include parents separating their own identity from that of the child and the enabling of the development of support and opportunities for individual family members outside the family system. Another task is the individualization of each family member.

4. *Companionship vs. isolation*—The stage of teenage children in the family. Important themes are separation and sexuality. The tasks are development of parent–child relationships based on the knowledge of the child's growing independence and a marital relationship based on companionship.

5. *Regrouping vs. binding or expulsion*—This is the stage of the children leaving home. The task is a regrouping on generational lines and development of an adult-to-adult relationship between parents and children.

6. *Recovery vs. despair*—The couple renegotiates a relationship that does not involve parenting children in the home. Parent–child relationships are also changed. The task then is renegotiation of relationships.

7. *Mutual aid vs. uselessness*—Parents are now retired. Couples often are grandparents. The task is to develop a mutual-aid system among the generations.[6]

A study of the family as a social system also includes the identification of that system's concerns and needs. Though the needs of individual members and subsystems contribute to the family system needs, the needs of the family system are different from those of the parts. The needs of the family system relate to what will enable the family to maintain itself as a system and still fulfill its responsibility to its members and to its environment.

Needs and how needs are met are typically influenced by diversity. Various cultures can define needs in different ways and may have different priorities for certain needs. For instance, the centrality of the family and the view of collective identity that is found in many African American families will tend to lead to defining needs in terms of the family or the community rather than defining them in terms of the individual. For example, developing a plan to finance a college education might be seen not so much as a need for the individual to acquire financial aid and work but as a family effort to ensure that funding is available. Family members might set aside savings or take on an extra part-time job to accomplish this. The community may see the financing of higher education as an important priority and engage in fundraising activities for this purpose.

Gender is another diversity factor that can influence need. Males might tend to define needs in more tangible ways, whereas females may see needs in terms of relationships. Males might emphasize the end result, whereas females may place a higher value on the process of meeting needs.

Of particular importance when working with families in which ethnicity and social class must be considered is use of a multisystem model. Here the focus is on the interacting level of family functioning (within the family, within the extended family, and with the various formal helping agencies involved). This type of approach will lead the worker toward more appropriate interventive strategies, whether they are strategies better suited to a particular ethnic situation or toward a choice that will bring about change in the larger system that negatively affects the family's healthy functioning.[7]

It is important to identify the strengths and challenges of the family in situation as a base for developing a professional relationship and for considering intervention into the transactions among family members and between the family and its environment. Through intervention into these transactions the social worker can enable families to meet the needs of the family as a system, as well as those of the individual members, and can help families improve social functioning. Strengths and challenges can be viewed quite differently by diverse families. As with needs, these can be defined quite differently by different cultures or by different genders. In general, members of the dominant white culture tend to devalue or are blind to many of the strengths within the cultures of people of color. In general, women are not valued as much as men and so their strengths are also devalued or overlooked. Likewise, challenges that are related to prejudice, discrimination, and oppression are typically denied or not even considered. The understanding of the family as a social system is a means of identifying its strengths and challenges and of planning for intervention.

Social Study: Family

I. Identifying Information

A. Names and Birth Dates of Family Members

Father:	Jorge Perez	Born: January 21, 1973
Mother:	Maria Perez	Born: April 2, 1974
Children:	Juan	Born: June 14, 1992
	Carmen	Born: July 20, 1993
	Arturo	Born: October 8, 1996
	Juanita	Born: December 7, 1999
	Jose	Born: February 25, 2003

Extended Family: Guadalupe Hernandez (maternal grandmother)
Born in Mexico. Date of birth uncertain.

B. Marriage: August 24, 1991. First marriage for both parents. Parents had dated since junior high.

C. Religion, Cultural/Racial Background: Catholic, attend regularly. Both parents are Mexican American, born in Texas.

D. Language Spoken in Home: Spanish and English.

E. Date of First Contact: October 1, 2007, Juan and Carmen were brought to the runaway shelter by sheriff's deputy after they were found walking on the side of the road late at night.

II. The Family as a System

A. Family Structure

Jorge dropped out of school in ninth grade and is employed as a laborer. He works long hours but barely makes enough money to meet the family's needs. Maria did not return to school when the couple was married just before she entered her senior year of high school. She has always stayed at home to care for the children and has never been employed outside of the home. Her mother, Guadalupe Hernandez, has lived with the family since her husband's death five years ago. She was born in Mexico and grew up in a migrant family. She married Felix Hernandez and they moved from Texas when Maria was twelve years old. Shortly after they arrived in the area, Jorge and Maria met and have been together since that time. Mrs. Hernandez understands and speaks some English but is most comfortable conversing in Spanish. Both Mr. and Mrs. Perez are bilingual.

Juan is fifteen and in tenth grade. He has been an average student until this year when he began skipping school and his grades plummeted. He has never been very active in extracurricular activities and does not especially like school. Juan feels that because his parents did not complete high school, it should be okay for him to drop out. He has had two minor problems with the law in the past six months, a curfew violation and a shoplifting complaint.

Carmen is fourteen and in ninth grade. She has always been a good student and very active in school activities. Carmen has never been in any trouble. However, since entering high school, Carmen has had a number of boys who are interested in dating her. Mr. and Mrs. P are opposed to this and expect that Carmen will follow the traditional expectations of waiting until she is fifteen to date and then only under chaperoned circumstances. She sees this as being "old fashioned."

Arturo is ten years old and in fifth grade. He is very affable and outgoing. Although he has been a good student, he is also somewhat of a class clown, which gets him into trouble periodically. He has not been in any trouble in the community.

Juanita is seven years of age and is in second grade. She is a good student, but is very quiet and shy. She rarely plays with the other children at school, and, if she does, it is generally with only one friend. She prefers to spend her recess reading and would actually prefer to stay inside where it is quiet.

Jose just turned four years old and is in Head Start. He also seems outgoing and happy. He shows an interest in learning and readily socializes with the other children.

There is generally good communication between Mr. and Mrs. P. Each fulfills traditional gender-based roles in the family with Mrs. H sharing many tasks with her daughter. Mr. P wants a clean house, well-cooked meals, and well-behaved children.

The children have had a close bond with each other until recently when both Juan and Carmen began to rebel against the expectations of their parents and grandmother. The younger children get along well with each other and there are few arguments. The parent–child system is primarily focused on mother–child, with Mrs. H serving as a surrogate mother of sorts. Mrs. P has experienced a loosening of the bonds of parental authority with her two oldest children but retains good control over the younger three. She has tried to elicit assistance from Mr. P, but his long hours at work limit the amount of time he has to devote to this. Mr. P, for his part, has tried ordering Juan and Carmen, which works while he is home but has little effect when he is not. Mrs. H has tried to intervene, but Juan and Carmen do not see her as an authority figure per se. They are fond of their grandmother but feel that her way, and that of their parents is the old way, and they want to do the same things that their friends are doing instead. The adults in this family expect to follow traditional family roles and ways of functioning. However, the two teens want to break away from this and, as a result, there are some serious cultural clashes occurring. While there is cohesion around protecting each other as family members, the two oldest children seem caught between loyalty to the family and their ethnic identity and the lure of what is seen as a more permissive attitude by the dominant Anglo culture. This has led to much more tension within the family system as the adults attempt to preserve traditional cultural expectations and their two teens seek to break away from those very traditions.

The family lives in an older two-story, five-bedroom home in a predominantly Hispanic neighborhood. Mr. and Mrs. P have a bedroom upstairs along with the children. Juan has his own room and the two girls and other two boys share a room. Mrs. H has a room off the dining area on the first floor that she uses as her bedroom.

Mr. P's parents are both alive and live in the area. He also has six mostly older siblings who live nearby. Mr. P's family has always been very close. The extended family get together

(continued)

regularly for every American and Mexican holiday and for other important family traditions. Juan and Carmen have begun resisting attending these events, especially since their aunts and uncles try to influence them to adhere to the family and cultural traditions.

Mrs. P has a sister in the area, but all four of her brothers have moved to other parts of the country in search of work. Her mother is not able to live with her sister because her home is much too small. Mrs. P's family has also been very close. She misses the family gatherings that they once had. When any of her brothers come to town, they make it a point to celebrate the occasion.

B. Family Functioning (see Figure 5.1)

There is good communication between Mr. and Mrs. P on the whole, although this has become strained by the need for Mr. P to work long hours and the couple's frustration at the rebelliousness of their teenage children. The communication between Juan and Carmen is good, but this tends to serve as an alliance against the parents. The two communicate very little with the rest of the family, and they try to be absent from home as much as possible, preferring to be with their friends. The younger children communicate well with each other and with their parents and grandmother except that Juanita tends to keep to herself a lot, preferring to read in her room. Mrs. P relies heavily on her mother for communication in the absence of her husband. This is almost exclusively in Spanish. Juan and Carmen understand and speak some Spanish but have drifted away from any serious effort to retain their language skills. The younger children show some interest in the Spanish language because they have had their grandmother living with them for a significant portion of their formative years. Thus, they have some proficiency in Spanish.

Mr. P makes all of the major decisions in the family; however, day-to-day decisions have to be made by Mrs. P because he is gone most of the time. Mrs. P usually consults with her mother when she is not able to delay a decision until her husband is available. Housekeeping standards are high, and Mrs. P and her mother do well at maintaining the home inside. The house needs some paint and some minor repairs, and Mr. P tries to get to these when he is not working. Parenting is left primarily to Mrs. P with assistance from her mother. However, recently Mr. P has become more involved with parenting and discipline with the two oldest children, but because he is frequently absent from the home, this has had minimal effect on them. This is a source of great frustration for Mr. and Mrs. P and Mrs. H as well. They are at a loss as to how to get their teens to respect their authority. They are worried that they will lose Juan to the streets and that Carmen will become sexually active and become pregnant. Mr. P has resorted to physical threats with Juan, but he wants to avoid crossing into physical confrontation. He is at a loss as to how to deal with his daughter's rebelliousness. The family is not in a position financially to reward or sanction behavior economically. Even if they were, it does not appear that the nature of the conflict would lend itself to this type of intervention. They have tried grounding, but the teens simply leave when Mr. P is not around.

There is an obvious bond of affection within the family despite this latest difficulty. This is especially true with the younger children. There has always been some stress in the family as a result of their poor economic situation. However, the strain in the relationships between the adults and the teenagers has increased the stress tremendously. Ordinarily, the adults in the family have found that turning to their faith has been the best way to cope with major difficulties. They also talk with each other and with extended family members. Usually, the family and extended family pull together whenever there is a crisis. However, the current situation has challenged their ability to cope in the usual ways. The children generally cope by either denying any problems and trying to forget about them or by going to their parents for help. Under the current circumstances, Juan and Carmen have turned instead to their friends, which in turn has driven them further away from their parents. The younger children do not discuss the situation and seem oblivious to it but are obviously watching and waiting to see what will happen.

C. Family Developmental History (see Figure 5.2)

This couple is very tied to their traditional Mexican American roots. It is these very traditions that are now being challenged by their two teenage children, who want to break away from this and become part of the dominant Anglo culture. The family is experiencing a great deal of stress concerning issues of acculturation. This is quite common as members of various ethnic groups assimilate into U.S. society. Earlier generations often seek to preserve their ethnic heritage, whereas younger generations either straddle between ethnic traditions and current trends in the larger society or they seek to break from the traditions of their parents.

Until this time, the two most significant events in this family have been the dropping out of school of Mr. and Mrs. P and the death of Mr. H. The fact that neither parent completed high school has frozen them in a life on the brink of poverty. The only thing that has kept them from going over the edge is the fact that Mr. P works as many hours as he can. Now he is stuck between working long hours and being gone from the family or cutting back on his hours so he can deal with the crisis at home. If anything were to happen that would prevent him from working, the family would be economically devastated. The death of Mr. H was a severe blow to everyone in the family. He was loved by all and is still mourned.

The family is in stage 4, companionship vs. isolation in Rhode's stages of family life. The important themes in this stage are teenagers who are in the midst of separation and sexuality. This describes the family as it struggles with the emerging independence and sexuality of the two oldest children. However, the cultural clashes that are occurring has created a crisis concerning resolving these issues.

III. Concern or Need

The family is receiving services as a result of Juan and Carmen running away from home. When they were picked up late at night by a sheriff's deputy they refused to return home and said they would run away from home again. The primary need is to reunite the family and reduce the stresses that have resulted in this home truancy. In addition, the family needs assistance in dealing with unexcused absences at school by Juan. They are also concerned about Carmen's desire to date, which is what precipitated the truancy. Carmen had decided to run away to be with an older boy she had recently met. Juan left with

(continued)

her to protect her. He was also upset about the fact that he wants to quit school and go to work. Customary disciplinary approaches have not been successful in dealing with the situation.

Mr. P might be able to improve his circumstances if he was able to complete high school or get a GED. Mrs. P could also benefit from this and might be able to relieve Mr. P of some of the burden of providing for the family.

Mrs. H needs to know that her grandchildren will value the heritage that she and her late husband tried to pass on to them. She is hopeful that the younger children will do this but is very concerned about Juan and Carmen and about their influence on the younger ones.

Juan needs to find a way to meet his need to belong with a positive peer group while also satisfying his parents' expectations of him. He needs to see that completing high school and having a skill are important to escaping from the poverty that his family has experienced.

Carmen has a positive peer group but needs to avoid becoming involved with males, especially older ones, until she is mature enough to manage a relationship. She needs to be able to negotiate with her parents around some agreement that will satisfy their need to know that she will abide by some of their traditions until she is old enough to decide for herself what she will retain from her heritage.

Arturo needs to continue to do well in school and not let his zest for life and sense of humor interfere with his success academically. Juanita needs some assistance in coming out of her shell. Her teacher is aware of this and has brought it to the attention of the parents, but they have not had the energy to focus on this because they are trying to deal with the situation at hand. Jose needs to continue to receive nurturing and support from his family and not have his needs overlooked because of the stress of the current situation.

The couple need support in preserving the strength of their relationship, which is being challenged by Mr. P's long hours at work and the strain of dealing with two rebellious teenagers. They need to maintain some separation between the demands of parenting and the intimacy in their marriage. As parents, they need to present a united front in dealing with the demands of parenting. A major aspect of this is the need for increased communication regarding discipline and a mechanism that will address the challenges at hand.

In terms of parent–child relationships, Mr. P needs help in reestablishing his parental influence over his older children, and Mrs. P needs support in disciplining Juan and Carmen when Mr. P is not home. Juan needs to find a way to meet his individual needs for peer relations and see the need to stay on track in school so he has a brighter future, while maintaining positive father–son and mother–son relationships. Carmen has similar needs, but these are focused on dating and boy–girl relationships. Mr. and Mrs. P need to be able to continue to maintain strong parent–child relationships with the younger children while dealing with the stresses of the relationships with Juan and Carmen.

The family needs some relief from the stresses of economic hardship and needs to find a way to preserve important aspects of their heritage while also recognizing the influence of the dominant Anglo culture. Mr. and Mrs. P were moderately successful in accomplishing this, although they have not enjoyed much economic success. Their children have all proven to be at least adequate students and their parents will need to encourage success at school if they hope to see a brighter future for them. At the same time, school and work bring the children in more contact with others who do not share their heritage and this will inevitably increase the tension between their heritage and other cultures.

IV. Strengths and Challenges for Meeting Needs

In addition to dealing with Juan's home and school truancy and getting into trouble and Carmen's home truancy and boy–girl relationships, the family wants assistance in dealing with the crisis around the cultural clashes that are occurring between the adults and the teens. They would like to have the stress reduced so that they can deal with the economic issues that they face. The parents want the teens to abide by their wishes and to adhere to the traditions of their heritage. The teens would like to have their parents accept their decisions to reduce their involvement with their ethnic traditions and to become more Anglo in their cultural activities. The parents are highly motivated to resolve the situation. The teens are much less motivated, fearing that the resolution will not be in their favor. There is the potential for change, but there are also major impingements. Both sides will need to be ready for some give and take. Regardless of what the parents do and even if they were to be successful at curbing the recent unrest, it is inevitable that the children will reach a point where they are able to make these decisions for themselves. The question will be how much influence will the parents have and will they be successful at retaining the important aspects of the traditions that they value the most. The teens need to realize that some of their parents' wishes with regard to adhering to traditions are in their best interests regardless of whether they are associated with their heritage. For example, Juan needs to stay out of trouble and in school if he is to put himself in a position of achieving economic success. Carmen needs to avoid getting overinvolved prematurely so that she can mature and make good decisions about her future. Within the family, the parents have a strong marriage, Mrs. H is able to provide emotional support and assistance with household tasks, and the family has retained a strong sense of love and care and concern. The extended family system on Mr. P's side of the family is intact and very supportive. There are resources available in the community such as adult education, job training, and family service agencies. The school is concerned and has some resources to support academic success. The turmoil in this family has not reached the point where irreparable harm has been done. This should add to the family's motivation and capacity for change. Many Hispanic families have successfully dealt with these same issues, which makes the family's expectations realistic, even though there are clearly some major differences between parents and teenagers. The main strengths of the family lie in their love for each other and their desire to maintain a positive family system. The challenges that they face are in large part cultural in nature, and, although these are substantial, they are not insurmountable. The most immediate need is to find a way to return Juan and Carmen home within the fourteen-day limit on their residential stay and have them stay home while the other issues are resolved. A referral to a family service agency will be needed for longer-term assistance.

■   IMPORTANT ELEMENTS OF THE ASSESSMENT   ■
PHASE WITH FAMILIES

Assessment is a complex process at the core of the change process with families and other client systems. The schemas that are identified in this chapter and in Part III are tools for gathering information, but care must be taken that relevant information that falls outside the schema is not overlooked. Assessment, although a creative process, is also scientific in that it is a manifestation of the scientific method. Some of its most important characteristics are as follows:

1. *Assessment is both product and process*—The stages of the assessment make up the process that the worker experiences in conducting an assessment. The social history is the product that is the outcome of the assessment. Table 5.2 presents a schema for the development of an individual social history. Table 5.3 presents a schema for the development of a family social history. A case example is included.

2. *Assessment is ongoing*—Assessment takes place throughout the life of the helping endeavor with families. During the early stages it is a primary focus. However, during later stages, when the work of doing something about need and of intervening into transactions among systems takes place, assessment is also a concern. As the family and worker engage in their work together, new information becomes available and new understandings emerge. These then become a part of the ongoing assessment.

3. *Assessment is twofold, focusing both on understanding family in environment and on providing a base for planning and action*—Information must be gathered about the family, its subsystems, and its members, about their interrelationship, and about their environment. Information should be collected about the need, blocks to need fulfillment, the situation, and people and systems significant to the need. It is also important to determine strengths, challenges, motivation for change, and resistance to change that are applicable to the family and the systems involved. When assessing the environment and large systems, it is important to gather information about the demography of the system and the situation being considered.

Information is gathered in many different ways. Of prime importance are the family's perceptions and feelings about the need or concern and the situation. Carefully attending to the family's story conveys respect and acknowledges that the family members are the "experts" regarding the family. The manner in which they tell their story, including nonverbal communication, provides important information.

Other sources of information may be previous case records and reports from other interested persons. If a worker uses information sources other than family members, the family should be aware of the use of these resources and give suggestions about sources for such information and permission for the worker to obtain the information from other people. The information being collected should always be clearly connected to the concern or need being worked on.

4. *Assessment is a mutual process involving both family members and worker*—The family is involved in all aspects of assessment to the maximum of their capacity. The primary content to be assessed arises from the worker's interaction with family members in the interview. One source of content is the information provided as the worker observes the family in the interview. Content also derives from observations of the family in life situations.

The worker discusses observations and other information with the family to establish the meaning of the facts or to gain an understanding of family in environment. The use of a mutual process in assessment is one means of empowering the family because it provides family members with a sense of value and worth and demonstrates that what they think and believe is important. Family members come to realize that they are not passive recipients of help but important partners in the work to be done.

5. *There is movement within the assessment process*—Movement usually occurs from observation of the situation to identification of information needed for understanding. This is followed by collection of information and an explanation of its meaning. The facts and their meanings about various parts are put together in order to understand the total situation.

6. *Both horizontal and vertical exploration are important*—In the early stages of assessment it is usually helpful to look at the situation horizontally; that is, the situation is examined in breadth to identify all possible parts, interactions, and relationships. The purpose of this horizontal exploration is to determine the block to need fulfillment and the strengths and resources in the family ecosystem that can be used to meet the need. Later, those parts identified as most important to the situation or to meeting needs are examined vertically, or in depth. The information-gathering process can move from horizontal to vertical and back to horizontal several times as the worker and family explore the need and the situation. Social workers should develop skill in determining when a horizontal approach is most appropriate and when a vertical approach is the one to use.

7. *The knowledge base is used in developing understanding*—The worker uses her knowledge base as one means for developing understanding of family in environment. An understanding of an individual family member takes into consideration factors of human development and diversity. An understanding of a family is related to what is known about family structure and process and its culture and diversity. An understanding of an agency considers knowledge of bureaucratic structures. An understanding of community calls for knowledge of economics and political science. An understanding of the ecosystem requires knowledge of systems theory and the exchange of matter, energy, and information among systems.

8. *Assessment identifies needs in life situations and explains their meaning and patterns*—Assessment makes use of the process of growth and change throughout the life cycle in specifying the need and what is blocking need fulfillment. (This idea is discussed more fully later in this chapter.)

9. *Assessment identifies family and ecosystem strengths with an eye toward building on those strengths during intervention*—Individuals and families grow from their strengths, not their limitations. A thorough assessment of physical, mental, emotional, and behavioral assets must occur in order to work with the family system to set goals, objectives, and tasks that have a high likelihood of success. Identification of individual and family strengths requires identifying resources present in the family system and the environment or situation that can be used to meet needs.[8]

10. *Assessment is individualized*—Human situations are complex; no two are exactly the same. Each assessment is different and is related to the differential situation of the family. Assessment takes into consideration the different parts of the situation and relates these to the unique whole that emerges. This is particularly true when working with families from populations that differ from the worker's ethnic or sociocultural orientation. It is critical to understand the situation and its meaning to the family system from the family's perspective, not the worker's.

11. *Assessment considers diversity*—Diversity is an important consideration in assessing the family. In many respects it determines the family in context. Ethnic and racial diversity and diversity regarding sexual orientation influence the structure and functioning of the family and also influence how the environment responds to the family. In addition, various cultures have different worldviews that affect how the family views and responds to the environment. Many cultures have norms, roles, and expectations that are determined by gender. Spirituality is heavily tied to culture. For many families diversity is the most important factor in understanding and working with the family.

12. *Judgment is important*—Many decisions must be made regarding each assessment. Decisions include what parts to consider, which parts of the knowledge base to apply, how to involve the family, and how to define the concern or need. The kinds of decisions that are made greatly affect the content and the interpretation of that content. The family system's view of the significance of events must be evaluated carefully; again, what the worker may consider unimportant from his frame of reference may be of great importance to the family system, or vice versa.

13. *There are limits to the understanding that can be developed*—No assessment is ever complete. It is impossible to gain complete understanding of any situation. It is also undesirable. Understanding takes time. Families in need are seeking help that often must be given quickly. The worker must decide what understanding is necessary to give that help and then be aware of new understandings that develop in giving the help. The worker must be comfortable with the uncertainty of limited understanding and learn to trust in the ongoing process of assessment.

The tasks of assessment, then, are (1) identification of the need or concern and of family and ecosystem strengths and resources, (2) identification of the information needed to further understand the need or concern and to determine appropriate means for meeting the need, and (3) collection and analysis of information. Decision making includes interpreting meanings, ordering information, and discovering relationships among parts of the situation. Decision making considers family members, needs, situations, family and ecosystem strengths, and relationships.

Judgment is an important component of assessment. Judgment is, in effect, decision making. According to Harriet Bartlett, "Professional judgment provides the bridge between knowledge and value, on one hand, and interventive action on the other. Assessment is its first application in practice."[9]

The schema that was presented in Table 2.2 provides a framework for community assessment. It is used to assess the community portion of the ecosystem when working with families. The generalist social worker must have knowledge and skill in assessing both the family and the community that makes up part of the family's ecosystem.

Values are very influential in the decision-making process. Our perceptions and thinking are affected by our values, which influence how much of a situation and what parts of a situation we perceive. We tend to screen out that which is not congruent with our values or our thinking. Because of our biases about how things should be, we may miss the unfamiliar or the different. In particular, as we have pointed out, the perception of what constitutes strength may be very different in various cultures. When working with families from different backgrounds, it is particularly important for the worker to be aware of how her values influence her decisions. Interpretations of meaning from the worker's value perspective may be invalid from the family's perspective.

For example, a worker who adopts a family theory emphasizing the nuclear family may have difficulty working with a Native American family whose orientation includes the extended family and the tribe. The worker might determine that family members are not being given appropriate opportunities for self-determination, whereas the family might feel the worker is overlooking the family member's responsibilities to family and tribe. The worker would be viewing the situation through her value perspective, which considers individuality to be of prime importance. The family would be viewing individual self determination as irrelevant and be more concerned with how they could better the lot of the collective group. Some resolution of such value-driven difference must take place before a worker and family can work productively together.

Harriet A. Feiner and Harriet Katz have pointed out how deeply held beliefs relating to women and family structure influence the judgments that are made in practice situations.[10] They noted that commonly held myths, such as that women should not compete with men and women should assume the nurturing role, can be detrimental when working with female family members who are struggling to become independent individuals. A discussion of gender competent practice was presented in Chapter 3.

Decision making is an important ingredient in professional judgment. Judgments are decisions based on reason and evidence, with the goal of identifying what is a fact, what is an assumption, and what is an inference. The influence that values have on assumptions and inferences is then considered and perceptions are analyzed. In addition, value conflicts and ethical dilemmas are assessed and included in the decisions that are made.

Decisions need to be made jointly with the family and with the family's needs, preferences, and strengths as primary considerations. Principles that can be used when making judgments in assessment include the following:

1. *Individualization and the uniqueness of each family*—Each person, family, and system in a situation is different. In order to assess effectively, the unique aspects of the family and its ecosystem need to be identified and understood. This understanding should be derived primarily from the family system.

2. *Participation*—Participation by appropriate family members in decisions and in the assessment process is an important means of developing an assessment that recognizes the family's needs and preferences. Further, it is extremely difficult to assess family strengths without participation by family members in some manner.

3. *Human development for family members and the family as social system*—Assessment recognizes the developmental process of individual family members and the family as a social system as a means to further the understanding of family members and the family system. One needs to be aware of the impact of cultural and ethnic influences on developmental stages for individual family members and the family as a system. One also needs to be aware of the developmental stages of the family system.

4. *Human diversity*—Recognition of the diverse aspects of individuals, families, systems, and cultural groups is another important component of assessment. This should take into account strengths that are unique to various populations, especially with respect to the family.

5. *Purposeful behavior*—Recognition that all behavior is purposeful leads to a search for understanding of the underlying meanings of behavior.

6. *Systemic transactions*—The assessment process identifies stressful and energizing life transactions, adaptive and maladapative interpersonal processes, and environmental responsiveness and unresponsiveness when seeking understanding of family in environment.

7. *Strengths and resources*—Identification and acknowledgment of the strengths and positive attributes of families and their environments are critical.

Through using the principles of individualization and the uniqueness of each family, participation, human and family development, human diversity, purposeful behavior, systemic transactions, and strengths and resources, the worker identifies with the family, the family's needs, and the family's preferences about what needs to be done. This, combined with an awareness of value influences and an appropriate choice of the knowledge to apply, leads to an assessment that yields a valid understanding of family in environment that is useful for planning intervention. Mary K. Rodwell, in presenting a model for assessment based on the naturalistic paradigm of research, described a model similar to the one discussed in this chapter when she stated, "The naturalistic framework frees social work to reach a deeper understanding of person–situation through a holistic assessment style and promotes a sophisticated inquiry into human relationships with social and physical environments."[11] We suggest that this model is valid for working with families, especially because it allows families to tell their own stories rather than using the worker's framework for determining how the change process is utilized.

■ STAGES IN THE ASSESSMENT PHASE WITH FAMILIES ■

Assessment is the first phase of the change process with families. It lays the foundation for the phases that follow. Each phase is a part of the change process as follows:

Assessment phase

>   Identify the initial concern or need
>   Identify the nature of the concern or need and decide if family work is needed
>   Identify potential strengths and resources in the family ecosystem
>   Select and collect information regarding the family and its ecosystem
>   Analyze the available information

Planning phase

>   Develop a plan with the family based on analysis of available information

Action phase

>   Take action with the family to implement the plan

Evaluation and termination

Evaluate results during each phase and after the plan is completed
Consolidate change at termination of service

The planning phase is covered in Chapter 6. The action phase is discussed in Chapters 7 and 8. The evaluation and termination phase are covered in Chapter 9.

The worker and the family must decide how family members are to be involved in the change process. This decision depends in part on how much energy and desire each member has for working on the situation. The family member's involvement hinges on her capacity, both cognitive and emotional, to work. For example, in a crisis situation, when the need for action is great and when the family is already overwhelmed, the worker will take a more active role in the work than in a situation in which there is less pressure for an early solution. It is not that the family in acute crisis is not involved in resolving the situation; rather, it is a matter of how the worker involves the members and to what extent the process is made explicit to them. Teaching the change process can be a strategy for involving family members.

Other considerations in determining each family member's involvement in the change process include status, age, and culture. As adults, parents are recognized as holding a higher status in the family with respect to decision making. They are often the primary source of information. Their roles and responsibilities are much greater than the children, so the responsibility for making and carrying out decisions regarding change will also be much greater in most cases. However, this might be different for couples who are elderly and who may need to have their adult sons and daughters involved in decision making and carrying out those decisions and in caring for them. Thus, age is also a factor.

In addition to considering older members of the family and their ability to make or carry out decisions, younger members may be limited by their age. Generally speaking, children who are very young will play little or no role in the change process, although they will be affected by the changes that are made. There is no set age at which children should not be included in the change process, but the ability of children younger than age seven is probably too limited and in fact might interfere with the process. Seven- to twelve-year-olds might be able to assist or participate in carrying out a decision but may be quite limited in their ability to freely participate in decisions beyond a simple level. This is partly because they are likely to be heavily influenced by the adults or older siblings and have limited experiences with independent decision making. Teens should definitely be involved because their participation can make or break the success of decisions about family change. Adolescent rebellion or movement toward emancipation can be difficult for the adolescent and the family as a whole and may very well be the primary reason the family is seeking help.

A difficult task in the change process is the specification of the need or concern. A member or members of the family bring an initial need or concern to the helping situation. Based on material discussed in the first few contacts with family member(s), the worker may realize that the presenting need is not the actual need. As the worker clarifies the reasons for the initial need or concern, he makes assumptions about the nature of the need or concern. Identification of theoretical knowledge used in thinking about family in environment is another way in which assumptions are created. As assumptions are identified, it is possible to determine the information needed to verify the preliminary formulation of the need or concern and to restate it if necessary. The need to be addressed is formulated after an understanding of "family in environment" or the family and its ecosystem is developed and after the available information has been analyzed.

When the diversity competent social worker uses naturalistic inquiry in family assessment and in formulating need, she lets the family tell their story about themselves. She allows them to define needs in terms of their view of themselves and the world. She checks with them about needs that they present along with other needs that might be experienced. She works with them on prioritizing needs within their culture or diversity.

Formulation of the need or concern is the basis for the next four stages of the assessment. Planning and action can be enhanced by the thorough and appropriate formulation of the need or concern. Three steps of formulating the need or concern are (1) identification of need, (2) identification of blocks to need fulfillment, and (3) formulation of the need in terms of removing the blocks to need fulfillment. Once the need or concern is identified, the worker and the family can proceed in considering the nature of that need or concern and potential strengths and resources in the ecosystem that would meet that need. This is followed by selection and collection of information and an analysis of the information available. It should also be remembered that the needs that concern the social worker are those that relate to social functioning and that planned change needs to build on existing strengths and actual or potential resources in the family and its ecosystem.

Identify the Initial Need or Concern

There are three steps that are taken in identifying the initial need or concern.

1. *Identify initial need*—The first source of material for identifying need is how the family tells their story. Who talks first, who talks to whom, who defers to whom, and who talks about what are some of the important considerations the worker notes. This may be dictated by cultural considerations and by family custom. The worker not only listens to the verbal content but also looks for nonverbal communication. The pronouns and words used, the tense of verbs, the tone and inflection all give clues to the meaning of the need. The worker also can note what is not said, what is omitted.

Needs must be considered within the context of the family's diversity. Whereas all human beings have some common human needs, different needs are associated with culture, gender, age, religion, sexual orientation, and so on. For instance, the dominant U.S. culture places great emphasis on the individual, but in African American, Asian, and Hispanic cultures, the family unit takes on a great deal of significance. As a result, individual needs must be seen in relation to the family. Talking about what is best for the individual without considering the family would be inappropriate. In Native American culture, ancestors, the spirit world, and the tribe are important considerations that supercede the individual. Workers should consult others beforehand and take time to weigh a decision before making the decision. Women tend to place more importance on relationships, so needs may be expressed in terms of significant relationships and the affect that decisions might have on them. Religious beliefs may require clients to pray or have a sense of peace with their spiritual self. Gays and lesbians may consider the need to have their sexual orientation either hidden or revealed and respected as part of the process. For those who are in partnerships, the affects of revealing their sexual orientation may have a negative impact on their partner's circumstances.

The skillful worker often has hunches about what is needed. These hunches are part of the art of social work, the creative nature of the work. Hunches are very useful, but they should be checked out with the family before they are given the power of fact. Hunches are generally based on the worker's experiences rather than the family's; it is, therefore, important to evaluate these ideas in light of the family's reality before sharing them verbally with the family.

As the worker begins to identify the family's need by using the material provided by family members, hunches or ideas that derive from the knowledge base, and information available to the worker from other sources, other systems significant to the situation can be identified. The needs of these systems in relation to the situation being considered should also be identified. Systems that are significant to the situation are those that are affected by the lack of need fulfillment, those that affect the situation, and those that may have resources for meeting the need.

One of the areas that warrants attention is the agency and the service delivery system. If the function of the agency does not include services that can enable the family to fulfill the identified need or needs, the family should be made aware of this. The nature of the service delivery system is sometimes an important factor in the lack of need fulfillment.

2. *Identify blocks to need fulfillment*—Once the need is identified, it is then possible to consider why that need is not being fulfilled. The social worker's past experience, values, and theoretical framework lead to assumptions about the reasons for the blockage. These preliminary assumptions must be checked. Additional information about the family and the situation may be needed. The family and the significant systems should be given an opportunity to provide their points of view. Written materials such as case records or descriptions of social systems involved may be useful.

From a diversity perspective, blocks to need fulfillment are often associated with the affects of prejudice, discrimination, and oppression. Whenever the worker is engaged in helping a member of a population at risk for these blocks, the worker should consciously examine potential blocks. There may be some reluctance to do so, particularly if the worker is a member of a more dominant group such as males working with females or white workers working with people of color. Collective guilt can come into play or a sense of guilt arising out of being a member of a culture, race, gender, and so on, that has engaged in prejudice, discrimination, and oppression. Guilt can also be associated with privileges that members of the dominant group enjoy that members of other groups do not. The worker might also be resistant because recognizing such blockages means that change needs to occur in how clients are treated by society and this would be a daunting task to say the least. Obviously, one worker is not going to change societal attitudes and actions. However, the actions of those in the immediate environment of the family may very well be changed. The diversity competent worker considers prejudice, discrimination, and oppression as blocks to need fulfillment in examining the needs of the family.

From an ecosystems strengths perspective, the location of the blockage is sought in the relationships among the significant systems or the subsystems or among family members. In this way, the needs of all systems are recognized and the problem is not considered the responsibility of only one system but is seen as interactive in nature.

Carel Germain and Alex Gitterman have identified three situations that seem likely to lead to problems in social functioning: (1) stressful life transitions, (2) communication and relationship difficulties, and (3) environmental unresponsiveness.[12] Assessment of family in environment to see if one of these conditions exists is one means of determining the nature of the blockage of need fulfillment.

Stressful life transitions can result from difficulties in carrying out the tasks of the developmental stages of individuals, of families, and of other social systems. Thus, the assessment must be concerned with identifying the developmental stage for individual family members and the family stage of development as well as the tasks that are not being carried out. Difficulties may result from lack of opportunity, including opportunity to fulfill tasks in ways congruent with one's cultural or diversity group.

Another potentially stressful life transition is status change. This includes such events as becoming a widow or widower, becoming unemployed, graduation from or dropping out of school, and becoming part of the work force. Change of status creates new role demands on people and on their families. Sometimes there has been no preparation for these demands. The widow with young children who returns to the work force confronts not only the demands of being a single parent and helping the family adapt to the loss of a father but also the demands of a job. Demands of the single-parent role and the work role may conflict or be overwhelming.

Closely related to stressful situations are crisis situations. When change is so great that families cannot cope and maintain a steady state, a crisis can result. The need is not only for a resolution of the situation but also for the family system to regain its steady state so that it can meet the expectations of its environment.

Other social functioning difficulties develop because a family member or the family as a system is not effectively communicating with or relating to other people and social systems. Some families from diverse cultures have considerable difficulty relating to the institutions of society and vice versa. For example, a school's lack of awareness of the needs of children from diverse cultures can undermine the ability of the parents to relate to the school and can result in unmet educational needs of the children. The family may not be able to use existing resources or they may not even know about them. The school may not be able to identify the strengths of the individual or family because of lack of understanding of cultural factors. The underlying issue is lack of accurate communication, which can result in relationship difficulties.

The needs of children from diverse cultures can result from the school's unresponsiveness to their needs. Environmental unresponsiveness is a third cause of stress and coping failure. Environmental unresponsiveness can take two forms: failure to provide the needed service or failure to provide the needed service in a manner in which it can be used by the diverse family. Examples of the latter failure include unrealistic expectations of the family or family member on the part of the social worker, providing the service in a way that requires the family to violate cultural values and norms, and expecting families to function with ease in a culturally foreign milieu.

3. *Formulate the need or concern*—Once the blockage to the need is identified, it is possible to formulate the concern. Formulation of the need or concern considers the need that is not being fulfilled, the block or blocks to the fulfillment of that need, and factors contributing to the block. It is important to be as specific as possible while still recognizing the transactional nature of social functioning.

The specification of need may be made in several ways. It may be that a concrete resource or service is lacking, such as sufficient income to meet the needs of a nutritious diet or health care. Need can also be specified in terms of psychosocial development needs. An example would be a physically challenged ten-year-old child who does not have the opportunity to develop daily living skills. This might occur because of lack of understanding of the child's need to feel competent or because the mother compensates for her guilt over the child's condition by "overcaring." Need can also be specified in terms of inadequate role fulfillment in the realms of parenting, marriage, or work or in terms of difficulty in life transitions. Another way of specifying need is in terms of relationships among family members and social systems.

In formulating the need or concern, the worker includes those that are associated with the diversity of the family. He does this in a way that captures the need from the perspective of family members. The best way to do this is to actively seek out the family members' versions of what their needs or concerns are. Paraphrasing and summarizing with a solid check out is important.

The next step in formulating the concern or need is a statement about what seems to be blocking the need fulfillment, including the recognition of relationships with potential resources. This statement needs to be clearly worded and must recognize the transactional aspects of the blockage.

The source of a blockage may be in attitudes and values, knowledge and understanding, behavior, coping skills, role overload, environmental expectations, ignorance of available resources, or lack of usable resources. Usually, the source of blockage is not one but a combination of circumstances. Formulation of the concern or need should recognize this complexity in stating need and specifying blockage to need fulfillment.

Identify the Nature of the Concern or Need and Decide If Family Work Is Needed

As the worker and the family proceed through the assessment phase, there are assumptions about the family in environment that play an important role in focusing the assessment. At the outset of assessment, the worker determines (1) what information is necessary to understand the situation and (2) what resources are available to meet the needs of the family and its ecosystem. In order to accomplish the first, the worker must make some assumptions about the nature of the concern or need. She uses her knowledge of human behavior in the social environment, of human and family development and diversity, and of Maslow's and Towle's systems of identifying needs to determine the underlying nature of the needs. For example, using Maslow's hierarchy, are the needs related to basic needs, such as food, clothing, shelter, or health care? Is the need related to safety and security, socialization, self-esteem, self-actualization, or cognitive understanding?[13] Using Towle's elements of need, does the need represent a need for emotional and intellectual growth, relationships, or spiritual well-being?[14] As a next step, the worker combines knowledge and creativity in speculating about what might be creating the need in the specific situation.

Identify Potential Strengths and Resources in the Family Ecosystem

Moving to the third step in the process, the worker might speculate about what would bring about the changes necessary to meet the needs. He begins by identifying potential strengths, abilities, assets, capacities, and resources within the family system and its ecosystem. How do the family members and family meet needs? What is going well? What works now or has worked in the past? How does the present circumstance represent a deviation from the family's typical pattern of meeting needs? The worker then formulates some assumptions about what is needed to develop, maintain, or restore the ecosystem to a steady state in which needs are met on a mutually satisfying basis.

The diversity competent worker prepares herself for working with diverse families by developing her knowledge about diversity (see Chapter 3). She is aware of the strengths of diverse families and seeks these in the families with whom she works. The worker listens for strengths and challenges as the family tells their story and points these out to them. She is committed to a strengths-based approach that views all families as having strengths and all environments as having resources.

In this part of the change process, the worker tries to be realistic while still allowing herself to speculate about what might be possible. One question that is invaluable in working with family systems is, What would it take to meet this need? This leads the worker to look at possibilities rather than looking at challenges and deficits.

Select and Collect Information Regarding the Family and Its Ecosystem

The assumptions that are made about the nature of the needs and the strengths and resources available in the family and its ecosystem are important to setting the stage for collecting information. Information is needed to determine whether the assumptions are true or if some other assumptions need to be made and checked out. The worker should not collect information without a purpose. The two main reasons for having information should be to assist the family in meeting its needs and to meet the bureaucratic demands of the agency or regulatory bodies. In the latter case, certain information may be collected to identify clients, to bill insurance or other third-party payment systems, to meet eligibility criteria, to meet basic standards of accepted professional practice, and so on. Care should be taken that information is gathered in a way that respects the family's right to confidentiality.

In order to achieve a thorough understanding of the situation, it is useful if the worker asks himself what he knows about who, what, where, when, and how. These five areas of questioning are typically used by reporters when they are covering a story. They are also useful to the social worker to ensure that he has covered all of the aspects of the situation. A sixth area relates to the question "Why," but this is covered in the analysis portion of the process.

Based on the assumptions made, the worker is able to select the information needed to understand the situation and to lay the groundwork for developing a plan to meet the needs of the family and its ecosystem. Using the various schema presented in this chapter and in Part III, the worker selects relevant parts of each schema, depending on the family system or subsystem and the parts of the ecosystem being considered. For example, in working with individual family members, Table 5.2, "Schema for Development of a Social History: Individual," is used as an overall guideline. Relevant parts of the family history schema are used as they relate to understanding the family member's interactions with his family, if this is important to understanding the situation and meeting the family member's need. Relevant parts of the community schema are used to assess the systems in the community that are impinging on the situation or that might be accessed in meeting the need. In working with the family, Table 5.3, "Schema for Development of a Social History: Family," is used as an overall guide for working with the family system. Table 5.4 is included in working with an ethnically diverse family. Relevant parts of the individual and subsystems schemas are used as needed.

In selecting and collecting information, the social worker considers diversity factors that are present in the situation. She seeks to find out how the family views their own diversity. This should include the influence of diversity on thoughts, feelings, and actions. It should also include the response to diversity by both the nurturing and sustaining environment and how these affect the family member's thoughts, feelings, and actions. The manner in which information is collected is also important. For the most part, naturalistic inquiry is the best approach to use. By taking the position that she does not know what she does not know, the worker allows the family to take the position of experts in their own lives, including their lives as diverse persons. It allows families to tell their own stories using their own words in a manner of their choosing. When the worker incorporates diversity in her selection and collection of information, she is better able to see the whole picture in full color, so to speak.

Analyze the Available Information

There are four general areas the worker must analyze as the work proceeds: (1) what the worker understands about family in environment and strengths and resources, given what is known; (2) what changes are needed, given what is known; (3) what further information is needed to better understand the situation; and (4) what further information is needed to bring about successful change.

As the worker analyzes these four areas, he uses critical thinking along with his knowledge base to gain insight into the family and its ecosystem. Throughout the process, he checks out his analysis with the family and with relevant parts of the ecosystem. Paraphrasing and summarizing are particularly valuable in this process. The worker asks the family if his perceptions about the situation are accurate and if there are other aspects that family members are aware of that might be important.

The worker asks family members for input into what changes are needed or desired. A good question to ask is, What would you like to see happen that would meet your needs in this situation? Or, If this situation was resolved and your needs were being met, what would it look like? The worker might address these questions to the family as a whole by asking, What would meet the needs of this family in this situation? Or, If this situation was resolved and everyone's needs were being met, what would it look like?

Analysis of information should lead the worker to an understanding of family in environment and potential strengths and resources that are sufficient to proceed with planning. It should answer the question "Why?" to the extent that the worker understands the situation from the family's perspective and is able to see what is blocking the need from being met. The worker and the family should be somewhat confident that the strengths and resources necessary to meet the need are present, either in the family and its ecosystem or in the worker's ecosystem (the service delivery system). If greater understanding is needed or if more strengths and resources must be found, then the analysis should indicate this, and the worker and the family should return to an earlier stage of the assessment process for more information.

Quite often the analysis or other stages of the assessment will uncover new or previously unknown needs or concerns that take precedence over the initial need. This can occur for many reasons, including reluctance by family members to reveal uncomfortable information before trust is established or lack of awareness by the family of the need or that the worker can assist in helping meet the need. In this case, the worker and the family return to stage 1 to reformulate the need and then proceed through the remaining stages. There is no need to start over. Rather, it is only necessary to gather information regarding this new need or concern.

In analyzing the available information, the worker uses her knowledge and skills, especially her knowledge of families and family theory, social systems theory, diversity, and ecosystems, to bring about an understanding of family in environment. She uses a diversity competent approach with naturalistic inquiry to understand the family's diversity from the family's perspective. She uses her practice wisdom and experience to help her understand the situation at hand and what might be done to meet the need. She uses her critical thinking skills to analyze the gaps between need and need fulfillment. She uses her creativity to uncover strengths and resources in the family, the family's ecosystem, and the service delivery system and to brainstorm with the family about what might work in meeting the family's needs. Thus, analysis is truly the heart of the thinking part of the social work process.

The diversity competent worker incorporates diversity into his assessment. He considers need within the context of the family's diversity group. Needs may vary according to different groups. How needs are defined, their importance, and how they are met can vary based on culture, gender, age, religion, and so on. Thus, the nature of the need may also be affected by diversity. Potential strengths and resources should be considered based on how diverse groups define them. The selection and collection of information should be conducted within the context of the family's diversity. This includes what information is collected and how and from whom it is collected. Finally, the information must be analyzed within the understanding and perceptions of the family's diversity. People's actions rely heavily on their perceptions. The unique perspective of each diverse group must be considered as the worker seeks to understand family in environment.

■   TRANSACTIONAL ASSESSMENT   ■

The transactional nature of human interaction, especially family interaction, is complex, and this complexity can cause difficulties in assessment. Transactional assessment depends to a great extent on the worker's creativity and ability to look at a complex situation and bring order and meaning to that complexity. Transactional assessment is particularly useful when considering possible plans of action with families and the effect those plans might have on the family, family members, family subsystems, and various systems involved in the situation of concern.

The worker needs to understand the strengths and resources within the family and the ecosystem. This includes understanding the transactions that are taking place. As discussed earlier, the types of exchanges that occur among systems involve matter, energy, and information. In analyzing a situation, the worker needs to know what matter is necessary and from where it comes. For instance, how does the family obtain food or clothing? Who is involved? What is obtained? Where, when, and how is it obtained? In terms of energy, the worker might consider which relationships family members find energizing and which drain energy.

Some frameworks for transactional assessment have begun to appear. An example is an ecosystems framework developed by Paula Allen-Meares and Bruce A. Lane. They identified variables to be considered and placed them in a three-dimensional framework that consists of kinds of data, data sources, and the system to which the data are related. Examination of the framework leads to the conclusion that in order to obtain the breadth of understanding needed for assessment, it is important to collect and place a wide variety of data in a framework that shows some relationship among the data.[15]

In considering the nature of transactional assessment, the generalist social worker needs tools for assessing the functioning, needs, and concerns of individuals, families, small groups, organizations, and communities. Three tools can be useful in transactional assessment: (1) the dual perspective, (2) mapping, and (3) social support network analysis.

The Dual Perspective

As discussed earlier, Dolores Norton's concept of **dual perspective** depicts the plight of many minority people. The dual perspective is "a conscious and systematic process of perceiving, understanding, and comparing simultaneously the values, attitudes, and behavior of the larger social system with those of the client's immediate family and community system."[16] When the two systems are not congruent in terms of norms, values, expectations, and ways of functioning, conflicting expectations can lead to misunderstanding among individuals, families, and cultural groups.

In making an assessment from the dual perspective, the worker looks for points of difference, especially for conflicting expectations between the two systems. The degree of difference and the number of characteristics that are different are important factors in judging the incongruity between the systems. Also important is how the systems perceive the difference and how the difference affects their functioning. This kind of an assessment calls not only for a general intellectual understanding of a specific cultural group but also for an understanding of the specific, immediate, environmental system of the person or group of persons. The dual perspective is a particularly useful tool in assessing the transactions of any specific cultural group or of those from a minority culture within the larger, dominant society. It is also useful with other forms of diversity.

When dealing with families and situations having values, cultures, and ways of functioning different from the dominant culture, it seems wise to use a dual perspective approach as part of the assessment process. Some determination of the extent and impact of the difference on families, family members, and systems should be made. When the difference is great or the impact significant, it is important to determine motivations, resistances, and appropriate interventive points to bring about adjustments in dominant social systems that affect the situation or affect need fulfillment. It is also important to determine with families if there are coping mechanisms that would be helpful in situations in which incongruencies exist between the two systems.

Use of the dual perspective can be illustrated by considering the characteristics of Puerto Rican culture. Sonia Ghali has identified these as an extended family structure with kinship through godparents; the importance of virginity for an unmarried woman; an emphasis on individualism and inner integrity; a fatalistic, submissive-passive approach to life situations; use of family, friends, and neighbors as the first sources of help; high respect for the advice of pastors and teachers of their own group; use of spiritualism; expectation that helping persons will use authority; belief in mysticism; use of the Spanish language; and an expectation that the wealthy will be paternalistic and benevolent toward the poor.[17] It is, of course, important to determine if these characteristics hold true for a particular Puerto Rican family. When these characteristics are compared with the characteristics of the majority society, a number of incongruities become apparent, including different language, different expectations about respect, different usage of expression, and so on. An assessment of the incongruities gives an understanding of the transactional influences on a Puerto Rican family.

Mapping

Mapping is a tool for pictorially representing the relationships of the significant parts of any situation. Mapping is a variation of the sociogram. First, the client or focal point of a situation is depicted with a circle. If this focal point is a family system, the relationships of the family members in that system are shown in the circle just as they are in the sociogram.

The other significant systems in the situation are placed around the circle representing the focal system. Various kinds of relationships are drawn, noting which family member in the focal system carries the relationship to these systems.[18]

Mapping can also be useful in assessing the role structure of a situation. The map can be examined for incongruities in role expectations, either within the focal system or with systems in the environment of that focal system. The map can be examined for role overloads and for missing roles.

Use of mapping makes apparent the transactional nature of the situation. It can also be useful in identifying strengths and resources available to the helping situation. Mapping is particularly helpful in understanding the relationships among the parts of an organizational or community system. It also can be used to depict the relationships among key persons in these larger systems.

Two other forms of mapping can be especially useful in working with families. These are the use of genograms and eco-maps. The genogram, a family tree that specifies significant information about each individual for at least three generations, is a useful tool for gaining an understanding of one's family (see the example). From studying a genogram one can identify the effects of such things as death, size of family, birth position in family, naming patterns, and major family behavior patterns, to name a few. This method of studying the family as a system can yield much previously unrecognized information and help a person see not only the place she has filled in a family but also how she has been influenced by the family.[19]

An **eco-map** can also be useful in understanding the family ecosystem. The family system is part of a larger environment. That environment has expectations for the family, which involve the functioning of the family as a system internally and responsibility toward other systems in the environment. In a society of cultural diversity, there are often conflicting expectations that should be identified. Impacts of prejudice and discrimination because of family diversity should be identified. It is important to determine the nature and extent of the influence of systems such as church, school, cultural group, extended family, and the like that impinge on the family or have expectations of responsibility for the family. It is also useful to identify environmental systems that may be resources to the family. As one way of gathering this information, Hartman and Laird developed the technique of developing an eco-map. (See the example.)[20]

Social Support Network Analysis

Closely related to the technique of mapping is the analysis of the social support network of a family or a family member. Mapping aids the identification of significant social support resources. A **social support network analysis** helps in specifying the nature of the supports and complements the map in the assessment process.

Elizabeth M. Tracy and James K. Whittaker have developed a Social Network Map for use in a research project. This grid can also be useful in assessing the social support network of a family or a family member. Areas to be considered in such an assessment include the area of life in which the support is given (e.g., work, school, etc.), the kind of support (e.g., concrete, emotional, informational, etc.), how often the support is given, whether the support is critical of or problematic to the support receiver, whether the support is in a reciprocal relationship with the support receiver, the closeness of the support to the support receiver, how often there is contact between the provider and receiver, and how long the receiver has known the support provider.[21]

With the goal of identifying and using resources or social supports that are either available or potentially available to families and family members, generalist social workers must develop assessment tools for analysis of social support networks.[22] This is particularly crucial when working with disadvantaged or oppressed populations because locating, developing, and using support networks are avenues to empowerment. It is increasingly important in a time of managed care and resource constraints to develop practice knowledge in this area.

SUMMARY

A social work family assessment is a picture (however incomplete) made up of all available facts and pieced together within a particular frame of reference for a particular purpose. It contains the following elements:

1. Identification of all the entities involved in the situation
2. Development of the needed understanding about each of these entities
3. Arrangement or ordering of these entities in such a manner that the role and relationship structure—the transactional nature in the situation—is seen
4. Identification of the need in the situation and of the blockage to need fulfillment
5. Identification of strengths and resources of individuals and systems present in situations, including previously successful efforts to meet needs
6. Identification of conflicting expectations of cultures in which the systems operate
7. Formulation of the concern or need from a transactional point of view
8. Identification of additional information needed, of the knowledge base to be used to enhance understanding, and of the values operating in the situation
9. Evaluation of the information available
10. Identification of relevant social policy, constraints in the situation, expectations of all involved, and actual and potential resources in the situation
11. Identification of possible impacts of potential change in the situation on all systems involved

Assessment is a core skill for any social worker. Like any other skill, it must be practiced if it is to be developed. Professional interaction and professional helping both are heavily dependent on skill in assessment.

QUESTIONS

1. Review the case example in the chapter. Identify additional information you would seek if you were asked to make an assessment of this family and their situation. What would you use as sources for each piece of information you have identified?

2. Review the material on interviewing in Chapter 4. How do you see the interviewing process used to assess the need or concern and situation with the family in the case example?

3. What issues do you think you should consider when working with a family? Identify those issues that may be unresolved or important to you personally in your own family situation and that may get in the way as you work with a family.

4. Discuss the differences when working with the family as a system as contrasted with working with individuals who may be family members. Why is it important to work with the family as a system rather than work with individuals in a family?

5. Do your own family social history. What did you discover about your family's structure, functioning, and development? What do you see as your family's strengths? Its challenges?

6. Think of someone you know who comes from a cultural background somewhat diverse from the commonly accepted majority group. Use the dual perspective to assess congruencies and incongruencies between that person's cultural or sustaining system and the societal system. Do you have any suggestions for dealing with incongruencies?

7. Use the mapping technique to develop a picture of some problematic situation for a family of which you are aware. What did you learn from the map that might be of use in resolving the situation?

■ SUGGESTED READINGS ■

Johnson, Louise C., and Yanca, Stephen J. *Social Work Practice: A Generalist Approach,* 9th ed. Boston: Allyn & Bacon, 2007 (Chapters 9 and 13).

Boyd-Franklin, Nancy. *Black Families in Therapy: Understanding the African American Experience,* 2nd ed. New York: Guilford Press, 2003.

Bricker-Jenkins, Mary, Hooyman, Nancy, and Gottlieb, Naomi. *Feminist Social Work Practice in Clinical Settings.* Newbury Park, CA: Sage, 1991.

Falicov, Celia Jaes. *Latino Families in Therapy: A Guide to Multicultural Practice.* New York: Guilford Press, 1998.

Fong, Rowena, and Furuto, Sharlene, Eds. *Culturally Competent Practice: Skills, Interventions, and Evaluations.* Boston: Allyn & Bacon, 2001 (Part II, Chapters 8–15).

Laird, Joan, and Green, Robert-Jay, Eds. *Lesbians and Gays in Couples and Families.* San Fransisco, CA: Jossey-Bass, 1996.

Lum, Doman. *Culturally Competent Practice: A Framework for Understanding Diverse Groups and Justice Issues,* 3rd ed. Pacific Grove, CA: Brooks/Cole, 2007.

Saleeby, Dennis. *The Strengths Perspective in Social Work Practice,* 4th ed. Boston: Allyn & Bacon, 2006 (Chapter 6).

Schiele, Jerome H. *Human Services and the Afrocentric Paradigm.* New York: The Haworth Press, 2000.

Sheafor, Bradford W., and Horejsi, Charles R. *Techniques and Guidelines for Social Work Practice,* 7th ed. Boston: Allyn & Bacon, 2006 (Chapter 11).

Silverstein, Louise B., and Goodrich, Thelma Jean, Eds. *Feminist Family Therapy: Empowerment in Social Context.* Washington, DC: American Psychological Association, 2005.

6

Planning with Families

LEARNING EXPECTATIONS

1. Understanding of the planning process with families.

2. Understanding of goals in social work and skill in developing goals and objectives with families.

3. Skill in choosing units of attention.

4. Skill in identifying strategies to use in specific practice situations with families, including choice of roles and tasks.

5. Understanding of the factors that affect a plan of action and skill in identifying these effects on specific practice situations with families.

6. Skill in identifying resources for use in planning with families.

7. Understanding of the importance of diversity in planning with families and the need for empowerment when planning with populations at risk of discrimination or oppression.

Planning is the bridge between assessment and actions focused on change with families. Often it is seen as a part of the assessment process. Although planning considerations are important in assessment, the emphasis at that phase is on assessing possible strengths and resources in the family and its ecosystem for planning. Planning and assessment with families are both such important aspects of the total process that each deserves separate consideration. Planning is based on assessment of the family and is the outcome of assessment. It is part of the change process, and as such it cannot be separated from other aspects of the generalist social work process except for study purposes. Planning with families is based on deliberate rational choices and thus involves judgments about a range of possibilities.

The assessment process with families helps develop an understanding of family in environment and identifies potential resources. The planning process with families translates the assessment content into goal statements that describe the desired results. Planning with families also is concerned with identifying the means to reaching goals, which includes identifying the focal system or unit of attention and the strategies, roles, and tasks to be used. It sequences tasks, specifies a time frame, and considers the costs involved.

Good planning with families includes using diversity competent practice for both the process and the product. Using naturalistic inquiry, listening to the family as members tell their stories, and allowing the family to take the lead in identifying needs and concerns will ensure that diversity is incorporated into the planning process and the product.

This chapter begins with an overall discussion of planning with families. It considers components that make up a plan, including goals, objectives, and tasks. There are factors to consider that affect the plan of action with families. Like assessment, planning is both a process and a product. Finally, we discuss the agreement between the worker and the family.

■   PLANNING WITH FAMILIES   ■

Planning with families, when related to social functioning, involves activity designed to enhance growth potential and adaptive capacity of the family and its members. It also is designed to increase the capacity of environments to respond to the family's needs.

Strategic thinking is the cognitive source of the plan. This implies a complicated process of developing a plan with parts that fit together, not by chance, but by choice. This process considers alternatives, evaluates their usefulness, and predicts outcomes of each. The plan considers both process and outcomes by specifying intermediate objectives as well as end goals.

Planning with families is a skill. The work of the process calls for a complex set of decisions. These decisions are informed by a broad body of knowledge about the nature of human systems, especially the family system and their ecosystem, and their functioning and of possible interventive strategies. In addition, social work, family, and community values must be considered. The worker's experiences in similar situations also inform the decisions. Planning with families links purpose to action. Intervention into the transactions among family members and between family members and social systems is the context of planning. The end goal is planned change. The plan is composed of specified, interrelated parts that have a logical relationship. The reason for each action is specified.

Because of the nature of the human condition, the uniqueness of each family, and the complexity of the social situation, it is virtually impossible to predict with certainty the outcome of a plan. However, a well-developed plan—one developed with flexibility for change as the process develops—has a better chance of achieving the desired outcome than action not based on such a process.

In developing a plan with a family, it is important to maintain a family-centered perspective and process. During the planning phase, it is easy to leave the family or its members out of the process. Until now, the worker has relied heavily on family members for information. The development of a plan implies that enough information has surfaced to begin acting toward change. Thus, workers may be tempted to take over and write the plan themselves. This happens all too often in practice. Sometimes it occurs because workers feel pressured to complete their paperwork. In other cases, workers may be eager to start the change process, which tends to be their primary focus, because they see themselves as change agents. Inexperienced workers or students may desire either to demonstrate their skills and abilities or to compensate for anxiety over their developing skills. Also, workers may feel uncomfortable with the family being in control of the helping process. However, when family members do not fully participate in the planning process, the chances of failure increase because they are deprived of an opportunity to become more empowered and to improve their problem-solving skills. In addition, their right to self determination is undermined.

Plans should either be written with the family present or should be reviewed with them before being finalized. Of course, a plan should not be made without the agreement of the family. A plan that does not have family members' consent results in the need to manipulate the family or its members into meeting the expectations of the worker. This would be against social work values and ethics. One way to tell if goals are being written by the worker instead of formulated with the family is to check for repetition. Over a period of time, workers who write goals for families will use the same or similar goals over and over and have difficulty individualizing plans.

The plan should be sensitive to the background and circumstances of the family. Individual family and cultural values and diversity need to be incorporated into the process. The best way to ensure that this happens is to use naturalistic inquiry, listen carefully to family members as they tell their stories, and have full participation by family members. In addition, the plan should build on the strengths of the family system and environment while seeking to overcome or strengthen areas in which there are barriers or challenges. Families from populations at risk of discrimination or oppression as a result of poverty, class, color, culture, marital status, family structure, national origin, religion, sex, gender, race, ethnicity, age, disability, or sexual orientation are especially in need of planning that empowers them and that recognizes the need to change the attitudes and stereotypes of others. Assertiveness in interactions with others on the part of both the family and the worker is likely to be needed. This should be built into the plan by identifying targets for change in the environment. Helping family members of these groups adapt to discrimination or oppression is not acceptable. Confronting discrimination and oppression through empowerment and advocacy is generally what is needed for true change to take place.

■   COMPONENTS OF A PLAN   ■

Because a **plan of action** relates to a complex human situation to be dealt with over time, identification of the components of a plan helps in managing the complexity of the plan. One formulation of a plan specifies three components: goals and objectives, units of attention, and strategies that include the roles of worker and family and the tasks to be performed.

Goals, Objectives, and Tasks

An important consideration when planning with families are differences between the ages and statuses of family members. As social workers, it is not appropriate to value one person or his or her needs over someone else. Social workers value all human beings. At the same time, when working with families, the worker needs to recognize that parents are responsible for raising their children and must make decisions for them until they are able to make their own. When working with families, social workers are inevitably faced with this dilemma: How to give credibility to goals that children might have while also respecting, and not undermining, parental responsibility and authority. This is especially difficult when the child is a teenager. The answer to this lies partially in understanding the different types of goals that are typically used with families.

The **goal** is the overall, long-range expected outcome of the endeavor. Because of the complexity of the overall plan, a goal is usually reached only after intermediate goals or **objectives** have been attained. **Tasks** are steps that the worker and the family need to take to reach the objective and achieve the goal. Goals and objectives may relate to the family, various family members, several different persons, or social systems involved in the situation. Goals and objectives develop out of assessment related to the needs of the family and various systems involved and the identification of the blocks to need fulfillment. They are generally related to the removal of a block or to developing new means of need fulfillment. This variation in types of goals allows the worker to include the goals of children as individual goals and relate them to the need for family support in achieving those goals.

It is challenging to write appropriate goals and objectives using an acceptable format. Social workers are prone to qualify or hedge their statements to allow for flexibility or individuality. Much of this comes from a desire to respect client self determination and to allow for unforeseen difficulties. However, planning calls for direct and definitive statements so that expectations and outcomes are clear and progress can be accurately measured. Otherwise, confusion will occur about who is responsible for what, and measuring progress and outcomes will be impossible. Although goal statements must be definitive, there is room for flexibility in that plans can be changed. When it is obvious that something is not working, the plan needs to be changed. However, the need for flexibility in planning should not obscure the need for clearly defined goals, objectives, and tasks.

Many social workers will see a variety of things that might be improved or changed as they assess the family in environment and will want to fix everything. Families can easily become overwhelmed by what may be received as a negative message about their well-being. It is best to keep things less complicated and focus on the main areas the family wishes to change and where change will likely make the biggest difference. A general guideline in working with individual family members is to limit the number of goals to no more than three at any given time during the process. For family members facing multiple barriers or difficulties, more goals may be necessary. However, the likelihood that an individual family member will remember to work on more than two or three goals at a given time is very low. Families may need more than three goals, depending on the size of the family and the complexity of its situation. However, no single member should be asked to keep track of more than two or three goals. For children and those who are under stress or have limitations, one or two goals may be the most they are able to handle at one time.

In developing a plan with a family system, the challenge is to balance the needs and goals of each individual with each other and with those of the system. The first task is to identify individual or personal goals for each member. Although the worker may have discussed these beforehand, it is important for members to state their goals to other members of the family. The next step is for the worker to assist the family in articulating a common goal that includes everyone in the system. This inclusion process helps to establish and reinforce a sense of belonging and teamwork and increases a sense of cohesion. It is sometimes difficult to develop an all-encompassing goal; thus, the worker should keep the goal simple and straightforward. For example, for a family a common goal might be to get along better with each other. Sensitivity to diversity and to at-risk populations is essential when planning with families, as is building on the strengths of individuals, the family system, and the environment. Once the family has established a common goal, the task is to assist them in finding ways to help each other achieve individual goals as well as to identify roles in helping the family to achieve its overall goal. The worker will need to use mediation and negotiation in helping the family in this process.

Goals should build on the strengths of individuals and the family as a whole, as well as the strengths and resources available in the larger ecosystem. In addition to personal or individual goals and a common goal for the family, there are two other types of goals that are important: mutual, or shared, goals and reciprocal goals. Mutual goals require two or more members to participate or act in certain ways regardless of the actions of others. An example would be a goal in which everyone agreed to use "I" statements when talking to each other in order to improve communication. If one person forgets, it does not excuse others from using the word *I* as a reminder. The respondent should not say, "You forgot to use 'I'!" Instead, he would need to say something like, "I would like to hear that in an 'I' statement." Reciprocal goals require different actions on the part of two or more members. An example would be a goal in which a parent agrees to cook the family's favorite meal and the family members agree to make a commitment to sit together as a family for that meal. Reciprocal goals may also be contingent. This is usually stated as "if–then." For example, parents can agree to give each child an allowance based on completion of certain chores. This might be stated as "If John cuts the grass when requested, then Mr. A will pay him $20.00."

Goals should also be based on the strengths of the family system as well as the strengths and resources of the environment. A strengths-based approach ensures that the plan is built on the existing capacities of the family and its environment. Without this, the plan might be based on skills the family has not mastered or cannot master or on resources that may not be readily available. The result would be a plan with a great deal of uncertainty, one that depends on too many "if's." The more uncertainty, the greater the chances of failure. Although building on strengths does not guarantee success, it increases the odds and provides the family with opportunities to act more immediately rather than waiting to acquire skills and resources.

There is a danger in setting goals that are too broad and general. Broad goals do not lead to the precision that is possible when the outcomes are more specific. It is helpful to specify a general goal that is a statement of the desired end and then develop specific short-term objectives. These short-term objectives can be placed in chronological order to facilitate a plan. In that case, the first objective must be reached before working on the second objective, and so on. Objectives should describe a specific desired change in individual family members, a subsystem of the family, the family as system, or social systems involved in the total situation. In effect, a miniplan, or a plan within a plan, is developed. This approach allows for evaluation of the progress toward the general goal and for adjusting the plan in progress when there is a change in the situation or because of previously unrecognized influences and consequences.

Care must be taken to express the objectives in terms of the behavioral outcomes desired rather than of how the goal will be reached. In other words, receiving a service is not a goal but rather a task designed to meet a need or achieve the goal or objective. Also, each goal and objective should have a specified date for its accomplishment. Objectives should be specific, concrete, and measurable. Goal statements are usually broader and more general than objectives. If objectives have specific statements about frequency, duration, and time frame, then the goal statement can be more broad. For example, the statement "The interaction within the family will result in positive feelings" is broad in that it does not specify how positive feelings will be measured or the time frame for completion. In developing more specific, measurable statements for objectives, it is helpful to think in terms of a sequence of questions—namely, who, what, how, where, and when. The "who" refers to the family member or members or the person or persons taking action and the targets of change. The person(s) taking action should appear first in both the goal statement and the objectives. The next word should be *will,* which conveys a positive, unequivocal statement about the desired state of affairs. Next comes a description of "what" and "how" the situation will appear if the goal or objective were accomplished or the need were to be met. Identifying "who" is the target of change may come next, if appropriate. "When" describes the time, frequency, or duration in which the action is to take place and the time frame for completion. "Where" specifies the place for the action. An example of an objective written using these guidelines follows:

Objective: The family will have at least one day of 100 percent positive interactions with each other at home by April 15.

"The family" is the "who." "Positive interactions" represents the "what." "At home" refers to both "where" and "when." The expected frequency is "100 percent." "At least one day" is the duration, and "by April 15" is the time frame. It is clear from this statement who will do what and where and when they will do it. There should be no confusion about expectations; both progress and outcomes are readily measurable.

Goals should be reasonably feasible; that is, there should be a good chance of reaching them. In thinking about feasibility, consideration is given to time and energy factors. Some questions that should be asked are, Do the worker and the client have the time available to work toward the specified goals? Is sufficient energy available? Are the needed resources available?

It is wise to state goals and objectives in terms of a positive outcome rather than in negative terms. That is, goals should be stated as "The family will" rather than "the family will not." When goals and objectives are positive, they help to focus on the desired outcome instead of being problem focused. This reinforces behavior that is needed to bring about change. In addition, a positive focus gives the family more hope that the situation can be resolved. Finally, it creates a "self-fulfilling prophecy" that is more likely to result in success than failure. People tend to engage in behavior that is based on a prediction or "prophecy" of what they expect to have happen, not necessarily what they want to have happen. "Self-fulfilling prophecy" means that one's own behavior contributes a great deal to the outcome. When family members are focused on behavior that is likely to bring about the desired change, they are more likely to succeed and are also more likely to receive positive reinforcement from each other and from their environment.

Family members can often be most helpful in evaluating the feasibility of a goal; thus, they should be involved in setting goals. This can motivate a family for the work needed to reach that goal. As the family reaches objectives, the members gain hope for reaching the overall goals.

As with all decisions in the social work process, decisions regarding goals are influenced by value judgments. The choice of goals or end states is based on what is desirable. What is desirable is a value judgment. Social work values also influence the means to the end, or the process and objectives involved in the process. Because people are seen as having the right to make decisions about themselves, workers should not use means in reaching goals that go against the family's desires and values. Workers should respect lifestyle, diversity, and cultural factors in the development of goals and objectives. The worker should constantly evaluate whether the chosen goals are appropriate. There must be flexibility in adjusting goals to changing situations as the plan is implemented.

Different situations call for different kinds of change and different kinds of goals. The kinds of change that should be considered are as follows:

1. *A sustaining relationship*—used when it appears that there is no chance to change the person in environment and when the person lacks a **significant other** who can give needed support or when a relationship with a significant other is threatened or has broken down

2. *Specific behavioral change*—used when a family member or members are troubled by specific symptoms or behavior patterns and are generally otherwise satisfied with the situation

3. *Relationship change*—used when the issue is a troublesome relationship

4. *Environmental change*—used when it is recognized that a part of the need is a change in some segment of the environment or in the transactions between family and environment

5. *Directional change*—used when values are conflicting or unclear, when a family system is unclear about goals or direction of effort, or when aspirations are blocked in a manner that makes unblocking very difficult or impossible

When setting goals with families, it is important to consider expectations of family members, of significant others in the family's environment, and of the worker. These three sets of expectations may be different because each party may see the situation differently or may have identified the need differently. The consistency and inconsistency among these goals must be identified and some reconciliation obtained. The family's goals are to be considered of prime importance, and the worker should point out to the family the environmental expectations and the consequences of not meeting these expectations. The worker's goals can be discussed and incorporated or discarded as jointly determined by the worker and the family.

In summary, goals and objectives for families should relate to meeting a need. They should be stated in terms of an outcome, be specific, and be measurable. They should be feasible and positive in direction and developed with the family to reflect the family's desires.

Units of Attention

The **unit of attention**, or focal system, is the system being focused on for the change effort. This is generally in relation to the overall goals, but there may be different units of attention in relation to specific objectives. A unit of attention is either a person, a social system such as the family or an organization, or the transactions between them. It may be the client system or a person or system that has a significant influence on the situation. In other words, units of attention are systems that are the focus of the change activity.

The unit of attention can be an individual family member; it can be several family members or a family subsystem working on meeting a common need or on similar individual family member needs; it can be an individual or system that in some way affects the family and its situation; or it can be a group of persons in a community concerned about services to meet the needs of a category of clients.[1] The interactions and transactions among various parts of the ecosystem can be a unit of attention.

In setting goals with the family, the units of attention may be within the family system or in the environment. Units of attention can be individuals, subsystems, or the family as a system. The unit of attention may include the structure, the functioning, or the development of the system or subsystems. Change may be focused on internal or external boundaries, relationships, cohesion, interactions, communication, decision making, roles or role performance, support, coping mechanisms, or various skills. Change may be focused on the growth and development of individuals, subsystems, or the family system as a whole.

The unit of attention may be in the environment. In particular it is important for the family to be able to access and use needed resources. With families that have experienced discrimination and oppression, this is vital. These families have limited access to necessary resources and little hope of changing the situation. The worker's role is to assist the family in gaining access to resources and to advocate for people's rights when there are barriers.

As the change process is divided into activity related to more specific objectives, several objectives and miniplans are often worked on at the same time. It is important to specify the unit of attention related to each miniplan. For example, the overall goal may be a more desirable living situation for a family. It may be necessary to have an objective that relates to understanding the family's situation. To develop this understanding, the focal system may be the family or its landlord as a source of needed information. Another objective may be that a potential landlord be prepared to meet the special needs of the family. The potential landlord then becomes a focal system.

Incorporating diversity into planning means identifying units of attention in the environment because the blocks to fulfilling need are often found in prejudice, discrimination, and oppression directed at members of populations who are at risk of experiencing these. In addition, the plan should include direct and indirect methods for empowering members of these populations. Often, this involves assisting families to change the interactions between themselves and the environment. The unit of attention in these types of goals is the relationship between family and environment. Some of this may be accomplished by helping families to change how they respond to prejudice, discrimination, and oppression. For this part of the goal, the family is the unit of attention. Some of it may be accomplished by intervening to change the attitudes and actions of the environmental system. For this part, the unit of attention is the environment.

Units of attention may be individuals, families, small groups of unrelated persons, organizations, or communities. Table 5.1 gives some indications and counterindications for the choice of each kind of system. It is important to specify appropriate units of attention for every goal and objective. Units of attention may be clients or other persons and social systems involved in the situation.

Strategy

Strategy is an overall approach to change in the situation. It involves roles for worker and family members, tasks to be done by each, and methods and techniques to use. It has been defined as "an orchestrated attempt to influence persons or systems in relation to some goals."[2] The term originated in a military context and relates to a battle plan. It also is used in a game context. Action in the game depends on the action of others. Strategy implies multiple causes. Action depends on the action of others; that is, there is anticipation and assessment of the actions and reactions of others rather than reliance on independent action. There is a recognition of the transactional nature of human social functioning.

The worker begins thinking about strategy by considering the thoughts, feelings, and actions of the client and his ecosystem. (Figure 7.1 depicts how these factors influence each other.)

Human systems are made up of individuals. Thus, thoughts, feelings, and actions are woven into the fabric of every human system. In developing a strategy, the worker considers thoughts, feelings, and actions of the family and of the members of human systems in the family's environment as aspects of the units of attention. The unit of attention is the system (individual, family, group, organization, or community) that is the focus of the change strategy. The intended change occurs by changing the thoughts, feelings, or actions of people in that system. The worker assesses the need to influence change in these elements and with the family selects the best option. For example, if the unit of attention is a family member, the worker discusses with the member ways in which various combinations of working with his thoughts, feelings, and actions would be preferred in meeting his need or addressing his concern. The worker also considers how changing transactions will influence these aspects of the ecosystem and will be influenced by them. As with other elements of the social work process, an understanding of the effects of diversity is included in developing and choosing the change strategy.

One final note, when the unit of attention is an individual or system other than the family system, the ultimate goal of the change strategy is to change the actions of that system or the family's interaction with that system so that the family system's need is met.

The interaction is an aspect of action. The worker and the family may accomplish this by changing thinking or feelings, but changes in action are what count. On the other hand, assisting a family member to change his feelings, thinking, or actions can be the goal of the change strategy if a family member is the unit of attention.

When a general strategy is used in many situations, it becomes a category of strategy. Some categories that have been identified are *consensus strategy, conflict strategy, demonstration strategy,* and *bargaining strategy.* Social work has developed a variety of approaches to practice. These may be called theories of practice or models of practice. These conceptualizations of practice (e.g., crisis intervention, conjoint family therapy, locality development) provide an overall approach to practice and thus may be considered strategies.

Some strategies provide a philosophical approach to the situation. For example, a social action approach assumes a lack of balance in the power structure and recommends that a conflict strategy be used to redistribute power. Value judgments as to the desirability of power redistribution often guide the choice of this strategy. Other strategies have theoretical bases. The socialization model, which is based in socialization theory, is an example. Most strategies have both value assumptions and knowledge assumptions as well as identifiable practice theory. Strategies are one means of tying the knowledge and value aspects of practice to the action.

In choosing strategies the worker must decide if the value and knowledge base of a particular strategy are congruent with his own values and worldview. The worker must decide if he possesses the knowledge needed for using the strategy. The worker must also determine if the values, explicit and implicit, in the strategy are congruent with those of the family and its situation.

Strategies should apply not only to the family's need but also they should correspond with the family's lifestyle. Much has been written about the necessity of understanding diversity group clients and their cultures and of applying this understanding to service delivery with these families. This literature recommends decisions that match the helping style to the lifestyle of the client.

For example, in discussing services for African Americans and Puerto Ricans, Emelicia Mizio and Anita Delaney noted that it is important to use strategies that recognize how racism and discrimination affect the lives of these families. They recommended the use of advocacy as a core strategy and the use of counseling strategies based on ecological and systems knowledge.[3] The authors' Native American students indicated that Siporin's situational approach and the functional approach are appropriate for their culture.

Different strategies and different kinds of service call for the social worker to fill different roles. The term *role* is used here in a somewhat different manner from the strict pattern-of-behaviors sense. Rather, the definition used is that of Robert Teare and Harold McPheeters: "A cluster of altruistic activities that are performed toward a common objective [goal]."[4] The **role** is the way the worker uses self in the specific helping situation. Role further depends on the function of the worker and the particular agency offering the service and its function. For example, in short-term, crisis-focused service, the caregiver role will be minimally used, whereas in a nursing home this may be an often-used role. Teare and McPheeters have identified twelve roles that may be part of the generalist repertoire that social workers fill:

1. *Outreach worker*—identifying need by reaching out to clients in the community; usually involves referral to services

2. *Broker*—enabling persons to reach appropriate services by providing information after assessing need of individual and nature of resources; also includes contact and follow-up

3. *Advocate*—helping clients obtain services in situations in which they may be rejected; helping expand services to persons having a particular need

4. *Evaluator*—gathering information and assessing client and community needs; considering alternatives and planning for action

5. *Teacher*—teaching facts and skills

6. *Behavior changer*—developing activities aimed at specific behavior change

7. *Mobilizer*—helping to mobilize resources to develop new services or programs

8. *Consultant*—working with other professionals to increase their skill and understanding

9. *Community planner*—helping communities to plan for ways to meet human need

10. *Caregiver*—providing support and care to persons when problems cannot be resolved

11. *Data manager*—collecting and analyzing data used in decision making

12. *Administrator*—planning and implementing services and programs[5]

There seems to be one additional role, that of coordinator. The coordinator enables several social workers, other professionals, or other service providers to function so that services are provided in a synchronized manner. The coordinator sees that all involved are aware of and take into consideration the work of all others as they provide service. This role may also be identified as the case manager role. (This is discussed in Chapter 8.) Another role is the enabler role. (See Chapter 7 for a discussion of enabling.)

Ronald Simons and Stephen Aiger discussed role choice in terms of client system characteristics and needs. The four client system characteristics they noted as important to consider when choosing the worker role are (1) the needs and desires of the client system, (2) the resources of the client system, (3) the expectations of the client system and of the worker regarding the client system, and (4) the client system's perceived expectations of the worker. Although they defined *role* somewhat differently from Teare and McPheeters, they identified particular situations and client systems' difficulties in which particular roles are important. A lack of resources calls for the broker role; a lack of opportunity, the advocate role; role inadequacy, the teacher role; unrealistic role expectations or behavior, the confronter role; conflicting role expectations, the mediator role; role transition stress, the empathic listener role; role indecision, the clarifier role.[6]

Usually, role and task are discussed in relation to the worker and the worker's functioning. However, role implies action and interaction by and with the family—a reciprocal relationship. Thus, in carrying out the plan attention needs to be paid to the family's functioning and tasks. The plan should specify the role or roles of the worker and consider the reciprocal role or roles of the family members. The tasks to be completed by family members and the worker should be specified. A task is a specific action or activity; it is the specification of what needs to be done.

The strategy is developed after tentative goals and units of attention relative to the goals have been identified. After the strategy has been identified, it is possible to develop the operational goal or goals and objectives and to become more specific about roles and tasks. Tasks and objectives are related.

Tasks are steps that are necessary to achieve the objectives and ultimately the goal. Tasks may be used to describe events that occur only once or are ongoing. They should cover the "who, what, how, where, and when" for the actions that are planned. This is generally the first place the worker appears in the plan. The exception would be cases in which the worker might be part of an objective by monitoring, prompting, or rewarding the family or a family member to assist in accomplishing objectives.

The tasks should be sequenced and a time for the completion of each established. This results in an overall time frame or time line for the service. It is important to specify the resources needed to carry out the plan and to indicate how those resources are to be obtained. This would include the time investment of the worker and family. Any monetary investment, such as fees or agency funds, should be specified. Other needed resources could be the use of an agency or community facility or service or the inclusion of other persons in the action system.

The plan is based on the information collected and the assessment of that information. It is developed with the fullest possible participation of the family. The plan is an agreement with the family outlining what the worker will do and what the family's responsibility in the endeavor is.

All plans of action should contain some mechanism for evaluating how well the goals of the plan are met. Evaluation, which is ongoing in the entire interventive process, is discussed in Chapter 9.

Plans should also contain some mechanism for specifying when various objectives are to be met or when specific tasks are to be completed. This can be as simple as specifying a date for the completion of each objective. When working on complex goals it is often useful to use a task-flow mechanism. Figure 6.1 shows an example of this type of time line.

The plan must be flexible. As the implementation of the plan progresses, new information is added that may result in a change of plan. The development of the plan calls for specificity. Specific plans are more likely to lead to service that is directed toward family needs and desires and that enhances accountability. Such plans allow for a breadth of possible decisions about the components of the plan, a mark of generalist social work as presented in this text.

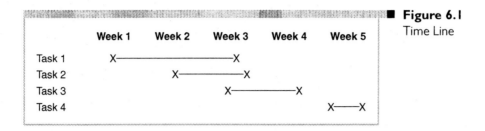

■ Figure 6.1
Time Line

When developing plans of action, it is usually advisable to consider several different plans and make choices based on an analysis of each plan and its suitability for the specific situation. This involves considering strengths and limitations of each plan. The chosen plan may be a synthesis of parts of several of the considered plans.

■ FACTORS AFFECTING A PLAN OF ACTION ■

Plans of action reflect the differential nature of social work. Each plan is specific to a situation and to the family involved. Each plan of action, with its component parts, should be different from every other plan of action. It is important to specify not only the components of a plan but also the various factors that affect the development of that plan. Seven factors that have considerable influence on the plan are (1) the community in which it is being carried out; (2) the agency sanctioning the plan; (3) the social need that the plan is a response to; (4) the worker involved in the plan; (5) the family involved in the plan; (6) diversity issues among members of all of these systems, along with issues related to disadvantaged or oppressed populations; and (7) the strengths and limitations of all of the above.

The Community

The community as a system is an important influence on the differential plan of action. The family is a part of a community; as such, the family reflects its characteristics. The community has expectations for the family. Any plan of action needs to consider the environment in which the plan takes place. What is feasible in one community may not be feasible in another.

The culture of a community is important to consider in planning. Attitudes about receiving help are particularly important, as are accepted coping mechanisms. In communities in which self-help and neighborliness are highly valued, the chosen plan of action may be one that strengthens and enables the natural helping system to function well rather than an extended social work service.

The community's service delivery system is another factor to be considered. An assumption is often made that the ideal service delivery system should be that of a large urban community with many specialized services. This assumption has led to the development of strategies specific to such situations. However, these strategies are sometimes inappropriate for small nonmetropolitan settings in which the service delivery system is different.[7] It is very different for rural areas where services are sparse or not available and where distance and travel are considerations for both the worker and families.

In the case example of the Perez family the following plan might be developed.

■ **Plan of Action**

A. Goal A: The Perez family will improve their communication.
   1. Objective A.1: The Perez family will use "I or we" statements at least three times each day for a week by November 15, 2007.
      a. Family task: The family will track the number of times they each use an "I or we" statement on a chart on the refrigerator and will report them to the worker during each session.
      b. Worker task: The worker will prompt the family to report on their progress in using "I or we" statements and will assist them to practice during each session.

B. Goal B: Juan and Carmen will return home and remain there for at least three months.
   1. Objective B.1: Juan, Carmen, and Mr. and Mrs. Perez will resolve the situation that led to the home truancy by January 1, 2008.
      a. Family task: Juan, Carmen, and Mr. and Mrs. Perez will attend family counseling sessions at Catholic Family Services and will work together to reach an agreement on Carmen's social life and Juan's school and community adjustment.
      b. Worker task: Worker will make a referral to Catholic Family Services, monitor progress, and work with the school regarding Juan and Carmen's adjustment.

■ **Unit of Attention**

At this point, the units of attention are the family as a system and a portion of the parent–child subsystem comprised of Juan and Carmen and their parents. The unit of attention will also be the school as the worker seeks to find ways for Juan and Carmen to be successful there.

■ **Strategy**

The social worker started out with a strategy of taking the direct practice action of getting the family to work together on a goal in order to reinforce family cohesion that might reduce the temptation for Juan and Carmen to leave. In addition, the use of "I or we" statements was intended to get the teens and their parents to talk with each other about their concerns. If they can do this, then they might improve their abilities to resolve issues before they become overwhelming.

    The worker decided to also use the indirect practice action of coordinating services by making a referral to a family service agency and also working with the school on the teens' adjustments there. The social worker knew that the high school has a co-op program that allows students to work and go to school. She intended to see if Juan could qualify for the program and this might satisfy his need to contribute to the family's economic needs while remaining in school. The worker also planned to meet with the principal regarding the school's taunting and teasing policy and to determine if Carmen might be able to connect with her counselor or the school social worker regarding a situation with a group of girls.

The Agency

In considering the influence of the agency on the plan of action, the worker is influenced by constraints and resources within the agency. Constraints may take the form of the kinds of service that can be offered, financial considerations, time priority factors, and the manner in which the agency is organized. Resources to be considered include people (staff expertise), structures, money, and expendable supplies that can be used by the worker and family to enhance the social work process or goal achievement. Skillful use of the agency system in service of the family is an important attribute of planning.

The agency is a component of the community, and, as such, it is an integral subunit of the community system. It is sanctioned by the community and must, at least in part, express its will. The agency depends on the community for resources. Social agencies seldom function without financial support from the community, which may be in the form of contributions or taxation. Other kinds of resources and support are also vital to providing services to clients. Planning must take into consideration the influence of community needs, values, and intentions for the service being delivered by the agency. It is important that the planning process recognize the influence of agency structure and functioning on service to families. This recognition gives both the worker and family a sense of the realities involved in the provision of service.

An additional factor to consider with respect to some organizations is the impact of managed care on how the agency and its workers function. Although managed care is currently most relevant for health care, mental health, and substance abuse, this approach may eventually be applied to other areas of human services. There are two primary situations in which social workers may be affected by managed care in their practice. The first is when the agency provides services that are reimbursed by a managed care organization under a prescribed insurance plan. The other is when a social worker is employed by a managed care provider. In the first case, the worker can be affected by the length of service that is approved for reimbursement and by the type of service considered reimbursable. In the second case, the worker may be responsible for assessing, referring, and monitoring the implementation of a managed care plan. Some managed care providers recognize that social workers possess valuable assessment skills and referral potential, especially in the areas of mental health and substance abuse treatment.

An important consideration is that the *NASW Code of Ethics* requires that social workers regard clients' concerns as primary. This means that regardless of the interests of themselves or their employers, social workers must do what is in the best interests of their clients. A major criticism of managed care is that managed care plans may limit what is available to clients or encourage less care by discouraging more expensive services. Social workers must not allow themselves to be influenced by any policies that do not allow workers to act in the best interests of clients regardless of the circumstances. Facing the challenges of these situations requires courage and the ability to act as a strong advocate.

The Social Issue

Societal attitudes and expectations about social issues vary. By sanctioning or developing means for control, amelioration, or prevention, these attitudes and expectations influence the task assigned to the agency. Some social issues are seen as a sign of illness or deviance, and some, as the result of environmental influences.

Elliot Studt has expressed this idea in her conceptualization of the field of practice. She pointed out "three organizing dimensions for describing a field of practice: social problem, social task, and social service system."[8] In thinking about the social issue, it is helpful to consider why the issue concerns the community and other social systems. Important are such questions as, How does the issue affect the general welfare of the community? Why does a community see a need for action? What is the condition of central concern? Also important is how the issue affects the social functioning of individuals and families. As these questions are answered and as social policy and programs are developed, the social tasks related to the specific social issues develop. The social task is what the community sees as needing to be done in order to resolve the social issue. Social tasks also include work needed to help the individual or family affected by the social issue. These tasks develop in part from the expectations of the various segments of the community—taxpayers, professionals, legislators, agents of social control, commercial interests, and so on. Thus, the social task is often unclear and subject to conflicting expectations. This is one of the reasons that accountability is difficult and that goal expectations are unclear.

For example, quite different attitudes are held about someone with a difficulty in social functioning that leads to breaking the law and someone whose difficulty in social functioning is the result of sudden illness. The former enters the corrections field of practice; the latter, the health care field. Social control concerns are greater in the corrections field because the strategy used must protect the community from further threat of danger from lawbreaking. Thus, punishment is often the strategy used. Treatment of illness is the prime concern in the medical setting, and concern with social functioning is in relationship to the illness. Society has considerable compassion for the person whose social-functioning difficulties arise from illness. The strategy chosen must allow for the treatment of the illness and provide means for coping with the resulting difficulties in social functioning. Social policy is often a reflection of societal concerns and attitudes about social issues. Relevant social policy must be considered in developing plans of action. Societal and individual attitudes as they relate to the issue being worked on by the worker and family are important influences on the planning process.

The Worker

Each worker is first a unique person. The worker's primary tool is the self. The worker brings herself as a person, as a professional, as an agency employee, as a member of one or more families, and as a member of the community to the social work endeavor. In planning with families, the worker should be aware of her own perceptions about families. These are shaped by her experiences with family life. In addition to her professional experiences, the worker also has personal ones. These include experiences with her family of origin in which she grew up as a child. They may also include one or more families to which she belongs or has belonged as a parent, a stepparent, or a spouse. The self is another factor influencing the plan of action.

Because of workers' individuality, because there is no one theory about the human situation or about families, and because there is no one way to achieve social work goals, workers have preferences about explaining the human situation, working with families, and practicing social work. One worker may find a structural approach more helpful and use this approach more extensively. Another worker may use a more eclectic theory base and find problem solving or a solution-focused approach useful. A third worker might find that an ecosystems strengths approach provides the most positive and comprehensive approach. Plans of action, though developed by worker and family together, reflect the worker's preferences, priorities, and skills.

As an agency employee, the worker is both constrained and supported. The worker is responsible and accountable to the agency for his work. The worker must function within the agency structure and is interdependent with others employed by the agency. As a member of the community, the worker is subject to pressures from that community. The worker's preferences and influences from both the agency and the community also affect the planning process.

When a social worker is employed by a managed care organization, it is essential that the worker be aware of relevant social work values and ethics. The *NASW Code of Ethics* includes a statement that the social worker should adhere to commitments made to the organization that employs him. However, another section refers to the fact that the social worker's primary responsibility is to clients. This can present a serious ethical dilemma in cases in which the family's needs are not being met by the organization. If the organization has responsibly informed the family of the limits on coverage for various services, then family members participated in the plan with knowledge of what would or would not be reimbursed. However, this requires family members to be astute consumers, which may not always be the case. It is the obligation of the social worker to inform clients of all of their benefits and rights under the plan as well as those that might be applicable by law. For instance, if a client is entitled to appeal a decision either within the organization or to regulatory bodies, the social worker must inform the client of this and assist in the appeal process. In addition, the social worker has an obligation to be knowledgeable about alternative resources that may be available to assist the family in obtaining the needed service.

When working in a system in which reimbursement is controlled by a managed care plan, the worker must know how to maximize client benefits to fit the needs of the client and to ensure that the client receives needed services. Besides being knowledgeable about the coverage the family has, the worker needs to be ready to advocate for the needed services. The worker also should be creative about linking the family to other community services that can make up for some of the shortcomings of the insurance plan. The worker must be efficient in planning and delivering services within the agency's mandate. Frequently, this means developing time-limited plans that are designed to maximize the impact of the intervention. The worker should be task oriented and outcome focused so that tasks are completed within the limited time frames imposed by the covered services.

Managed care situations necessitate very careful planning to ensure an effective outcome within the limited time frames generally imposed by the insurance plan. This requires accurate assessment and the development of a plan that is task and solution focused. The restricted time frame can severely undermine the ability of the worker to develop and maintain a helping relationship that will carry the process through to a successful completion. It is imperative that family members be made aware of the limitations of their coverage and the need for immediate action. Otherwise, the family may misinterpret the worker's urgency as a lack of caring. In addition, a limited time frame is no excuse for ignoring the need to include the family in planning and decision making. Client self-determination is still relevant and must be central to any approach used by a professional social worker. Helping families make choices within the context of their situation, advocating for maximum use of their benefits, and using all of the resources at their disposal are the keys to successful planning in managed care situations. Including the family in this process ensures that the worker and the family are working together rather than working against each other. As mentioned previously, an ecosystems strengths approach can be an effective and efficient means of delivering services. It emphasizes using the family's own natural helping and support systems. Developing existing strengths and resources is the focus, rather than seeking to change the overall structure. However, a potential drawback in using this approach is that some managed care systems may not recognize certain worker activities as reimbursable. Again, advocacy and connecting tasks to an approved plan may be necessary to achieve reimbursement.

The Family

The family in its uniqueness brings much to the worker–client interaction. The family comes from a community, a neighborhood, and one or more diverse groups. Family members bring their biological, psychosocial, spiritual beings. Family members have self-images, roles in the family and the community, values, hopes, and expectations. The family has rights—the right to service, the right to participate, the right to fail. Family members carry a reference group's expectations as well as the results of interactions with meaningful persons in meaningful situations. The family has strengths, modes of adaptation, and ways of coping. Family members bring a particular set of motivations, capacities, and opportunities. This uniqueness will support some interventive strategies and eliminate others. Even more important, the family will have unique expectations and goals for the service. The family may have preferences about the way of working on the need with the worker. The family's needs are unique, and the plan must be unique in its response to those needs.

The roles of family members in the plan depend on several factors. Among these factors are the roles of family members in their life situations (parents, children, employees, etc.), each family member's role in the agency or organization (patient, inmate, student, etc.), and the role the worker has chosen (the family's role must be reciprocal to it). The family is a vital part of the factors influencing the plan of action.

Diversity and Populations at Risk

Important considerations in developing a plan are the similarities and differences among members of the various systems involved. (The earlier discussions of diversity, especially in Chapter 3, should be reviewed for a better understanding of its implications for planning.) Diversity is an important factor in planning because it permeates the process and affects the worker, family, and agency. For instance, the family might find it difficult to accept help from an agency that has a negative reputation among members of its ethnic or racial group. Alternatively, overcoming this barrier might represent an even stronger commitment on the part of both the family and the agency. Both may realize a benefit in forging a relationship with each other. The agency may see the experience as an opportunity to build a bridge to a part of the community that has felt alienated from its services. The family may see it as a new resource that until now was not accessible.

As mentioned earlier, families who are members of populations at risk of prejudice, discrimination, and oppression need to have a plan that reflects empowerment and a means of addressing these issues. As discussed in earlier, various diversity competent approaches need to be incorporated into the plan. When working with African Americans, Asians, and Hispanics, family and cultural traditions are important considerations. Women may desire to change relationships or at the very least may want to consider the impact of change on significant relationships. People who are aging may be concerned about losing their independence or they may have transportation or health care needs that have to be addressed. These approaches should not be applied as stereotypes but are intended to be used as potential areas for exploration with the family.

The use of naturalistic inquiry should continue during the planning phase. Its use in planning means that the worker looks to the family for guidance in developing a plan that is appropriate with respect to the family's diversity. As the worker gains competence in working with a specific diverse group, she might make suggestions that are consistent with the needs of that group. However, even then she should be sure to get feedback from the family about the appropriateness of the plan. She could ask questions that are specific to the family's diversity, such as, Could you describe what this situation would look like if it were resolved and you were feeling good about the results? What would it mean to you to have this need met? How would this fit with who you are as a (woman, African American, Hispanic, Native American, gay person, lesbian, etc.)? What types of considerations need to be made for you to feel comfortable with this plan? How would your community view this? What are some of the approaches to meeting this need that are used within your culture (or group)? Who else needs to be involved in developing a plan?

The answers to these types of questions should open up a discussion about diversity that need to be incorporated into the plan. Both the types of goals and means of achieving them should be part of this discussion. We do not think that it is wise to prescribe specific approaches to be used with families of each diverse group. The situation is much more complicated than using a step-by-step process. Besides, this would be inconsistent with using naturalistic inquiry. Using a prescribed approach implies that the worker knows what she does not know as opposed to taking the position that she does not know what she does not know. Instead of a prescribed approach, a dialogue about diversity needs to take place that leads to a diversity competent plan that is specific to the family. Another reason for taking this approach is that quite often families members may be members of more than one diverse group. In addition, each family has unique experiences as members of a diverse group or groups.

Diversity factors in the community at large play an important role in planning. The more homogeneity there is in the culture of a community, the more expectations tend to be standardized. The positive side is that homogeneity creates cohesion and community pride in a common heritage and traditions. The negative side is that there often is less tolerance for those who are "different." However, valuing "sameness" does not mean that "differentness" is bad. People can come to realize that there is strength in variety and diversity, but overcoming fear and prejudice is not easy. When the community is relatively homogeneous, there will likely be options for planning that are influenced by community expectations. These expectations may require certain expected behaviors but not tolerate others that deviate from the norm. Similarly, certain behaviors may not be tolerated because they are outside of the bounds of what the community will accept. This situation is probably more common in rural communities and in neighborhoods that have strong ethnic identities.

Communities that are more heterogeneous may be more tolerant of a wider range of behaviors but only to the extent that their citizens have been able to overcome their prejudices. Unfortunately, the gap between many ethnic and racial groups and the dominant Caucasian culture in the United States more often has resulted in devaluing diversity, even to the extent of open prejudice and oppression. When there is a gap between the expectations of the dominant culture and those of the person's ethnic or familial system, the client can feel she is in a double bind: No matter what she does she will be judged in a negative way by someone. In planning, the worker needs to discuss the implications of diversity and of prejudice and oppression so that the client is not set up for failure.

People of color have cultural roots and beliefs that are highly family centered. Thus, the fundamental approach in working with people of color needs to be family centered. Goals and objectives should be constructed with the family as the primary focus. Even individual goals should incorporate the effects of the goal on the family and the effects of the family on the goal. It is much better to include the family in the means of accomplishing the goal than to see a goal as an individual accomplishment. This approach fits quite well with using an Afrocentric approach with African American families and in family approaches that are recommended in working with Hispanic/Latino, Native American, and Asian families.

Strengths and Challenges of the Systems Involved

Each of the systems described brings both strengths and challenges to the work to be done. A primary consideration in good planning is building on strengths while addressing challenges. Sometimes, challenges constitute barriers that need to be circumvented or overcome. However, the place to begin is with a strengths-based approach. The worker needs to identify the capacities and potential of the agency, the community, the situation involving the social issue, the worker, the family and its immediate environment, and the diversity factors that might come into play.

To be successful in using a strengths-based approach, the worker must be highly self-aware and sensitive to his own perceptions as well as those of others in systems involved in the situation at hand. When using a problem-focused approach, there is a tendency to perceive the situation in terms of what is going wrong. This can easily lead to blaming, especially blaming the family for having the problem. The implication is that because the situation is caused by the family, all that is needed is for the family or family members to change. Besides, changing a system seems a more daunting task than individual change or changes in the family.

The person in environment or family in environment and a strengths approach dictate that all aspects of the situation need to be considered during assessment. Similarly, all aspects of the situation need to be incorporated in planning for change. A strengths-based approach involves basing a plan on the abilities and capacities of family members and systems. Instead of requiring the family and systems to develop new skills and abilities as a prerequisite for change, the plan is based on what the family and systems are already able to do. Everyone involved should be able to contribute to change by using skills already possessed.

Finally, a strengths approach clearly fits best with two of the cardinal values of social work, namely, the belief in the value and worth of every individual and the belief in self determination. In addition to valuing people inherently as human beings, a strengths approach orients the worker and the family toward abilities, thus valuing the contribution families can make toward bringing about change. A strengths approach gives families the tools they need to exercise self determination and recognizes that the family and family members are major forces in their own lives. As people are able to make decisions for themselves, they also need to see themselves as acting to make those decisions a reality. Highlighting their strengths helps them realize how they can make self determination a reality rather than merely an abstract concept.

■   THE PLANNING PROCESS WITH FAMILIES   ■

Planning is a joint process with the family. Students and new workers often find it difficult to decide where to start and how to determine priorities, time frames, tasks, and other aspects of the plan. In setting a goal, the worker can take several approaches. One approach is to take the preliminary statement of need or concern and turn it into a goal. In the case example, if the need statement is "The family needs to build positive relationships with each other," then a goal can be formulated by changing the *needs* to *will have*. Thus, the goal becomes "The family will have positive relationships with each other."

Sometimes the worker or the family may have difficulty in clearly articulating a need in a way that lends itself to converting it into a goal statement. A second way to formulate a goal is to ask the family, What would your life be like if this need were met (or this concern resolved)? If they are able to answer, then they have given the worker a goal with which to work. The worker should follow this up with questions such as, What would each of you be doing? What would other family members (or others outside the family) be doing? If the worker and the family can find feasible answers to these and related questions, then a goal can be formulated. The goal might be "The family will feel positive about each other and their relationships."

The next set of questions should relate to setting objectives. If the worker and the family have a clear understanding of the current situation and they have formulated a goal, then they know where the family is and where it wants to go. They have a direction they can take for the work to be done. The objectives should serve as intermediate steps toward the goal and should measure the progress toward the goal. A good way to determine these steps is to ask the family questions such as, What could you do this week (in two weeks, etc.) that would make a difference? or What could you do this month (in two months, etc.) that would make a difference? In the case example, a family member might say something about saying something nice to each other. The worker could develop this into the objective that was identified in the case example. The next questions might be, What would it take for that to happen? What do you need to do? What do other people need to do? What do I (the worker) need to do to help? What would you be willing to do if you received a positive response? What would you consider a positive response? What would make it worthwhile for you to change? What resources do you need? Where might we find those resources? The answers to these questions can be developed into tasks similar to those in the case example.

This approach fits well with becoming diversity competent. It relies on the family to articulate goals, objectives, and tasks that are appropriate for its culture or diversity group. If these components of the plan came from the worker, they would reflect the worker's values and perspective. To ensure that the plan is consistent with the diversity of the family, the worker should ask about important factors that are related to their diversity. For example, the worker might ask family members about the importance of the family in their particular ethnic group. She might ask about roles and how they are determined or about the way decisions are made.

The worker develops a plan in consultation with the family. She uses an approach that is family centered. She respects the family as the experts in their own lives and communicates an expectation that they are capable of resolving the situation and getting their needs met. She shows confidence in the family's ability to exercise self determination. She puts herself in the role of facilitator. She demonstrates how the family can use the change process for themselves so they can learn to use it in other areas of family life. As the worker uses this approach with the family, she builds a positive helping relationship and empowers them to act on their own behalf to bring about change that they desire in their life situation.

Agreement between Worker and Family

When the worker and family have worked together in assessment and in developing the plan of action, an agreement develops between them as to what needs to be done and who should do it. This agreement may take the form of a **contract.** The contract may merely be an understanding between worker and family, or it may be a formal, written, signed agreement. The form the agreement takes will depend in part on what is best for a particular family and in part on agency practice and policy.

Contracting is an accepted part of the worker–family interaction in many agencies. However, the use of contracts has been challenged in two ways. Pamela Miller asserted that contracts fail to recognize that the service provider is a professional using empathy as an important ingredient of the service. She called for a covenant approach, which implies that the worker has a gift of service for the client.[9] Tom Croxton pointed out that the use of the term *contract* is inaccurate because it lacks an important ingredient—legal implications. This inaccurate use can lead to misunderstandings, vagueness, and even conflict.[10]

Thus, instead of *contract,* the term *agreement* may better describe the worker–client decision. However, *contract,* as used in social work, has never been assumed to have a legal connotation. The concept of contract, as developed in social work literature, seems best to describe an agreement about the plan in the generalist social work sense. A contract or agreement can be thought of as an understanding between the worker and the family about the work to be done.

Agreements are easiest to develop with motivated, trusting families. They are very useful with disorganized or forgetful family members who need reminding about the work to be done or about their responsibility for carrying out tasks. Agreements can be more effective if written, but sometimes this is not necessary or even desirable. For the resistant or distrustful person, a signed paper may be a barrier, whereas a verbal commitment might be helpful. For a family in crisis, it may be best to quickly get to the work of helping and delay or eliminate the step of a formal agreement. A quick verbal agreement may be all that is necessary. The agreement should be flexible and appropriate to the specific family and their situation. It should be a tool to enhance the work together, not a mechanistic procedure to fulfill some outside, imposed requirement. However, regardless of whether the agreement with the worker is written, the plan that is entered into the case file should still be reviewed with the family. Generally speaking, when working with families that have a lot of conflict, it is best to develop the agreement in writing, otherwise it is likely to become one more thing about which the family can argue.

Planning and contracting are means for making clear the who, what, where, when, and how of the social work endeavor. They are means for individualizing the social work process to the family in situation and also provide tools for accountability and evaluation. Planning and contracting tie knowledge about the family in environment to the work of doing something to change the situation for the family. Planning expands opportunity for accomplishing the desired change.

SUMMARY

The following principles for developing a plan of action can give guidance to the planning process:

1. Each plan of action is a part of an overall social work process. This implies

   It is based on personal–social need and the needs of the family and its subsystems.

   It is developed through a change process that is based on a strengths approach.

   It recognizes the impact of diversity on all aspects of the planning process and incorporates into the plan the strengths of the family, the individuals, and the systems involved.

   It is dynamic, changing as new knowledge leads to reassessment of situations; reformulation of need; and development of new goals, strategies, and tasks.

2. Each plan of action clearly indicates

   The goal toward which it is aimed. This goal should be directly related to personal–social needs, the needs of the family and its subsystems, and should be stated in terms of a positive outcome. Objectives should be clearly stated in positive terms and be observable and measurable.

   The unit(s) of attention that are included in the plan.

   The strategy to be used and the role of worker, the family and each of its members, and others and the tasks to be performed by all concerned.

3. The plan of action takes into consideration the community in which the action system functions. This includes the awareness of community expectations, norms, values, service delivery system, and resources.

4. The plan of action reflects the agency's or organization's "way of doing business." Community influences and agency organization structure, functioning, and development all contribute to this "way of doing business."

5. The nature of the social issue is recognized as an important variable in the development of the plan of action.

6. The worker's contribution to the plan of action is based on professional knowledge, values, and skill. It involves the ability to assess and determine the usefulness of various resources as well as the capacity for professional judgment and the ability to make appropriate choices from among various possibilities.

7. The family brings uniqueness to the situation. This includes a perception of the need, a set of values, unique motivation, capacity, opportunity, and goals.

8. The plan of action is the outgrowth of the worker–family interaction. Everyone contributes from their perspective regarding the family in environment. Planning sometimes results in a contract or agreement between worker and family.

9. The plan of action considers the availability of the resources needed to carry out the plan and the feasibility of reaching the goals.

10. The plan of action includes a time line.

11. The plan contains a means for evaluation.

The diversity competent worker develops a plan that incorporates the diversity of the family. She explores goals and objectives that are comfortable for the family given their diversity. The worker realizes that the feasibility of a plan requires that it be consistent with both the family's values and those of their race, culture, religion, and so on. She includes ways of helping that are consistent with those that are expected within the family's diverse group. She incorporates natural helpers whenever possible.

QUESTIONS

1. Set a goal for your family or a family that you know that can be reached in a week. Write it in outcome terms and identify two objectives that relate to the goal. Identify a task for each objective.

2. What do you see as the advantages of being very clear about the identification of the unit of attention?

3. Using three of the roles identified by Teare and McPheeters, discuss the complementary client role and possible tasks for the family or a family member and worker.

4. In developing a plan of action for a family, discuss some considerations that exist in a community with which you are familiar.

5. Identify how diversity might affect the plan and the planning process if you are working with a family of color? Women in a family? A gay or lesbian family? A family with a member who is physically or mentally disabled?

6. Identify at least three strengths that could be considered in planning with a family of color? Women in a family? A gay or lesbian family? A family with a member who is physically or mentally disabled?

SUGGESTED READINGS

Johnson, Louise C., and Yanca, Stephen J. *Social Work Practice: A Generalist Approach,* 9th ed. Boston: Allyn & Bacon, 2007 (Chapters 10 and 13).

Miley, Karla Krogsrud, O'Melia, Michael, and DuBois, Brenda L. *Social Work Practice: An Empowering Approach,* 5th ed. Boston: Allyn & Bacon, 2007 (Chapter 11).

Rothman, Jack, and Sager, Jon Simon. *Case Management: Integrating Individual and Community Practice.* Boston: Allyn & Bacon, 1998.

Rothman, Juliet. *Contracting in Social Work.* Chicago: Nelson-Hall, 1996.

Saleeby, Dennis. *The Strengths Perspective in Social Work Practice,* 4th ed. Boston: Allyn & Bacon, 2006.

Sheafor, Bradford W., and Horejsi, Charles R. *Techniques and Guidelines for Social Work Practice,* 7th ed. Boston: Allyn & Bacon, 2006 (Chapter 12).

CHAPTER

7

Direct Practice Actions with Families

LEARNING EXPECTATIONS

1. Understanding of diversity competent practice actions with diverse families.
2. Understanding of how to enable families to use available resources.
3. Understanding of strategies for empowering and enabling families.
4. Understanding of the nature of crisis and of the crisis intervention process.
5. Understanding of the nature of support.
6. Understanding of the place and use of activity in helping families.
7. Understanding of the use of mediation within the family.

Following planning, the next step in the generalist social work process with families is action. Different families with different needs in different situations require different kinds of action on the part of the worker. For some situations, the actions of the assessment and planning phases provide the help needed so the family can take action for change. Sometimes help comes through the development of the worker–client relationship. This relationship then frees the family to engage in problem-solving activity with the worker. In other situations, action on the part of the worker is required. This action can be helpful in the development of relationships and in assessment. Actions by the worker may be needed to implement the plan or when barriers arise. The social worker may use various kinds of activity with people and with systems other than client systems as a part of the helping process.

Both direct and indirect practice actions are relevant for working with families. The work can be focused on individual family members, the family, or a subsystem as the client system. The environment can also be the unit of attention in the change process. Direct actions are the focus in this chapter. Indirect actions, which are used with systems in the family's environment and involve changing the actions and interactions of people in those systems, are covered in Chapter 8. The worker has a dual focus when the family is the client system. She uses actions in helping the family to achieve its goals while also helping the family to acquire skills in using these actions. Helping families to use the change process gives them the power to bring about change on their own in the future. This brings true meaning to the social work value of self determination.

In understanding direct practice actions, we return to Figure 2.1 and use an adaptation, Figure 7.1, to illustrate how various direct practice actions are aimed at assisting the family in changing thoughts, feelings, or actions. This is not intended to be an exhaustive list of all interventions used by social workers. However, it depicts the primary direct practice actions used by generalist social workers in helping clients. Most of these direct practice actions may be used with members of human systems in the environment along with other approaches that are discussed later in this chapter and in subsequent chapters on family subsystems.

Influence is included in parentheses in Figure 7.1 as a way of recognizing that the worker has influence on the family. However, the use of influence as a planned strategy with clients has many complications for the social worker because it tends to undermine self determination. Thus, it should only be used as a last resort when families are in crisis or are headed for disaster or are truly stuck. Influence as a planned strategy is commonly used as a direct practice action with organizations and communities and as an indirect practice action on behalf of the family. The use of influence as an indirect practice action is discussed in Chapter 8.

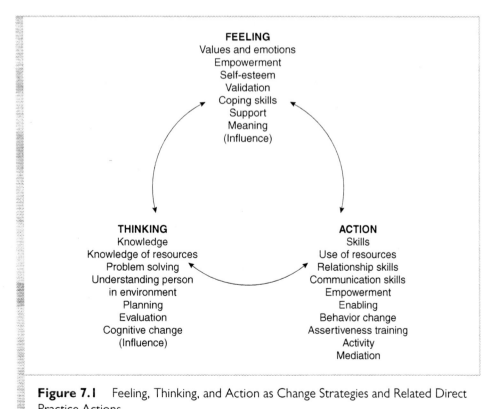

Figure 7.1 Feeling, Thinking, and Action as Change Strategies and Related Direct Practice Actions

Social workers need to be aware of the variety of theories available to guide their helping efforts. An in-depth study of these theories is beyond the scope of this book.

One of the marks of a generalist practitioner is the capacity to choose from a wide variety of possibilities the action most appropriate for the specific situation. Social work action falls into two primary classifications: **direct practice** (action with clients) and **indirect practice** (action with people and systems other than clients). Direct practice primarily involves action with individuals, families, and small groups. Direct practice is focused on change in either the transactions within the family or small-group system or in the manner in which individuals, families, and small groups function in relation to persons and societal institutions in their environment.

Indirect practice involves those actions taken with persons other than clients in order to help clients. These actions may be taken with individuals, small groups, organizations, or communities as the unit of attention.

Direct practice falls within the following categories:

1. Diversity competent practice actions with diverse families
2. Action taken to enable development of relationships
3. Action taken to enable development of understanding of person in environment
4. Action taken in the planning process
5. Action taken to enable the family to know and use available resources
6. Action taken to empower or enable families
7. Action taken in crisis situations
8. Action taken to support the social functioning of families
9. Action taken that uses activity with families as the base of help
10. Action taken to mediate within the family
11. Action taken in using a clinical model of social work

In this chapter, diversity competent practice actions, actions related to the use of resources, to empowerment and enabling of people, to crisis intervention, to support, to the use of activity, and to mediating are discussed. Action taken to enable the development of relationships and of an understanding of person in environment and action taken in the planning process have already been discussed, but are reviewed briefly here. Action taken in using clinical models of social work is beyond the scope of this book.

Action also depends on the skills of the worker. The *NASW Code of Ethics* mandates that social workers only practice in areas in which they have competence. Depending on the service goals and the usual ways the agency delivers service, workers more often use certain kinds of action than others. Skill in using the various types of action develops through use over time. In order to help diverse families with various needs, social workers can be most effective when they are skilled in using a variety of actions and choose the action best suited to the family and the situation. The generalist practitioner's repertoire includes actions for working with individuals, groups, families, organizations, and communities. Often, several types of action are needed to reach identified goals. There is overlap among possible actions or strategies, and often the worker creatively combines strategies or makes alterations to better respond to specific situations. The art of social work comes into play when action becomes the focus of service. In deciding which kinds of action to take in a particular situation, several principles can be used:

1. *Economy*—The action chosen should require the least expenditure of time and energy by both the family and worker. Generally, a worker helps the family do for itself whatever is possible to do with help, and does for a family only what they cannot do for themselves.

2. *Self determination*—The action that is most desirable to the family should be used whenever possible. The action of the worker is planned with the family during the planning phase of the helping process.

3. *Individualization*—Any action taken should be differentially adapted to the strengths, needs, and characteristics of the particular family member or family system. The worker should creatively adapt the action to the family's characteristics and situation.

4. *Development*—The action of the worker depends, in part, on the developmental stage of the family system and its members. Different kinds of help are appropriate at different stages of development of the individual and the family.

5. *Diversity*—The action is consistent with the culture and diversity of the family. Diversity competent practice involves delivering services in a manner that is acceptable within the norms and expectations of the culture or diverse group with whom the family identifies.

6. *Interdependence*—The action of the worker depends in part on the action of the family. The activity of the family and the family's capacity to change should always be considered. The actions of the worker, the family, and family members should be complementary.

7. *Focus on service goals*—The action should be related to the goals for the service as developed by the worker and family together during the planning stage.

Following through with the spirit of naturalistic inquiry, the worker continues to employ the basic aspects of this approach throughout the action phase. If the worker has been successful in employing naturalistic inquiry, he should have an assessment that incorporates diversity as it applies to the family. He should also have a plan that reflects the family's perspective on their diversity, including goals, objectives, and tasks that are appropriate for the diversity of the family. Using naturalistic inquiry during the action phase means that the worker consistently dialogues with the family about the actions that are taken. Before he or the family takes action, he discusses who, what, where, when, how, and why. Who is going to take what action? Where and when will it take place? How will it be carried out? Why are we doing this? In addition, the worker confirms that the action is something that the family approves so that it is consistent with their diversity or other factors. When the action takes place over time, the worker carries on a dialogue about the action with the family. He checks to ensure that the family is in agreement and that the action is appropriate for them and the situation at hand. When the action is completed, he discusses the family's level of comfort with the results and with the means by which the results were achieved.

Most of the actions that follow can be used with members of diverse groups. The actions identified here are those that are used by a generalist practice social worker. The actions are broad enough so that specific approaches may be subsumed under one or more of them. Thus, specific approaches that may be used with members of diverse groups can generally be categorized under one or more of these actions or may require a specific focus as the action is taken. For instance, an Afrocentric approach is mainly one that focuses on the unique contributions of African Americans and takes a worldview that values and incorporates

African traditions. As the worker works with her African American families, she seeks out information about how help is given and received within the African American community.

■ DIVERSITY COMPETENT PRACTICE ACTIONS ■ WITH DIVERSE FAMILIES

Diversity competent practice actions with diverse families require the worker to learn practice actions that will facilitate successful completion of the plan in a manner that is expected within their culture or diverse group. As we saw in Chapter 3, knowledge that is needed to understand diverse families is itself quite diverse. Similarly, ways of seeking and receiving help also varies. The foundation of diversity competent practice is the use of naturalistic inquiry, which has been described earlier. The application of this approach to direct practice actions means a continuation of the process in which the family is the source of what fits best for them. Thus, much of what comprises diversity competent practice actions with diverse families is really a process or a "how" rather than a "what." It is more of a how to work with the family rather than a what to do with the family in terms of a specific approach. Just because the family is diverse, does not mean that the worker should automatically assume that a certain approach is prescribed. For example, although an Afrocentric approach may be used with many African American families, some may not be comfortable with it.

In diversity competent practice, the worker explores with the family actions that are consistent with the diversity of the family as well as individual preferences as a unique family. She does not impose her own or society's view of what the family should do but seeks to find what fits with the family system. Most of the direct practice actions that follow this section can be used with any family, including those who are diverse. However, how they are used may be different based on either diversity or the unique family with whom the action is occurring.

Gender Competent Practice Actions

In Chapter 3 we discussed the use of a feminist-informed approach in becoming a gender competent social worker. This approach seeks to encourage gender equity while avoiding the temptation to impose this on families. Some of this can be accomplished by

CASE EXAMPLE

From the case example of the interview with the Perez family in Chapter 4, the following is an example of diversity competent practice.

Jane began the interview by formally addressing the parents using Mr. and Mrs. This demonstrates respect for their status as parents. Jane clarified whether they would need to use Spanish or English and apologized for not being bilingual. She addressed Mr. P first, respecting his role as the head of the family. Later, he indicated that she could address her questions directly to his wife and children. Jane used naturalistic inquiry in having the family tell their story. She allowed the family to be the expert and to teach her about how they functioned and what they experienced.

modeling actions and interactions that represent equality in relationships. Some of it can be accomplished by incorporating equality into goals and objectives. When the worker helps the family construct shared goals, she is encouraging equality in their relationship. When the worker seeks to balance the actions of each party in carrying out reciprocal goals, she is encouraging equity. When the family agrees to assist individuals with individual goals, they are allowing for greater empowerment of that family member. The very act of a female social worker assisting the family to meet its needs is in itself a model for greater gender equity, especially if she can work with a family in a way that models this for them.

As we indicated earlier, the decision regarding the encouragement of gender equity lies with the wife. If she wishes to continue with a patriarchal family system, then the worker should respect this as self determination. If she wishes to change it, then the worker acts in a manner that helps her to do so while minimizing risks to her and her family.

One of the difficulties in working with families from certain cultures is the strict boundaries between male and female role expectations. This generally results in the male being in the role of head of the household, called a *patriarchal system.* This system may be viewed as oppressive toward women. Most of these cultures define a "good husband" or a "good father" as a man who incorporates the needs and best interests of his wife and children into his decision making. He is obligated to see that the needs of his wife and family are met. This places tremendous pressure on him when faced with limited resources. Some men use their dominant position to meet their own needs or suppress the needs of other family members. Within their culture, this is a deviation from the "good husband and father" role. The worker can assist the husband to define this role within his culture and then work with him to obtain the resources that are necessary to carry this out. She might also help him to see that sharing his power is not necessarily a sign of weakness but may indeed be a sign of strength. In many respects, liberating females from their gender-based roles also means liberating males from their's. There are generally advantages to this as there are also disadvantages for both males and females. For instance, even though cooking and cleaning and housework may be seen as drudgery, some people may not experience these as such. In addition, males who rely on females to provide these services are essentially placing themselves in dependent positions. Those who learn to do these things for themselves are much more independent. Relying on wives to do most of the child-rearing deprives husbands of the pleasure of closely bonded relationships with their children. Assuming the role of primary disciplinarian can also result in more distant relationships if it is not accompanied by other child-rearing experiences.

Cross-cultural work with families is much more complicated when the work is also cross-gender. If the worker is female and the family system is patriarchal, it can be very difficult for the worker to gain credibility. Naturalistic inquiry can be especially helpful in these cases. Asking questions and giving the role of cultural guide to the family allows the process to unfold. The family will be more comfortable with a discussion of its cultural background if the focus is on strengths. Actively incorporating cultural customs and values into the plan is vital. This lays the groundwork for action that is culturally appropriate. It is important for the family to take pride in its cultural heritage and to use that heritage as a source of strength.

As we examine various direct practice actions with families, we identify ways in which these actions might be used in gender competent practice.

CASE EXAMPLE

From the case example of the Perez family, the following is an example of gender competent practice.

As Jane worked with the Perez family, it became apparent that Mr. P was not in favor of his wife's hope that Carmen would go to college after graduating from high school. Mrs. P had also brought up the possibility of finishing school and finding work. Mr. P felt that a woman's place was at home taking care of the household and the family and it was the man's responsibility to provide for his family. Jane did not challenge this directly but asked Mr. P about how he saw his roles as husband and father. She asked him which was more important for him, providing for his family or spending time with them. He indicated that both of them were important, but if he had to make a choice he would not be able to see his family starve or be without necessities so he would have to work. Jane decided to use an example of how other families cope with providing for their economic needs. She compared the incomes of two families, one with one income and another with two. She asked if Mr. P might think about what differences it would make in his family if they were able to increase their income by 25, 50 and 75 percent. What could they do with the additional income? She asked Mr. and Mrs. P to make up a list using each of the figures based on Mr. P's income.

At the next session, Jane discussed the list with Mr. and Mrs. P. They had worked out various plans to pay their debts first. The next option gave them an opportunity to save more money and to consider moving to a newer, larger home. The third option would allow them to buy a better car and perhaps keep the old car for Mrs. P to drive and later Juan when he got his license. It would also allow Mr. P to cut back on his hours and have more time for the family. As Mr. P realized these possibilities, he began to reconsider his position. Jane asked him if his real obligation was to see to it that his family had the best opportunity for economic success and suggested that it was in his power to decide to share the responsibility of providing for the family with his wife. Jane pointed out that they already had formed a very successful partnership as husband and wife and as parents so sharing roles that are involved would simply be another step in developing that partnership further. Mrs. P expressed her need to have Mr. P more involved with the children so he could influence them as the they grew into adults. She described how painful it was for her to watch him work so hard and how worried she was that he was overextending himself. She worried that he might be sacrificing his health or that he might fall asleep driving home after such long hours. He admitted that he was often tired and had to roll down the windows and turn up the radio on some nights.

At the next session Mr. P announced that they had a family meeting to discuss Mrs. P going work or finishing school. The children were enthusiastic about the idea of having their father around more. As a result, he had decided to give this plan a try to see if it could work.

In working with the family, Jane used an informed feminist approach rather than challenging Mr. P directly. She found a way for him to adhere to his cultural values while also opening some doors for the women in the family. Later, she showed Mr. P some statistics comparing incomes for high school graduates, college graduates, and those who did not complete high school. Mr. P was aware of his limited opportunities and did not want to see the same thing happen to his children. This allowed him to decide to support Mrs. P and Carmen with their educational hopes and he also saw the need to get his son Juan to consider his own options.

Diversity Competent Practice Actions with African American Families

In Chapter 3, we introduced the use of an Afrocentric approach in working with African American families. As with gender competent practice, there are both *what* and *how* aspects to an Afrocentric approach. *What* refers to the content and *how* refers to the process that is used. Using this approach, the worker should first become familiar with its principles and their application. The use of naturalistic inquiry with the family will help the worker to decide with the family what portions, if any, of this approach would be appropriate to use. Of particular relevance are the concepts of collective identity, connectedness, and spirituality. Some families may feel that they need to strengthen one or more of these areas.

Collective identity requires that the worker incorporate work with the family or at least consider the family in the work that is done with individual African American clients. Individual identity is tied to the family. In working with African American families, individual goals should also reflect this. The worker assists the family in mobilizing itself to meet needs and accomplish goals together. For many families, there is an important emotional aspect to this work, which intensifies their experience.

Connectedness means that working with African American families also means incorporating their community into the work. Connectedness also refers to the core of African American spirituality and worldview. All things are seen as spiritually connected. The worker explores this spirituality and connectedness with the family and helps the family to use these in the work. The worker looks for how various changes affect family members, family subsystems, and the family as a system and the relationships among these and the family's relationships with community systems. Where these relationships have broken down, he assists the family in restoring them. Where they have been weakened or are threatened, he seeks to assist the family in strengthening them. Where they do not exist, he helps the family to develop them.

Another aspect of using an Afrocentric approach involves both the history of African Americans and the history of the family itself. The worker uncovers the family's experience with prejudice, discrimination, and oppression and its awareness of the struggle for justice and equity by African Americans. The worker relates these to the family's situation and points out the family's strengths in dealing with these issues and in many ways overcoming them. At the same time, the worker also identifies barriers created by these and works with the family to overcome those barriers. This nearly always includes empowerment strategies and advocacy, which are discussed later.

Diversity Competent Practice Actions with Hispanic/Latino Families

Working with Hispanic/Latino families begins with developing an understanding of the specific cultural background of the family. As discussed in Chapter 3, Hispanic/Latino culture is quite varied. The experiences, customs, and even language of people of Mexican, Puerto Rican, Central or South American, or Cuban descent are different in some ways from each other. A language barrier between the worker and the family is one of the more common difficulties. This is mainly with newer immigrants and older members of the family. The best option for working with families that are monolingual or have limited proficiency is to use a bilingual worker. The next best option is to use a professional interpreter. Sometimes neither of these are available so the worker has to work with what is available. This might be a family member, a friend, or an indigenous worker. Children should not be used unless there is an emergency.

Another consideration in working with Hispanic/Latino families is the issue of documentation status. Recent estimates of undocumented people in the United States are about 11 million. Many of these are of Hispanic/Latino descent. In addition, Hispanic/Latino family members who are citizens or who have documentation may have relatives and family members who do not or they may have relatives and family members who wish to immigrate. Their fear is that the worker will discover those who are undocumented and he will inform the authorities. The worker is not obligated to inform authorities about undocumented clients or family members. In fact, the obligation to maintain confidentiality would prohibit this. The worker needs to make this clear to the family. Social workers should help families receive assistance that they need regardless of their citizenship or legal status. The worker should assist those who are undocumented to obtain proper documentation if possible. Social workers who routinely work with Hispanic/Latino families should be familiar with these issues and resources that are available to families.

■   ACTION TO DEVELOP RELATIONSHIPS   ■

Actions taken to develop relationships are essential to any form of family work. Relationship is the key element in working with families. Well-functioning families have healthy, well-functioning relationships. Often, direct practice actions with families as the client system or the unit of attention involve developing, repairing, restoring, or strengthening relationships among its members as either the primary need or concern or the means by which the primary need or concern will be met.

A good relationship requires the ability to do three things: (1) communicate effectively, (2) make decisions and solve problems, and (3) resolve conflict constructively. Effective communication begins with the use of "I" statements (statements that begin with the word "I"). The use of the word "we" or "we" statements are important when working with cultural groups that place a high value on family. A successful process for decision making and problem solving needs to be one that the parties agree on and results in everyone's needs being met. The ability to resolve conflict in a constructive manner is using a win–win approach, as opposed to win–lose.

In constructive conflict resolution, a willingness to negotiate and compromise is a must. The parties should stick to the issue and stay in the present, not the past. Using "I or we" statements will tend to encourage expression of feelings. "You" statements tend to create defensiveness and can easily lead to name calling and attacking the other person. These situations are related to win–lose. Changing the subject, talking about the past, attacking the other person, using or threatening violence are ways that people use to win at the other person's expense. It is crucial to avoid violence and threats of violence. The problem with win–lose in family systems is that someone has to be a loser, which does not lead to a successful family outcome.

The social worker uses her knowledge and skills in developing relationships to build a relationship with the family and to assist family members in strengthening relationships with each other. She models effective communication and teaches and guides members in communicating effectively with each other. When inappropriate or harmful interactions occur, the worker

CASE EXAMPLE

From the case example of the Perez family, the following is an example of direct practice actions to develop relationships.

Jane made a home visit for the first session after Juan and Carmen returned home to accommodate Mr. P's work schedule and to have an opportunity to observe the family's natural environment. She found that although the furnishings were older and well worn, the home was warm and comfortable. The younger children were somewhat boisterous at having a visitor. It was also a pleasure for her to meet Mrs. P's mother, Mrs. Hernandez. Jane apologized for not being bilingual and Mrs. H said that was okay, they would manage. She expressed appreciation for Jane's work in keeping Juan and Carmen safe and returning them home. Since the entire family was together, it was decided that this would be a good opportunity to have a family meeting. Jane asked Mr. P if he knew what each of his family members felt were their positive feelings about the family, and about what each of them might be concerned. Mr. P asked his wife to respond and then his mother-in-law and in turn asked each child. It was clear from their responses that there was a lot of love in the family. Concerns were more diverse, but one that seemed to be common was the arguments about Juan and Carmen's behavior. It was decided that improving communication might reduce the incidences of arguing, at least this seemed like a good place to start. Jane suggested a quick way to improve communication might be to use the words "I or we" when family members were communicating with each other. Some of the younger children chuckled at this and so Jane followed up on this by suggesting the family use a chart to keep track of it. The children noted that they had a chart on the refrigerator for chores. They laughed at the prospect of having a chart that would include their parents and grandmother. Mr. and Mrs. P and Mrs. H smiled and agreed to participate. Jane spent some time helping each family member practice using "I or we" statements and working on how to remind each other in a respectful way.

helps those involved to restructure the interaction. For instance, calling someone a derogatory name generally occurs because the person is angry. The worker asks the person what he was thinking and feeling before he called the other person a name. As the reasons for the name calling emerge, the worker asks for a direct statement about the person's real feelings using "I" statements. The person might say, "I feel hurt and angry because. . . ." Behind negative interaction in families is unmet need. Family members need positive relationships to grow and develop and succeed. Good communication skills, an effective decision-making/problem-solving process, and constructive conflict resolution are necessary for maintaining positive relationships.

■   ACTIONS TAKEN TO ENABLE UNDERSTANDING   ■
OF PERSON IN ENVIRONMENT AND PLANNING

Actions to enable the family to use the change process include helping them to use assessment and planning whenever they have needs or concerns. Helping families to learn to use the change process is important for their long-term success in meeting needs. This approach should be included mainly when the family (or subsystem) is the client system. When a family develops a better understanding of itself and its environment, it has learned the first step in the change process—assessment. This understanding allows the family to change the interactions between itself or its members and the environment. In an ecosystems strengths approach, need represents an imbalance in the transactions in the ecosystem. Changing the transactions is necessary to meet the need. Understanding the ecosystem is critical to restoring balance and meeting need. It helps the family identify strengths and resources within the family system and in the environment.

Understanding family in environment is the foundation for successful planning. Families can learn planning skills as they work together on resolving the current situation. Teaching planning skills is an important direct practice action with all client systems. The actions that follow can be learned in order to facilitate implementation of plans the family formulates and to remove barriers.

■   ACTION TO ENABLE FAMILIES TO   ■
USE AVAILABLE RESOURCES

For some families the major block to meeting need is a lack of resources. Sometimes these resources are available, but the family is not aware of or does not know how to use them. Sometimes the resource is not responsive to some families. In a complex and diverse society, not all resources are amenable to all clients. One part of the generalist social worker's understanding of a community is knowing which resources can meet the needs of which clients. An important part of the social worker's interventive repertoire is the ability to match the family with resources and to enable the family to use the available resources.

Enabling families to know and use resources is especially important when working with diverse families. Experiences with prejudice and discrimination often results in families becoming marginalized and isolated. Members of diverse groups may not be aware of resources or may not feel welcome in using them. The way in which resources are made available or services delivered may not fit with the culture or diversity of the family. In practice with diverse families, the social worker uses naturalistic inquiry to find out what the family knows about resources that are available. She explores experiences that the family has had or has heard from others regarding the use of those resources. She incorporates this into the actions she takes in enabling the family to use resources.

To help families use the available resources, workers should have knowledge and skill in four areas: (1) knowledge of the service delivery systems of the community in which they practice and the community in which the family lives and functions, (2) knowledge of and skill in the use of the referral process, (3) knowledge of the appropriate use of the broker and advocate roles and skill in filling these roles, and (4) knowledge of how to empower families to take charge of their life situation. The social worker takes action to enable families to use available resources, with the purpose of enabling families to meet their needs and thus enhance their social functioning and coping capacity.

The Service Delivery System

When identifying components of the service delivery system, workers usually begin by identifying social service agencies and services provided by other professionals. A broader view needs to be considered. Within many neighborhoods, communities, and ethnic groups, a helping network outside the formal system exists. This **natural helping system** becomes known to social workers as they come into contact with diverse clients and groups in the community. There is, however, much to be learned about how to work cooperatively with this system.

The natural helping system is made up of a client's family, friends, and coworkers. These are the people to whom a person in need goes for help first. When clients come to a social worker, they have probably first tried to get help from these natural helpers. The use of the natural helping system has particular importance in working with diverse cultural groups. Past experiences with discrimination and oppression has led many people of color to rely on systems in their immediate environment for assistance. Often the relationship between the client and this system may need to be strengthened or restored or the systems themselves may need to be strengthened and supported in providing help. Social workers can sometimes strengthen or support the natural helping attempts rather than take over the helping function completely. The extended family has always been an important part of the helping system for many ethnic groups and in small towns and rural areas. For example, among Native Americans the extended family is so important that if a social worker fails to involve this system in the planning process, the family may not be able to use any help offered. Ross Speck and Carolyn Attneave have developed a method of working with extended families called network therapy, or **networking,** which involves and supports the extended family in helping a family member in need.[1] A **network** is an association of systems that operates through mutual resource sharing.

The work of Eugene Litwak and Ivan Szelenyi supports the use of family, neighbors, and kin as a helping resources.[2] They consider neighborhood ties to be useful because of the speed of response to need. With such ties, the person seeking help has personal, immediately available contact. The person in need is continually observed, and help is provided quickly when situations change. Family or kin are particularly helpful because of the long-term relationships that exists. For example, they are a resource for the care of children when a parent dies or when individuals face long-term medical care or institutionalization. Friendship networks are useful because of the strong emotional element and aspect of free choice.

Also part of the natural helping network are natural helpers in the community, community benefits, and self-help groups. **Natural helpers,** sometimes called indigenous helpers or healers, are those persons who possess helping skills and exercise them in the context of mutual relationships. These are usually individuals who make helping a part of their everyday life. They are hardworking people who are optimistic about being able to change; mature, friendly people who often have had the same needs as those they are helping; trustworthy people who keep confidences; and people who are available and share a sense of mutuality with others. They usually have had similar life experiences and have similar values as the person they are helping. Members of neighborhoods, small communities, or ethnic groups usually know who these people are. For example, in the Hispanic community the *curandero* is considered the indigenous healer to be consulted when someone needs mental or medical treatment. However, it is often difficult for professional people to identify these healers without help from those who are a part of the community system.

Alice Collins and Diane Pancoast have discussed effective methods for working with natural helpers.[3] They believe that social workers should not try to train natural helpers or make them paraprofessionals. Rather, social workers should recognize natural helpers as valuable resources and support them in their unique ways of helping. This requires recognition of natural helpers' capacity and competence to help and calls for a consultative relationship.

Community benefits, fundraising events organized for someone who has had a catastrophe such as a fire, illness, or death of a family member, is another example of the natural helping system at work. Many cultural groups are more comfortable with this form of support than with support from a formal organization. The challenge to the worker is to use organizational skills in working with the family's native community while at the same time ensuring that leadership and responsibility for the benefit reside in the culture. Some of the suggested guidelines that follow concern working with natural helping systems.

Self-help groups may also be considered a part of the natural helping system. Mutual aid is related to the responsibility people feel for one another. One means of carrying out this responsibility is the voluntary small group, often of spontaneous origin, that develops for people who have similar problems. Groups are important in developing connectedness to others at a time when isolation may be experienced. They are useful in encouraging growth and redefinition of self. Some also work for change regarding social issues that affect group members. In these groups those who have lived through problems help those who currently experience the problem. Help is given by modeling, positive reinforcement, and emphasis on the here and now. These groups can be used with individual family members or with the family as a whole. Examples of such groups are Alcoholics Anonymous, Alanon and Alateen, cancer support groups, and life-transition groups such as widow-to-widow groups.[4]

The relationship between self-help groups and formal human service organizations is often problematic because each has different ways of functioning. Such variables as the client group on which service is focused, the need for resources outside the system, and the relationship of helper to those receiving help usually differ significantly. Also, relationships among self-help groups and human service organizations vary. Yeheskel Hasenfeld and Benjamin Gidron have identified five relational patterns: competition, referral, coordination, coalition, and co-optation. The ideal relationship would be one of coordination or coalition.[5] Regardless of relational patterns, to maximize the use of self-help groups, social workers must be aware of the relational pattern that exists and, when appropriate, work to facilitate a different pattern.

In working with all natural helping systems, social workers must be aware that these systems are primary groups that use informal, personal means of interaction. Attempting to work with natural helping systems using the strategies and techniques of formal bureaucratic systems often blocks any meaningful interaction or coordination. Two results that can occur are as follows: (1) The natural helping system may stop helping and allow the formal system to do the helping; in this situation the natural helping system is destroyed. (2) The natural helping system may withdraw from the formal system and go underground; in this situation the social worker is unable to coordinate and cooperate, and the two systems may offer help that does not allow the family to use both systems effectively. The consultative, enabling stance seems to be the most appropriate approach to functioning with natural helping systems. Social workers must be creative in linking formal and informal networks if the assistance of the natural helping system is to be maximized. It is most important to maintain communication without interfering with the functioning of either the formal or informal systems.

The formal service delivery system includes not only social service agencies but also organizations that either have an interest in specific projects or have resources for their members. The American Legion may be able to provide certain resources for a veteran or his family, particularly if that veteran is a member of the organization. The Lions Club has concerned itself with visual problems and might help in obtaining glasses for a client. Other organizations may have resources, such as used clothing stores, that can provide necessary items for families. The social worker should be aware of these organizational resources.

To help families use the resources of various community institutions and professionals, the social worker needs a good understanding of the available services and resources and how to access these resources. Acquaintance with other professionals, such as teachers, ministers, and doctors, can help the worker learn of resources. Skill in coordination, consultation, and team functioning is often important in helping families use resources.

Service delivery by social service agencies takes different forms. Agencies use many kinds of workers to deliver different services. MSWs often deliver clinical services; BSWs are used in many ways to support families and family members, to help with meeting needs, and to provide concrete services; paraprofessionals may be used to provide some services. Indigenous workers, who are skilled in working with their particular cultural groups, are another resource. Although they often have no formal education relative to social work, indigenous workers have knowledge of the sociocultural group being helped. Homemaker or chore services may be provided by paraprofessionals or indigenous workers. Volunteers provide some services.

Service may be provided in an agency office only or by outreach to people in need. Agencies may provide only counseling or clinical social work, or they may provide concrete services or resources such as food or money. Some agencies station workers in small communities or in neighborhoods not easily accessible to the main office. Others use a "circuit-riding" approach to servicing clients in remote areas. In this approach, the worker visits an area on a scheduled frequency to meet with clients. With limited populations or for some highly specialized services, the client leaves the community to obtain service. Social workers must have knowledge of how agencies deliver services and what resources they have if they are to help families find needed resources. Some agencies may not deliver services in a manner that is usable by some families. Workers need to be aware of agency limitations so that they do not add to clients' frustration by referring them to services that are unattainable or institutions that are unresponsive.

The first step in enabling families to use resources is a thorough knowledge of the resources available. The second step is choosing the appropriate resource for the family. This choice is based on matching family needs and lifestyle with a resource that can meet the needs in a manner congruent with the family's lifestyle and culture. Family involvement in the choice is essential for matching and linking the family to the resource. In addition, workers may use indirect practice strategies to work for change in the relational patterns characterizing segments of the service delivery system so that client need can be better met. (See Chapter 8.)

Referral

Referral is the process by which a social worker enables a family to know and use another resource. In addition, the referral process involves supplying the referral agency with information that may be helpful in providing service to the family and then following up on the usefulness of the service to the family. The worker must obtain written permission from the family, usually called a release of information, before sharing any identifying information about the family with an outside service.

Referral is used when the family's needs cannot be met by services provided by the agency that employs the worker or when a more appropriate service is provided by another agency. The worker uses knowledge of the potential resources and knowledge of the way service is delivered to match potential clients and potential services so that the service is acceptable to and usable by clients. The referral service may be used in conjunction with the service a worker is providing or as the primary service.

Referrals are made only with permission of the family. The worker and family discuss the potential service, and the worker helps the family make the initial contact with the new agency, if necessary. This can be done by giving a phone number or directions for reaching the agency or by making suggestions about how to approach the agency. Sometimes it is helpful for a worker to call the agency for the family or go to the agency with the family for the first contact. The worker must make sure the family has the resources needed to access and utilize the service, including transportation, access to a telephone, financial resources, and daycare.

The worker and family also discuss the information that would be helpful to the agency. After receiving the family's permission and obtaining a written release of information, a worker provides this information to the worker at the new agency. It is often helpful if the two workers know each other and can discuss the family's needs.

An often-overlooked final step in referral is follow-up. In determining whether the family is receiving the services sought, the worker gains information about the appropriateness of the service for the family and other families who may have similar needs. This enables the worker to make appropriate referrals in the future. If the family has not been able to use the service, the worker must advocate for the family or assist them in receiving the needed service elsewhere or determine why they were unable to use the service. Skill in referral is a necessary tool for all social workers.[6]

Broker and Advocate Roles

In enabling families to use available resources, two primary roles are used: the broker role and the advocate role. It is important for the social worker to understand the difference between these two roles and to choose the one most appropriate to the situation. The **broker** helps a person or family get needed services. This includes assessing the situation, knowing the alternative resources, preparing and counseling the person or family, contacting the appropriate service, and ensuring that the family gets to the resource and uses it.[7] The goal is to expedite the linkage of family to the needed resource. This involves giving information and support, teaching families how to use resources, and negotiating with the agency.

The role of advocate consists of "pleading and fighting for services for clients whom the service system would otherwise reject."[8] For example, a lesbian couple may be denied housing because of their relationship, or a family member with HIV or AIDS may be denied medical treatment. The worker as advocate seeks different interpretations or exceptions to rules and regulations, points out clients' rights to services, and removes blocks to receiving or using an agency's services.

Advocacy might be considered an indirect practice action because the unit of attention is not the client system. It is included here because it is so important in ensuring that the family receive the services that it needs and for which it is eligible. In addition, the worker takes the opportunity to teach family members how to advocate for themselves. It is especially important for parents as the adults in the family to learn how to do this for themselves, their children, and the family system.

In the advocacy role, the worker speaks on behalf of the family. Before engaging in advocacy, a worker must first be sure that the family desires the worker to intervene in this manner. Then the worker must carefully assess the risks involved for the family if advocacy is used. This includes consideration that any action taken might cause problems for the family or block access to the resources. The family should clearly understand the risks involved and be motivated to use the service if it is obtained. Case advocacy, advocacy for a single family, is most effective when used to obtain concrete resources for which the family is eligible. It is also useful when people and systems impinge on a family's functioning. To be a case advocate, social workers must be comfortable with conflict situations and knowledgeable about the means for conflict management. They must be willing to negotiate and be aware of the value of withdrawing application for service if the best interests of the family are not being served. Families must have considerable trust in the worker before they will be willing to allow the worker to advocate for them.

The worker uses the advocate role only when the broker role is not effective. Whenever possible, it is better for the family to act on their own behalf in order to strengthen their belief in themselves as well as gain a sense of empowerment. There are times, however, when an advocate stance must be taken in order to enable families to obtain needed services. *Cause advocacy* is used to serve groups with similar difficulties. Both case and cause advocacy are important actions on behalf of families who are members of populations that are at risk of prejudice, discrimination, and oppression. Case advocacy is used when barriers to resources and services exist for individual clients. Cause advocacy addresses issues on a larger scale. Mediation with the family and the environment as an alternative to advocacy is discussed in Chapter 8.

■   ACTION TO EMPOWER AND ENABLE FAMILIES   ■

Empowerment and enabling involve validation of feelings, positive reinforcement, feedback, assertiveness, and cognitive and behavioral change. The family can learn to use these actions to build strong members. These actions are primarily used when the family is the client system and the unit of attention in the change process. The most powerful validation, reinforcement, and feedback come from one's parents. The fundamental basis for good self-esteem is love and acceptance from one's parents. Unconditional love for being, not doing, allows the child to internalize unconditional acceptance of himself or herself as a human being who has worth. This is not unconditional acceptance of the child's behavior. It is the parent's responsibility to socialize the child so that he learns what is acceptable and not acceptable behavior. The message is, "I love you as a person no matter what you or I feel, think, or do. However, your behavior is a separate matter. I do not have to love or even like your behavior and neither does anyone else." The worker helps the parent to use validation and reinforcement and feedback to build healthy self-esteem in the child while also shaping appropriate behavior. She also helps the family to appropriately use cognitive and behavioral change strategies in meeting each others' needs.

Empowerment

Most clients can benefit from being able to take an active role in changing the situations impinging on their functioning. Empowerment is "a process of increasing personal, interpersonal, or political power so that individuals can take action to improve their life situation."[9]

From the case example of the Perez family, the following is an example of direct practice actions to enable families to use resources.

In referring Mr. and Mrs. P along with their son Juan and their daughter Carmen to Catholic Family Services, Jane recognized the need to find a resource for providing family counseling that could also fit with the family's spirituality. In addition, Jane agreed to work with the school regarding resolving situations there that were difficult for Juan and Carmen. She was able to obtain information regarding the co-op program for Juan but met with resistance regarding Carmen's experience of being ridiculed about her dark hair and complexion. It appeared that the school personnel were downplaying the importance of dealing with the situation. Jane was able to make an appointment with the principal about Carmen's situation. Jane pointed out that this was clearly a violation of the school district's antidiscrimination policies and could result in suspensions. He agreed and referred Jane and the family to the assistant principal who was responsible for discipline and for maintaining the school's antidiscrimination policy. Jane went with Mrs. P and Carmen to discuss the situation. Carmen was concerned that if the girls were suspended things would get worse. The assistant principal suggested that they try the peer mediation program that the school sponsored. They agreed to try it.

Juan's situation was complicated by the requirement that students have a 3.0 average to be in the high school co-op program and be a junior. Juan had an average above that before he started skipping and letting his grades slip. He was also too young to get a job in fast food or retail. When Jane met with Juan and his family, she discussed this option with him but indicated that he would have to wait until next year and in the meantime he would have to get his grades back up. He agreed to try and also indicated that he had gone on a class visit to the skill center and was very interested in a program that trained students in computer graphics for mechanical and architectural design. He would need to maintain a 2.5 average and could co-op through the skill center with a local business his senior year if he made it into the program and completed his junior year. He seemed very excited about this. Jane pointed out the need to have a good math background and Juan admitted that he had let his math skills slide, not seeing much use for math. Jane said she would look into arranging for a tutor through the school. Juan was concerned about how it would look if he had a tutor. Jane said there should be a way to be discreet about it. Jane felt that Juan's trouble in the community would probably be taken care of by ensuring that he was involved in positive activities at school and had an opportunity to work.

When Mr. and Mrs. P decided that Mrs. P would look into going to work or finishing school, they asked Jane where to start. Because Mrs. P was older and had not worked outside of the home, Jane thought that finishing school or getting a GED might be the best option first. She noted that the local community college had a GED preparation program that was computerized so people could start any time and work on their own. Mr. and Mrs. P noted that their computer was very old and they did not have Internet access in their home. Jane explained that Mrs. P could use a computer at the library or at the college. She also connected Mrs. P with a program at the college for returning homemakers. They were able to get her an inexpensive recycled computer that the college made available to students. Mrs. P decided to work on getting her GED by the next spring and then looking for work through the homemakers program at the college.

In this example Jane connected the family with a number of community resources and acted as a broker in doing so. She acted as an advocate on Carmen's behalf when the school personnel initially failed to respond to her concerns. Jane explored resources, identified eligibility requirements, made referrals, and coordinated services.

Empowerment has been suggested as a strategy of choice when working with members of minority groups, populations at risk, and women.[10] Empowerment is particularly useful in the contemporary world in which power is an all-pervasive issue and in which the gap between haves and have-nots is growing dramatically. Empowerment means providing clients with the supports, skills, and understanding needed to allow them to take charge of their own lives and use their power in situations in which they have felt powerless.

Those caught in feelings or situations of powerlessness often lack knowledge of how to negotiate systems, feel hopeless that any change is possible, and may lack the self-esteem necessary for engaging in change activity. Empowerment involves assisting clients in negotiating systems. It involves motivating, teaching, and raising self-esteem so clients believe they are competent individuals with the skills needed for negotiating community systems and that they deserve the resources necessary for healthy social functioning. Empowerment enables clients to receive the benefits of society and increases their capacity to work toward resolving the conditions preventing them from providing for their needs.

According to Ruth J. Parsons, a literature search confirms that the important ingredients of an empowerment strategy are support, mutual aid, and validation of the client's perceptions and experiences. When these ingredients are present, there is a heightened degree of self-esteem, more self-confidence, and a greater capacity to make changes or take action. An empowerment strategy calls for building collectives; working with others in similar situations; educating for critical thinking through support, mutual aid, and collective action; and competency assessment, or identification of strengths and coping skills.[11]

Thus, the use of groups, particularly mutual aid groups, enhances this action strategy. Silvia Staub-Bernasconi pointed this out and called for a focus on consciousness development, social and coping skills training, networking, and mediation. Also, empowerment calls for work with power sources and power structures.[12] This strategy is congruent with the generalist social work model presented in this text. The strong emphasis on maximal family involvement in assessment, planning, and action to meet goals is an important ingredient of empowerment. Teaching families about meeting needs and about the nature of the systems in their environment is a part of empowerment.

A technique useful in an empowerment strategy is consciousness raising, which involves giving the family information about the nature of the situation, particularly the various environmental forces affecting family functioning. This work can heighten family member's understanding of self in relationship to others. Workers must feel comfortable with the anger that can result from using this technique and be able to help families use anger in ways that further the work at hand. When the time is appropriate, it is also important for the worker to help family members move beyond anger into other responses. It is hoped that the family can gain a more realistic view of the situation and then take advantage of change possibilities.

Groups are powerful adjuncts to consciousness raising. It is helpful for family members to see others struggle with new understandings and to see the work of a group be of benefit. The group can be involved in collective action and thus enhance a sense of individual power. The group can also be a support system for mutual aid. Participation in a group can lead to enhanced self-esteem and can help family members learn new skills. Conciousness raising can also be used within the family system. As members tell their stories and share their perceptions and as parents and elders share the family heritage with younger members, new understandings can emerge about the family and its culture.

The nature of the relationship between worker and family is an important consideration when using this strategy. Using an empowerment approach requires establishing mutual respect, building on family strengths, sharing information and knowledge of resources in a sense of partnership, and considering the family as the "expert" on their own situation. Because the worker may be viewed as yet another person with power over the family, the social worker needs to act as a colleague or a member of the family rather than as a detached professional. This requires the worker to shift his frame of reference from that of an expert to that of a collaborator.[13] As the worker demonstrates belief in the family and points out competencies, the family will gain a sense of value and worth and a belief that they have the ability to bring about change.

Another valuable technique that can be an adjunct to an empowerment strategy is work focused on reducing self-blame and blame within the family system. The family needs to see that the difficulties they are facing often have their source in the functioning of systems in the environment or in the functioning of the family as a system. The worker can help the family take responsibility for changing the environment by teaching specific skills for environmental change. Although the worker may also work for environmental change through advocacy and mobilization of resources, it is important that the family participate; otherwise, the feelings of inadequacy may be further reinforced.[14]

Empowerment is not a strategy that is used in isolation from other strategies. Instead it aims to reduce helplessness so that families can take charge of their lives.

Enabling

Enabling or helping families reach their goals may seem similar to empowerment, but there are subtle differences. **Enabling,** the broader term, refers to helping a family carry out an activity otherwise not possible. This term recently has taken on negative connotations when used with regard to alcohol and other addictions. For example, a spouse whose actions support the addictive behaviors of the partner is often called an enabler. As used in this text, enabling has a positive connotation in that the action being supported is desirable.

Sometimes in the process of empowering or enabling the family or its members, the worker may need to work directly with the family members to enhance positive thinking and actions. Often, the family member has had experiences that reinforce a negative view of herself or her situation. She may be frustrated or may have learned that it is safer to predict failure than to hope for success. The family member may blame herself or others for the situation or be blamed by the family. She may engage in self-defeating thoughts or actions. When the worker senses that this is happening, he can assist the family or family member in changing thoughts or actions so that the member can successfully meet goals and carry out the plan. The thinking part of this strategy is called a cognitive approach or intervention. The action part refers to behavior. Some theorists have combined these two approaches into what is called a *cognitive–behavioral approach.*[15]

The basic idea behind this approach is that thoughts lead to feelings and behavior. Negative thoughts lead to negative feelings and negative reactions, and positive thoughts lead to positive feelings and positive behavior. The BSW-level social worker is not generally trained to use this approach in a clinical model of practice. However, it is important to be able to work with the family member to develop positive thinking and actions as she carries out the plan. The plan contains behaviors that the family or its members have agreed to do. These behaviors are stated in the objectives and tasks. If the family member does not think she can accomplish something, she is unlikely to do so. The worker asks the member what she thinks about the situation and about the proposed goals, objectives, and tasks. The worker listens for thoughts that might be barriers to success. The worker helps the family member to see how her thinking can have either a positive or a negative influence on carrying out the plan. A good set questions to ask are as follows: (1) What do you think will happen if you do this? or What were you thinking when that happened? (2) What do you want to have happen? (3) What could you do to make that happen today? This week? This month? (or Next time?) (4) What could you tell yourself that would make you feel more confident in doing that? (5) What kind of payoff or reward could you identify that would help you to remember to do that?

An important technique in empowering or enabling clients that uses a cognitive–behavioral approach is assertiveness training. In this technique, the worker assists the family member to become more assertive about meeting her needs. The worker will generally engage in practicing and role-playing assertive behaviors in situations in which the family member needs to advocate for herself. It is important that the worker help her differentiate between assertiveness and aggressiveness. Assertiveness is the positive expression of oneself and is marked by the use of statements that begin with "I." Aggressiveness is imposing one's thoughts or feelings on others and is generally marked by statements that begin with "You."

Sometimes families need to be able to use a behavioral approach in their relationships with others or within the family. This is especially valuable for parents who need to influence their children's behavior. This is covered in greater detail in Chapter 12. Social workers are generally uncomfortable using negative reinforcement or punishment to modify behavior because doing so usually violates social work values and ethics. In addition, family members may have experienced a great deal of punishment and negative reinforcement in their lives. The use of extinction and positive reinforcement tends not to be a violation of social work values and ethics. Basically, **extinction** involves ignoring an undesirable behavior to eliminate it. The parent should be warned that the initial response of the child will be to increase the behavior in order to receive the customary attention. However, persistently using this technique generally results in the desired goal.

Positive reinforcement is giving a reward for or recognizing the desired behavior. Parents can give positive reinforcement whenever they observe the desired behavior, or they can make an agreement beforehand with the child to reward certain behavior. The strongest reinforcements are those that are identified by the person receiving them. If a reinforcement is given too frequently, it is more likely to change the behavior more quickly, but the strength of the reinforcement tends not to last very long. On the other hand, if the reinforcement is infrequent or seen as unattainable, it will have little impact on changing behavior. Sometimes a smaller reward or a symbol can be used on a more frequent basis and a larger reward given less often. An example of this would be a star chart where the child receives a star that he can put on a chart for each day of the week. When he earns enough stars, he is rewarded with a toy. In this way the stars serve as positive reinforcement on a day-to-day basis, and the toy serves as a longer-term reward.

Positive feedback is a form of positive reinforcement that is extremely important in developing and maintaining positive relationships. Family members may not have received much positive support in their lives. Thus, they may not be able to give much positive support. Whenever the worker sees dissatisfaction with a relationship, she should look for the absence of positive feedback. The worker can suggest ways to give positive feedback and ways to receive it. Generally, giving positive feedback results in getting positive feedback in return, although this may take some time if the other person has become accustomed to negative feedback or no feedback at all. Feedback is an important part of parenting. Parents need to give consistent messages about the behavior they expect from their children and then follow up with positive or negative feedback. Positive feedback tends to be the strongest form of reinforcement a parent can give a child.

Actions that assist family members to engage in positive thinking and positive behavior are important to empowering and enabling them. The ability to be assertive may be needed for the member to advocate or speak up for herself. Positive reinforcement and feedback are essential to good parenting and to developing and maintaining successful relationships. The worker incorporates these tools into her work in empowering and enabling families to carry out their plans.

■   ACTION IN RESPONSE TO CRISIS   ■

Frequently, the family is in a crisis when the service is initiated. Unmet need can create a crisis situation. In systems theory, when one part of the system experiences stress or unmet need, it affects other parts of the system. Situations in which families may experience a crisis include financial woes, health problems, relationship difficulties, trouble with the law, and the like.

CASE EXAMPLE

From the case example of the Perez family, the following is an example of actions to empower and enable.

■ Action to Empower and Enable

As Jane worked with the Perez family, she allowed them to take the lead in identifying their needs and assisted them in meeting those needs. She helped to empower Mrs. P in pursuing her desire to finish school and obtain employment. She empowered Mr. P to make a decision about supporting his wife in doing this in a way that felt comfortable for him culturally. She worked at empowering and enabling Juan and Carmen to be successful at school. She was able to get the family mobilized in improving their relationships in a way that made them feel good about their family. Jane also was able to get them to replace some of their negative interactions with more positive ones. She helped Mrs. P become more assertive. She could also have helped Mr. and Mrs. P to get better responses from the children by using positive reinforcement and positive feedback.

During a crisis, the family's normal coping mechanisms are overwhelmed. The worker helps the family to restore its coping abilities by developing and working on a plan that will meet needs and resolve the crisis. When faced with a crisis, there are two types of families: those that pull together and those that pull apart. Of course, nearly every family wants to be one that pulls together. The idea of pulling together can be used as a motivation for change. When inappropriate or destructive actions occur, the worker can ask how those fit or contribute to the family pulling together. He can follow this up with a discussion of what actions would do this.

Families use many coping mechanisms as well as the resources of the natural helping systems and community institutions before coming to a social worker. They often are under considerable stress and may be in a state of crisis. If the family or a family member is in a state of crisis, it is important that the social worker be able to recognize this situation and respond appropriately. Crisis intervention is a model of social work practice that provides a knowledge base and guidelines for crisis response. All generalist social workers should develop knowledge of and skill in working with people in crisis. The major goal of action in response to crisis (*crisis intervention*) is resolution of the crisis and restored social functioning. If, after this goal is reached, the worker and the family then decide there is some other goal they want to work on together, another kind of action is taken.

Recognizing Crisis

A **crisis** exists when a stressful situation or a precipitating event causes a system such as an individual or family to develop a state of disequilibrium, or to lose its steady state. Coping mechanisms that have worked in past situations no longer work, despite a considerable struggle to cope. A person or family continually in a state of disorganization is not in crisis; working with such a situation requires a different kind of action.

Crisis is usually a part of the life experience of all people. Workers seeing clients in crisis should assume that these people were functioning adequately before the crisis event and should view the helping role as restorative rather than remedial. It is important not to base an assessment of clients' normal ability to function on the behaviors and coping mechanisms displayed during the crisis.

A crisis situation can develop because of situational and developmental factors. Situational factors include illness of the individual or close family members, death of a close family member, separation or divorce, change of living situation or lifestyle, and loss of a job. These situational factors call either for assuming new roles and responsibilities or for changing the established way of functioning with others. Sometimes these factors cause considerable stress only temporarily; after a period of instability and trying new coping methods, the result is a new and comfortable way of functioning. At other times, an additional stressful situation precipitates the crisis situation.

Developmental stress arises from the unsettled or stressful feelings that may occur as families or family members move from one developmental stage to another. This movement requires new ways of functioning. Adolescence is a time of stress, a time of new concerns and a time when needs may not be fulfilled. As young persons learn to deal with their sexual drives, make career decisions, and develop new relationships with parents, they may become overwhelmed and crisis can develop. Families may also experience a crisis as they move from one stage to another. The birth of the first child calls for new patterns of social functioning, thus creating additional stress and sometimes crisis.

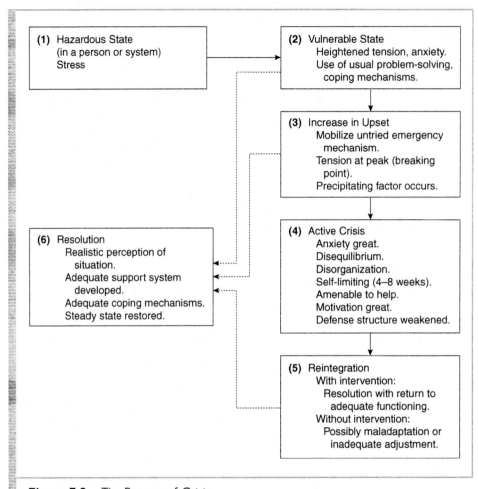

Figure 7.2 The Process of Crisis
Note: Dotted line indicates that Resolution can occur after states 2, 3, or 5.

Figure 7.2 provides an overall view of the crisis process. The hazardous state, the vulnerable state, and increase in upset are precrisis states that are often resolved by the usual means of coping and help from personal support systems. When these means do not bring about resolution, people can move into a crisis state, and crisis intervention becomes an appropriate strategy for action.

Responding to Crisis

When working with families or family members in crisis, the worker needs to be aware of the time element of crisis. The true crisis situation generally lasts a maximum of four to eight weeks. After that time people find new ways of **coping.** Without appropriate help during the crisis stage, the result may be a reduced capacity for effective social functioning. Thus, help for people in crisis must be immediate and sometimes fairly intensive.

The worker has two crucial tasks: (1) to develop an understanding about the person or family in crisis and what precipitated the crisis and (2) to develop the helping relationship. In developing an understanding, the worker searches for the precipitating event—the event that pushed the person or family into crisis—as well as the nature of the underlying stressful situation. The worker also determines what the family has tried to do to resolve the stress (the coping mechanisms used) and encourages the family to share how they feel about the situation.

The worker forms a helping relationship by actively responding to the family's concern or need. Together they explore the situation and determine the reality of the family's perceptions. The worker supports the family's strengths by acknowledging the coping attempts and makes specific suggestions for other means of coping. The worker shares with the family her understanding of the situation. The worker communicates realistic hope that the crisis can be resolved and that she will help the family through this difficult time. Family members are encouraged to express feelings about the situation. The worker is sensitive to the family's anxiety and to the possibility of depression in family members. If excessive anxiety or depression develops, the worker helps the family seek the services of a competent mental health professional. The worker also links the family to other needed resources.

Through the work together in the four- to eight-week period of crisis, the family usually discovers new coping mechanisms, and the crisis is resolved. In the latter part of this period, the worker can often enhance the family's problem-solving and coping skills and thus prevent future crises. Working with families in an intensive, fairly directive manner during the crisis helps prevent future social-functioning difficulties and restores the family to a state in which they can manage in an effective manner.

When family systems experience crisis, generally there are certain members that experience the crisis more intensely than others. The worker supports those members who are coping better to assist those family members who are not coping so well. Often the crisis in families revolves around relationship difficulties. When this occurs, the worker focuses the work on those relationships but also uses relationships that are functioning well as strengths in resolving these difficulties. She does this by identifying what is working well and what it will take to use these skills in rebuilding, repairing or restoring the relationships that are at risk.

CASE EXAMPLE

■ Action in Response to Crisis

The interview that is used as a case example in Chapter 4 is a good example of direct practice actions in response to crisis. (See the case example of an interview with the Perez family in Chapter 4). The family was in a crisis over the tension between Juan and Carmen and their parents, which reached a head with the childrens' truancy from home. Jane was able to get them to express their feelings and reach at least a temporary resolution that allowed the teens to return home.

ACTION THAT IS SUPPORTIVE

Support has been a universal part of helping. As Lois Selby accurately put it, "It is as old as man's humanity to man."[16] Supportive means are a part of every generalist social worker's repertoire, yet support is a concept that has received little attention in social work literature. Beulah Roberts Compton pointed out that social work attitudes toward support historically have limited its use to chronic clients or to those for whom no other treatment is possible.[17] There is a prevailing notion that support is hardly worth the social worker's time. This notion seems to have developed as social workers emulated psychiatry and its worldview.

Support is an important aspect of healthy family functioning. Most of us place a high value on having the support of our family. When we have it, we feel that we can face almost anything. When we do not, we may despair or look to others to make up for the loss. Support may be used when the family is the client system or the unit of attention. When working with individual clients, especially those in crisis, establishing support from the family is often a vital action.

For couples, having the support of one's spouse or significant other makes all the difference in the world. Sharing a life together means sharing happiness and unhappiness. When couples are at odds with each other, they are using their power and energy against each other instead of using it to deal with life's challenges. The worker shows them how disagreements can be used to either weaken or strengthen their relationship. Unresolved issues and destructive interactions will weaken it. Constructive conflict resolution can strengthen it. The couple can feel a deeper understanding and appreciation of each other when they successfully face an issue together. Commitment to the relationship will be stronger as a result. In the end, a disagreement can be seen as an opportunity to demonstrate one's love by allowing the other person to have his or her way. However, this must be done with no strings attached; otherwise, it will be manipulation.

Florence Hollis identified sustainment as one of the procedures of social work practice.[18] Her use of the term *sustainment* seems very close to the notion of support and is primarily expressed by nonverbal means. Hollis identified some of the components or techniques of sustainment as expression of the client's abilities and competencies, expression of interest, desire to help, understanding of a client's situation and feelings about that situation, and use of encouragement and reassurance. Reassurance should be realistic. Emphasis should be on the feeling component and support for the acceptability of having feelings about the situation of concern.

Contemporary social work sees support as an acceptable function. Social work literature recognizes the use of support as a means of helping people cope with difficult situations and thus grow. However, little has been written that identifies the nature of support; there seems to be an assumption that social workers know what support is. The use of support seems to be an idea in the domain of practice wisdom of social work knowledge.

Judith Nelson defined supportive procedures as "those intended to help clients feel better, stronger, or more comfortable in some immediate way."[19] She has identified four kinds of support: (1) *protection,* which includes giving directions and advice, setting limits, and giving structure to complex or overwhelming situations; (2) *acceptance,* which includes making clients aware that the worker is with them in their struggles, confirming the worth of the person, and communicating understanding of clients' feelings and situations; (3) *validation,* which includes showing clients ways they are effective and competent persons, giving feedback, providing hope, communicating praise and approval, and encouraging clients in their coping efforts and role performance; and (4) *education,* which includes teaching clients how to cope and function effectively, providing needed information, socializing clients to new roles, and helping clients develop self-knowledge. One of the ways of teaching is modeling effective methods of coping.

Not only is Nelson's classification useful for identifying what support will best meet a client's needs, it also is important in identifying which aspects of a client's functioning the worker desires to support. Two other useful ways to identify the specific area of social functioning that needs support might be in terms of coping tasks or life roles. Using the coping-task approach, the worker identifies the task or tasks a client confronts when coping with a life situation (e.g., acceptance of the limitations of chronic illness). Using the life-role approach, the worker identifies the client's limitations, difficulties, and strengths in carrying out a life role. For example, if the client has difficulty following through with disciplinary procedures as a parent, the worker might first note areas in which the client does follow through, such as meal preparation. The worker then helps the client determine what skills she uses to complete that task and teaches her how to use the same motivations and skills when disciplining her child. This approach builds on the client's strengths rather than weaknesses and reinforces the idea that the client has problem-solving skills useful in various situations.

When using support as an interventive strategy, the worker identifies the family's need (as in all social work practice). This assessment emphasizes the family's perception of the situation and the family's realistic expectations in attempting to fulfill the need. Feelings of threat or deprivation are particularly important to note. The assessment should also consider the family's capacity for hope, the family's strengths, and the support the environment can provide.

The worker then decides what behaviors and attitudes can be supported to enable the family to get the need met. A decision is made about the specific kind of support to provide. Sometimes it is useful to provide the family with concrete resources or tangible services as a means of demonstrating the worker's care and concern. Using a supportive approach, the worker tries to develop a climate for helping that is accepting, understanding, comfortable, and validating and in which the family feels free to discuss concerns and feelings openly. The worker expresses interest and concern, encourages and praises the client for appropriate efforts, expresses realistic confidence in the family's ability to cope and to carry out life tasks, guides the family, and provides needed structure for the family's work.

Problems can arise from the inappropriate use of support. For one thing, there is always a danger that the family will become overly dependent on the worker. Thus, the worker must guard against unrealistic expectations on the part of the family and avoid helping when the family can do things themselves or when the environment can provide the support. Workers need to be aware of their tendencies to be overly protective or to make up for the wrongs families have suffered. The worker also needs to be aware that an evaluative tone can create resistance in the family and thus be counterproductive.

Although worker support is an important component of the social work endeavor, the worker also should focus on helping the family build an adequate support system within the family and with the family's natural environment. Support from other family members is one of the most powerful tools in coping and change efforts. When people feel that they have the support of their families, they are often able to face some of the most difficult challenges. There is a feeling that as long as I have my family behind me, I can face almost anything. One way to motivate families to increase their power and strength is to use the same approach discussed under crisis and point out that when faced with adversity, there are fundamentally two types of families, those that pull together and those that pull apart. As we pointed out under crisis, nearly every family wants to be a family that pulls together. Once they have committed themselves to this, then the worker encourages family members to make their actions fit with that commitment, especially when an action is counterproductive. Support from relatives, friends, family, ministers, churches, and so on is essential to healthy functioning. If these systems have not been adequate or have broken down, the worker should assist the family in rebuilding or strengthening these relationships as a means of resolving the current situation as well as meeting future needs. Building a support system is especially important for diverse families at risk of prejudice, discrimination, and oppression.

In the past, many social workers have become accustomed to spending extra time in a supportive role with clients. However, managed care and limitations on services have reduced the time available for such extra support services. Social workers need to be certain from the beginning that adequate support systems are in place for the family, especially in a situation in which time limits are placed on the service. If support is needed from more formal support systems, then developing a relationship with those systems must be a priority.

Small groups have been found to be effective for providing support. These support groups are of particular value for use with caregivers,[20] those who have family members suffering from chronic or life-threatening conditions,[21] and those who have had a common debilitating experience.[22] The worker should be aware of support groups and self-help groups that are available in the family's area. If a group is needed, the worker may initiate setting up a group through his own agency if appropriate or may approach another agency whose services might potentially include such a group. In the era of managed care and limited services, agencies need to sponsor these groups as a means of providing support beyond the time limits of service. If agencies collaborate and share this task, then the burden of committing staff and resources will not be overwhelming. For instance, a health care agency might agree to sponsor a group for cancer patients and their families, the local senior agency may sponsor a support group for caregivers, and the local substance abuse program may sponsor Alcoholics Anonymous or Alateen, and Al-Anon groups.

Properly used, support can produce growth, not only maintain the status quo. It provides positive reinforcement and can give families strength to live and to grow in difficult situations. Support should be a part of the generalist social worker's interventive repertoire.

CASE EXAMPLE

■ **Action That Is Supportive**

Jane used a supportive approach from the very first session with the Perez family. She was able to develop a climate that was accepting, understanding, comfortable, and validating. In working with Mrs. P, Jane connected her with a program at the local community college for homemakers returning to school. The program functioned as a support system for women wishing to complete their education after being away from school for extended periods of time. The program had both a mentoring component and a support group as part of its services.

■ USE OF ACTIVITY AS AN INTERVENTIVE ■ STRATEGY WITH FAMILIES

Activity is doing something or performing tasks as opposed to talking about what to do or about feelings and ideas. Activity can take the form of helping family members carry out normal life tasks. It can also take the form of activity constructed by the worker to enhance the helping process, such as role-playing a difficult situation, or in a family session, using an activity that requires cooperation.

Activity can be used with families, but it is usually limited to when the family is the client system. "Homework assignments" help to carry over the work that is done in family sessions to everyday life. Once family members begin to use the work from the sessions, they can build on their success. The worker asks members to describe in detail what happened and how they felt about it. If they feel good about the change, the worker discusses what it would take to make this happen more frequently.

Activity is a means for influencing change in the ways family systems and individuals function. Through action, family members learn many of the skills needed for adequate social functioning. Socialization of family members to the ways of their society and culture (that is, life experience) relies heavily on the use of action. Activity is a means for developing social-functioning skills and also for enhancing self-awareness. Activity leads to accomplishment, which in turn enhances self-esteem and a positive sense of self. Activity also has usefulness in developing an assessment. As the worker observes the family in action, the family's interactional and communication patterns become evident. The worker can also assess the family's competence in functioning and the quality of the functioning by observing the family in action.

Traditionally, activity has been used in certain segments of social work, notably in the use of games and crafts in social group work. The use of play therapy with children has been another use of activity. Milieu therapy (use of the setting) in institutions also uses activity (as discussed later in this chapter). Some family therapists help families plan family activity. Workers dealing with chaotic families have found activity to be very useful.[23] Literature on the ways people learn emphasizes experiential learning involving activity. Activity has been a major technique in working with children and is considered valuable in working with "action-oriented" persons.

Activity is also useful in a variety of other helping situations and can be used as a technique for meeting many needs of families. It enhances physical development and neuromuscular control and stimulates intellectual growth. Activity can be an acceptable release for feelings and emotions, teach patterns of behavior and provide self-discipline, enable acceptance by peers, and increase status. It can provide opportunity for making and carrying out decisions, for forming relationships, and for resolving conflict. Activity can also encourage the development of new interests, skills, and competencies. It can enhance social functioning by enabling movement along the normal growth processes and can be useful with persons who may be at risk of not developing. This risk is often related to lack of opportunity, and activity can provide needed developmental opportunities. In this sense, it can be a preventive approach.

Activity can be broadly defined as anything that involves action by the family or its members. This includes structured activities that are a part of individual, subsystem, or family meetings. It includes activities that the worker may participate in as a leader or facilitator. It also includes actions that the family needs to take in order to accomplish various tasks associated with the plan. As we pointed out, some practitioners refer to these latter activities as "homework" in that the family agrees to carry out certain tasks between sessions. There may be practice or role-plays that take place within the session to prepare the family for the work to be done outside the session. For example, in improving family communication, the worker might ask the family to try to use "I" statements when they are speaking with each other. The worker has them use "I" statements throughout the session and allows family members to catch each other when they forget to use "I" statements. However, they have to use an "I" statement when doing so. When there has been enough practice and a sufficient level of proficiency, the family is asked to try this at home. The family then reports back at the next meeting. It is essential to build activity into the work with the family so that the family can "own" the work to be done. The more active a family is in accomplishing the goals in their plan, the more competent they will feel. Activity is especially helpful to family members who are depressed. Movement toward a goal brings hope and a sense of accomplishment.

Care should be taken in how activity is incorporated into work with families from populations that have been oppressed or experienced discrimination or excessive control from others. If activities are imposed on these families, it adds to their feeling of being controlled. The type of activity should enhance opportunities for choice, decision making, and empowerment. The way in which the activity is presented and carried out should also include these elements. Of course, family members should be allowed to decline to participate at any time with any activity without fear of negative consequences.

Social workers must plan activity carefully. This calls for an expanded knowledge of the nature of action and skill in its use. Robert Vinter has identified three aspects of activity: (1) the physical space and social objects involved in the activity, (2) the behaviors essential to carry out the activity, and (3) the expected respondent behavior because of the activity. Before deciding to use any activity, a worker should assess these three aspects as they relate to the specific activity. Some dimensions discussed by Vinter that influence the action include (1) its prescriptiveness as to what the actors are expected to do, (2) the kinds of rules and other controls that govern the activity, (3) the provision the activity makes for physical activity, (4) the competence required for persons to engage in the activity, (5) the nature of participation and interaction required, and (6) the nature of rewards that are inherent in the activity.[24]

It is also important to assess family or family member's capacity and use of activity. Areas particularly important to consider include the following:

1. *The family's particular need and interests*—Need should be identified before deciding to use activity. Interest can be identified by considering the family's stated desires, skills, and interests.

2. *The capacity of the particular family member to perform the tasks required in the activity*—An understanding of age-group characteristics is important, as is understanding of the usual activities of a family's cultural or other diversity subgroup.

3. *The family's motivation and readiness to use the particular activity*—Some families cannot participate in certain activities because of cultural taboos. Others, who are work oriented, may not be able to join in activity that appears to be play. Families need to have an opportunity to make choices among possible alternatives. Activity that is relevant to the family's lifestyle is usually the activity most useful to them.

4. *The ability of the family's internal and external support systems and community to accept and support the activity being used*—Consideration should also be given to these factors.

A third kind of analysis that workers using activity should carry out is related to its use in a specific situation and includes

1. The materials, equipment, and resources needed to carry out the activity
2. The time and capacity required of the worker to help the family carry out the activity
3. The climate and environment in which the activity will be carried out (the environment's ability to allow the activity and its support for carrying out the activity)
4. Directions for carrying out the activity
5. Precautions and safety measures that need to be taken in carrying out the activity
6. Adaptations of the activity that may be needed

Based on the four kinds of assessments discussed previously, a decision is made to use a particular activity. In preparing to implement the activity, the following tasks may need to be carried out:

1. *An activity may need to be tested or carried out to determine if all aspects are understood*—It is usually best not to use an activity with families that the worker has not pretested. Adaptations should be made as necessary.

2. *All supplies and equipment must be obtained*—Rooms or other areas must be obtained. Responsibility is allocated for specific tasks to either the worker, other staff, or family members.

As the activity takes place, the worker should be supportive and positive, show rather than tell, and set appropriate limits. It is also important to discuss the process and outcome of the activity with the family after its conclusion.

In using activity as an interventive strategy, the criteria for "good activity" should be kept in mind:

1. Good activity grows out of the needs and interests of the family.
2. Good activity takes into consideration age, cultural background, and other diversity factors of the family members.
3. Good activity provides experiences that enable or enhance the physical and psychosocial development of family members.
4. Good activity is flexible and offers a maximum opportunity for participation.

Because the possibilities for the use of activity are vast and varied, it is beyond the scope of this book to provide information about the use of specific activity. Social workers can make use of literature from the field of recreation, structured group or family experiences, and various forms of family or group work to gain knowledge about the use of specific activity.[25]

In using activity, the worker employs a creative approach and adapts the activity to the particular family or family member's need. The creative use of activity can be a powerful influence for helping families. Its use calls for skill and understanding on the part of social workers.

■ **Use of Activity as an Interventive Strategy with Families**

Jane used an activity of sorts in getting the Perez family to use "I or we" statements. She had them set up a charting system for keeping track of their use of "I or we" statements. This was also a homework assignment for them. If Jane were to be called on to work with the younger children in the family, she might have had them engage in an activity such as coloring a picture of the family and then telling a story about the picture. The family also decided to use Sunday afternoons as a time to set aside for a family activity.

■ **ACTION AS MEDIATION WITHIN THE FAMILY** ■

Mediation within the family system is critical to successful family work, whether the family is the client system or the unit of attention. When the worker takes sides, he loses credibility with the other side. Taking sides increases conflict and competition by creating the illusion of winning the worker over to one's side. In any work that involves ongoing relationships, the worker must take and be given the position of mediator. The worker helps the two sides reach common ground and resolve their differences. He engages in a dialogue of negotiation and compromise, asking questions such as, What would you like to do with this? What do you want to see happen? What would satisfy you? What would you be willing to do? As the issues emerge, the worker asks each party about the give and take that is necessary to reach a compromise, If he does . . . , would you be willing to . . .? What would it take to get you to . . .? Would you be willing to . . .?" While mediating and negotiating a compromise, the worker is also modeling how family members can do this among themselves. The worker can also use mediation when there is a block to accessing resources.

William Schwartz described mediation strategy in terms of the client and systems in the environment.[26] We cover this form of mediation in the next chapter. In this chapter we are concerned with mediating within the family system among members of the family. The worker's concern—and the focus of the mediation action—is the social functioning of both the family system and members of the family. The transactional system within the family is the concern, the target for change.

In overcoming blocks in the family's transactional system, the worker and the family both have tasks. The purpose of mediation is not for the worker to be an advocate and challenge one or the other family member but to help them reach out to each other so that together they can achieve a common goal. The worker helps or enables each of the family members to accomplish the tasks necessary to reach an agreement.

The worker has three major tasks to accomplish when mediating within the family: (1) to help the family member reach out to the other family member(s), (2) to help the family member(s) respond to each other, and (3) to encourage family members to identify a common goal and do the work needed to reach that goal.

In helping the family members to reach out to each other, the worker first points out common interests and goals of the family members and the family system. The worker also identifies the blocks that seem to be preventing them from reaching these goals. The worker challenges these blocks by pointing out ways they can be overcome and the advantages to the family of overcoming them. The worker tries to give the family a vision of what can happen if they find a means of working together. In doing this, the worker reveals her own commitment and hopes for a family that can work together for the common good. Through this the worker gives hope to the family. The worker helps the family define what needs to be done in the reaching out, and together they decide how they can do it.

When helping family members to respond to a member reaching out, the worker points out their common interests and concerns and the obstacles that seem to prevent cooperative functioning. The worker tries to help the family system mobilize its concern and its resources for helping. The worker can point out information that will enhance the family's understanding of the situation. In some situations (e.g., divorce) a social worker may be engaged as a mediator on initial contact. Both parties immediately are seen as clients under these circumstances.

In using a mediation strategy, the worker negotiates a contract or agreement with the family members as to the work (tasks) each will do in attempting to overcome problems. The worker helps them carry out their tasks by helping them adhere to the contract, clarifying what is expected in the situation, and requiring that they do their tasks.

Schwartz and Zalba have identified a four-step process for working with clients when using a mediative strategy:

1. *"Tuning in"*—The worker gets ready to enter the process of transactions in the situation.

2. *Beginning together*—The worker helps the various individuals involved to reach out to one another and identify what needs to be done. Contracts are negotiated.

3. *Work*—This is doing what needs to be done.

4. *Transitions and endings*—This consists of leaving the situation, ending the work together, and the worker separating from the situation.[27]

Ernesto Gomez has adapted the four steps or phases of work for use with Chicano clients. He places particular emphasis on the tuning-in phase. He notes that in this phase it is very important to "tune in" to the culture by focusing on how culture may be affecting the situation. This includes concern for linguistic and other cultural practices as they relate to specific needs in the situation for which help is sought. As the work begins together, a cultural assessment helps to pinpoint how cultural factors contribute to the situation and how the culture can provide resources for dealing with the difficulty.[28] This approach can be useful when working with diverse families.

When working in a mediation mode within the family, the units of attention are the family's transactional system and the family members involved. Each is helped to acknowledge the common interests and to become aware of the feelings, needs, and demands of all. This requires that the worker be aware of the rules and roles within the family. The worker provides focus and structure for the work to be done. Based on his knowledge and understanding, the worker also supplies ideas and suggestions as to how the family might better work together. Clarification and problem solving are important tools of the endeavor.

■ **Action as Mediation within the Family**

Jane took a mediating role within the Perez family from the very beginning and throughout the work. She did not take sides but maintained her neutral position as she helped Juan and Carmen and Mr. and Mrs. P to uncover the issues that precipitated the home truancy and was able to help them reach a point where the teens were able to return home. Jane used a mediating approach in helping Mr. P and Mrs. P come to an agreement about Mrs. P's desire to finish school and work. She also used this approach at family meetings in reaching an agreement to work on improving communication by increasing the use of "I or we" statements.

SUMMARY

The choice of which kind of action generalist social workers take with a family should be based on the principles of economy, self-determination, individualization, development, interdependence, and focus on service goals. The choice also depends on the skill of the worker and the worker's interventive repertoire. The dimensions of using action follow:

Action to enable families to use available resources requires a thorough knowledge of the service delivery system, skill in use of the referral process, and skill in the use of the broker and advocate roles. The service delivery system includes the informal helping network as well as the formal system.

Action that enables families to bring about change in their environment and its institutions allows for empowerment of powerless people.

Action that enhances positive thinking and positive actions on the part of families enables them to use strengths in themselves to bring about change.

Action in response to crisis calls for skill in recognizing a crisis situation. Response to a crisis should be immediate and active.

Action that is primarily supportive is focused on particular positive behaviors and attitudes. It guards against overdependence and can promote growth.

Action in the form of activity is especially useful when working with action-oriented persons.

Action is a tool. When using activity, the worker considers the family's lifestyle and characteristics. Also to be considered are the inherent characteristics of the activity and the process for carrying it out.

Action can have a mediation purpose, which is essential for working with families. The worker needs to assume and must be granted a position that does not require taking sides. This allows the worker to help the family to work together.

QUESTIONS

1. What are some factors you would consider when making a choice about the kind of action to take with a family?

2. As a representative of a formal system (an agency), how would you go about helping a family use an informal system to obtain a resource they need?

3. Empowerment has been considered of particular importance when working with women, people of color, and populations at risk. Why do you think empowerment is important in such situations?

4. Consider a situation that you are facing and describe a negative thought or feeling you have about it. Change the thought to a positive one that predicts a successful resolution and describe the feeling that accompanies it. How would acting on the positive thought change your behavior in that situation?

5. Describe the crisis process in a situation in which you have been involved. What was most helpful in the resolution of the crisis?

6. Name some situations in which you believe support is an appropriate action for a social worker to take with families.

7. Choose an activity that you think will be helpful in a specific situation. How did you go about choosing this activity? How should it be structured and presented?

8. In what kinds of situations would the mediating model be appropriate in working with families? When would it not be appropriate?

■ SUGGESTED READINGS ■

Johnson, Louise C., and Yanca, Stephen J. *Social Work Practice: A Generalist Approach,* 9th ed. Boston: Allyn & Bacon, 2007 (Chapters 11 and 13).

Dobson, Keith, Ed. *Handbook of Cognitive–Behavioral Therapies,* 2nd ed. New York: Guilford Press, 2000.

Edwards, Richard L., Ed. *Encyclopedia of Social Work,* 19th ed. Washington, DC: NASW Press, 1995 ("Crisis Intervention: Research Needs," "Direct Practice Overview," "Natural Helping Networks," and "Women: Direct Practice").

Ellis, Albert. *Better, Deeper, and More Enduring Brief Therapy: The Rational Emotive Behavioral Therapy Approach.* New York: Brunner/Mazel, 1996.

Epstein, Laura, and Brown, Lester. *Brief Treatment and a New Look at the Task-Centered Approach,* 4th ed. Boston: Allyn & Bacon, 2002.

James, Richard, and Gilliland, Burl. *Crisis Intervention Strategies,* 5th ed. Pacific Grove, CA: Brooks/Cole, 2005.

Lantz, Jim. "Cognitive Theory and Social Work Treatment" in *Social Work Treatment,* 4th ed. Francis J. Turner, Ed. New York: Free Press, 1996.

Miley, Karla Krogsrud, O'Melia, Michael, and DuBois, Brenda L. *Social Work Practice: An Empowering Approach,* 5th ed. Boston: Allyn & Bacon, 2007 (Chapters 12–14).

Norman, Elaine. *Resiliency Enhancement.* New York: Columbia University Press, 2000.

Reid, William. *The Task Planner: An Intervention Resource for Human Service Professionals.* New York: Columbia University Press, 2000.

Roberts, Albert R. *Crisis Intervention Handbook: Assessment, Treatment, and Research.* Oxford, New York: Oxford University Press, 2005.

Sheafor, Bradford W., and Horejsi, Charles R. *Techniques and Guidelines for Social Work Practice,* 7th ed. Boston: Allyn & Bacon, 2006 (Chapters 6 and 13A).

Worell, Judith, and Remer, Pam. *Feminist Perspective in Therapy: An Empowerment Model for Women.* New York: Wiley, 1996.

8

Indirect Practice Actions with Families

LEARNING EXPECTATIONS

1. Understanding of the use of mediation with the family and the environment.
2. Understanding of influence and its use.
3. Understanding of environmental manipulation as a strategy.
4. Understanding of action to coordinate services.

In the generalist approach to social work practice, the worker is involved not only in direct work with clients but also in work with individuals, small groups, agencies, and communities on behalf of the family and its members. This work has often been characterized as indirect practice. It is very often work with the agency and community systems. This is sometimes described as *macropractice* when the work that is done with these larger systems involves them as a client system or when the target of change is a larger system in the environment. A discussion of individual or family needs points out the historic cause–function debate in social work. That discussion also noted two kinds of need: private troubles and public issues. Work with individuals and families usually falls in the function and private-trouble domain of response to need, whereas work focused on agencies and communities tends to fall in the cause and public-issue domain.

One of the identifying characteristics of the generalist social worker is the worker's ability to respond to both private troubles and public issues. Furthermore, the generalist social worker identifies both the private troubles and the public issues inherent in any practice situation and then decides on the appropriate focus of the action for change. This focus may be on private-trouble (individuals and families) or on social issue (agency and community) concerns. Often the focus may call for work with both private parties and the public. Thus, the generalist practitioner must possess knowledge and skills for indirect as well as direct practice and be able to combine the two when appropriate. As we will see, it is possible to change the interactions between members of these systems and the family or its members without the necessity of bringing about change in these larger systems.

Indirect practice actions are used with families as client systems; as units of attention; or on behalf of individual members, subsystems, or the family as a system. Indirect actions are aimed at bringing about change in the environment. Indirect actions can be learned by family members so they can act on their own behalf in the future. This chapter discusses four approaches that may be used in indirect practice, particularly with families:

1. Action that involves the use of mediation between the family and the environment
2. Action that involves the use of influence
3. Action designed to change the environment
4. Action relative to coordination of services

■ ACTION AS MEDIATION WITH THE FAMILY ■ AND THE ENVIRONMENT

Sometimes as the worker and family explore the family's needs, concerns, and situation, it becomes apparent that the way in which the family or its members and a system in the their environment interact is not effective. Often the situation is of a conflictual nature. For example, a mother seems unable to communicate with a probation officer so that they can work together in setting limits for her son. The mother is afraid of the authority represented by the probation officer and does not respond to his suggestions. The probation officer is frustrated and believes the mother is indifferent to her son's need for limits. The worker knows this is not the case. In such a situation a **mediation strategy** can be useful.

William Schwartz described this strategy as "to mediate the process through which the individual and his society reach out for each other through a mutual need for self-fulfillment"[1] and as "helping people negotiate difficult environments."[2] The worker's concern—and the focus of the mediation action—is the social functioning of both the client and the system. The transaction between the two is the concern, the target for change.

Mediation is basic to an ecosystems approach to social work practice with families. This approach views need as arising out of incongruity between the family and systems in its environment. Restoring or developing a balance between the needs of the family and its members and the needs of systems in their environment is necessary for the situation to be resolved. A mediating role allows the worker to work with the family and individuals or groups in their environment without taking sides. Mediation bridges the gap between direct practice actions, or work done directly with the family, and indirect practice actions, or work on behalf of families with systems in the environment.

William Schwartz and Serapio Zalba and Lawrence Shulman have written extensively about this type of action and strategy.[3] Shulman has identified three blocks in the interactions of clients with environmental systems:

1. *The complexity of systems*—The development of institutions and the bureaucratizing of their functioning has made it less possible for people to understand how to approach these systems or to use the resources they provide. These complex systems seem strange, impersonal, and often overwhelming to many clients.

2. *Self-interest*—The self-interest of systems often is in conflict with the interests of others or of the larger system of which they are a part. When such self-interest is predominant, it is necessary to make that system aware of the interdependence, and thus of the mutual interest, necessary for the functioning of the larger system.

3. *Communication problems*—Often, the inability of systems to work together is a result of a lack of communication or of inaccurate communication and thus of misconceptions about the other.[4]

In overcoming these blocks, the worker and family both have tasks. The purpose of mediation is not for the worker to be an advocate and challenge one or the other system but to help the family and the larger system reach out to each other so that together they can achieve a common goal. The worker helps or enables each of the two systems to accomplish the tasks necessary but does not do the work leading to the goal. That work belongs to the family and the environmental system.

The worker has three major tasks to accomplish: (1) to help the family reach out to the environmental system, (2) to help the environmental system respond to the family, and (3) to encourage both the family and the environmental system to do the work needed to reach the common goal.

In helping the family to reach out to the environmental system, the worker first points out to the family the interests and goals they have in common with the environmental system. The worker also identifies the blocks that seem to be preventing the family from reaching these goals. The worker challenges these blocks by pointing out ways they can be overcome and the advantages to the family of overcoming them. The worker tries to give the family a vision of what can happen if the family and the environmental system find a means of working together. In doing this, the worker reveals her own commitment and hopes for a society in which people and institutions work together for the common good. Through this, the worker gives hope to the family. The worker helps the family define what needs to be done in the reaching out, and together they decide how family members are to do it. The worker is careful to define the limits of what may be expected so that the family does not develop unrealistic expectations.

When helping the environmental system to respond to the family's reaching out, the worker points out their common interest and concerns and the obstacles that seem to prevent cooperative functioning. The worker tries to help the environmental system mobilize its concern and its resources for helping. Where appropriate, the worker can provide the environmental system with information that will enhance its understanding of the situation. In a sense, both the family and the environmental system are clients. In some situations (e.g., divorce) a social worker may be engaged as a mediator on initial contact. Both parties immediately are seen as clients under these circumstances.

In using this strategy, the worker negotiates a contract or agreement with the family and, when possible, with the environmental system as to the work (tasks) each will do in attempting to overcome problems. The worker helps both carry out their tasks by helping them adhere to the contract, clarifying what is expected in the situation, and requiring that they do their tasks.

When working in a mediation mode, the units of attention are both the family and the environmental systems involved. Each is helped to acknowledge the common interests and to become aware of the feelings, needs, and demands of all. This requires that the worker be aware of the rules and roles within the situation. The worker provides focus and structure for the work to be done. Based on his knowledge and understanding, the worker also supplies ideas and suggestions as to how the systems might better work together. Clarification and problem solving are important tools of the endeavor.

Although the mediation strategy was developed to use with small groups, it has proven equally effective in working with individuals and families and is particularly useful with institutionalized individuals.[5] It is often useful in situations in which empowerment is a goal.

■   ACTION INVOLVING THE USE OF INFLUENCE   ■

"Reality demonstrates influence, not control" best describes the worker's affect on a situation. The social worker does not have complete control and cannot guarantee a specific outcome when working from an interventive–transactional stance. Clients and others involved in the situation maintain the ability to decide what their behavior will be in the situation. This ability makes control by the social worker impossible except in those areas in which she has been given the authority to control certain aspects of the client's behavior, such as in some institutional situations, some work with children, protective service work, and probation and parole work.

Influence has been defined as "the general acts of producing an effect on another person, group, or organization through exercise of a personal or organizational capacity."[6] Influence is powerful. It can produce change, persuade or convince, overcome obstacles, motivate, and bring about attitudinal changes. The social worker's input is to create a climate favorable for the needed work, heighten the motivation of those needing to do the work, "provide a vision"[7] for the work to be done together, and reduce the resistance involved.

Influence is an important aspect of working with families and on behalf of families. As the social worker works with families, the influence for change is heavily based on the worker–family interaction, particularly on the relationship between worker and family members. In indirect practice, the worker often works with individuals and small groups in order to meet needs of families either as small systems (the family or its members) or as collectives (community segments affected by a dysfunctional delivery system or a social problem). Relationship remains an important aspect of influence, although other factors (such as the knowledge and expertise of the worker and the material resources and services the worker might have available) are also important. The worker's status and reputation are also sources of influence. All these influences are used when the work together is collaborative and cooperative in nature. Sometimes persuasive techniques must be used for the other system or systems involved to become convinced that a collaborative or cooperative approach is of value to all concerned. Sometimes cooperation and collaboration are not possible, and confrontation, bargaining, and even coercion are necessary to reach the desired goals.

Sometimes the social worker initiates and participates in the action on behalf of families. Sometimes mediation is called for between systems. At other times the social worker stimulates others to carry out the action. Regardless of who takes the action, some means of legitimizing any action taken must be sought. The social worker does not act in isolation but as a representative of an agency. Sometimes the social worker can act with or through an organization to which she belongs. Without the support of legitimization, the worker lacks the influence needed to support the change effort. Without legitimization, ethical issues can come into play. Influence is used as an indirect practice action with individuals and environmental systems on behalf of the family, as is environmental change and coordination of services. Generally, indirect practice actions are intended to be used to bring about changes in the actions of systems. Changes in feeling and thinking may be used as tactics in accomplishing this, but changing actions is the basic strategy.

Generally, the worker uses influence on behalf of the family and refrains from using it with the family except in a crisis situation or as a last resort, when they are truly stuck. The use of influence in family work typically takes place when the client system is an individual and the family (or subsystem or members) is the unit of attention. In that case, the family is considered part of the environment, and influence can be used to bring about change on behalf of the client. For example, if the client has been alienated from her family but needs assistance, the worker might contact the family (with his client's permission) in an effort to restore the relationship or at least agree to work at it. Influence includes bringing about changes in the thoughts, feelings, and especially the actions of individuals and systems in the environment.

Quite often, when people or staff in other agencies know that there is a worker involved with a family, this changes the way that they act. People may give more credibility to the family's need because the worker has done so. They may be willing to defer to the worker because of her position or authority. Workers in other agencies may do this as a matter of policy or as a professional courtesy. Workers are more conscious of their work when a fellow professional is also involved. The majority of workers are conscientious and hardworking, regardless of the circumstances. However, the worker will naturally want to make a good impression on fellow professionals, and this fact alone can influence change on behalf of the family. For example, if the worker calls for services on behalf of the family whose situation requires immediate action, it increases the likelihood that the family will receive services more quickly. Similarly, accompanying a family member to an agency sends a strong message about the importance of the service.

The use of influence has potential ethical problems. The worker should only use influence with the family when absolutely necessary. This also applies to influencing other systems. The worker should not routinely use his influence as a shortcut or to gain favor for his family over other clients. This undermines client empowerment and self-determination. It can lead the other agency to see the worker in a negative light over time, limiting his ability to obtain services when he has a family who really needs immediate attention. Other agencies will expect reciprocity when they have clients who need immediate or special attention. A worker who abuses his influence may build up expectations with other agencies that cannot be met by him or his agency.

An important base for influence is the skill and knowledge of the social worker in developing and using relationships with a variety of persons in a variety of situations. Influence can be exerted by those who know about and can use a planned change process. Influence derives from understandings about human development, human diversity, the variety of social problems, and the availability of services and resources.

Social workers use not only their own base of influence but also that of other people with whom they are working. When working for change in situations, in organizations, and in communities, **influentials** or people with influence are very useful. Influential people may be elected or appointed to positions of authority, are respected and looked up to, have control over resources and information, and are involved in important decision making. They often are people who control from behind the scenes. Values are another important factor to consider in relationship to influence. People are more apt to be influenced for change when the change is within their value system and provides something that is important to them.

Workers need to be aware of the nature of the power and influence they wield in relationships with clients. Influence can be an inherent outgrowth of the power differential in the worker–client relationship. Every effort needs to be made to guard against the potential for abuse of power with clients. In addition to professional expertise, which workers possess by virtue of their skill, values, and knowledge base, certain personal characteristics may also contribute to a worker's influence with a client.

Families and family members do have some choice of whether they will be influenced. To be influenced, people must have at least some motivation for change. Some factors that affect willingness to be influenced include discomfort with the situation and a belief that it can be changed, a desire to gain position or resources, and a desire to change the situation for someone else.

According to Nora Gold, "Social workers can be very useful as motivators to their clients by increasing their sense of competence and control and helping them to recognize the power in 'seeing oneself as a potential force in shaping one's ends; and changing oneself with making whatever changes must come about.'"[8] Gold's quote is from none other than Helen Harris Perlman, the originator of the problem-solving approach in social work. This statement is very close to describing a process of enabling.[9]

Resistance is the opposite of motivation and is sometimes a sign that other influences on a person or family are stronger than the need for change. Barriers to change—to accepting influence—can be cultural in nature. Ideologies, traditions, and values are all part of cultural influences on situations. Barriers also may be social in nature. The influence of a person's family or peer group, the norms of the situation, or the reputation of the change agent can be social barriers to change. Or the barrier may be organizational in nature: a competitive climate or an organizational climate that considers procedure rather than people. Family communication patterns can be a barrier to change. Personal barriers such as fear, selective perception, or lack of energy and skill also affect an individual's capacity to accept influence and to change. All of these barriers may be part of the transactive nature of relationships in a helping situation.

The influence process is carried out in a relationship with one or more of the systems involved in the transaction. This relationship is transactional in nature in that it is affected by other relationships. The relationship between the social worker and the system being influenced is a major source of a social worker's influence. A major task in the social work endeavor is to foster the kind of relationships that allow the worker to bring other sources of influence to bear on the situation. As the worker applies these various sources of influence to the situation, change takes place in the relationships among the subsystems involved. The worker's knowledge and skillfulness as well as social work values guide the decisions about what sources of influence to use and how to use them.

There are also ethical considerations regarding the use of influence. Of particular importance is concern about the difference between influence and manipulation, control, or abuse of power. Clients and others typically do not understand the limits of the social worker's span of control and ascribe more authority to the worker than is legally allowed. Clients may believe that the worker can withhold an income maintenance check if they do not do what they think the worker wants them to do. Such situations can become complex when the client acts according to what she believes the worker wants rather than what the worker has said. Workers can use their ascribed authority to control clients. However, this negates the value of self-determination and also raises concerns about who has the right to do what and on what grounds.[10] In the contemporary situation, social work values, such as the right to self-determination and confidentiality, are often limited by agency mandates, statutory reporting laws, or other constraints of practice.

All three of the following questions can be used to determine if influence is being used within social work values:

1. Whose needs are being met by the use of the influence? If it is the family's needs, it is within the social work value system. If it is the worker's needs, it is not.
2. Have the goals been established by the worker and family together as part of a collaborative process?
3. Has freedom of choice for all concerned been considered and maintained to the maximum extent possible?

Influence is a major consideration for the social worker to take into account in planning and implementing interventions in transactions among people and their systems. Because a power differential often exists between social workers and their clients, attention must be given to prevent misuse of influence. Influence, or use of self, when used within the social work value system serves as an enabling function.

■   ACTION TO CHANGE THE ENVIRONMENT   ■

Environmental manipulation is the strategy that brings about alteration in the environment of a family as a means of enhancing the family's social functioning. Specifically, three factors in the environment are considered as appropriate targets for change: space, time, and relationships.

Environmental change has been a strategy of social work since the time of Mary Richmond. The term *environmental treatment* appears in the work of Florence Hollis, who discussed treatment of the environment as bringing about change in the situation of the client.[11] Max Siporin defined situational intervention as "actions that alter structural, cultural and functional patterns."[12] In discussing "change in behavioral setting," Siporin pointed out that "an environment has profound effects on the behavior, feelings, and self-images of the people who inhabit or use that setting."[13]

Richard Grinnel and Nancy Kyte reported a study of the use of environmental modification by social workers in a large public agency. The authors stated that this is a much more intricate technique than is widely believed.[14] This may be related in part to the fact that the environment is a complex system that transacts with clients and impinges on their functioning.

Environmental psychology provides some of the knowledge needed to understand the impact of the environment on individuals.[15] This knowledge relates the effects of crowding on individuals, the need for privacy, distance as it relates to different kinds of relationships, territoriality, and other aspects of individual functioning. As this field develops, social workers should gain more understanding about the use of this strategy.

Carel Germain and Alex Gitterman, in *The Life Model of Social Work Practice,* placed considerable emphasis on the ecological aspects of human functioning. They differentiated between the social and physical environments, pointing out that people in the environment not only can provide resources for clients but also can affect the client's behavior by their responses to that behavior. When considering the physical environment, both the "built world" and the "natural world" are included.[16] Although social workers have long used the strategy of environmental manipulation, the knowledge base has remained in the realm of practice wisdom or common sense. Carel Germain and Alex Gitterman provided a beginning knowledge base to use when manipulating the environment.

In using an ecosystems strengths approach, action takes place to change the transactions within the family or between the family and formal and informal systems in the immediate environment. In identifying the immediate environment, both proximity and relationships are important. For an individual, the family is often a primary system in the immediate environment. School or places of employment are important systems for individuals and families, as are the neighborhood, extended family, friends, and other significant individuals or systems. The first choice in working with families is for the family itself to be able to mobilize these systems to assist them in meeting their needs. However, often the relationship between the family and significant individuals and systems in their environment needs to be developed, enhanced, or restored. This may be the reason needs are not being met and the family requires assistance from the social worker. In working on behalf of the family, the worker may need to have contact with these significant individuals or systems and take actions that will develop, enhance, or restore important relationships.

As we pointed out earlier, mediation is an important action with systems in the environment. Mediation can be used with both formal and informal systems. Other important skills are improving communication, bargaining, negotiation, problem solving, and conflict resolution. Either the worker may work jointly with the family and systems in the environment, or she may work separately with each. When working separately, the goal is usually to move toward some kind of joint effort to resolve the situation.

The social worker uses his communication skills to facilitate good communication. (These skills were covered in Chapter 4.) He models good communication and asks people to change their communication patterns to reflect good communication.

Decision-making and problem-solving skills involve the ability to work together to develop a plan that will resolve the situation. Because the social worker is familiar with various models of problem solving, she can assist families and members of their ecosystem in doing this. In addition, the worker can assist them to develop an ongoing process of reaching decisions or solving problems.

Bargaining, negotiation, compromise, and conflict resolution are used when unresolved differences persist. These approaches involve identifying the needs and concerns of the parties involved and finding ways to meet those needs. As needs are identified, the worker elicits responses to need from others. He may ask those involved in the situation to give and take in order to have their needs met. He may suggest ways of reciprocally meeting needs between parties. Throughout the process, the worker attempts to reach a mutually beneficial arrangement that can be sustained over time. Some questions that might be used are as follows: (1) What would you like to see happen in this situation? What would meet your needs? What would it take to satisfy you? (2) What would you be willing to do to resolve this? (3) Would you be willing to . . . ? (4) If . . . , then would you be willing to . . . ? (5) What do you want to do with this? These questions are designed to move people toward having their needs met by meeting the needs of others in their ecosystem. When needs are balanced, then the ecosystem is balanced.

When planning for change in the environment, a worker can use the variables of relationship, space, and time as a framework. Relationships should be influenced to enhance the competence of family members. This can be illustrated by considering the situation of a person with physical disabilities. If those in this person's environment provide care so that the person makes few decisions and little use of the physical capacity she possesses, she will feel less competent. If caregivers encourage appropriate self-reliance, however, her competence will be enhanced.[17]

Changes in time, space, and relationships are relevant in family work. Relationships were discussed earlier under direct practice actions. With indirect practice actions, the relationships between family members and the environment are the focus. Reviewing these earlier sections and the discussion of interaction in Chapter 4 gives the worker a foundation for working on these relationships. In an ecosystems strengths approach, family needs may involve incongruity in the transactions among family members and the environment. If one or more members of the family experience unmet need from the environment or excessive demands, it affects other family members as others try to cope or meet the need. Changing the transaction to meet the need not only returns balance to the individual and his ecosystem but also restores balance to his family system by reducing the stress in his family.

Changes can be made in the spatial aspects of a family's environment. Space should be appropriate for the people who occupy it. According to Irene Gutheil, some of the factors important when considering physical space are the features of a space and whether they are fixed or can be changed through modifying the design of the building and placement of furniture. Also important are issues of territory, personal space, crowding, and privacy.[18] These concerns are particularly important in residential situations but should also be considered in evaluating offices and other areas where services are provided.

For people with physical disabilities, physical barriers can be a block to relative self-sufficiency. A sense of competence is enhanced when barriers are removed. The physical environment should provide for the privacy a person needs. The effects of color and light in influencing feelings and behavior should be considered.

The activity to take place in the space and the manner in which people interact during the activity are important considerations. There must be provision for appropriate closeness of people; being too close or too far apart can lead to discomfort and cause people to withdraw.

Spatial arrangement that allows for eye contact is important in working with families. A circle arrangement encourages people to talk to one another, as each can see everyone else. Room arrangements in which all individuals face a speaker discourage group interaction and encourage attention to the speaker only. Social workers can use their understandings of families and their needs and of spatial arrangements to determine how space can be changed to enable people to function more adequately.[19]

When a social worker working with a family arranges chairs at the meeting space to bring about interpersonal interaction or certain seating configurations among family members, she has manipulated space and created environmental change. The way the physical environment of a social agency is arranged can make people feel comfortable or uncomfortable and can cause undesirable behavior or enable constructive activity. Physical arrangement can sometimes make the difference in whether the family uses the services offered or fails to get needs met.[20]

Changes in space can range from accommodating the family for an office visit to assisting in major moves, such as changing the place of residence for the family or for one of its members. When the family decides to make a move from its current residence, the worker may need to assist in locating other living options, especially in instances of limited finances or that involve government funding. The family may need access to resources to assist with security deposits and other costs. Families may experience discrimination and need to have their rights protected.

Placement of a child in a residential treatment facility is a form of environmental change. The facility uses the milieu (the arrangement of the space, program, and staff relationships) to help the child. Milieu therapy involves attitudes and relationships of the persons who occupy the space as a therapeutic tool. Hospitals, nursing homes, and other institutions can make use of milieu therapy.[21]

The social worker may become involved in accessing day programs or in arranging for residential, institutional, or alternative placement for one of the members of the family. This is common in child welfare, mental health, disability services, health care, aging services, delinquency services, corrections, and similar settings. Social work services can include making referrals and securing placement, providing services to the family while the member is in care, or providing aftercare services. Social workers also may provide services within a program.

Any environmental change should be preceded by a thorough study and assessment of the situation, with particular emphasis on relationship, space, and time factors that may be impeding the family's social functioning. Attention should be given to how culture and lifestyle prescribe the use of the physical environment and time so that the plan does not conflict with the family's culture and lifestyle.

Time factors can be changed in service of families by changing the schedule for activity. There is a time for physical or mental activity and a time for quiet in people's lives. By considering the family's needs at various times, the social worker uses the time allotted in ways that are congruent with the family's needs. For example, when children have been in school all day, after school they are usually ready for physical activity rather than for sitting quietly. When working with a mother, the worker should realize that times when family demand is high are not times the mother can reflect on her own needs. The timing of appointments should take into consideration the time rhythms of the family's life. Institutions often develop schedules to meet staff desires rather than considering the daily rhythms of those being served. Social workers can be alert to these time elements and work for changes in schedules so that service to individuals and families can be facilitated.[22]

Changes in time with family work generally mean flexibility in scheduling, which is much more difficult with families than with an individual. Family size, the ages of its members, and environmental demands, such as work or school, affect the time that members have available to meet and to carry out various tasks. Not only must the visits with the worker be coordinated but also scheduling services and activities can be complicated. Working with families generally involves more involved scheduling and arrangements.

When using the strategy of environmental manipulation, the worker assesses the situation and plans to bring about change in relationships, space, and the use of time. In planning for change it is essential that the worker use her understandings about relationships, space, and time. The social worker also should be creative in structuring environments to support the family's efforts in social functioning.

ACTION TO COORDINATE SERVICES

Coordination is the working together of two or more service providers. Coordination of activity can be focused on a client system, such as an individual or family (microlevel coordination), or it can be focused on persons in a particular category, such as persons with AIDS or developmental disabilities (macrolevel coordination).

Coordination of services can be used on behalf of the family as a system or on behalf of family members. When a family is in crisis or faces severe or multiple needs, it may require assistance in coordinating needed services. This is a common situation with social workers who work in the settings mentioned previously. Case management is usually the model that is used. This is discussed later. Child welfare cases involve families who are having difficulty in meeting children's needs or are abusive. In the majority of cases, there are multiple needs experienced by the family and by individual members. The worker may assume initial responsibility for coordinating services, with the expectation that the family will eventually assume responsibility or will experience a reduction in the need for services. Various family preservation models have emerged since the 1970s that are designed to prevent out-of-home placement of children. These are mainly short-term, intensive, in-home services.[23] Given the tremendous rise in costs, various alternative models to residential and institutional care have evolved for the mentally ill, developmentally disabled, or mentally retarded. The juvenile and adult corrections systems have seen similar efforts. Services for aging individuals are becoming more community based and will inevitably require more alternative services as the costs of residential and institutional care mount. All of these services require the social worker to provide coordination or to participate in situations where another worker is the primary coordinator of service.

When the family is the client system and coordination of services is needed, the worker involves the family with the process as much as possible. Over time, some families will be able to do this for themselves. Others will no longer need the array of services. Still others will require some assistance over an extended period of time. When working with an individual, the worker attempts to involve the family in the process if this is possible and the client is agreeable. The assumption is that the family will be an important and more consistent source of ongoing assistance in securing services. For some clients, this may not be so, but in most cases, the family remains an important resource. Sometimes all that is needed is for the worker to mobilize the family or give information to key members. Other times, the worker may supplement what the family provides, or she may find resources for the family that will ease some of the burden.

Collaboration and coordination are often used as if they were synonymous, but, as used in this text, there is a difference between the two. **Collaboration** is the working together, or teamwork, of two or more helpers using a common plan of action. Coordination does not imply a common plan of action; in fact, there may be two or more plans of action. Collaboration and teamwork are two kinds of coordination. In this section several other methods of coordination are presented.

For coordination to be effective, there must be a spirit of working together toward a desirable end. For example, this end could be a common goal, such as maintaining in the community a person with chronic mental illness. This would require coordination of different services provided by different agencies, such as socialization and vocational rehabilitation services as well as housing services, medical monitoring services, income maintenance services, and the like. Public social services as well as mental health and vocational rehabilitation units and perhaps other agencies would all need to be involved.

In another example, the end may be the common goal of providing a range of services to a particular community to enable it to meet the needs of its aging members. This might involve coordination of the services of the senior citizens' center, the public health nursing agency, public social services, and the variety of other services available in the community. The goal would be not only to help specific older clients but also to enable existing services to more appropriately respond to the needs of all older persons. The common end would be a network of needed services that would be usable by a broad range of older persons.

An important aspect of coordination is the mutual satisfaction of all concerned. The persons or agencies involved need to believe that it is advantageous to coordinate their services with others. This feeling of common benefit leads to open exchange and feelings of satisfaction, which are necessary for productive relationships. Coordination can involve a range of resources broader than those of formal social service agencies. It can involve professionals from a variety of disciplines: service providers of community institutions such as schools and churches; community self-help group leaders; and the informal resources of friends, family, and work colleagues.

One factor that can hinder coordination relates to the differing perspectives on families and family members' needs held by those of different professional disciplines. A doctor might see an older person's frail health status as the primary need. A social worker might consider this person's lack of a support system as the main issue. A senior citizens' center director might identify the need for socialization to prevent isolation. Each professional would advocate for a different need for the client. The physician might push for a nursing home placement. The senior citizens' center director might want to involve the client in the activities of the center. The social worker might attempt to develop an individualized support system after ascertaining the client's desires.

Each profession has its own societal task to perform, its own way of functioning, and its own values and knowledge base. When social workers work with other disciplines, it is important to have an understanding of the other professions' perspectives. Issues of concern to other professions and areas of overlapping interest and service should also be identified. The social worker should also be aware of potential tensions among professionals.

The expectation that every professional thinks or should think in the same ways about a family or a family's needs is a major block to coordination. Understanding differences is a first step to working together in a coordinated manner. This understanding aids in identifying the distinctive capacities of each professional that can be used in developing a coordinative relationship and can lead to respect and acceptance. Respect for and acceptance of another profession's contribution are necessary components of coordinative action.

When coordinating resources and activities from the informal arena, it is important to be aware of the different ways formal and informal resources function. Eugene Litwak and Henry Meyer pointed out the differences in functioning of the primary group (natural systems) and the bureaucracy (formal system). *Primary systems* are diffuse, personal, have an affective bond, and call for face-to-face contact. They can best deal with nonuniform, relatively unique events. They are adaptable and flexible and have the capacity to respond quickly. *Formal systems* tend to be impersonal, specific as to what they can do, and operate within rules and regulations. They function with professional and technical expertise and deal with large numbers of people in an impartial manner. Both kinds of service systems are important and should be coordinated. An important contribution of Litwak and Meyer is what they called the *balance theory of coordination.* According to this theory, the important aspect of coordination is communication. If the two types of systems (formal and informal) are too far apart, communication does not take place. If they are too close together, their differences hinder each other's functioning. There is a midpoint of social distance between the two systems at which each system can function best. (The midpoint is the point at which the two systems can communicate with each other but are not so close that the functioning of either system is impaired.)[24]

Social workers who get to know community influentials and natural helpers in relatively informal community groups can develop relationships that will facilitate coordination with the informal system. If individuals who function in the informal system know the social worker, they will be more apt to consult with her or to refer someone to her. Social workers in turn can discuss common concerns in the informal settings in which these helpers are more comfortable.

Another consideration is the difference between the ways in which men and women communicate. Traditionally, women tend to seek cooperation when communicating, whereas men tend to be more competitive. Women tend to be more comfortable in relatively less structured settings, whereas men are drawn to settings with more formal lines of communication. The natural helping system seems to be more often a female system. The formal system, although staffed with both men and women, functions in a formalized manner that is more akin to traditional male communication. Male social workers should be particularly aware of differences in communication styles when working with the informal helping system.

Coordination can be carried out through several mechanisms. One is to locate those who serve a similar population in a common setting, often called a multiservice center. This can be done by either locating the agency or the individual service deliverers (e.g., family service worker, community health nurse, income maintenance worker) representing a variety of agencies in a common setting close to those needing service. It is assumed not only that this will make services more accessible to clients but also that close proximity will encourage sharing among the professionals.

Another means of linking services has been an information and referral service; this can serve as a coordinative mechanism, depending on its means of functioning and on the capacity of those who staff it. If the emphasis is on providing information about services, the coordinative function will probably not be carried out. If the emphasis is on referral and enabling clients to access needed services, then a coordinative service is enhanced by follow-up and evaluation of the service delivered. Evaluation can also lead to identification of unmet needs and of needed services that are not available and thus to program development. A coordination approach that merits special consideration is case management.

Case Management

Case management has received considerable attention as a coordinative approach to service delivery. It has been found to be useful in the fields of child welfare, mental health (particularly with the chronically mentally ill), developmental disabilities, and gerontology. Its use is often indicated when a family or a family member needs a range of services from several social service or health providers. Provision for such services is supported by federal legislation.[25]

Although the process of case management has been identified in a varying manner from field to field, a common thread has emerged. According to Karen Orloff Kaplan, the process contains five components: (1) case identification; (2) assessment and planning; (3) coordination and referral; (4) implementation of services; and (5) monitoring, evaluation, and reassessment.[26]

In case management with families and family members, assessment and planning involve consideration not only of the family's and family members' needs but also of the resources available within the family's informal network of relationships and in the immediate community. Assessment is carried out with maximum family member input and involves identifying the needed resources and weaving them into a plan that is congruent with the family's culture, desires, and lifestyle. This weaving together can be described as developing a *complementary resource pattern*. The case manager provides an integration so resources are not duplicated or at cross-purposes, and the family can sense a holistic concern for need fulfillment.

The case manager reaches out to the various resources to obtain their cooperative input and to provide the information needed for coordinating services. The case manager may need to creatively develop a new resource or modify an existing one. Often the case manager provides a part of the needed service. Regular monitoring is another task of the case manager.

Several case management models have been developed, usually addressing service in a particular field of practice (e.g., child welfare, services to older adults). One developed by Jack Rothman seems to depict the process most thoroughly and clearly. This model begins with access to the agency through outreach or referral and proceeds through intake and assessment, which may have both short- and long-term psychological, social, and medical components to goal setting. From this point a variety of options are possible: intervention planning, resource identification and indexing, and linking clients to formal agencies or informally to families and others. Counseling, therapy, advocacy, and interagency coordination, including policy considerations, may also be used but are outside the process loop and are used only when needed. Monitoring, reassessment, and outcome evaluation are also within the loop. Rothman noted that the process is meant to be used flexibly and is cyclical in nature.[27]

Two goals are often discussed in relation to case management: continuity of care and maximum level of functioning. *Continuity of care* is important because many of the clients who benefit from the use of this approach need services for an extended period of time, if not for the rest of their lives. This care may need to be provided in a range of different community and institutional settings. A holistic plan for services is considered desirable, and case managers can often provide the desired continuity. *Maximum level of functioning* is important because many clients with whom this approach is used operate at a less-than-independent level of functioning. Because of the multiple needs involved, they may not be functioning at the highest level of which they are capable. A case management approach provides an overview that can lead to planning, which encourages a maximum level of functioning.

Stephen P. Moore noted that case management should be an enabling and facilitating activity. A major thrust is to ensure that formal service complements family care and other informal helping rather than competing with or substituting for such care. This can add to the complexity of the service. The case manager may not only need to consider the current and potential strengths, limitations, and ways of functioning of the informal care system but may also need to develop a potential for help within these systems. He may need to provide support and other services to the informal system to enable it to perform as the needed resource. It is important to be aware of the stresses on the informal system as well as the needs of the helping system.[28]

Case management calls for the social worker to use both direct and indirect approaches. It is truly generalist social work practice in that it weaves together a variety of strategies so that the range of needs of clients with multiple challenges can be met. Coordination is a major concern of the case manager.

CASE EXAMPLE

From the case example of the Perez family, the following are examples of indirect practice actions.

■ **Action as Mediation with the Family and the Environment**

When Jane intervened with the school for Carmen as described in Chapter 7, she acted as an advocate when she went to the principal about the situation. However, she took a mediating position and was able to identify the options that were available. Had she come on too strong, the principal might have responded defensively and also resisted her efforts. This would have required Jane to advocate with the superintendent and, if that was not successful, perhaps the board of education. As this escalated, it may have been more difficult to resolve the situation. As it was, obtaining the support of the principal meant that Jane and Mrs. P and Carmen were able to try to resolve this through the assistant principal. Ironically, they agreed to use the peer mediation program at the school to try to bring the situation to a successful resolution.

■ **Action Involving the Use of Influence**

When Jane first tried to schedule an appointment with the principal, she encountered difficulty in doing so. Jane went to her supervisor who discussed the situation with the agency director. The director contacted the school and was able to arrange an appointment. The director and influential people in the school district and the community had worked together to develop the runaway shelter and program. The school was heavily involved in providing interim educational services to students while they stayed there and were very invested in having home truancy services available to their own students.

The agency that operated the home truancy program has several programs under its umbrella that serve youth and their families. In starting the runaway shelter and services, the agency director approached her board of directors, which included several influential people in the community, about the need for these services. Before she did this, she gathered data from the juvenile court regarding repeat home truants and the incidence of other delinquent activity. She also researched the professional literature on effective programs for home truancy. The director pointed out to the board that runaway youth were ending up in the juvenile home if they refused to return home or their parents refused to take them back. While in the juvenile home, they were exposed to delinquent youth who were involved in more serious trouble, including criminal activity. Some of the youth who were home truants would later end up back in the youth home for more serious crimes that they had learned about when they were previously in detention. Some had committed those crimes when they ran away after their stay. For example, some youth had learned how to break into homes or steal cars. Both male and female home truants had learned about prostitution. Some youth made follow-up contacts with delinquents and began hanging around with them, getting involved in drugs and criminal activity. Thus, the director pointed out that the current response at the time was inadequate and even harmful. Her board agreed and some of the influential members contacted other influential people in the community and formed a task force. The task force included the juvenile court judge and representatives from local youth and family service agencies, the educational systems, law enforcement, the business community, and some active community volunteers. The task force contacted the state representative and state senator and received support. After more than a year of work, they were successful in obtaining a grant to start the program and funding from the state to operate it.

■ Action to Change the Environment

To a great extent the work of the task force in establishing a runaway shelter was a form of environmental change. The results of their work changed the type of environment in which runaways who were not able to return home right away were housed. The program at the shelter and the follow-up services are aimed specifically at preventing home truancy and reducing the incidence of recidivism, especially regarding involvement in more serious problems such as drugs and delinquency.

Environmental change includes changes in time, space, and/or relationships. With the Perez family, over the long term, if Jane were successful at helping the family to improve their economic situation, the family might be able to move to a home that met their needs more adequately. This is an example of spatial change. If Jane were to have the entire family come to the agency for some sessions, she might have to rearrange her office or meet in another area to accommodate them. These are also forms of spatial change. When Jane accommodated Mr. P's work schedule by visiting their home in the evening, this was a form of temporal change or environmental change related to time. Her work with the family to reduce arguing and improve communication was environmental change regarding relationships as was Jane's work with the school.

■ Action to Coordinate Services

From the very beginning, Jane helped the family to coordinate the array of services that were available. The family went from being somewhat isolated to receiving services from Jane and her agency, Catholic Family Services, several programs in the school, and the local community college. Jane assisted with making contact and accessing these services and monitored them throughout her involvement with the family.

SUMMARY

The generalist social worker engages in direct and indirect practice actions to facilitate successful completion of the plan or to assist in removing barriers to success. Indirect actions are actions the worker takes on behalf of the family or its members. These actions are aimed at either changing some aspect of the environment or the interaction between the family and its environment. The dimensions of using indirect action follow:

Action can have a mediation purpose, which can be useful when the family and environment are not interacting in a functional manner. The worker helps the family and environment reach out to each other so they can fulfill common needs.

Action can involve influence and its use. The social worker may use influence with other individuals and systems to change the response to the family. The worker may also seek to influence people who are influential in order to modify, improve, change, or bring about new services for families.

Action can involve changing the environment. This may include action to manipulate the environment or to have the family or a family member move to a different environment.

Action to coordinate services is used to assist families or family members when they are overwhelmed by the need for multiple services.

QUESTIONS

1. Describe a situation where mediation might be needed between a family and a system in their environment. How would you go about mediating this situation?
2. Describe a situation where a social worker might be need to influence a person or a system in the environment on behalf of a family or family member. How would you go about using influence in this situation?
3. Describe a situation where environmental change or manipulation might be needed on behalf of a family or family member. How would you go about doing this?
4. Describe a situation where a family might need assistance in coordinating services. How would you go about assisting the family?

SUGGESTED READINGS

Johnson, Louise C., and Yanca, Stephen J. *Social Work Practice: A Generalist Approach,* 9th ed. Boston: Allyn & Bacon, 2007 (Chapters 11 and 13).

Miley, Karla Krogsrud, O'Melia, Michael, and DuBois, Brenda L. *Social Work Practice: An Empowering Approach,* 5th ed. Boston: Allyn & Bacon, 2007 (Chapters 13 and 14).

Netting, Ellen F., Kettner, Peter M., and McMurtry, Steven L. *Social Work Macro Practice,* 2nd ed. Boston: Allyn & Bacon, 2004.

Sheafor, Bradford W., and Horejsi, Charles R. *Techniques and Guidelines for Social Work Practice,* 7th ed. Boston: Allyn & Bacon, 2006 (Chapters 6 and 13B).

Evaluation and Termination with Families

LEARNING EXPECTATIONS

1. Understanding the importance of and skill in the use of evaluation in generalist social work practice with families.
2. Understanding of the use of research techniques in the evaluation process with families.
3. Understanding of the place of the termination process in generalist social work practice with families.
4. Understanding of the components of the termination process with families.
5. Understanding the transfer process with families.

Evaluation and termination are covered together in this chapter. Although each is distinctive in many ways, they are also linked to each other. In the successful completion of a change process, evaluation provides a basis for termination by determining that the goals have been achieved and the need has been met. Evaluation occurs throughout the change process. At the same time, unplanned termination can occur at any point during the process and for a variety of reasons. The worker must be prepared to respond to the needs of the family and its members, even when unplanned termination occurs. Thorough, ongoing evaluation provides the worker with important knowledge in determining a response to planned and unplanned termination.

It is important that the worker and the family have developed a plan in which progress toward meeting needs and overcoming barriers can be measured. Otherwise, the work can seem aimless rather than being focused on suitable outcomes. An essential ingredient for change is hope. As the family is able to see progress, they are able to feel more hope that the situation will change for the better. If the plan is based on strengths the family possesses, then progress will be made sooner and the overall plan will have greater chance of success. The family will feel more empowered because they are acting on abilities and capacities they already have. As the family is able to see progress, they will experience positive reinforcement for change. Even the completion of tasks can be very uplifting for family members.

As an ongoing part of the social work process, **evaluation** is the means for determining if the goals and objectives of the social work endeavor are being reached. It also involves looking at the means being used to reach goals and objectives. Evaluation identifies spinoffs (unexpected outcomes), both negative and positive, from the helping activity. Evaluation should be continuous, but it becomes particularly important as each step is completed. Evaluation should occur during assessment to see that all needed information has been collected, that the information is valid and reliable, and that appropriate conclusions about the meaning of the information and about family in situation have been drawn. During and after planning, there should be evaluation to determine if the plan is complete and feasible. During and after action has been carried out, evaluation should be used to determine if there is progress toward the desired goals and if they have been reached. Evaluation is also an important part of the termination process.

Evaluation, then, is finding out if what is expected to happen is really happening. It measures progress toward achieving goals and objectives. It looks at completed work and determines which methods and strategies worked and why. It is an opportunity to check with clients and significant others to see how it is going from their viewpoint. Evaluation of one's work is a professional obligation for every social worker and should be a continuous process.

Programs and agencies are obligated to carry out, on an ongoing basis, evaluation of the mission, purpose, and goals of the agency and its programs. Evaluation is necessary if social workers and the agencies for which they work are to be accountable to clients, support sources, and the general public. Social workers participate in evaluation in some way, regardless of their place in the agency hierarchy.

This chapter considers various kinds of evaluation, techniques used in evaluation, and evaluation during each phase of the change process.

The final stage of the social work process is **termination**, or the ending stage. Although ending the process is often slighted, it is nevertheless an important aspect of the social work endeavor. Termination is planned from the beginning of the work together. A social work relationship that focuses on meeting the needs of the family terminates when those needs are met. The time line that is a part of the plan of action specifies the anticipated time for termination.

In termination, it is important to consider the background of the family system and the reasons for termination. Life is full of beginnings and endings. The end of one experience usually signals the beginning of another. Termination work can enhance the family's social functioning. Any ending can arouse strong feelings. These feelings can be used as a means for growth, or they can be denied or suppressed, perhaps to arise and interfere with later social functioning.

In considering termination, two areas are discussed: (1) kinds of termination and reasons for families' and workers' terminating a helping relationship and (2) content of the termination process—dealing with feelings, stabilizing change, and evaluating with families.

KINDS OF EVALUATION

Planning for evaluation when developing a plan of action is one way of ensuring that the plan of action is carried out in a way that yields maximum information to the worker, the family, and the agency. If the information to be used in evaluation is identified before the social work process begins, there is a better chance that such information will be available for use in evaluation.

The worker and the family need to develop a plan in which progress toward meeting needs and overcoming barriers can be measured. Otherwise, the work can seem like it has no purpose rather than being focused on outcomes. An essential ingredient for change is hope. When the family is able to see progress, they feel more hope that the situation will change for the better. Plans based on strengths the family possesses will have greater chance of success. The family feels more empowered because they are acting on abilities and capacities they already have. When the family sees progress, they experience positive reinforcement for change. The completion of tasks can raise hope for family members.

Evaluation is important for measuring progress toward change. In order to plan effectively and efficiently for evaluation, an understanding of the various kinds of evaluation and some of the means for carrying out the evaluative process is useful. Evaluation serves many purposes and takes a variety of forms. In its most simplified form, it is a worker thinking about what has happened and why it happened. During the termination phase of the social work process, the worker and family together determine if the goals set out in the contract have been reached and then discuss what enabled the goal attainment. Evaluation involves discussing what has been helpful to the family and what could have been done differently.

Program evaluation is more complex, generally involving statistical data or other research methodology. Evaluation may be summative or formative. **Summative evaluation** is concerned with outcomes and effectiveness. **Formative evaluation** is concerned with looking at the process of the work, at how the work during the various steps in the service influenced the final outcome. Such evaluation would look at such things as the nature of the relationship, the content of sessions, or the setting in which the work took place. Both types are important in social work practice and should be included in the evaluation process.[1] This section points out a variety of other ways of looking at evaluation. The kind of evaluation employed in part depends on the stage of the social work process or on the program or agency need for data related to accountability.

One way to develop an understanding of evaluation is to consider various classification schemes used relative to evaluation. The first classification to be considered is whether the evaluation is of a particular case, of a program within an agency, or of the agency itself. When considering a specific case, evaluation focuses on whether the goals set by the worker and client system together were attained. Evaluation of the process of the work should focus on how the various components of the plan of action contributed to reaching the goal. Evaluation of the process of work is a joint endeavor of the worker and the client system because the client system is usually the best source of information about goal attainment and about the process of the work together. Workers often do some additional thinking about family in situation and how the family and their situation relate to other families with whom the worker has worked. This is done so that the worker can develop an understanding of how to approach future families who may be in similar situations.

Program and agency evaluations determine effectiveness of agency functioning. These kinds of evaluation are often concerned with efficiency of service provision and usually are not as personalized as a case evaluation is.

Program evaluations serve four purposes. First, they are necessary to meet the requirements of outside funding and accreditation bodies. Second, they can provide indications of client satisfaction. Third, they can provide information that can be used in developing new practice knowledge and worker competence. Fourth, program evaluations can document the need for new services or service effectiveness to other service providers, funding sources, and the general public.

A second classification is qualitative versus quantitative evaluation. With quantitative data, an effort is made to measure satisfaction by using numbers and averaging the responses of those surveyed. The advantage of this procedure is that statistical computations can be used to determine whether the outcome is the result of random error or is likely to be associated with the service. The disadvantage is that the data may not be very meaningful because they lack the richness of individual experiences. Qualitative data tend to derive from asking people to relate their experiences. This has the advantage of providing a comprehensive picture of service from the client system's perspective. However, gathering qualitative data is more time consuming and thus more costly than quantitative data collection. In addition, samples of the client population tend to be smaller, and the data are more difficult to analyze. The contemporary service delivery system has been highly influenced by organizational management trends and the use of a quantitative base for evaluation. Clinical practice has also been influenced by behavioral psychology and its emphasis on measuring behaviors. The trend toward computerization of information and records also supports the demand for quantitative data. However, most social workers maintain that not all information can be dealt with in a quantitative manner because of the qualitative factor in human functioning. Although behaviors can be measured, feelings and emotions cannot, at least not directly. Qualitative measures are better mechanisms for evaluating these factors. Most client surveys should include both quantitative and qualitative data acquisition in order to tap the advantages of each of these methods.

Clinical versus management evaluation is the third classification. Although this classification might be closely related to the quantitative–qualitative classification (management generally uses quantitative data; clinical generally uses qualitative data), the application of these two types of evaluation is quite different. Management evaluation is used to make internal staffing and program decisions and to substantiate need for services and resources to support services. Clinical evaluation is limited to use by professional persons (worker and supervisor) and the client system involved in the situation being evaluated. Because of the different usage, different information is sought for use in different types of evaluation, and different kinds of outcomes are expected. Sometimes data are used for both types of evaluation, which is more efficient in that it avoids collecting two sets of data. It can be difficult, however, to use the same information for two different purposes. Management evaluation is apt to call for statistical data, data that can be broken down into categories of problems. Clinical evaluation is usually concerned with the type of need or concern dealt with and specific information as to how the need and its resolution are affected by the client and her situation. This information loses some of its meaning when converted to categories or statistics.

The fourth classification is that developed by Michael Key, Peter Hudson, and John Armstrong,[2] who identified a hard line–soft line continuum. Hard-line evaluation focuses on aims and objectives that are set before the implementation of programs. Some degree of scientific objectivity is involved in this type of evaluation. Soft-line evaluation is based on impressions and opinions. Each approach yields different kinds of information. The worker needs to determine whether hard-line information will adequately provide for the evaluation needs and tell the necessary story. If not, then soft-line information should be used either to tell the story or to supplement the hard-line information.

Each type of classification points out a different dimension of evaluation. Each evaluative effort can be classified along a continuum related to each of the four classifications. When choosing evaluation methods and techniques, it is important to consider the requirements of the situation being evaluated, keeping all four possible classifications in mind (case or program/agency, quantitative or qualitative, clinical or management, hard or soft), and to choose methods that match the requirements of the situation.

■ SINGLE-SYSTEM DESIGN AND RESEARCH TECHNIQUES IN EVALUATION ■

Many research techniques are very useful in carrying out evaluations because evaluation and research share common considerations and concerns. The main reasons that social workers need to be familiar with research and evaluation techniques in practice are (1) to evaluate the success or failure of their services, (2) to evaluate themselves and their strengths and limitations as practitioners, (3) to evaluate the potential use of various approaches and techniques found in professional literature or obtained through training programs, and (4) to evaluate programs in order to make them more effective while maximizing the efficient use of resources and to report these results as a part of accountability. This last area is covered in the next section.

The purpose of this discussion is to point out the relationship of practice and research when evaluating social work practice and to discuss a few research methods and techniques that are particularly suited for evaluation of practice. The research techniques chosen for discussion are single-system design and goal-attainment scaling.

Single-system design is a research method that fits very well with problem solving, the change process, or any solution-oriented approach. It is a natural follow-up to the measurable goals and objectives that were identified in Chapter 6. Other variations of single-system design are not covered here. A more comprehensive study of single-system research is beyond the purview of this text.

Single-system design can be used with any size client system. It is a variation of time series design, in which a series of measurements are made over time. With single-system design, the same system is measured over time. The system can be an individual, a family, a group, a program, an organization, or a community.

Social workers favor using single-system design rather than the traditional experimental design because of ethical considerations. The simplest traditional experimental design uses a control group and an experimental group. Participants are randomly assigned to each group in order to avoid biasing the outcome. The experimental group receives services, and the control group does not. Differences between the two groups at the end of the experiment are assumed to be caused by the service. Statistical methods are typically used to estimate the probability that the results were due to error rather than the service. The problem with this approach is that it is unethical for a social worker to withhold services to clients, especially if the client would benefit from the service.

Occasionally, social work evaluators can develop a research project using a traditional experimental design in which the control group consists of clients on a waiting list for service. The control group might also be offered service at a later time. However, it is nearly impossible to randomly assign clients to a waiting list, and so these designs are considered quasi-experimental.

In single-system design, no one is refused service for experimental purposes. There is no need to apply statistical methods or to use random assignment to ensure that the control and experimental groups are equivalent. Instead, the client system serves as its own control group by measuring a target behavior, condition, or event before the intervention or service begins and then measuring the same thing during and/or after the intervention or service.

In single-system design, families can be informed and can consent to the evaluation by participating in the process itself. Throughout the change process, the family participates as partners in change efforts. Including family members in measuring and evaluating change is essential to sound ethical practice. Researchers who are "purists" would be highly critical of this approach. Their concern would be that one would have difficulty in determining whether the intervention or some other influence brought about the change. They would be especially concerned that family members would "contaminate" the process by doing something out of the ordinary that would either enhance or sabotage the results. However, practitioners are interested in assisting families in changing their circumstances rather than in maintaining purity in research design. If the purpose is to measure the family's goals, then the concerns of the "purists" are irrelevant.

If the worker needs to use the results to determine the effectiveness of an intervention method, a service, a program, or the like, then greater care needs to be taken to control for bias. For most purposes it is sufficient for the worker to limit claims of success or failure to the situation at hand. Another option is to be scrupulous in describing how the evaluation was designed and carried out, allowing others to decide for themselves the validity or reliability of the results.

The research technique of **single-subject design** is useful when working with an individual family member. Single-system design is used when evaluating the family system. During the assessment phase, a baseline is established for family members' behaviors. Interventive methods, goals, and measurable objectives related to a desired change in behavior are identified. At specific points during the intervention, the target behavior is measured to determine the progress toward reaching the goal. After completion of the intervention, a final measurement is made to determine the extent to which the goal has been reached. The proponents of this method claim that measurable results or outcomes of the intervention can be obtained. It is felt that use of single-system design provide a reliable means of validating practice. It is also a critical part of developing what is called "practice wisdom," which consists of benefits gained through experience in the field. The more the social worker adds empirical evidence to her experience, the greater her confidence in practice decisions.

Critics of single-system design believe that the range of applicability is very limited because the technique is only useful within a behavioral framework for social work practice. They also believe that there are qualitative questions that are not addressed by this methodology. Questions also are raised as to the lasting quality of the change when measurements are made during and directly after intervention. Is the planned intervention the cause of the desired change, or have other factors, either in the treatment situation or in the environment, contributed to the change?[3] The major contribution of single-system design is its focus on goals and outcomes and the provision of a methodology for measuring outcomes, which moves evaluation toward the hard end of the soft–hard continuum.

The simplest single-system design involves a pretest before intervention and a posttest afterward. Another variation involves several measurements during the baseline period, with continued measurement during the intervention. This is typically called AB design, where A represents time when the intervention is not taking place and B represents time when it is.

Careful attention should be paid to measurement in all single-system designs. In order to ensure validity and internal reliability, measurement must be as consistent as possible. A good way to monitor this is to pay attention to the who, what, where, when, and how of measurement. To be consistent, the same person or group (who) needs to measure the same thing (what) with the same client system (who) at the same place (where) and time (when) using the same instruments or observation techniques (how). Any variation in any of these circumstances will raise doubts about the validity and reliability of the data or information; that is, whatever is being observed or measured may change because the person sees or interprets it differently or because the time and place are different. If what gets measured or how it gets measured changes, then the worker is actually comparing two different things that may not be related at all. The worker will have to prove that the relationship exists before the results can be used with any confidence.

It should be noted that measuring lack of progress is as important as measuring progress. Evaluation is not simply a matter of measuring success but also of measuring failure. Finding out that something is not working allows the family and the worker to change the plan. If the worker finds that certain techniques or approaches do not work in certain situations or with certain families, he has added important information to his practice wisdom. In addition, with managed care it is essential that the worker be as effective and efficient as possible. There may be little if any room for error before the family's benefits or reimbursement are cut off or exhausted. To prevent financial hardship for the family or the agency, the worker must be focused on resolving the situation and will need to establish time frames and track progress quickly and with a minimum of effort.

As mentioned previously, single-system design can be used with any size client system. As long as what is being examined can be observed and measured, change can also be measured. Indications of the effectiveness of an intervention, service, or program can be determined, with some caution regarding the generalizability of the results. Extra caution should be used to protect the consistency of measurement when larger client systems are being evaluated and when ongoing or long-term evaluation is planned.

A technique often used with the single-subject design is **goal-attainment scaling.** When using this technique, the goals are set so that the outcomes can be measured on a five-point scale. The five points on the scale are (1) most unfavorable outcome thought likely, (2) less-than-expected outcome, (3) expected outcome, (4) more-than-expected outcome, and (5) most favorable outcome thought likely. Allowance for recording several goals is made by the development of a grid, with goals on one axis and levels of predicted attainment on the other axis.[4]

The major strength of goal-attainment scaling is that it allows for several measurements of success and failure to reach an outcome. By specifying a continuum of outcomes, the technique includes a growth factor. It also offers an evaluative mechanism (the five points on the scale) that can be converted to symbolic codes needed for computerization of data. The grid provides a quickly read summary of the outcomes of a specific episode of service.

The major limitations of goal-attainment scaling relate to the time needed to set up the scales for measurement. Some social workers believe the time spent in setting up the scales would better be used in working with the family. Also, some desired outcomes are very difficult to specify in the manner needed in this technique. Goal-attainment scaling also has some of the same limitations of single-system design, such as questions about the relationship of the change to the intervention, the emphasis on the outcome of goals, and the sustainment of the change over time.

Other forms of evaluating practice outcomes include *task-achievement scaling (TAS)*. Two of the major contributors to this approach are William Reid and Laura Epstein, who have written about task-centered practice.[5] Joel Fischer and Kevin Corcoran have compiled a sourcebook of more than 320 *rapid-assessment instruments (RAIs)* that can be used quickly in assessing numerous client conditions. RAIs generally have the additional advantage of being able to be used over and over with the same client while retaining their validity and reliability.[6] *Individualized rating scales (IRSs)* can be used for developing what are called self-anchoring scales.[7]

One of the most common uses of research for practitioners is for professional development activities. Professional social workers must increase their professional knowledge and skills and should aspire to contribute to the knowledge base of the profession. This means that social workers must be committed to continuing education throughout their careers. Usually, this takes the form of attending in-service events, workshops, conferences, and training programs along with researching and reading professional literature. To be a competent consumer and user of new techniques, the social worker must be able to evaluate the quality of the material presented and its applicability to various clients, practice settings, and circumstances. A solid foundation and knowledge base in the area of research and evaluation is required in order to accomplish this. In addition, competent and appropriate supervision is needed when trying new approaches or techniques.

Social work has become more professional and demands for accountability have increased, especially from managed care systems. This has led to an increased expectation for research and practice to become more closely associated with each other. Social workers are expected to become more knowledgeable about the effectiveness of their approaches. However, it is not enough to evaluate the effectiveness of interventions. As research has expanded, social work has begun to develop an approach called evidence-based practice, which is also called best practices. This approach calls for identifying from research approaches that are most likely to succeed with various clients experiencing certain needs or concerns in various settings. In the Appendix we propose incorporating these along with practice wisdom and an empowerment approach into what we call good practices.

In aspiring to contribute to the knowledge base of the profession, not every social worker will have an opportunity to write or publish an article or a book. However, opportunities to make contributions occur on a daily basis. These include sharing articles and educational materials with colleagues and other professionals, conducting in-service training and workshops, sharing practice wisdom through peer or formal supervision, and networking with other social workers and human service professionals. These daily contributions are fundamental to how social workers have functioned from the very beginning of the profession.

■ SOME CONSIDERATIONS ■ REGARDING EVALUATION

The social worker engages in evaluation throughout the change process. The first five stages of the change process comprise the assessment phase. As the worker adds new information to her assessment, she evaluates that information to see how it helps in her understanding of the situation. She checks out her perceptions and interpretations with the family. Agreement means she can have more confidence in the information in building a foundation for change. Disparity means negotiating an understanding with the family.

Validity and reliability are two important concepts from research that are also relevant for evaluation. **Validity** refers to the accuracy of the information. **Reliability** is concerned with whether repeated measurement would yield the same results. In using naturalistic inquiry for diversity competent practice, knowledge is considered to be tentative. That is, what we think we know we consider to be fluid and not fixed. In practice situations, information is exchanged within the context of human interaction. Thus, the information includes interpretation and perception that is subjective. Yvonne Lincoln and Ergon Guba described negotiated outcomes and negotiated meanings and interpretations as important in naturalistic inquiry. In a person in environment approach, the worker is interested in understanding "reality" from the client's perspective. The worker seeks to understand the meanings and interpretations of the client. The worker also realizes that the client's willingness to disclose his true thoughts and feelings depend on the quality of the helping relationship and the level of trust.[8]

Because we are concerned about the family's interaction with their environment, it is not necessary and probably impossible to know with certainty the objective accuracy of the information. What is important is that the worker has an understanding of the family members' interpretations and perceptions of the information. The question is not whether family members should feel or think what they do. The question is what do they feel or think and how does that influence their actions. Validity is established when there is an understanding between the worker and the family member regarding the family member's perception of herself, her environment, and the interaction between herself and her environment.

Reliability in practice situations relates to how well the understanding the worker and family have about a given situation will carry over in time or in similar situations. In other words, does the same thing happen over and over again whenever the same situation arises? Does the same thing happen in situations that are similar? If so, then we can be more certain that we understand family in environment. If there is inconsistency, then we need to explore our understanding further with the family. However, in naturalistic inquiry and diversity competent practice, the worker refrains from making judgments or drawing absolute conclusions from her observations. In other words, inconsistency does not represent deception. Rather, it represents a lack of understanding on the part of the worker or a lack of mutual understanding or the trust in the relationship may not be sufficient for the family to openly reveal their thoughts and feelings.

We believe that family members will reveal what they can about themselves. If the family member does not trust the worker, she would be foolish to reveal things about herself that might cause her harm. None of us would do this until we could feel that we trusted the other person. Instead of making judgments about the family member, the worker takes responsibility for not having established sufficient trust and seeks ways of improving trust in the relationship.

One of the advantages of working with the family is the fact that the worker has multiple sources of information. When there is agreement from more than one source, the worker is more confident of the validity of the information. This is called **triangulation,** a term that comes from geometry and telemetry. It is used in tracking animals that have radio collars attached to them. Researchers only need to establish two directional signals, and they can locate the position of the animal by plotting the track from which the signal is emanating. The animal will be located where the two lines or tracks intersect. Triangulation of information occurs constantly as family members confirm or contradict each other's stories.

Evaluation with families is more complex than evaluation with individual clients because families have members of varying ages who have different interactions with systems in the environment. Additionally, the worker must evaluate the family as a system. This involves evaluating family structure, functioning, and development along with evaluating interactions within subsystems. Also, as with other situations involving clients, the social worker must work within the culture, diversity, and value system of the family. The best way to ensure diversity competence is to include the family in the evaluation process. The worker relies on naturalistic inquiry. He asks questions about how the family's structure, functioning, and development are viewed within the cultural system. Frequently, families in the United States are multicultural, as couples from different cultures have children. Questions will need to be answered with respect to the relevant cultural backgrounds. The worker asks questions about how the family perceives or experiences attitudes held by the larger society toward the family and its circumstances. The worker is interested in how help is viewed, whether his assessment is accurate, and what kinds of goals and actions are acceptable within the cultural or diversity systems. This gives him a sense of whether the help and the services are likely to be effective and appropriate.

The age and developmental levels of family members are factors that need to be considered in terms of their involvement in evaluation and the means by which evaluation is conducted. Young children or family members who have significant disabilities may not be able to participate or they may need to be observed to determine the effects of the actions that are taking place. On the other hand, adults and teenagers are generally quite capable of giving feedback either formally or informally. Ideally, evaluation includes all of the members of the family who are or were involved in receiving services.

■   EVALUATION DURING PHASES OF THE CHANGE PROCESS   ■

The process of evaluating the family during various phases of the change process and at the end will vary. Some workers may choose to use more formal mechanisms such as inventories at strategic intervals or at the end of a phase. Most workers do informal evaluation in which they take stock of the situation and decide where the process is and where it might need to go.

During assessment, the worker checks with the family regarding the information that she receives. She confirms the accuracy of the information and clarifies discrepancies. She regularly asks about how complete or comprehensive it is by asking questions such as, Is that everything we need to consider regarding this matter? Are there other concerns that anyone would like to discuss? Do we have a complete picture of what is happening? Are we ready to proceed?

In understanding need with families, the worker approaches the situation from an ecosystems perspective and seeks an interpretation that is based on incongruity between the family and systems in the environment. What the family or its members need or want to have happen is not happening.

The worker looks for blocks to fulfilling need. He considers the nature of the need and makes assumptions about why the need is not being met. He makes assumptions about potential strengths and resources in the family, the environment, their interactions, and the worker's own ecosystem. Throughout these stages of the assessment, the worker constantly evaluates the information he has, the assumptions he has made, and the information he needs to determine whether his assumptions are supported and his understanding appropriate.

The worker selects and collects information that is used to further her understanding of family in environment and of strengths and resources in the ecosystem. The selection of information is based on her assumptions. The worker evaluates information that she needs to check her assumptions and the degree to which the information she collects supports those assumptions. Verification of assumptions adds to understanding. Assumptions that are not verified are either discarded or remain in question if more information is needed.

Evaluation of the analysis is critical. The worker must determine whether he has sufficient information to proceed or if he needs to gather more information. At some point, the analysis yields enough information to provide a basis for the plan. These are judgments that the worker must make. They involve evaluating the quality of his understanding of family in environment and strengths and resources. A major source of feedback is the family along with other sources of information in the environment. When his understanding is consistent with the family's and is supported by information from the environment, the worker and the family have a high level of confidence in the decisions that are made. Minor discrepancies or differences that can be accounted for as variations in perception mean keeping the door open for more information, but the work can usually proceed. Major discrepancies mean that more work on assessment needs to be done. The worker checks with the family to decide if they are ready to proceed with developing a plan.

During planning the worker needs to evaluate with the family the degree to which the goals and objectives will address the needs of the family and of individual family members. The worker should solicit this feedback from each family member that is involved with each goal and objective. The worker should evaluate the quality of the goals, objectives, and tasks. As described in Chapter 6, the worker determines with the family if the goals are feasible. She looks at the objectives to see if they are clear, measurable, and aimed at accomplishing the goal. If so, then the objectives can be used to measure progress toward completion of the goal. She looks at both the objectives and tasks to decide if they clearly identify who, what, where, when, and how in terms of the work to be done. She should also ask each family member if they understand the tasks that they have agreed to accomplish in meeting the objectives and ensure that each member is committed to carrying out those tasks. Finally, the worker and the family agree on the plan and develop a mechanism for monitoring progress and completion.

If the worker is meeting with the entire family or a subsystem of the family, he usually will check with them about progress toward goals and objectives at the beginning of each session as the work proceeds and actions take place to achieve the goals and objectives. This is followed by a discussion of what is working and what is not and what kinds of adjustments might need to be made. Thus, as actions take place, the worker evaluates their effectiveness. Is the plan working? If not, why not? What needs to be done to change the plan or remove barriers to success? Does the action need to be modified? Are new actions needed? Should the plan be scrapped and a new or an alternative plan be implemented? Is there a need to return to a stage of the assessment that should be modified? Is there a new need that takes precedence over the initial need? The answers to these questions require the worker and the family to constantly monitor and evaluate their work as they proceed with the change process.

On completion of the plan, the worker and the family evaluate the results. The first questions are, Are we done? Did it work? Was the need met? If measurable objectives were set, the first question has been answered. If the family or family member no longer experiences the need or concern, then the next two questions have been answered. If the need is still there, then the worker and the family need to evaluate what went wrong and return to an earlier stage of the process, perhaps even back to the beginning.

As with assessment and planning, evaluation consists of both process and product. The product of evaluation is typically very informal. The worker may enter into the case record her observations or the feedback she receives from the family. Upon termination, some agencies may require a termination summary that includes some form of formal or informal evaluation. This may be a formal instrument or simply an evaluation by the worker regarding whether the termination represented a successful outcome. Increasingly, agencies are conducting client satisfaction surveys to receive direct and more formal feedback from former clients regarding their services. Evaluation as a part of termination is discussed later in this chapter.

KINDS OF TERMINATION

For families who are successful at achieving their goals, ending their work with the worker signals a resolution of their difficulties and greater independence. It may also trigger anxiety over the ability to succeed without the worker's assistance. For workers leaving an agency for another job or for students graduating from college, the end of an experience in one setting can be accompanied by excitement and anxiety at the prospect of a new phase in their career path. This represents the ambivalence frequently related to termination.

Because human beings are mortal, it is the nature of all relationships to end. Dwelling on this fact might lead some people to avoid relationships for fear of the pain or loss associated with the ending. This fear can obscure the need to be free to enjoy relationships with others and go on to other phases in life. Many clients have experienced pain, loss, abandonment, or rejection in some of their significant relationships. Often patterns of loss have been handed down from one generation to the next. Overcoming the results of these experiences may be the central issue that needs to be resolved in the social work process. Thus, termination issues can be a focus of the change process itself. Termination of the worker's involvement is inevitable. Helping clients to successfully terminate is essential to solidifying any change that has taken place. Thus, handling a termination is an important skill for social workers to develop.

Termination is an aspect of social work that is often given inadequate consideration. Endings can be painful for workers as well as for families. Workers sometimes make decisions about the desired goals of service that prolong the time of service beyond what the family desires.[9] This has resulted in many unplanned terminations (those in which the client fails to keep appointments). According to William Reid, research has shown that

1. Recipients of brief, time-limited treatment show at least as much durable improvement as recipients of long-term, open-ended treatment.
2. Most of the improvement associated with long-term treatment occurs relatively soon after treatment has begun.
3. Regardless of their intended length, most courses of treatment turn out to be relatively brief.[10]

There is a growing emphasis on short-term service. This service considers the family's desires and expectations in the planning to a greater extent than in long-term service. Plans are much more specific, with specific goals and time frames for reaching those goals. Goals are measurable, making it easier to know when the purpose of the service has been fulfilled, the goals met, and the contract satisfied. The ending is more apt to be planned by the worker and the family rather than the family deciding that the worker's help is no longer needed.

Termination can take place at any point in the process: when the goals set by the worker and family have been reached and the family feels comfortable in carrying out those goals without help from the worker; when families feel that sufficient help has been given so they can meet the need or deal with the problem on their own; when it becomes apparent that no progress is being made or that the potential for change is poor; or when a worker or an agency does not have the resources needed by the family or does not have the sanction of the agency to deliver the service needed. This last condition may result in a referral, which is discussed in Chapter 7. Sometimes families terminate because the systems on which they depend are threatened by the possibility of change.

If a worker is leaving an agency, termination activity may result in transfer to another worker within an agency or referral to another agency for continued service. It may result in a decision by the new worker and the family to work on another goal or use another strategy in reaching an elusive goal and thus continue with a new plan of action. However, termination usually results in separation of the family from both the worker and the agency.

Termination is an expectation discussed with families from the beginning of the work together; it is planned for by the worker and the family together. When a worker senses that the family is not using the help being offered, or when the family is missing appointments or in other ways indicating that termination may be advisable, it is time to discuss the possibility of termination. This is done to maximize the benefit that can come from a planned termination and to minimize feelings of anger and guilt that might interfere with seeking help in the future. Many times what a client wants is someone to talk to about his need. This discussion can lead to a better understanding of the need, identification of resources, or planning what can be done about the need. The client does not always need or want any other interventive activity from a social worker or a social agency. Figure 9.1 shows the place of termination in the social work process.

When the worker–client system relationship is terminated because the worker is ending employment or being transferred to a new position, special consideration should be given to the family's feelings. In some cases this is also a good time for the family to

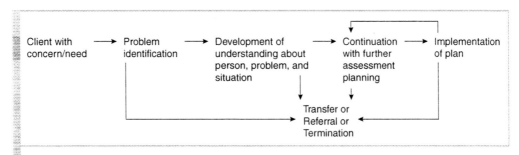

Figure 9.1 Termination and Its Place in the Social Work Process

terminate with the agency as well. At other times, the decision is made to transfer the family to a new worker. Family members may be angry because the worker is breaking an agreement. They may feel deserted or may have a reawakening of old feelings about previous separations. The worker may experience feelings of guilt about leaving the family and breaking the agreement. The worker also may be absorbed in plans for a new job or in the demands of a new situation. When transfer becomes necessary, it is important to recognize and deal with feelings that may impede the continuation of service to the family.

When a worker engages in the termination process with a family because he is leaving his current position, it is important to bring family members' feelings into the open, however painful. Sometimes family members can also deal with previous painful separations in this process. The worker should be prepared to accept the family member's anger and resentment and, whenever possible, should help the family accept the new worker. A useful technique is for the worker to introduce the family to the new worker and for all three to discuss the work that has been done and the possibilities for future work. After this session, the worker and the family should have a last session so that they can terminate their relationship.

Whenever a worker takes over a case from a former worker, feelings about termination should be discussed with the individual, family, or group. Clients need time to adjust; if they are rushed, they will not be ready to accept help from the new worker. Beginnings and endings occur together. How the previous relationship ended will determine whether unresolved issues will create barriers or negative expectations for the next relationship. Allowing the family to talk through these feelings can be a strong bridge to building a new helping relationship. For this reason, the worker should discuss with a new family any previous experiences they may have had and their feelings about that experience.

In order for a social worker to be effective in terminating with families, she needs to be aware of some blocks to effective termination that arise because of her feelings and attitudes. There may be a tendency for the worker to hang on to certain families. This may arise because the worker is reluctant to terminate relationships that she has enjoyed. Other reasons for hanging on may be that the worker expects more of the family or the situation than is warranted or that she is ambitious and is seeking "the perfect case." Sometimes a worker wants to compensate for what the family may have suffered. Awareness of these feelings and a focus on the family's needs and goals can prevent these blocks to effective termination.

The nature of the worker–client relationship is another factor. Any time a close working relationship develops, both the worker and family members may have strong reactions to termination. When this is the case, more time must be allowed for the termination process so that feelings of loss can be handled.

It should not be assumed that all family members view termination as loss; some, especially those mandated to service, may view termination with relief. Other family members view the work together as a necessary interlude in their lives but are pleased that they have gained understanding and coping skills so they can get on with the business of living without further help from the worker.

Research by Anne E. Fortune, Bill Pearlingi, and Cherie D. Rochell indicated clients can have positive feelings about termination. They can feel pride and a sense of accomplishment in what they have been able to do. This study has limitations because it was carried out with a limited group of voluntary practitioners in a limited geographic area. Also, case selection may have been limited to those for whom there was success.[11]

Howard Hess and Peg McCartt Hess pointed out differences in termination, depending on context. The nature of the relationship required in the work and the expected ongoing relationships with others who have been a part of the process affect the impact of termination. Hess and Hess discussed the difference between termination of the one-to-one relationship and the formed group, in which the loss is not only of the worker but also of other group members.[12] In the family and the friendship group, the only person terminating is the worker. The authors also note the differences in termination when the strategy has been counseling, education, or resource mobilization. The nature of attachment and the impact of termination are different in each of these situations. The content of the termination phase will be different in each situation.

Termination with families is likely to be much different from individual termination, although individuals in the family may express feelings similar to those of individual clients. For families, termination generally represents the end of the social work process experience but not the end of their relationship with one another. This is especially true if the worker has been successful at reinforcing and strengthening the positive functioning of the family system by supporting appropriate family roles and relationships and positive interaction with the family's environment. At such times, successful termination brings good feelings as well as a desire to terminate. It is not unusual for family members themselves to conclude that they are ready to try things on their own. They may announce at the beginning or at the end of a meeting that they do not intend to return. If the worker has been tuned in to the family, he may be able to plan for it.

If worker and family have developed the habit of consciously terminating each session together, they have developed a good base on which to conduct the final termination of work together. Summarizing each session—what has been done and what is to be done—should give the family a good sense of the process and how much time there is before the work is completed and termination takes place. Planning termination should help avoid a surprise ending and the feelings of desertion that can go with such endings. Evaluating at the end of each session should give the worker an understanding of the family's sense of the work together and allow for corrections so that unplanned or precipitous termination does not take place. What has been done in a small way at the end of each session can then be done in a more complete manner at the end of the work together.

Because the family goes on after termination, less time may be needed to resolve any remaining issues. At the least, members should be given an opportunity to express how they feel about terminating. For children, this might be structured in terms of what they liked best and least about meeting and what they will miss most and least about not meeting. Sometimes an informal celebration may take place, such as going out to dinner or having a picnic, to mark this significant event in the life of the family. Generally, the worker does not participate in these events.

Issues related to diversity need to be included in termination. Family values and experiences as well as cultural values, attitudes, and beliefs play an important role. The ultimate termination is death, and family and cultural attitudes and beliefs about death often reflect attitudes and beliefs about termination in general. The worker should be aware of the stages of termination and be sensitive about individual and family experiences with termination and about cultural mores.

In many cultures, there are customs such as gift giving when termination occurs. Even without this, some families will want to give the worker a gift as a sign of appreciation. This presents some ethical dilemmas for the worker because the social worker should not benefit from her service to the family except through compensation from her agency or through the financial arrangements that were made ahead of time. Gift giving can also signify "the repayment of a debt" by the family, which would be a misunderstanding of the social work relationship. Expensive gifts should clearly not be accepted. Inexpensive ones might be allowed by an agency's policies. In either case, the worker should discuss the situation with the family and with her supervisor to ensure an ethical outcome.

For people at risk, termination can represent a crisis in their quest for power and control over their lives and for acceptance and recognition. Empowerment that was gained during the intervention may be ascribed to the worker, and inner doubts and anxieties about the family member's own abilities may arise again. Helping families and their members solidify their gains and assert and advocate for themselves without the support of the worker are major issues during termination with people who have experienced discrimination or oppression. Clients need to know that the fight against discrimination and oppression is both personal and collective. Efforts to connect clients to groups engaged in this cause should be made during the intervention to ensure continuation of support.

Continued success by the family after termination rests to a great degree on the extent to which the plan was based on strengths and resources within the family and their environment and on building strength in areas in which challenges and barriers exist. The family's success also rests on the degree to which the worker helped them learn new skills while resolving their situation and was able to assist them to experience social work values as a part of the helping relationship and as something integral to their everyday life. This is what represents true social work and differentiates it from other human service professions. If clients feel more valuable as human beings based on inherent worth, if they are able to exercise greater self determination and control over their lives, and if they can access appropriate resources to meet socially accepted needs, then they have truly been empowered. This means that the social work intervention has been successful not only on a short-term basis but at a deeper, more significant, and long-term level.

■   PLANNED TERMINATION WITH INDIVIDUAL   ■
FAMILY MEMBERS

Individual family members may experience termination in a very personal way. They may have derived a great deal of satisfaction from the relationship. They may also be vulnerable to feeling pain, loss, abandonment, or rejection. Helping them to resolve these issues is important in determining how permanent any changes might be. Throughout the intervention, the worker should be aware of the affect of relationships and termination on each family member. He should note how family members handle termination in other areas of their lives. Sensitivity to the family member's attitude toward termination is fundamental to planning for successful termination.

When the worker has been able to support independence and interdependence instead of dependence, she has already begun to prepare the family for termination and for life without the social worker's involvement. However, family members may want to give credit to the worker for the work that was done. Statements that they may make can be extremely flattering, such as "You were wonderful. Thank goodness that we found you. We don't know how we could have made it without you." The worker should resist the temptation to accept accolades or credit. To do so will undermine the family's sense of empowerment and the need to recognize who did the work. The social work plan identifies clients as the primary force behind change, and clients deserve credit and recognition when they are successful at achieving their goals and objectives. If they had not done what they needed to do, then no real change would have taken place.

At its worst, crediting the worker with the change is a form of magical thinking in which the family makes the worker "the savior." The worker should quickly dispel the myth that he is the only one who could have helped them. He should credit the family for their courage in facing their difficulties and for the hard work they did in resolving the situation. If there were things that the worker did that were especially helpful, he should point out that such help is available from other social workers who practice the way he does.

Planned termination with family members who experience an intense reaction should allow enough time to resolve issues related to feelings of termination. These may be similar to, and as intense as, a grief process. Thus, the worker should plan for at least three or four sessions to work through unresolved issues. In the end, family members should have access to positive feelings and a sense of accomplishment as opposed to feeling abandoned or rejected. Some families stop meeting rather than face the feelings associated with termination. In these instances, the worker should follow up with them and offer an opportunity to experience an appropriate termination process. If they refuse, the worker should at least make a follow-up contact at a later date to ensure that the family is still open to receiving help if needed. Unplanned termination initiated prematurely by families should be handled similarly, except that families should be offered a transfer or a referral if it is feasible.

Planned termination can include time-limited services imposed by design, regulations, funding sources, limited resources, or other circumstances. The advent of managed care has resulted in limitations on the amount of services that are reimbursed by insurance companies. Although this is viewed by those companies as a form of efficiency and cost savings, in essence it is rationing services for the benefit of the insurer. Managed care can place social workers in the awkward position of either denying continuation of services when they believe continued service is needed or continuing services without receiving reimbursement. At times, the existence of the agency can be threatened by reduction in revenue. Refusing needed services is a violation of the *NASW Code of Ethics*. Social workers should consider becoming active in organizations that advocate for providing services based on client needs or for decision making on services by those without a financial stake in limiting services. Allowing service decisions to be made by bureaucrats or to be arbitrarily set by diagnosis is not acceptable for clients or social workers.

In the era of managed care, termination is an issue from the onset of service. Social workers need to become proficient in providing brief and time-limited services. Family members are not as likely to invest themselves as significantly in a relationship when termination is an ever-present issue. When there is a significant investment, some form of brief follow-up may be needed to smooth the transition. Workers need to develop extensive referral networks for posttermination services. Social workers should be aware of the benefits and rights of clients and ensure that families are so informed. Workers should be prepared to advocate for needed services and to assist families in appeals processes and other advocacy actions. Finally, social workers should be open to greater use of natural helpers and nontraditional services, such as self-help and support groups.

■   COMPONENTS OF TERMINATION   ■

Allen Pincus and Anne Minahan identified three major components of the termination process: disengagement, stabilization of change, and evaluation.[13] As with other aspects of the social work endeavor, these are intermingled in practice and are separated only for purposes of discussion and study.

Disengagement

Endings bring about a cessation of relationships. If relationships have been meaningful, feelings are aroused. An unplanned termination leaves family members to deal with these feelings on their own, which results in a sense of unfinished business. It is assumed that the family is aware that termination will take place when goals have been reached. Nevertheless, when faced with actual termination, family members and the worker should acknowledge the reality of their feelings.

These feelings will vary from happiness to loss. Some common expectations about feelings of loss at termination have been identified. The initial reaction is often one of denial, either of the reality of termination or of the feelings associated with it. Denial is a defense mechanism used to avoid painful feelings. An indication of this mechanism is the phenomenon of flight. This phenomenon is manifested by a family not keeping appointments after termination is discussed. The temptation is for the worker to let the family go and to assume that they want to deal or not deal with the termination feelings in this manner. However, it is important for the worker to elicit feelings at this point so that the family and the worker can move through the termination process.

The next stage is usually a period of emotional reaction. Feelings or emotions may arise from fear of loss or of the unknown. There may be feelings of sadness or grief over the impending loss as well as anger. There may be a return of feelings associated with old wounds from previous disappointments and separations. There can be regression to old patterns of behavior. Regression may be a family member's attempt to say that she is not ready for termination. At this stage it is important for the worker to accept the family member's feelings and to help her examine these feelings and the fears, anxieties, and past experiences that are the source of the feelings. Acceptance and help in examining feelings enables the family member to work through the feelings. In a sense, the family member is helped to go through a process of mourning and is enabled to disengage from the relationship in a helpful manner.

Another means of dealing with disengagement is reminiscing about or reviewing what has been done in the work together. Doing this can help family members see the positive aspects of the work together and develop the understanding that growth often has pain associated with it. At this time, workers also should try to minimize any guilt the family members may have about the work together.

Clients sometimes introduce new problems when termination approaches. The worker and family together need to examine why these new problems have been introduced and whether there is a valid reason for continuing the service with a focus on the new problems or whether the family can work on these problems in other ways.

Clients' feelings about termination vary as to intensity and nature. If the intensity of the relationship or the period of time involved has been minimal, the feelings about termination will usually be less than if the relationship has been intense or of fairly long duration.

Clients who are not involved voluntarily may be relieved that service is terminating. Clients with feelings of success or satisfaction about the service will have different kinds of feelings about termination from those whose service experience has not been as positive. Clients who have had significant losses or separations in their lives—particularly if they have not had opportunities to deal with feelings about those losses—will have different feelings about separation from those clients for whom loss has not been as significant. The client's capacity for independence or need for dependence will also influence feelings. A significant factor in the way a client deals with termination is what is happening in his life as a whole at that point in time. If a client is called on to cope with many changes or other demands, termination may either be more difficult or may come as a relief.

The social worker needs to develop skill in disengaging from relationships with families. This should be done with consideration for, and sensitivity to, a family member's feelings and needs. A useful technique for disengagement is to taper off involvement with the family as feelings are dealt with and other work of termination is completed. Appointments may be set further apart or more emphasis placed on what the family member is to do for herself.

The worker needs to develop self-awareness about her own reactions to separation and loss. If the worker has difficulty with these tasks, she will be less able to help the family deal with the tasks of separation. The worker may wonder how to react to the intense feelings of family members that may arise in the process of termination. These feelings may be related not only to loss or grief but also to dissatisfaction about what the worker and family have been able to do together. Everyone tends to ignore or downplay feelings that are uncomfortable. If, because of their own discomfort, workers do not adequately encourage family member's feelings about termination and about their work together, they will fail to allow the family to learn management of feelings in coping with life tasks.

The work of disengagement, then, is related not only to the immediate social work situation but also to past and future losses of family members and social worker. In helping the family disengage, the worker is helping family members deal with past losses and unresolved feelings about those losses. Also, the family and its members are being provided with coping mechanisms for dealing with future loss, with understandings for dealing with grief and loss that are part of human functioning. To bypass or minimize the disengagement process is to lose an opportunity for growth.

Stabilization of Change

In helping family members deal with the feelings of termination and disengagement from the relationship, the family and the worker often review what has happened in the work together. This is useful in stabilizing the change that has taken place and helps family members understand how they have grown and what has led to the growth. This gives them guidelines on how future needs or concerns might be approached and dealt with. It enables them to know they have resources that can help them to make it on their own and what those resources are.

One way to work on stabilization of change is to review what has occurred. The time together should be seen as one step, an important step, of the growth that results in better coping with life tasks. This view implies there are other steps to be taken, not with the worker but through new relationships or in ongoing responses to life situations. Continued growth is one way of stabilizing the change that has taken place. The worker and family discuss the next steps and how they can go about taking these steps. They then plan ways of obtaining needed supports and resources they can use in taking these steps.

Together, the worker and the family explore possible ways for dealing with situations similar to the one that brought the family to the agency for help. They consider how the learning that has taken place can be transferred to other situations. The worker and family may identify other resources in the family's environment that would be useful in coping with life situations. These may be natural helpers or other community systems, such as recreation programs, groups of people with similar concerns, and the like. These resources can be substitute or replacement support systems.

Usually, the worker offers the family the option of returning to the agency if future situations become overwhelming. It is important for the family to know that the agency makes the service possible and that even if the worker is no longer available, the agency will provide someone else to help. The family needs to be aware that workers come and go but that the agency continues to provide the service. This awareness is particularly important for the family who may be terminating service against the advice of the worker.

Stabilization of change can be encouraged by discussing possible goals for further growth and resources that can be used to enable growth. This discussion can examine how change took place as the worker and family worked together. The process that was used can be examined, and the worker can maximize the family's understanding of this process. Through the work of stabilizing the change, the worker supports within the family a sense of accomplishment and competence. The family members' fears are recognized and examined, and suggestions are made about how to deal with them.

Stabilization of the change is an important stage in growth and change. Without conscious efforts to carry out the tasks involved in stabilization, the family's capacity to sustain the desired change may be reduced.

Evaluation

The third component of termination is evaluation. As discussed earlier, evaluation is an ongoing part of the social work endeavor and a particularly important component of the termination phase.

As the worker and family engage in evaluation during termination, the major focus is on the goals set as a part of the plan of action and on the family's needs or needs of family members as identified in the assessment process. The major question to be answered is, Did we accomplish what we set out to do? If the goals were achieved and the needs met, then the purpose of the service has been accomplished. If the goals were met but a need or needs remain troublesome, then the goals may not have been the right goals or other goals must be met as well.

Evaluation at termination is focused on whether goals have been achieved and needs met. This includes evaluating the family's ability to continue to meet its needs as a system and the needs of its members. The worker asks the family to evaluate the service. He asks what was helpful, what was not helpful, and what would have been helpful. If appropriate, he asks everyone to respond to these questions. With younger children, it may be necessary to rephrase these questions. Questions about what it was they liked best or least and what they will miss the most or the least are likely to elicit this feedback.

Any spinoffs or unexpected consequences of the work together should be noted. This aspect of evaluation is useful for both worker and family in that it helps the family better understand how to meet needs in the future. It helps the worker gain greater understanding of the helping process and of means for working with families.

The worker's openness to evaluating what has happened involves a certain amount of risk because the worker's mistakes and limitations may come to light. The family may be overly critical or display undue dissatisfaction, which may be one way family members express negative feelings related to termination. The worker needs to accept these feelings without becoming defensive and carefully examine with family members the negative feelings and sort out current feelings from past feelings of abandonment or unrealistic dissatisfaction. Perhaps one of the reasons workers have not put sufficient emphasis on the termination process is that it is a time for examining the performance of the worker. This is a threatening experience but one that is essential for good social work practice.

Competence in guiding the termination process is one way of influencing client satisfaction over the work together. The family reviews what has happened, acknowledges improvement or progress, discovers their part in the process and how the experience may be transferred to other life experiences, and assesses how they can continue their growth.

The social work endeavor is terminated through the interwoven activities aimed at disengagement, stabilization of change, and evaluation. Through these activities the family and its members are helped to deal with feelings so that these feelings will not inhibit future social functioning. The family and its members are readied to continue to grow and to cope with activities of living and with the environment and its expectations.

CASE EXAMPLE

From the case example of the Perez family, the following is an example of evaluation and termination.

Jane met with the Perez family at the agency to finalize their work and terminate services. The family brought some baked goods with them. Jane thanked them for the food and said that she would share it with the staff. Although receiving gifts is not typically ethical for social workers, Jane knew that refusing it would be taken as an offense in the family's culture and by sharing it with the staff she was not personally benefiting from this. The family had invited Jane to join them for a celebration dinner, but she declined saying that was against agency policy and that they should celebrate this together as a family. The family sat down together to review what had occurred since they began working together. Juan and Carmen are doing well in school and Juan has stopped hanging around with a negative crowd. Carmen and the group of girls who were harassing her were able to resolve the situation through peer mediation. She has made some new friends and is on the junior varsity soccer team. Juan's grades have risen and he is on track to qualify for both the co-op and the computer graphics programs; unfortunately, he will not be able to do both next year. He is leaning toward the computer program with the hope of co-oping his senior year. Mrs. P has joined the homemakers program at the local community college and has started working on her GED. Mrs. P's mother watches the children while she is gone. Mr. P is still working long hours because Mrs. P has not started working as yet. They decided that she might be able to get a position with better pay if she got her GED first. In an effort to restore more family togetherness, the family plans a family event for every Sunday after church. Sometimes Juan and Carmen balk at this, but thus far it seems to have helped in bringing the family closer.

(continued)

Jane asked each family member to say what they felt was helpful, what was not help-ful and what might have been helpful in terms of her services. For the younger children she restated this in terms of what they liked, did not like, and would have liked to have happen. She explained that this would be helpful to her in improving her services to other families. Mr. P said that he felt a great deal of pride in his wife and children for what they have accomplished. It is important for him to know that things are going well when he is not there. He feels that his reward will come later when his wife goes to work and he can spend more time with the family. He feels that spending Sunday afternoons together has been a big step in that direction. He did not think that there was anything Jane did that was not helpful or could have been more helpful. Mrs. P thanked Jane for helping her to realize some of her dreams. She admitted that she had some fears that her husband would not be receptive and doubted Jane's approach would work but it turned out well. Juan said that he liked the options that he has at school although he still does not like go-ing. He wishes that he could work and still be in the computer graphics program and he might look for a part-time job when he turns sixteen. Juan stated that he initially did not like working with a female worker and would have preferred a male social worker, espe-cially one who was Hispanic. He admitted that Jane could not help that. He said that he thought Jane's initial approach was mostly on the side of his parents and he felt that she was not as evenhanded as she might have been. However, he feels good about the way things have turned out. Carmen felt that everything has gone well and she would not change anything. The younger children and their grandmother agreed. The younger chil-dren especially enjoyed having the "I and we" chart on the refrigerator with all their names on it, including their parents and grandparent. They still laughed about that. Jane told the family that they would be receiving a satisfaction survey in the mail from the agency and asked that the family fill it out and return it and they agreed.

Mrs. P stated that she did not know what they would have done without Jane's help. She said that they could not have done it without her. Jane said that was very flattering but that it was not she who did the work, it was the family. She pointed out that if the family was able to work with her then they could work with other workers. She told the family that if they needed assistance in the future that she or another worker would be available or they would find someone who would meet their needs. The family said their good-byes and left for their celebration dinner.

SUMMARY

This chapter has considered evaluation as an ongoing part of the social work process. It has discussed various kinds of evaluation and their usefulness. The use of research tools in the evaluative process was explained. Evaluation during each stage of the change process was discussed. Evaluation is a skill that all social workers must possess and a process that all so-cial workers must engage in if they are to adhere to the ethical principles of the social work profession. The diversity competent worker incorporates diversity into her evaluation both in terms of content and process. She is careful to include those factors that are relevant to her client's diversity and evaluate the process in a manner that is consistent with that diversity.

The last phase of the social work process is termination. It is planned from the beginning of the process. Termination may lead to transfer of the client to another worker. There are three components of termination work: disengagement, stabilization of change, and evaluation. Social workers who engage the family in a well-thought-out termination process strengthen the family's capacity for social functioning in the future. They also enhance their own professional capacity through evaluating with the family what led to the desired outcome. Termination is an integral part of the total social work process.

Termination is highly value laden and has many cultural nuances. The diversity competent worker is aware of these nuances and seeks to become aware of how they affect his client. He incorporates this into his terminations and seeks to make the process as comfortable and growth-enhancing as possible.

QUESTIONS

1. How do the change process and single-system research design fit with each other?
2. What are some ethical concerns that social workers might have with respect to the use of the traditional experimental method and with other research designs?
3. Discuss your feeling about losing a relationship with someone who is important to you.
4. Discuss some of the reasons why families may terminate prematurely.
5. How can a worker appropriately deal with issues during termination?

SUGGESTED READINGS

Johnson, Louise C., and Yanca, Stephen J. *Social Work Practice: A Generalist Approach,* 9th ed. Boston: Allyn & Bacon, 2007 (Chapter 12).

Bloom, Martin, Fischer, Joel, and Orme, John G. *Evaluating Practice: Guidelines for the Accountable Professional,* 5th ed. Boston: Allyn & Bacon, 2006.

Fortune, Anne E. "Termination in Direct Practice" in *Encyclopedia of Social Work,* 19th ed. Richard L. Edwards, Ed. Washington, DC: NASW Press, 1995 (pp. 2398–2404).

Ginsberg, Leon. *Social Work Evaluation: Principles and Methods.* Boston: Allyn & Bacon, 2001.

Miley, Karla Krogsrud, O'Melia, Michael, and DuBois, Brenda L. *Social Work Practice: An Empowering Approach,* 5th ed. Boston: Allyn & Bacon, 2007 (Chapter 16).

Sheafor, Bradford W., and Horejsi, Charles R. *Techniques and Guidelines for Social Work Practice,* 7th ed. Boston: Allyn & Bacon, 2006 (Chapter 14).

Tripodi, Tony. *A Primer on Single-Subject Design for Clinical Social Workers.* Washington, DC: NASW Press, 1994.

Weinbach, Robert W. *Evaluating Social Work Services and Programs.* Boston: Allyn & Bacon, 2005.

Yegidis, Bonnie L., and Weinrich, Robert W. *Research Methods for Social Workers,* 5th ed. Boston: Allyn & Bacon, 2006.

Generalist Practice with Family Subsystems

Part III presents some applications of our generalist social work practice model as it applies to various types of family systems that the worker is likely to encounter. The chapters are devoted to examining the application of the Johnson/Yanca model to family subsystems. Our practice experience and research indicate that subsystems are the main focus for most family work, especially parent and parent–child subsystems for generalist social workers. However, it seems that family texts tend to assume that the worker is conducting family therapy and is working with the entire family as a unit in the room during the process. Our experience indicates that most family work, especially for generalist social workers, is not family therapy and is focused on one or more of the subsystems in the family.

In family systems theory, subsystems are based on the four types of relationships that might be present in a family system. These are the marital or couple relationship, the relationship between the two parents, the relationships between each parent and each child along with the overall relationship between the parent subsystem and the children, and the relationships among the siblings in the family. Of course, not all families have all of these relationships or subsystems present. In addition, the presence of these may change over time and other forms may also appear. These include stepfamily relationships and relationships with extended family and fictive kin.

Chapter 10 presents the application of the Johnson/Yanca model of generalist practice with couples. It includes a table that provides a guideline for deciding whether to work with various family subsystems. The chapter proceeds to consider interaction and engagement with couples and follows the phases of the change process: assessment, planning, direct and indirect practice actions, and evaluation and termination with couples. Finally, there is a discussion of generalist practice with couples who are older.

Chapters 11, 12, and 13 follow the same format as 10 in presenting our generalist social work practice model in working with parents, parent–child, and sibling subsystems respectively. Each chapter presents the application of the model of generalist practice by examining interaction and engagement with the respective subsystem followed by the phases

10

Generalist Practice with Couples

LEARNING EXPECTATIONS

1. Understand the application of the generalist practice model to working with couples.

2. Understand interaction and engagement with couples.

3. Understand assessment as a process and a product with couples.

4. Understand planning as a product and a process with couples.

5. Understand direct and indirect actions with couples.

6. Understand evaluation and termination with couples.

This chapter begins examining the change process with family subsystems. We begin with couples because marriage and marital types of relationships are the foundation of family life. These are the relationships that make family life possible. When these relationships go well, they provide a solid foundation for family functioning. When these relationships do not go well, then families often find themselves compensating for the loss of that foundation. We are not saying this to pass judgment on divorce, single parenthood, stepfamilies, or any other form that families take. We are simply recognizing that couples who have a solid relationship provide some great advantages for their families. Unfortunately, this has proven elusive for many families. We will use the terms *couple* and *marital system* interchangeably to include marriage and marital types of relationships, including live-in relationships, committed gay or lesbian relationships where marriage is not available, significant relationships that produce children, and the like. The term *marital system* will be used to refer to the couple as part of a family system. The term *couple* will be used as a generic term or will tend to be used to refer to the relationship within the marital system.

As discussed previously, there is a need to differentiate between the relationship that a couple has with each other and the relationship that they have as parents. These are separate roles that need to be identified and kept separate from each other. When functioning within the marital system, the couple fulfill roles as spouses to each other regardless of whether they are married. In these roles the couple have needs and expectations that must be met within their relationship. When functioning as a member of the parent system, the couple need to work together to fulfill roles and expectations as parents of offspring. This includes meeting the needs of the children in the family and dealing with issues that arise as they raise the children. In other words, they are working together to meet needs, demands, and expectations from outside of their relationship. The couple needs to function as a united parental system for this to be accomplished. We focus on this in Chapter 11. However, this is one of the greatest challenges a couple will face if they are raising children. Unresolved differences regarding parenting, child-rearing, and stepparenthood are often major factors in threatening a marriage or marital type relationship. We discuss the need to do this in this chapter and will follow up with this in the next chapter.

This chapter covers the change process with couples. Generally, working with couples as parents is quite common, but marriage counseling is usually reserved for professionals with special training and is not typically provided by generalist social workers, especially at the BSW level. However, reality often dictates that the social worker assist couples with strengthening their relationship in order to function well as parents and to strengthen the family system. In rural areas, the worker may be the only realistic option available regardless of her level of education or training. Distance, travel time, or lack of transportation may make it unlikely or even impossible for couples in rural areas to access a marriage counselor. In other areas, services to couples may be difficult to access or may be beyond their reach financially. More urban areas may have a high demand for services with waiting lists. Another difficulty is that traditional insurance companies do not cover marriage counseling. They require that the person receiving treatment be diagnosed with a mental condition. It may be possible to do this and still do conjoint work with a partner, but this is not always the case.

This chapter provides a basic approach to working with couples that focuses on building relationship skills that are necessary for a successful relationship. These skills can and should be used by the worker with all forms of important relationships. Some of these were introduced in Chapter 4 and others were discussed in Chapter 7. The basic skills necessary are good communication, a problem-solving/decision-making process that works, and a process for resolving conflict. These are skills that every social worker must have in their repertoire to begin with and so any social worker can use these skills to assist couples in strengthening their relationship.

The change process with couples follows the same stages that were outlined for families in Part II. We begin with interaction and engagement. The chapter also considers assessment, planning, action, and evaluation and termination with couples. There is overlap between this chapter, chapters in Part II, and those that follow in Part III. As we pointed out in Chapter 5, examining the change process with the family as a system and with subsystems of the family are separated in this text for learning purposes. This is done so that the student or practitioner can achieve a better understanding of how to work with family subsystems, which is likely to be the focus of most of their work with families. However, the material on family subsystems here in Part III is also used in working with the family as a system, especially when subsystems and relationships are part of the focus of the work.

Similarly, working more exclusively with a family subsystem does not exclude the need to understand the family as a system. As a result, the information from the family social history schema should be added to the schemas for development of a social history for each subsystem here in Part III as indicated. In addition, the units of attention for parts of the plan for a family subsystem may be parts of the family system, the whole system, or the interactions that occur within various parts of the family system. Direct and indirect practice actions that are identified with working with the family system may also be used when working with subsystems and vice versa. On those occasions when the worker is working with all or most of the family system, issues related to family subsystem structures, functioning, and development are likely to arise and the worker will need to use the relevant material from Part II or Part III. Thus, it is important to view the material in Parts II and III as integrated with each other and only separated here for learning purposes.

■ INTERACTION AND ENGAGEMENT ■
WITH COUPLES

Working with couples involves working with two individuals and their relationship with each other. In this work, the social worker must be cognizant of her role and the roles of her clients. As we pointed out in Chapter 4, whenever a worker is working with more than one client, the client is the system as a whole as well as each individual in that system. This means that the worker must take and be given the role of mediator. She cannot take sides and still serve the individuals and the system as a whole. At the same time, it would be inappropriate and unethical to sacrifice the needs of any of the individuals involved. If the needs of the individuals are not met, then it leaves the system unbalanced and will eventually lead to further difficulties. Instead, the worker must work with the client system to meet both individual needs and the needs of the relationship. This is what it takes to have a strong relationship.

As with all generalist practice, the worker might start out working with an individual or individuals, a family, or a subsystem before it is decided that working with the couple or marital subsystem is necessary or the best approach. Working with couples may also begin with the couple presenting themselves for service. However, for the generalist social worker it is more likely that she will start with an individual or with parental, parent–child, or family work and then discover that the couple needs to strengthen their relationship before this work can be done. Situations that begin with an individual and lead to working with a couple most often involve one of the partners receiving services that leads to working with the relationship or a child receiving services and discovering that the marital system is experiencing challenges or difficulties to which the child is reacting. Table 10.1 gives an overview of some of the indications and counterindications for working with family subsystems.

When a social worker works with a couple on their relationship, he must remain neutral if he is going to be able to help them. In order to do this, the worker should insist on conjoint sessions. Individual sessions tend to raise mistrust and often lead to secrets that will cause the worker to lose his neutrality. Any secrets between the worker and one of the partners will result in a "special" relationship with that partner, which destroys the worker's neutrality. If individual sessions must take place, the worker needs to have an understanding that the contents cannot remain confidential from the other partner. If the worker has already met individually with either partner, then he may need to have or at least offer an individual session

Table 10.1   Indications and Counterindications for Working with Family Subsystems

Subsystem	Indications	Counterindications
Marital/Couple	Difficulty in couple interaction. Trend toward family or marital breakup. A member undercuts change efforts of the other member. A member needs to respond to individual need of other member. Information gathering or giving regarding marital/couple relationship. Need for understanding or strengthening marital/couple interaction to understand or support individual or family functioning. Couple needs to examine role functioning, decision making, communication or conflict. Chaotic families with a need to restore order and marital/couple subsystem needs strengthening or support Couple's choice	Significant impairment of a member of marital/couple subsystem prevents participation Need for individual help precludes work with marital/couple Worker cannot deal with destructive interactions within marital/couple subsystem
Parental	Major difficulties exist in couple interaction regarding parenting. One member undercuts parenting efforts of the other member. Information gathering regarding family. Information giving regarding parenting. Need for understanding parental interaction to understand individual or family functioning. Couple needs to examine role functioning, decision making, communication or conflict regarding parenting. Chaotic families with a need to restore order and parental subsystem needs strengthening or support Couple's choice	Irreversible trend toward family or marital breakup Significant impairment of a member of parental subsystem prevents participation Need for individual help precludes work with couple as parents Worker cannot deal with destructive interactions within marital/couple or parental subsystem
Parent–Child	Major difficulties exist in parent–child interaction. A parents need to develop or improve relationship with a child or step-child. Need for understanding parent–child interaction to understand individual or family functioning. Family/couple choice	Irreversible trend toward family or marital breakup Significant impairment of a parent or child prevents participation Need for individual help precludes work with parent–child subsystem Worker cannot deal with destructive interactions within parent–child subsystem

(continued)

Table 10.1   Continued

Subsystem	Indications	Counterindications
Sibling	Major difficulties exist in sibling interaction.	Irreversible trend toward family breakup
	Siblings or step-siblings need to develop or improve relationship with each other.	Significant impairment of a sibling prevents participation
	Need for understanding sibling interaction to understand individual or family functioning.	Need for individual help precludes work with sibling subsystem
	Family/couple choice	Worker cannot deal with destructive interactions within sibling subsystem

or two with the other partner. The worker should also have the partner with whom he met individually give an overview of what was discussed. If individual work needs to take place before conjoint work can be successful, then the first choice is to have that work be done with a different worker. If this is not possible, then the choice is to do the individual work with the other partner present or develop an agreement to avoid any discussion about the relationship or the other partner in the individual sessions. In the latter instance, the success of the work will depend on the ability of the absent partner to trust the worker.

It is not unusual for one of the partners to refuse service while the other partner seeks assistance with the relationship. When this occurs, the worker should warn him or her that doing so can increase the threat to the relationship because one partner is seeking change whereas the other is not. At the same time, taking a systems approach, the worker can assist a partner to change his or her half of the relationship and doing so may change the way the other partner acts in the relationship. However, in working with an individual partner, the focus must be on that individual and his or her part of the relationship. Meeting to discuss the other partner is essentially complaining because a person can really only change him- or herself.

As the first meeting begins, the social worker must engage the couple and establish a working relationship. This must be done within the context of the customs and culture of the couple. It may not always be clear what this is even if the worker has some familiarity with the race or ethnicity of the couple. As we described earlier, using naturalistic inquiry is a sound approach for nearly any situation, but it is especially helpful when working cross-culturally. Using this approach, the worker observes her clients and mirrors their verbal and nonverbal approach. People are often more cautious during an initial contact, so the worker might begin slowly with some small talk. Commenting about the weather or some recent event (preferably something positive) can break the ice. If the couple has come to the agency, the worker might inquire whether they had any difficulty finding the office. She might then ask what brings them in for service or she might begin by discussing what has transpired in working with a family member or members that lead up to the decision to meet them as a couple. In some cases she may have already met either one or both of them in providing services. If it is a home visit, the worker should explain how she was referred and ask about their understanding of the referral.

When the worker starts working with a couple, he should begin with a discussion of his background and training and any limits he might have in working with them. If it appears that his skills and abilities are commensurate with the work to be done then the work can begin. If this is not the case, then a discussion regarding a referral should be undertaken.

If a referral is not possible, then it may be necessary for the worker to provide the services that are within her capacity and then reevaluate the situation at a later date. Often when clients experience some relief from the situation that brought them into service, they do not feel the need for further service. At times, this relief releases energy for change that can also lead to changes in other areas without formal intervention. Sometimes people decide not to change or will only go so far before they decide to end their involvement. Other times, people simply need to gain an understanding of their situation and what might be done about it and then they proceed on their own. Quite often in working with couples, assisting them in acquiring new or strengthening existing relationship skills gives them the tools they need to resolve matters on their own. Sometimes couples want to know that it is okay to stay together even though they are faced with difficulties in their relationship. This is quite common with respect to infidelity. Research indicates that the majority of marriages and probably most marital type relationships will experience at least one incident of infidelity during the course of the relationship. Some of these are never discovered or disclosed. However, most of the one's that are exposed, do not result in a termination of the relationship. Obviously, there is a lot of work to be done in these situations, but some couples simply need reassurance that they do not have to end their relationship along with some guidance on how to proceed. We cover this further later in this chapter.

If the decision is to work together, then the worker should begin a discussion about cross-cultural issues. Again using naturalistic inquiry, the worker explores how help is viewed, given, and received within the culture or diversity of the couple. He looks for commonality between the couple and areas of differences as well as commonality and differences with his own diversity. He uses common areas to bridge some of the differences and notes areas for further exploration or negotiation and compromise with regard to differences. Most importantly, the worker asks questions and takes the position that he does not know what he does not know. He allows the couple to be experts with regard to their own lives and their diversity. When the worker is able to get the couple to talk about their culture or diversity and about themselves, he has begun the real work toward engagement. Showing an interest in people gives them a feeling of respect and importance. It contributes to a sense of value and worth as an individual, the most basic cardinal value of social work. Once the worker has a sense of the diversity factors involved and the reasons for working together, he begins to explore the relationship. The assessment process has begun.

ASSESSMENT WITH COUPLES

As with families, assessment with couples involves both process and product. The change process follows similar steps taken in assessment with families as described in Chapter 5. The social history for a couple follows a similar format as the family social history presented in Table 5.3. Table 10.2 contains elements that should be added to the family history format as part II.D. In addition, the term *couple* should be substituted for *family* for parts III and IV of Table 5.3. Relevant portions of the individual social history should be added from

Table 5.2. Making these changes will convert the family social history to one that is focused on the marital or couple subsystem.

The assessment phase is the process that is used to set the stage for change. The assessment product is the social history. A supplemental schema for the social history of a marital/couple subsystem is outlined in Table 10.2. It includes an assessment of the structure, the functioning, and the development of this family subsystem.

As is the case with families, the purpose of assessment with couples is to gain an understanding of the couple and their situation and lay the groundwork for change by identifying the strengths and resources in the ecosystem. In this way, the assessment spans all three dimensions of time—past, present, and future.

Assessment as a Process

As mentioned earlier, working with couples may begin with working with an individual or a family or another family subsystem. The decision to work together as a couple may come at any point in the change process, but typically it will come during either assessment or planning. Whenever the decision is made, the social worker establishes a relationship with the couple and begins to gather information about the presenting need or concern as it relates to them as a couple. Generally, this is related to the indications for working with the marital/couple subsystem identified in Table 10.1. It is best to formulate these needs and concerns in a format similar to the following:

> Mr. and Mrs. Jones need to strengthen their relationship.

If the need or concern relates to a family matter, the following format might be used:

> In order to help their blended family to grow together as a family, Mr. and Mrs. Jones need to strengthen their relationship.

The nature of the need or concern relates to areas that may be causing the need to arise and assumptions about resolution of the situation. This step allows the worker and the couple to speculate about the work to be done. It may include focusing on the relationship, focusing on how the couple meets each others needs within their relationship, or how they deal with their ecosystem (including their family) as a couple. Some examples of these are as follows:

> If Mr. and Mrs. Jones can maintain a healthy marriage that is separate from their other roles in the family, they will be able to help their blended family grow together as a family.
>
> If Mr. and Mrs. Jones take time to nurture their marriage, they will strengthen it and be more satisfied with their relationship.
>
> If Mr. and Mrs. Jones give each other a hug and a kiss each morning and evening they will feel more satisfied with their relationship
>
> If Mr. and Mrs. Jones set aside time each day to talk about their individual needs and their relationship, they will feel more intimate as a couple.

If Mr. and Mrs. Jones improve their communication, decision making, and conflict resolution as a couple, they will be more effective in their roles as parents and stepparents in the family.

If Mr. and Mrs. Jones set aside time each day to talk about their concerns at work, they
will feel more support for dealing with issues at their workplaces.

In identifying the nature of the needs and concerns, the worker is able to gain a better understanding of the couple and their situation. This also provides a focus for selecting and
collecting information.

As the social worker gathers information about the couple and their situation, he looks
for potential strengths and resources in the marital/couple subsystem and their ecosystem.
As we discussed with families, change needs to be based on a solid foundation. Abilities
and capabilities in one area of their life are signs of potential in other areas. For instance, if
one of them feels that he or she has a good relationship with a friend or a relative, then the
elements of that relationship can be examined to determine its relevance for improving the
marital relationship. Or, the ability to work together in dealing with certain situations can
be used to build abilities in other areas of their relationship.

The selection and collection of information are driven by the first three steps of the assessment phase. As much as possible, the social worker does not collect information that will not be
used in the changed effort. The exception to this is information that is necessary to complete a
case file, obtain reimbursement, or meet similar bureaucratic requirements. The worker gathers
information about the need or concern and that which is necessary to understand the couple and
their situation. She gathers information about the assumptions that were made in the second step
to determine if these are accurate or feasible. She explores potential strengths and resources to
decide whether these can be used to develop a plan to meet needs and address concerns.

Analysis of the information that is collected is done both independently and jointly. The
worker analyzes the situation and the information he has to gain sufficient understanding of person in situation or "couple in situation" in this case. As with any form of family work, he must
analyze five general areas as the work proceeds: (1) what he understands about couple in environment and strengths and resources, given what is known; (2) what changes are needed, given
what is known; (3) what further information is needed to better understand the situation; (4) what
further information is needed to bring about successful change; and (5) what are some potentially successful change strategies that can be used to meet the needs and address the concerns.

Assessment as a Product

The product of the assessment is the social history. Depending on the setting and various
bureaucratic requirements, different structures and information may be required in the social history. In some settings, it may be a more informal than formal document. Table 10.2
along with modifications from Table 5.3 contains the information required in the typical social history. Various settings may emphasize certain areas or have additional areas of concern such as health, mental health, or substance abuse.

The first two parts of the social history involve demographic and background information.
The worker gathers information that she needs to understand the situation. Part I focuses on
family members and other persons relevant to the situation. Part II considers the family as a

Table 10.2 Supplementary Schema for Development of a Social History for Couples

I. Identifying Information (as needed by agency)
(This is the same as Table 5.3.I.)

II. (Parts A, B, and C are the same as Table 5.3.II.)
   D. The couple as a subsystem of the family (note the strengths, resources, and challenges for each section)
      1. Structure and form of current and past marriages and significant relationships
         a. Identify all persons within the current functioning family subsystem. Include members of past marriages and significant relationships. Describe the couple as individuals and each person relevant to the situation using appropriate parts of "Schema for Development of a Social History: Individual" (Table 5.2).
         b. Subsystems—Describe the relationship and functioning of the marital system and its influence on and the influence from parental, sibling, and parent–child subsystems.
         c. Cohesiveness as a couple—Describe the manner in which the couple maintain their relationship system, boundaries, and relatedness. Include the issue of connectedness and separateness, rules and norms for their relationship, and emotional bond.
         d. The couple's environment—Describe the couple's
            1) Living situation—current and past situations during other marriages and significant relationships.
            2) Socioeconomic status and how the couple maintains this.
            3) Community or neighborhood and the couple's relationship with the community or neighborhood. Include community organizations and institutions important for the couple and the nature of the relationship with these. Describe community and neighborhood resources and responsibilities and impingements for this couple in this community.
            4) Extended family, including involvement with, significant persons in, strength of the influence of, and resources, responsibility, and impingements from it on relationship.
      2. Functioning as a couple
         a. Communication patterns and skills
         b. Decision-making and problem-solving patterns and skills
         c. Conflict resolution patterns and skills
         d. Role performance and satisfaction and how these are established and maintained
            1) Work and housekeeping standards and practices
            2) Parenting and childcare standards and practices
            3) System member support; growth encouragement, care, and concern
         e. Couple's customary adaptive and coping mechanisms
         f. Intimacy as a couple
      3. Development of the relationship—history
         a. Brief history of the relationship from dating and courtship until current situation
         b. Roots, influence of cultural group and previous generations on the couple
         c. Significant events in the life of the couple, including previous marriages and significant relationships, especially live-in relationships and relationships that have produced children
         d. Developmental stage of the relationship

III. The concern or need
(This is the same as Table 5.3.III. with "couple" replacing "family" as the focus)

IV. Strengths and Challenges for Meeting Needs
(This is the same as Table 5.3.IV. with "couple" replacing "family" as the focus)

system and the couple as a subsystem of the family. Part II.D focuses on the two individuals as a couple. This part is divided into considering the structure, functioning, and development of the relationship.

Understanding the structure of current and former relationships is an important aspect of assessment with couples. This is often influenced by culture, diversity, and sociological factors. In contrast to most areas of the world where there is relative homogeneity with respect to culture between couples, the United States has experienced a great deal of variation. Cross-cultural relationships are more the norm than are shared cultural relationships. This sets up a great deal of variation with respect to roles and expectations. However, most couples seem unaware of this. In relationships where both partners have a common culture, it is more likely that couples will have common expectations with respect to their roles and that of the other. Most cultures have common expectations for the roles of males and females in a relationship. They are likely to have had common experiences growing up that reinforce these roles, especially with respect to their experiences in watching their parents' relationship. There are also likely to be common expectations with regard to child-rearing and various tasks within the family system. Couples in cross-cultural relationships tend to have the opposite experience in that it is less likely that they will share these expectations and experiences. As a result, there is a much greater need to communicate around these areas and to negotiate and compromise.

For biracial or multiracial couples, difficulties include prejudice and discrimination on the part of society along with meeting the challenges of developing a successful cross-cultural relationship. Developing an understanding of a partner from a different culture is challenging. Fighting prejudice and discrimination can be either a divisive factor in a relationship or something that unites the couple and makes their relationship stronger. For many couples, problems with extended family members are even greater than those that come from outside the family.

Couples who are gay or lesbian also face intense prejudice and discrimination on the part of society. They also have numerous legal barriers such as not being able to be legally married or not having their marriage recognized by the state in which they reside. It is often difficult for them to receive coverage for benefits for their partners. Holding hands or displaying affection can bring on anything from rude looks or remarks to violence.

Unmarried couples have become much more common during the past several decades. Unmarried heterosexual couples have gained much more acceptance than same-sex partners. These relationships range from postdating relationships and trial marriages to long-term relationships. There may be a series of these types of live-in relationships without any marriage, before marriage, or between marriages.

Single parents may experience intermittent live-in relationships. These also may be a series of live-in relationships without any marriage, before marriage, or between marriages. The involvement of children in these situations tends to create a great deal of stress for both the couples and the children.

Couples receiving services from generalist social workers include foster parents and adoptive parents. Foster parents may need to work out the details of how they will handle the fostering of children. Adoptive couples who are not able to conceive children need to resolve issues around their infertility and will need to prepare themselves for becoming adoptive parents. Many of these marriages do not survive, so working with adoptive couples to solidify their relationship is essential for a long-term successful adoption.

Couples can experience more than one of these characteristics in any given relationship. In addition, there can also be a series of these relationships with any of these variations over time.

All of these factors can increase or decrease the cohesion that couples experience in their relationship. Couples with strong relationships will use challenges to strengthen their relationships. Each time a challenge is faced, they believe that if they can face what they have faced in the past, then they can face other challenges ahead. They are able to establish an emotional bond that carries them through hard times. They have worked out the details of being a couple and are comfortable with each other. They trust and rely on each other.

The environment may or may not be supportive for a couple. An environment that is hostile or threatening adds stress. Financial difficulties are one of the major threats to a relationship as are difficulties with in-laws. Unfortunately, even strong environments with many resources may not provide sufficient support for couples, especially when people in that environment are hostile toward, or not accepting of, some of the variety or diversity previously mentioned such as biracial or gay or lesbian couples, unmarried couples, single parents, and the like.

The functioning of the couple as partners is an important consideration. This is the heart of the assessment with families and their subsystems, especially couples. The most important relationship most people have as adults is with a spouse or partner. The essential skills that are necessary for a strong successful relationship are communication skills, decision-making or problem-solving skills, and the ability to resolve conflict in a constructive rather than a destructive manner.

Other considerations regarding functioning as a couple include how the partners are able to perform in the roles that are necessary for functioning within their relationship and in the family. To be happy, couples must be satisfied with their own and their partners performance in these roles. In addition, working together on the stresses and strains within and outside of their relationship is important.

In most U.S. marriages or marital type relationships, intimacy is generally considered vital. This includes both emotional and physical closeness along with meeting each other's sexual needs. This can be a delicate area for social workers to explore. There are inventories that are effective in assessing these and other areas of marital relationships. The worker can discuss intimacy with a couple in incremental steps. Asking more general questions will usually give some clues as to the state of affairs in terms of intimacy. For instance, the worker might inquire about how satisfied each partner is with their ability to discuss their thoughts and feelings. The worker can also explore the degree to which the couple is able to express love and affection for each other. As these questions are answered, the worker gets a sense about the appropriateness of inquiring about satisfaction with their sexual intimacy. Generally speaking, couples who have difficulty with positive responses to verbal intimacy, expressions of love, and showing physical affection are more likely to have one or both partners also dissatisfied with their sexual intimacy. However, couples who feel positive about these areas are more likely to feel positive about their sexual relationship or at least they are more likely to feel free to discuss their sexual satisfaction. As with many other areas in working with couples, the worker needs to approach this using naturalistic inquiry and asking questions about how love and affection are expressed within the couple's culture or cultures. The worker also needs to get a sense about cultural taboos regarding even discussing sexuality and be sensitive to this.

Constructing an eco-map will give both the worker and the couple a snapshot of their current situation. The eco-map was covered in Chapter 5. When constructing one with a couple, it should still include all members of the household but the emphasis on energy flow should be on the couple as individuals and as a couple.

It is important to assess the development of the relationship over time. It is not necessary to discuss every detail. This would be too time consuming and unproductive. However, exploring how the relationship began, what attracted them to each other, and how they decided to marry or live together are valuable in understanding them as a couple. It can also highlight some things that are now missing from the relationship. Exploration of the influence of culture was discussed earlier because it also influences structure. It is also helpful to have the couple describe their experiences with their parents' marriages or marital type relationships. Significant events in their life as a couple and as individuals can yield insight into current thoughts, feelings, and actions within their relationship. Finally, the worker needs to identify the stage of development for the relationship and the family. The family stages of development were discussed in Chapter 5.

Although most family developmental systems revolve around stages of development for children, there are also typical developmental stages for marriage or marital type relationships without considering children. Some of these are lifelong relationships and others might be a series of two or more relationships with or without marriage. Generally, relationships begin with some sort of dating. One exception would be an arranged marriage or perhaps a "catalog bride." A couple could continue dating either each other or others indefinitely. If the dating becomes more serious, a commitment to have an exclusive relationship is generally the next step. This is generally either a courtship or a live-in arrangement. Some couples move in together without a courtship period, others do so during a courtship, and some do not live togther until they are married. Some live-in relationships continue on in the same way as a marriage without the legal commitment.

Whether the couple is married or living together, there is usually a "honeymoon period." This usually consists of a time when couples try to act in a positive loving way with each other while also adjusting to life together. They are more likely to set aside differences and overlook negatives for the sake of being happy with each other. This period can last anywhere from a few days to years, but most of the time it is probably three to six months. The end of the honeymoon period is usually marked by the first major disagreement that threatens the relationship. It is at this point that reality sets in and a couple must decide if it is worthwhile working on their relationship. This is the point at which they realize that love will not conquer all, in fact it will not get them past dirty dishes or dirty clothes. Of course, some couples do not make it past the courtship or live-in period or the preparations for the marriage. Others may not be able to make it out of the parking lot at the church or reception. This is a critical point for the relationship. Each partner must decide whether they are going to stay and work things out, stay and fight things out, or leave. Leaving might lead to terminating the relationship or to a temporary separation followed by a reconciliation. Some couples experience a series of these. A separation followed by a reconciliation generally results in another honeymoon period except that after the first each one is more tenuous.

Couples who continue after the honeymoon period generally settle into some kind of routine. In happy relationships, the routine includes working on their relationship and working things out as they face adversity. In unhappy relationships, the routine is usually either a somewhat distant relationship with little work and few rewards or a relationship where the couple has decided to fight it out rather than work it out. Of course, couples can experience any of these during the course of their relationship.

During midlife, either partner or both may experience gratification in terms of their lives and their relationship or there may be what is commonly referred to as a "midlife crisis." This is typically a period of reexamination that is prompted by the realization that life is not forever and that half or more of one's life is over. The question to be answered is whether I am satisfied with where I have been and where I am going or do I need to do something different before it is too late. The trigger for this is often a birthday (turning forty or fifty), the death or physical decline of a parent, or the emancipation of children.

Couples who continue on into their sixties and beyond (or marry or remarry during this period) will experience their own and their partners' aging process. Erik Erikson saw this as a period of integrity versus despair in which one either felt positive about one's life and accepted aging and death or one experienced regret and despair.[1] Betty Friedan wrote a book entitled *The Fountain of Age* that considered what it takes to age well.[2] For the most part, successful aging seems most associated with acceptance and involvement. Most couples who continue to enjoy good health and financial security report positive feelings about their aging. However, as health declines or if finances are limited, then the couple must face these challenges. Eventually, if a couple remains together long enough, one of them will experience the death of the other. Of course, death may come at any time during the course of a relationship. Some people remain widowed for the rest of their lives and others begin the cycle all over again with someone else.

The remainder of the schema for a social history of a couple examines the two purposes discussed earlier. Part III involves gaining an understanding of the couple and their situation as these relate to the need or concern. Part IV involves identifying strengths and resources and challenges for meeting needs or addressing concerns. Once the worker and the couple have accomplished these purposes sufficiently, then planning for change can begin. Assessment itself continues throughout the work. Every time the worker works with the couple, she learns something new that adds to her understanding. In successful work, the couple also learns something about themselves as individuals and as a couple.

■   PLANNING WITH COUPLES   ■

Planning with couples is similar to planning with families, which was described in Chapter 6. As with assessment, planning is both a process and a product. The planning process for couples is somewhat different from that for families because couples should be recognized as equal partners, and in families, children are not considered to be peers of their parents. Planning with couples is a joint process, with the worker acting as a facilitator, mediator, and negotiator. Planning is intended to meet the needs of each partner and to strengthen their relationship by meeting the needs of the relationship. It is extremely important that each of the couple take responsibility for expressing his or her own needs and grant the worker the position of speaking for the relationship. This does not mean that the worker dictates his own version of the relationship. Each partner expresses what he or she would like to experience in the relationship. It is the worker's responsibility to find ways of connecting each partner's version and to explore what it will take to make those versions reality.

In areas where each partner's desires for the relationship overlap or are similar, the social worker helps the couple to find common goals and objectives. In areas that are different, reciprocal goals and objectives may be negotiated. In areas of conflict, negotiation and compromise are necessary.

The product of the planning process is the service plan. Depending on the setting this may be called other names, but essentially this is where the goals, objectives, and tasks are written down at least in the case file. Because many couples who need assistance complain about arguing. It is usually best to have each partner keep a written version of the plan so that it is less likely to become a point of contention. An example of this is as follows:

Goal: Mr. and Mrs. Jones will improve their communication.

Objective: Mr. and Mrs. Jones will use "I" statements with each other at least three times a day for three consecutive days by August 15.

Clients Task: Mr. and Mrs. Jones will maintain journals of their "I" statements and bring their journals to sessions with the worker.

Worker Task: Worker will assist Mr. and Mrs Jones in monitoring and practicing "I" statements during conjoint sessions.

■   DIRECT PRACTICE ACTIONS WITH COUPLES   ■

As with families, direct practice action with couples refers to actions that are taken in working with the couple. Indirect practice actions are those that are taken on behalf of a couple. Direct practice falls within the following categories of actions taken: (1) to enable development of relationship, (2) to develop an understanding of couples in environment, (3) to plan with couples, (4) to enable couples to know and use available resources, (5) to empower or enable couples to strengthen their relationship, (6) to resolve crisis situations, (7) to use support in working with couples, (8) to use activity with couples, (9) to mediate with couples and between couples and a system in their environment, and (10) to use a clinical model of social work with couples. These actions are similar to those described for working with families, and there are areas where they overlap. The development of a relationship was described in Chapter 4 and earlier in this chapter. Development of understanding of person in environment as this relates to couples was covered under assessment with couples and planning was covered in the previous section. Action taken in using a clinical model of social work with couples is beyond the scope of this book and is typically covered in advanced graduate-level social work courses.

Action taken to enable couples to know and use available resources is similar to the description for families in Chapter 7. The main point with couples is to help them to be informed about resources that are aimed at assisting couples. These include marriage counseling, marriage enrichment, and other relationship-building activities, along with tangible and intangible resources for the family.

Action Taken to Empower or Enable Couples to Strengthen Their Relationship

Empowering and enabling couples takes two tracks. One is to engage in activities that will empower and enable them as individuals and the other is to do so as a couple. Empowering and enabling as individuals was covered in Chapter 7. In working with couples, these actions are focused on the relationship. The ideal situation for a happy relationship is to have two happy individuals sharing their happiness with each other. Anything other than this will not make for a happy relationship. One partner might be happy at the other's expense, but these arrangements tend not to last. At the very least, one's happiness is on shaky ground.

A solid relationship built on mutual happiness and satisfaction is the only way to ensure long-term personal happiness for couples. The worker assists each partner to build self-esteem and to exercise control over his or her life. She helps them as individuals and as a couple to change irrational thinking, negative feelings, and self-defeating or negative actions. Partners can be very powerful forces in facilitating individual change. They can assist with carrying out changes between sessions and can reinforce positive outcomes through positive feedback. This is discussed further under support and under activity.

Empowering and enabling as a couple means strengthening their relationship. As indicated earlier and in the schema in Table 10.2, the basic elements of a successful relationship are good communication, an effective problem-solving and decision-making process, and the ability to resolve conflict constructively. As discussed in Chapter 4, good communication begins with the use of "I" statements. Getting the couple to use the word "I" to begin each sentence is essential. The use of "you," directly or implied, tends to create defensiveness in the other person and distracts from self-expression. When a person uses the word "I," he is discussing his own thoughts, feelings, or actions. The next word after "I" is a verb that describes something about that person. This is the purpose and essence of communication which is intended to let someone else know what we are thinking, feeling, or experiencing.

Effective communication also involves listening. Good listening focuses on what the other person is saying, not on what we want to say next. Because misunderstanding or miscommunication is common (as discussed and illustrated in Chapter 4), it is important to reflect on what is heard before responding. This lets the sender of the message know that she has been heard and gives her a chance to correct misconceptions. Reflective listening skills include paraphrasing, summarizing, and reflecting thoughts, feelings, and meanings. Once it is clear that the message is understood as it was intended, then the listener can respond most appropriately to the message. This is a much more tedious way to communicate than what people are used to doing. We generally take short cuts and assume that we know what the message is or what is meant by it and then we proceed to respond to what we have perceived. It is unrealistic to think that couples would use this method routinely in their everyday conversations. It is better to teach them to use it during discussions of important or sensitive issues or when a topic arises that may lead to conflict or during a conflict.

Couples can also be taught to use code words that will signal these important or sensitive topics or other times when a special skill is needed. For instance, they might use terms such as *quality talk* or *quality discussion* to refer to the need to use reflective listening. One of them could say, "I think we need to use some quality talk to discuss this matter." The use of code words needs some preparation and practice in order to be effective, but it can be a useful shortcut to more effective communication.

Problem solving and decision making are lumped together here because they involve basically the same process. The main difference is that problem solving may at times involve more negotiation and compromise when the problem represents a difference between the two parties. For the sake of discussion, we use the term *decision making* here to refer to both of these processes. Important aspects of decision making include structure, process, and product. The structural aspect refers to who makes what decisions. Nearly all couples divide certain decisions between them based on who is responsible and available. For instance, most couples rely on the parent on the scene to deal with their children's behavior unless there is a major problem. Most rely on the person who does the shopping to decide what brand of a product to buy. In many cultures, the responsibility is prescribed by gender-based roles. However, because most U.S. couples have more than one cultural background, some agreement may need to be reached about these prescribed roles. For more important decisions, a more formal structure is typically needed. Egalitarian couples generally use some kind of joint decision making structure in which they are both involved. True egalitarianism would mean equal power in this arrangement. However, equal power does not always mean that the decision making is fair. If one person is much more affected by the decision than the other, then a fairer method would be to take that into consideration. Most successful egalitarian couples will develop a method for doing so.

In many cultures, major decision making is more exclusively the purview of one of the partners, usually the husband or male partner. This is known as *paternalism*. However, for decision making to be effective there must be at least tacit agreement about its structure and process. The social worker shows respect for the couple's right to decide on these matters, even if it does not agree with her own views. If a partner agrees that his or her partner should make the important decisions, then the worker works with the couple around making this effective for them. Self determination includes the right to decide this. However, if there is disagreement about who decides what, then some kind of mediation or negotiation will be required in order to avoid destructive consequences. This is very difficult work. As we discussed in Chapter 3, the worker needs to respect the culture of her clients. However, there may be no easy way to reconcile differences when a couple have more than one culture. Even when a culture is shared, it does not mean that both will have had the same experience. There is also no guarantee that either partner will decide to retain his or her cultural prescriptions. In most paternalistic cultures, the definition of a good father and husband includes the requirement that the man act in the best interests of his partner and family, even over his own self-interests. Men who make decisions that benefit themselves, and who do not consider the wishes, desires, and needs of his partner or family, are actually acting against this prescribed role. One way to work around an impasse over this type of decision making is to point out that sharing decision making means sharing responsibility for the results of decisions and also the responsibility for carrying them out as well. This can relieve a great deal of stress related to individual as opposed to joint decision making. Another approach is to point out that sharing power is generous and may even be seen as a powerful act itself.

The decision-making process refers to how decisions are made or the method of actually making a decision or solving a problem. There is a range of processes from impulsive decision making to more methodical methods. Some couples may even avoid making a decision and allow circumstances to take their course without taking any action. These couples tend to be seen in a negative light by workers and others. They may be viewed as uncaring, uninvolved, indecisive, not competent, chaotic, resistant, lazy, or with other negative terms. In reality they may be depressed, overwhelmed, stressed, fearful, or perhaps unaware of how to go about making decisions or solving problems effectively. It is remarkable that decision-making and problem-solving skills are not typically taught by parents or teachers. Most people are left with watching their parents or others and trying to figure out how they do it then emulating them. Social workers should assume that couples want to make good decisions but are somehow being blocked from doing so. Removing the blockage then becomes the goal of the work to be done.

Couples who make decisions impulsively are also seen in a negative light. Their actions that result from impulsive decisions may be seen as incompetent, chaotic, unintelligent, risky, inexplicable, or with other negative terms. Often a series of decisions will appear disordered and not well connected. Their rationale for a decision often appears unrealistic and based more on wish fulfillment.

Couples can be more methodical and still be ineffective in making good decisions. The more extreme example would be a couple who overanalyze situations and fail to make a decision or act because they are still mulling it over. They might take extended periods of time to make simple decisions and are overwhelmed by more complex ones. These couples might appear to be similar to those who avoid making decisions.

Good decisions are defined as those that result in positive or desirable outcomes for people who are involved or affected by the decision without serious negative consequences to themselves or others. The best way to achieve this is to use some form of the change process as presented in this text. This process is in essence the scientific method applied to everyday life. In using the scientific method, a scientist assesses a phenomenon and what is known theoretically about it. He then creates a hypothesis, tests it, and observes the results. This is evaluated to determine how the results compare with the hypothesis and the theory underlying it. In the change process, the social worker assesses and observes her client system in its environment. This is the assessment. She works with the client system to develop a hypothesis based on theories about human behavior and social work practice methods. This is the plan. The worker then assists her client system in implementing the plan. This is the action phase or testing of the hypothesis. She evaluates the results to determine whether the plan worked. This is the same as comparing results with what was the predicted outcome of the hypothesis. Some scientists, and even some social scientists, have criticized social work as not being very scientific. Actually, we use the scientific method to assist our clients in improving their lives. As much as possible the social worker teaches the change process to her clients and tries to work herself out of a job. Helping clients improve their decision-making and problem-solving skills is essential to enhancing their independence and effectiveness. In working with couples, the worker can help them to adopt all or portions of this method so that it fits with what they are comfortable. A simplified version of this can be remembered by the acronym "Apple PIE" or a saying such as: "Making decisions or solving problems is as easy as Apple PIE." The "Apple" stands for "A" which represents assessment. The "P" represents planning. "I" is the implementation of the plan or the action phase. "E" is evaluation. So in simple terms, the couple needs to remember to assess, plan, implement, and evaluate.

Conflict resolution was discussed in Chapter 7. With couples, it is important to reinforce the need to avoid violence and destructive interactions. It should be pointed out that the only acceptable result of a disagreement is a win–win situation. Win–lose means somebody has to be a loser. With couples, this means that either the party who loses is a loser or he or she is married to or living with a loser. In either case, the relationship cannot be a happy one. Basically the lesson here is that destructive interactions have long-term destructive consequences for long-term relationships. We suggest that couples use rules for handling disagreements. These include the following:

1. Create win–win situations. Nobody wants to be a loser or be married to or living with one.
2. No violence or threats of violence. This is simply another form of win–lose.
3. Use "I" statements for every sentence. Avoid using "you" and attacking the other person.
4. Stick to the subject. This is another form of win–lose. Do not change the subject until it is resolved.
5. Stay in the here and now. Bringing up the past is another form of win–lose. Do not bring up the past without permission.

6. Remember that this is the person you love and who loves you. Show respect. Express your anger, but also protect them from it.

7. If you cannot control your anger, walk away and come back to discuss the matter when you feel more in control.

It is helpful if couples realize that having disagreements is normal and these can be constructive rather than destructive. In fact, couples who do not have disagreements may be in more serious trouble than those who do. Generally, this means that they are not dealing with important matters in their relationship and either one or both are saving up negative feelings for a guilt-free divorce or worse.

Negotiation and compromise are important for successful conflict resolution. However, these cannot really be used until the anger subsides. When angry feelings become attached to an issue, it is not likely to be something a person will give up very easily. However, once the anger is gone, then the importance of the position that was taken may be considerably reduced. Examples of negotiation and compromise were discussed in Chapter 7. This is the give and take that are required in any long-term successful relationship. The best way for the worker to teach skills in negotiation and compromise is to model these skills in her work with the couple. This is especially relevant for the planning phase of her work with them. As the worker develops goals and objectives, she starts by asking each partner to identify a desirable outcome. She then asks each partner what he or she would be willing to do to make that happen. If it is a common or shared goal or objective, the worker elicits what each partner might do or what they might do collectively. For a reciprocal goal or objective, the worker asks if each would be willing to do something if the other partner would do certain things. After modeling this, the worker helps the couple to use these methods with each other directly by coaching them and giving feedback.

In addition to working on relationship skills, the social worker can enable couples to strengthen their relationship by increasing intimacy and closeness. As mentioned previously in assessment, after a period of time couples often fall into a routine that may not include things that made the relationship worthwhile in its early stages. The worker can assist in identifying these and incorporating them into their everyday lives. It is usually a matter of setting aside time to be together as a couple, including showing affection, talking about inner thoughts and feelings or events, setting goals, laughing and having fun, and the like. The worker might feel uncomfortable in discussing sexual aspects of the relationship, but even this can be discussed at least at the level of bringing out a discussion about pleasure and satisfaction. Serious problems with sexual function and dysfunction should be referred to a specialist.

Another important aspect of enabling the strengthening of a couple's relationship is the need for positive self-talk and positive reinforcement from each other. What people say to themselves about themselves and about others has a great deal of influence over feelings and actions. Using a cognitive–behavioral approach, the worker explores thoughts and self-talk with each partner. He supports positive self-talk about oneself and challenges negative self-talk, especially negative thinking that contributes to low self-esteem. The worker assists the couple to correct negative thinking about each other and their relationship. Quite often, people will interpret statements or behavior or the lack of certain statements or behaviors as a sign of something negative without checking out their perceptions with other people. The worker teaches the couple to check out their thoughts, feelings, and actions with each other and to use feedback to clear up misconceptions. He helps them to give positive reinforcement to each other to build positive self-esteem and a more positive relationship. The worker teaches them to use "I" statements in giving both positive and negative feedback.

Action Taken in Crisis Situations

In dealing with crisis situations, the worker assists the couple in mobilizing their coping skills. If the crisis lies outside of their relationship, the task is to come together as a couple and work together as a team in managing their thoughts, feelings, and actions to resolve the situation. Sometimes when people are faced with a difficult situation, they lash out at the people around them instead of reaching out to them for help. Some couples may not have learned how to deal with difficulties together and use their relationship to cope. It may be a revelation for them to find out that they both have the same feelings about what is happening. The primary task for the worker is to help the couple to tap into their power as a couple. The true test of the strength of a relationship is not determined by its ability to handle positive experiences. The true test lies in its ability to handle adversity. When couples are able to deal with a difficult situation and not only survive but also feel closer as a couple, then they feel that they can face other adversity as long as they do so together.

If the crisis is within their relationship, then they will need to work on restoring their equilibrium. Generally, a crisis in the relationship represents a serious threat to the continuation of the relationship. This can range from a situation where one party is thinking about ending the relationship to an actual separation. The best way for the generalist social worker to deal with this is to refer the couple to a professional marriage counselor. As mentioned earlier, this may not always be possible or there might be a lag between when the referral is made and when the couple can be seen or the worker is faced with an immediate situation that must be dealt with right now. These can be very scary situations for the worker, especially if there is a threat of violence or suicide. Any threat should be taken seriously, especially when it involves the break up of a relationship. Even if a threat to life has not been made, the worker should assess this and take steps to make sure that everyone is safe. The removal of guns and weapons from the home may be necessary. Although meeting jointly with the couple is preferred under most circumstances, a major crisis in the relationship may require meeting individually to assess the danger and to take steps to ensure safety. If threats are made, the worker has an obligation to inform the person against whom the threat is made. This is called a duty to warn. Some states have laws that cover this. There are also legal precedents for it. An immediate threat of violence or suicide requires intervention by law enforcement. The emergency services at the community mental health center should also be involved if the threat includes suicide.

If the crisis comes without warning and the worker has to deal with it immediately, the primary approach is deescalation. The discussion should be focused on reducing the level of anger and tension and not on reasons to stay or leave. The worker will need to at least negotiate a "cooling off" period to remove the immediate threat. Empathy and support become important tools in this endeavor. It is essential that the worker remain calm even though that is not how she feels. In this situation, professional training dictates that she not act on her feelings but rather on her training. Acting calmly is more likely to produce calm in others. Acting afraid or angry will tend to escalate feelings in others. The worker calmly listens and empathizes with feelings and encourages verbalization as opposed to acting on those feelings. Generally, during a crisis, the person feels overwhelmed, so the worker needs to be more in charge and give directions. The worker states that it is okay to have feelings and to verbalize them but it is not okay to act on them if those actions would be harmful. She directs the person toward taking actions that will resolve the situation in a positive way instead of making it worse. She points to the need for rational decision making and gives hope for future times when the person will feel better. The worker should not promise that the relationship will continue but should focus on coping with the situation at hand.

Suicidal clients should be evaluated for hospitalization or medical attention for depression. Under no circumstances should they be left alone. Arrangements should be made to have a friend or relative around if there is a delay in having them evaluated.

Any time the influence of drugs or alcohol are present, the worker's goal should be the removal of himself and other parties from the situation until the person is no longer under the influence. Reasoning with someone who is under the influence of drugs or alcohol tends to be fruitless and mood swings can be very unpredictable. In cases of extreme influence, either detox or the intervention of law enforcement may be necessary.

In situations with lower risk, the worker should negotiate a temporary resolution of the immediate situation until the couple can be seen by a marriage counselor. If seeing a marriage counselor is impossible, the worker should inform the couple of her limitations and offer to work on improving their relationship skills so that they are better prepared to work on their relationship issues. The worker can offer to mediate some of the issues for them if she feels able to do so. Mediation is discussed later.

Action Taken to Use Support in Working with Couples

The use of support in working with couples is similar to that which was discussed in Chapter 7 for working with families. However, the focus is on building support between the two partners within their relationship. Receiving support from one's partner is extremely important. Knowing that one's partner is backing us up, gives us a feeling that we can accomplish whatever we set out to do. On the other hand, a lack of support becomes a barrier that may seem insurmountable. Students know all too well how much the support of their family means to them. When you have it, you feel good about your endeavors in school. When it is missing, you may not have anyone with whom you can share your triumphs and challenges.

As mentioned earlier, support is important in terms of bringing about individual changes in thoughts, feelings and actions. The worker can teach and coach the couple to give each other support between sessions for changes that are worked on during sessions. Individual change is accelerated and solidified when the environment supports that change. On the other hand, individual changes generally occur slowly if at all and may not be long lasting when people in the environment do not support or actively oppose those changes. Usually, the most powerful force in the environment for supporting or opposing change for adults is their partner. Thus, working with couples can be very successful for both individual and relationship change when a positive working relationship is established and the change is supported by both partners.

Support from one's partner can be for almost anything, but it is especially important in terms of vital roles. These would include the roles of spouse or lifelong partner, parent or stepparent, employee, student, brother or sister, son or daughter, grandparent, and the like. Receiving positive feedback and expressions of support for these roles from one's partner raises self-worth and confidence and increases the fulfillment of these roles in positive ways. However, all too often support that was given early in the relationship may wane or not be expressed. Couples may feel that they are being taken for granted by their partner. The social worker assists the couple in providing open and honest support for each other on a regular basis. He checks with each partner on areas in which he or she would like to receive support and helps the couple to incorporate this into their relationship. The worker might have to model this first and then coach the couple in saying and doing things that are supportive. It is important that the recipient interpret statements and actions as being supportive so this might need to be discussed. The conversation might include the following questions: What do you do to support your partner in carrying out the role of . . . ? Did you know that he was trying to support you when he said or did that? Would you be willing to accept that as a sign of support? What would you like your partner to say or do to support you in this? Would you be willing to do that? or What would it take for you to do that? As the work progresses, the worker looks for ways to encourage support and coaches the couple in requesting and receiving support so it becomes overt rather than assumed.

Action Taken That Uses Activity with Couples

Just as with families, activities can be effective in working with couples. As with other direct practice actions, activities need to be focused on the relationship. Activities form the base for most marriage encounter, marriage enrichment, and other relationship building services. These may be offered either individually or in group formats. Group sessions are generally structured around variations of discussion (D) and activity (A). The most common structure is DAD or discussion–activity–discussion. The exercise is presented and discussed. This is followed by the activity or exercise. Then a debriefing or discussion follows. The activity itself may involve discussion or actions between each couple. In marriage encounter sessions, couples are sent back to their rooms for the exercises or activities. For other types of marriage or relationship enrichment sessions, couples may either stay in the room or leave for a period of time. In group formats couples may be asked to volunteer to share their experiences during the debriefing. In couple sessions, the debriefing focuses on the experience and relating it to their relationship and their everyday lives.

To be successful, it is essential that any work that is done be transferred over to the everyday life of the couple. The most effective way to do this is to give "homework assignments" in which couples practice the skills and implement the changes that are discussed. We consider this to be another form of activity. The worker usually needs to structure these assignments during the joint session. It is wise to engage in some practice and coaching until the partners feel comfortable enough to try it on their own. Taking some pressure off may be important, especially for those couples who find themselves in situations where they are having a lot of arguments. The risk in these situations is that the homework may become simply one more thing to argue about. One way to take pressure off is to tell the couple that they might not be ready for this. If they are not, then they can blame the worker instead of each other. Actually, this is a win–win for the worker because she is either right that they are not ready or they are ready and they use the homework to improve their relationship. In fact, some couples may take this as a challenge and put extra effort into proving that they are ready.

One of our favorite homework assignments for couples is the same as that which was identified in Chapter 7 in working with families. This is the use of "I" statements to improve communication. The importance of getting couples and families to do this cannot be overstated. It is the single most important element in effective communication. It is also essential for avoiding arguments and for avoiding destructive interactions when disagreements occur. It is much more difficult to go from using "I" to start a sentence to calling the other person a name or saying something derogatory. On the other hand, it is much easier to get there when we start with the word "you" either directly or implied. Using "you" to start a sentence tends to make it a blaming statement or at the very least it creates a defensive stance in the other person because we are going to say something about him or her. Using "I" means that we are going to say something about ourselves. This is much less threatening and is the real reason for communication to begin with.

In getting couples to use "I" statements as a homework assignment, the social worker gives them permission to remind each other to do so. However, they must also use an "I" statement when they do this. They cannot say "You forgot to use 'I' " or variations of this because this is a "you" statement. Couples may be puzzled about how to do this. If they are, the worker helps them to use either a direct "I" statement or a code word that might be used as a reminder. An example of a good direct "I" statement would be, "I would like to hear that in an 'I' statement."

Sometimes the worker may be able to get couples to use humor in reminding each other about their homework assignments. In fact, reminding each other about "homework" may be somewhat humorous itself. Using code words or statements can be quite humorous. For instance, when one of the partners brings up the past, especially during a disagreement, calling this a "museum trip" can be a humorous way to remind each other of the need to stay in the here and now. Using humor to improve relationships can be very effective provided it is not derogatory or at one party's expense.

Action Taken to Mediate with Couples and between Couples and Their Environment

These actions provide both an important direct service to couples and a transition to indirect practice actions. Mediation with couples is essential as the basic approach in working with them. It is also important in helping them to work out difficulties in their relationship. Mediating with systems in the environment is an indirect practice action that was covered in Chapter 8. Mediation requires that the worker not take sides but remain neutral and facilitate effective and constructive interactions between the two parties.

As mentioned earlier in Chapter 7 and in this chapter, using a mediating approach with families and with couples is essential in any situation where the social worker is working with multiperson client systems. Without the ability to maintain a neutral position, the worker will get caught up in disagreements and will become a pawn to be manipulated in games of rivalry and destructiveness. The basis for sibling rivalry is to win the favor of the parent and to use that position to win the competition with other siblings. Similar rivalries will exist in other family subsystems when the worker takes sides or is perceived to be doing so. If a couple perceives that the worker can be won over to either partner's side, then the worker can really only have a worker–client relationship with one of them. She cannot serve the needs of the relationship. The worker must make the need for a mediating position clear from the very start and should remind the couple of this throughout the work.

An effective approach to use in developing and maintaining a mediating role is to have the couple visualize their relationship as a triangle made up of "you," "I," and "we." The "you" and the "I" represent the two partners as individuals. The "we" represents their relationship. In geometry, the triangle is the strongest figure because you cannot bend the angles without breaking one of the legs. By the same token, a triangle is only as strong as its weakest leg. A strong marriage or marital type relationship calls for two strong individuals getting their needs met within a strong relationship that is itself strengthened by meeting the needs of the relationship. In using this approach, the worker has each partner take responsibility for his or her own individual needs and the worker must be granted the position of advocating for the relationship. His basic position is to ask the question, What will it take to make this relationship work? He continuously asks this question in various forms along with ancillary questions such as the following: How will this help strengthen your relationship? What could you do to make this relationship better in this situation? What outcome would strengthen your relationship? What do you need out of this relationship? What do you need from your partner? Would you be willing to . . . in order to make this relationship stronger or better?

As the worker asks these types of questions, he facilitates good communication by having the partners talk with each other about their needs and about their relationship. He helps them to negotiate agreements and alliances. He supports efforts to build honesty, trust, and intimacy.

In some states, social workers may receive training as mediators. Mediation can be used in a wide variety of situations, including with couples who are separated and going through divorce. In addition to providing formal mediation, mediation techniques can be used with couples in facilitating changes in their relationship. In formal mediation the two parties are generally in separate rooms and the mediator goes back and forth between them with offers to resolve the issue. In using mediation techniques with a couple, the worker would typically meet jointly with the two partners. The discussion might include the following questions: What do you want to do with this? What would be an acceptable resolution for you? What would you be willing to do to resolve this? What do you need from your partner to resolve this? Would you be willing to . . . in order to resolve this situation? If your partner does . . . , would you be willing to . . . ?

The worker continues with this line of questions in an effort to move the partners to a middle ground where each party is satisfied that he or she can live with the results. This is not a process where either side is happy with the resolution. They might be happy that it is resolved, but each side will have to give something in order to make this work.

■ INDIRECT PRACTICE ACTIONS WITH COUPLES ■

Indirect practice actions with couples are similar to those that are used with families in Chapter 8, except the focus is on the relationship as a couple. Indirect practice actions include the following: actions that (1) involve the use of influence, (2) are designed to change the environment, and (3) are relative to coordination of services. These actions are not usually used as frequently with couples as they are with families and with parents or parent–child subsystems and will only be briefly summarized here.

Action That Involves the Use of Influence

Influence is an important consideration in working with couples. The social worker needs to be aware of the influence that she has with the couple. She is careful to limit her influence so that the partners feel free to make their own decisions and not decisions that they think the worker wants them to make. The worker is cognizant of the fact that they have to live with the results of their decisions. To an extent, the worker uses influence to persuade the couple to work out their differences when she mediates.

As with families, the worker is free to use influence on behalf of a couple. This generally is not as common as using influence on behalf of the other family subsystems. Most work with couples tends to be within the subsystem between the partners. The work to be done is to improve the relationship so that their needs are met within the relationship, and they feel more empowered in influencing their environment. Working with a couple who are older may involve influencing other family members and systems to assist them with planning and decision making with regard to health care, elder care, and services that are needed to maintain their independence. This might also be the case if the couple were experiencing acute or chronic health care issues, mental or physical disability, poverty, or other situations where services from various agencies are needed. Mediation and advocacy are the most common forms of influence used in most instances. The worker might also use contacts with influential people to build support for services that are not available.

Action Designed to Change the Environment

Actions designed to change the environment are mainly used to either assist the couple to change their existing environment or to move to a new environment. In changing their existing environment, there may be aspects of their home or neighborhood that are stressful. Perhaps the couple are having difficulty in maintaining their home or residence. It may not be affordable or it could be in disrepair. There may be disagreements about housekeeping chores or standards. Getting couples to become more empowered to influence change in their environment may be needed. A goal in working with couples is often to get them to harness their energy to deal with the world around them, rather than wasting their energy on negative interactions between them. Most of the time, a couple that is able to do this will be able to make these changes on their own or with some assistance. However, some couples are never able to come together and do this or may only be able to do so intermittently. These couples will need assistance when they encounter obstacles that are beyond their ability to overcome, either in the environment or within their relationship or both.

If a change to a new environment is necessary, the social worker may become involved in assisting with this. Most couples are capable of doing this on their own, but some will need assistance. For couples who are older, this is most often a result of mental or physical limitations that are brought on by aging. It is these very limitations that make it difficult for the couple to make a decision and to implement it.

Action Relative to Coordination of Services

As mentioned previously, there are times when it may be necessary for the social worker to coordinate services on behalf of couples. The first choice is for the couple to be able to manage these services on their own. However, circumstances might dictate that the worker act on their behalf. This generally occurs when the couple is either temporarily unable to manage these tasks or there is a chronic circumstance that interferes with their ability to do so. These services can range from information and referral to full case management.

When another agency is the best fit for the services needed by the couple, the worker makes a referral and follows up to make sure that the appropriate services are received. The referral process was discussed in Chapter 7.

When couples are in crisis, the worker will need to be much more direct and involved in the work to be done. If the nature of the crisis produces an impairment in functioning for either or both partners, then the worker will need to either marshal resources in the ecosystem to take over managing services or provide this himself. Couples may have other family members that can assist them during a crisis. For couples who are older, this is most often their adult sons and daughters. Sometimes, old issues among adult siblings will get in the way of assisting their parents. This is covered in more detail in Chapter 13.

The generalist practice social worker may temporarily step in to coordinate services or she might work for an agency where this is part of her responsibility. The most common types of agencies where case management is a primary service are mental health, health care, and aging services. These agencies are set up to do both temporary and long-term case management.

CASE EXAMPLE

The following are examples of direct and indirect practice actions with a couple.

Sue is a social worker at a domestic violence program. She has been working with a Caucasian couple after Mrs. Jones came to the shelter with her two young children. Mr. Jones had been drinking and becoming verbally abusive. One night he came home and hit her and pushed her down after they argued about money problems and his drinking. Mrs. J left the next day and came into the shelter. When Mr. J found out, he was desperate to find her. He was able to find out from some relatives that she was at the shelter and he contacted Sue in a panic. She talked with him briefly about his feelings and assessed that he could be depressed and possibly suicidal. She said that she could not work with him at this point because she was working with his wife. Sue referred him to a crisis center where he met with a crisis worker, Tamika.

Tamika started out by discussing the situation. She asked Mr. J if he felt okay about talking with an African American female. He admitted that it was not his first choice but now that they had started he did not want to start all over with someone else and tell his story all over again. Tamika assessed that Mr. J was anxious and distraught over losing his family. He admitted that he had thought about suicide but denied any current ideation. She asked him if he had a plan and he said that he had guns in the house, a pistol and a hunting rifle. Tamika was able to get him to agree to give the guns and ammunition to his brother for now. She began to discuss his options with him, pointing out that if he was willing to try counseling his wife might agree to give their marriage another try. As they talked, Tamika was able to get Mr. J to calm down. He admitted that he had been drinking the night of the incident but denied having a "drinking problem." Tamika wondered if he made an effort to stop drinking and went to some counseling and AA meetings, his wife might take that as a sign that he was serious about changing. He balked at this but said that he would think about it. Now that he was calmed down, it seemed to Tamika that he was getting anxious to leave. She got him to sign a safety contract in which he promised to remove his guns from the home and to not harm himself or anyone else without seeing someone at the crisis center first. Tamika had him agree to call her the next day and she made an appointment to see him again two days later. Before he left, Tamika had him sign a release of information so she could talk with Mr. J's brother to confirm that he had the guns and with Sue at the domestic violence program. After Mr. J left, Tamika called Sue about the situation.

Sue could not reveal information about Mrs. J without a release, but Tamika was able to inform Sue about what she had accomplished. The next day Tamika heard from Mr. J and confirmed with him and with his brother that the guns had been removed. He said that he was feeling better and had not had a drink since he had been at the crisis center. Tamika praised him for this and encouraged him to go to AA and one of the counseling programs about which she had given him information. He said that he was still thinking about it and would see her the next day. She informed Sue of the situataion.

As Sue worked with Mrs. J, it became apparent that she was probably going to return to her husband and try it again. Sue agreed to help her to do so in as safe a manner as possible. Sue wanted to empower and enable Mrs. J as much as possible under the circumstances so she respected her right to make her own decisions. Mrs. J stated that she felt that she probably needed to change some things that she was doing to make their relationship better.

Sue met with Mr. and Mrs. J to discuss expectations. She explained to them that in order to help them as a couple she would need to be able to take a neutral position and be allowed to speak for what would benefit their relationship. She recognized that Mr. J might be more uncomfortable with trusting her because she already had been working with his wife. To try to balance this, she offered him the opportunity to have a separate individual session. Mr. J declined and said that he wanted to give this a try. Sue said that she was not a licensed marriage counselor, but the agency did provide couple counseling related to domestic violence and so that would need to be their focus. She indicated that a referral to a marriage counselor would be necessary but that it might take awhile to get an appointment. Meanwhile they could look for ways to provide a safe and healthy situation. They agreed.

Mr. J started by saying that he would do anything to get his family back. He said he was upset with what his wife had said and was drunk at the time. Sue pointed out that being upset or drunk was not an excuse for acting out violently or threatening someone. She asked Mr. J what he thought would have happened if he had done what he did with someone outside of the family. Mr. J looked down and said that he probably would have gone to jail. Sue told him that he could have gone to jail for what he did to his wife and that she could still press charges if she chose to do so. He continued to look down and did not say anything for about a half a minute. Finally, he looked up at Sue then his wife and apologized. She said that his apology was not enough, he needed to do something about his drinking because she was tired of living poor and being scared of what would happen when he came home. Mr. J became defensive and started to blame his wife for "nagging" him. Sue stepped in and said that the discussion seemed to be headed in the wrong direction. She recognized that Mrs. J had a right to expect her husband to act appropriately but there might be a better way to get at these issues. She asked if they would try something that should improve their communication. She asked them to try to remember to use "I" to begin every sentence. Sue went over the problems with "you" statements and the need to use "I" to express thoughts and feelings. They agreed to try it. Sue went back to their discussion. She had them practice using "I" statements as they talked. Several times she had to stop them and coach them in using "I" sentences. They agreed to practice this outside the sessions as they communicated with other people. It

(continued)

was decided that each would keep a journal to keep track of their ability to use "I" statements. Mrs. J expressed her anxieties over unpaid bills, calls from bill collectors, and fears about Mr. J's temper. Mr. J admitted to being frustrated at not making enough money and worried about paying the bills. He said that having a few beers with his friends was his way of letting off some steam. He felt that if she would simply leave him alone when he got home everything would be okay. Sue wondered if that would be enough. She pointed out how spending money on alcohol compounded the money problems and was like adding gasoline to a fire with Mr. J's temper. She stated that it looked to her like Mr. J was going to have to choose between alcohol and his family. Initially, Mr. J was in denial about how alcohol was affecting the situation but later relented when his wife said she wanted him to quit drinking. Sue gave him a list of alcohol treatment programs and AA meetings in the area. He indicated that he did not think he needed it but would try it if it meant getting his family back.

Sue met with the Joneses a few more times before they were able to get into a marriage counselor. She was able to get them started by working with them on communication, problem solving and decision making, and conflict resolution. She had given Mr. J a list of agencies providing marriage counseling. Initially, Mr. J had trouble finding one because his insurance did not cover marriage counseling. Sue was able to refer them to a family service agency with a sliding fee scale. Mrs. J decided not to return home until they had a few sessions. She moved out to stay with her sister across town temporarily until her return home. Sue worked with her on a safety plan that included either staying with her sister or coming into the shelter if she felt threatened.

While she was at the shelter, Mrs. J had been searching for a job and found one. She was able to use the shelter's children's program for childcare and later when she moved out to her sister's home, her sister agreed to care for them. Sue worked with Mr. and Mrs. J on coordinating the various services they were receiving. Mr. J had begun alcohol counseling and AA. Mrs. J needed assistance in locating childcare and arranging transportation when she returned home so she could keep her job. Mr. and Mrs. J were also going to marriage counseling.

In working with Mr. and Mrs. J, Sue and Tamika provided a full range of social work services. Sue was able to get them started on strengthening their relationship by working on communication, problem solving and decision making, and conflict resolution. She showed them the use of the change process in problem solving and decision making. Sue empowered Mrs. J by respecting her decisions and supported her in carrying them out. She arranged for Mr. J to receive crisis intervention when he was in crisis and Tamika took steps to ensure that he was safe and did not harm himself or others. Sue used activity when she had Mr. and Mrs. J practice using "I" statements during sessions and outside sessions, along with keeping a journal on using "I" sentences. Sue took a mediating position in her work with them. She used influence with Mr. J to get him into alcohol treatment but did not use threats or manipulation in doing so. Tamika used environmental change when she had Mr. J remove the guns from the home as a safety measure. Finally, Sue helped the couple to coordinate the services that they were receiving and acted as a broker when she made referrals for those services.

■   EVALUATION AND TERMINATION WITH COUPLES   ■

Evaluation and termination with couples are quite similar to that which was described for families in Chapter 9. Evaluation is a constant process throughout the work. It occurs during assessment and as new information arises during each contact. Evaluation is built into planning and is used during the action phase. It is used to determine the outcome of the work and during termination.

The worker evaluates the validity and reliability of the information collected for assessment and information that arises throughout the change process. With couples, triangulation of the data is built into the process because the worker is generally working with both partners at the same time. When there is agreement between the two partners, the worker can usually rely on the accuracy of the information. When there is disagreement, the worker discusses the situation in an effort to reach a consensus about it. Sometimes a disagreement will persist. When this occurs, the worker might suggest that the couple agree to disagree about their perception of the situation. Over time, the difference in perception may disappear or it might need to be revisited, especially as new information comes to light. In general, when there is a difference in perception, the worker can assume that the actual situation is somewhere between the two positions that the partners are taking.

If there is a reason to believe that one partner has more to gain or lose relative to the difference in perception, then it may be safe to assume that his or her perception is probably skewed in that direction. It is important that the worker not assume that either party is "lying" or "not telling the truth." We all have a tendency to perceive the world around us in a manner that fits with our self interest, and we will not be totally honest until we feel that we can trust and that it is safe to do so. Even then it may be too painful for us to examine certain issues. This is simply human nature.

Evaluation is built into every plan. Objectives must be measurable so they can be evaluated. Evaluating objectives tells the worker and the couple when the goal has been reached. It is also used to measure the progress toward the goal.

Evaluating the actions that are taking place to achieve the objectives tells the social worker and the couple what is working and what is not working. Plans are hypotheses or educated guesses about what might work. The worker and the couple need to monitor areas that are successful and those that are not. When actions produce positive results, the work proceeds as planned. When the results are negative or the work is not productive, then it generally signals a need to either remove a barrier to change or go back and try something different. This might be "plan B" or a new plan, at least for that particular goal.

As the goals are reached, the worker and the couple need to evaluate whether the need has been met or the concern addressed. If so, then they should assess whether the work is done and if the helping relationship should continue. If the work has been completed and there are no other pressing needs that the couple cannot meet on their own, then the worker and the couple can proceed to termination. Thus, evaluation is used for planned termination.

Evaluation is also used within the termination process. The worker should receive feedback about what was helpful, what was not, and what would have been helpful. This gives him an opportunity to evaluate his skills and to improve his ability to provide services to couples in the future. The couple also need to evaluate and own their new skills and abilities.

This validates the work they have done and gives them confidence in working together in the future.

As with families and other client systems, various forms of unplanned terminations often take place. At the very least, when the couple drops out of service, the worker should do some follow-up to ensure that they either receive services elsewhere or the door is open for them to return. When the termination is initiated by the worker or the agency, the worker ensures that a smooth transfer takes place to another worker in the agency or to another agency. The ideal way to do this is to have at least one joint session with the new worker. However, this is often not possible, so the worker must prepare the couple for receiving services from a different worker. She does this by reinforcing the fact that they are the ones who have done the meaningful work and if they can work with her, they can work with another worker in completing the change process that they have undertaken.

■   GENERALIST PRACTICE WITH COUPLES   ■
WHO ARE OLDER

Although there may be occasions when the generalist social worker works on relationships with couples who are older, much of this work typically revolves around helping them to make the adjustments that are necessary during the aging process in order to maintain their quality of life. This generally includes accessing resources, making decisions about living arrangements, and dealing with losses.

Maintaining quality of life during the aging process is the overall goal in working with people who are older. As we get older, we lose some of our physical strength and abilities. We are not able to do everything that we did when we were younger. In addition, some people who are older develop physical or mental conditions that limit their abilities or require treatment and accommodations. Generalist social workers have the knowledge and skills necessary to assist with these needs. They are able to assist in accessing both routine and specialized resources that are needed to support living at home. Generalist social workers are found working in community-based aging services such as case management services, congregate meal sites, meals on wheels, foster grandparent programs, and volunteer opportunities for people who are retired. Generalist social workers can assist couples in setting up and carrying out home care plans if these are needed for a medical condition.

Generalist social workers also have the knowledge and skills necessary to assist people who are older in making and carrying out decisions about their living arrangements. During recent years, a whole new set of options have become available to people who are older. For many couples it is no longer necessary to choose between living at home or in a nursing homes. There has been an increase in home care services to assist people who are able to live in their own homes. There are apartments and condominiums that cater to people who are older. Group care has expanded beyond adult foster care to include assisted living facilities. There are retirement communities some of which have a full continuum of care from apartment living to assisted living to nursing home care. Other options are almost sure to develop as the baby boomers age. Unfortunately, the availability of many of these options are based on financial circumstances. So it is incumbent on the worker to become familiar with eligibility requirements and the financial aspects of various options and to find creative ways of using resources to improve access to these options.

Probably the two most difficult situations in making decisions about living arrangements are when a couple who is older decide to leave the family home if they have lived there for an extended period of time and when a decision needs to be made about dependent care for a spouse who is disabled. Both of these situations are really about grief and loss, which will follow. In the first situation the couple may be able to make this decision together or it may fall on one of them to do this if the other is not able to participate. In the former case, the worker helps the couple to identify the advantages and disadvantages of moving and the various options that are available. It is especially important for the worker to explore all of the options that are available. He supports them in dealing with the anticipated losses that are generally connected to memories. Sometimes adult sons and daughters may object for these same reasons. This is discussed in later chapters.

In situations involving decisions about dependent care for a spouse who is disabled, the decision often falls on the shoulders of the spouse who is not disabled. This is especially true when it is a mental disability. The spouse may receive assistance with the decision from adult sons and daughters and this is also covered in later chapters. When the spouse makes the decision on his or her own, the worker uses a similar approach to that previously discussed in terms of developing a full spectrum of options and weighing the advantages and disadvantages of each one. The worker then supports the spouse in making and carrying out the decision.

Generalist social workers can work with people who are older to deal with losses that they experience during the aging process. Losses range from loss of one's abilities to the loss of friends and relatives. Elizabeth Kübler-Ross proposed five stages of the grief process.[3] She applied these to the grief process associated with death and dying, but they can be used to understand any loss. Successful completion of the grief process allows people to go on after the loss. It also allows them to have access to positive memories without having to experience the emotions associated with the loss all over again. However, people can get stuck at any of the stages in which case they do reexperience these emotions and are not able to complete the grief process. The worker will usually use support and cognitive–behavioral approaches during this time.

The first stage is generally characterized as denial.[4] We cannot believe that the loss has occurred. No, it's not possible. Are you sure? People who are stuck here may continue to deny or avoid dealing with the loss. They may refuse to accept it or deny that it has taken place. They typically avoid thinking or talking about it. They never allow themselves to experience any of the pain that is associated with it. They may exhibit symptoms of shock or posttraumatic stress disorder. The worker can assist with this stage by providing support that is needed to deal with the pain and to let the person know that she is not alone, the worker will be there with her. The worker can also help to get the person to begin to deal with loss by confronting irrational thinking about the loss and the grief process itself.

The next stage is usually anger.[5] Why did this have to happen? It is not fair. Why did God do this? The person may get angry at someone for dying. At the very least, he is angry that the loss has occurred. The worker provides support for expressing anger appropriately and validates those feelings by reassuring the client that it is okay to be angry.

Bargaining usually occurs either before or after anger or sometimes along with it. We wonder if we could do something to reverse the loss or wonder if we could have prevented it.[6] Some people may try to bargain with God to do this. The worker needs to listen and provide support for the feelings while avoiding support for the idea that bargaining will be successful.

Reframing the client's statements generally helps with this. The worker might say things such as, You wish this had not happened or It is difficult to accept this or You want God to take this pain away. This allows the client to own her feelings while avoiding giving false hopes.

The next stage is experiencing the grief itself along with the pain of the loss.[7] Once again the worker needs to use support and encourage the client to express his feelings. Crying often accompanies this stage and the worker needs to support the fact that it is okay to cry. The worker tries to get the client to let go of these feelings.

The final stage is resolution. The feelings have been expressed and now the person can look back and accept the loss and go on with her life.[8] It is not a matter of forgetting as with denial but a matter of remembering, perhaps with fondness. People generally have to revisit their grief and loss several times before they reach complete resolution. This is why the first year after the death of a significant person is so important. The grief process is typically revisited on important dates and anniversaries during the first year and perhaps later.

SUMMARY

Generalist social work practice with couples varies according to the setting and circumstances involved. In urban areas, the availability of MSW social workers who specialize in marital and couple counseling is an important resource. However, many insurances do not cover this form of counseling and so the cost may make it difficult for couples to use this service. Rural areas often do not have these services readily available. In addition, marital or couple counseling is typically provided in an office setting and not at home or in the community. Thus, generalist social workers may find themselves working with couples in many of these circumstances.

Generalist social workers can provide important assistance to couples by helping them to improve their relationship skills, including communication, decision making and problem solving, and conflict resolution. Crisis intervention may be necessary when couples are faced with the potential breakup of their relationship. The mediation role is essential for any form of practice with client systems comprised of more than one person.

Generalist practice with couples who are older usually revolves around issues related to aging. The goal is to maintain quality of life in the least restrictive environment. Assistance with health care and alternative living arrangements is often needed.

QUESTIONS

1. Describe the marital or couple relationship(s) that you observed growing up in your family of origin. Assess the strengths and challenges.
2. Describe any marital or couple relationship(s) that you have experienced as an adult. Assess the strengths and challenges.
3. Using Table 10.2 and relevant parts of Table 5.3, develop a social history for yourself or a couple whom you know.
4. Describe some of the variations you might expect to find in marital relationships for members of diverse groups.
5. How would you go about working with a lesbian couple? A gay couple?

■ SUGGESTED READINGS ■

Johnson, Louise C., and Yanca, Stephen J. *Social Work Practice: A Generalist Approach,* 9th ed. Boston: Allyn & Bacon, 2007 (Chapters 8, 11, and 13).

Gutheil, Irene A., and Heyman, Janna C. "Working with Culturally Diverse Older Adults" in *Multicultural Perspectives in Working with Families,* 2nd ed. Elaine P. Congress and Manny Gonzalez, Eds. New York: Springer, 2005.

Laird, Joan, and Green, Robert-Jay, Eds. *Lesbians and Gays in Couples and Families.* San Fransisco, CA: Jossey-Bass, 1996. A "must have" text for anyone practicing with gay and lesbian couples and families.

Mattaini, Mark A. *Clinical Interventions with Families.* Washington, DC: NASW Press, 1999 (Chapter 6).

Perlman, Helen Harris. *Relationship: The Heart of Helping People.* Chicago: University of Chicago Press, 1979.

Silverstein, Louise B., and Goodrich, Thelma Jean, Eds. *Feminist Family Therapy: Empowerment in Social Context.* Washington, DC: American Psychological Association, 2005.

11

Generalist Practice with Parents

LEARNING EXPECTATIONS

1. Understand the application of the generalist practice model to working with parent subsystems.

2. Understand interaction and engagement with parents.

3. Understand assessment as a process and a product with parents.

4. Understand planning as a product and a process with parents.

5. Understand direct and indirect actions with parents.

6. Understand evaluation and termination with parents.

In our study and our practice, the two most common forms of family work for generalist social workers are with parent subsystems and with parent–child subsystems. In fact, these are the most common forms of family work for most social workers, including those engaged in clinical practice. The exceptions to this might be clinicians who specialize in family work with the entire family system or those who specialize in marriage counseling. However, our research and our own practice experience indicate that this is generally not very common. Unfortunately, most family texts assume that the worker is working with the entire family rather than focusing on subsystems within the family.

This chapter examines working with parent subsystems. Chapter 12 focuses on working with parent–child subsystems. It may seem somewhat redundant to separate these two subsystems, but we will see that they have important differences. For instance, working with parent systems focuses on the relationship between the parents with regard to parenting, which is intragenerational. Working with parent–child subsystems requires an intergenerational focus. In fact, the parent–child subsystem is the only relationship system that is intergenerational. In addition, the parent–child subsystem is often the main area of focus for blended families in which stepparent and stepchild relationships are usually important to the success of the family system. However, it is the strength of the parent relationship that generally determines this issue.

As we mentioned in Chapter 10, working with parent subsystems is also different from working with couples. When the social worker works with couples, she focuses on the husband–wife or marital or partner relationships. She is concerned with how the partners relate to each other and how they are able or unable to meet each other's needs within their relationship. These are very different roles from the roles of mother and father or stepmother and stepfather or what might be called surrogate parent in the case of unmarried couples living together with children or other types of parent figures. When partners relate to each other in the parental role, they are concerned with meeting the needs of children in the household. Couples often allow these roles to overlap or become intertwined. This is inappropriate and potentially very harmful to success in both subsystems. In a traditional intact nuclear family, the marriage exists before children are born and is intended to continue after children leave the family as adults. Thus, the marriage must stand on its own and be nurtured and strengthened. Couples who allow the demands of parenting to interfere with this often find themselves with little in common other than child-rearing. This is a recipe for divorce. In blended families, the issue of parenting becomes a primary focus from the start, and most second or subsequent marriages or partnerships fail because of the inability of the partners to separate these roles and to develop both a strong marital relationship and a strong parenting system. We discuss this further later in this chapter and then follow up with focusing on building parent–child relationships in the next chapter.

Before we begin, we would like to share some assumptions that we make when working with parents. The first is that love and nurturing and support are essential ingredients for good parenting. This does not mean that the parent approves of whatever behavior the child presents. In fact, love and acceptance of the child as a person should be separated from approval and disapproval of the child's behavior. The message should be, I love you for who you are, not what you do.

The second assumption is that positive parenting is far superior to negative parenting. We define positive parenting as parenting that expresses clear positive expectations for children and then gives clear feedback about the extent to which those expectations are met. Negative parenting is seen as expressing expectations in a negative way. This is usually followed by criticism or punishment. Positive parenting focuses on what parents want from their children. It begins with statements such as, I expect you to. . . . Negative parenting focuses on prohibitions or "don'ts." Parents who employ positive parenting will need to express some prohibitions, but they give their children an expectation of what to do when they find themselves in those situations. Parents who use mainly negative parenting only give the "don't" side of the message.

The third assumption is that successful parenting is based on consistency. Regardless of the choice of parenting styles and techniques, children are more likely to respond favorably to consistent expectations along with consistent feedback and discipline.

The fourth assumption is that there are fundamentally three types of parenting styles. One style is the authoritarian or controlling parent who takes the approach that can be characterized as "I am going to control your behavior if it's the last thing I do." This approach generally either fails to control the child's behavior or succeeds in generating resentment or inadequacy. This style of parenting tends to set the child up to become a dependent adult rather than an independent one or it results in the child becoming rebellious. The second style can be called laissez faire or permissive. The laissez faire parent takes a "hands off" approach giving little direction or feedback or discipline. The permissive parent is similar to the laissez faire parent but is mainly lenient with regard to expectations and discipline. The third style is one we like to call the "reasonable" parent. This style tends to have reasonable expectations based on age and development. Expectations are clear and change as children grow up with the expectation that they will become independent adults capable of making their own decisions. There are reasonable positive and negative consequences for positive and negative behaviors. Of course, our bias is toward this third style, but these styles are not necessarily qualitatively different from each other. They are probably on a continuum with the first two being at the extremes and the third somewhere in the middle. There are probably various combinations of these styles in every household. However, we believe that the closer parents get to the third style, or the reasonable parent, the better they will have prepared the child to function in U.S. society as an independent or interdependent adult. These styles are heavily influenced by culture. A more authoritarian approach may be expected in some cultures. Adult interdependence, especially with respect to the family, is also common in some cultures. The diversity competent social worker works within these cultural frameworks but also discusses the advantages and disadvantages of each so that parents can make an informed decision about what approach is desirable.

These four assumptions comprise what we consider to be good parenting practices. Recently, social work has begun to develop what is called "best practices," which refer to using practices that have been proven to be effective through research. Other terms for this are *evidence-based practice* or *empirical practice*. In our companion text *Social Work Practice: A Generalist Approach*, 9th ed., we offered our own version of good practices, which are shown as applied to families in the Appendix. Borrowing from that concept, we will use the term *good parenting practices* throughout this text to refer to parenting practices that reflect love and care and concern with a positive, consistent approach that is reasonable in terms of expectations and consequences.

This chapter examines the change process with parents. It includes working with parents as a dyad and in groups. Generalist social workers frequently work both directly and indirectly with parents as well as with parent–child subsystems. Relationship skills are obviously important to good parenting. This was covered earlier in Chapter 4 and in Chapter 10 and will not be repeated here. However, we will refer to these relationship skills throughout the chapter and will relate them to the development of a strong parent subsystem. The change process with parents uses the same phases that were outlined for families in Part II. We begin with interaction and engagement. The chapter also considers assessment, planning, action, and evaluation and termination with parents. As mentioned earlier, there is overlap between this chapter, chapters in Part II, and those in Part III. The social worker needs to become proficient at developing skills that are focused on each of the subsystems in the family as well as with the family as a whole.

■   INTERACTION AND ENGAGEMENT   ■
WITH PARENTS

As mentioned earlier, with all generalist practice the worker might start out working with an individual or individuals, a family, or a subsystem before it is decided that working with the parent subsystem is necessary or the best approach. Working with parents may also begin with the parents presenting themselves for service, but it is much more likely that one or more children will be the focus of attention first. Situations that begin with an individual and lead to working with the parents most often involve a child receiving services and finding that the parent subsystem needs to be strengthened in order for the work to be successful. In most child welfare cases the parent or parents are the focus of attention to begin with as a result of neglect or abuse. Table 10.1 gives an overview of some of the indications and counterindications for working with parents and other family subsystems.

Working with parents as a dyad involves working with two individuals and their relationship with each other as parents. As is the case with any form of family work, the social worker must be aware of her role and the roles of the parents. As we pointed out in Chapters 4 and 10, whenever a worker is working with a system or a subsystem, the client is the system or subsystem as a whole as well as each individual in that system. This means that the worker must take the role of mediator and must be given that role by members of the system. She cannot be seen as taking sides and still serve the individuals and the system as a whole. In addition, it would be inappropriate and unethical to sacrifice the needs of any of the individuals involved. When the needs of the individuals within the system are not met, then the system will be out of balance. This will eventually lead to further difficulties. The worker must work with the parent subsystem to meet both individual needs and the needs of the relationship. A strong relationship requires that needs be met throughout the system, establishing a balance or equilibrium.

The social worker often finds himself working with single parents. In these cases, there are several options available. He may work directly with the parent on parenting skills, parenting style, or specific parenting techniques that are needed to resolve the situation at hand. The worker may also have the parent join a parenting group or class. If the noncustodial parent is available, the worker should seek to include him or her in the work. Unfortunately, all too often this relationship may be the primary reason that work is necessary. Parents who continue to fight out the divorce through their children are visiting their problems on their children. This may require skills that are beyond those that the generalist social worker possesses. However, as we pointed out for couples, if the worker is the only realistic option, then he should do what he can to assist. If the relationship is too volatile, the worker can attempt to bring about change by working with each party individually and mediate some kind of arrangement.

Sometimes there may be two parents in the home, but one may refuse to participate or may not be available because of work or other obligations. When this occurs, the social worker should do what she can to assist in strengthening the parent subsystem. The reason for the absence of the second parent is important to the likelihood of success in working with only one partner. If the parent is generally absent from the home, then the parent who is present may be functioning as a single parent even though there is a second parent. This situation arises when one parent works long hours or the afternoon/evening shift or is out of town for extended stays. Some couples work different shifts and so neither are available very often at the same times. There may be third parties involved in childcare or the children may attend before- and/or after-school programs. If the parent refuses to participate, it may be a sign of much deeper difficulties and could indicate that the marital relationship is at risk. There may also be cultural expectations that make child-rearing a primarily gender-based role. The special challenges in these situations are related to the need to develop consistency with respect to parental expectations and discipline.

Engagement and interaction with the parents should follow the same pattern established in earlier chapters and should be culturally and diversity competent. Cultural competence is especially important because child-rearing is heavily value laden and generally dictated by cultural norms. The social worker should yield the role of expert with regard to cultural aspects of parenting. However, there are some basic principles that should not be compromised. Parenting practices that are emotionally or physically harmful or that constitute neglect or abuse are never acceptable. In fact, the worker is obligated by law and his code of ethics to report these to Child Protective Services. The issue of physical discipline and spanking will be taken up later in the chapter.

Using a diversity competent approach that includes naturalistic inquiry, the social worker proceeds with engagement in a similar manner as was described in Chapter 10 with couples. The worker observes the parents and mirrors their verbal and nonverbal approach. The worker might begin slowly with some small talk. She might try to break the ice by commenting about the weather or some recent event, preferably something positive. If the meeting is at the agency the worker might inquire if they had any difficulty finding it. If this is the first meeting, she might then ask what brings them in for service. However, if there has been some initial work with a child as was pointed out earlier, then the worker might begin by discussing what has transpired in working with the child or a family member or members that lead to the decision to meet them as parents. In these cases she may have already met either one or both of them in providing these services. If the first meeting is a home visit, the worker should explain how she was referred and ask about their understanding of the referral.

A diversity competent approach allows parents to tell the story of their approach to parenting. Most parents in the United States have a multiethnic or multicultural background, so parenting approaches and styles tend to be quite diverse. This can cause disagreements and inconsistency with regard to parenting. Some parents only need to understand the source of these differences and will then be able to negotiate a common understanding. Others will need more intense services to sort out the differences between them. In using a naturalistic approach to diversity competence, the worker seeks to have an open dialogue, free from preconceived notions about what style or approach to parenting is "best." In order to do this, the worker must understand his own biases about parenting, which inevitably are based on his own experience as a child and may include his own experiences as a parent. Examining and understanding these experiences must take place as part of the worker's preparation for family work. However, this work is never really finished and becomes a part of one's professional development as the worker becomes more skilled at working with families. The worker needs to understand the influence of the larger society on his attitudes toward and perceptions of parenting. He also needs to understand the effects of these influences on the parents.

In listening to the parents' stories, the diversity competent social worker looks for areas of common ground as well as areas of difference. She seeks to clarify these and reach an understanding regarding the work to be done. Most people are highly sensitive about their parenting. It is almost as if it is worse to be seen as a "bad parent" than it is to be seen as a "bad person." Perhaps this is because the consequences of being a "bad parent" will generally be paid by the children. Using an unbiased approach is essential to forming a successful helping relationship. Parents need to feel valued and accepted as human beings before they will be willing to trust the worker, and without trust, permanent change is not likely to take place.

Regardless of their cultural background, parents usually have at least one area of agreement regarding the outcome of their parenting. Parents want their children to grow up to be happy and successful adults. Disagreements tend to occur around the definition of success, how it will be achieved, how long it will take, and how to get there. However, the fact that there is general agreement about the outcome can be used to bring parents together and motivate them to change their parenting. The areas of disagreement become areas for negotiation and compromise. At times, the greatest challenge may be the desire on the part of the children to achieve success that is defined by the larger society as opposed to how success is defined within the family's culture. These are clearly among the most difficult situations to resolve. Ultimately, children become adults and are free to make their own choices about this. The inevitability of this fact can be used to help parents find a way to parent that allows for the inclusion of highly valued cultural norms. Forcing these on their children is unlikely to be successful in the long run and may even push the children away from their cultural heritage. Developing a healthy self-image includes valuing oneself within the context of one's cultural heritage. Thus, this work often becomes bicultural work in which parents are encouraged to help their children become bicultural so they can have the best of both worlds.

■ ASSESSMENT WITH PARENTS ■

As with families and couples, assessment with parents involves both process and product. The change process follows similar steps taken in assessment with families and with couples as described in Chapter 5 and will not be repeated here. The social history for parents follows a similar format as the family social history presented in Table 5.3. Table 11.1 contains elements that should be added to the family history format as part II.D. In addition, the term *parents* should be substituted for *family* for parts III and IV of Table 5.3. Relevant portions of the individual social history should be added from Table 5.2. Making these changes will convert the family social history to one that is focused on the parent subsystem.

This description of the assessment phase is the process that is used to set the stage for change. The product of the assessment is the social history. A supplementary schema for the social history of a parent subsystem is outlined later in Table 11.1. It includes an assessment of the structure, the functioning, and the development of this subsystem of the family.

As is the case with families and couples, the purpose of assessment with parents is to understand the "parents in situation." The assessment should lay the groundwork for change by identifying strengths and resources in the ecosystem. The assessment spans all three dimensions of time—past, present, and future. The understanding of parent in situation examines the past and present. Laying the groundwork for change focuses on the future.

Assessment as a Process

As mentioned earlier, family work may begin with working with an individual, the family system, or a family subsystem. The decision to work with the parent subsystem may come at any time during the change process. Typically, it will come as a result of working with children. When the decision is made, the social worker begins by establishing a relationship with the parents and also begins to gather information about the presenting need or concern as it relates to them as parents. This is generally similar to the indications for working with the parent subsystem identified in Table 10.1. These needs and concerns can be formulated similar to those identified in Chapter 10, only the focus is on the parenting relationship:

> Mr. and Mrs. Jones need to strengthen their relationship as parents.

If the need or concern relates to a family matter, the following format might be used:

> In order to help their blended family to grow together as a family, Mr. and Mrs. Jones need to strengthen their relationship as parents.

As with families and couples, the nature of the need or concern refers to areas that may be causing the need to arise and assumptions about what would resolve the situation. The worker and the parents speculate about what is possible and what needs to be done. It may include focusing on their relationship as parents, on how they provide support for each other in parenting, or on how they deal with their ecosystem (including their family) as parents. Some examples of these are as follows:

> If Mr. and Mrs. Jones can agree on a positive approach to parenting, they will be able to help their blended family grow together as a family.
> If Mr. and Mrs. Jones improve their communication, decision making, and conflict resolution, they will be able to improve their ability to successfully parent the children in their blended family.
> If Mr. and Mrs. Jones set aside time each day to talk about their parenting and issues that arise with the children, they will strengthen their ability to successfully parent the children in their blended family.

In identifying the nature of the needs and concerns as parents, the social worker gains a better understanding of parents in situation. This provides structure for selecting and collecting information.

As the social worker gathers information about parents in situation, she looks for potential strengths and resources in the parent subsystem and their ecosystem. These are generally found in areas where the parents have reached common ground about parenting and the means by which this was achieved. Strengths are also found in overcoming adversity or disagreement. As with families and couples, permanent change should be based on a solid foundation. Abilities and capabilities in one area of life are signs of potential in other areas. The ability to work together in dealing with various situations can be used in their parenting abilities.

The selection and collection of information are focused on information gathered in the first three steps of the assessment phase. The social worker should limit the information collected to that which is needed to bring about change. Of course, as we mentioned earlier, some information needs to be gathered to complete the case file and meet bureaucratic requirements. The worker gathers information so he can understand the need or concern and the parents and their situation. He gathers information about the assumptions that were made in the second step to assess their accuracy or feasibility. He explores potential strengths and resources to determine whether these can be used to develop a plan to meet needs and address concerns.

Analysis of the information that is collected is done by the worker independently and jointly with the parents. The worker analyzes information to gain an understanding of person in situation or "parents in situation." The worker's analysis with any form of family work includes five general areas as the work proceeds: (1) what she understands about parents in environment and strengths and resources, given what is known; (2) what changes are needed, given what is known; (3) what further information is needed to better understand the situation; (4) what further information is needed to bring about successful change; and (5) what are some potentially successful change strategies that can be used to meet the needs and address the concerns.

Assessment as a Product

The product of the assessment is the social history. Different structures and information may be required in the social history depending on the setting and various bureaucratic requirements. Some settings may use a more informal format rather than a formal document. Table 11.1 is a supplementary schema representing information required in the typical social history. Of course, various settings may require more information about certain areas or have additional areas of need or concern such as education, health, mental health, or substance abuse.

Table 11.1 Supplementary Schema for Development of a Social History for Parent Subsystems

I. Identifying Information (as needed by agency)
(This is the same as Table 5.3.I.)

II. (Part A, B, and C are the same as Table 5.3.II.)
D. The Parents as a subsystem of the family (note the strengths, resources, and challenges for each section)
1. Structure and form of current marriage or relationship and past marriages and significant relationships, especially those that produced children.
a. Subsystems—Describe the relationship and functioning of the parent subsystem and relevant aspects of marital, sibling, and parent–child subsystems or other subsystems.
b. Cohesiveness as parents—Describe the manner in which the parents maintain their relationship system, boundaries, and relatedness as a couple and as parents. Include the issue of connectedness and separateness, rules and norms for their relationship, and emotional bond.
c. The parents' environment—Describe the parents':
1) Living situation
2) Socioeconomic status
3) Nature of community or neighborhood and the parents' relationship with the community or neighborhood. Include community organizations and institutions important for the parents and the nature of the relationship with these. Describe community and neighborhood resources and responsibilities and impingements for these parents in this community.
4) Extended family: involvement with; significant persons in the extended family; strength of the influence of this family system; and resources, responsibility, and impingements from it.

(continued)

Table 11.1 Continued

2. Functioning as parents and as a couple
   a. Communication patterns and skills
   b. Decision-making and problem solving patterns and skills
   c. Conflict resolution patterns and skills
   d. Role performance and satisfaction
      1) Work and housekeeping standards and practices
      2) System member support; growth encouragement, care, and concern
   e. Parenting and childcare standards and practices. Identify the parenting style of each parent. Identify commonalities and differences in style and techniques. Identify expectations of each other and of the children. Identify feedback mechanisms and disciplinary systems.
   f. Parents' customary adaptive and coping mechanisms
   g. Intimacy as a couple
   h. Construct an eco-map for the parents. Include important elements that effect their functioning as parents and as a couple.
3. Development of the relationship–history
   a. Brief history of the relationship from dating and courtship until current situation
   b. Roots, influence of cultural group and previous generations on parenting
   c. Significant events in the life of the couple including previous marriages and significant relationships, especially live in relationships and relationships that have produced children
   d. Developmental stage of family life
   e. Brief history of parenting experiences

III. The Concern or Need
   (This is the same as Table 5.3.III. with "parents" replacing "family" as the focus)

IV. Strengths and Challenges for Meeting Needs
   (This is the same as Table 5.3.IV. with "parents" replacing "family" as the focus)

Demographic and background information is covered in the first two sections of the schema. Parts I and II focus on the parents as individuals. Part II.D examines the parent subsystem of the family. The focus is on the parents as parents. It includes the structure, functioning, and development of the relationship as parents.

Understanding current and former experiences with being parented and with parenting is an important aspect of assessment with parents. This is heavily influenced by culture, diversity, and sociological factors. The United States has experienced a great deal of variation in culture and this has resulted in a great deal of cultural variation within most family systems. For most areas of the world there is much more homogeneity with respect to culture between parents. Cross-cultural relationships are more the norm in the United States than are shared cultural relationships. Thus, there is much more variation with respect to roles, parenting styles, child-rearing practices, and expectations. Most parents are not aware of this variation. There tends to be an assumption that they will have substantial agreement regarding parenting and child-rearing when in fact they are likely to have areas of disagreement. If the parents have a common culture, they are more likely to have common expectations regarding roles and expectations for parenting. Most cultures have common expectations for these roles and for child-rearing practices. Parents are more likely to have had common experiences growing up that reinforce parenting roles and practices. Parents in cross-cultural relationships are more likely to have had different expectations and experiences. As a result, these parents have a greater need to communicate about parenting and child-rearing and to negotiate and compromise in order to reach common ground.

Biracial or multiracial parents must deal with prejudice and discrimination on the part of society toward themselves as a couple as well as face the challenge of raising their children to cope with these difficulties. They also must meet the challenges of developing a successful cross-cultural relationship and incorporate parenting styles and child-rearing practices that are comfortable for each of them while still maintaining some consistency regarding expectations and discipline with their children. Developing an understanding of each other as a partner and as a parent from a different culture is challenging. Some parents are able to use their fight against prejudice and discrimination as a source of strength and unity. Others experience these as a more divisive factor in their relationship. For many of these parents, difficulties with extended family members can be an even greater challenge than those that come from outside the family.

Parents who are gay or lesbian face very intense prejudice and discrimination on the part of society. Among the challenges they face are numerous legal barriers to marriage. It is difficult for them to receive benefits including medical coverage for their partners. They face difficulties with producing and acquiring children to raise. Some have children from previous relationships or must seek out formal or informal surrogate mothers. In these cases, courts have tended to award custody to the other parent based solely on sexual orientation. Some parents who are lesbian opt for artificial insemination. Adoption is available in some states but is often difficult to achieve, especially for those who are open about their sexual orientation. Even when adoption occurs, most states prohibit the partner from being a legal adoptive parent.

Unmarried couples have become much more common and often include full- or part-time custody of children from previous relationships. Raising children born out of wedlock has gained much more acceptance than it had in the past. Some couples will have one or more children before they are married. Some never marry but function as if they were and others go their separate ways with a wide range of levels of involvement with their children on the part of the noncustodial parent. The relationships of unmarried couples who have children range from postdating relationships and trial marriages to long-term relationships. There may be a series of these types of live-in relationships without any marriage, before marriage, or between marriages. Some may produce children. Others may be short or long term, quasi- or pseudo-stepparent situations.

Single parents may experience long-term single parenthood and others may have intermittent live-in relationships without any marriage, before remarriage, or between marriages. The children and the parents, stepparents, and quasi- or pseudo-stepparents in these situations tend to experience a great deal of stress as a result of the uncertainty of parental responsibility and authority in these situations and the lack of a blood relationship with at least some of the children. The absent biological parent sometimes plays an important role in encouraging and maintaining difficulty with parenting for the single parent regardless of whether a quasi- or pseudo-stepparent is present in the home.

Generalist social workers may provide services to foster parents and adoptive parents. Workers assist foster parents with handling the challenges of parenting foster children. Social workers work with adoptive parents on issues related to their infertility and help prepare them to raise an adopted child. Many infertile marriages do not survive, so working with these parents to solidify their relationship is essential for long-term success in adoption.

Parents can experience more than one of these situations in any given relationship or they can have a series of any of these relationships with any of these variations over time. These situations can either increase or decrease the cohesion that parents have in their relationship as parents and as a couple. Some will use challenges to strengthen their relationship and others will experience a decline in that strength. Parenting is challenging enough even under the best of circumstances. It is imperative that parents develop relationship and coping skills that will meet their needs and those of their children.

Parents may or may not receive much support from the environment. Generally, there is a great deal of variation of support from various parts of the environment. Some relationships may be very supportive and others very stressful. Financial difficulties are one of the major threats to a relationship and are quite common for parents raising children. In an agrarian society, children tend to be an economic asset, contributing to the family's economic activity. In industrial and technological societies, children are an economic liability because they do not contribute to the financial well-being of the family. In fact, the demand for a more educated work force tends to prolong dependence well into adulthood. Parents may experience difficulties with in-laws who may interfere or be critical of parenting and child-rearing. Unfortunately, some environments are hostile toward the variety or diversity of family forms such as biracial or gay or lesbian couples, unmarried parents, single parents, and the like.

The functioning of the couple as partners and as parents is an important consideration. Although we mentioned that these roles need to be separated, the skills that are necessary to develop and maintain a relationship are essentially the same. The content and focus are the main differences. Essential skills necessary for any successful relationship are communication skills, decision-making or problem-solving skills, and the ability to resolve conflict in a constructive rather than a destructive manner. For parents, these skills are critical in terms of sorting out similarities and differences in parenting styles and child-rearing practices and in reaching an agreement on the who, what, where, when, how, and why of parenting. Consistency in parenting means both parents having the same expectations, expressing those in clear messages to the children, giving similar feedback regarding the same types of behavior each time they occur, and providing the same consequences (positive reinforcement and discipline) each and every time over time. This requires good, ongoing communication. It requires that the parents reach decisions and solve problems together so they do not undermine each other. It means that conflict needs to be resolved in a positive manner. Although it can be helpful for children to see their parents disagree and work out their differences so they can learn to do this, parenting issues should probably be settled in private so a united front can be maintained. Otherwise, children will tend to exploit these differences to serve their own purposes. This is not really deviousness, it is simply natural for children to want what they want when they want it.

Parents need to develop an understanding of and an appreciation for the roles that each play in the family system as a couple and as parents. Happy couples tend to be satisfied with their own and their partner's performance in these roles. Agreement on work and housekeeping standards and practices need to be developed and maintained with consistent positive feedback and expressions of appreciation. Otherwise, the partner who performs the role easily can feel that he or she is being taken for granted. Parents need to feel that they are supported by each other. There needs to be growth in the relationship along with encouragement, care, and concern.

Parenting and childcare standards and practices are critical aspects of a social history for parents. The social worker should develop an understanding of the parenting style of each parent. He should help them to identify commonalities and differences in style and techniques. He should explore their expectations of each other and of the children. Feedback mechanisms and disciplinary systems should also be discussed.

Adaptive and coping mechanisms for parents refer to the ways in which each parent is able to adapt to and cope with the changes and challenges of parenting. Some people are more rigid than others and find that adapting to change is difficult and stressful. Others relish the variety and diversity that change brings with it. Coping with the stresses and strains of parenting often means taking time out. This is where it is important for the parents to support each other. It is nice to know that someone is there to step in when needed. If there are difficulties in doing this, then there may actually be added stresses and strains.

Intimacy was discussed in Chapter 10 and relates primarily to the parents' relationship as a couple. The importance to parenting is less direct but still significant. Couples who share a satisfying intimate relationship have an extra store of good will that can serve them well in meeting the demands of parenting. By the same token, a less-than-satisfactory intimate relationship can mean that parenting is less fulfilling and the demands of parenting are more taxing on the relationship. A satisfying intimate relationship is also likely to be a sign that the couple have been successful at developing good communication, effective problem solving and decision making, and constructive conflict resolution. Thus, these skills are available to them in sorting out the challenges of parenting.

An eco-map will give the worker and the parents a picture of their current situation in terms of the flow of energy into and out of the family system and the parent subsystem. The eco-map was covered in Chapter 5. When constructing one with parents, it should still include all members of the household but the emphasis should be on the parents as individuals, as a couple, and as parents. Special attention needs to be paid to issues that are likely to generate stress on parenting, stress on children, and strengths and resources available for parenting.

It is important to assess the development of the relationship over time both as a couple and as parents. It is not necessary to cover every detail. However, it can be very insightful to explore the development of an intimate relationship and parenting experiences as well as experiences that influence parenting. This generally helps to understand the current situation and may also uncover areas of potential strengths. Having experience with successful and satisfying relationships, especially those related to parenting, is a sign that either one or both parents are capable of developing or restoring these relationships. The lack of success or satisfaction may be a sign that some basic skill building will be needed. Fortunately, parenting is learned and is not an innate quality or trait. Exploration of the influence of culture is important to understanding the roots of expectations around parenting and child-rearing. It offers the parents an opportunity to examine these and decide what they want to keep and what they would like to change. It also takes some of the mystique out of these. Most people learn parenting from the way in which they were parented. However, we generally do not know where it comes from or originates. This is especially true in multicultural societies. In a homogeneous society, everyone knows where it comes from (the culture), and everyone is more likely to have more in common with each other in terms of how they were parented. In multicultural societies, parenting and child-rearing practices come from more than one culture, both within and outside of the family. As a result, the typical couple is not likely to have a clear understanding of the source of their knowledge about parenting and child-rearing. Significant events in their lives as parents and as individuals can assist in highlighting influences that may explain current parenting practices. In particular, some experiences may enhance parenting ability and others may impair it. Finally, the worker needs to identify the stage of development for the relationship and the family. The family stages of development were discussed in Chapter 5.

The next section should contain a brief history of the parenting experience. Depending on how the worker has responded to other parts of the schema, this may be a summary of all parenting experiences for each parent along with their experience together or it may be limited to the latter.

The genogram may or may not be added to this schema. It can be helpful in terms of looking at family patterns and previous parenting experiences. It can also be tailored to parenting and child-rearing practices to see how these patterns have been established on each side of the family.

Part III focuses on the need or concern that initiated the work with the parent subsystem. The worker should include needs and concerns for individuals, subsystems, and the family as a whole, even if these are not the focus of the current work. Identifying the pattern of needs in the family gives the worker and the parents a view of the stresses and strains and also helps to identify strengths, particularly with respect to the ability of the parents and the family system, to meet needs in the family.

Part IV identifies strengths and challenges within the ecosystem including the family, the parent subsystem, and the environment. Parts III and IV are where the two purposes of the assessment are examined. The first purpose is to gain an understanding of the parents and their situation as these relate to the need or concern. The second purpose is to identify strengths and resources for meeting needs or addressing concerns and challenges that might create barriers to meeting needs. Once these purposes have been sufficiently fulfilled, planning for change can begin. As mentioned earlier, assessment continues throughout the work. The worker learns something new and adds to her understanding every time she meets with the parents. If the work is successful, the parents also learn something about themselves and their parenting.

■   PLANNING WITH PARENTS   ■

Planning with parents is similar to planning with families, which was described in Chapter 6, and may have some similarity to planning with couples, which was described in Chapter 10. Similar to assessment, planning is both a process and a product. The planning process with parents has some relationship to planning with families because planning with families will generally include parenting and child-rearing practices in some form. It is different from planning with couples because working on their relationship should be kept separate and distinct from other forms of family work. Work with couples should take place in private, totally separate from the family. However, some parent work can take place with the children present. To some extent there is overlap between working with parent subsystems and working with parent–child subsystems. The primary task in working with the parent subsystem is developing a consistent and effective system of parenting that both parents can agree with and support. The result of this work is then implemented through the parent–child subsystem. Thus, the goals in planning with parents are focused on their relationship as parents and their ability to function in that role.

As with couples, planning with parents is a joint process with the worker acting as a facilitator, mediator, and negotiator. The plan should address the needs of each partner as a parent; should strengthen their relationship as parents; and should result in a unified, functional parent subsystem. In the process of developing a plan, each parent takes responsibility for expressing his or her own needs as a parent. The worker should be given the position of mediator. In this role the worker helps them to identify common ground and differences. These differences are then negotiated until an agreement is reached. This approach works best within the context of an egalitarian relationship. Some cultures dictate that one of the parents be the dominant figure in determining parenting and child-rearing practices and their implementation. One way to help these parents in moving to at least a shared role relationship in terms of parenting is to point out some of the advantages in sharing these roles. Having one parent in charge will undermine the power of the other parent in supervising and disciplining the children, but when parents share this power, then there are no weak spots for the children to exploit. In addition, when one is in charge, then ultimately that person is also responsible for the outcome. Raising children is difficult enough without dividing the power that parents need to be successful. Sharing this role means that each parent has the support of the other and there is always someone "in the bull pen" to assist when either parent feels stressed.

The product of the planning process with any client system is the service plan. Various settings have different terms for this, but essentially this is where the goals and objectives are written down in the case file. In order to assist parents in becoming more consistent in their parenting, it is generally helpful for each parent to keep a written version of the plan. An example of a parenting plan is as follows:

Goal: Mr. and Mrs. Jones will improve their relationship as parents.
Objective 1: Mr. and Mrs. Jones will use "I" statements when communicating with each other as parents at least once a day for one week by August 15.
  Clients Task: Mr. and Mrs. Jones will maintain journals of the use of "I" statements in discussing parenting and will bring their journals to sessions with the worker.
  Worker Task: Worker will assist Mr. and Mrs. Jones in monitoring and practicing "I" statements during conjoint sessions.
Objective 2: Mr. and Mrs. Jones will use an effective parental decision-making process with each other at least three times in one week by August 15.
  Clients Task: Mr. and Mrs. Jones will maintain journals of their parental decision making and will bring their journals to sessions with the worker.
  Worker Task: Worker will assist Mr. and Mrs Jones in negotiating, monitoring, and practicing parental decision making during sessions with the worker.

■ DIRECT PRACTICE ACTIONS WITH PARENTS ■

As with families and couples, direct practice actions with parents are actions that are taken in working with the parents. Indirect practice actions are those that are taken on behalf of the parents. Direct practice includes actions taken (1) to engage in diversity competent actions with parents, (2) to enable development of relationship, (3) to develop an understanding of parents in environment, (4) to plan with parents, (5) to enable parents to know and use available resources, (6) to empower or enable parents to strengthen their relationship, (7) to resolve crisis situations, (8) to use support in working with parents, (9) to use activity with parents, (10) to mediate with parents and between parents and a system in their environment, and (11) to use a clinical model of social work with parents.

These actions are similar to those described for working with families and with couples. There are areas where they overlap with items that were discussed earlier. Diversity competence was covered in Chapters 3 and 5. The development of a relationship was described in Chapters 4 and 10 and earlier in this chapter. Development of understanding of person in environment

CASE EXAMPLE

Jamilla is a young African American social worker who is employed as a foster care and adoption worker. Her position puts her in contact with parents in several different venues. As a foster care worker, Jamilla works with both foster parents and biological families. She also trains foster parents. As an adoption worker, Jamilla conducts adoption studies for prospective adoptive parents, arranges the placement of adoptees, and supervises the adoption for one year. Because she is young, single, and not a parent, sometimes she finds that parents do not always respect her abilities right away. Working with white, Hispanic, and Asian parents also creates cross-cultural and cross-racial challenges. Following are examples of the work that she does.

■ **Diversity Competent Practice Actions with Diverse Families**

Jamilla often works with parents whose race and culture are different from hers. Her foster parents, biological parents, and adoptive parents include parents who are white, African American, Hispanic, and Asian. This can present numerous challenges for her as she tries to work with each family in a way that reflects diversity, competent practice. Fortunately, her social work education included an approach to diversity competence that allows her to learn from each family with whom she works. Jamilla uses naturalistic inquiry in working with the parents on her caseload. She listens to each person's story and tries to maintain an open mind at all times. Jamilla studied her own family as part of her coursework. She finds that she learns more about herself and her own family as she works with each family. She also has learned to understand diversity in families from both a broad and individual perspective. Jamilla realizes that diversity competence is a lifelong process that requires constant learning and growth.

Included on Jamilla's caseload are a small number of families whom she works with on a prevention basis. These are families where a complaint was filed, but it was decided that a case did not need to be opened if the family agreed to work with the agency. One of the families was an Hispanic couple who had been referred to protective services by a visiting nurse who found an open pair of scissors in their daughter's crib. When Jamilla began working with them, she asked about the scissors and found out that they had placed them in the crib as a cross because they did not have a small crucifix. It was intended to be something that would protect their daughter. Jamilla understood this as part of their spirituality and felt that the whole incident had been caused by a lack of understanding about their culture. She felt that the nurse and the protective services worker were a bit overzealous and did not take the time to understand this. Jamilla worked with the couple on getting a free crucifix from their church and also referred them to a nutrition and well baby program.

as this relates to parents was discussed under assessment and planning was covered in the previous section. Action taken in using a clinical model of social work with parents is beyond the scope of this book and is typically covered in advanced graduate-level social work courses.

Action Taken to Enable Parents to Know and Use Community Resources

Action taken to enable couples to know and use available resources is similar to the description for families in Chapter 7 and for couples in Chapter 10. However, special attention should be paid to this with regard to the role of parent. As the adults in the family system, parents are responsible for providing basic needs and ensuring that family members, especially children, are safe; receive proper care; and have their physical, social, psychological, emotional, economic, and educational needs met. In order to accomplish this, parents need to be knowledgeable about various systems in the community. Chapter 2 contains a schema for a community study that outlines many of these systems. Most parents are able to provide adequately for themselves and their children through income from employment and by learning to negotiate these community systems on their own and through knowledge gained from their social support network. However, parents who have weak support systems or who are faced with unusual or excessive needs may not be able to meet these needs. The social worker assists these parents in strengthening their support system and accessing resources in the community.

There are similarities between the direct actions and indirect actions that a social worker can take with parents and families. The primary difference is that direct actions are actions that the worker takes directly with the parents. These actions are designed to facilitate or enhance knowledge and skills that parents need in acquiring resources and building strengths. Indirect actions are actions taken with systems on behalf of parents. The worker uses these in emergency situations, when the parents are unable to act on their own behalf or that of family members, or when systems are not responsive to the parents and influence is required to make them more responsive.

The first action taken under this category relates to knowledge that is necessary to access resources. Parents who are isolated or have weak social support systems may simply be unaware of resources that are available. These can range from tangible to intangible resources. Examples of tangible resources are furniture, appliances, and other goods necessary for setting up a household. They might include inexpensive housing, assistance with rent or security deposits, and food and commodities. Intangible resources generally refer to services that are available. These could include counseling or parenting skills training as individuals, couples, or in a group. Services to children can refer to educational, psychological, health, and mental health services. Knowledge about resources and services should include knowledge about locations and how to access services.

In order to assist parents in knowing and using resources, the social worker needs to be knowledgeable himself. Typically, workers will acquire this knowledge as they provide services to families. The knowledge should include types of resources, service area, eligibility criteria and the process of determining eligibility, and key contacts within the organization. Some of this knowledge can be obtained from resource manuals within the agency and from other agencies, telephone books, professional staff within the agency and from other agencies, professional experiences, and libraries. Many libraries either have hard copies of community resource materials or will have this information available

■ **Action Taken to Enable Parents to Know and Use Community Resources**

In her work with biological and foster parents on her caseload, Jamilla is constantly enabling them to use community resources. A primary responsibility is for her to act as a broker and refer these parents for services. She refers parents to counseling and parenting classes. She gets biological parents to work on their education and refers them to employment training programs. Jamilla helps parents to network with each other to locate inexpensive sources of food, clothing, and entertainment for their families. She helps biological parents to find and access resources to provide suitable housing.

online. Reference librarians can be very important resources in searching for this information.

In addition to knowledge, the social worker should also be prepared to assist parents in using the resources that are available in the community. Several skills are important in this process. These include organizational skills as well as assertiveness. Parents may need to learn to be advocates for themselves and for their children. Effective communication and problem-solving skills are important. These are skills that a professional social worker uses every day and can be taught to parents so that they can be more effective in developing and carrying out plans to use community resources.

Action Taken to Enable or Empower Parents

Enabling and empowering parents are two skills that are needed in assisting them to use community resources. These are also important for them within the parenting relationship. It is our belief that strong parenting requires two strong individuals working together in a strong relationship. Thus, these activities should be intended to empower and enable them as individuals, as a couple, and as parents. Empowering and enabling as individuals was covered in Chapter 7 and as couples in Chapter 10. We assume that enabling and empowering activities are aimed at assisting parents to be loving, positive, and consistent "reasonable" parents who engage in good parenting practices as described earlier in this chapter. Enabling is making it possible to engage in actions as a parent. The empowering aspect refers to increasing power to take action. Enabling is seen as assisting parents in developing skills necessary for parenting. Empowering refers to increasing confidence and strength as parents so they can use those skills.

Enabling and empowering as parents means strengthening each parent and their parenting relationship. Generally speaking, when two parents are working in concert with each other, each parent is more empowered. Each feels more confident and positive about their parenting. On the other hand, when parents are at odds with each other or are uncertain about where the other parent stands, then at least some of their power is negated. We view empowering parents as empowering them to use good parenting practices. We believe that this approach produces children who grow up to be empowered adults. It is inappropriate to use power as parents to dominate or to undermine the potential of children.

As mentioned earlier, fortunately parenting is learned and as such can be relearned if inappropriate. Social workers frequently find themselves working with parents to change or improve their parenting. This can be difficult for those workers who are younger and who have not been parents. They can expect to be challenged for their lack of experience. Being parented or having babysat is generally not going to be good enough in terms of establishing credibility. It is best to not be defensive and instead admit that one does not have experience. At the same time, the worker should express a willingness to listen to the parents' concerns and to work with them on finding ways to be more effective. The worker can also offer knowledge about child development, access to resources, and professional training in various parenting techniques.

Social workers work with parents in the home, at the office, and in groups. The first task in working with parents is to establish their goals for parenting. These are often expressed in terms of the immediate situation, such as having their children obey them in a certain situation. Although it is appropriate to work with them on these issues, it is helpful if the worker can establish a long-range goal, such as raising their children to be responsible, independent adults. Once this is established, the worker has an important reference point with which to work. She can ask the parents how their current approach fits with this long-range goal. She can ask them to come up with an approach that will fit better with it. She can also suggest ways that might be a better fit. This is a key ingredient in successful work with parents.

There are a number of good quality parenting curricula available that can be effective in teaching parenting skills. They all have some strengths, but they also all have some weaknesses. The real strength in most good ones lies in teaching parents to problem solve and to be consistent. The primary weakness that is inherent in all of them is that parents are unlikely to completely discard their current parenting in favor of a totally new approach. At best, they will probably use bits and pieces, which may be more or less effective in bringing about successful parenting. Workers who use an ecosystems strengths approach are in a good position to help parents take advantage of these strengths while minimizing this primary weakness. An ecosystems strengths approach is inherently eclectic in that it works with the strengths that are present, seeks to build on them, and utilizes resources available in the ecosystem. The worker uses what is present and what is available to build on what is possible. As the worker assesses the parents in situation, he looks for strengths and challenges in their parenting. Using our conception of good parenting practices, the worker assesses the bond between parent and child. He offers assistance in overcoming barriers to expressing love and affection, and care and concern. He works with parents to turn negative statements and expectations into positive ones. He helps them to practice so that their parenting becomes more consistent. The worker assists the parents in setting appropriate expectations along with a system of positive and negative consequences that are appropriate for the situation. He draws on his knowledge of various parenting approaches and techniques to find one that might fit with what the parents are already doing. If he is not aware of any that are close, he researches new ones that might fit. It is critical to involve the parents in making a decision about what might work.

There are times when the worker might be faced with parents whose approach is so extreme that a new one is needed. This is most likely to occur with parents who are abusive and with some who are neglectful. In these cases, teaching parenting skills is usually not enough to bring about change. Personal and couple counseling or therapy may be needed beforehand or concurrently with teaching new parenting skills. These parents are typically duplicating the inappropriate parenting that they received and require insight into this before they can make permanent changes in their parenting. Some parents may not be capable of this insight or change. If they cannot make the necessary changes to their parenting, then the courts may need to terminate parental rights for the safety and well-being of the children.

In enabling parents to use good parenting practices, the social worker helps them to develop effective relationship skills, including good communication, effective problem solving and decision making, and constructive conflict resolution. This has already been covered in previous chapters and will not be repeated here. However, we should mention how these are used in good parenting practices. Parents who have a strong relationship are able to use their relationship to be more effective as parents. They use their relationship skills to communicate and make decisions about their parenting style and techniques. They use their problem-solving skills in ironing out issues and concerns that arise. They resolve conflict in a manner that strengthens their relationship rather than weakens it. Communication is also important in implementing parenting practices. Good parenting practices require communicating clear expectations and giving clear feedback. They require making good decisions about positive and negative consequences for behavior. They include helping children to develop good communication, decision-making and problem-solving skills, and conflict resolution skills. Thus, good parenting practice and good relationship skills go hand in hand with each other.

An important aspect of positive parenting is the need to use good behavior management techniques with children, particularly positive reinforcement. Some parents overemphasize punishment in their parenting and neglect using the most powerful tool they have as parents. Punishment tends to be limited in its ability to control or eliminate negative behavior. Its main effect is to provide a consequence for behavior, which is appropriate, but often parents use it in an effort to extinguish a behavior. Although punishment is an important aspect of discipline, parents should be encouraged to express their expectations regarding appropriate behavior and then give their children positive feedback when they meet the parents' expectations. This is much more powerful in establishing appropriate behavior. If punishment is necessary, it should be administered consistently, be relatively brief, and should include feedback regarding parental expectations for appropriate behavior.

There is a great deal of controversy about the use of physical punishment, in particular spanking. We are not prepared to take sides in this controversy. Besides, it has been our experience that this decision is rarely placed in the hands of the social worker. For the most part, it is a parental decision and the worker is generally left with making suggestions. The exception to this is when the parents have been abusive. In these situations, parents need to realize that their own inability to control their behavior means that physical punishment needs to be off limits. Working with parents who decide to use physical punishment means helping them to set limits. Physical punishment should be limited to spanking with the open hand on the child's posterior. It is probably ineffective once the child reaches six or seven years of age so the parents need to find substitute consequences before that time. Generally, time out, grounding, or depriving the child of some pleasurable item or activity are effective in providing consequences for inappropriate behavior.

The best way for parents to deal with inappropriate behavior is to eliminate it before it occurs or immediately after the first time. Children are much less likely to engage in inappropriate behavior if they are told by their parents what behavior is expected ahead of time, and they consistently receive positive feedback or reinforcement when they exhibit the expected behavior. Some parents wonder why they should reward their children for doing what they are supposed to do. Our response is to ask them if they would go to work if they did not get paid. Most parents respond that they would not. Well for children, their "pay day" comes when they receive positive recognition from their parents. It takes some time and energy and practice to do this, but the pay off can be great in terms of more positive interaction between parents and children and less time spent on punishment and correction. The first time an inappropriate behavior occurs when using this approach, parents should avoid using punishment and instead they should use a corrective response. They should discuss the situation with the child and explain why the behavior is not appropriate, what behavior is expected, and what the consequences are if the inappropriate behavior continues. For young children, this may need to be repeated several times along with administering the negative consequence.

Above all, parents need to communicate love and affection to their children and not assume that they know they are loved. Establishing a baseline of unconditional love is essential for children to develop positive self-images. This was discussed in Chapter 1 and will be discussed again in the next chapter on parent–child subsystems. One important aspect of this is to separate love and acceptance as a person from accepting or not accepting behavior. When children experience unconditional love and acceptance from their parents, they are able to internalize this and love and accept themselves, even though they are not perfect. They can feel good about themselves as human beings and good about others as well.

Enabling and empowerment of parents of teenagers can be challenging. During the teen years, children are moving from childhood to adulthood. Half the time they act and want to be treated as adults and then other times they want the irresponsibility of childhood. Many cultures have rites of passage that recognize when children become adults. These are often associated with puberty. However, in industrial and technological societies, a more educated work force is needed. In the United States, this has extended dependency well into the teens, and even into the twenties for those attending college. This sets up an extended period during which emancipation into adulthood may become a power struggle between parents and their offspring.

Additional stresses are experienced by parents and children of paternalistic cultures in which the father is expected to be the primary, and often the sole, decision maker. Teens and young adults in these families are generally bicultural and are usually caught between the tug of the dominant culture toward freedom, independence, and more individualistic lifestyles, and the paternalistic, family-oriented expectations of their culture of origin. These power struggles can become very dramatic and emotional. These parents often need assistance in formulating a plan to maintain vital or highly valued aspects of their culture while compromising in less important areas so that their sons and daughters can develop healthy bicultural lifestyles. For these families, at best, the choice of living in the United States brings with it the inevitability of a bicultural system for their families over time. At worst, they might see a total rejection of their culture by younger family members. A few immigrant groups have been successful at developing enclaves that perpetuate their culture over a longer period of time, but most will eventually be faced with the prospect of maintaining a bicultural existence. Planning for this gives parents more influence over the outcome.

Parenting teens means helping them to move from childhood to adulthood. The measure of maturity for young adults is the ability to balance freedom with responsibility. Social workers need to assist parents in planning and carrying out a strategy for doing this with their teens. Ideally, parents should discuss this process with their children as they enter adolescence and remind them of it as they progress toward adulthood. Parents should map out with the adolescent the steps that will be taken in this process and the expectations for behavior along the way. This way teens can see that their parents are partners in the emancipation process and not obstacles.

If parents have not communicated a map to emancipation, then the worker can assist the parents and teen in doing so. Generally, this begins with convincing them that they really have the same goal, an independent adult who makes good decisions. The disagreement is actually about how they are going to get there and what it is going to look like in the meantime. If they all agree on the eventual goal, the worker can help them negotiate how to get there. The key is for the parents to see the value in gradually shifting responsibility for decisions over to the teen so he or she can practice making decisions before striking out into the "real world."

Single parents have a rather daunting task in raising and emancipating their children. They have to do it solo, often while having less time because of work, and perhaps without the cooperation of noncustodial parents who may even undermine their efforts. The best situation for single parents is to be able to work together with noncustodial parents even though they are not living together. Ironically, this requires the same skills that are needed to maintain a good relationship as a couple, good communication, effective problem solving and decision making, and constructive conflict resolution. Parents who are successful at developing this in their parenting relationship can overcome many of the challenges of single parenthood. Parents who cannot will struggle with these challenges. Parents who continue to fight the divorce long after the court date is passed will visit their problems on their children. Working with single parents who do not have the support of their counterpart involves helping them to develop an alternative support system. It also means working with them on consistency and sorting out issues related to "parentifying" older children as substitute parents when they are not at home. The majority of single-parent households are headed by women and so the social worker often needs to assist the family in acquiring resources to sustain itself in the face of scarcity.

Parents of blended families face the task of blending their parenting techniques and styles into an effective and consistent system. Because most couples have multiethnic backgrounds, it is likely that parents of blended families have differences in parenting and child-rearing styles just as other parents we have identified. However, a complicating factor is the difference in history for both parents and children. They do not share a common history, and they need to build a new one together. This begins with the parents building a new relationship with each other as parents. Unfortunately, many parents in this situation do not take the time needed to solidify their relationship as a couple or as parents. The social worker helps them by giving them permission to do so and by working with them on constructing an approach to parenting with which they can both feel comfortable. This can require a great deal of give and take and will also require patience in implementing their decisions. Parents who fail in this effort are placing their relationship at grave risk because most second (or subsequent) marriages fail as a result of issues related to children from previous relationships.

■ **Action Taken to Enable or Empower Parents**

Enabling and empowering parents are major direct practice actions that are necessary for Jamilla's practice. Biological parents on her caseload often feel that they are powerless to change their situation. Getting them to act and to see that they are able to make changes is generally the first hurdle. Those who are able to take these steps can be successful in following through so that their children are returned and their case can be closed. Those who are not may have their children back, but then they often recycle back through the system. Parents who are not able to change may eventually lose their parental rights.

An important aspect of enabling in child welfare is teaching parents to use good parenting practices. Biological parents, foster parents, and adoptive parents all must have the knowledge and skills necessary to engage in good parenting practices.

Action Taken in Crisis Situations

As with crisis situations in the family and with couples, the social worker works with the parent subsystem to mobilize their coping skills. Crises within the parent subsystem may include dealing with a strain or breakdown in the relationship, coping with emergencies related to their children, and maintaining their parenting in the face of serious adversity. If the crisis is within their relationship as parents, then they will need to work on restoring their balance and equilibrium. Often a crisis in the parental relationship either represents a serious threat to the marital relationship or is caused by a threat to the marital relationship. Working on the marital relationship was covered in Chapter 10.

A strain or a breakdown in the parental relationship may be brought on by fundamental differences in parenting styles or by an episode in parenting in which there is serious disagreement about how to handle it. In either case, the social worker needs to work from a mediating position to negotiate an agreement. In doing so, the worker takes the opportunity to introduce good parenting practices as a principle around which the parents may be able to find common ground. Often the roots of these types of disagreements come from experiences parents had as children. Parents may seek to duplicate those experiences. They may be trying to meet cultural expectations. In other cases, parents may be trying to avoid repeating inappropriate parenting by their parents. After exploring the root of the disagreement, the worker attempts to reach an agreement regarding the use of good parenting practices. If the parents agree, then the discussion can turn to ways in which the parenting style or the resolution of the specific situation can be modified to fit with those principles. If there is disagreement about the use of good parenting practices, then the worker may need to use a broader approach. If the parenting approach is not inappropriate or harmful, she might negotiate a compromise. However, if the approach is inappropriate or harmful, then counseling may be indicated in order to work through underlying issues that may be driving the situation. For example, a parent, who experienced harsh punishment or even severe physical punishment as a child, might use similar techniques, especially when faced with a lack of satisfactory responses from his own child. The attitude might be, "My parents did this with me and I turned out okay." Another attitude might be, "That is not as bad as what my parents did with me." In either case, parents may not see that the actions of their parents were

■ Action Taken in Crisis Situations

Child welfare services often require crisis intervention. A protective services investigation may be a crisis in and of itself for all involved. Situations that require removal of the children from their home are crises for the children, the biological parents, and the foster care system. Social workers who are involved in these situations need to be knowledgeable about crisis intervention techniques so they can stabilize the situation as soon as possible. There may also be crises once a child is placed in care. Health emergencies may arise. Children may run away or get into trouble. Biological families may continue to experience difficulties. The following might be a typical crisis situation calling for the removal of children from the home.

Joe is a social worker employed in child protective services. He has been assigned to investigate a complaint from the school regarding the Gray family after the children were found to have head lice for the third time this school year. The children are typically dressed in dirty clothes and are eager to eat the free breakfast and lunch for which they qualify at school. Joe went to the school to interview the children. They were very guarded and it was obvious that they did not want to talk with him. They denied any problems at home. Joe left to make a home visit. He knows the neighborhood where they live is one with homes that are older and not well kept. As he drives down the street, he notices several abandon homes, some of which have been partially burned out. The Gray home has long grass and is littered with broken toys and a couple of cars that do not appear to be in operating condition. Joe knocks on the door and a disheveled woman answers. He announces who he is and asks to come in. Once inside Joe is appalled by the condition of the home. There are piles of clothes, newspapers, and objects throughout the house. Joe notes the piles of dirty dishes in the kitchen and sees roaches scurrying around. The smell is overwhelming and Joe has to breathe through his mouth. He checks the refrigerator and finds that it has rotten food and nothing that is edible. Similarly, the cupboards have a few canned goods and little else. Joe snaps several pictures. He asks Mrs. G to step outside. He questions her about her situation. She says that she has fallen on hard times and has several chronic conditions that prevent her from maintaining the household. Her husband left her several years ago and she has not seen or heard from him since. Joe noticed that her eyes were glazed and there were tracks on her arm. He suspected substance abuse and asked if she was using. He warned her that he would find out what was going on so it was best to come clean with him. She admitted to having been addicted as a result of pain from her medical condition but denied any current use. However, it was obvious that she was still using. The family is on assistance, which was recently reduced because Mrs. G failed to comply with work requirements.

Joe left and return to the office to prepare a petition to remove the children from the home. He made copies of the digital pictures he took and prepared his report. He contacted Jamilla to ask for foster care placement for the three children. Jamilla indicated that she did not have a home for all three and would have to split them up, placing two in one home and one in another. After obtaining the order, Joe returned to the school with Jamilla to pick up the children. When they were told what was happening, they began to cry. Kelly, the middle child, age nine, said she was not going and ran out of the office and out of the building. Joe gave chase and Jamilla stayed with the other two trying to calm them down. When Joe caught up to Kelly, she was walking briskly toward home. He told her that this was going to be a temporary arrangement until they could get her mother back on her feet and the house cleaned up or move them to a different home. She stopped and said she never liked the house they were in and asked why they could not stay there while this was happening. Joe indicated that it was not safe to do so and that he wanted to get her mother some help. Kelly broke down and started to cry. She sobbed about her mother using drugs and how scared she was. She said that sometimes her mother would be passed out and she could not wake her. Kelly worried that her mother might die. Joe did his best to reassure Kelly that they would try to get her mother into treatment, but meanwhile the children would have to stay with another family. Kelly returned with Joe to the school where Jamilla had calmed the other two children down. They were upset they would not be together, but were assured that there would be visits and some possibility of being reunited sometime soon.

inappropriate to begin with. The worker must keep in mind the need to report suspected abuse to child protective services if parents are acting in a manner that would constitute abuse.

During the course of raising children, various emergencies may arise. Children experience medical emergencies, accidents, and life-threatening situations. Sometimes parents are overwhelmed when faced with these situations. The death of a child is probably the most difficult situation anyone can face and it tends to affect parents for the rest of their lives. Having a child with a major disability is also a crisis. Many marriages do not survive these situations. When faced with these and other crises, parents need to rely on each other and on their support system for help in coping. If the parents can do this and make it through the period of feeling overwhelmed, it can strengthen their relationship both as parents and as a couple. However, if they get stuck, it can drive a wedge between them that may never heal.

Similar difficulties may arise when parents are faced with serious adversity. Health problems, accidents, extended absences, substance abuse, or disability on the part of the parents can seriously undermine the parent subsystem. Unemployment, financial hardship, homelessness, or incarceration are also serious threats. Temporary situations may only need brief support or intervention to restore the well-being of the parents and their relationship. Long-term or permanent situations will require more extensive work. The task for the worker is generally twofold: to provide assistance in overcoming or coping with the adversity itself and to help the parents maintain effective parenting in the face of the adversity.

The social worker assesses the crisis situation and the coping skills of the parents. He acts to strengthen these skills or add new ones to restore a healthy equilibrium. He encourages support from the family's support network and taps into sources of support from the human service delivery system in the community.

Action Taken to Use Support in Working with Parents

The use of support in working with parents is similar to that which was discussed in Chapter 7 for working with families and in Chapter 10 for couples. The need for support during crises was discussed in the previous section. The focus in this section is on building support between the two parents within their relationship as parents. It is important that parents feel supported by each other as they face both day-to-day parenting and the challenges of parenting over time. Nothing is more encouraging than knowing that the parents are together as partners in these endeavors. Similarly, nothing is more discouraging than being alone or knowing or feeling that our partner is not there to support us.

As with other actions mentioned earlier, it is important for parents to reach an agreement on parenting style and child-rearing techniques. If there is a lack of agreement, then the worker uses other actions to assist parents in developing or restoring it. However, even when there is agreement, parents may not act in a supportive manner with each other. Often this is associated with a lack of confidence in parenting. When parents seek to replicate parenting that they experienced as children, they tend to be much more confident in its effectiveness, and consequently, much more confident in using it themselves or supporting their partner in using it. However, when there is a difference in how they were parented, even if it is more positive, parents tend to have less confidence. This is also the case when parents are trying to change their parenting. We call this "defensive parenting." Essentially, the parents may know more about what not to do than what to do. As a result, they are less likely to stick with something new and are more likely to revert to something old or to jump around to something else. The lack of consistency then becomes a problem in terms of effectiveness. To be effective, parents need to be consistent in similar situations over time. Lack of consistency can extend to failing to support each other in challenging situations.

Sometimes one parent clearly had superior parenting as a child or his or her parenting skills are superior to the other parent. Similarly, one of the parents may have experienced clearly abusive, neglectful, or inappropriate parenting as a child, whereas the other parent had appropriate parenting. In these cases, the social worker should help the "defensive parent" to "borrow" his or her partner's "parent." Once again, the fact that parenting is learned means that new ways of parenting can be learned.

In strengthening or establishing supportive parent subsystems, the social worker encourages positive feedback and expressions of support. This raises self-worth and confidence and increases the fulfillment of parental roles in positive ways. However, support may not be given consistently over time or may not be expressed. Parents may take for granted that they are supporting each other without expressing their support. The social worker assists the parents in providing open and honest support for each other on a regular basis, preferably daily. She checks with each parent on areas in which he or she would like to receive support and helps them incorporate this into their relationship. The worker might have to model expressions of support first and then coach the parents in saying and doing things that are supportive. It is important that the parents interpret statements and actions as being supportive so this might need to be discussed. The conversation might be similar to that which was presented in Chapter 10: What do you do to support your partner in carrying out the role of parent (stepparent)? Did you know that he/she was trying to support you when he/she said or did that? Would you be willing to accept that as a sign of support? What would you like your partner to say or do to support you in this? Would you be willing to do that? or What would it take for you to do that?

As the work on parenting progresses, the worker looks for ways to encourage support and coaches the parents in giving, requesting, and receiving support so it becomes overt and consistent.

■ **Action Taken to Use Support in Working with Parents**

Jamilla's agency sponsors support groups for foster parents, for biological parents, and for adoptive parents. Jamilla is primarily responsible for the foster parent support group. They meet once a month and generally have a speaker, a video, or some type of training program. The parents find it helpful to share information and phone numbers with each other. They have formed an informal childcare network to cover for each other when needed. Some of them go together to buy food in bulk quantities to save on their food bill. There is also a mentoring program for newer foster parents to receive assistance from veteran families. This has been extended to include foster parents mentoring biological parents in an effort to speed up the return of their children and to improve the opportunities for success.

The support group for biological parents has been up and down in terms of attendance. Jamilla helps out the regular worker and acts as a liaison from the foster care group. Jamilla invites foster parents to the biological parents support group periodically to share ideas about raising children, stretching dollars, and finding good childcare. It was one of those sessions that sparked the idea of extending mentoring to biological parents.

Jamilla also runs the adoptive parents group, which includes prospective parents, parents whose adoption is undergoing the year of supervision that is required, and some veteran adoptive parents who have stayed on to help out. This group is very active, planning family outings and keeping up with various legislative issues while also providing assistance and guidance to new and prospective parents.

Action Taken That Uses Activity with Parents

Just as with families and couples, activities can be effective in working with parents. Activities form the base for most parenting classes and services. These may be offered individually, as a parent dyad, or in group formats. As with other activity groups, sessions are generally structured around variations of discussion (D) and activity (A). The most common structure is DAD or discussion–activity–discussion. Whether the worker uses an individual, dyad, or group format, the parenting skill or technique is presented and an exercise is discussed. This is followed by the activity or exercise. Then a debriefing or discussion follows, generally focused on the application of the parenting technique. The activity itself usually involves role-plays or practicing the skill or technique.

It is essential that any work that is done be transferred over to the everyday life of the parents. "Homework assignments" are used to practice the skills and implement the changes that are discussed. These are another form of activity. The worker should work with the parents to structure these assignments during the session. She coaches them as they practice until they feel comfortable enough to try it on their own. As with couples, taking some pressure off may be important, especially for those parents who find themselves in situations where they are having a lot of disagreements. The homework may become one more thing to argue about. As we suggested in Chapter 10, one way to take pressure off is to tell the parents that they might not be ready for this. If they are not successful, then they can blame the worker instead of each other. This is a win–win for the worker because she is either right that they are not ready or they are ready and they use the homework to improve their parenting skills. Some parents may take this as a challenge and put extra effort into proving that they are ready.

■ **Action Taken That Uses Activity with Parents**

Jamilla's agency offers parenting classes for parents in the community and for those whose children are in foster care or who are court-ordered to attend classes for various reasons. There are series for parents of young children, parents of elementary age children, and parents of teenagers. There are several different curricula that are used over the course of a year so that parents who do not find one helpful can try another. All of the formats use homework assignments that are intended to have parents practice the skills being taught. This is an example of the use of activity with parents.

As with any ongoing relationship, parents need to develop and practice good relationship skills, including good communication, effective problem solving and decision making, and constructive conflict resolution. These were covered in earlier chapters. The social worker teaches parents these skills and has them practice using them during and between sessions.

Action Taken to Mediate with Parents and between Parents and Their Environment

Actions taken to mediate provide both an important direct service to parents and a transition to indirect practice actions. Mediation with parents is the basic approach used in working with them. Mediating with systems in the environment is like an indirect practice action except that in mediation both sides are involved in the work. Mediation requires that the worker remain neutral and facilitate effective and constructive interactions between the two parties.

As mentioned earlier, using a mediating approach is essential in any situation where the social worker is working with multiperson client systems. The ability to maintain a neutral position allows the worker to avoid getting caught up in disagreements. Rivalries similar to sibling rivalries can arise when the worker takes sides or is perceived to be doing so. If parents perceive that the worker can be won over to either partner's side, then he cannot serve the needs of the relationship. The worker must establish the need for a mediating position from the very start and should remind the parents of this throughout the work.

In Chapter 10, we discussed an effective approach to use in developing and maintaining a mediating role by having the couple visualize their relationship as a triangle made up of "you," "I," and "we." In working with parents, the worker can use the same approach, only she might change the labels to "mother," "father," and "parents." In using this approach, the worker has each partner take responsibility for his or her own role and the worker must be granted the position of advocating for the relationship. As with couples, the worker's basic position is to ask a similar question, "What will it take to make this parenting relationship work?" She continuously asks this question in various forms along with ancillary questions such as the following: How will this help strengthen your parenting and your parenting relationship? What could you do to improve your parenting or make this relationship as parents better in this situation? What outcome would strengthen your parenting or your parenting relationship? What do you need out of this relationship that would make your parenting better? What do you need from your partner that would improve your parenting? Would you be willing to . . . in order to make this relationship as parents stronger or better?

The worker asks these types of questions and facilitates good communication by having the parents talk with each other about their needs as parents and about their parenting relationship. He helps them to negotiate agreements and alliances regarding parenting styles and child-rearing techniques. He supports them in building honesty and trust.

Mediation can be used in a wide variety of situations, including with parents who are separated and going through divorce. In formal mediation the two parties are generally in separate rooms and the mediator goes back and forth between them with offers to resolve the issue. In using mediation with parents, the focus would be on parenting and child-rearing issues that need to be resolved in an effort to avoid further difficulties in raising the children as divorced or separated parents. In using informal mediation techniques with parents, the worker would typically meet jointly with the two partners. The discussion might be as follows: What are some of the parenting or child-rearing concerns for each of you? What do you want to do with this? What would be an acceptable resolution for you? What would you be willing to do to resolve this situation for your child/children? What do you need from your child's mother/father to resolve this? Would you be willing to . . . in order to resolve this situation for your child/children? If your child's mother/father does . . . , would you be willing to . . . for the sake of your child/children?

The worker continues with this line of questions focusing on the need to resolve these issues for the sake of the child or children. The worker seeks to move the parents to a middle ground where each party is satisfied that he or she can live with the results and uphold his or her part of the agreement. This is not necessarily a process where either side is completely happy with the resolution but one in which the child or children can survive and, hopefully, thrive.

CASE EXAMPLE

■ Action Taken to Mediate with Parents and between Parents and Their Environment

Jamilla and her coworkers have learned to use a mediation approach in working with parents and families. They teach their parents to use this with children in settling arguments. When there are disagreements about child-rearing practices or discipline, they use a mediation approach and help the parents to negotiate an agreement about what they will do. They know that an important key to good parenting is consistency. So the fact that the parents agree is often more important than what they agree on. The workers use similar examples of questions as were given in the chapter in assisting parents to come to an agreement.

There have been numerous times when Jamilla has had to mediate between her foster parents or her biological parents on her caseload and various organizations in the community. For instance, in seeking substance abuse treatment for Mrs. Gray from an earlier example, Jamilla found that the best treatment program for her type of addiction had a policy that participants had to be drug free for five days before they could enter the program. In other words, they did not provide detox. The detox unit did not want to accept her because she was not a good candidate after having been there several times. Jamilla was able to have a meeting with them and Mrs. G in which Mrs. G indicated that getting her children back would be a strong motivation for her to get off and stay off drugs. The detox unit relented and decided to admit her.

■   INDIRECT PRACTICE ACTIONS WITH PARENTS   ■

Indirect practice actions with parents are similar to those that are used with families in Chapter 8 and couples in Chapter 10, except the focus is on the parental roles. Indirect practice includes actions that (1) involve the use of influence, (2) are designed to change the environment, and (3) are relative to coordination of services.

These actions can be used quite frequently with parents.

Action That Involves the Use of Influence

Influence is an important consideration in working with parents. Depending on her role and the situation, the social worker may have more or less influence. When serving in roles associated with child welfare services, the worker has a great deal of authority, and, as result, she may also have a great deal of influence. Child protective services workers can remove children from parental custody with court approval. Later, they may recommend foster care, return to parental custody, or they may seek to influence the court in terminating parental rights in extreme or chronic cases of neglect or abuse. Foster care workers arrange visitation, coordinate services, and recommend continuation in foster care or return to the parents. Adoption workers approve couples for adoption, match children with adoptive parents, supervise the adoption, and recommend that it be made permanent. Other social workers who work with the parents can influence these decisions. In these situations, the worker has considerable influence and must balance this with her responsibilities to her clients. Sometimes it is difficult to define the client system under these circumstances. Is the client system the child (or children)? Is it the parents? Is it the family system? Depending on who is defined as the client system, the worker might have very different recommendations.

In situations related to child welfare, the federal government has mandated the use of a family preservation approach. This obligates workers to diligently seek ways of restoring the family while protecting children as the first option. At the same time, workers must develop permanency planning within a relatively short time after children enter foster care. Permanency planning means that children should not remain in temporary care indefinitely but should have a plan that leads to a permanent home with their parents, a relative, or in an adoptive home. Sometimes these two mandates conflict with each other. For instance, parents who are not able to maintain, develop, or restore a suitable environment for their children or who take a long time to do so may find themselves faced with deadlines that they cannot meet. Parents experiencing severe or chronic difficulties are very vulnerable to this. Probably the most common situations of this are parents with substance abuse conditions. Alcoholism and drug addiction are common or complicating factors in child abuse and neglect. At the same time, these conditions do not lend themselves to quick and sustainable cures.

We support the concept of family preservation. In our practice experiences, the best chance for many children to experience permanency is with their own parents. Certainly, children prefer that option, even many of those who have experienced severe neglect or abuse. All too often, workers do not do the really difficult work that needs to be done to ensure that children have the best opportunity to return home to their parents. It is incumbent on every social worker to make sure that every needed service is provided in an effort to restore the family.

As pointed out earlier, young workers and those who are not parents may find their credibility in question when working with parents. In these cases, the worker needs to work at establishing some influence with parents. The influence is most likely to come from persistence, the ability to provide tangible resources, or from technical expertise gained from education and training.

Whether the social worker has more or less influence, he needs to be aware of the influence that he has with parents. He is careful to limit his influence and allow parents to make their own decisions and rather than making decisions that they think the worker wants them to make. The worker is aware that most parenting goes on behind closed doors so it is important that good parenting practices be developed and maintained when he is not there and after he closes the case. To an extent, the worker uses influence to persuade the parents to engage in good parenting practices as described earlier.

As with families and couples, the worker is free to use influence on behalf of parents. This includes developing and securing resources to support good parenting practices. If parenting classes or groups are not available, the worker uses her influence to start them if it is within the purview of her agency or to get another more appropriate agency to offer these services. She supports parents in feeling more empowered in influencing their environment. The worker might also use contacts with influential people to build support for services that are not available.

CASE EXAMPLE

■ Action That Involves the Use of Influence

The state chapter of NASW asked Jamilla to testify before a state legislative committee that was set up to consider recommendations for improving the child welfare system. They wanted social workers who worked directly with families to testify so that the legislators would have an opportunity to hear real stories about what was working and what might need to be changed. Jamilla met with the legislative liaison and the lobbyist for NASW beforehand to get some idea about what to expect. She knew that she needed to tell the stories on behalf of her families while also maintaining their confidentiality. They were able to help her with this.

When the day came for her testimony, Jamilla was nervous but also anxious to represent the needs of her families and her coworkers across the state. She told the legislators about some of the great things that were happening with her foster parents and how they were mentoring some of her biological families. She also identified the need for better reimbursement and more funds for training for workers and for foster parents. While she was at the state capitol, Jamilla was able to meet with her state representative and her state senator to reinforce some of the needs that she identified in her testimony before the legislative committee. It was exciting to have the opportunity to influence people who were influential. She now understood how important it was to write letters and to contact legislators about issues that were relevant for her clients and her profession.

■ Action Designed to Change the Environment

The removal of the Gray children from their home was an example of an action to change their environment. After Mrs. G went through detox and completed the substance abuse program, she needed to secure new housing for herself and her children. Jamilla assisted with that process, helping her to secure funds for a security deposit and the first month's rent. She was also able to help Mrs. G obtain furnishings through local charities. The home that Mrs. G rented is in a better area of town than the previous house. The children made several visits to the home before a return to their mother was arranged. Jamilla had to be sure that Mrs. G was maintaining her recovery and also able to maintain her home.

Another example of environmental change occurred when Jamilla was working with an adoptive couple who were interested in adopting a child who was in a wheelchair. They found that their home needed several alterations to make it more accessible. Jamilla was able to have their story aired on a local television program and there was also a news article. Donations came rolling in. A local service for people who were older agreed to build a ramp. Several contractors donated time and materials to widen doorways and lower counter tops. These alterations in the home environment made it possible for the family to accommodate their new member.

Action Designed to Change the Environment

Actions designed to change the environment are mainly used either to assist parents in changing their existing environment or to move to a new environment. Much of what was discussed under this heading in Chapter 10 is also relevant for working with couples as parents. To a great extent, environmental change is a key to dealing with difficult behaviors by children. By changing how they parent, parents are changing the environment of their children.

The most common form of neglect occurs when parents do not maintain a clean household with adequate food and other necessities. In these cases, the worker should work with the parents to alter their actions and to provide a safe and healthy environment for their children. Some programs provide homemaker services for parents who are not able to do this. Sometimes workers get directly involved and organize a cleanup effort for parents who are overwhelmed by their circumstances. The residence may need repairs that are beyond the ability of the parents. In extreme circumstances or when the residence has been condemned, workers may need to become involved in helping parents find different housing. In any case, workers may need to help parents set up a system for maintaining their household.

Parents of children who are delinquent or exposed to drugs and crime because of the neighborhood may need to move to a safer environment with fewer negative influences. They may need assistance in doing this, especially financial assistance for deposits, utilities, and so on.

Action Relative to Coordination of Services

As mentioned previously, there are times when it may be necessary for the social worker to coordinate services on behalf of parents. The first choice is for the parents to be able to

■ Action Relative to Coordination of Services

The staple of Jamilla's work in child welfare is case management and coordinating services. It is her primary function in foster care with both foster parents and biological parents on her caseload. With the Gray family, Jamilla coordinated the services to Mrs. G in receiving substance abuse treatment and later in securing new housing. While the children were in foster care, she provided case management in assisting the foster parents in caring for the children. She helps her foster parents to find doctors and dentists that will accept medicaid. She assists in obtaining schools records and meeting the children's academic needs. She works with foster parents on childcare and transportation needs. Her position entails ensuring that the full range of needs are met for the families with whom she works.

manage necessary services on their own. However, parents' circumstances might be overwhelming for them, requiring the worker act on their behalf. This occurs when parents are either temporarily unable to manage these tasks or there is a chronic circumstance that interferes with their ability to do so. As with couples, these services can range from information and referral to full case management.

The worker makes a referral and follows up to make sure that the appropriate services are received when another agency is the best fit for the services needed by the parents. The referral process was discussed in Chapter 7.

When parents are in crisis, the worker needs to be more direct and involved in the work. When the crisis produces an impairment in functioning for a single parent or both parents, then the worker needs to mobilize resources in the ecosystem to take over managing services or provide this herself. Parents may have members of their extended family who can assist them during a crisis. For parents who are elderly, this is most often their adult sons and daughters. As mentioned earlier, sometimes issues among adult siblings will get in the way of assisting their parents. This is covered in detail in Chapter 13.

As we mentioned in Chapter 10, the generalist practice social worker may temporarily coordinate services or he might work for an agency where this is part of his regular responsibility. Common types of agencies where case management is a primary service include mental health, health care, and aging services, which perform both temporary and long-term case management.

■ EVALUATION AND TERMINATION WITH PARENTS ■

Evaluation and termination with parents are quite similar to that which was described for families in Chapter 9 and for couples in Chapter 10. Throughout the change process, evaluation is a constant process. Evaluation occurs during assessment and as new information is revealed during subsequent contacts. Evaluation is an important part of planning and is built into each objective. It used during the action phase to measure the effectiveness of the intervention and progress toward achieving goals and objectives. Evaluation is used to determine the outcome and completion of the work and during termination.

As with families and couples, it is important that the worker evaluates the validity and reliability of the information she collects during assessment and throughout the change process. When she works with two parents, triangulation of the data is built into the process because the worker has two sources of information. When there is agreement between the two parents, the worker can usually rely on the accuracy of the information. When there is disagreement, the worker needs to discuss the situation in an effort to understand and clear up the discrepancy. Sometimes a disagreement or discrepancy will continue. In these circumstances, the worker can suggest that the parents agree to disagree about their perceptions of the situation. Over time, the difference in perception may disappear or it might need to be revisited, especially as new information comes to light. When there is a difference in perception, the worker can generally assume that the actual situation is somewhere between the two descriptions that the parents are offering.

If there is a reason to believe that one parent has more to gain or lose by taking a certain position, then the worker might assume that the parent's perception is probably skewed in that direction. It is important to avoid labeling either party is "lying" or "not telling the truth." It is human nature to perceive the world around us in accord with self-interest. It is natural for us to be guarded about what we say until we establish trust and feel safe in doing so. Even after establishing trust and safety, certain issues may be too painful to discuss.

As mentioned earlier, evaluation is built into every plan. Evaluation is used to measure progress and determine completion of goals and objectives. The worker and the parents evaluate the actions that are taking place to achieve the objectives to determine what is working and what is not working. Plans are hypotheses or educated guesses about what might work. The worker and the parents need to monitor actions to determine whether their hypotheses or educated guesses are accurate in terms of meeting the parents' needs. When there are positive results, the work proceeds as planned. If the results are negative or not productive, then either a barrier needs to be removed or the plan needs to be changed or a new plan needs to be developed.

As goals are reached, the worker and the parents evaluate whether the need has been met or the concern addressed. If so, then they decide if the work is done or if it needs to continue. If the work has been completed and no further work is necessary, they can proceed to termination. Evaluation is an essential aspect of planned termination.

Evaluation also occurs within the termination process. As with couples and families, the worker should solicit feedback about what was helpful, what was not, and what would have been helpful. This helps the worker evaluate his skills and improve his ability to provide services to parents in the future. The parents also need to evaluate themselves and own their new skills and abilities. Owning their new skills and abilities provides validation for the work they have done and raises their confidence in working together in the future.

As mentioned earlier with families and other client systems, various forms of unplanned terminations often take place. If the parents drop out of service, the worker should follow up to ensure that their needs have been met. If they have not, then the worker should offer to help them receive services elsewhere or, at the very least, she should make sure that the door is open for them to return. When termination is initiated by the worker or the agency, the worker or agency needs to do everything possible to ensure a smooth transfer takes place to another worker in the agency or to another agency. The preferred way to accomplish a transfer is to have at least one joint session with the new worker. If this is not possible, the worker should prepare the parents for receiving services from a different worker. She reinforces the fact that the parents are the ones who have done the meaningful work. She reassures them that if they can work with her, they can work with another worker in completing the change process that they have undertaken.

■ GENERALIST PRACTICE WITH PARENTS IN GROUPS ■

Working with parent groups is very popular as a method of delivering services. There are a number of curricula that are available to assist in this process. In general, parent groups are classified as structured and unstructured and time limited or ongoing. Typically, time-limited groups are more structured than ongoing groups. The structure for parenting groups is most commonly provided by a curriculum. Some are more didactic than others. Some use videos to illustrate skills and concepts or to present scenarios for discussion. Others use written material and some use both. Group sessions are generally structured with variations of activities or presentations (A) and discussions (D). Simple sessions would typically be discussion followed by the activity or presentation followed by another discussion. So the structure would be D–A–D. More complex curricula could be a series of discussions and presentations or activities, or D–A–D–A–D, and so on.

Ongoing parent groups tend to be less structured with the agenda set at each meeting based on what the membership decides to discuss. These types of groups could be classified as problem-solving/decision-making groups or as skill-building groups or as support groups. The first type uses the group to generate ideas about how to handle parenting concerns. The second focuses on developing parenting skills. Parent support groups bring parents together to support each other as they face difficult situations, including groups of parents whose children are ill with various diseases or with cancer or parents of children who are delinquent or have substance abuse issues. Of course there is overlap between these types of groups, with each type often looking like one of the others as they seek to deal with parenting issues. Another type of group is self-help groups. The most well known is Parents Anonymous, a group for parents who have abused or neglected or are at risk of abusing or neglecting their children. This type of group functions very similar to Alcoholics Anonymous only the focus is on preventing child abuse and neglect. Another group is Parents without Partners for single parents. Generalist social workers can be found working directly or indirectly with these various parent groups. They may be the group leader or facilitator or they may serve as hosts or referral sources.

■ GENERALIST PRACTICE WITH PARENTS WHO ARE OLDER ■

There are several types of situations in which generalist social workers are likely to work with parents who are older and who still have some type of parenting activities. One involves situations in which the parents are caring for a dependent adult son or daughter.

Another situation might be one in which grandparents are parenting grandchildren either full time or part time. Part-time care may be provided so that the parents can work. When parents are caring for dependent adult sons or daughters or when grandparents are parenting grandchildren on a full-time basis, there are similarities in that the care may become quite challenging over time and long-term planning is needed. A third situation is when parents who are older have an adult son or daughter die.

When parents have children who are mentally or physically disabled, they may continue to provide care throughout their life span. Parents may also provide care for children who are impaired later in life as a result of accident, injury, or disease. As parents age, their ability to provide the care that is needed can be challenged by either increased need for care or diminished capacity to do so.

A situation that is becoming more common is grandparents raising their grandchildren. This may occur as a result of death, disability, incarceration, neglect, abuse, or desertion by the parent. Added features here include the reason for the situation and helping grandparents and grandchildren cope with this while not letting it interfere with their abilities to form strong relationships. Grandparents may find that their age is a concern in terms of maintaining their own health and well-being and a fear that they will be disabled or die before they finish raising their grandchildren. They also face the possibility of their son or daughter returning to take the children away, especially when these arrangements are informal and not court ordered. However, even when a court is involved, it may decide to return custody to the parents even if the grandparents object. The generalist social worker may be working with the grandparents and grandchildren around any or all of these issues. He keeps in mind the fact that his first obligation is to the most vulnerable clients, in this case the children. He works to maximize their safety and well-being.

These situations call for workers to maximize access to resources for parents who are older or for grandparents. Parents and grandparents who are in these situations may need assistance with the care itself, such as nursing assistance, respite from the constant demands of care, financial assistance, and similar services. The worker advocates and secures resources as needed. She negotiates and mediates with parties that are directly and indirectly involved with the situation. Working with people in these situations also calls for workers to provide support for the emotional strain involved. Probably the best way to do this is by a referral to or sponsoring and facilitating support groups for parents who are older and are in these situations.

In addition to needs for providing care, parents who are older and grandparents parenting grandchildren worry about what will happen if either one or both of them are incapacitated or die. Workers need to assist parents or grandparents who are older to develop both short-term and long-term care plans. Short-term plans should include respite care and emergency plans that may need to be made for crises that may occur. Long-term plans can be implemented in the event of death or incapacitation of the parent or grandparent.

The situation involving the death of a son or daughter can occur any time during the life span, but some parents live so long that they outlive their offspring or death can be caused by accidents, illnesses, and even homicide. These situations typically cause an especially intense and longer-term grief process. The grief process itself was covered in the previous chapter and will not be repeated here. However, the worker may need to work with the parents for an extended period of time. This is also a situation where it is often best to provide an opportunity for a support group.

SUMMARY

One of the most common forms of generalist social work practice with families is work-ing with parents. A version of good parenting practices is presented in the chapter. These good parenting practices form a base from which generalist practitioners can operate in working with parental subsystems. It is important for the worker to promote, support, and reinforce a positive relationship between parents in their role and relationship as parents. It is also important for parents to separate their marital or couple relationship from their role as parents, otherwise they are at an increased risk of undermining their relationship as a couple.

Generalist practitioners may work with parents as dyads especially when making home visits. They may also work with parents in groups. The most common forms of this type of group work involve a structured curricula. There are several good quality parenting curricula available that can be used for this purpose. Stepparenting is especially challenging and has become quite common. Difficulties with stepparenting is the most frequent reason for divorce in stepfamilies.

Generalist social workers may also work with parents who are older. The most com-mon types of these situations are when the worker is providing services to families with adult sons or daughters who are disabled, to grandparents who are parenting grandchildren, and to parents who have an adult son or daughter who dies.

QUESTIONS

1. Describe the parental relationship(s) that you observed growing up in your family of origin. Assess the strengths and challenges.
2. Describe any parental relationship(s) that you have experienced as an adult. Assess the strengths and challenges.
3. Using Table 11.2 and relevant parts of Table 5.3, develop a social history for yourself, your parents, or a parent or parents whom you know.
4. Describe some of the variations you might expect to find in parenting for members of diverse groups.
5. How would you go about working with a lesbian couple as parents? A gay couple as parents?

SUGGESTED READINGS

Johnson, Louise C., and Yanca, Stephen J. *Social Work Practice: A Generalist Approach*, 9th ed. Boston: Allyn & Bacon, 2007 (Chapters 8, 11, and 13).

Cox, Carole B. "Grandparents Raising Grandchildren from a Multicultural Perspective" in *Multicultural Perspectives in Working with Families*, 2nd ed. Elaine P. Congress and Manny Gonzalez. New York: Springer, 2005.

Gordon, Thomas. *Parent Effectiveness Training: The Proven Program for Raising Responsible Children*. New York: Three Rivers Press, 2000.

Hayslip, Bert, and Hicks-Patrick, Julie. *Custodial Grandparenting: Individual, Cultural, and Ethnic Diversity.* New York: Springer, 2006.

Klass, Carol Speekman, *The Home Visitor's Guidebook: Promoting Optimal Parent and Child Development.* Baltimore, MD: Paul H. Brookes, 2003.

Mattaini, Mark A. *Clinical Interventions with Families.* Washington, DC: NASW Press, 1999 (Chapter 7–9).

Webb, Nancy Boyd. *Culturally Diverse Parent–Child and Family Relationships: A Guide for Social Workers and Other Practitioners.* New York: Columbia University Press, 2001.

There are a number of good quality approaches and curricula for working with parents. The American Guidance Service has several curricula for parenting groups including the following (see www .agsglobe.com and click on "Parenting/Class Mgmt").

Dinkmeyer, Don Sr., McKay, Gary D., and Dinkmeyer, Don Jr. *The Parent's Handbook: Systematic Training for Effective Parenting.* Circle Pines, MN: American Guidance Service, 1997.

Dinkmeyer, Don C. *Parenting Young Children: Systematic Training for Effective Parenting (STEP) of Children under Six.* Circle Pines, MN: American Guidance Service, 1997.

Dinkmeyer, Don Sr., McKay, Gary D., and Dinkmeyer, Don Jr. *Parenting Teenagers: Systematic Training for Effective Parenting of Teens.* Circle Pines, MN: American Guidance Service, 1998.

CHAPTER

12

Generalist Practice with Parent–Child Subsystems

LEARNING EXPECTATIONS

1. Understand the application of the generalist practice model to working with parent–child subsystems.
2. Understand interaction and engagement with parent–child subsystems.
3. Understand assessment as both a process and a product with parent–child subsystems.
4. Understand planning as both a product and a process with parent–child subsystems.
5. Understand direct and indirect actions with parent–child subsystems.
6. Understand evaluation and termination with parent–child subsystems.

As we stated earlier, in our study and our practice, the two most common forms of family work for generalist social workers are with parent subsystems and with parent–child subsystems. This chapter examines working with parent–child subsystems. Working with parent–child subsystems is intergenerational in focus. The parent–child subsystem is the only relationship system in the family system that is intergenerational. The parent–child subsystem is often the main area of focus for blended families in which stepparent and stepchild relationships are usually important to the success of building a new family system.

Working with parent–child subsystems overlaps with working with parents, but it also is different. When the social worker works with parents, she focuses on the relationship between mother and father or stepmother and stepfather or between unmarried parents living together with children. She is concerned with how they meet the needs of children in the household. In blended families, the issues of parenting and stepparenting become a primary focus from the start. Failure to establish successful stepparenting relationships are major factors when most second or subsequent marriages or partnerships fail.

Before we begin, we would like to review the assumptions that we made in Chapter 11 regarding what we call good parenting practices. The first assumption is that love and nurturing and support are essential ingredients for good parenting. This includes relationships between stepparents and stepchildren. Although love may or may not exist in these relationships, respect must be present for success. Nurturing and support from parents to the stepparents and from the stepparents to the stepchildren are important ingredients for building positive relationships. It is also important for parents to nurture and support the development of a positive relationship between their children and their partners.

The second assumption is that positive parenting is far superior to negative parenting. Positive parenting involves parenting that expresses clear positive expectations for positive behavior for children and then gives clear feedback about meeting expectations. Negative parenting is expressing negative expectations along with the use of criticism or punishment. Positive parents focus on what they want from their children.

The third assumption is that successful parents are consistent in terms of their expectations and their feedback and discipline.

The fourth assumption is that the "reasonable" parent is the best parenting style. The reasonable parent has reasonable expectations based on age and development. Expectations are made clear to children. Expectations also change as children grow up. The goal is for children to become independent adults capable of making their own decisions. Reasonable parents use reasonable positive and negative consequences for positive and negative behaviors. As discussed earlier, the diversity competent social worker works within cultural frameworks but also discusses advantages and disadvantages of various parenting styles so that parents can make an informed decision about what approach they wish to use.

This chapter examines the change process with parent–child subsystems in the family. It includes working with these subsystems as parents and children age and when step-relationships exist. Generalist social workers frequently work both directly and indirectly with parent–child subsystems. Relationship skills are obviously important to working with any subsystem in the family. This was covered earlier in Part II and in Chapter 10 and will not be repeated here. We refer to these relationship skills throughout the chapter and relate them to the development of successful parent–child relationships. The change process with parent–child subsystems uses the same phases that were outlined for families in Part II. It begins with interaction and engagement. It continues with assessment, planning, action, and evaluation and termination. As mentioned earlier there is overlap between this chapter and earlier chapters as well as chapters in Part II. The social worker needs to become proficient at developing knowledge and skills focused on each of the subsystems in the family as well as those necessary for working with the family as a whole.

■ INTERACTION AND ENGAGEMENT WITH ■ PARENT–CHILD SUBSYSTEMS

As mentioned earlier, with all generalist practice the worker might start out working with an individual or individuals, a family, or a subsystem before it is decided that working with the parent–child subsystem is necessary or the best approach. It is likely that one or more children will be the focus of attention first. This leads to identifying the parent–child subsystem as needing to be strengthened in order for the work to be successful. Table 10.1

gives an overview of some of the indications and counterindications for working with parent–child subsystems and other family subsystems.

When a worker is working with the parent–child subsystem, the client is the subsystem as a whole as well as each individual in that system and the relationships between parents and children. In order to be effective, the worker needs to take the role of mediator and must be given that role by the parents and children in the subsystem. As with other subsystems and with the family system, he cannot be seen as taking sides and still serve the individuals and the system or subsystem as a whole. It would also be inappropriate and unethical to sacrifice the needs of any of the individuals involved. Whenever the needs of individuals within a system are not met, the system will be out of balance, eventually leading to further difficulties. To establish a balance or equilibrium, the worker should work with the client system to meet both individual needs and the needs of the relationship.

Social workers often work with single parents. Single parents face special challenges in parenting and in maintaining parent–child relationships. It is more common for the single parent to be the mother, which creates challenges in terms of maintaining the financial viability of the family. In the process of doing so, most women must overcome the effects of discrimination that results in lower wages and benefits, placing an undue burden on making up for lost income from the father. Child support tends to be inadequate in doing so. The demands of meeting financial needs can lead to less time and energy available to devote to parent–child relationships. Children growing up in single-family homes often feel like they have lost much of their childhood. Older children are frequently called on to fill in for the absent parent by taking on caregiving of younger children and by taking additional responsibility for household tasks. This shifting back and forth from a parentlike role to the role of child when the parent is home can create a great deal of stress in both the sibling and parent–child subsystems. There are also additional issues around the noncustodial parent that may need to be included in the work to be done.

As with couples, parents, and families, this work may require skills that are beyond those that the generalist social worker possesses. However, if the worker is the only realistic option, then she should do what she can to assist. When relationships are too volatile, the worker may be better off working with each party individually while mediating some kind of arrangement.

Besides working with parent–child subsystems in families with intact marriages, social workers also work with subsystems in blended and diverse families. These include stepfamilies, adoptive families, foster families, and families of same-sex partners. Whenever at least one parent is not the biological parent, there are additional issues that need to be resolved. A primary issue is the legitimacy of parental authority. Underlying this are often doubts about genuine love and acceptance along with bonding and attachment issues. Throughout this chapter, we refer to parent–child relationships with the understanding that we are referring to any form of parent–child relationship, including all of these types.

Perhaps the greatest challenge in establishing a relationship when working with the parent–child subsystem is the fact that both the worker and the parents are adults and the child is not. This disparity creates a need to have two different types of relationship while maintaining a mediating position. It requires a type of triangular relationship in which the worker establishes a relationship with the parent and with the child and then she encourages changes in their relationship with each other that is intergenerational. Sometimes this can be accomplished by seeing the parent and the child separately and then bringing them together to work with each other.

Engagement and interaction with parent–child subsystems can be especially challenging when working with families from cultures in which parental authority is emphasized. This takes on added stress when the children are exposed to U.S. culture, which may clash with values held by the parents. This calls for both cultural competence and skills at working cross-culturally. The worker should follow the same pattern established in earlier chapters regarding cultural and diversity competence. The social worker should yield the role of expert with regard to cultural aspects of parenting and child-rearing. However, there are some basic principles that should not be compromised. Parenting practices that are emotionally or physically harmful or that constitute neglect or abuse are never acceptable. In fact, the worker is obligated by law and his code of ethics to report these to Child Protective Services.

Using a diversity competent approach that includes naturalistic inquiry, the social worker proceeds with engagement in a similar manner to that described in earlier chapters. The worker observes the parents and children and mirrors their verbal and nonverbal approach. She might begin slowly with some small talk. With children it is usually safe to begin by talking about school unless that is the reason for the referral. If there has been some initial work with other family members, then the worker might begin by discussing what has transpired in that work that led up to the decision to meet the parent–child subsystem. The worker may have already met some family members in providing these services.

A diversity competent approach allows parents and children to tell their own stories about their family. In using a naturalistic approach to diversity competence, the worker seeks to have an open dialogue, free from preconceived notions about what is happening in the family. In order to do this, the worker must understand the effects of his own background as a child and as a parent on his attitudes toward relationships between parents and children. Examining and understanding these experiences should be an important part of the worker's preparation for working with families. As we have pointed out, this work is never really finished and becomes a part of one's professional development. The worker needs to understand the influence of the larger society on himself and on the families with whom he works.

In listening to the parents and children tell their stories, the diversity competent social worker looks for common ground and for differences. The worker tries to clarify these and reach an understanding regarding the work to be done. One assumption that needs to be discussed is that parents generally want to see their children grow into happy, healthy, competent adults. This is also generally a desire that children have. Areas of disagreement typically revolve around how they are going to get there, how long it will take, what will it look like once they get there, and what will it look like during the process. These can all become topics for discussion and negotiation.

As discussed in Chapter 11, at times the greatest challenge may be the desire on the part of the children to achieve success as defined by the larger society rather than success as defined within the family's culture. These are clearly among the most difficult situations to resolve. Ultimately, children become adults and are free to make their own choices about this. The inevitability of this fact can be used to help parents find a way to relate to their children that preserves highly valued cultural norms while sacrificing some that are less highly valued. Forcing certain norms or values on their children is unlikely to be successful in the long run and may even push the children away from their cultural heritage. Developing a healthy self-image includes valuing oneself within the context of one's cultural heritage. Thus, this work often becomes bicultural work in which parents are encouraged to help their children become bicultural so they can have the best of both worlds.

■   ASSESSMENT WITH PARENT–CHILD SUBSYSTEMS   ■

As with families, couples, and parents, assessment with parent–child subsystems involves both process and product. The change process follows similar steps as those taken in assessment described in earlier chapters and will not be repeated here. The social history for parent–child subsystems follows a similar format as the family social history presented in Table 5.3. Part II.D from Table 11.1 should be added to identify relevant parts of the parent subsystem. Table 12.1 contains elements that should be added to the family history format as Part II.E. In addition, the term "parent–child subsystems" should be substituted for "family" for Parts III and IV of Table 5.3. Relevant portions of the individual social history should be added from Table 5.2. Making these changes will convert the family social history to one that is focused on the parent–child subsystem. This description of the assessment phase is the process that is used to set the stage for change. The product of the assessment is the social history. It includes an assessment of the structure, the functioning, and the development of this subsystem of the family.

As is the case with families and their other subsystems, the purpose of assessment with parent–child subsystems is twofold. First, the social worker needs to understand the "parent–child subsystem in situation." She needs to understand the parent, the child, and the situation in order to be able to help. She does not need a complete understanding but enough to assist in meeting and resolving the situation. Second, the assessment provides a foundation for change by identifying strengths and resources in the ecosystem. The assessment spans past, present, and future. The understanding of parent–child subsystem in situation assesses the past and present, laying the groundwork for change, which is in the future.

Assessment as a Process

As mentioned in earlier chapters, family work may begin with working with an individual, the family system, or any family subsystem. The decision to work with the parent–child subsystem may come at any time during the change process. Typically, it will come as a result of working with children. When the decision is made, the social worker typically begins by establishing a relationship with the parent and also begins to gather information about the presenting need or concern as it relates to him or her as a parent. The worker might then establish a relationship with the child and gather information about the presenting need or concern from his or her perspective. This is generally similar to the indications for working with the parent–child subsystem identified in Table 10.1. The needs and concerns can be formulated similar to those identified in Chapters 10 and 11, except the focus is on the parent–child relationship:

> Josh and his stepfather need to strengthen their relationship.

If the need or concern relates to a family matter, the following format might be used:

> In order to help their blended family to grow together as a family, Josh and his stepfather need to strengthen their relationship.

As with families and other subsystems, the nature of the need or concern examines areas that may be causing the need to arise and assumptions about what would resolve the situation.

The worker and the parent and child speculate about what is possible and what needs to be done. This may include focusing on their relationship, focusing on how they meet each other's needs, or how they deal with their ecosystem (including their family). Some examples of these are as follows:

> If Josh and his stepfather can agree on a positive approach to their relationship, they will be able to improve it and help their blended family grow together as a family.
>
> If Josh and his stepfather improve their communication, problem solving, and conflict resolution, they will be able to improve their ability to get along with each other and work together.
>
> If Josh and his stepfather set aside time each day to talk about their needs or concerns that arise, they will strengthen their ability to get along with each other and work together.
>
> If Josh and his stepfather set aside time each day to talk about their concerns, they will feel more support from each other for dealing with issues as they arise.

In identifying the nature of the needs and concerns in the parent–child subsystem, the social worker gains a better understanding of the situation, which provides structure for selecting and collecting information.

As the social worker gathers information about parent–child subsystem in situation, she looks for potential strengths and resources in the subsystem and in their ecosystem. These are generally found in areas where the parent and the child have been successful at building a relationship with each other or with other family members or with people outside of the family. Strengths are also found in overcoming adversity or disagreement. Permanent change needs to be based on a solid foundation. Abilities and capabilities in one area of life are signs of potential in other areas. Having positive relationships demonstrates a capacity for building positive relationships in other areas of our lives.

Selection and collection of information focuses on information gathered in the first three stages of the assessment phase. The social worker should limit the information that is collected to whatever is needed to bring about change. Some additional information will be needed to meet bureaucratic requirements. The worker seeks to understand the need or concern and the situation. He gathers information about the assumptions that were made in the second stage and assesses their accuracy or feasibility. He explores potential strengths and resources to develop a plan to meet needs and address concerns.

Analysis of the information occurs independently and with the parent and the child, either separately or jointly. The worker analyzes information to gain an understanding of the situation. As mentioned previously, the worker's analysis includes five general areas as the work proceeds: (1) what she understands about the parent–child subsystem, the ecosystem, and strengths and resources, given what is known; (2) what changes are needed, given what is known; (3) what further information is needed to better understand the situation; (4) what further information is needed to bring about successful change; and (5) what are some potentially successful change strategies that can be used to meet the needs and address the concerns.

Assessment as a Product

The product of the assessment is the social history. The setting tends to dictate different structures and information required in the social history. Some settings may use a more informal format rather than a formal document. Table 12.1 is a supplementary schema representing information required in a typical social history for the parent–child subsystem. Various settings may require more information about certain areas such as education, health, mental health, or substance abuse.

Demographic and background information is identified in the first two sections of the schema and are the same for the family social history as well as other subsystems. Parts I and II focus on the parent and the child as individuals. Parts II.D and II.E examine parental and the parent–child subsystems of the family, respectively. The focus is on each subsystem. It includes the structure, functioning, and development of the relationship.

Understanding current and former experiences is an important aspect of assessment. Parenting and parent–child relationships are heavily influenced by culture, diversity, and

Table 12.1   Supplementary Schema for Development of a Social History for Parent–Child Subsystems

I. Identifying Information (as needed by agency)
(This is the same as Table 5.3.I.)

II. (Part A, B, and C are the same as Table 5.3.II. Part D is the same as Table 11.1.II.D)
   E. The parent–child subsystem—Structure and form of current relationship. Structure and form of other current and past parent–child relationships for the parent and for the child
   1. Subsystems—Describe the relationship and functioning of the parent and the child with other subsystems.
   2. Cohesiveness as a subsystem—Describe the manner in which the parent and child maintain their relationship system, boundaries, and relatedness. Include the issue of connectedness and separateness, rules and norms for their relationship, and emotional bond
   3. Communication patterns and skills for the parent and the child individually, with each other, with other family members and with people outside of the family system
   4. Decision-making and problem solving patterns and skills for the parent and the child individually, with each other, with other family members and with people outside of the family system
   5. Conflict resolution patterns and skills for the parent and the child individually, with each other, with other family members and with people outside of the family system
   6. Role performance and satisfaction with each other and within and outside of the family system
   7. System member support: growth encouragement, care, and concern
   8. Identify commonalities and differences between the parent and the child. Identify expectations. Identify feedback mechanisms and disciplinary system.
   9. Parent and child customary adaptive and coping mechanisms with each other and within and outside of the family system
   10. Intimacy and closeness as parent and child

III. The Concern or Need
(This is the same as Table 5.3.III. with "parent–child subsystem" replacing "family" as the focus)

IV. Strengths and Challenges for Meeting Needs
(This is the same as Table 5.3.IV. with "parent–child subsystem" replacing "family" as the focus)

sociological factors. There is a description of these in previous chapters and it will not be repeated here. However, there are some unique aspects that are relevant for parent–child subsystems that will be identified.

Generally the more common issues that require focusing on parent–child subsystems are difficulties in getting the child to respond to parental expectations, parental disappointment with a child, a desire by parents to resolve difficulties between the child and other systems (school, neighborhood, etc.), stepparent–stepchild relationships, and conflicts that arise as a result of differences between the family's culture and the larger culture to which the child is exposed. All of these issues are affected both directly and indirectly by culture and diversity. They are further complicated when there are differences in culture and diversity within the family and between stepparents and stepchildren. This increases the need to use a diversity competent approach that includes naturalistic inquiry.

The social history for parent–child subsystems is similar to that for parental subsystems with some changes and additions. Understanding the parental subsystem is important for understanding the context in which the parent–child subsystem functions. It is also important for understanding the structure and development of the parent–child subsystem, especially for blended families. We will not repeat that portion of the assessment here, but refer the reader to this material in Chapter 11 for review.

The portion of the social history that is unique to the parent–child subsystem has been added under III.E. When assessing this subsystem, the worker should discuss the structure, form, functioning, and development of the current relationship as well as other current and past parent–child relationships for both the parent and the child. This will give the worker some idea of successes and difficulties that each has experienced. Successes are signs of potential strengths. Difficulties may be contributing to the current situation. If the relationship has been positive in the past or if either one or both have similar current or past relationships that have been successful, it demonstrates a capacity to build such a relationship in the current situation. The worker can also help identify what made those relationships successful so that these aspects can be utilized in the current relationship. The worker should include an exploration of the parent's own parent–child experiences when he or she was a child. A comprehensive examination should include thoughts, feelings, and actions for each member of the subsystem.

Past difficulties with building a positive parent–child relationship may influence some of the difficulties in the current relationship. The pattern from earlier relationships may be repeated. Both current and past relationships tend to shape expectations for other relationships. As we respond to these expectations, our behavior can actually bring about what we predict. This is generally called a self-fulfilling prophecy.

The cohesiveness of parent–child relationships refers to how relationships and boundaries are maintained. Some questions to ask here are how each one sees and experiences the relationship, interactions and activities that occur, expectations and responses to expectations, and feelings that they have for each other. The worker should discuss how connected or separated they feel. What are the rules and norms for their relationship? How attached or bonded are they?

Examination of the communication system is vital for working with any relationship. The worker needs to assess the skills and abilities of members of the subsystem. Typically, adults will have more advanced skills than children, especially younger ones. However, this is not always the case. Adults can be limited in their communication skills or they may experience blockages to using these skills in certain situations. For instance, a father might feel that he was not able to communicate with his father when he was grow-ing up. As a result, he may feel at a loss as to how he can communicate with his son now that he is a father. Stepfamily relationships can be so complex that communication skills that are functional in other relationships may not be sufficient for these. At the same time, skills and abilities in communicating in other relationships demonstrate the capacity to communicate and may be useful if applied to the parent–child relationships that are the focus of attention.

Decision-making and problem-solving skills and abilities are another vital area when working with relationships. Without these skills, communication will erode over time be-cause people will tend to withdraw from conflict by not talking about issues that may lead to conflict. When they do talk about these issues, it typically leads to an eruption of feel-ings that have been pent up over time. This serves to reinforce the need to avoid these is-sues setting the stage for the next eruption. Good decision making and problem solving leads to resolution of issues and concerns, reducing the likelihood of conflict and opening the door to more communication about important needs and concerns. As with other skills and abilities, demonstrating these with current or past relationships shows a capacity to use them in the current parent–child relationship.

Conflict resolution skills and abilities are the third leg of the triad of relationship skills. Conflict needs to be resolved in a constructive rather than destructive manner. The basic elements of this have been covered earlier. They include negotiation and compro-mise, using "I" statements, creating win–win situations instead of win–lose, and avoid-ing violence and threats. In assessment, the worker explores how members of the subsystem deal with conflict within their relationship and with others outside their relationship.

In addition to serving the needs of the current relationship, these three skill areas are important for children to learn as they grow into adults. They are especially important dur-ing adolescence and young adulthood when issues around independence and emancipation generally arise. If good basic skills in communication, decision making and problem solv-ing, and conflict resolution can be established early on and nurtured and grown between par-ents and children, children will be prepared to handle adult relationships effectively. In some respects, the teen years are a testing ground for these skills, but they need to be used in age-appropriate ways before that time. It is much more difficult to establish these during ado-lescence and adulthood if the foundation has not been laid earlier. To a great extent this is frequently part of the difficulty in establishing parent–child relationships between steppar-ents and stepchildren, with unmarried partners and unrelated children, and with older adopted or foster children.

Culture plays an important role in establishing these skills and influences rules and norms for family relationships, especially between parents and children. It is important for the worker to gather information about these as she works with the subsystem. As with other family relationships, bicultural and cross-cultural situations tend to create much greater complexity in understanding and working with stepparents and stepchildren.

Role performance and satisfaction refer to how each member of the parent–child sub-system performs in their role as parents or children and how satisfied they are with their own and each other's performance. Consideration should also be given to other roles that each play within the family and outside of the family system. The ability to perform in other roles can be used to develop satisfactory role performance in the current relationship.

The worker should assess the support that parents and children receive from each other, from other family members, and from their ecosystem. He includes support that encourages growth and development, especially on the part of the parents, but also by other family members. He assesses the degree to which the parent, the child, and other family members show care and concern for each other.

Assessing commonalities and differences within the parent–child subsystem lays some of the groundwork for change. Commonalities can be built on and differences can be bridged or respected. These areas are especially relevant for stepfamily relations and when working with adoptive and foster families. The worker identifies expectations of the parents and children. What do they expect from each other? To what extent are these expectations similar to or different from each other? How are expectations communicated and what is the response? How and what kind of feedback is given and how is it typically received? What positive or negative consequences are there? These are some of the questions that the social worker explores to gain an understanding of the subsystem.

Assessing coping mechanisms used by members of the parent–child subsystem gives the worker a picture of what might work or not work for them in dealing with stress within the subsystem. How do the parents and children cope with stress within the subsystem? How do they cope with stresses within the family? With individuals and systems outside of the family system? Coping mechanisms are vital in dealing with stress and avoiding crises.

Assessing intimacy and closeness may be more nonverbal in some respects. Although the worker can ask about this, she also needs to look for ways in which affection and other signs of closeness are expressed. Some might assume that biological parent–child relationships are naturally closer with love and affection, but this is not necessarily the case. Some parents may not be able to express their love. Some may not love their child at all. On the other hand, stepparents may love their stepchildren. However, some may have difficulties expressing this and some stepchildren may not readily accept it. The worker considers these and other possibilities as she assesses this area of the parent–child subsystem.

Part III of the social history focuses on the need or concern that initiated the work with the parent–child subsystem. Whether he is working with the family as a whole or with subsystems, the worker should include needs and concerns for individuals, subsystems, and the family as a whole, even if these are not the focus of the current work. Identifying the pattern of needs in the family gives the worker information about the stresses and strains and also helps to identify strengths, particularly with respect to the ability of the parents, the children, and the family system to meet needs in the family.

Part IV of the social history identifies strengths and challenges within the ecosystem, including the family, the parent–child subsystem, and the environment. Parts III and IV are where the two purposes of the assessment are examined. The first is to gain an understanding of the parent–child subsystem and their situation as these relate to the need or concern. The second purpose is to identify strengths and resources for meeting needs or addressing concerns and challenges that might create barriers to meeting needs. Once these purposes have been met, planning for change can begin. As mentioned throughout the text, assessment continues during all phases of the change process. The worker learns something new and adds to his understanding every time he meets with the parents and children. If the work is successful, the parents, children, and family also learn something about themselves as individuals and as members of the family system.

■ PLANNING WITH PARENT–CHILD SUBSYSTEMS ■

Planning with parent–child subsystems is similar to planning with families and other family subsystems as described earlier with some important differences related primarily to inter-generational differences. Similar to assessment, planning is both a process and a product. The planning process with parent–child subsystems involves both parents and children and their relationships with each other. Although child-rearing practices should be decided by the parental subsystem, these are implemented in the parent–child subsystem. As a result, the parental relationship affects the parent–child relationship and vice versa. This is true for all types of families, but it has particularly important ramifications for stepfamily relations. When planning with parent–child subsystems, the worker typically includes both parents in decid-ing issues related to child-rearing. In addition, children's input is limited because they are not adults and do not have the same authority or responsibility. However, as children grow toward adulthood, the relationship should become more equal as parents yield responsibility for de-cision making in preparation for independent adulthood. Generally, the best approach to use is for parents to come to an agreement about how much independence and responsibility is appropriate for various age levels and then share this with the child at regular intervals. Birth-day celebrations can become graduations to higher levels of autonomy.

Some parents favor total or at least considerable parental authority throughout child-hood. Often there are cultural influences that dictate this approach. Unfortunately, this does not usually prepare children very well in terms of functioning as independent adults in U.S. society. Thus, parents need to consider the fact that childhood generally makes up only a small portion of the average person's life, typically 20 to 25 percent. The primary respon-sibility of parents is to prepare children for the other 75 to 80 percent of their lives. Ex-ploring with parents their vision for their children's future is a good way to assist them in developing a parenting style that will fit with that vision.

Once child-rearing practices are established, they provide a framework for planning with parent–child subsystems. Goals and objectives are discussed within this framework. In other words, children should not be given the same autonomy and status as parents, but their needs and concerns should be taken into consideration and met within the framework of the child-rearing practices established by the parents. Thus, what can be negotiated are the specifics related to the situation at hand, such as expectations and specific positive and negative consequences.

In addition to working on the effects of child-rearing practices on the parent–child sub-system, the social worker often finds herself working on the relationship itself. The focus is on how parents and children relate to each other. How can they act, interact, express thoughts and feelings, and show affection in a way that meets needs and strengthens the re-lationship? What are the barriers to meeting needs and what are they willing to do to over-come those barriers? Once again stepfamilies as well as adoptive and foster families have special challenges to face in these areas. Cultural influences also must be considered.

Throughout the planning process, the worker takes the role of facilitator, mediator, and negotiator. The plan should address the needs of each member of the parent–child subsys-tem and should strengthen their relationship.

As we pointed out earlier, the product of the planning process with any client system is the service plan. Various settings use different terminology for this, but essentially this is where goals and objectives are entered into the case file. In order to assist parents and children in following through with their part of the plan, it is generally helpful for each member to keep a written version of it. An example of a parent–child plan is as follows:

Goal: Bill and his mother will improve their relationship.
Objective 1: Bill and his mother will use "I" statements with each other at least three times a day for three consecutive days by August 15.
Clients Task: Bill and his mother will maintain journals of their "I" statements and bring their journals to sessions with the worker.
Worker Task: Worker will assist Bill and his mother in monitoring and practicing "I" statements during conjoint sessions.
Objective 2: Bill and his mother will use an effective decision-making process with each other at least three times in one week by August 15.
Clients Task: Mr. and Mrs. Jones will maintain journals of their decision making with each other and bring their journals to sessions with the worker.
Worker Task: Worker will assist Mr. and Mrs Jones in monitoring and practicing decision making during sessions with the worker.

■ DIRECT PRACTICE ACTIONS WITH ■ PARENT–CHILD SUBSYSTEMS

As with families and other family subsystems, direct practice actions with parent–child subsystems are actions that are taken in working directly with parents and children and their relationship. Indirect practice actions are taken on behalf of parent–child subsystems. Direct practice includes actions that (1) engage in diversity competent actions with parents and children, (2) enable development of the relationship, (3) develop an understanding of parent–child subsystems in environment, (4) plan with parents and children, (5) enable parents and children to know and use available resources, (6) empower or enable parents and children to strengthen their relationship, (7) resolve crisis situations, (8) use support in working with parents and children, (9) use activity with parents and children, (10) mediate with parents and children and between parent–child subsystems and a system in their environment, and (11) use a clinical model of social work with parents and children.

These actions are similar to those described for working with families and with other family subsystems. There are areas where these overlap with areas that were discussed earlier. The development of relationships was described in Chapters 4, 10, and 11 and earlier in this chapter. Development of understanding of person in environment as this relates to parent–child subsystems was discussed under assessment. Planning was covered in the previous section. Action taken in using a clinical model of social work with parent–child subsystems is beyond the scope of this book and is typically covered in advanced graduate-level social work courses.

Action Taken to Enable Parent–Child Subsystems to Know and Use Community Resources

Action taken to enable parent–child subsystems to know and use available resources is similar to that described for families in Chapter 7, for couples in Chapter 10, and for parents in

Chapter 11. Most of this work is done with the parents, especially with regard to providing basic needs and ensuring that family members, especially children, are safe; receive proper care; and have their physical, social, psychological, emotional, economic, and educational needs met. There are community resources for children and teens that can play an important role in building character, providing guidance, and providing healthy positive outlets for them. Generally, it is up to the parents to provide the support for involvement in these activities. However, the worker may play a key role in reducing resistance on the part of the child or teen to accessing or using these resources.

Another category of community resources are those that provide opportunities for families to engage in positive activities. These can be formal and informal. Formal activities are those that are specifically structured for and aimed at families. They can range from social or community events, such as fairs and excursions, to church related activities or clubs that offer family events and activities. Informal resources are those that are available, but the family structures its own involvement. Examples might be picnicking at a park, going to the zoo, camping, and so on. The more opportunities that parents and children have to enjoy each other, the better the chance of building strong successful parent–child relationships.

As with earlier discussions of actions with families and other subsystems, the first action taken by the worker relates to knowledge that is necessary to access resources. Parents and children who are isolated or have weak social support systems are typically unaware of available resources. The worker needs to be able to acquire knowledge about formal and informal resources and be creative about assisting families in using them, especially regarding informal opportunities. Knowledge about resources and services should include knowledge about locations and access to them.

Knowledgeable social workers acquire their knowledge about resources as they provide services to families and as they accumulate personal experiences in the community. The worker is constantly looking for ways to improve his services to his clients, even when he is not engage in actual work. He notices what other families are doing to enjoy themselves and looks for ways to include his families in similar activities. The knowledgeable worker also accumulates knowledge about the use of formal resources through colleagues, resource manuals, the media, and similar sources that have been identified in earlier chapters.

Action Taken to Enable or Empower Parent–Child Subsystems

Enabling and empowering parent–child subsystems are skills that are needed in assisting them to use community resources and in developing and maintaining positive parent–child relationships. Empowering and enabling as individuals was covered in Chapter 7, as couples in Chapter 10, and as parents in Chapter 11. We see enabling and empowering activities as aimed at assisting parents and children to be loving and positive in their relationships with each other. Enabling refers to making it possible to engage in actions and develop skills as a parent or child. Empowering refers to increasing power to take action or use skills. Enabling is assisting parents and children in developing skills necessary for successful relationships. Empowering refers to increasing confidence and strength in using those skills.

It is important that parents work in concert with each other using good parenting practices that were identified in Chapter 11. These will not be repeated here, but the reader is encouraged to review them and keep them in mind as a context for using the actions that follow. The worker should ensure that good parenting practices are in place first before she begins working on the parent–child subsystem. Without this in place, it is highly unlikely that any approach to change will be successful. Parents need to have confidence in themselves and each other before they can feel safe in changing their parent–child interactions. They cannot be looking back over their shoulder wondering where their partner is or if they have their support.

There are aspects of developing parent–child relationships that need to be discussed because of the intergenerational nature of them and differences in status. Essentially, the younger the child, the more responsibility falls on the parent to develop and model good relationship skills for the child. In fact, a general rule to follow is the younger the child, the more the worker works with the parents. Thus, in enabling and empowering parents, the social worker should work with them on developing their relationship skills and on teaching these to their children. This includes good communication, decision making and problem solving, and conflict resolution. Some parents may not be aware of the need for developing these skills or of their role in modeling them for their children. Probably, the most important communication skill that can be taught easily to children is the use of "I" statements. This is the basic building block of good communication. Good listening skills are also basic but are a bit more difficult to teach. However, the power of modeling as parents cannot be underestimated. Helping parents with their own skills and getting them to use them with each other and with their children are fundamental to enabling development of good parent–child relationships.

There are various structures for working with parent–child subsystems. Most revolve around variations of individual and joint portions of sessions. Some workers will see the parent then the child and then bring them together. Others will do parent then child then parent sessions. Still others prefer only joint sessions. The first two tend to be more common. It is rare that one would see the child or teen first because the child or teen may be reluctant to discuss issues that the parent would want to discuss.

In terms of enabling and empowering children in parent–child subsystems, the social worker needs to model good communication and relationship skills, just as the parents need to do this. This means good listening, encouraging the use of "I" statements, and the like. The worker seeks to form an adult–child relationship that is also somewhat of a partnership. This is similar to the relationship he seeks to build with parents, only the parent relationship is adult–adult as partners in seeking solutions. With younger children, communication needs to be more simple and at their level of development. Working with older teens usually calls for a more adult–adult approach that recognizes their approaching independence. Adult–child relationships are generally characterized by some kind of recognition for the difference in status. Some young clients might use the terms Mr., Mrs., or Miss along with the first name of the worker. So instead of Miss Smith, the child might use Miss Sue to refer to the worker. Much of this is culturally determined. Some cultures dictate more formal forms of address between children and adults and others allow for other forms.

Part of the worker's adult–child relationships with children might model parent–child relationships as long as such relationships do not take the place of parent–child relationships. This modeling mainly takes place when the worker works jointly with parents and children. However, the primary goals in joint sessions should be to coach parents and children or to mediate with them around building a stronger, successful relationship. The worker enables and empowers parents and children as she encourages them to engage in healthy, positive interactions that meet each other's needs. The greatest needs within this and other family subsystems are for love, acceptance, and affection. Nothing enables or empowers people more than knowing that their family loves them and accepts them for themselves. Often the expression of love, acceptance, and affection is blocked or not expressed. For stepfamilies and adoptive and foster families, love, acceptance, and affection need to be developed. For abusive and neglectful families, the underlying causes of the abuse or neglect must be resolved and its effects overcome before parents and children can build healthy relationships.

When working individually with younger children, the worker may use games or puppets or other forms of play to draw out the child's story. Play is where children work out their issues and concerns. Fantasy can also create rich areas for growth and change. Restorying or replaying successful outcomes of difficult situations can bring new solutions to the situation at hand.

Working with younger adolescents can be challenging in developing relationship skills. Their swings from childlike to more adult behaviors and moods make it more difficult to work with them. The worker needs to assess this throughout each session and may even label it so that the young adolescent can confirm how he is feeling and gain a better understanding of himself. At the same time, the worker needs to consistently appeal to the side that is striving toward adulthood and encourage behavior that reflects this. In the end, successful parent–child relationships between young adolescents and their parents are typically based on parental support for greater autonomy and responsibility that is consistent with their age and developmental levels. Similarly, successful worker–client relationships with younger adolescents are also built on this approach.

The basic approach to enabling and empowering is to replace negative thoughts, feelings, and actions with positive ones. This is commonly known as a cognitive–behavioral approach to change. The assumption is that everyone wants to have positive family relationships. However, some families may not be able to express or exhibit these. Barriers may include a lack of knowledge or experiences, a history of negative experiences, cultural restrictions, and the like. The worker seeks to find ways of helping the parents and children to replace negative thoughts with positive ones. One approach to use is to examine how negative thoughts influence negative feelings, which produce negative actions. The worker then seeks to find out how the parents and children would like to experience their relationship. She identifies positive behaviors that each would like to see in each other. She explores how their own actions might bring about those positive behaviors. The worker helps them to restructure their thoughts and feelings in a way that would facilitate exhibiting that behavior.

Another related approach is to get parents and children to predict positive responses from each other so that their thoughts, feelings, and actions are consistent with eliciting those responses from each. The worker explores how predicting a positive response might affect their thoughts and feelings. She develops scenarios to help them to practice these new experiences and coaches them in acting them out.

A third approach the worker can use is to get parents and children to "act as if" they had a positive relationship, especially in terms of acting as if they love each other. The worker has them identify actions that others would take as signs of love and positive feelings. He contracts with them to exhibit these behaviors at frequencies that they feel they can do so. Generally, this approach needs to begin with parents. The worker asks the parents how often they could see themselves engaging in certain actions, such as showing affection, expressing appreciation or saying "I love you," at certain frequencies, such as once, twice, three times a day or week, and so on. He asks them to specify the actions and plan on strategic times and places when they could exhibit them. Some good times to do this are first thing in the morning, when the child comes home from school, when the parent or stepparent comes home from work, at bedtime, or when the parent or child is leaving the house. He warns them that initially they may not get the response they would like and encourages them to stick with it for a period of time. The worker also coaches the children in how they might respond to actions they would like to see from their parents and identifies behaviors the children might exhibit to bring those about.

These approaches typically begin in sessions with parents and children in which the worker helps them to discuss and practice these behaviors. As they gain a sense of confidence in being able to exhibit them, the worker structures some activities outside of the sessions and has them report back their experiences. Later, she develops less structured activities outside of the sessions that would lead to more positive interaction to reinforce these experiences. Once parents and children have at least one or more positive experiences, the worker can help them identify thoughts and feelings that were associated with those experiences. She works with them on finding ways to increase and expand those experiences and to reinforce them.

Action Taken in Crisis Situations

As with crisis situations in the family and with other subsystems, the social worker works with the parent–child subsystem to mobilize their coping skills. Crises within this subsystem may include dealing with a strain or breakdown in the relationship, coping with emergencies related to the family or another subsystem, and maintaining their relationship in the face of serious adversity. If the crisis is within their relationship, then they will need to work on restoring and strengthening it. Often a crisis in the parent–child relationship reflects a serious threat to the marital relationship. Strained marital relations may lead to children taking sides or may result in children being included in the stressful interactions. This is commonly referred to as *triangling*, in which a third party is included in a relationship that should only include the marital partners. In the worst case scenarios, parents use children to fight with each other or to get back at their partners. Some parents actively seek to have their children take their side. In stepfamilies, these divisions can be quite pronounced. In these families, stresses between stepparents and stepchildren can be a serious threat to the marital relationship. The basic approach to crisis intervention in families was presented in Chapter 7. Working on crises in the marital relationship was covered in Chapter 10. Working on crises with parents was discussed in Chapter 11.

A strain or a breakdown in the parental–child relationship is generally related to disagreements between parents and children regarding child-rearing and discipline, relationship issues between them, or stresses within or outside the family. In any case, the social worker needs to work from a mediating position to assist in restoring their coping mechanisms and in reaching a resolution to the crisis. The worker also takes the opportunity to introduce changes that will result in improving the relationship and strengthening it so the parents and children are better prepared to handle crises in the future.

As we mentioned in Chapter 11, various emergencies may arise during the course of raising children. Children experience medical emergencies, accidents, and life-threatening situations. Although these situations can be overwhelming for parents, they can also become opportunities for bonding and attachment, especially for stepfamilies and adoptive and foster families. This all depends on how the situation is handled. If the parent can reach out and support the children and the family during the crisis, then their relationship is likely to be strengthened by having faced adversity together. Unfortunately, not everyone reacts to crisis in a way that builds relationships. Some people withdraw or flee from crisis situations. They can do this either physically or psychologically. In the latter case, people become detached rather than investing themselves. Some people may even become critical or blaming when crises arise. Rather than focusing on resolution, they look for causes and someone to blame. The social worker needs to assist parents and children in establishing positive coping mechanisms in the face of these crises.

Crises may also arise when parents are faced with serious adversity, such as health problems, accidents, extended absences, substance abuse, disability, unemployment, financial hardship, homelessness, or incarceration. When these are temporary situations, parents and children may only need assistance with establishing temporary coping mechanisms. Long-term or permanent situations require more extensive work. In these instances, the worker needs to provide assistance in overcoming or coping with the adversity itself, and he needs to help the parents and children maintain or restructure their relationship to effectively cope in the face of the adversity.

The social worker assesses the crisis situation and the coping skills of the parents and children. She assists them in strengthening these skills or adding new ones to resolve the situation and restore a healthy equilibrium. She encourages support from the family's support network along with support systems for the parents and the children. The worker accesses sources of support from the human service delivery system in the community as needed.

Action Taken to Use Support in Working with Parent–Child Subsystems

The use of support in working with parents is similar to that which was discussed in Chapter 7 for working with families, Chapter 10 for couples, and Chapter 11 for parents. The need for support during crises was discussed in the previous section. This section focuses on building support in the parent–child relationships. It is important that parents feel supported by each other and that children feel supported by their parents and stepparents. Nothing is more encouraging for parents than knowing that they are together as partners. Nothing is more important for children than knowing that they have support from their parents. Similarly, nothing is more discouraging than feeling that one is alone or that one does not have a partner or parents there to support us. As adults, most support needs to come from the parents as opposed to support coming from children. However, when sons and daughters become adults, this gradually shifts as parents age and may experience a decline in physical or mental abilities. An argument could be made that stepchildren need to support the efforts of their stepparents in establishing a positive parent–child relationship in blended families.

For parents to feel supported by their partners, it is important for them to reach an agreement on parenting style and child-rearing techniques. This was covered in the previous chapter and will not be repeated here. However, the reader is encouraged to review this material as a context for considering the effects of having or not having agreement on how parents and stepparents approach relationships with children in the family. Nowhere is this

more important than in the area of parental expectations and discipline. Parents .
gether on these issues are more likely to be consistent and those who are not will .
nearly impossible to be consistent.

For children, having the support of one's parents makes all the difference in the world. It
allows the child to grow and develop socially, emotionally, and psychologically. Parental support tends to build self-confidence, self-esteem, and self-assurance. One caveat to this is the
need for parental support for appropriate rather than inappropriate actions. Some parents go
overboard and take the position "not my kid" when faced with issues raised by other adults,
including teachers, neighbors, and even law enforcement officials. These parents are fostering irresponsibility instead of responsibility. Parents who are themselves engaged in illegal activities are directly or indirectly supporting illegal activities on the part of their children.

In strengthening or establishing supportive parent–child subsystems, the social worker
should encourage positive feedback and expressions of support on the part of both parents
and children. This is fundamental to raising self-worth and confidence. However, support
may not be given consistently over time or may not be expressed. The social worker assists
the parents in providing open and honest support for each other and for their children on a
regular basis. She checks with each parent and child on areas in which he or she would like
to receive support and helps to incorporate this into their relationship. The worker should
be prepared to model expressions of support first and then coach the parents and children
in saying and doing things that are supportive. The conversation might be similar to those
presented in Chapters 10 and 11 as follows: What do you do to support each other? Did you
know that he/she was trying to support you when he/she said or did that? Would you be willing to accept that as a sign of support? What would you like your parent/child to say or do
to support you in this? Would you be willing to do that? or What would it take for you to
do that? As the work with parent–child subsystems progresses, the worker encourages support and coaches the parents and children in giving, requesting, and receiving support so it
becomes consistent.

Action Taken That Uses Activity with Parent–Child Subsystems

Just as with families, couples, and parents, activities can be effective in working with parents and children. It is essential that the work that is done be transferred over to everyday life.
"Homework assignments" are used to practice the skills and implement the changes. These
are a form of activity. The worker works with parents and children to structure these assignments during the session. He coaches them as they practice until they feel comfortable
enough to try it on their own. As mentioned earlier, activities can be formal or informal. Formal activities for families typically have parent–child interaction built into the experience.
Informal activities will typically require more planning to ensure a positive outcome.

The social worker uses the phases of the change process when working with parents
and children on activities. This has the added benefit of reinforcement for learning the
change process. The worker helps the parents and children to identify desirable activities.
She coaches them in planning for the activity and, if necessary, contracts with them on
specifics, such as who, what, where, when, and how. The worker provides assistance with
information, referral, and accessing resources and helps them to remove barriers. She helps
them to anticipate the experience by identifying what each member would like to get out of

it. Afterward, the worker discusses the experience and helps the family to evaluate positive and negative aspects that need to be duplicated or changed, respectively.

As with any ongoing relationship, parents and children need to develop and practice good relationship skills, including good communication, effective problem solving and decision making, and constructive conflict resolution. The social worker teaches these skills and has parents and children practice using them during and between sessions.

Action Taken to Mediate with Parent–Child Subsystems and with Their Environment

Actions taken to mediate are provided directly to parents and children and are a transition to indirect practice actions. Mediation is the basic approach used in working with any multiclient system or subsystem. As we said before, mediating with systems in the environment borders on an indirect practice action except that in mediation both sides are involved in the work. In mediation the worker remains neutral while facilitating effective and constructive interactions between the two parties.

Maintaining a neutral position allows the worker to avoid getting pulled into the middle of disagreements. Taking sides typically leads to more intense conflict or losing the ability to relate well with whomever feels left out. The worker can only serve the needs of the relationship if members see him as being neutral. The worker must establish a mediating position from the very start and should remind the parents and children of this throughout the work.

In Chapters 10 and 11, we discussed an effective approach to use in developing and maintaining a mediating role by having the family members visualize their relationship as a triangle made up of "you," "I," and "we." The worker has each person take responsibility for his or her own needs and the worker assumes responsibility of advocating for the relationship. The worker's basic position is to ask questions such as, What will it take to make this relationship work? She continuously asks this question in various forms along with ancillary questions such as the following: How will this help strengthen your relationship? What could you do to improve your relationship in this situation? What outcome would strengthen your relationship? What do you need out of this relationship that would meet your needs? What do you need from your parent/child that would help you to strengthen your relationship? Would you be willing to . . . in order to make this relationship stronger or better?

The worker asks these types of questions and facilitates good communication by having the parents and children talk with each other about their needs and about their relationship. He helps them to negotiate agreements. He supports them in building honesty and trust and strengthening their relationship.

■ INDIRECT PRACTICE ACTIONS WITH ■ PARENT–CHILD SUBSYSTEMS

Indirect practice actions with parent–child subsystems are similar to those that are used earlier with families, couples, and parents. Indirect practice includes actions that (1) involve the use of influence, (2) are designed to change the environment, and (3) are relative to coordination of services.

These actions tend to be used more frequently with parents.

Action That Involves the Use of Influence

Influence is an important consideration in working with all client systems. The social worker may have more or less influence, depending on her role and the situation. The worker's influence in child welfare situations and with family preservation approaches was discussed in the previous chapter and will not be repeated here. An important consideration with regard to influence is the fact that the worker is an adult and the children are not. This difference in status in and of itself leads to the potential for the worker to have much more influence. Of course, some influence is unavoidable. What the worker needs to ensure is that influence is used in a positive way to improve the child's circumstances. It should not be used to undermine the child's self-esteem or self-interests. The child should be encouraged to participate in decision making, taking into consideration age and developmental level.

The social worker needs to be aware of the influence that he has with parents. He tries to limit his influence and allow parents to make their own decisions. The worker uses influence to persuade the parents to engage in good parenting practices as described in the previous chapter.

As with families and other subsystems, the worker is free to use influence on behalf of parents and children. This includes developing and securing resources to support positive parent–child experiences. If family activities are not available, the worker uses her influence to initiate them within the purview of her agency. She promotes family-oriented activities and services through her work and her personal life. She supports families and empowers them in influencing their environment. The worker uses her contacts with influential people to build support for activities and services for parents, children, and families that are not available.

Action Designed to Change the Environment

Actions designed to change the environment are mainly used to either assist families in changing their existing environment or to move to a new environment. Much of what was discussed under this heading in previous chapters is also relevant for working with parents and children. To a great extent, environmental change is a key to dealing with difficult situations between parents and children. For instance, changing how parents act changes the environment of their children.

In cases of neglect, the worker works with parents to maintain a clean household with adequate food and other necessities. He assists parents in altering their actions to provide a safe and healthy environment for their children. He arranges for homemaker services if appropriate. Some workers may get directly involved and organize a cleanup effort. The worker helps the parents to arrange for needed repairs or, in extreme circumstances or when the residence has been condemned, he becomes involved in helping parents obtain different housing. The worker helps parents set up and follow through with a system for maintaining their household.

Another situation that involves changing the environment is when children are placed in alternative forms of care. This is generally associated with delinquency, abuse or neglect, or becoming orphaned. These are covered in the Appendix under "Good Practices with Families Experiencing Crime and Delinquency" and "Good Practices with Families Experiencing Child Abuse and Neglect."

The social worker may also be involved with environmental change with parents who are older and need care that cannot be received at home. This is covered later in this chapter, in the next chapter, and in the Appendix under "Good Practices with Families with Members who are Older."

Children who are delinquent or exposed to drugs and crime because of the neighborhood may need to move to a safer environment with fewer negative influences. The family may need assistance in doing this, especially regarding financial assistance for deposits, utilities, and so on.

Action Relative to Coordination of Services

As mentioned earlier, sometimes it is necessary for the social worker to coordinate services on behalf of parents and children. The first choice is for the parents to be able to manage this on their own. However, when parents are overwhelmed, the worker acts on their behalf. This may be a temporary situation or a chronic circumstance that interferes with the parents' abilities to act on their own. These services can range from providing information and referral to full case management. When appropriate, the worker makes a referral and follows up to make sure that the needed services are received. The referral process was discussed in Chapter 7. In crisis situations, the worker is more direct and involved in the work. The worker mobilizes resources in the ecosystem to take over managing services or provides this herself.

For adult sons and daughters, it may be necessary to coordinate services for aging parents. If the adult children live nearby, the worker helps them learn about resources and works with them on developing a system for maintaining their parents' well-being. For families who are unable or unwilling to do so, the worker either provides this if it is part of his agency's service delivery system or he refers the family to such an agency.

As we mentioned previously, the generalist practice social worker may temporarily coordinate services or this may be part of her regular responsibilities. Common types of agencies where case management is a primary service are mental health, health care, and aging services, which do both temporary and long-term case management.

■ EVALUATION AND TERMINATION WITH ■
PARENT–CHILD SUBSYSTEMS

Evaluation and termination with parents and children are similar to that which was described for families in Chapter 9. Evaluation is constant throughout the change process. Evaluation is also used to determine the outcome and completion of the work and during termination. It is important that evaluation be geared toward the age and developmental level of the client. When working with children, the worker uses language that is appropriate for the child. Otherwise, the information is not reliable and the evaluation is not valid.

As with other forms of family work, the worker evaluates the validity and reliability of the information he collects. When he works with parents and children, triangulation of the data is built into the process because the worker has more than one source of information. When there is agreement between more than one source, the worker can rely more on the accuracy of the information. When there is disagreement, the worker discusses the situation to understand and clear up the discrepancy. Sometimes a disagreement or discrepancy represents differences in perceptions of the situation. Over time, these differences may disappear or they may need to be revisited as new information is gathered. Differences in perception generally reflect various aspects of the actual situation. The worker may assume that the actual situation is somewhere between the descriptions that are offered.

If there is a reason to believe that either the parents or the children have more to gain or lose by presenting a certain position, then the worker might assume that their perceptions are probably skewed in that direction. As we pointed out earlier, the worker should avoid labeling either party as "lying" or "not telling the truth." It is natural for us to perceive the world around us in a manner that fits with self-interest. Most people are guarded about what they say until trust and security is established. Even then, certain issues may be too painful to discuss.

Evaluation is built into every plan and is used to measure progress and determine completion of goals and objectives. The worker, parents, and children evaluate progress toward achieving objectives and determine what is working and what is not. Positive results indicate the plan is working. Negative or unproductive results indicate a barrier needs to be removed or the plan should be changed or a new plan should be developed.

When goals are reached, the worker, parents, and children evaluate whether needs have been met. They also need to decide whether the work needs to continue. When the work has been completed, then they can proceed to termination.

Within the termination process, the worker solicits feedback about the change process. He seeks to find out what was helpful, what was not, and what would have been helpful. This helps him evaluate his skills and improve services to parents and children in the future. The parents and children also need to evaluate themselves and their new skills and abilities.

As mentioned earlier with families and other client systems, various forms of unplanned terminations often take place. When clients drop out of service, the worker follows up to ensure that their needs have been met. If necessary, the worker offers a referral for services elsewhere or ensures that they feel free to return. When termination is initiated by the worker or the agency, the worker needs to ensure a smooth transfer to another worker or to another agency. It is preferable to have at least one joint session with the new worker. If this is not possible, the worker prepares the parents and children to receive services from a different worker. She reinforces the fact that they are the ones who have done the real work and assures them that if they can work with her, they can work with another worker in using the change process.

GENERALIST PRACTICE WITH OLDER PARENT–ADULT CHILD SUBSYSTEMS

As children grow into adults and parents become older, changes occur in the parent–child relationship. There are also changes that are needed in the services the generalist social worker provides. The nature of these changes revolves around the need to transition from parent–child to adult–adult relationships and the need to transition from parents meeting their children's needs to adult sons and daughters assisting parents who are older meet their needs.

As adolescents and young adults strive toward independence, it often puts a strain on their relationships with parents. Sometimes these situations call for services from MSW social workers who specialize in family therapy or counseling. However, in rural areas or when home visits are the primary form of service delivery, the generalist social worker may encounter these situations and have to work with them. When this occurs the worker helps the parents and their sons or daughters to use or improve their relationship skills, including communication, problem solving and decision making, and conflict resolution. She assists them by mediating and helping them to negotiate an understanding about where they are and where they need to go with their relationship and their situation.

Similar situations can arise when adult sons and daughters return home after emancipation. This is not unusual when they experience a crisis such as divorce or the loss of a job. Sometimes they move back home with a spouse or with children. In urban areas, this work is more often done by MSW social workers specializing in counseling. However, in rural areas and in situations where the worker makes home visits, the generalist social worker may find herself working with these situations. When this occurs, the worker falls back on her skills in helping families develop and use good relationship skills, including communication, problem solving and decision making, and conflict resolution. These are basic tools for any effective relationship. The worker assists the family in using the change process—assessment, planning, action, and evaluation. Important issues to work through typically include defining roles, rules, and expectations; establishing housekeeping standards and responsibilities; reaching an understanding about financial arrangements; and establishing a time frame for leaving.

Some adult sons and daughters may not leave the home at all, for example, those with physical or mental disabilities that prevent them from becoming independent. In other instances, a parent or parents may move in with an adult son or daughter for financial reasons or because of mental or physical disabilities, or an adult son or daughter may move in with his or her parents who are older for the same reasons. It is not unusual for generalist social workers to be faced with these situations. In urban areas with more services, specialized services may be available to work with these situations. In more rural areas or when services are delivered in the home, it is more common for generalist social workers to become involved.

When the worker and the family assess the need for assistance with these situations, the worker helps them identify how they would like their relationship and their living arrangement to be. If there is some agreement on this, the worker proceeds with a plan to bring it about. If there is disagreement, then the worker mediates an acceptable arrangement. Often one issue revolves around helping the parents accept the fact that their son or daughter is now an adult and should be treated accordingly. Another aspect may be getting the adult son or daughter to accept more responsibility and act more adult.

With parents who are older, adult sons or daughters may experience difficulty in having their parents understand the need for assistance or the need to move into assisted living or nursing home care. Often there are issues regarding their safety and well-being. At the same time, the parents desire to maintain their independence is in conflict with ensuring their well-being. These are difficult situations for social workers who believe in self-determination while also valuing life and quality of life. Generally, if the person who is older is capable of making his or her own decisions, the worker respects that right. However, if there is a mental impairment, such as dementia, the worker helps the family or a guardian to obtain either power of attorney or guardianship and conservatorship in order to make decisions on that person's behalf. Typically, the spouse assumes these roles and takes responsibility for making decisions if he or she is able. If not, then an adult son or daughter may do so. If there are no relatives available, a public guardian is usually the only option. Generalist social workers who work for hospitals and services for the aging are often involved in these types of situations and in helping the family or guardian secure the necessary resources or facilities to ensure proper care. Sometimes the worker may need to mediate with the family when there are disagreements about these issues or about care and living arrangements.

Sometimes issues arise over grandparent–parent–child relationships. This is especially the case in families of divorce and adult sons and daughters living with parents with custody of their children or those who are noncustodial parents with visitation. Most often the issues concern parenting practices. The worker should promote good parenting practices and also help the parties to reach an understanding and agreement regarding their respective roles.

CASE EXAMPLE

The following are examples of direct and indirect practice actions with a parent–child subsystem.

Sam is an African American social worker in an intensive program designed to divert delinquent youth from out-of-home placement. Most of the youth and their families on his caseload are also African American. However, recently he was assigned a white youth and his family. Sam picked Bill Stewart up at the youth home to take him home. He talked with Bill as they rode home. At first Bill seemed quite distant and guarded. Gradually, he warmed up and began telling Sam about his family. Bill lives with his mother and two sisters. His parents are divorced and his father lives out of state so he does not get to see him very much. The family lives in an area that is made up of poor and working-class white households and is known as an area that does not welcome African Americans. When Sam pulled up in front of the house, he could see several neighbors peering at them. Bill's mother had been quite friendly over the phone, but she seemed somewhat cold and distant on meeting him. She looked around outside as she let them into the house. Sam sensed that she was uncomfortable with the fact that he was African American. As they sat down at the kitchen table to talk about the program and about Bill, Sam asked about their ability to work with him. Mrs. Stewart admitted that they had not worked with "your kind" before and that she was concerned about what the neighbors might think about having an African American man coming to their home. Sam said that he could see what she was talking about when he got out of the car earlier. Mrs. S was from the South and had moved here with her husband when he got a job at a local factory. After they were divorced, he was laid off, but was able to transfer to another plant out of state. Bill had reacted negatively to the divorce and began getting into trouble at school and later in the community. He had been on probation for shoplifting and later for breaking and entering. The latest incident involved stealing a car. She said that she was at her wits end with him and was not sure if she could manage him at home. She had tried sending Bill to live with his father, but that only lasted a few months before he was kicked out of school and his father sent him back.

Mrs. S felt that Bill did not show her much respect and although they were poor she was doing the best she could under the circumstances. She started yelling at Bill for getting into trouble and he yelled back about her not being around and going out to the bar with other men. Sam intervened and asked if this was typical of their disagreements. They confirmed this. He noted that the argument seemed to deteriorate as each of them became more accusatory. He asked if they would be willing to try something that might help them to communicate better. Mrs. S said okay and Bill shrugged his shoulders and said "whatever." He asked them to try using the word "I" to start every sentence. He explained how "I" statements forced people to talk about themselves, but that "you" statements tended to be blaming and created defensiveness. They agreed to try and so for the rest of the session Sam had them practice this. He modeled how to correct each other when they forgot to use "I" and helped them to rephrase their communication. Sam proceeded to gather information for a social history.

As they were talking, Sam noticed that Bill was hanging his head. He asked Bill about what had been happening, and Bill admitted he had been in some trouble but that he was "just messin' around." Sam asked if Bill knew were he would be five to ten years from now if he kept "messing around." Bill said he would probably be in jail or prison. Sam asked if that was okay with him. Bill said no. Sam said that they would have some work to do if Bill was going to turn things around. For one thing, Bill was going to have to get serious about school and find some other way to have fun and get things he wanted. After covering information for a social history, Sam asked Mrs. S about whether she thought they could work together. She said that she liked the way he talked with Bill and that Sam "did not seem to be like other black folks" that she knew, so they could give it a try.

As Sam worked with Bill and his mother over time, he used most of his social work skills. He worked with them on strengthening their relationship by improving their communication. In working with Bill and his mother, Sam had used support, crisis intervention, and mediation. He showed them how to improve their problem solving and decision making along with conflict resolution. He worked with Mrs. S on different ways to respond to Bill and his behavior. Sam was able to get Mrs. S to attend a parenting skills course, which helped her to become even more effective. She began using more statements about her expectations of Bill and then giving him feedback on how he responded. She was also more careful about giving positive feedback, which she realized she did not do. Sam was able to get Bill back in school and Bill participated in social skills training and an employment preparation program through Sam's agency. Because Bill stayed out of trouble and progressed at school and in the program, the agency's employment program was able to place him in a job after school and on weekends. Mrs. S had admitted that she could use some help to quit smoking and later with her drinking. Sam got her and Bill into a smoking cessation program and Mrs. S started going to AA. Sam helped Mrs. S find a program to finish a GED and she was able to find work that paid more and had benefits. Sam also helped with getting the Friend of the Court to pressure Mr. S to make his child support payments on a more regular basis. Thus, the family was able improve their financial situation. In his work, Sam provided support and was able to empower and enable Bill and his mother. He gave them homework assignments to work on their relationship and for Mrs. S to improve her parenting. A change in environment would have taken place if Bill had been placed out of home, but this became unnecessary because he made good progress. As he provided services and made referrals, Sam assisted with coordinating the various services that the family received.

When it came time for Bill to graduate from the program, Mrs. S thanked Sam for all he had done. Mrs. S said that she had come close to asking for a new worker that first day, but she was glad she did not. Sam said that all he did was open a few doors for them, but they were the ones who had to do all the work.

SUMMARY

In addition to working with parent subsystems, a common form of generalist social work practice with families is working with parent–child subsystems. The version of good parenting practices presented in Chapter 11 is also used as a base for generalist practitioners working with parental–child subsystems. It is important for the worker to promote, support, and reinforce a positive relationship between parents and children. It is also important for parents to develop healthy relationships with each of their children, but they must do so without undermining their parental relationship.

Generalist practitioners may work with a parent–child subsystem as a dyad or they may work in triads or other combinations, depending on the need or concern and the situation at hand. Stepparent–stepchild relationships are especially challenging and have become much more common. Difficulties with stepparent–stepchild relationships is the most frequent reason for divorce in stepfamilies.

As children grow into adults and parents become older, changes occur in their parent–child relationship. There are also changes in the services provided by the generalist social worker. These changes revolve around the transition from parent–child to adult–adult relationships and the transition from parents meeting their children's needs to adult sons and daughters assisting parents who are older meet their needs.

QUESTIONS

1. Describe the parent–child relationship(s) that you observed and experienced growing up in your family of origin. Assess the strengths and challenges.
2. Describe any parent–child relationship(s) that you have experienced as an adult. Assess the strengths and challenges.
3. Using Table 12.1, Table 11.1, and Table 5.3, develop a social history for yourself, your family, or a parent–child subsystem that you know.
4. Describe some of the variations you might expect to find in parent–child relationships for members of diverse groups.
5. What are some needs or concerns that might arise in working with a lesbian couple regarding parent–child relationships? A gay couple regarding parent–child relationships? How would you go about working with these situations?

SUGGESTED READINGS

Johnson, Louise C., and Yanca, Stephen J. *Social Work Practice: A Generalist Approach,* 9th ed. Boston: Allyn & Bacon, 2007 (Chapters 8, 11, and 13).

Cox, Carole B. "Grandparents Raising Grandchildren from a Multicultural Perspective" in *Multicultural Perspectives in Working with Families,* 2nd ed. Elaine P. Congress and Manny Gonzalez, Eds. New York: Springer, 2005.

Gordon, Thomas. *Parent Effectiveness Training: The Proven Program for Raising Responsible Children.* New York: Three Rivers Press, 2000.

Hayslip, Bert, and Hicks-Patrick, Julie. *Custodial Grandparenting: Individual, Cultural, and Ethnic Diversity.* New York: Springer, 2006.

Klass, Carol Speekman, *The Home Visitor's Guidebook: Promoting Optimal Parent and Child Development.* Baltimore, MD: Paul H. Brookes, 2003.

Mattaini, Mark A. *Clinical Interventions with Families.* Washington, DC: NASW Press, 1999 (Chapters 7–9).

Webb, Nancy Boyd. *Culturally Diverse Parent–Child and Family Relationships: A Guide for Social Workers and Other Practitioners.* New York: Columbia University Press, 2001.

There are a number of good quality approaches and curricula for working with parents that are relevant for establishing positive parent–child or stepparent–stepchild relationships. American Guidance Service has a number of curricula for parenting approaches including the following (see www.agsglobe.com and click on "Parenting/Class Mgmt").

Dinkmeyer, Don Sr., McKay, Gary D., and Dinkmeyer, Don Jr. *The Parent's Handbook: Systematic Training for Effective Parenting.* Circle Pines, MN: American Guidance Service, 1997.

Dinkmeyer, Don C. *Parenting Young Children: Systematic Training for Effective Parenting (STEP) of Children under Six.* Circle Pines, MN: American Guidance Service, 1997.

Dinkmeyer, Don Sr., McKay, Gary D., and Dinkmeyer, Don Jr. *Parenting Teenagers: Systematic Training for Effective Parenting of Teens.* Circle Pines, MN: American Guidance Service, 1998.

CHAPTER

13

Generalist Practice with Siblings

LEARNING EXPECTATIONS

1. Understand the application of the generalist practice model to working with sibling subsystems.
2. Understand interaction and engagement with siblings.
3. Understand assessment as a process and a product with siblings.
4. Understand planning as a product and a process with siblings.
5. Understand direct and indirect actions with siblings.
6. Understand evaluation and termination with siblings.

This chapter examines working with sibling subsystems. Working with sibling subsystems is less common than working with other family subsystems. The more common types of work with this subsystem are working with intense sibling rivalry, helping stepsiblings adjust in blended families, and assisting adult sons and daughters making decisions for parents who are older.

Working with sibling subsystems overlaps with working with parents in that parents are often either indirectly or directly involved in what occurs among siblings. In cases of sibling rivalry, the relationship and favor of the parents are the targets of the rivalry. The influence of biological parents is important to resolving issues among stepsiblings. The focus of adult sons and daughters of parents who are elderly is on the well-being of the parent or parents. Thus, working with sibling subsystems frequently involves working with parent and/or parent–child subsystems. Of course as with other subsystems, the primary focus is on the relationship among siblings.

Before we begin, we would like to review how the assumptions that we made in Chapter 11 about good parenting practices affect working with siblings. The first assumption was that love and nurturing and support are essential ingredients for good parenting. Parents who are able to provide this will reduce the likelihood of more intense sibling rivalry. Parents and stepparents who are loving, nurturing, and supportive with each other, with their biological children, and with their stepchildren send the message that there is plenty of these to go around and that they expect similar actions and feelings from the children. Parents need to nurture and support the development of positive relationships among their children. Parents who were loving, nurturing, and supportive with their children are more likely to have this reciprocated when they have to rely on their adult sons and daughters for nurturing and support later in life.

The second assumption was that positive parenting is far superior to negative parenting. Positive parenting is parenting that expresses clear positive expectations for children and gives clear feedback about meeting expectations. When parents express positive expectations for sibling relationships and give clear feedback about meeting those expectations, sibling rivalry tends to be reduced and stepsibling relationships are more likely to be positive. Parents tend to reap what they have sown when adult sons and daughters are placed in the position of caring for them or making decisions for them.

The third assumption was that successful parents are consistent in their expectations and their feedback and discipline. Parents can influence sibling rivalry and stepsibling relationships by how they parent.

The fourth assumption was that the "reasonable" parent is the best parenting style. This includes clear and reasonable expectations of children based on their age and development. Reasonable parents use reasonable positive and negative consequences for positive and negative behaviors. Reasonable parents have a better chance of raising reasonable children.

This chapter considers the change process with sibling subsystems in the family. It includes working with siblings over the life span and when step-relationships exist. Generalist social workers do not frequently work with sibling subsystems. Probably the most frequent occurrences are with adult sons and daughters caring for and making decisions for parents who are elderly. As with any subsystem in the family, relationship skills are very important. This was covered in Part II and in earlier chapters of Part III and will not be repeated here. We will refer to these relationship skills throughout the chapter and will relate them to the development of successful sibling relationships. The change process with sibling subsystems uses the same phases that were outlined in earlier chapters. Interaction and engagement are the beginning of the process. It continues through assessment, planning, action, and evaluation and termination. The material in this chapter overlaps with earlier chapters. The effective family social worker develops knowledge and skills regarding each of the subsystems in the family along with those that are necessary for working with the family as a whole.

■ INTERACTION AND ENGAGEMENT ■
WITH SIBLING SUBSYSTEMS

As mentioned earlier, in generalist practice the worker might start out working with an individual, a family, or a subsystem before it is decided that working with the sibling subsystem is best. In many forms of family work, it is not unusual for one or more children to be the focus of attention first. Thus, sibling subsystems may be the initial focus of attention before it is decided that other subsystems need work. Table 10.1 gave an overview of some of the indications and counterindications for working with sibling subsystems and other family subsystems.

As with other subsystems, working with the sibling subsystem means the client is the sibling subsystem as a whole as well as each sibling in that system and the relationships between siblings. As with any multiclient system, the worker needs to take the role of mediator and must be given that role by the siblings. If she is seen as taking sides, she will not be able to serve the individual siblings or the sibling subsystem as a whole. In any circumstance, it is inappropriate and unethical for a social worker to sacrifice the needs of people. When the needs of individuals within a system are not met, the system is out of balance. This eventually leads to further difficulties. The worker should work with the sibling subsystem to meet both individual needs and the needs of the relationships so that a balance or equilibrium is established and maintained.

As with other subsystems and families, working with sibling subsystems may require skills that are beyond those of the generalist social worker. However, when the worker is the only real option, he does what he can to assist. With highly volatile relationships, the worker may work with each sibling separately while mediating an arrangement.

Besides working with families with intact marriages, social workers also work with blended and diverse families, including stepfamilies, adoptive families, foster families, and families of same-sex partners. Issues in these families generally revolve around love, acceptance, belonging, and attachment. Although these are typically focused on the relationship with parent figures, siblings can reinforce these or undermine them.

A challenge in establishing relationships with the sibling subsystems made up of children is the fact that the worker is an adult and the children are not. Similar feelings and behaviors may arise with the worker as those that are exhibited with parent figures. Although this can interfere with forming relationships, it also presents opportunities to demonstrate how to resolve those issues. In addition, the worker typically will coach the parents in reinforcing these changes.

Engagement and interaction with stepsibling subsystems can be especially challenging when working with blended families where members are from cultures that are different from each other. This calls for both cultural competence and skills at working cross-culturally. The diversity competent social worker gives the role of expert to family members. She observes her clients and mirrors their verbal and nonverbal approach. With children it is usually safe to begin by talking about school or their favorite activity or something that they enjoyed recently.

The diversity competent worker allows children to tell their own stories about themselves and their family. The worker encourages an open dialogue without preconceived notions about what is happening in the family. To do this, the worker needs to understand the effects of his own childhood on his attitudes toward parents and children. The worker also needs to understand the influence of the larger society on himself and on the families with whom he works.

■   ASSESSMENT WITH SIBLING SUBSYSTEMS   ■

As with families and other family subsystems, assessment with sibling subsystems includes process and product. The change process follows similar steps as those taken in assessment described in earlier chapters and will not be repeated here. The social history for sibling subsystems follows a similar format as the family social history presented in Table 5.3. Table 13.1 contains elements that should be added to the family history format as part II.F. In addition, the term "siblings" should be substituted for "family" for parts III and IV of Table 5.3.

Relevant portions of the individual social history should be added from Table 5.2. Making these changes will convert the family social history to one that is focused on the sibling subsystem.

This description of the assessment phase is the process that is used to set the stage for change. The product of the assessment is the social history. A schema for the social history of sibling subsystems is outlined in Table 13.1. It includes assessment of the structure, the functioning, and the development of this family subsystem.

As is the case with families and their other subsystems, the purpose of assessment with sibling subsystems is twofold. First, the social worker needs to understand the "sibling subsystem in situation." She needs to understand each sibling along with the overall family system and the situation in order to be able to help. She does not need a complete understanding, but she needs to understand enough to assist in meeting and resolving the situation. Second, assessment provides a foundation for change by identifying strengths and resources in the ecosystem. It spans past, present, and future. Assessing the past and present involves understanding of the sibling subsystem in situation. Assessing strengths and resources lays the groundwork for change in the future.

Assessment as a Process

As mentioned in earlier chapters, family work may begin with working with an individual, the whole family, or any family subsystem. The decision to work with the sibling subsystem may come at any time during the change process. Typically, it will come as a result of working with either parents or children. When the decision is made, the social worker generally begins by discussing the situation with the parents if the sibling system is made up of children. For adult siblings, usually one of the siblings has contact with the worker and serves as the initial source of information. The worker begins by gathering information about the presenting need or concern. Later, he establishes a relationship with the children or other adult siblings and gathers information about the presenting need or concern from their perspective. The presenting needs or concerns are generally similar to the indications for working with the sibling subsystem identified in Table 10.1. The needs and concerns are formulated similar to those identified in Chapter 10, only the focus is on the sibling relationship:

> The siblings in the Smith family need to strengthen their relationship.

If the need or concern relates to a family matter, the following format might be used:

> In order to help their blended family to grow together as a family, Joshua, Tiffany, and Cedric need to strengthen their relationships.

As with families and other subsystems, the nature of the need or concern is examined to identify areas that may be causing the need to arise. Assumptions are then made about what might resolve the situation. The worker and the parents and children or the adult siblings speculate about what is possible and what needs to be done. This may include focusing on their relationship, focusing on how they meet each other's needs, or how they interact with their ecosystem (including their family). Some examples of these are as follows:

> If Joshua, Tiffany, and Cedric can agree on a positive approach to their relationships, they will be able to improve them and help their blended family grow together as a family.

If Joshua, Tiffany, and Cedric improve their communication, problem solving, and conflict resolution, they will be able to improve their ability to get along with each other and work together.

If Joshua, Tiffany, and Cedric can establish effective communication and problem solving regarding their mother's needs, they will be able to agree on the care that she needs and her living arrangement

By identifying the nature of the needs and concerns in the sibling subsystem, the social worker has a better understanding of the situation providing structure for selecting and collecting information.

As the social worker gathers information about sibling subsystem in situation, she identifies potential strengths and resources in the subsystem and in their ecosystem. These are generally found in areas where the siblings have built successful relationships with each other or with other family members or with people outside of the family. Strengths include overcoming adversity or disagreement. Permanent change is based on a firm foundation. Abilities and capabilities in one area of life can potentially be used in other areas. Positive relationships in one area demonstrate a capacity for building positive relationships in other areas.

Selection and collection of information are based on information gathered in the first three stages of the assessment phase. The social worker limits the information collected to whatever is needed to bring about change. Additional information will be needed to meet bureaucratic requirements. The worker seeks to understand the need or concern and the situation. He gathers information about the assumptions that were made in the second stage and assesses their accuracy or feasibility. He explores potential strengths and resources to develop a plan to meet needs and address concerns.

Analysis of the information occurs independently and with the parents and the siblings or with the adult siblings, either separately or jointly. The worker analyzes information to understand the situation. As mentioned previously, the worker's analysis includes five general areas as the work proceeds: (1) what she understands about the sibling subsystem, the ecosystem, and strengths and resources, given what is known; (2) what changes are needed, given what is known; (3) what further information is needed to better understand the situation; (4) what further information is needed to bring about successful change; and (5) what are some potentially successful change strategies that can be used to meet the needs and address the concerns.

Assessment as a Product

The product of the assessment is the social history. The setting tends to dictate different structures and information required in the social history. Some settings may use an informal format rather than a formal document. Table 13.1 is a schema representing information required in a typical social history for the sibling subsystem. Various settings may require more information about certain areas, such as education, health, mental health, or substance abuse.

Demographic and background information is identified in the first two sections of the schema and is the same for the family social history as well as other subsystems. Parts I and II focus on the parents and the children as individuals. Part II also examines subsystems of the family with an emphasis on the sibling subsystem. It includes the structure, functioning,

Table 13.1   Supplementary Schema for Development of a Social History for Sibling Subsystems

I. Identifying Information (as needed by agency)
(This is the same as Table 5.3.I.)

II. (Part A, B, and C are the same as Table 5.3.II, Part D is the same as Table II.1.II.D, and Part E is the same as table 12.1.II.E.)
   F. The Sibling Subsystem—Structure and form of current relationship. Structure and form of other current and past sibling relationships for each sibling.
      1. Subsystems–describe the relationship and functioning of each sibling with other subsystems.
      2. Cohesiveness as a subsystem–describe the manner in which the siblings maintain their relationship system, boundaries, and relatedness. Include the issue of connectedness and separateness, rules and norms for their relationship, and emotional bond.
      3. Communication patterns and skills for the siblings individually, with each other, with other family members and with people outside of the family system.
      4. Decision-making and problem-solving patterns and skills for the siblings individually, with each other, with other family members and with people outside of the family system.
      5. Conflict resolution patterns and skills for the siblings individually, with each other, with other family members and with people outside of the family system.
      6. Role performance and satisfaction with each other and within and outside of the family system
      7. System member support: growth encouragement, care, and concern
      8. Identify commonalities and differences between the siblings. Identify expectations. Identify feedback mechanisms.
      9. Siblings customary adaptive and coping mechanisms with each other and within and outside of the family system
      10. Intimacy and closeness as siblings

III. The Concern or Need
(This is the same as Table 5.3.III with "siblings" replacing "family" as the focus)

IV. Strengths and Challenges for Meeting Needs
(This is the same as Table 5.3.IV with "siblings" replacing "family" as the focus)

and development of relationships. Understanding current and former experiences is important to understanding the current situation.

As we identified earlier, the more common issues that require focusing on sibling subsystems are sibling rivalry, stepsibling relationships, and adult sons and daughters making decisions for parents who are elderly. These issues can be affected both directly and indirectly by culture and diversity. They are further complicated when there are differences in culture and diversity within the family between parents, between stepparents and stepchildren, and among stepsiblings. This increases the need to use a diversity competent approach that includes naturalistic inquiry.

The social history for sibling subsystems is similar to that for other subsystems with some changes and additions. Understanding the parental and parent–child subsystems is important for understanding the context in which the sibling subsystem functions. It is also important for understanding the structure and development of the sibling subsystem, especially for blended families. We suggest that the reader review this material in Chapters 11 and 12.

The portion of the social history that is unique to the sibling subsystem has been added under II.F. When assessing the sibling subsystem, the worker considers the structure, form, functioning, and development of the current relationships as well as past sibling relationships. This yields a picture of successes and difficulties that each sibling has experienced. Successes are signals of potential strengths. Difficulties contribute to the current situation. If the sibling relationship has been positive in the past or if there are similar current or past relationships that are or were successful, it demonstrates a capacity to build such a relationship. The worker can identify what has made those relationships successful so these aspects can be used in the current relationship. A comprehensive examination should include thoughts, feelings, and actions for each member of the sibling subsystem.

Past difficulties with building positive sibling relationships may be related to the difficulties in the current relationship. Patterns from earlier relationships may be repeated. Various current and past relationships tend to shape expectations for other relationships. As people respond to their expectations, they can actually generate a self-fulfilling prophecy as we pointed out in the previous chapter.

The cohesiveness of sibling relationships refers to how relationships and boundaries are maintained. The worker should seek to find out how each sibling sees and experiences his or her relationships with other siblings. What interactions and activities occur? What are their expectations? What are the responses to expectations? What feelings do the siblings have for each other? How connected or separated do they feel? What are the rules and norms for their relationship? How attached or bonded are they?

As we have mentioned repeatedly, examination of the communication system is vital for working with any relationship. The worker assesses the skills and abilities of each sibling. Typically, adult siblings will have more advanced skills than younger siblings. However, adults can have limited communication skills or they may experience barriers to good communication in certain situations. For example, stepfamily relationships can be complex. Communication skills that are functional in other relationships may not be so in stepfamily relationships. However, the use of good communication skills in other relationships demonstrates the capacity to communicate and may be applied to sibling relationships.

Other vital areas when working with relationships are decision-making and problem solving-skills and abilities. Without these skills, communication will be affected by the tendency to withdraw from conflict. People tend to avoid talking about issues that may lead to conflict. The more these issues are avoided the more pent up and intense the feelings become leading to greater difficulty in expressing them. This reinforces the need to avoid these issues, setting the stage for further difficulty. Effective decision making and problem solving resolves these issues by reducing the potential for conflict. This allows for more communication about important needs and concerns. As with other skills and abilities, demonstrating these with other relationships shows a capacity to use them in sibling relationships.

Conflict resolution skills and abilities are the third set of relationship skills. Constructive resolution of conflict allows people to maintain positive relationships with open and honest communication. The basic elements of this have been covered earlier, including negotiation and compromise, using "I" statements, creating win–win situations, and avoiding violence and threats. The worker assesses how siblings deal with conflict with each other and with others. These three skill areas are important for children to learn as they grow into adults. These are especially critical in strained or tenuous relationships such as those within stepfamilies, or families with unmarried partners and unrelated children, and with adoptive or foster families.

Role performance and satisfaction refer to how each member of the sibling subsystem performs in their roles as brother, sister, stepbrother, or stepsister and how satisfied they are with their own performance and each other's. Age difference is an important factor here with different expectations for older versus younger siblings. Being oldest, middle, or youngest each carry with them differences in role expectations throughout the formative years. In some families these differences continue to be exhibited even into adult relationships with siblings. The worker should also explore other roles that each play within and outside of the family system. The ability to perform in other roles demonstrates good potential for developing satisfactory role performance in sibling relationships.

The worker assesses the support that siblings receive from each other, from other family members, and from their ecosystem. He looks for support that encourages growth and development. He assesses the degree to which siblings and parents show care and concern for each other.

Assessing commonalities and differences within the sibling subsystem lays some of the groundwork for change. Commonalities can be built on and differences can be bridged or respected. These areas are especially relevant for stepfamily relations and when working with adoptive and foster families. The worker identifies expectations of the siblings. What do they expect from each other? To what extent are these expectations similar to or different from each other? How are expectations communicated and what is the response? How and what kind of feedback is given and how is it typically received? What positive or negative consequences are there? These are some of the questions that the social worker explores to gain an understanding of the sibling subsystem.

Assessing coping mechanisms used by members of the sibling subsystem gives the worker a picture of what might work or not work for them in dealing with stress. The worker considers how siblings cope with stress in their relationship with each other and with stress from outside of the sibling subsystem. In most families, siblings band together to deal with difficulties. Younger siblings are protected and nurtured. However, in some families siblings act individually and it is each person for him- or herself. Younger siblings end up at the bottom of the pecking order and may even be exploited. The worker assesses how each sibling copes with stress within the sibling subsystem. She identifies how siblings cope with stresses within the family and with individuals and systems outside of the family system. Successful coping mechanisms help siblings deal with stress and avoid crises.

As with other forms of family work, assessing intimacy and closeness can be done verbally but may be more nonverbal in some respects. The worker asks about intimacy and closeness, but he also looks for ways in which affection and other signs of closeness are expressed. Some people assume that biological sibling relationships are naturally closer, but this is not always the case. Sibling rivalry can result in angry feelings or ambivalence about sibling relationships. Stepsibling relationships can generate similar feelings. The closeness among siblings can be a powerful force for positive change. On the other hand, lack of closeness can be a significant barrier. Closeness or the lack of it can be carried into adulthood and is particularly important when adult siblings are placed in the position of making decisions for parents who are elderly.

Part III of the social history focuses on the presenting need or concern and its relationship to the sibling subsystem. Whenever the social worker is working with the family or a family subsystem, she includes needs and concerns for individuals, subsystems, and the family as a whole. The pattern of needs in the family helps the worker to identify stresses and strains as well as strengths.

Part IV of the social history identifies strengths and challenges within the ecosystem, which includes the family, the sibling subsystem, and the environment. Parts III and IV are where the two purposes of the assessment are considered. Part III leads to an understanding of the sibling subsystem and its situation as these relate to the need or concern. Part IV identifies strengths and resources for meeting needs and challenges that might create barriers to meeting needs. Once an understanding is reached and strengths and resources are identified, planning for change can begin. As mentioned throughout the text, assessment continues throughout the change process. The worker increases his knowledge and understanding every time he meets with family members. As the work progresses, family members also learn about themselves as individuals and as members of the family system.

■   PLANNING WITH SIBLING SUBSYSTEMS   ■

Planning with siblings is similar to planning with other family subsystems with some important differences related primarily to age. Planning is also both a process and a product. Planning needs to take into consideration the ages of the siblings. Planning with adults or older adolescents is different from planning with children. When planning with younger siblings, the worker should consider their level of understanding and abilities. The wording of the plan needs to be understandable and the content should be age appropriate. In addition, parents will generally need to be involved in at least knowing about the plan and perhaps monitoring it or providing reinforcement. It is particularly important that the plan is consistent with parental expectations and child-rearing practices as well as incorporating cultural considerations.

In the planning process, the worker acts as facilitator, mediator, and negotiator. Examples of the process have been presented in Chapter 6 and will not be repeated here. The reader should review this material in developing an understanding of the planning process with each family subsystem. The plan itself should address the needs of each member of the sibling subsystem and should strengthen their relationships. It also addresses needs and concerns related to the ecosystem.

Planning with adult siblings often involves developing plans for the care of parents who are older. Some of this was discussed in previous chapters in Part III. Developing and carrying out plans in these situations requires good communication and an attitude of cooperation. Joint decision making and consensus are the preferred ways of accomplishing good planning in these situations. So the worker needs to facilitate this with the adult siblings. She should help them to build or strengthen this approach when it is missing or weak. The worker may need to mediate and negotiate when conflict exists about either the content of the plan or the process that is used to develop it.

The product of the planning process is the service plan. Various settings use different terminology to refer to the plan, but this is where goals and objectives are identified. In order to assist siblings in following through with their part of the plan, each member should have a written version. An example of a sibling plan is as follows:

Goal: Joshua, Tiffany, and Cedric will improve their relationship.
Objective 1: Joshua, Tiffany, and Cedric will use "I" statements with each other at least three times a day for three consecutive days by August 15.
Clients Task: Joshua, Tiffany, and Cedric will maintain journals of their "I" statements and bring their journals to sessions with the worker.
Worker Task: Worker will assist Joshua, Tiffany, and Cedric in monitoring and practicing "I" statements during joint sessions.
Objective 2: Joshua, Tiffany, and Cedric will use an effective problem-solving process with each other at least three times in one week by August 15.
Clients Task: Joshua, Tiffany, and Cedric will maintain journals of their problem solving with each other and bring their journals to sessions with the worker.
Worker Task: Worker will assist Joshua, Tiffany, and Cedric in monitoring and practicing problem solving during sessions with the worker.

■ DIRECT PRACTICE ACTIONS ■ WITH SIBLING SUBSYSTEMS

Direct practice actions with sibling subsystems are actions that are taken in working directly with siblings and their relationship. Indirect practice actions are taken on behalf of siblings. Direct practice includes the following categories: (1) engage in diversity competent actions with siblings, (2) enable development of relationship, (3) develop an understanding of sibling subsystems in environment, (4) plan with siblings, (5) enable siblings to know and use available resources, (6) empower or enable siblings to strengthen their relationship, (7) resolve crisis situations, (8) use support in working with siblings, (9) use activity with siblings, (10) mediate with siblings and between sibling subsystems and a system in their environment, and (11) use a clinical model of social work with siblings.

These actions are similar to those described for other forms of family work. There are areas that overlap with areas discussed earlier. The development of relationships was described in Chapter 4 and in earlier chapters in Part III as well as in this chapter. Development of understanding of person in environment as this relates to sibling subsystems was discussed under assessment. Planning was discussed in the previous section and in earlier chapters. Action taken in using a clinical model of social work with sibling subsystems is beyond the scope of this book and is typically covered in advanced graduate level social work courses.

Action Taken to Enable Siblings to Know and Use Community Resources

Actions that enable sibling subsystems to know and use available resources are similar to the description for families in Chapter 7 and for other subsystems in earlier chapters in Part III. As with parent–child subsystems, most of this work is done with the parents if the siblings are children, especially in providing basic needs and ensuring safety; receiving proper care; and having physical, social, psychological, emotional, economic, and educational needs met. In addition, there are community resources for children and teens that can play an important role in building character and providing guidance and healthy positive outlets for them. Generally, parents will need to provide the support for involvement in these activities. However, the worker can play a role in lowering resistance to accessing or using these resources.

The importance of community resources that provide opportunities for families to engage in positive activities was identified in Chapter 12. Not only do these provide opportunities for parents and children to enjoy each other but they can also be important in building strong successful sibling relationships.

To accomplish these actions, the worker needs to have knowledge about accessing resources. Families that are isolated or have weak social support systems are generally unaware of resources that are available or how to access them. The worker needs to be knowledgeable about formal and informal resources and creative about assisting families in using them.

Social workers generally acquire knowledge about resources as they provide services and accumulate personal experiences in the community. The worker is constantly looking for ways to improve his knowledge and skills, even when he is away from work. He observes other families enjoying activities and suggests ways for his families to enjoy similar activities. The social worker accumulates knowledge about the use of formal and informal resources from colleagues, resource manuals, the media, and other sources.

In working with adult siblings regarding their parents who are older, some families are able to identify and access resources that are needed. Sometimes one or two of the adult siblings will take responsibility for this or it is shared in different ways. For instance, one sibling might research various options for providing care at different levels while another does the financial planning to ensure that there are sufficient funds to pay for various options. Whenever possible, the worker should seek to develop and support this kind of teamwork.

Action Taken to Enable or Empower Siblings

Enabling and empowering siblings will assist them in using community resources and in developing and maintaining positive relationships. Empowering and enabling was covered in Chapter 7 and earlier chapters in Part III. Enabling and empowering activities are aimed at assisting siblings to be loving and positive in their relationships with each other. Enabling makes it possible for siblings to engage in actions and develop skills. Empowering increases their power to take action or use skills. Enabling assists siblings in developing skills necessary for successful relationships. Empowering increases confidence and strength in using those skills.

An important aspect of enabling siblings is the need for parents to model, support, and reinforce positive behaviors and relationship skills. With younger children, it is often essential for the worker to work primarily with the parents. Enabling and empowering parents helps them to develop their relationship skills and teach these to their children so that siblings can maintain good relationships with each other. This includes good communication, decision making and problem solving, and conflict resolution. Good parental modeling is very important for siblings in developing their skills and abilities. Although earlier modeling may not have been as positive, it is never too late to change to a more effective approach. There is no substitute for success. Relationships with teens can be turned around dramatically when parents are able to use good relationship skills. In turn, these skills can be used by siblings with each other. Generally speaking, sibling relationships are affected by other relationships in the family subsystem. They also have an effect on and are affected by peer relations outside the family.

For the most part, the social worker will work with siblings in joint sessions. Because parental expectations and actions have an effect on sibling relationships, it is typically necessary to also work with the parents on influencing more positive interactions among siblings. Sessions with parents may be separate but may also include siblings. It may also be necessary to meet individually with siblings, but the worker needs to be careful that these are balanced among them. In working with adult siblings, joint sessions are preferable but may not be practical. So, it is important for the worker to reach an understanding that the content of individual sessions should be shared with other siblings who are not present.

In terms of enabling and empowering children in sibling subsystems, the social worker should also model good communication and relationship skills, just as the parents do. She models good listening and encourages the use of "I" statements. The worker seeks to form an adult–child relationship similar to a partnership. She uses more simple communication with younger siblings that is appropriate for their level of development. When working with older teens, the worker uses a more adult–adult approach that recognizes their approaching independence. As with parent–child subsystems, the worker encourages some kind of recognition for the difference in status in adult–child relationships. In Chapter 12, we pointed out that some young clients might use the terms Mr., Mrs., or Miss along with the first name of the worker. So the child might use Miss Sue to refer to the worker. This is often culturally determined with some cultures dictating more formal forms of address between children and adults and other cultures allowing other forms. The worker should investigate these issues as she begins her work with families.

The primary goals in joint sessions should be to coach siblings or to mediate with them around building stronger, successful relationships. The worker enables and empowers them when he supports healthy, positive interactions that meet each other's needs. The greatest needs within the family and its subsystems are for love, acceptance, and affection. Receiving unconditional love and acceptance from one's family is probably the most enabling and empowering force people can experience. Expressions of love, acceptance, and affection may be blocked or not expressed. For stepfamilies and adoptive and foster families, love, acceptance, and affection needs to be developed, especially among step and nonbiological siblings. With abusive and neglectful families, the underlying causes of the abuse or neglect may need to be resolved and its effects overcome before siblings can build healthy relationships.

When working with younger siblings, the worker may use games or puppets or other forms of play to draw out their stories. As we pointed out earlier, children work out issues and concerns through play. The worker helps siblings to restory or replay successful outcomes of difficult situations and bring new solutions to the situation.

In working with adult siblings, the worker may work with them individually or jointly. The most efficient and effective approach is working jointly provided there is not an overwhelming amount of hostility. If there is, then individual work may be necessary either temporarily or, on occasion, throughout the process.

As with other forms of family work, the basic approach to enabling and empowering is the replacement of negative thoughts, feelings, and actions with positive ones. This is a cognitive–behavioral approach to change. It is assumed that positive sibling relationships are desirable for everyone, but in some families siblings may be unable to develop these on their own. There may be barriers created by a lack of knowledge or experiences, a history of negative experiences, cultural restrictions, and so on. The worker seeks to find ways of helping siblings replace negative thoughts, feelings, and actions with positive ones. He helps them examine how negative thoughts produce negative feelings, which produce negative actions. He helps siblings to identify how negative actions produce negative outcomes. He asks them how they would like to experience their relationships and identifies positive behaviors that each would like to experience. The worker identifies actions that might bring about those positive behaviors. He helps siblings to restructure thoughts and feelings that would be more likely to elicit that behavior.

Another related approach is to get siblings to predict positive responses from each other so that their thoughts, feelings, and actions are consistent with eliciting those responses. The worker explores how predicting a positive response affects thoughts and feelings. She helps them practice these new experiences by developing scenarios and coaches them in acting these out.

The worker can use an approach in which siblings or stepsiblings "act as if" they had a positive relationship, especially in terms of acting as if they love each other. Using this approach, each sibling describes actions that he or she and others might take as signs of love and positive feelings. The siblings agree to try to do these things at frequencies with which they feel comfortable. The worker coaches and has them practice these behaviors and then checks back with them on their experiences. The worker might also encourage parents to recognize and reinforce these efforts.

Typically, these approaches require some discussion and practice before they can be used outside of sessions with the worker. As the siblings gain some confidence in using these different approaches, the worker can structure scenarios outside of the sessions and then examine their experiences. Later, less structured activities can be used to determine whether more spontaneous behavior arises. Once siblings have at least one or more positive experiences, the worker discusses thoughts and feelings that were associated with those experiences and works with them on finding ways to increase and expand positive experiences and reinforce them.

In working with adult siblings, the worker may be successful in helping them to set aside their differences for the sake of their parent or parents. One way to do this is to have them compartmentalize their relationships with each other as siblings and their relationships as adult sons and daughters. In other words, the worker helps them to shift the focus from their current or past relationship with each other to their relationship with their parent or parents. Being an adult son or daughter is a different role from that of adult brother or sister. Some people are capable of doing this, but others may not be.

Action Taken in Crisis Situations

As with other crisis situations in the family, the social worker works with siblings to use their coping skills and develop new ones as needed. Crises with the sibling subsystem most often are generated by emergencies related to the family. Actions are focused on using the relationship to face serious adversity. Occasionally, a crisis may occur within the sibling relationship that requires restoring and strengthening it. This is more likely to occur with adult sibling relationships or relationships among adolescent siblings. A crisis can be generated by a serious threat to the marital relationship. Strained marital relations may lead children to take sides or be included in the stressful interactions. This can lead to great stress in sibling relationships, especially in stepfamilies. In stepfamilies, stresses between stepsiblings can produce a serious threat to the marital relationship if the marital pair is not able to solidify their relationship and deal effectively with the children. With adult siblings the crises are typically around medical emergencies and the need for changes in elder care for their parent or parents. The basic approach to crisis intervention in families was presented in Chapter 7. Working on crises in families or other subsystems was discussed in respective previous chapters.

The social worker works from a mediating position to assist in restoring coping mechanisms and in reaching a resolution to the crisis. With younger siblings it is typically critical to involve parents in this work. With adult siblings, the worker provides support and assists them in mobilizing themselves to deal with the situation at hand. The worker introduces changes that will result in improving relationships and strengthening them so siblings are better prepared to handle crises in the future. She may also connect the family with services or resources that will ameliorate the current situation or future crises.

As we mentioned earlier, various family emergencies may arise such as medical emergencies, accidents, life-threatening situations, health problems, extended absences, substance abuse, disability, unemployment, financial hardship, homelessness, incarceration, and so on. Although these situations can be overwhelming for families, they can also increase bonding and attachment, depending on how the situation is handled. If the family can pull together during the crisis, then their relationship will be strengthened by facing adversity together. Sometimes the sibling group is the greatest source of support in the face of these crises. Siblings can come to rely on each other as they face a common challenge together. If the family fails to pull together or it pulls apart, then family relationships may become more difficult. The social worker needs to assist family members to establish positive coping mechanisms in the face of these crises.

The social worker assesses the crisis and the coping skills of the siblings. He facilitates strengthening these skills or adding new ones. He works with them to resolve the situation and restore a healthy balance or equilibrium. He encourages support from the family's support network along with support systems for family members. The worker accesses appropriate resources from the human service delivery system in the community.

Action Taken to Use Support in Working with Siblings

The use of support in working with parents was discussed in Chapter 7 and earlier chapters in Part III. The need for support during crises was discussed previously. Now let us focus on building support within and for sibling relationships. It is important for siblings to feel that they are supported by each other and by their parents along with experiencing support from outside of the family, especially from peers and the school. Support from adult siblings can be vital later in life, particularly as siblings face making decisions and carrying them out for parents who are elderly. Sometimes siblings come to rely on each other in old age and some may even choose to live together or become caregivers or guardians.

As we pointed out in Chapter 12, children need to have the support of their parents to grow and develop socially, emotionally, and psychologically. Parental support builds self-confidence, self-esteem, and self-assurance. The social worker encourages positive feedback and expressions of support from parents. This is fundamental to positive self-worth and confidence. Siblings who feel good about themselves are in a stronger position in terms of building positive relationships with their siblings and stepsiblings. The worker models support and then coaches the parents and children in saying and doing things that are supportive. Samples of this were presented in Chapter 12. She encourages support and coaches the parents and siblings in giving, requesting, and receiving support.

Action Taken That Uses Activity with Siblings

Just as with families and family subsystems, activities can be effective in working with siblings. This is important in helping them to transfer changes to everyday life. The worker uses "homework assignments" to have them practice skills and implement changes. He structures these assignments during the session and coaches siblings as they practice until they feel comfortable enough to try them on their own. Activities can be formal or informal. Formal activities are structured to provide certain experiences that promote certain outcomes. Informal activities are less structured and are designed to provide an opportunity for positive interactions.

The social worker uses the same phases as the change process when using activities, reinforcing learning to use the change process. The worker helps the siblings identify desirable activities and coaches them in planning for the activity. She provides information and referrals and helps to access resources and remove barriers. She has them identify what each member would like to experience and then helps them to evaluate positive and negative aspects.

As with any ongoing relationship, siblings need to develop and practice good relationship skills, such as communication, problem solving and decision making, and conflict resolution. The social worker teaches these skills and has siblings practice them during and between sessions.

Action Taken to Mediate with Siblings and with Their Environment

As with other types of family work, actions taken to mediate can be used directly with siblings and are also used as indirect practice actions. Mediation is an essential approach when working with any multiclient system or subsystem. In mediation, the worker is neutral and facilitates effective and constructive interactions among members of the system or subsystem. If the worker can maintain a neutral position, he can avoid taking sides in disagreements. Taking sides tends to generate more intense conflict and leads to difficulty in working with those who are on the other side. Neutrality allows the worker to focus on the needs of the relationship. The worker needs to establish a mediating position from the beginning of his work and should remind the siblings of this throughout the work.

In earlier chapters, we presented an approach in which family members visualize their relationship as a triangle made up of "you," "I," and "we." Each person takes responsibility for his or her own needs and the worker assumes responsibility for considering the needs of the relationship. The worker takes the position, What will it take to make this relationship work? She continuously asks this question in various forms along with ancillary questions that are similar to those identified in the previous chapter such as, How will this help to strengthen your relationship? What could you do to improve your relationship in this situation? What outcome would strengthen your relationship? What do you need out of this relationship that would meet your needs? What do you need from your brother/sister that would help you to strengthen your relationship? Would you be willing to . . . in order to make this relationship stronger or better? For adult siblings, deciding about concerns regarding their parents who are older, the worker might ask, What does your mother/father need from the two (or more) of you right now? Will you do it?

The worker facilitates good communication by having the siblings talk with each other about their needs and about their relationship. With adult siblings, he helps them identify the needs of the parents who are older. He helps siblings to negotiate agreements and supports them in strengthening their relationships.

■ INDIRECT PRACTICE ACTIONS WITH SIBLINGS ■

Indirect practice actions with sibling subsystems are similar to those that were described earlier with families and other subsystems, especially parent–child subsystems. Indirect practice includes actions that (1) involve the use of influence, (2) are designed to change the environment, and (3) are relative to coordination of services. These actions tend to be used more frequently by parents on behalf of siblings.

Action That Involves the Use of Influence

Influence is an important aspect in working with all client systems. The social worker tends to have more influence with sibling subsystems that are made up of children because of her status as an adult. Regardless of the situation, some influence is unavoidable and should be used in a positive way to improve the situation. The ethical worker takes steps to ensure that her clients are free to participate in decision making at a level appropriate to their age.

As with any client system, the worker is free to use influence on behalf of his clients. This includes developing and securing resources to support positive outcomes. He advocates on behalf of families within his agency, with other organizations, and with the community. He supports and empowers families in influencing their environment. The worker uses contacts with influential people in the community to support resources for parents, children, and families.

Action Designed to Change the Environment

Actions designed to change the environment refers to assisting families in changing their current environment or moving to a new one if necessary. Environmental change is often a key ingredient in reducing sibling rivalry and creating a positive atmosphere for dealing with difficult situations such as building a positive stepfamily system. Most often the change is brought about by the parents. For stepfamilies, at least one set of stepsiblings may either have to move to the other stepsiblings' home or they visit on a regular basis. This creates environmental changes for both sets of stepsiblings.

Environmental change is frequently the central issue in working with adult siblings making decisions for parents who are elderly. When parents cannot care for themselves, their sons and daughters may be faced with assisting them in changing the environment to ensure that their needs are met. If one parent is mentally sound, then he or she will generally make these decisions. However, if the parent or parents are mentally incapacitated, then the decisions about environmental change falls on the siblings. Depending on the circumstances and the availability of resources, the range of options can be anywhere from home-based care or care in the home of a son or daughter to nursing home care. Retirement communities, adult foster homes, assisted living facilities, and adult day activity programs are included in this range of options. In working with adult siblings, the worker may need to assist them in locating and accessing resources and in making decisions about the proper care.

In cases of neglect or abuse, the generalist social worker may function as a protective services worker who investigates and substantiates the allegations. Generalists also serve as foster care workers, licensing and supervising foster homes, working with foster children in the homes, and working with parents to achieve a level of functioning that would allow for the safe return of their children.

Generalist social workers can also be found working with delinquents. In working with delinquents, the worker may facilitate placement outside of the home in foster care, group homes, or residential settings when necessary. In other instances, the worker might assist families with children who are exposed to drugs and crime because of their neighborhood. He may need to help the family move to a safer environment with fewer negative influences. The family may need financial assistance for deposits and utilities or access to other resources in order to accomplish this.

Action Relative to Coordination of Services

As mentioned earlier, sometimes the social worker acts to coordinate services on behalf of parents and children. It is best if the parents can manage this on their own. But if they are overwhelmed or unable to do so, the worker acts on their behalf. The situation may be a temporary or chronic. Services range from providing information and referral to full case management. The worker makes referrals and follows up to ensure that services are received. The referral process was discussed in Chapter 7. In crisis situations, the worker is more involved and either mobilizes resources in the ecosystem to take over managing services or provides this herself.

As mentioned previously and in Chapter 12, adult sons and daughters may be need assistance with coordinating services for aging parents. The worker provides information about resources and works on developing a system for maintaining their parents' well-being. If the siblings are unable or unwilling to participate in coordinating services or if the needs are too complex, the worker either provides this if it is an appropriate function within her agency's service delivery system or she refers the siblings and parents to such an agency.

As we have already mentioned, generalist practice social workers may temporarily coordinate services or this may be part of his regular duties with his organization. Agencies that typically provide case management include mental health, health care, and aging services. This may include either temporary or long-term case management.

■   EVALUATION AND TERMINATION WITH SIBLINGS   ■

Evaluation and termination with siblings follow similar patterns to those which were described for families in Chapter 9 and for other subsystems in Part III. Evaluation occurs throughout the change process and is also used to determine the outcome and completion of the work leading to termination. As we pointed out in the previous chapter, evaluation needs to be geared to the age and developmental level of the client. When working with younger siblings, the worker uses language that is age appropriate. The information is not reliable and the evaluation is not valid if the child does not understand the language or concepts that are used.

Throughout the change process, the worker evaluates the validity and reliability of the information she receives. When she works with siblings, triangulation of the data is built into the process because there is more than one source of information. In addition, when working with siblings, parents will frequently provide another source of information. Agreement between more than one source indicates greater accuracy of the information. Disagreement indicates a need to gather more information to understand and clear up the discrepancy. A disagreement or discrepancy may simply indicate differences in perceptions. Sometimes these differences may disappear over time or are cleared up as new information arises. As we pointed out, differences in perception generally reflect various aspects of the actual situation. The worker can usually assume that the actual situation is somewhere between the descriptions that are presented.

If there is a reason to believe that any of the siblings have more to gain or lose by presenting a certain position, then the worker might assume that his or her perceptions are probably skewed in that direction. This should not be labeled as "lying" or "not telling the truth" because it is natural for humans to perceive the world through the lens of self-interest. People are generally guarded about what they say until trust and safety is assured. However, there may be some issues that are too painful to discuss.

Evaluation is an important aspect of every plan, measuring progress and determining whether goals and objectives have been met. The worker and siblings evaluate progress and determine what works and what does not. Good progress is an indication that the plan is working. Negative results or poor progress are indications of a barrier or the need to either change the plan or develop a new one.

When goals are completed, the worker and siblings evaluate whether needs have been met and if the work needs to continue. When the work has been completed, then they can proceed to termination. During termination, the worker solicits feedback about the effectiveness of his services. He asks for feedback about what was helpful, what was not, and what would have been helpful. This helps him improve his skills. The siblings should also evaluate themselves and their new skills and abilities.

As mentioned earlier, various forms of unplanned terminations often take place. Clients who drop out of service should be contacted to ensure that their needs have been met. If appropriate, they should be offered a referral for services elsewhere or it should be made clear that they are free to return. When termination is initiated by the worker or the agency, the worker should try to ensure a smooth transfer to another worker or agency. It is best if at least one joint session can be arranged with the new worker. If this is not possible, the worker prepares the siblings to receive services from a different worker by reinforcing the fact that they are the ones responsible for the changes that have occurred. She assures them that if they can work with her, they can work with another worker in using the change process.

The following are examples of direct and indirect practice actions with siblings.

Sara is a social worker at an agency that provides services to people who are older. She makes home visits to clients and monitors their needs. Recently, one of her clients, Mrs. Smith, had a fire at her senior high-rise apartment because she left food on a lit stove burner. Although the fire was not serious, it was a signal that something might need to be done to ensure the safety of her client. Mrs. S, a widow, had been showing signs of dementia and now it seemed that she might need to be in a setting where there was more supervision. Sara had been working with Mrs. S and her family for the past year. Sara visited Mrs. S in the hospital where she was recovering from smoke inhalation. She met with the doctor and the hospital social worker who confirmed what Sara was thinking in terms of Mrs. S needing to be in a supervised setting. Sara contacted Mrs. S's family to discuss their mother's situation. Mrs. S has two adult daughters and a son. Carol is the oldest and she lives quite far away in another state. She is married with two children and works as an executive for a major corporation. Mary is also married and has two children. She lives in the area and has been very active in assisting her mother. She works but has been able to take time off most of the time when her mother needed to be taken to an appointment. Joe is the youngest and also lives in the area. He is divorced and lives alone. Joe works at a factory and gets out of work at 3:00 P.M. He has not been involved in assisting his mother very much. On occasion, when Mary was unable to take her mother to an appointment, she would ask Joe and he would grudgingly agree to do it, but it has been difficult to get him to do things voluntarily.

Carol came to town to visit her mother and Sara was able to meet with the three siblings. They had already been told by the doctor and the hospital social worker that their mother was going to need to move to a safer environment. Sara met with them to discuss their options. They had already started the process of discussing what to do, but they were in a quandary. When their meeting began, Mary was crying, Carol was looking out the window, and Joe was sitting in a chair looking down at the floor. Sara introduced herself to Carol whom she had not met. Sara asked Carol how she was doing and Carol said not so well because they had just had an argument about what to do for their mother. Sara asked them to sit down and talk about the situation. There was silence at first, but gradually Sara got them to talk. She took a mediating position and did not take sides. She also used her skills with crisis intervention and, after providing understanding and support for each person, she began to discuss their options for resolving the situation.

Although both Carol and Mary expressed a desire to have their mother live with them, it did not appear that this would be a viable option for either of them. Prior to moving into the senior apartment, Mrs. S had told Carol that she did not want to move away to a large city so far from where she lived and that she did not want to be a burden to any of them. So moving in with Carol would be going against their mother's wishes although Carol's company has elder care available through an adult day activity center nearby. Mary and her husband both work and it would be a major financial hardship for her to quit to care for her mother. In addition, their home is quite small and it would be difficult to accommodate Mrs. S. Joe also needed to work and his mother would be left alone while he was gone unless they had some sort of caregiving arrangement. It was obvious that Joe did not want to take on this responsibility. Sara presented the family with potential options. Mainly these consisted of arranging care in one of their homes with some combination of home care and care at a local adult day activity program, adult foster care, an assisted living facility, or a nursing home. The Smith family was totally against the nursing home option. Mary was also against adult foster care because she had talked with other families at a support group and they had found that supervision was not as secure as assisted living. Although home care might be an option, Joe was the only one who had room for this and it did not appear that this was a viable long-term option. So it looked like assisted living was the best plan if Mrs. S could not live with one of them. Mary had already been able to have her mother give her power of attorney so she could conduct her business for her. Carol had used her skills to ensure that her mother had the financial security to afford this option. Sara said she would contact the local facilities to determine which ones might have an opening.

Sara found that none of the facilities had an immediate opening but one was expecting to have one in about a month. She had the siblings visit the facility and they were pleased with it. Sara helped them discuss this move with their mother, and she seemed compliant with it although she wanted to be sure that she could still see several of her close friends and could still attend her church on Sundays. Carol had to return to her job so Sara worked with Joe and Mary on a temporary living arrangement and on the admissions process while they awaited the opening. Mary moved her two children into one bedroom and had her mother stay with her. They arranged for a combination of time at the adult day activity program and an in-home respite caregiver so that Mary could still work. Joe agreed to pick his mother up from the adult day program after work and have her stay with him until Mary got off from work. When the opening occurred and Mrs. S moved in, Sara assisted the family in making the move. Carol came back to town to be there as well. They thanked her for all of her help with their mother. Sara congratulated them on working together so well and they said that they felt good about the process and how things turned out. They indicated that although their relationships had been strained at times in the past, they were glad that they were able to come together and work this out for the sake of their mother.

During this process, Sara was able to use most of her social work skills. She enabled the siblings to use community resources. She used crisis intervention and support. She helped them strengthen their relationships. She used mediation in helping them settle their disagreements and had mediated with the day activity program when there was a problem with Mrs. S wanting to leave several times during the day. The move to the assisted living facility was an action designed to change the environment. Sara assisted with coordinating the activities needed to have Mrs. S admitted to the facility and she assisted in arranging and coordinating services needed to provide care beforehand.

SUMMARY

This chapter examined working with sibling subsystems. This type of family work is less common than working with parent or parent–child subsystems. The more common types of work with the sibling subsystem are working with intense sibling rivalry, helping stepsiblings adjust in blended families, and assisting adult sons and daughters making decisions for parents who are older.

The effects of good or poor parenting practices on the sibling subsystem are an important consideration in generalist practice with siblings. Generally, the worker assists siblings with improving their relationships by working on effective communication, decision making and problem solving, and conflict resolution.

Adult sons and daughters are typically thrust into the role of decision makers when parents are not able to make decisions for themselves or are not able to carry them out. Some families find this very difficult to do. Generalist social workers working in hospitals and nursing homes, and providing services to people who are older are often called on to provide assistance in these matters.

QUESTIONS

1. Describe the sibling or stepsibling relationship(s) that you observed or experienced growing up in your family of origin. Assess the strengths and challenges.
2. Describe any adult sibling relationship(s) that you have observed or experienced as an adult. Assess the strengths and challenges.
3. Using Table 13.1 and relevant portions of Tables 5.3, 11.1, and 12.1, develop a social history for yourself and your siblings or a sibling subsystem that you know.
4. Describe some of the variations you might expect to find in sibling relationships for members of diverse groups.

SUGGESTED READINGS

Johnson, Louise C., and Yanca, Stephen J. *Social Work Practice: A Generalist Approach,* 9th ed. Boston: Allyn & Bacon, 2007 (Chapters 8, 11, and 13).

Brazelton, T. Berry, and Sparrow, Joshua D. *Understanding Sibling Rivalry: The Brazelton Way.* Cambridge, MA: Da Capo Press, 2005.

Ingersoll-Dayton, Berit, Neal, Margaret B., and Ha, Jung-hwa. "Collaboration among Siblings Providing Care for Older Parents," *Gerontological Social Work* 40, 3 (2003), pp. 51–66.

Lang, Frieder R., and Fingerman, Karen L. *Growing Together: Personal Relationships across the Lifespan.* New York: Cambridge University Press, 2004.

Levitt, JoAnn, Levitt, Marjory, and Levitt, Joel. *Sibling Revelry: Eight Steps to Successful Adult Sibling Relationships.* New York: Dell, 2001.

Safer, Jeanne. *The Normal One: Life with a Difficult or Damaged Sibling.* New York: Free Press, 2002.

Sanders, Robert, and Campling, Jo. *Sibling Relationships: Theory and Issues for Practice.* New York: Palgrave Macmillan, 2004.

Sonna, Linda, *The Everything Parent's Guide to Raising Siblings: Eliminate Rivalry, Avoid Favoritism, and Keep the Peace.* Avon, MA: Adams Media, 2006.

Good Practices with Families with Special Challenges

■ A MODEL FOR GOOD PRACTICES IN GENERALIST ■ SOCIAL WORK PRACTICE

There is a need to incorporate knowledge gained from research and from practice into working with families. The approach presented here recognizes both of these needs. We are calling it good practice methods for generalist practice. **Good practice** is broadly defined as accepted practice in the field or setting or with a population that is based on empirically based practice, practice experience, and the empowerment of clients. So, in addition to acquiring knowledge and skills through empirical means, the social worker uses her practice wisdom. Good practice also incorporates social work values into each intervention, in terms of both process and content. Good practice uses the skills of the worker in service to the family. Our model for good practice is as follows:

1. The worker takes responsibility for developing the knowledge, values, and skills needed to serve her families.
2. The worker shares her knowledge and skills with her families as they proceed through the change process.
3. Together the worker and the family decide what will be used in facilitating the change process.
4. The worker and the family evaluate the outcome and make decisions accordingly.

These steps are applied throughout the change process as the worker and the family develop an assessment and a plan, then take actions to carry out the plan.

This appendix describes good practice methods typically used by generalist social workers with families experiencing special challenges. The good practice methods provide suggestions for practice in various settings that typically use generalist social workers to provide services.

Case Management

Case management is one of the most common forms of practice for generalist social workers. It can be used with any client or family experiencing the challenges discussed here and with those who are in need of multiple services, including many families experiencing poverty. For these families, accessing and using resources are critical to survival and to improving their quality of life.

Source

Case management seems to have grown out of the roots of social work practice, in particular what was called casework. The traditional form of casework is derived from the Charity Organization Societies, which sought to alleviate poverty and other social ills by working with individuals and families. The settlement house movement offered a different approach, which focused on environmental change through social action and advocacy. Modern case management developed during the 1960s to 1980s, when deinstitutionalization of the mentally ill and developmentally disabled necessitated the coordination of community services for those who were vulnerable. A major contributor to the formalization of this approach is Jack Rothman.

Underlying Assumptions

The purpose of case management is to ensure that people receive services that they need. The growing complexity of human services makes it difficult for most client populations to negotiate the system. Vulnerable populations find it impossible without assistance. Vulnerable populations can live and have their quality of life enhanced when they receive the services they need within the community. Without this coordination, these populations are more likely to use more costly services such as hospitals and residential care.

Practice Theory

Several models have evolved, but all of them include various forms of assessment, planning, and coordination of services. Case finding, intake, and referral are included in most models as is reassessment. Brokering, mediation, and advocacy are used to access necessary services with the latter two coming into play when barriers are experienced.

Practice Usage

Case management is used with any client or family, but reimbursement tends to be limited to more intensive services to vulnerable populations. These include people who are mentally ill, developmentally disabled, mentally retarded, elderly, medically fragile, children, child welfare clients, and so on.

Suggested Resources

Orloff Kaplan, Karen, "Recent Trends in Case Management," in *Encyclopedia of Social Work*, 18th ed. (Supplement), Leon Ginsberg, Ed. (Silver Springs, MD: NASW Press, 1990), pp. 60–77.

Roberts, A. L., and Greene, G. J., Eds. *Social Worker's Desk Reference* (New York: Oxford University Press, 2002). See Jack Rothman, "An Overview of Case Management"; Joseph Walsh, "Clinical Case Management"; Jannah H. Mather and Grafton H. Hull, Jr., "Case Management and Child Welfare"; David P. Moxley, "Case Management and Psychosocial Rehabilitation with SMD Clients"; Charles A. Rapp, "A Strengths Approach to Case Management with Clients with

Severe Mental Disabilities"; W. Patrick Sullivan, "Case Management with Substance Abusing Clients"; Candyce S. Berger "Social Work Case Management in Medical Settings"; Carol D. Austin and Robert W. McClelland, "Case Management with Older Adults"; and Brian Giddens, Lana S. Ka'opua, and Evelyn P. Tomaszewski, "HIV/AIDS Case Management."

Rothman, Jack. *Guidelines for Case Management: Putting Research to Professional Use* (Itasca, IL: F. E. Peacock, 1992), and *Case Management: Integrating Individual and Community Practice* (Boston: Allyn & Bacon, 1998).

■ GOOD PRACTICES WITH FAMILIES WITH MEMBERS ■ WHO ABUSE SUBSTANCES

Substance abuse has a devastating effect on families. It interferes with role performance and has a negative effect on relationships. When parents abuse substances, it takes away from their ability to engage in good parenting practices and to provide for the family. People who are abusing substances tend to make poor decisions because their thinking and their judgment is impaired. The cost of purchasing drugs or alcohol takes away resources from the family. The effects of these substances can impair the ability to maintain employment.

Although alcohol is clearly the most frequently abused substance, cocaine, crack, and methamphetamine have become the scourge of many families and communities. Addiction to these substances often leads to serious crimes and prostitution. Stealing and dealing are common problems associated with addiction. Families can become prisoners in their own households when members become addicted. Nothing is safe. Families may be forced to evict members who are addicted in order to preserve their assets and belongings as well as their sanity. Of course, this is painful for both the family and the person who is addicted to one or more substances.

Description of Practice Areas

The practice areas in chemical dependence include prevention, outpatient treatment, and inpatient or residential treatment. In many settings, there also tends to be some separation between services aimed at alcohol dependence and those that are targeted at dependence on other drugs. However, services tend to be similar under each.

Good practice with chemical dependence is founded on various combinations of professional treatment and the twelve-step system provided by Alcoholics Anonymous and various offshoots if it. Some programs offer only one or the other, but most offer a combination.

An important aspect of good practice in this area is the acceptance that recovery from chemical dependence is a lifelong process. Relapse is prevalent and can occur at any time, even after many years of abstinence and recovery. This may be difficult for some professionals to accept. It is also difficult for families to deal with it. The idea of "cure" is so ingrained in U.S. medicine that maintenance is generally not valued as much.

Client and Family Needs

The most obvious need in U.S. society is to curb the use of chemicals that alter the mind. These come in the form of both legal and illegal products that permeate U.S. culture. Alcohol, nicotine, and caffeine are legal drugs that are consumed by the majority of U.S. citizens daily. Pharmaceutical companies market various chemical products on television and radio. The use of marijuana, cocaine, and methamphetamine has been categorized as epidemic. Although the use of these illicit drugs are clearly a major social and health problem in the United States, the use of legal drugs is by far the most pervasive problem. Hundreds of thousands of people die each year from conditions caused by the use of tobacco and alcohol. Thousands more die in accidents caused by alcohol. The vast majority of people in jail or prison were either drunk or high when they committed their crimes or they committed their crimes to get drunk or high. Incarceration has become the favored method of "treatment" for chemical dependence in the United States.

Families with members who are chemically dependent need support and assistance in coping with and overcoming the effects of this challenge. They need to understand the difficulties associated with these problems and what they can do to assist the family member to recover and maintain their recovery.

Services to Clients and Families

Good practice in chemical dependence generally includes active prevention programs along with the use of a full spectrum of services. Prevention needs to be aimed at children and adolescents as well as adults. It should be in the schools, in the media, and throughout the community and it must be ongoing. The most common forms of prevention tend to be those that provide information about the physical, mental, and environmental consequences of chemical dependence. Some programs offer ways to resist the pressure to use drugs and alcohol.

Good practice in treating chemical dependence should include the availability of both outpatient and inpatient or residential services along with supportive services for the family. It should include a combination of professional counseling and therapy and variations of the twelve-step program. It should offer both individual and group formats and be available to voluntary and involuntary clients. It should support abstinence while also focusing on eliminating overt and covert mechanisms that support continuing use and building skills and support systems for recovery. These include physical, mental, and environmental factors.

Good practices should also include the family in the process of recovering and maintaining recovery. Programs such as Al-Anon and Alateen for family and friends of alcoholics are invaluable in helping families to understand and cope with the challenges of chemical dependency. They also help families to learn how to work with family members to support their recovery.

Suggested Resources

There are many Websites devoted to this subject. Those that seem most relevant for good practice are Alcoholics Anonymous (alcoholics-anonymous.org), Narcotics Anonymous (na.org), Al-Anon and Alateen (al-anon.alateen.org) for family and friends of alcoholics, the Substance Abuse and Mental Health Administration (samhsa.gov and ncadi.samhsa.gov), the U.S. National Library of Medicine and the National Institutes of Health (nlm.nih.gov/medlineplus/substanceabuseproblems), the National Institute on Alcohol Abuse and Alcoholism (niaaa.nih.gov), the National Council on Alcoholism and Drug Dependence (ncadd.org), and the Partnership for a Drug-Free America (drugfree.org). Recent publications include the following:

Craig, R. J. *Counseling the Alcohol and Drug Dependent Client: A Practical Approach* (Boston: Allyn & Bacon, 2004).

Fisher, G. L., and Harrison, T. C. *Substance Abuse: Information for School Counselors, Social Workers, Therapists, and Counselors*, 3rd ed. (Boston: Allyn & Bacon, 2005).

Johnson, J. *Fundamentals of Substance Abuse Practice* (Pacific Grove, CA: Brooks/Cole, 2004).

Lewis, J. A. *Substance Abuse Counseling*, 3rd ed. (Pacific Grove, CA: Brooks/Cole, 2002).

McNeece, C. A., and DiNitto, D. M. *Chemical Dependency: A Systems Approach*, 3rd ed. (Boston: Allyn & Bacon, 2005).

■ GOOD PRACTICES WITH FAMILIES EXPERIENCING VIOLENCE ■

When families experience family violence of any kind, it tends to break down the very essence of what families need to be—safe, nurturing environments that support the growth and development of their members. Violence destroys the sense of safety and is definitely counter to nurturing. This entry will concentrate on domestic violence services.

Description of Practice Areas

Good practice for generalist social workers in domestic violence services includes prevention, dissemination of information, and services to victims and perpetrators. Prevention can include early intervention with children to prevent family violence; policy changes that promote intervention by the police, prosecution, and courts; and similar initiatives. Dissemination of information is essential because victims are often isolated and controlled by their perpetrators. Publicizing facts about domestic violence, raising awareness, and informing victims about accessing services are critical in reaching victims. Services to victims should include outpatient and residential components along with support for legal matters. Services to perpetrators include treatment to reduce the risk of further violence.

Client and Family Needs

Although victims of domestic violence can be either male or female, the overwhelming majority of victims served by domestic violence programs are women. In addition to physical abuse, victims are typically abused emotionally and psychologically as well. They may be threatened with death if they attempt to leave. Some may even be killed. Victims of domestic violence have a range of needs as they progress toward establishing a life that is free of violence. The first need is to be safe. In some instances, the removal of the perpetrator along with a personal protection order may be sufficient to protect the victim from further harm. However, it is often necessary for the victim to be removed from the home or residence and steps may need to be taken to keep her from being found by the perpetrator. This might mean moving in with friends or relatives or entering a shelter. In more extreme cases of danger, the victim may need to be moved out of town, out the area, or even out of state. Domestic violence programs have developed networks that make these options possible.

A major consideration for women who are mothers are their children. Domestic violence is closely related to child abuse and oftentimes mothers will decide to leave when the abuse begins to be directed at the children or when they realize the effects of the abuse on their children. Most mothers leave with their children. This can complicate their ability to secure temporary shelter with friends and relatives. Domestic violence shelters readily accept families, but space can become an issue at times. Other complications associated with children are school and recreation. Children may not be able to attend their regular school because of the ease with which the perpetrator can locate them and ultimately their mother. Adjusting to a new school under these circumstances can be quite difficult. Children also need to be entertained and be able to play. While in a shelter, these activities need to take place under supervision.

Families who leave perpetrators of violence may literally leave with the clothes on their backs. So those who leave permanently are usually starting over with practically nothing.

Assistance with legal matters is another need. Both criminal and civil proceedings may be involved. Victims need support and advocacy in order to persevere in securing justice for themselves and their children. They are often faced with financial barriers in covering the cost of legal representation, and it may be difficult to obtain pro bono services from attorneys.

Perpetrators of domestic violence need to eliminate violence or the threat of violence from their behavior and establish healthy patterns of behavior in relationships. Accepting responsibility is usually the first step. Alternatives to violence classes, substance abuse treatment, and mental health treatment are usually necessary in order to reverse long-standing and underlying patterns of domination and violence in domestic partnerships.

Services to Clients and Families

Good practice in domestic violence services requires courage and fortitude. Some perpetrators are not beyond threatening workers who assist their victims. Quite often, victims decide to return to their abusing partners. In fact, victims may return multiple times before they decide to leave permanently. Women are especially vulnerable in part because of the disparity between male and female income levels. It is much more difficult for women to obtain employment that will support themselves and their children. The costs of childcare and setting up a new residence is daunting for even the strongest person. Securing child support and alimony may be difficult if it ends up revealing the victim's whereabouts.

Knowledge of the cycle of violence is necessary for good practice. Lenore Walker developed this concept in her book, which is cited later. The cycle begins as tension builds and an incident of abuse occurs. This is followed by making up and then a period of calm before tension begins to build toward another incident (see domesticviolence.org/cycle.html for an adaptation of this). Good practice includes educating both victims and perpetrators regarding this cycle. With victims, it is important for them to break the cycle by either taking steps to ensure that their partner receives treatment or by leaving their partner and establishing their independence. They also need to become aware of the potential to become involved in future relationships that become abusive. If they can recognize the signs ahead of time, they can avoid these types of relationships. Educating perpetrators of abuse involves helping them to break the cycle by changing their thoughts, feelings, and behaviors during any stage of the cycle. Anger management can be particularly useful in this process.[1]

Empowerment and strengths-based approaches are essential in providing domestic violence services. Victims need to recover personal power that is lost through the victimization process. Empowerment means helping victims to restructure their thoughts, feelings, and behaviors to increase their power and control over their physical, psychological, emotional, social, and economic well-being. Group work and the use of support and consciousness-raising are typically employed along with personal counseling. This can occur on either an outpatient or residential basis. Advocacy and legal representation is vital. A positive relationship with law enforcement, prosecuting attorneys, and the courts needs to be built and maintained. Case management and referrals are also part of the core of services. Access to a full spectrum of services is important. Service gaps tend to lose clients. When clients are lost because a service is not available, it can easily become a life and death situation.

Suggested Resources

The National Council against Domestic Violence provides information and resources. Their website is ncadv.org. The National Domestic Violence Hotline also provides information and referral at ndvh.org. The U.S. Department of Justice provides information at usdoj.gov/domesticviolence/htm. Recent publications include the following:

Hines, Denise A., and Malley-Morrison, Kathleen. *Family Violence in the United States: Defining, Understanding, and Combating Abuse* (Thousand Oaks, CA: Sage, 2005).

Potter-Efron, R. T. *Handbook of Anger Management: Individual, Couple, Family, and Group Approaches* (Binghampton, NY: Haworth, 2005).

Stith, S. M. *Prevention of Intimate Partner Violence* (Binghampton, NY: Haworth, 2005).

Walker, L. *The Battered Woman* (New York: Harper and Row, 1979).

Wilson, K. J. *When Violence Begins at Home: A Comprehensive Guide to Understanding and Ending Domestic Abuse* (Alameda, CA: Hunter House, 2005).

■   GOOD PRACTICES WITH FAMILIES REQUIRING   ■
CHILD WELFARE SERVICES

Generalist social workers are quite prominent in various roles in the child welfare system. They are found working in child protective services, which is responsible for investigating child abuse and neglect complaints. These workers have to make decisions about whether abuse or neglect might be substantiated. If there is sufficient evidence, they need to decide about the risk to the children and whether to pursue removal from the home or allow the children to remain. Removal from the home or supervision in the home involves a court process with which they must be familiar.

Generalist social workers provide services through the foster care system. They are typically involved in recruitment, training, licensing, and supervising foster homes. They also supervise the care of children while they are in foster care. In addition, workers are involved in permanency planning, which includes adoption services.

Description of Practice Areas

Child welfare includes child protective services (CPS), foster care, and adoption. CPS is the responsibility of the public welfare system. It includes investigation of complaints regarding child maltreatment, including physical, educational, and medical neglect; and physical, sexual, and emotional abuse. Private agencies may provide prevention and family preservation programs. Foster care is used when children cannot remain in their own home because of an ongoing risk of maltreatment. It is considered to be a temporary arrangement until the risk is removed or parental rights are terminated and a permanent plan is implemented. If family reunification is not possible, then permanency planning generally requires an effort to place children for adoption. Adoption services include domestic, foreign, and specialized adoptions.

Client Needs in CPS

Good practice in CPS begins with a thorough investigation. Protection of the child from harm is coupled with the need to preserve the family unit if possible. The long-term interests of children are to have parents who are able to provide for their needs. Removal from the home should be undertaken as a last resort if necessary to protect the child from further harm. The worker assesses the situation and the risk of future maltreatment. Several inventories have been developed to assist in assessment along with structured interview formats. Generally, the more cooperative the parent or guardian is the lower the risk. Higher risk is associated with substance abuse, criminality, and poverty.

Services in CPS

The alleviation of risk factors is the focus for services. A comprehensive treatment program for substance abuse is required whenever that is present. Parenting classes and improving the family's economic well-being can reduce risks. The social work intervention role is case manager to ensure the effective use of resources. Social workers may also provide counseling, substance abuse treatment, and parenting classes. Risks are reduced when the parent admits to the maltreatment and acts to alleviate the risks.

Working in CPS can be risky for the worker. The use of teams and police protection may be necessary, especially when removing children from their home. Workers should use cell phones, a system of tracking their location, and regular check-ins. Risks are considerably elevated if there are drugs or alcohol or criminal activity in the home. Urban settings may include elevated criminal activity in the neighborhood. In rural settings, isolation and distance reduce law enforcement's ability to respond to emergencies.

Client and Family Needs in Foster Care

Foster care is used when it is determined that children have to be protected from further harm as a result of neglect or abuse and their parent or parents are either the source of the risk or are not able to protect the children from further harm. Generally, the first choice is to place children with relatives. In these cases, similar services are provided as would be the case if the children were in nonrelative foster care. If a relative is not available or it is determined that the children would not be safe, then regular foster care is needed. While in foster care, children have a full spectrum of needs, including physical, social, emotional, and educational needs. The foster parents need support in assisting children to adjust to living with them and in arranging for services such as medical, dental, mental health treatment, and educational planning and placement. There is a special need to balance assisting the child to adjust to temporary care while preserving the relationship with the parents and siblings so reunification can take place if possible. The biological parents need assistance in overcoming the circumstances that has resulted in their loss of custody.

Services in Foster Care

Good practice in foster care involves recruitment and training of foster parents and case management activities associated with maintaining children in care and with reunifying the family. The worker provides support for the foster parent in arranging for services, arranges appropriate visitation with the biological family, and provides case management services necessary for successful reunification if appropriate. The latter often includes such services as parenting skills, counseling, homemaker services, referrals for job training, and so on. Referrals to appropriate community services are needed such as mental health, health care, dental care, and so on. A family preservation model is used in foster care as it is with CPS. In addition, a psycho-education model is typically used to teach parenting and social skills.

Client and Family Needs in Adoption

Adoption is intended to provide children with a permanent home. It also meets the needs of adoptive parents who wish to have the opportunity to raise children. For infant adoption, pregnant mothers need assistance in making decisions about their pregnancy, especially regarding their emotional response to the pregnancy and to the possibility of terminating the pregnancy or the decision to adopt. Older children need to be prepared to bond with new parents who are not their biological parents. Prospective adoptive parents need to be prepared for the challenges of bonding to and raising a child who is not biologically theirs. Some prospective adoptive parents may wish to add to their existing families. They will need assistance in helping their family to adjust to an adoptee. Some parents are single and the challenges of being a single parent must be addressed. Some couples may be gay or lesbian. They will need assistance in overcoming the additional prejudice and discrimination that they will face. They also need assistance in helping the child to deal with these issues.

Adoption Services

Good practice in adoption services includes recruitment, assessment, training, matching, supervision, and knowledge of the legal process. Infant adoption generally involves infertile couples seeking to adopt and little if any recruitment of parents is needed. Most adoption agencies have long waiting lists of couples wishing to adopt healthy white infants. The primary service here is providing problem pregnancy counseling to mothers who are considering adoption and ensuring that they receive appropriate health care. The worker helps the pregnant mother make a decision to keep the child and raise it, to terminate the pregnancy, or to offer for adoption. In the first instance, good practice means assisting the mother to prepare for the child both emotionally and practically.

Adoption of older children, minorities, and those with special needs requires recruitment. This can take many forms including the use of the media, contact with churches and community groups, advertizing, and so on. After recruitment, assessment and screening needs to take place. Adopting older children and those with special physical or emotional needs has many additional challenges for which parents need to be prepared. Prospective parents should view adoption as meeting their needs and not so much as an altruistic act for which the child will be grateful. The latter is a prescription for a failed adoption because altruism will not last very long in the face of difficult parenting experiences.

Social workers need to do background and reference checks as part of screening and assessment to ensure that the parents are appropriate for consideration. The worker generally provides a series of training programs where the adoption process and the role of adoptive parent is discussed. These may be individual or in group formats. One or more home visits are made to determine the suitability of the living arrangements. Social workers gather information and develop a family social history.

Workers are involved in matching prospective parents with children. Matching is especially important for older children, cross-racial adoption, and those children with special needs, in fact it is the key ingredient in successful adoption. Usually, these adoption arrangements are made between two agencies. States are required to list children who are available for adoption. Children in these categories have most often become available through the CPS system in which parental rights have been terminated. Foster parents are given first choice of adoption if the child has been placed with them for a sufficient length of time. There are also national listings available. The child's worker lists important characteristics and needs and, in many cases, includes a picture. The worker for the prospective adoptive parents seeks out information from the parents about their desires and looks for potential matches. When a potential match is found then visits are arranged. Generally, a mutual agreement between parents, child, and workers need to take place for a permanent move to be made. In some jurisdictions, the worker may prepare and file the necessary legal documents. In others, the worker provides the family history and other information to an attorney for managing the legal aspects. The worker then provides supervision before finalization, generally for one year.

Adopting children from foreign countries generally involves an organization that specializes in this area with a local social worker providing all of the services previously described except the matching process, which is usually performed by the organization. One of the challenges with this type of adoption is helping Caucasian parents to have realistic expectations for raising children of color. This is also the case for any form of cross-racial adoption. Being able to see themselves as the parent of a child of a different race is a part of this process. In addition, consideration needs to be given to maintaining ethnic and cultural awareness and identity for the child. Parents also need to be prepared for the prejudice and discrimination that they and their child will face in U.S. society.

The model of practice most commonly used in adoption services is psycho-education. In working with adjustments to foster care a behavioral approach is often used with younger children.

Suggested Resources

The NASW has developed NASW Standards for Child Welfare, which is available at socialworkers.org/practice. The Child Welfare League of America (cwla.org) has a number of publications in this area, including *CWLA Standards of Excellence for Services to Strengthen and Preserve Families with Children, CWLA Standards of Excellence for Family Foster Care,* and *CWLA Standards of Excellence for Adoption Services.* Recent publications include the following:

Berg, I., and Kelly, S. *Building Solutions in Child Protective Services* (New York: Norton, 2000).
Brittain, C., and Hunt, D. *Helping in Child Protective Services: A Competency-Based Casework Handbook* (New York: Oxford University Press, 2004).
DePanfilis, D., and Salus, M. *Child Protective Services: A Guide for Caseworkers*, 3rd ed. (Washington, DC: U.S. Department of Health and Human Services, http://purl.access.gpo.gov/GPO/LPS33451, 2003).
Ellis, R. A., Dulmus, C. A., and Wodarski, J. S. *Essentials of Child Welfare* (Hoboken, NJ: Wiley, 2003).
Kluger, M., Alexander, G., and Curtis P. *What Works in Child Welfare* (Washington, DC: CWLA Press, 2000).

■ GOOD PRACTICES WITH FAMILIES EXPERIENCING ■ CRIME AND DELINQUENCY

Families experiencing crime and delinquency may receive a variety of services including those rendered by generalist social workers. Although some social workers are found in adult corrections, they are much more likely to work with juvenile delinquents and their families. However, workers may work with families in which one or more members are currently involved in criminal activity, are involved in the criminal justice system, or have criminal records.

Exploring criminal records and activities is an important consideration whenever the worker works with a family. The presence of criminal activity places children at very high risk of engaging in criminal or delinquent activity themselves. It also presents a risk for the worker.

Description of Practice Areas

The primary practice areas for generalist social workers in youth and delinquency services are community-based services and residential care. Community practice involves promoting growth and development, prevention, and juvenile probation. There are further subdivisions within delinquency services between youth who commit crimes and those who are classified as status offenders. Status offenses are only offenses because of the age or status of the offender. Status offenses include home truancy, school truancy, and incorrigibility (failure to obey the reasonable and lawful commands of one's parents). Residential care ranges from foster care and group homes to state training schools.

Client and Family Needs

All youth need their basic needs met along with the need to grow and develop according to the stages of development. A glance at Erikson's stages of development will show that children experience five stages of development before they reach young adulthood. Each stage presents challenges for successful growth and development. All children and youth need opportunities to complete the tasks of each stage.[2] Some will need assistance in overcoming barriers.

An important task in delinquency services is balancing the needs of youthful offenders against the need to protect society from victimization. This task has become increasingly more difficult, especially in many urban areas, as youthful offenders have become involved with drugs, gangs, and guns. Delinquency seems to stem from a combination of family experiences and environment, with a number of theories about its etiology. Boys from fatherless homes seem to be especially vulnerable as are youth whose families are engaged in various criminal enterprises. Additional risk factors are similar to those in families experiencing neglect or abuse as identified previously. In many cases the difference between children who enter the child welfare system and those who enter the delinquency system is age, with younger children entering the former and older children the latter. So, substance abuse in the family increases the risk along with the presence of neglect or abuse. Growing up in a neighborhood with high crime and delinquency increases the risk regardless of the presence or absence of a father. Poverty is also a risk factor. There is evidence that untreated attention deficit hyperactivity disorder may also increase a youth's risk. For some delinquents, the threat of punishment is sufficient to deter them from further criminal activity. Others need a meaningful relationship with an adult who genuinely cares about them and their future. Some need a positive peer group to whom they can relate along with positive activities that meet their needs for attention and for access to resources. Many need positive experiences at school in order to have access to legitimate employment opportunities. Their family's circumstances are important factors in providing for these needs.

Girls are more often brought to the attention of the court for status offenses than are boys. Girls do engage in criminal activity, but they tend to be less violent and aggressive. One of the factors that influences the greater use of status offenses with girls is the concern over sexual activity and pregnancy. Thus, there tends to be a double standard in delinquency. Some families are more concerned about these types of behaviors than other families and this will tend to determine whether the girl comes to the attention of the authorities. There are also differences in court involvement with status offenses in urban areas. In larger cities with higher crime rates, the system tends to be overwhelmed with cases involving criminal activity and, as a result, status offenses are not considered a high priority.

Services to Clients and Families

Good practice in youth and delinquency services for generalist social workers ranges from providing growth and development activities to prevention services to juvenile probation to residential care. Examples of growth and development activities are youth recreation, scouting, youth groups, Boys and Girls Clubs, and similar programs. Prevention programs include drug prevention, gang prevention, runaway services, diversion programs, and similar youth initiatives. Juvenile probation involves working within the court system to assess, plan, and intervene with youthful offenders. Residential care involves the rehabilitation of offenders away from their homes and communities. This includes foster care, group homes, open and closed residential facilities, and boys' and girls' state training school programs.

Good practice in probation services follows the change process presented in the text: assessment, planning, intervention, and evaluation. Generally, the juvenile probation officer provides the court with a social history that identifies functioning at home, at school, and in the community. A recommendation is also made to address the balance between the needs of the youth and those of society. The worker then carries out the decision of the court. Probation includes monitoring, case management, and often some form of counseling with regard to avoiding further delinquent activity. The success of juvenile probation work relies heavily on the family. Families are the primary source of supervision and juvenile probation officers generally rely on the family to monitor and report on the activities of the juvenile on probation.

Diversion from residential care involves intensive services that is generally focused on the youth and the family in an effort to avoid the human and financial costs of care. The financial costs of out-of-home placement are substantial. Intensive counseling and case management along with crisis intervention and close monitoring are usually the services that are provided. Generalist social workers provide counseling and case management to youth and their families who are placed in various forms of residential care, which is intended to temporarily remove the youth from a situation that is promoting further delinquency or which is intended to protect society from the youth.

Generalist social workers may have primary responsibility in serving the needs of families with members who are incarcerated. It is more typical for workers to be involved in some other capacity with a family and find that a member is currently in jail or prison. The worker needs to support the family in coping with this situation. This can include meeting both emotional and tangible needs. Families typically experience loss and embarrassment. Children are usually subjected to teasing and taunts. There may be financial difficulties. Transportation for visitation can be a major problem for families on limited incomes without a car or with one that is not reliable.

Suggested Resources

NASW has developed *NASW Standards for the Practice of Social Work with Adolescents*, which is available at socialworkers.org/practice. Information and resources are also available through the National Criminal Justice Reference Service at ncjrs.org., the Office of Juvenile Justice and Delinquency Prevention at ojjdp.ncjrs.org, and the National Council on Crime and Delinquency at nccd-crc.org. Recent publications include the following:

Bartollas, C., and Miller, S. J. *Juvenile Justice in America* (Upper Saddle River, NJ: Pearson/Prentice Hall, 2005).

Glicken, M. D., and Sechrest, D. *The Role of the Helping Professions in Treating the Victims and Perpetrators of Violence* (Boston: Allyn & Bacon, 2003).

Heilbrun, K., and Goldstein, N. E. Sevin. *Juvenile Delinquency: Prevention, Assessment, and Intervention* (New York: Oxford University Press, 2005).

Jackson, M. S., and Knepper, P. *Delinquency and Justice* (Boston: Allyn & Bacon, 2003).

Rapp-Paglicci, L. A., and Dulmus, C. N. *Handbook of Preventive Interventions for Children and Adolescents* (Hoboken, NJ: Wiley, 2004).

■   GOOD PRACTICES WITH FAMILIES WITH   ■
MEMBERS WHO ARE MENTALLY DISABLED

Much of the responsibility for providing care and coordinating services for people who are mentally disabled is taken on by families. Some families do not do very well with this because of their own circumstances or because they do not have the necessary knowledge and skills or because they are overwhelmed with the situation. People with mild retardation can develop skills necessary for independence, but those with more severe conditions will need some form of care throughout their lifetimes.

Families with members who are psychotic or with members who are mentally retarded face many challenges, especially if the retardation is profound or when psychotic symptoms interfere with forming or maintaining a relationship. Mental impairments generally limit the ability to think and interact, so the relationship may also be more limited.

Description of Practice Areas

The primary practice areas for generalist social workers in mental health are case management, partial hospitalization, inpatient, clubhouses, emergency services, assertive community treatment, day activity programs, sheltered workshops, supported employment, and residential care. Generalist social workers can be found in each of these areas. Typically, outpatient therapy is provided by MSW social workers with clinical expertise along with psychologists and psychiatrists. Thus, therapy is not covered here, but these other areas of practice are discussed. Because there is considerable overlap with regard to clients who use these services, the organization for this method will focus on clients with severe or chronic mental health care needs and those who are mentally retarded.

Client and Family Needs

There are two primary types of clients who utilize most of the services provided in the areas of practice identified. The first are people who have symptoms of major mental illness and the second are people who are mentally retarded. The two main types of clients who experience major mental illness include people who experience various psychotic symptoms and those who experience serious symptoms of depression. Most of the first type of clients are diagnosed with some form of schizophrenia. The latter are those whose depression places them at risk of suicide. These are typically people who are diagnosed with major depression or with bipolar disorder. People who experience anxiety are a third major area of service, but they generally receive services through outpatient treatment and medication, so they are not covered here. Generally, people with acute or chronic psychosis or depression need support in meeting the full spectrum of needs identified by Maslow[3] and by Towle[4] when their symptoms are active and interfering with their cognitive functioning. Many people with these conditions will fluctuate in terms of their abilities to function and meet their own needs and so their need for various services will also fluctuate. However, some are never able to experience relief from having symptoms and will need ongoing support. Because these conditions are often either chronic or cyclical, maintaining full employment can be difficult. This limits many of the resources that are available, such as income and health insurance. In turn, this affects the quality of life and puts people at high risk of living in poverty. There are no cures for these conditions. Although people can recover from major depression, they are typically at risk of experiencing periodic episodes in the future. Many people are able to function with pharmacological treatment, but some may not experience full or continuous benefit. Thus, in addition to needing support for meeting their full spectrum of needs at various times, people with these conditions need constant monitoring of their medication regimen.

People who are mentally retarded need support for a full spectrum of needs depending on the extent to which their mental or physical symptoms affect their independence. Their conditions are almost always chronic, but their levels of functioning and independence may be increased with consistent support. People with these conditions face similar challenges as those who are mentally ill in that their conditions can present barriers to accessing services. In addition, those with fragile health conditions may need substantial medical monitoring and services.

Families with members who are mentally ill or mentally retarded are most often their primary source of support. Thus, the social worker needs to support the family in coping with the situation and in accessing resources.

Services to Clients Families

Good practice in mental health for generalist social workers often includes providing case management to clients who are experiencing acute or chronic symptoms. Case management in the mental health system follows the typical model for case management identified in Chapter 8. Case managers provide assessment, planning, coordination of services, and crisis intervention. For clients and their families with acute or chronic mental illness and those who are mentally retarded or physically disabled, these services are vital in advancing their quality of life and in ensuring that their basic needs are met. Case managers monitor medication and health needs and ensure that clients have access to psychiatrists and doctors. Case managers ensure that periodic medication reviews take place and that the medication is effective in maximizing their clients' abilities to function. For clients who are physically or developmentally disabled, case managers ensure that they receive the necessary health care needed to address their conditions. They meet with clients in the office and on home visits to determine whether basic needs are being met. They arrange for participation in any of the programs mentioned previously as needed. A primary goal is to assist clients in maintaining themselves in the least restrictive environment. In other words, case managers try to help clients maintain a maximum level of independence. This can range from complete independence with employment and their own homes or apartments to residential care in a group home or in foster care. In between these extremes, clients may be in supported or semi-independent living situations or they might live with their families. Case managers assist in arranging for changes in living circumstances when the client's condition or situation require such change. This may mean movement toward more or less independence depending on the client's abilities at a given time.

Generalist social workers are employed in all of the services mentioned previously under practice areas. In inpatient settings, they provide supportive and habilitation services such as coping skills, training in life skills, activities, and so on. These are generally provided in a group format. The same types of services are provided in partial hospitalization. Typically, the main difference between these two types of settings is that clients go home at night when they are attending a partial hospitalization program. Day activity programs offer socialization and training in social skills as well as assistance with personal care. Some are designed for people who are mentally ill, but most are for people who are mentally retarded or developmentally disabled. Clubhouses have begun to substitute for partial hospitalization and day activity programs. These are operated by the participants, with support available from staff who are usually social workers. Generalist social workers also provide supportive services in sheltered workshops where clients who cannot function in a competitive employment situation are able to learn work skills and receive payment for their work, which is often done on a piecework basis. In supported employment, clients receive support services such as coaching in a competitive employment situation. Emergency services staff provide crisis intervention and assessment for inpatient hospitalization. All community mental health programs must provide this service twenty-four hours a day, seven days a week, every day of the year. Social workers are frequently used to staff this service. In urban areas, emergency services and crisis centers may be housed independently or in hospitals with emergency rooms and inpatient units. Usually, rural areas cover crises at the office during business hours and rely on hospital emergency rooms after hours. Inpatient units are usually located in a more urban area at a distance. In rural areas, staff carry beepers or cell phones for coverage after hours and talk over the phone or meet with clients in the emergency room. Assertive community treatment teams are designed to meet the needs of people who are chronically mentally ill and who have a history of multiple or long-term psychiatric hospitalizations. The team approach is used to prevent hospitalization or shorten the client's stay when he is hospitalized. It is generally made up of a doctor, a nurse, and one or more social workers. Some teams may also have a psychologist. It provides twenty-four-hour response to a small group of patients as well as intensive case management on a frequent basis, daily if necessary. Residential care provides a range of options from independent or semi-independent living to group or foster care. Independent living generally consists of the client living in some sort of supported living arrangement, but staff are not on site. Generally, a case manager visits and maintains contact to ensure that the client's needs are met. In semi-independent living, usually clients live alone or with a roommate in an apartment and staff are available on site to assist them. In foster care, clients live with a family or in an adult foster home. In a group home, clients live together with staff who work in shifts to provide supervision and basic needs. Social workers provide case management services to most of these groups of clients.

Good practice in mental health settings must include crisis intervention skills, the ability to assess for hospitalization, and suicide assessment and intervention. A model for crisis intervention was presented in Chapter 7. Because each state has its own mental health code, assessment for hospitalization varies somewhat from state to state. However, at the very least, all states and good practice dictate that hospitalization occur when the client's condition results in immediate danger to himself or others. Voluntary hospitalization means that the client is able to sign himself into the hospital. It also means he can sign himself out. Involuntary hospitalization requires that a petition for hospitalization be initiated. Petitions are usually permitted to be signed by an adult, a law enforcement officer, or a health care professional who has direct knowledge of the situation. All social workers, but especially those working in mental health settings, should be knowledgeable about their state with regard to the process of hospitalizing people who are mentally ill, both voluntarily and involuntarily.

Good practice by generalist social workers in mental health settings nearly always involves case management to ensure that necessary services are received. A thorough understanding of the *Diagnostic and Statistical Manual of Mental Disorders: DSM-IV* is also needed to work effectively in mental health settings. Cognitive–behavioral approaches, pharmacological treatment, and psychosocial rehabilitation are typically used in various aspects of providing mental health services.

Suggested Resources

NASW has developed *NASW Standards for Social Work Case Management*, which is available at socialworkers.org/practice. The American Association of Suicidology has excellent resources available at suicidology.com. The Crisis Intervention Network has resources listed on its website at crisisinterventionnetwork.com. Recent publications include the following:

American Psychiatric Association. *Diagnostic and Statistical Manual of Mental Disorders: DSM-IV* (Washington, DC: American Psychiatric Association, 1994).
Bentley, K. J. *Social Work Practice in Mental Health: Contemporary Roles, Tasks, and Techniques* (Pacific Grove, CA: Brooks/Cole, 2002).
Holt, B. *The Practice of Generalist Case Management* (Boston: Allyn & Bacon, 2000).
Jacobs, D. G. *Harvard Medical School Guide to Suicide Assessment and Intervention* (San Francisco, CA: Jossey-Bass, 1999).
Roberts, A. R. *Crisis Intervention Handbook: Assessment, Treatment, and Research* (New York: Oxford University Press, 2005).
Stout, C. E., and Hayes, R. A., Eds. *The Evidence-Based Practice: Methods, Models, and Tools for Mental Health Professionals* (Hoboken, NJ: Wiley, 2005).
Thyer, B. A., and Wodarski, J. S. *Handbook of Empirical Social Work Practice, Volume 1, Mental Disorders* (Hoboken, NJ: Wiley, 2004).

■ GOOD PRACTICES WITH FAMILIES ■ WITH MEMBERS WHO ARE OLDER

It is quite common for generalist social workers to work in settings serving people who are older. These workers can be found at every level of living situation, including local aging services. Generalist practitioners are ideally suited to assist people who are older and their families in every facet of service delivery.

Description of Practice Areas

The primary practice areas in providing services to people who are aging are related to maximizing their independence and maintaining people in what is called the least restrictive environment. In order to provide for the needs of people at various stages of independence, a continuum of care is needed. At the highest level of independence, people who are elderly receive support for living in their own homes, condominiums, or apartments. Those who have needs for lower levels of care may either receive services directly to meet those needs or may have caregivers who receive services to support their caregiving. Those who have intermediate needs may live in community living facilities. Those with more advanced needs will likely need nursing home care. Social workers provide valuable services at all these levels.

Good practice methods in aging services begins with an understanding of the aging process. In addition, the worker must come to terms with his own aging and mortality and be able to provide support when client's experience grief and loss. A commitment to maintaining people's dignity in the face of declining abilities is a must. People who are experiencing increased dependence need reassurance that their status as adults will be respected.

Client and Family Needs

There are common areas of concern in delivering services to people who are elderly at all levels of care. These are related to Maslow's hierarchy of needs. At each level of care, the worker seeks to ensure that as many of these needs are met within the context of the client's mental and physical status as possible. The degree to which various levels of need are met determines the quality of life for the client. If the ecosystem is not functioning in a way that maximizes the client's quality of life, then the worker either marshals resources to do so or seeks to change to a higher or alternative level of care that will fulfill this need. If we consider Maslow's hierarchy of needs with regard to working in aging services, we can see where meeting basic or physiological needs means ensuring survival. Safety needs may relate to being safe from becoming a victim of crime or abuse or the need to be safe from injury. It also relates to the need for quality medical care to maintain one's health. These first two levels of need tend to drive much of the work that is done in aging services. The third level is also important. Maintaining a connection with others and meeting social needs regarding belonging and love are necessary for maintaining our mental health and this can also affect physical well-being. The other levels of Maslow's hierarchy for people who are older are primarily determined by how people are treated by those around them, the extent to which the environment provides opportunities and stimulation, and the extent to which people are able to come to terms with their own aging and mortality.[5] These are also important considerations in providing services to this group of clients and their families.

Services to Clients and Families

Most people who are elderly and living on their own do not receive services unless they experience a temporary need such as a medical emergency. They rely on themselves, their families, and their friends and neighbors for assistance if anything is needed.

In general, good practice in aging services requires the ability to provide support and assistance with grief and loss. As we age, we lose or experience decline in various physical abilities. With each loss we need to grieve in order to reach acceptance and resolution. Otherwise, the losses can accumulate to the point where it interferes with our quality of life. The stages of the grief process were discussed in Chapter 10.

Services to people who are elderly and living independently revolve around maintaining independence and enhancing their abilities to meet higher-level needs for socialization, esteem, self-actualization, and cognitive understanding. Proper nourishment and medical care are two major areas of focus with regard to basic needs. Congregate meal sites are available in all urban and most rural areas. In addition to meals, these sites provide opportunities to socialize and engage in activities. Case managers provide assessment and referral for medical needs and various programs designed to meet needs.

Generalist social workers provide a wide variety of services to families caring for a member who has dementia. Much of this is aimed at preserving the ability of the family to provide care. Social workers have designed and carried out training programs for professional and family caregivers as well as training programs to train other trainers. They design, implement, and operate adult day activity programs that allow family caregivers to work or receive respite. Social workers are found working in home health care agencies, assisted living facilities, retirement communities, and nursing homes.

The options of living situations are much more plentiful for people who are older than for any of the other populations requiring assistance with adult daily living tasks. Optional living situations include home-based services, adult day activity programs, retirement communities, adult foster care, assisted living facilities, and nursing homes. There has been a dramatic increase in retirement communities in the past few years. Some of these have a full continuum of living options from individual apartments to assisted living facilities to nursing homes. These generally require a substantial investment of assets along with various levels of monthly payments.

Suggested Resources

The NASW has developed *NASW Standards for Social Work Services in Long-Term Care Facilities, NASW Standards for Social Work Case Management,* and *NASW Standards for Social Work Practice in Palliative and End of Life Care,* which are available at socialworkers.org/practice. Recent publications include the following:

Berkman, B., and D'Ambruoso, S. *Handbook of Social Work in Health and Aging* (New York: Oxford University Press, 2006).

Berkman, B., and Harootyan, L. *Social Work and Health Care in an Aging Society: Education, Policy, Practice, and Research* (New York: Springer, 2003).

Friedan, B., *The Fountain of Age* (New York: Simon and Schuster, 1993).

McInnis-Dittrich, K. *Social Work with Elders: A Biopsychosocial Approach to Assessment and Intervention,* 2nd ed. (Boston: Allyn & Bacon, 2005).

National Institute on Aging, U.S. Administration on Aging. *Resource Directory for Older People* (Bethesda, MD: U.S. Department of Health and Human Services, National Institutes of Health, Administration on Aging, 2001).

Roberts, A. L., and Greene, G. J., Eds. *Social Worker's Desk Reference* (New York: Oxford University Press, 2002). See Arnold, E. M., "End-of-Life Counseling and Care: Assessment, Interventions, and Clinical Issues"; Brownell, P., "Elder Abuse"; and Giddens, B., Ka'Opua, L. S., and Tomaszewski, E. P. "Case Management with Older Adults."

action The process of carrying out a plan developed through the assessment and action phases of the social work process.

action system System of people and resources involved in carrying out tasks related to goals and strategy of the helping endeavor.

activity Doing something or performing tasks as opposed to talking about what to do or talking about feelings or ideas.

agency The organization that employs the worker and manages resources used to help the client.

assessment Ongoing process of the social work endeavor that develops an understanding of person in situation to use as the basis for action.

best practices Engaging in practice activities that are based on research and is intended to increase successful outcomes.

blended family A family in which the parents have had previous relationships and have children from those relationships, as well as possibly having children from the present relationship.

boundary Point at which the interaction around a function no longer has the intensity that interaction of system members or units has. For example, when considering who is a member of a family system, the boundary is the point that divides those who are continually interacting around family concerns and issues and those who have little or no input into family functioning.

broker A social work role in which the worker provides the client with information about available resources and helps link the client with the resource.

case management A method for coordinating services in which a worker assesses with a client which services are needed and obtains and monitors the delivery of the services.

client system An individual, family, group, organization, or community that has either sought help from a social worker or is served by an agency employing a social worker.

closedness A quality of social systems that describes the lack of ability of the system to allow information or individuals to permeate the system's boundary.

collaboration The working together of several service providers with a common client toward a common goal.

community Immediate environment of worker, client, and agency that is manifest as a social system.

concern A feeling that something is not right. Interest in, regard for, and care about the well-being of self and other persons.

congruity A situation in which the interactions or transactions within an ecosystem are balanced, resulting in mutual benefit for the person and the environment.

contract An agreement, verbal or written, between worker and client about the work to be done together. Goals, objectives, and tasks to be carried out by worker and client are specified.

coordination The working together of two or more service providers in activity focused on a particular client or focused on persons in a particular category (e.g., the aged). Coordinative mechanisms include colocation of services, networking, linking, case management, collaboration, and a team approach.

coping Efforts to deal with some new and often problematic situation or encounter, or to deal in some new way with an old problem.

crisis A state of disequilibrium or a loss of steady state as a result of stress or a precipitating event in the life of a person who usually has a satisfactory level of functioning.

cultural competence The ability to provide services to clients from a particular cultural group in a manner that is consistent with the norms and customs of that culture.

deductive learning Moving from theory to hypothesis to testing hypothesis to see whether the theory is supported.

diagnosis A term borrowed from the medical field. It relates to developing a statement as to the nature of the client's need and the situation related to that need. A more contemporary term is *assessment*.

diagnostic approach A historic model of social work practice that places a primary emphasis on diagnosis. The contemporary model is usually referred to as the *psychosocial approach*.

direct practice Action with individuals, families, and small groups focused on change in either the transactions within the family or small group or in the manner in which individuals, families, and small groups function in relation to individuals and social systems in their environment.

diversity competence The ability to provide services to clients with a particular diversity factor in a manner that is acceptable within that diversity group.

dual perspective Process of consciously perceiving, understanding, and comparing simultaneously the values, attitudes, and behaviors of the larger social system and those of the immediate family and community system.

ecological perspective A way of thinking about practice that involves a focus on the client's surrounding environment.

eco-map A diagram depicting the interactions between the family and the environment.

ecosystem A system of systems including the person(s) and all of the interacting systems in the environment along with the transactions among the person(s) and systems.

ecosystems perspective An approach that examines the exchange of matter, energy, or information over time among all the systems in a person-in-environment approach.

ecosystems strengths approach A blend of the ecological and strength perspectives with the problem-solving approach to form a process for facilitating growth and change.

empirically based practice Practice that is based on knowledge that has been tested by empirical or scientific methods and found to be effective.

empowerment A process for increasing personal, interpersonal, or political power so that individuals can take action to improve their life situations.

enabling Making it possible for an individual or system to carry out some activity they might not be able to engage in without support or help.

engagement The establishment of a helping relationship between the worker and the client system.

entropy The quality of systems that describes the loss of energy and the capacity to carry out necessary functions.

environmental demands Expectations that people or social systems in an individual's or social system's environment place on themselves relative to their social functioning.

environmental manipulation A strategy to bring about change in a client's environment in order to enhance the client's social functioning.

equifinality The capacity of two systems to achieve identical goals when they are starting from different conditions.

equilibrium A fixed balance in a social system among the various subsystems and their functioning. Tends to represent a quality of stability and closedness.

evaluation Collection and assessment of data about the outcomes of a plan of action relative to goals set in advance of implementing that plan.

extinction The technique of ignoring undesirable behavior as a way of eliminating it.

family systems theory The application of social systems theory to the family. The family as a system is seen as having structure, functioning, and development and is comprised of subsystems.

feedback A special form of input that gives a system information on the effects of its output on other systems.

feeling An intuitive sense of a situation or solution to a problem. Facts have not been sought. More of an emotional process than a cognitive one.

felt need A need identified by a client.

feminist perspective An approach related to redistribution of power that addresses discrimination; useful in working with women and minority groups.

focal system The primary system on which the social work process focuses in the change activity also called the unit of attention.

formative evaluation Evaluation that looks at the process of the work.

functional approach A historic model of social work practice that places emphasis on the role and tasks of the social worker in the helping situation rather than on a client's deviance or illness.

gemeinshaft A characteristic of communities that demonstrates a sense of "we-ness" and informal functioning.

generalist practice Practice in which the client and worker together assess the need in all of its complexity and develop a plan for responding to that need. A strategy is chosen from a repertoire of responses appropriate for work with individuals, families, groups, agencies, and communities. The unit of attention is chosen by considering the system needing to be changed. The plan is carried out and evaluated.

genogram A pictorial assessment mechanism for showing intergenerational relationships and family characteristics.

gesellschaft A characteristic of communities in which individuals tend to relate through institutions and other formal structures.

goal The overall, long-range expected outcome of an endeavor.

goal-attainment scaling An evaluation technique that not only specifies goals but also specifies outcomes at five levels: expected, more desirable, most desirable, less than desirable, and least desirable.

good practice Broadly defined as accepted practice in the field or setting or with a population that is based on empirically based practice, practice experience, and the empowerment of clients.

holon A system that is part of a larger system and is made up of several smaller systems. Often the system of focus.

homeostasis Fixed balance in a system that allows some permeation of the system's boundary by ideas and individuals, yet maintains the capacity of the system's structure to remain stable.

human development perspective A way of viewing human need that sees people as developing over the life cycle.

human-diversity approach A way of viewing persons in situations that considers culture, race, gender, age, sexual orientation, and disabling conditions as they affect human functioning. It views human behavior as highly relative to the social situation in which persons function.

incongruity A situation in which the interactions or transactions within an ecosystem are out of balance, resulting in unmet needs for the person or the environment.

indirect practice Action taken with persons other than clients in order to help clients.

inductive learning Moving from making observations of phenomena to searching for patterns that may lead to theory development. It means adopting an open-minded inquisitive approach, laying aside preconceived notions, and listening to the experiences of the client.

influence General acts of producing an effect on another person, group, or organization through exercise of a personal or organizational capacity.

influentials Persons in a community or an organization who have power or authority.

input Matter, energy, or information that enters a system.

interactional process The process by which a worker and a client work together on a concern or need in an environment.

interactional skill The capacity of social workers to relate to both clients and significant others, both individuals and social systems, in such a manner as to be helpful and to support the work at hand.

interface A point of contact between two systems where transactions occur.

intervention Specific action by a worker in relation to human systems or processes in order to induce change. The action is guided by knowledge and professional values as well as by the skill of the worker.

interventive repertoire The package of actions, methods, techniques, and skills a particular social worker has developed for use in response to needs of individuals and social systems.

interview The structure for operationalizing the interaction between worker and client.

knowledge Picture of the world and the place of humans in it. Ideas and beliefs about reality based on confirmable or probable evidence.

mapping A pictorial assessment mechanism that shows the relationship of subsystems to each other or the relationship of a system to other systems in its environment.

mediation strategy A strategy in which a worker helps a client and a system in the immediate environment to reach out to each other and find a common concern or interest and to do the work necessary to bring about a desired change.

medical model Used in medical field and often appropriated by social workers. Characterized by a process of study, diagnosis, and treatment.

multifinality A situation when two systems start from identical conditions and reach different end states.

multiperson client system A client system that is made up of more than one person such as a family, group, organization, or community.

natural helpers People who possess helping skills and exercise them in the context of mutual relationships, as opposed to professionals trained in certain helping skills who are not part of a client's immediate community.

natural helping systems A client's friends, family, and coworkers. Those in an individual's informal environment to whom one turns in time of need.

naturalistic inquiry An inductive learning process that begins with the position that one does not know what one does not know, which leaves one open to hearing the client's story without preconceived notions.

need That which is necessary for a person or a social system to function within reasonable expectations, given the situation that exists.

negative entropy The efficient use of energy by a system and the addition of energy to the system from the outside.

network A loose association of systems. Not a social system but an entity that operates through mutual resource sharing.

networking Development and maintenance of communication and ways of working together among people of diverse interests and orientations. One means of coordination.

objectives Intermediate goals that must be reached in order to attain the ultimate goal.

openness A quality of social systems that describes the capacity of the system to allow information and individuals to permeate the system boundaries easily.

output Matter, energy, or information that is produced by a system.

person in environment (or person in situation) The focus of the social work endeavor; not only on the person or the environment but on the complex interaction of the two as that interaction affects both person and social situation.

plan of action The way or method for carrying out planned change in the social work endeavor. It is structured and specifies goals and objectives, units of attention, and strategy.

problem (in social work) A social functioning situation in which need fulfillment of any of the persons or systems involved is blocked and in which the persons involved cannot by themselves remove the block to need fulfillment.

problem-solving process A tool used by social workers to solve problems in a rational manner. It proceeds through identifiable steps of interaction with clients. These steps include identification of the problem, statement of preliminary assumptions about the problem, selection and collection of information, analysis of information, development of a plan, implementation of the plan, and evaluation.

process A recurrent patterning of a sequence of change over time in a particular direction.

professional relationship A relationship with an agreed-on purpose, a limited time frame, and in which the professional devotes self to the interest of the client.

psychosocial approach See *Diagnostic approach.*

referral The process by which a client is made aware of another service resource and helped to make contact with that resource to receive a needed service.

relationship Cohesive quality of the action system. Product of interaction between two persons.

reliability The extent to which repeated measurement would yield the same results in evaluation.

role A function with a specific set of behaviors or responsibilities.

scientific philanthropy Systematic, careful investigation of evidence surrounding the need for service before acting on the need.

self-help groups Voluntary groups in which members with common problems help each other.

significant others Those persons in an individual's social network who have importance to, or impact on, the system being worked with.

single-subject design A research method used when the *n* (number of subjects) is one. Comparisons are made from baseline data, with progress toward goals being measured.

single-system design A research design in which a single system—individual, family, group, program, organization, or community—is measured over time.

skill A complex organization of behavior directed toward a particular goal or activity.

social history A form of assessment of individuals or families. It includes information (historical and current) needed for understanding and working with clients.

social support network analysis Specification of the nature of an individual's or family's support network. Both pictorial and written depictions are used.

social system A system composed of interrelated and interdependent parts (persons and subsystems).

social work process A change process carried out with clients to meet needs related to social functioning that clients cannot meet without help. It is conceptualized as study, assessment, planning, action, and termination/evaluation.

solution-focused interventions An approach that focuses on quickly finding a successful solution and empowering clients for change.

special populations Refers to specific groups of people such as women, members of a particular minority group, those with a particular disabling condition, and so on. These groups may need special consideration when providing services.

steady state State of a system's functioning that provides a balance between stability and adaptive change.

strategy An overall approach to change in a situation. Includes defining roles and tasks for both worker and client.

strengths approach An approach to social work practice that emphasizes the strengths and capabilities of the client system and the resources within the client's natural environment.

summative evaluation Evaluation concerned with outcomes and effectiveness.

support The use of techniques that help clients feel better, stronger, and more comfortable in some immediate way.

tasks Steps necessary to achieve a goal.

team A group of persons, often representative of various professions, who work together toward common goals and plans of action to meet the needs of clients.

termination The last phase of the social work process when the emphasis is on disengagement, stabilization of change, and evaluation.

thinking Use of a cognitive process to sort out information or to engage in a problem-solving process.

throughput The processing of matter, energy, or information by a system from input to output.

transaction The exchange of matter, energy, or information among persons or systems within an ecosystem.

treatment Term used for action segment of the social work process. Very often used in clinical social work.

triangulation Gathering data from multiple sources of information to establish validity and reliability. When there is agreement from more than one source, the worker is more confident of the validity and reliability of the information.

unit of attention The system or systems on which the change activity is focused; also called *focal system.*

validity The accuracy of information or data.

values What is held to be desirable and preferred. Guides for behavior.

NOTES

Chapter 1

1. For a fuller discussion of COS and Mary Richmond's work see James Leiby, *A History of Social Welfare and Social Work in the United States* (New York: Columbia University Press, 1978), chap. 8.
2. See Ann Hartman and Joan Laird, *Family-Centered Social Work Practice* (New York: Free Press, 1983), pp. 11–22.
3. Hartman and Laird, *Family-Centered Social Work Practice,* p. 18.
4. Leiby, pp. 127–135.
5. Leiby, *A History of Social Welfare and Social Work,* p. 127 ff.
6. From personal discussion with Bert N. Adams, professor of sociology (emeritus) University of Wisconsin, Madison, July 4, 2006. Also from Bert N. Adams, *The Family: A Sociological Interpretation* (Fort Worth: Harcourt Brace & Co., 1995).
7. Joan W. Stein, *The Family as a Unit of Study and Treatment.* Monograph One (Region IX Rehabilitative Research Institute, University of Washington, School of Social Work, 1969), chap. 2.
8. From quote in Stein, *The Family as a Unit of Study and Treatment,* p. 27.
9. For a summary of this approach, see Louise C. Johnson and Stephen J. Yanca, *Social Work Practice: A Generalist Approach,* 9th ed. (Boston: Pearson, 2007), pp. 409–410.
10. For a summary of this approach see Johnson and Yanca, *Social Work Practice,* p. 405.
11. Leiby, *A History of Social Welfare and Social Work,* p. 284.
12. Leiby, *A History of Social Welfare and Social Work,* op cit.
13. For a summary see Johnson and Yanca, *Social Work Practice,* p. 414.
14. Eleanor Reardon Tolson and William J. Reid, Eds., *Models of Family Treatment* (New York: Columbia University Press, 1981).
15. Hartman and Laird, *Family-Centered Social Work Practice,* op cit.
16. Ann Hartman, "To Think about the Unthinkable," *Social Casework* 58 (October 1970): 467–474.
17. Genevive Dehoyos and Claigh Jensen, "The Systems Approach in American Social Work," *Social Casework* 66 (October 1985): 498–497.
18. See Carel B. Germain, Ed., *Social Work Practice: People and Environments* (New York: Free Press, 1976); Carol H. Meyer, Ed., *Clinical Social Work in the Eco-Systems Perspective* (New York: Columbia University Press, 1983); and Carel B. Germain, *Human Behavior in the Social Environment: An Ecological View* (New York: Columbia University Press, 1991).
19. Dennis Saleeby, Ed., *The Strengths Perspective in Social Work Practice,* 2nd ed. (New York: Longman, 1997).
20. Ibid., p. 12.
21. Ibid., p. 15.
22. Ronald C. Federico, "Human Behavior and the Social Environment within a Human Diversity Framework," in *Educating the Baccalaureate Social Worker: A Curriculum Resource Guide,* vol. 2, Betty L. Baer and Ronald C. Federico, Eds. (Cambridge, MA: Ballinger, 1979).
23. Dolores G. Norton, *The Dual Perspective* (New York: Council on Social Work Education, 1978).
24. John F. Longres, "Toward a Status Model of Ethnic Sensitive Practice," *Journal of Multicultural Social Work* 1, 1 (1991): 41–56.
25. Kenneth L. Chau, "Social Work with Ethnic Minorities: Practice Issues and Potentials," *Journal of Multicultural Social Work* 1, 1 (1991): 23–39.
26. Elaine P. Congress, "The Use of Culturagrams to Assess and Empower Culturally Diverse Families," *Families in Society* 75, 9 (November 1994): 531–540.
27. Sharon Berlin, "Better Work with Women Clients," *Social Work* 21 (November 1976): 492–497.
28. Norton, *Dual Perspective.*
29. See Carol Meyer, "The Ecosystems Perspective: Implications for Social Work Practice," in *The Foundations of Social Work Practice,* Carol Meyer and Mark Mattaini, Eds. (Washington, DC: NASW Press, 1995), pp. 16–27.

Chapter 2

1. Mary E. Richmond, *Social Diagnosis* (New York: Russell Sage Foundation, 1917; reprint, Free Press, 1971).
2. Ibid., p. 357.
3. Helen Harris Perlman, *Social Casework: A Problem-Solving Process* (Chicago: University of Chicago Press, 1957).
4. Ibid., p. 4.

5. Ibid., p. 171.

6. Ibid.

7. Florence Hollis, *Casework: A Psychosocial Therapy* (New York: Random House, 1964); and Ruth Elizabeth Smalley, *Theory for Social Work Practice* (New York: Columbia University Press, 1967).

8. Hollis, *Casework*, 2nd ed. (1971).

9. Carol H. Meyer, *Social Work Practice: A Response to the Urban Crisis* (New York: Free Press, 1970).

10. Harriett M. Bartlett, *The Common Base of Social Work Practice* (New York: NASW Press, 1970).

11. Max Siporin, *Introduction to Social Work Practice* (New York: Macmillan, 1975); Beulah Roberts Compton and Burt Galaway, *Social Work Processes* (Homewood, IL: Dorsey Press, 1975); Howard Goldstein, *Social Work Practice: A Unitary Approach* (Columbia: University of South Carolina Press, 1973); and Allen Pincus and Anne Minahan, *Social Work Practice: Model and Method* (Itasca, IL: F. E. Peacock, 1973).

12. Pincus and Minahan, *Social Work Practice*, p. 103.

13. Ibid., p. 247.

14. See Catherine P. Papell and Beulah Rothman, "Social Group Work Models: Possession and Heritage," *Journal of Education for Social Work* 2 (Fall 1966): 66–77; and Jack Rothman, "Three Models of Community Organization Practice," in *National Conference on Social Welfare Social Work Practice* (New York: Columbia University Press, 1968), pp. 16–47.

15. Robert W. Roberts and Robert H. Nee, Eds., *Theories of Social Casework* (Chicago: University of Chicago Press, 1970).

16. For a fuller development of the model see Louise C. Johnson and Stephen J. Yanca, *Social Work Practice: A Generalist Approach*, 9th ed. (Boston: Pearson, 2007).

17. Harriett M. Bartlett, *The Common Base of Social Work Practice* (NASW Press, 1970).

18. For another formulation of the knowledge base, see Betty L. Baer and Ronald Federico, *Education of the Baccalaureate Social Workr: Report of the Undergraduate Curriculum Project* (Cambridge, MA: Ballinger, 1978), pp. 75–78.

19. Betty L. Baer and Ronald Federico, *Education of the Baccalaureate Social Worker: Report of the Undergraduate Curriculum Project* (Cambridge, MA: Ballinger, 1978), pp. 75–78.

20. See *Educational Policy and Accreditation Standards* (Washington, DC: Council on Social Work Education, 2001), pp. 9–12.

21. Dennis Saleeby, Ed., *The Strengths Perspective in Social Work Practice*, 2nd ed. (New York: Longman, 1997), pp. 12, 15.

22. Ferdinand Tönnies, *Fundamental Concepts of Sociology (Gemeinschaft und Gesellschaft)*, trans. Charles P. Loomis (New York: American Books, 1940).

23. Floyd Hunter, *Community Power Structure* (Chapel Hill: University of North Carolina Press, 1953).

24. Eugene Litwak and Ivan Szelenyi, "Primary Group Structures and Their Function: Kin, Neighbors, and Friends," *American Sociological Review* 34 (August 1969): 465–481; Phillip Fellin and Eugene Litwak, "The Neighborhood in Urban American Society," *Social Work* 13 (July 1968): 72–80; and Eugene Litwak, *Helping the Elderly* (New York: Guilford Press, 1985), chap. 8.

25. Roland L. Warren, *The Community in America* (Chicago: Rand-McNally, 1963).

26. Dennis E. Poplin, *Communities*, 2nd ed. (New York: Macmillan, 1979), chap. 2.

27. Louise C. Johnson, "Human Service Delivery Patterns in Non-Metropolitan Communities," in *Rural Human Services: A Book of Readings*, H. Wayne Johnson, Ed. (Itasca, IL: F. E. Peacock, 1980), pp. 55–64.

28. Louise C. Johnson, "Services to the Aged: Non-Metropolitan Service Delivery" (unpublished paper delivered at NASW Symposium, Chicago, IL, November 1985).

29. Padi Gulati and Geoffrey Guest, "The Community-Centered Model: A Garden Variety Approach or a Radical Transformation of Community Practice?" *Social Work* 35 (January 1990): 63–68.

30. Barbara Oberhofer Dane and Barbara L. Simon, "Resident Guests: Social Workers in Host Settings," *Social Work* 35 (January 1990): 63–68.

Chapter 3

1. Martha Ozawa, "Demographic Changes and Their Implications," in *Social Work in the 21st Century*, Michael Reisch and Eileen Gambrill, Eds. (Thousand Oaks, CA: Pine Forge Press, 1997), Chapter 1, pp. 8–27.

2. Delores Norton, *The Dual Perspective* (New York: Council on Social Work Education, 1978).

3. W. Nichols, "Portfolio," unpublished analytical paper (University of Vermont, Burlington), as cited by Marty Dewees in "Building Cultural Competence for Working with Diverse Families: Strategies from the Privileged Side," *Journal of Ethnic and Cultural Diversity in Social Work* 9, 3 (2001): 41.

4. James V. Leigh, *Communicating for Cultural Competence* (Boston: Allyn & Bacon, 1998), pp. 31–33.

5. Barbara F. Okum, Jane Fried, and Marcia L. Okum, *Understanding Diversity: A Learning-as-Practice Primer* (Pacific Grove, CA: Brooks/Cole, 1999), chaps. 2 and 3.

6. Doman Lum, *Culturally Competent Practice: A Framework for Understanding Diverse Groups and Justice Issues* (Pacific Grove, CA: Brooks/Cole, 1999).

7. Jerry V. Diller, *Cultural Diversity: A Primer for the Human Services* (Belmont, CA: Brooks/Cole and Wadsworth, 1999), p. 14.

8. Yuhwa Eva Lu, Doman Lum, and Sheying Chen, "Cultural Competency and Achieving Styles in Clinical Social Work: A Conceptual and Empirical Exploration," *Journal of Ethnic and Cultural Diversity in Social Work* 9, 3/4 (2001): 6.

9. Ibid., p. 7.

10. Dewees, "Building Cultural Competence for Working with Diverse Families, pp. 33–51.

11. Gargi Roysircar Sodowsky, Richard C. Taffe, Terry B. Gutkin, and Steven L. Wise, "Development and Applications of the Multicultural Counseling Inventory," *Journal of Counseling Psychology* 41 (1994): 137–144.

12. Lu, Lum, and Chen, "Cultural Competency and Achieving Styles in Clinical Social Work," p. 7.

13. Lum, *Culturally Competent Practice,* chap. 6.

14. Nan Van Den Bergh and Lynn B. Cooper, Eds., *Feminist Visions for Social Work* (Silver Springs, MD: NASW Press, 1986), introduction, pp. 1–28; and M. Bricker-Jenkins and N. Gottlieb, *Feminist Social Work Practice in Clinical Settings* (Newberry Park, CA: Sage, 1991).

15. Mary Bricker-Jenkins in *Social Work Practice: A Generalist Approach,* 9th ed., Louise C. Johnson and Stephen J. Yanca (Boston: Allyn & Bacon, 2007), p. 408.

16. Shelley A. Haddock, Toni Schindler Zimmerman, and David MacPhee, "The Power Equity Guide: Attending to Gender in Family Therapy," in *Marriage and Family Therapy* 26, 2 (April 2000): 153–170.

17. Schiele, Jerome H., "The Contour and Meaning of Afrocentric Social Work," *Black Studies* 27, 6 (July 1997): 805.

18. Ibid.

19. Vanessa D. Johnson, "The Nguzo Saba as a Foundation for African American College Student Development Theory," *Black Studies* 31, 4 (March 2001): 416–417.

20. Peter Bell and Jimmy Evans, *Counseling the Black Client: Alcohol Use and Abuse in Black America,* as cited by Ruth McRoy "Cultural Competence with African Americans" in *Culturally Competent Practice: A Framework for Understanding Diverse Groups and Justice Issues,* Doman Lum, Ed. (Pacific Grove, CA: Brooks/Cole, 2003), p. 222.

21. Vanessa D. Johnson, "The Nguzo Saba as a Foundation for African American College Student Development Theory," *Black Studies* 31, 4 (March 2001): 416–417.

22. Valerie Borum, "An Afrocentric Approach in Working with African American Familes," in *Multicultural Perspectives in Working with Families,* 2nd ed., Elaine P. Congress and Manny J. Gonzales, Eds. (New York: Springer, 2005), p. 252.

23. Ibid., p. 253.

24. Ibid., p. 252.

25. Ibid., p. 252.

26. J. P. Butler (1981) as cited by Borum, in "An Afrocentric Approach in Working with African American Families," p. 252.

27. Johnson, "The Nguzo Saba as a Foundation for African American College Student Development Theory," pp. 416–417.

28. M. K. Ho (1987) as cited by Roy A. Bean, Benjamin J. Perry, and Tina M. Bedell, "Developing Culturally Competent Marriage and Family Therapists: Guidelines for Working with Hispanic Families," *Marital and Family Therapy* 27, 1 (January 2001): 43–54.

29. Ibid.

30. Bean, Perry, and Bedell, "Developing Culturally Competent Marriage and Family Therapists," pp. 43–54.

31. Celia Jaes Falicov, *Latino Families in Therapy: A Guide to Multicultural Practice* (New York: Guilford Press, 1998), p. 149.

32. Ibid., p. 150.

33. Ibid., pp. 150–151.

34. We have chosen to use the term *Native American* rather than *American Indian,* the term imposed by European settlers. It should however be noted that various native persons use either term as their preference or other terms such as *First Nations People.*

35. Larry J. Zimmerman and Brian Leigh Molyneaux, *Native American North America* (Norman: University of Oklahoma Press, 1996). This book provides an excellent summary of characteristics of tribes in various regions of North America.

36. Ibid., p. 20.

37. This excellent essay is found in *Native Universe: Voices of Indian Americans*, Gerald McMaster and Clifford E. Tratzer, Eds. (Washington DC: National Museum of the American Indian, Smithsonian Institution in association with National Geographic, 2004).

38. See John F. Longres, *Human Behavior in the Social Environment* (Itasca, IL: F. E. Peacock, 1990), pp. 40–247.

39. The material on relationship is based on Louise C. Johnson's experiences working with and dialoguing with Native Americans, students, and others as director of the social work program at the University of South Dakota.

Chapter 4

1. Nick F. Coady, "The Worker–Client Relationship Revisited," *Families in Society* 74 (May 1993): 293.

2. Carl Hartman and Diane Reynolds, "Resistant Clients: Confrontation, Interpretation, and Alliance," *Social Casework* 68 (April 1987): 205–213.

3. Edith Ankersmit, "Setting the Contract in Probation," *Federal Probation* 40 (June 1976): 28–33.

4. Charles R. Horejsi, "Training for the Direct-Service Volunteer in Probation," *Federal Probation* 37 (September 1973): 38–41.

5. Helen Harris Perlman, *Relationship: The Heart of Helping People* (Chicago: University of Chicago Press, 1979), p. 2.

6. Ibid., p. 24.

7. Ibid., p. 62.

8. See Lawrence M. Brammer, *The Helping Relationship: Process and Skills*, 3rd ed. (Englewood Cliffs, NJ: Prentice-Hall, 1984); and Beulah Roberts Compton and Burt Galaway, *Social Work Processes*, rev. ed. (Homewood, IL: Dorsey Press, 1979), chap. 6.

9. Compton and Galaway, *Social Work Processes*, p. 224.

10. See Anthony N. Maluccio, *Learning from Clients: Interpersonal Helping as Viewed by Clients and Social Workers* (New York: Free Press, 1979).

11. See Felix P. Biestek, *The Casework Relationship* (Chicago: Loyola University Press, 1957) for a full description of the seven principles.

12. Ann Templeton Brownlee, *Community, Culture and Care* (St. Louis: C. V. Mosby, 1978), chap. 3.

13. Joel Fischer, Diane D. Dulaney, Rosemary T. Frazio, Mary T. Hadakand, and Ethyl Zivotosky, "Are Social Workers Sexists?" *Social Work* 21 (November 1976): 428–433.

14. Joanne Mermelstein and Paul Sundet, "Education for Social Work in the Rural Context," in *Educating for Social Work in Rural Areas: A Report on Rural Child Welfare and Family Service Project of the School of Social Work*, Lynn R. Hulen, project coordinator (Fresno: California State University, June 1978).

15. Louise C. Johnson, Dale Crawford, and Lorraine Rousseau, "Understandings Needed to Work with Sioux Indian Clients" (unpublished paper).

16. Joanne Mermelstein and Paul Sundet, "Worker Acceptance and Credibility in the Rural Environment," in *Rural Human Services: A Book of Readings*, H. Wayne Johnson, Ed. (Itasca, IL: F. E. Peacock, 1980), pp. 174–178.

17. Janet Kirkland and Karen Irey, "Confidentiality: Issues and Dilemmas in Rural Practice," in *Second National Institute on Social Work in Rural Areas Reader*, Edward B. Buxton, Ed. (Madison: University of Wisconsin—Extension Center for Social Studies, 1978), pp. 142–149.

18. Yvonne L. Fraley, "A Role Model for Practice," *Social Service Review* 43 (June 1969): 145–154.

19. Adapted from Brett A. Seabury, "Communication Problems in Social Work Practice," *Social Work* 25, 1 (January 1980): 40–44.

20. Floyd W. Matson and Ashley Montagu, *The Human Dialogue: Perspectives on Communication* (New York: Free Press, 1967), p. 6.

21. See Lawrence Shulman, *The Skills of Helping: Individuals and Groups*, 2nd ed. (Itasca, IL: F. E. Peacock, 1984), chaps. 2 and 4.

22. See ibid., pp. 65–72, for discussion of this task.

23. See Doman Lum, *Culturally Competent Practice: A Framework for Understanding Diverse Groups and Justice Issues* (Pacific Grove, CA: Brooks/Cole, 1999).

24. Ibid., p. 155.

25. Ibid.

26. James W. Leigh, *Communicating for Cultural Competence* (Boston: Allyn & Bacon, 1998), p. 19.

27. Ibid., chap. 8.

28. Ibid., chap. 5.

29. Ibid., p. 19.

30. Lum, *Culturally Competent Practice*, pp. 152–154.

31. This triad is based on the work of C. B. Truax and R. R. Carkhuff, *Toward Effective Counseling and Psychotherapy* (Chicago: Aldine, 1967). For an excellent discussion of this material, see Eveline D. Schulman, *Intervention in the Human Services*, 2nd ed. (St. Louis: C. V. Mosby, 1978), chap. 8.

Chapter 5

1. For further discussion, see Curtis Janzen and Oliver Harris, *Family Treatment in Social Work Practice* (Itasca, IL: F. E. Peacock, 1980), pp. 6–12.
2. Ann Hartman and Joan Laird, *Family-Centered Social Work Practice* (New York: Free Press, 1983), chap. 10.
3. Janzen and Harris, *Family Treatment*, pp. 12–16.
4. Hartman and Laird, *Family-Centered Social Work Practice*, chap. 8.
5. Janzen and Harris, *Family Treatment*, pp. 15–20.
6. Based on Sonya L. Rhodes, "A Developmental Approach to the Life Cycle of the Family," *Social Casework* 58 (May 1977): 301–311.
7. See Joseph D. Anderson, "Family-Centered Practice in the 1990's: A Multicultural Perspective," *Journal of Multicultural Social Work* 1, 4 (1992): 17–29; and Rocco A. Cimmarusti, "Family Preservation Practice Based upon a Multisystems Approach," *Child Welfare* 71 (May–June 1992): 241–256.
8. Ann Weick, Charles Rapp, W. Patrick Sullivan, and Walter Kisthardt, "A Strengths Perspective for Social Work Practice," *Social Work* 34 (July 1989): 350–354; and Florence Wexler Vigilante and Mildred Maileck, "Needs–Resource Evaluation in the Assessment Process," *Social Work* 33 (March–April 1988): 101–104.
9. Harriet Bartlett, *The Common Base of Social Work Practice* (New York: NASW Press, 1970), p. 159.
10. Harriet A. Feiner and Harriet Katz, "Stronger Women—Stronger Families," *Affilia* 1 (Winter 1986): 49–58.
11. Mary K. Rodwell, "Naturalistic Inquiry: An Alternative Model for Social Work Assessment," *Social Service Review* 61 (June 1987): 231–246.
12. Carel B. Germain and Alex Gitterman, *The Life Model of Social Work Practice* (New York: Columbia University Press, 1980), chap. 1.
13. Abraham H. Maslow, *Motivation and Personality*, 3rd ed. (New York: Harper-Collins, 1987).
14. Charlotte Towle, *Common Human Needs*, rev. ed. (New York: NASW Press, 1957).
15. Paula Allen-Meares and Bruce A. Lane, "Grounding Social Work Practice in Theory: Ecosystems," *Social Casework* 68 (November 1987): 315–321.
16. Dolores Norton, *The Dual Perspective* (New York: Council on Social Work Education, 1978), p. 3. Also see Dolores G. Norton, "Diversity, Early Socialization, and Temporal Development: The Dual Perspective Revisited," *Social Work* 38 (January 1993): 82–90.
17. Sonia Badillo Ghali, "Culture Sensitivity and the Puerto Rican Client," *Social Casework* 58 (October 1977): 459–468.
18. Hartman and Laird, *Family-Centered Social Work Practice*, chap. 10.
19. Ibid.
20. Hartman and Laird, *Family-Centered Social Work Practice*, chap. 11.
21. Elizabeth M. Tracy and James K. Whittaker, "The Social Network Map: Assessing Social Support in Clinical Practice," *Families in Society* 71 (October 1990): 461–470; and Elizabeth M. Tracy, "Identifying Social Support Resources of At-Risk Families," *Social Work* 35 (May 1990): 252–258.
22. Also see Charles Froland, Diane L. Pancoast, Nancy J. Chapmen, and Priscilla J. Kimboko, *Helping Networks and Human Services* (Beverly Hills, CA: Sage, 1981); and James K. Whittaker and James Garbarino, *Social Support Networks: Informal Helping in the Human Services* (New York: Aldine, 1983).

Chapter 6

1. This formulation is similar but not identical to a format developed by Ruth R. Middleman and Gale Goldberg, *Social Service Delivery: A Structural Approach to Social Work Practice* (New York: Columbia University Press, 1974), chap. 1.
2. Fred M. Cox, John L. Erlich, Jack Rothman, and John E. Tropman, Eds., *Strategies of Community Organization*, 4th ed. (Itasca, IL: F. E. Peacock, 1987), p. 258.
3. Emelicia Mizio and Anita J. Delaney, Eds., *Training for Service Delivery to Minority Clients* (New York: Family Service Association of America, 1981).
4. Robert J. Teare and Harold L. McPheeters, *Manpower Utilization in Social Welfare* (Atlanta, GA: Southern Regional Education Board, 1970), p. 34.
5. Ibid.
6. Ronald L. Simons and Stephen M. Aiger, "Facilitating an Eclectic Use of Practice Theory," *Social Casework* 60 (April 1979): 201–208.
7. For a discussion of nonmetropolitan service delivery, see Louise C. Johnson, "Human Service Delivery Patterns in Non-Metropolitan Communities," in *Rural Human Services: A Book of Readings*, H. Wayne Johnson, Ed. (Itasca, IL: F. E. Peacock, 1980), pp. 55–64.
8. Elliot Studt, *A Conceptual Approach to Teaching Materials* (New York: Council on Social Work Education, 1965), pp. 4–18.

9. Pamela Miller, "Covenant Model for Professional Relationships: An Alternative to the Contract Model," *Social Work* 35 (March 1990): 121–125.

10. Tom A. Croxton, "Caveats on Contract," *Social Work* 34 (March–April 1988): 169–171.

Chapter 7

1. Ross V. Speck and Carolyn L. Attneave, *Family Networks* (New York: Pantheon, 1973).

2. Eugene Litwak and Ivan Szelenyi, "Primary Group Structures and Their Function: Kin, Neighbors, and Friends," *American Sociological Review* 34 (August 1969): 465–481.

3. Alice H. Collins and Diane L. Pancoast, *Natural Helping Networks: A Strategy for Intervention* (Washington, DC: NASW Press, 1974).

4. Alan Gartner and Frank Riessman, *Self-Help in the Human Services* (San Francisco: Jossey-Bass, 1977).

5. Yeheskel Hasenfeld and Benjamin Gidron, "Self-Help Groups and Human Service Organizations: An Interorganizational Perspective," *Social Service Review* 67 (June 1993): 217–236.

6. For a good discussion of effective referral, see Elizabeth Nicholas, *A Primer of Social Casework* (New York: Columbia University Press, 1960), chap. 9.

7. Robert J. Teare and Harold L. McPheeters, *Manpower Utilization in Social Welfare* (Atlanta, GA: Southern Regional Education Board, 1970), p. 34.

8. Ibid., pp. 34–51.

9. Lorraine M. Gutierrez, "Working with Women of Color: An Empowerment Perspective," *Social Work* 35 (March 1990): 149–153.

10. Barbara Bryant Solomon, *Black Empowerment: Social Work in Oppressed Communities* (New York: Columbia University Press, 1976); and "Social Work Values and Skills to Empower Women," in *Women, Power, and Change*, Ann Weick and Susan T. Vandiver, Eds. (Washington, DC: NASW Press, 1980), pp. 206–214.

11. Ruth J. Parsons, "Empowerment: Purpose and Practice Principle in Social Work," *Social Work with Groups* 14, 2 (1991): 7–21. Also contains an excellent case example.

12. Silvia Staub-Bernasconi, "Social Action, Empowerment and Social Work—An Integrative Theoretical Framework for Social Work and Social Work with Groups," *Social Work with Groups* 14, 2 (1991): 35–51.

13. Karla Krogsrud Miley, Michael O'Melia, and Brenda L. DuBois, *Generalist Social Work Practice: An Empowering Approach* (Boston: Allyn & Bacon, 1995), p. 31.

14. Good discussions of techniques are found in Gutierrez, "Working with Women," and in Solomon, "Social Work Values."

15. The approach that follows is a simplified version of cognitive and behavioral approaches. Also see Albert Ellis, *Better, Deeper, and More Enduring Brief Therapy: The Rational Emotive Behavioral Therapy Approach* (New York: Brunner/Mazel, 1996); Judith Beck, *Cognitive Therapy: Basics and Beyond* (New York: Guilford Press, 1995); Jim Lantz, "Cognitive Theory and Social Work Treatment," in *Social Work Treatment*, 4th ed., Francis J. Turner, Ed. (New York: Free Press, 1996); Mark Mattaini, *Clinical Practice with Individuals* (Washington, DC: NASW Press, 1997); and Bruce Thyer and John Wodarski, *Handbook of Empirical Social Work Practice* (New York: Wiley, 1998).

16. Lois G. Selby, "Supportive Treatment: The Development of a Concept and a Helping Method," *Social Service Review* 30 (December 1956): 400–414.

17. Beulah Roberts Compton, "An Attempt to Examine the Use of Support in Social Work Practice," in *Social Work Processes*, 5th ed., Beulah Roberts Compton and Burt Galaway, Eds. (Pacific Grove, CA: Brooks/Cole, 1994), pp. 472–479.

18. Florence Hollis, *Casework: A Psychosocial Therapy* (New York: Random House, 1972), pp. 89–95.

19. Judith C. Nelson, "Support: A Necessary Condition for Change," *Social Work* 25 (September 1980): 388–392.

20. Patricia Ferris and Catherine A. Marshall, "A Model Project for Families of the Chronically Mentally Ill," *Social Work* 32 (March–April 1987): 110–114.

21. James Kelley and Pamela Sykes, "Helping the Helpers: A Support Group for Family Members of Persons with AIDS," *Social Work* 34 (May 1989): 239–242.

22. Carolyn Knight, "Use of Support Groups with Adult Female Survivors of Child Sexual Abuse," *Social Work* 35 (May 1990): 202–206.

23. See Elizabeth McBroom, "Socialization and Social Casework," in Roberts and Nee, *Theories of Social Casework*, pp. 315–351.

24. Robert Vinter, "Program Activities: An Analysis of Their Effects on Participant Behavior," in *Readings in Group Work Practice*, Robert Vinter, Ed. (Ann Arbor, MI: Campus Publishers, 1967).

25. See Ruth R. Middleman, "The Use of Program: Review and Update," *Social Work with Groups* 3 (Fall 1980): 5–23. The Suggested Readings in this text contain many important sources for this material as well.

26. William Schwartz, "The Worker in the Group," in *Social Welfare Forum 1961* (New York: Columbia University Press, 1961), p. 154 and William Schwartz, "On the Use of Groups in Social Work Practice," in *The Practice of Group Work*, William Schwartz and Serapio R. Zalba Eds. (New York: Columbia University Press, 1971), p. 5.

27. Schwartz and Zalba, *The Practice of Group Work*.

28. Ernesto Gomez, "The San Antonio Model: A Culture-Oriented Approach," in *Our Kingdom Stands on Brittle Glass*, Guadalupe Gibson, Ed. (Silver Spring, MD: NASW Press, 1983), pp. 96–111.

Chapter 8

1. William Schwartz, "The Worker in the Group," in *Social Welfare Forum 1961* (New York: Columbia University Press, 1961), p. 154.

2. William Schwartz, "On the Use of Groups in Social Work Practice," in *The Practice of Group Work*, William Schwartz and Serapio R. Zalba (New York: Columbia University Press, 1971), p. 5.

3. See Schwartz and Zalba, Eds. *The Practice of Group Work;* and Lawrence Shulman, *A Casebook of Social Work with Groups: The Mediating Model* (New York: Council on Social Work Education, 1968), and *The Skills of Helping Individuals and Groups*, 2nd ed. (Itasca, IL: F. E. Peacock, 1984).

4. See Shulman, *The Skills of Helping Individuals and Groups*, pp. 9–10.

5. See Shulman, *A Casebook of Social Work with Groups*.

6. Irving Spergel, *Community Problem Solving* (Chicago: University of Chicago Press, 1969), p. 106.

7. William Schwartz, "The Social Worker in the Group," in *The Social Welfare Forum Proceedings* (New York: Columbia University Press, 1961), p. 157.

8. Nora Gold, "Motivation: The Crucial but Unexplored Component of Social Work Practice," *Social Work* 35 (January 1990): 49–56.

9. Helen Harris Perlman, *Social Casework* (Chicago: University of Chicago Press, 1957).

10. See Charles S. Levy, "Values and Planned Change," *Social Casework* 53 (October 1972): 488–493, for another discussion of these factors.

11. Florence Hollis, *Casework: A Psycho-Social Therapy*, 2nd ed. (New York: Random House, 1972), pp. 81–85 and chap. 9.

12. Max Siporin, *Introduction to Social Work Practice* (New York: Macmillan, 1975), p. 302.

13. Ibid., p. 305.

14. Richard M. Grinnel, Jr., and Nancy S. Kyte, "Environmental Modification: A Study," *Social Work* 20 (July 1975): 313–318.

15. See Robert Sommer, *Personal Space* (Englewood Cliffs, NJ: Prentice-Hall, 1969); Edward T. Hall, *The Hidden Dimension* (New York: Doubleday Anchor, 1969); and William H. Itlleson, Harold M. Proshansky, Leanne G. Rivlin, and Gary H. Winkel, *An Introduction to Environmental Psychology* (New York: Holt, Rinehart and Winston, 1974).

16. Carel B. Germain and Alex Gitterman, *The Life Model of Social Work Practice* (New York: Columbia University Press, 1980).

17. For additional discussion, see Anthony N. Maluccio, "Promoting Competence through Life Experience," in *Social Work Practice: People and Environments*, Carel B. Germain, Ed. (New York: Columbia University Press, 1979), pp. 282–302.

18. Irene A. Gutheil, "Considering the Physical Environment: An Essential Component of Good Practice," *Social Work* 37 (September 1992): 391–396.

19. See Carel B. Germain, " 'Space': An Ecological Variable in Social Work Practice," *Social Casework* 59 (November 1978): 515–529.

20. For further consideration of this topic, see Brett A. Seabury, "Arrangement of Physical Space in Social Work Settings," *Social Work* 16 (October 1971): 43–49; and Thomas Walz, Georgina Willenberg, and Lane deMoll, "Environmental Design," *Social Work* 19 (January 1974): 38–46.

21. See Richard E. Boettcher and Roger Vander Schie, "Milieu Therapy with Chronic Mental Patients," *Social Work* 20 (March 1975): 130–139.

22. Carel B. Germain, "Time: An Ecological Variable in Social Work Practice," *Social Casework* 57 (July 1976): 419–426.

23. See Jill Kinney, David Haapala, and Charlotte Booth, *Keeping Families Together: The Homebuilders Model* (New York: Aldine de Gruyter, 1991); and Insoo Kim Berg, *Family-Based Services* (New York: Norton, 1994).

24. Eugene Litwak and Henry F. Meyer, "A Balance Theory of Coordination between Bureaucratic Organizations and Community Primary Groups," *Administrative Science Quarterly* 11 (March 1966): 31–58; and *School, Family and Neighborhood: The Theory and Practice of School–Community Relations* (New York: Columbia University Press, 1974).

25. Karen Orloff Kaplan, "Recent Trends in Case Management," in *Encyclopedia of Social Work*, 18th ed. (supplement), Leon Ginsberg, Ed. (Silver Spring, MD: NASW Press, 1990), pp. 60–77.
26. Ibid., p. 62.
27. Jack Rothman, "A Model of Case Management: Toward Empirically Based Practice," *Social Work* 36 (November 1991): 520–528.
28. Stephen T. Moore, "A Social Work Practice Model of Case Management: The Case Management Grid," *Social Work* 35 (September 1990): 444–448.

Chapter 9

1. For further discussion of this balance, see Beulah Compton and Burt Galaway, *Social Work Processes*, 5th ed. (Homewood, IL: Dorsey Press, 1994), chap. 16.
2. Michael Key, Peter Hudson, and John Armstrong, "Evaluation Theory and Community Work," in *Strategies of Community Organization*, 3rd ed., Fred M. Cox, John L. Erlich, Jack Rothman, and John E. Tropman, Eds. (Itasca, IL: F. E. Peacock, 1979), pp. 159–175.
3. See Roy A. Ruckdeschel and Buford E. Farris, "Assessing Practice: A Critical Look at the Single-Case Design," *Social Casework* 62 (September 1981): 413–419.
4. Thomas J. Kiresuk and Geoffrey Garwick, "Basic Goal Attainment Scaling Procedures," in *Social Work Processes*, 2nd ed., Beulah Roberts Compton and Burt Galaway, Eds. (Homewood, IL: Dorsey Press, 1979), pp. 412–421.
5. See William Reid and Laura Epstein, Eds., *Task Centered Practice* (New York: Columbia University Press, 1977); Sharon Berlin and Jeanne Marsh, *Informing Practice Decisions* (New York: Macmillan, 1993); and Catherine Alder and Wayne Evens, *Evaluating Your Practice: A Guide to Self-Assessment* (New York: Springer, 1990).
6. See Joel Fischer and Kevin Corcoran, *Measures for Clinical Practice*, 2nd ed., two vols. (New York: Free Press, 1995). There are also several reference texts available containing assessments for families, groups, organizations, and the like.
7. See Martin Bloom, Joel Fischer, and John Orme, *Evaluating Practice: Guidelines for the Accountable Professional* (Boston: Allyn & Bacon, 1995); and Joel Fischer and Kevin Corcoran, *Measures for Clinical Practice*, 2nd ed., two vols. (New York: Free Press, 1995).
8. See Yvonne S. Lincoln and Ergon G. Guba, *Naturalistic Inquiry* (Beverly Hills, CA: Sage, 1985), as cited in James V. Leigh, *Communicating for Cultural Competence* (Boston: Allyn & Bacon, 1998), p. 18.
9. See William J. Reid and Anne Shyne, *Brief and Extended Casework* (New York: Columbia University Press, 1969).
10. William J. Reid, *The Task Centered System* (New York: Columbia University Press, 1978), p. 5.
11. Anne E. Fortune, Bill Pearlingi, and Cherie D. Rochell, "Reactions to Termination of Individual Treatment," *Social Work* 37 (March 1992): 171–178.
12. Howard Hess and Peg McCartt Hess, "Termination in Context," in *Social Work Processes*, 5th ed., Beulah Compton and Burt Galaway, Eds. (Belmont, CA: Wadsworth, 1994), pp. 529–539.
13. See Allen Pincus and Anne Minahan, *Social Work Practice: Model and Method* (Itasca, IL: F. E. Peacock, 1973), chap. 13.

Chapter 10

1. Erik H. Erikson, *Childhood and Society* (New York: W. W. Norton, 1950), chap. 7.
2. Betty Friedan, *The Fountain of Age* (New York: Simon and Schuster, 1993).
3. Elizabeth Kübler-Ross, *On Death and Dying*, (New York: Macmillan, 1969).
4. Ibid.
5. Ibid.
6. Ibid.
7. Ibid.
8. Ibid.

Appendix

1. Lenore Walker, *The Battered Woman* (New York: Harper and Row, 1979).
2. See Erik H. Erikson, *Childhood and Society* (New York: W. W. Norton, 1950).
3. See Abraham H. Maslow, *Motivation and Personality*, 3rd ed. (New York: Harper-Collins, 1987).
4. See Charlotte Towle, *Common Human Needs*, rev. ed. (New York: NASW Press, 1957).
5. See Abraham H. Maslow, *Motivation and Personality*, 3rd ed. (New York: Harper-Collins, 1987).

INDEX

Note: Bold numbers indicate pages on which key terms are introduced.